SEX, SECTS AND SOCIETY

*'Pain and Pleasure': A Social History of
Wales and the Welsh, 1870–1945*

Russell Davies

University of Wales Press
Cardiff
2018

www.uwp.co.uk

British Library Cataloguing-in-Publication Data.
A catalogue record for this book is available from the British Library.

ISBN 978-1-78683-213-9
eISBN 978-1-78683-214-6

The University of Wales Press acknowledges the financial support of the Welsh Books Council.

Typeset by Eira Fenn Gaunt, Pentyrch.
Printed by CPI Antony Rowe, Melksham.

Contents

Contents

Diolchiadau – Acknowledgements

To Kylie Evans for once more transforming hieroglyphics into a typescript.

To the anonymous reader who reviewed the volume in an early draft and made valuable improvements.

To the staff at the University of Wales Press for their guidance and advice. The errors that remain in the volume are mine, and mine alone. (Why is it that in the proofing process errors are invisible, but seconds after publishing they glare at you with gleeful malevolence?)

To all those researchers working to find a cure for MS, thank you – please hurry up.

To Wales (whatever that is) and the Welsh (whoever you are).

I Cati, Beca a Guto, pob lwc wrth ichi greu Cymru'r dyfodol.

I Nerys, Betsan a Ffion, ac er cof am fy Nhad, John Haydn Davies (1926–2017), oedd yn drysorfa o straeon o'r cyfnod 1870–1945.

Introduction
'To Begin at the Beginning'

Parod yw dyn i liwio'r cread â'i ofidiau ei hun.

(Man is ever ready to fill creation with his own worries.)

Tegla Davies, *Gŵr Pen y Bryn* (1923).

Set in the mountain vastness that inspired the national identity of Ceiriog, O. M. Edwards and countless others is the Arts and Crafts Movement's gem of St Mark's Church, Brithdir. Forlorn and forgotten, its congregation long gone to glory, its architectural and artistic riches are under the care of the Friends of Friendless Churches – an organisation whose title often evokes a sympathetic or sentimental 'Oh'. In the graveyard's quiet earth is the grave of Sir Eric Ommanney Skaife (1884–1956). Of all the achievements of this Sussex-born, Sandhurst-trained career soldier, diplomat, civil servant, committed churchman and convinced conservative, a couplet in Welsh carved on the gravestone emphasises the most important:

> Yng Nghymru yr oedd fy nghalon,
> Yn ei thir hi mae fy ngweddillion.

> (My heart was in Wales
> And in her soil are my remains.)

Skaife learnt Welsh whilst a prisoner in Germany during the First World War and became an ardent eisteddfodwr, a vice-president of Urdd Gobaith Cymru and a generous patron of many aspects of Welsh language culture.

Across the same mountains are scattered the ashes of another person who is not always allowed into the Welsh Valhalla. Bertrand Russell (1872–1970) was the scion of an even more elite family than Skaife's. Russell's ancestors participated in every great British political event from the Dissolution of the Monasteries in 1536–40 to the Great Reform Act 1832. This philosopher, logician, mathematician, historian, writer, social critic, political activist and Nobel laureate had a deep attachment to Wales. Born in Trellech, Monmouthshire, after his career, Russell retired 'home' to Wales and lived out his long life in Plas Penrhyn, Penrhyndeudraeth.

Were they Welsh? Should their tales be considered as part of the story of Wales? Or were these nothing more than the desires of two people to wait the final trumpet in a tomb with a view? But their emotional attachment to the country would seem to suggest that a positive answer was appropriate. At the very least the couplet written in a Welsh country churchyard and the ashes scattered over the hillsides confirm the complexities of Welsh national identities. The private realms of belonging and being are often the preserve of the novelist or the literary critic but history too can provide valuable insights into a person's national identity.

This is the second of two volumes of the history of Wales in the period 1870–1945 under the collective title of *Pain and Pleasure*. 'Where, when, what was Wales and who were the Welsh?' are more than the monosyllabic questionings of children. As ever with such precocious utterings they help to point towards deeper human truths that reveal how complex and contradictory the answers can be. There are almost as many answers to the questions as there were people within and without Wales who claimed some affiliation and attachment to the nation.

To many Wales was God's Acre, gently watered by 'gwlith a glaw Rhagluniaeth' (the dew and rain of Providence). Its people had the piety of a chosen elect. But closer examination reveals that the spiritual life of Wales was not without its darker side, for the Welsh too were a people who walked in the darkness of superstition. After the revivalistic enthusiasm and excitement of 1905 and all that abated, there was an ebbing of the sea of faith. Wales experienced a disenchantment of the world, a dechristianisation and a desacralisation of the nation. One of the most fundamental factors behind these processes is that over the years 1870–1945, Wales and the Welsh, despite hardship and hardscrabble existences, experienced a remarkable transformation in the wealth of the nation and the longevity of the people. Life expectancy almost doubled. People were no longer terrified that they could scent the Grim Reaper's breath. This decline in fear must be one of the most remarkable transformations in Welsh history.

The Welsh were one of the few people who thanked their maker that they were a musical nation and included musicality as one of the characteristics of their national identity. In the 1940s Ealing film comedy *A Run for Your Money*, two miners on a trip to a rugby international in London are scandalised by a 'No Music' sign in a bar. The inference clearly was that such a prohibition would be impossible in Wales.[1] The prohibition in Wales, of course, would have been over the sale of alcohol in the first place. The Welsh Sunday Closing Act (1881), the first legislation to treat Wales as a separate nation since the Acts of Union in the sixteenth century, sought to prohibit the sale of alcohol on a Sunday. It was perhaps the first step of the tortuous journey along the long and winding road to devolution. The long, dry Sunday became a feature of the Welsh Sabbath. It was testimony to the strength of the temperance movement and religion within Wales. Yet, for every person who signed the pledge, there was another who developed a strategy to assuage a Sabbath-long thirst.

Appropriately for the 'land of song' and the 'musical nation', one of the signifiers and symbols of national identity that Wales acquired in the period 1870–1945 was a national anthem. Sung in response to the 'Hakka' war dance performed by the New Zealand rugby tourists in 1905, 'Hen Wlad Fy Nhadau' quickly replaced its closest rival for anthemic status – 'God Bless the Prince of Wales' – a process undoubtedly assisted for a 'Nonconformist nation' by the transformation of the portly prince into Edward the Caresser.

Despite the anthem's evocation of a land of masculine bards, minstrels and warriors the nation's cartoonic characterisation was often feminine. In an age of Empire the portly and pugnacious figure of Dame Wales elbowed out Britannia as John Bull's perfect

3

partner. J. M. Staniforth in particular had great fun in portraying this female Falstaff. In a series of cartoons in the 1900s and 1910s, chunky, dumpy, portly, roly-poly Dame Wales was invariably dressed, or rather draped, in that other invented tradition, the 'national costume' of stovepipe-style hat and 'brethyn cartref'. If all Welsh women dressed like the Dame then the woollen mills of Wales would have been booming at the twentieth century's turn for an entire week's production of wool would be needed to cover her. Cartoons and humour convey so much. One of Staniforth's cartoons in the *Western Mail*, 19 February 1915, shows Dame Wales watering the quickly growing plant of 'The Welsh Guards' with 'Welsh Enthusiasm', whilst the uniformed John Bull admiringly watches over the garden wall. It captures the proud moment of the emergence of another national institution, the moment when Wales was allowed her own national regiment. This national recognition, if such it was, that so inspired Lloyd George and his recruiter-in-chief the Revd John Williams, Brynsiencyn, came at a terrible price. Gehenna and Carthage sacrificed children to appease their Gods, Wales offered her sons as cannon fodder to attempt to impress her neighbour. Dame Wales suffered as much from Stockholm syndrome as schizophrenia.[2]

Symbols and stereotypes of national identity abounded in the period 1870–1945. To some Wales was best represented in the mountains and in the west where the language and literature had lingered in a tradition that flowed back to the sixth century. Others, such as Aneurin Bevan, argued that the turbulent experience of industrial Wales, especially the south, was the crucible in which a brave new Wales was forged. The stereotypes dealt reassuringly in black and white. Wales was divided into two mutually hostile and exclusive groups – that of a Welsh-speaking, nationalist, Nonconformist rural west and an English-speaking, socialist, industrial south Wales. But the lived reality was far more contradictory and complex as individuals with their ideals, ideas and identities moved across boundaries. The Welsh, as Declan Kiberd said of the Irish, were 'both imperial and counter-imperial, sometimes seemingly in the same gesture'.[3] The years 1870–1945 were a period in which Wales could be construed as central to the imperial project, making a special contribution, as the *Western Mail* claimed, on 8 August 1916, to 'the progressive, civilizing and Christianizing mission of the British Empire.' But as Emrys ap Iwan, Saunders Lewis and others argued, Wales was subject to a variety of 'internal' imperialism that hampered as much as it helped Welsh culture. Dr Ernest Jones in an article on 'The Welsh Inferiority Complex', published in *The Welsh Outlook* in March 1929, made short shrift of the complex but noted the multiple aspects of a people's identity.[4] Claims made for homogeneity and the unanimity of such groupings invariably broke down under scrutiny into myriad fragments, significant exceptions and many alternative competing identities. Indeed, as another commentator noted, in most 'mature national communities there is a criss-crossing of loyalties that make up the fabric of people's individual and collective lives.'[5] Sacred concerns such as religion shaped identities, so too did secular loyalties such as class, clan, ethnicity, gender, or race.

In the so-called battle of the sexes, Dame Wales and her sisters who shouldered the burdens whilst their menfolk went off to fight for Queen or King and Country greatly advanced the cause of equality between the sexes. By the 1920s, there were feminists, such as Lady Rhondda, who were insisting that equal partnerships between men and women would achieve the one single, all-encompassing 'human sex', which was only incidentally divided into male and female. In the land of the 'human sex' the differences and inequalities between men and women would finally dissolve and the result, according to the Russian-born anarchist Emma Goldman, would be 'true companionship and oneness'. To prove her argument, Goldman married an Ammanford collier, James Colton, in 1925, prompting *The New York Times* to comment that 'cupid was armed with a coal pick when he dug his way into the heart of Emma Goldman'.[6]

There is a strong claim that Wales experienced a sexual revolution in the years 1870–1945. The joys of sex were propounded in cinemas, literature, photography and the theatre. Propriety dictated that the audiences for the screenings of the 'VD movies' *Damaged Goods* (1911) and *The Dangers of Ignorance* (1928) should be segregated (men attending at 4.30 and 8.30 p.m., women at 2.30 and 6.30 p.m.

at Cardiff), but the lessons were discussed by both the puritanical and prurient. Bertrand Russell in his *Marriage and Morals* (1929) and *The Conquest of Happiness* (1930) set out to loosen the bonds of contemporary morality to allow the physical satisfaction of the sexes as an important aspect of marriage. Dr Ernest Jones, Freud's biographer and the greatest explicator of his ideas, took his master's views further in emphasising the importance of the sexual satisfaction of women. Jones complained that even after Freud, sexuality was still too phallocentric. The clitoris, he argued, had an important part to play. People just needed to find it. Of all the stepping stones in the long march of female emancipation, this surely is one of the most important.

Some of the profounder battles in the years between 1870 and 1945 were the attempts of the religious, the respectable, the rich and the educated to control and contain the expression of people's emotions. The collective effects of a damp climate, a harsh theology and overcrowded houses supposedly doused the ardour of the Welsh people. But despite its portrayal as a solemn, moral land, in which duty had defeated desire, Wales, in reality, had diverse expressions of love. It also had its rowdier, raucous and raunchy aspects. Rural Wales, often portrayed as a pious paradise of strict morality, was in actual fact the venue for some remarkably dangerous liaisons and a broad range of sexual behaviour. Examination of the sexual peccadilloes and practices of rural Wales disproves Oscar Wilde's glib witticism 'that anyone can be good in the countryside, there are no temptations there'.

It is ironic that in this highly moral land one of the most persistent characters of many villages was the prostitute. Herds of harlots hunted their customers in rural market squares. In seaports around Wales, jams of tarts, fanfares of prostitutes and flourishes of strumpets could be found, pursuing their prey, persuading, promising pleasure or perversion. In the 'roaring' 1920s and the amoral 1930s, Gwen and Augustus John, Rhys Davies, Emlyn Williams, Lloyd George, Dylan Thomas, Evan Morgan, Norman Lewis, Arthur Machen, Ivor Novello, Goronwy Rees, Marged Howard-Stepney, Jean Rhys, Emrys Williams, Roald Dahl and many others had a moral incontinence that led to a bewildering series of 'till dawn do us part' relationships.[7] Yet these serial adulterers were outlasted and outlusted by that remarkable 'Queen of Bohemia' – Tenby-born, Nina Hamnett. Such was her lust for life that she was considered excessive, even in an age of moral excess and amongst a social group in which infidelity and immorality were the norm. Nina was the good time that was had by all.

Welsh-language authors were also no strangers to the ways of all flesh. In 1924, the precociously gifted Prosser Rhys won the crown at the National Eisteddfod for his 'pryddest' 'Atgof', a searing examination of homoerotic and homosexual love. In 1926, Gwenallt's great poem 'Y Sant' (the Saint) provided a psychological examination of lust in a character who was anything but saintly. Whilst, in 1930, Saunders Lewis's novel *Monica* told the sorry tale of a prostitute who 'neidiodd o bechod i bechod' (leaped from sin to sin) without any sign of remorse or regret, until she contracted venereal disease. Monica would probably have been at home in the raunchy establishment described in Rhys Davies's novel *Black Venus* (1944), a brothel somewhere on the outskirts of a large town in south Wales. In recounting such a diversity of emotional and sexual experience we run the risk, somewhat rare for a history book, that this will be a bodice-ripper with footnotes.

It is a sad fact that one aspect of the Welsh national character that has been completely forgotten is humour.[8] The laughter of the past has been silenced. The portraits of eminent Welsh people show solemn, sombre men whose brows are furrowed in permanent frowns and rather grumpy and frumpy-looking old women in their black bonnets and bustles. Caradoc Evans once claimed that 'two subjects are privileged from jest – The Holy Scriptures and the Welsh people'. The writer Gwyn Thomas echoed his view with his recollection of interwar Wales that 'our only concession to gaiety was a striped shroud.' But the Welsh were not all obsessed with earnestly being important. A rich tradition of sardonic and sarcastic, gentle and guileful humour runs through these years. In the 1880s, several guidebooks to 'ffraethineb' were published and republished to ensure that the Welsh people always looked on the sunny side of life. Several comedians made it their professional concern to create laughter and levity.[9]

Though much humour was universal to the human condition, there was a strong Welsh dimension to it. When the circus visited Merthyr Tydfil in 1879, members of the cast were surprised when some of the audience at the 'St George and the Dragon' masque cheered for the dragon. Welsh humour was, and is, different to English humour, and Welsh humour was also subtly different to that expressed in Cymraeg. In mild and malign ways, the differences between English and Welsh, Cymraeg and the emotive term 'Anglo-Welsh', between Cymro and the even more emotive term 'Cymro di-Gymraeg', as well as the contrasts between Hwntw and Gog, were delineated in jokes.

Welsh religion had a lighter side, for it was not wholly obsessed with cheerless texts from the Book of Job of worms devouring flesh. Not all ministers were lamenting Jeremiahs or manic street preachers. Some ministers rejoiced at the Song of Songs and revelled in the Song of Solomon, and added humour to their sermons. In 1874, Morgan Powel declared in *Trysorfa y Plant* – 'Yr wyf yn ymwybod trwy brofiad fod tipyn o chwerthin iachus yn well na physic' (I know from experience that a little healthy laughter is more beneficial than medicine).[10] However hard denominational magazines emphasised the respectability of religious people and chapels, their humour contained a substantial element of cynicism that often provided a corrective to behaviour that was considered to be too ostentatiously pious. The tradition of 'y noson lawen' (the happy night) provided several opportunities for communities to express their solidarity and laugh at life and its turnings.

Laughter and levity, sex and sensuality are just a few of the diverse ways through which the Welsh faced life. The evidence of love letters, gravestones and court reports indicates that emotional life in Wales was far more diverse and dissipated than the traditional portrayal. Powerful economic, political and social forces operated at deep structural levels. The Welsh people reacted to these in myriad ways that were often different to those that their religious, political and moral leaders claimed. It is the pursuit of such diversity that makes history such an entertaining pleasure.

I

'Dygwyl y Meirwon' (Festival of the Dead): Death, Transcendence and Transience

Gwell inni anghofio'r rhai a aeth i'w hir hun,
Y rhai hawdd eu cofio
A'r cof amdanynt
Yn wefr ac yn wae.

(We had better forget those who have gone to their long rest,
Those easy to remember
The memory of them
A thrill and woe.)

Gwilym R. Jones, 'Dygwyl y Meirwon', in Gwynn ap Gwilym
and Alan Llwyd (eds), *Blodeugerdd o Farddoniaeth Gymraeg yr
Ugeinfed Ganrif* (Llandysul, 1987), p. 135.

'Glyn cysgod angau': the valleys of the shadow of death

Glyw' di hi'n canu? Yr un
           hen gloch
Ag a ganai'r bore gwyn
Pan ddest i'm cyfarfod â gwrid ar
           dy foch
I'r Eglwys yn ymyl y llyn;
Roedd hi'n canu'n bereiddiach
           bryd hynny, Sian,
Fel y cofi'n dda mi wn,
Ac 'roedd mwy o aur yn dy
           fodrwy, Sian,
Nag sydd ynddi'r bore hwn.

Y dydd pan ddilynem ni elor Gwen
I'w bedd yn y fynwent lwyd,
Ti gofi'r offeiriad mewn llaeswysg
           wen
Yn ein cwrddyd yn ymyl y glwyd;
Oes, mae deugain mlynedd er
           hynny, Sian,
A bu llawer tro ar fyd,

Ond bydd deigryn hiraethus yn
           gwlychu 'ngrân
Man y cano'r gloch o hyd.

Mae'n heinioes, anwylyd, yn
           dirwyn i ben,
Ac awr y noswylio'n nesáu,
A'r gloch oedd yn canu ddydd
           angladd Gwen
Fydd yn canu pan gleddir ni'n dau;
A phwy fydd ei hunan yn ymyl
           y tân
Yn dlawd a digysur ei fyd?
Fe fyddai'n drugaredd – oni
           fyddai, Sian? –
Pe galwai'r hen gloch ni'r
           un pryd.

Do you hear it ringing? That same
           old bell
That rang the white morn
When veiled you came to meet me
In the church near the lake;
She sang sweeter then, Sian,
As you well remember I know,
And there was more gold in your
           ring, Sian,
Than there is this morning.

The day we followed Gwen's coffin
To her grave in the grey cemetery,
You will remember the priest
           in white
Meeting us at the gate;
Yes, forty years have passed since
           then, Sian,
And the world has turned several
           times,
Yet still a tear wets my cheek

Whenever I hear the bell.

Our lives, my dearest,
           draw to a close,
And the hour for sleep encroaches,
And the bell that rang on Gwen's
           funeral morn
Will ring when we both die;
And who will be alone at the
           fireside
Poor and uncomforted?
It would be a mercy – would
           it not, Sian? –
If the bell rings for us both at the
           same time.

'Cloch y Llan' (The Church Bell),
William Williams (Crwys) (1875–1968),
Cerddi Crwys (Wrexham, 1926).

Crwys's elegy written in a Welsh country churchyard is a melancholic and mournful musing on life. It is, perhaps, one of the saddest poems written in the period 1870–1945. It is also one of the sweetest love poems. Two souls have shared their joys and sorrows on a single journey. Like Falstaff, the aged narrator 'has heard the chimes at midnight', even so, he still sounds calm and controlled. Together the long and winding road has led the couple to the inevitability of death and inescapable separation.

It is impossible to write about death. What we have are the attitudes of the living to death, to dying and to the dead. The historical imagination cannot be sparked for no first-hand testimony except the fraudulent, no artefact, even the humblest, exists from those who have experienced 'Ynys Afallach' (The Island of Avalon) as the Celts christened their magical land of the dead.[1] Obituaries of Robert Graves appeared in the press when he was reported as having been killed during the First World War.[2] Gordon Evans of Llanddewi Brefi had a memorial service when it was reported that he had been lost when his ship was sunk by the Japanese in 1940. Yet both survived.[3] The reports of these 'deaths' were much exaggerated, neither Evans nor Graves provided any evidence of a journey into Christina Rossetti's 'silent land'. Winifred Coombe Tennant (1874–1956), in her capacity as Mrs Willett, was the most prolific spirit medium of the 1920s and 1930s. How reliable a guide to the afterworld she was, we will never know,[4] for temporal historians do not have access to the extraterrestrial archives to discover how great an adventure death was, is and will be. We must approach the subject of death therefore with caution, but one striking fact is clear: *timor mortis* lost much of its terror over the years between 1870 and 1945 as death's grip on the Welsh loosened.

Proverbs, those pessimistic distillations of peasant and proletarian wisdom still warned 'rhag angau ni thycia ffo' (from death flight will not avail), 'Gaeaf las, mynwent fras' (a mild winter, a full cemetery), and 'pob hirnychdod i angau' (every long affliction leads to death). But the image of death as a sentinel changed. The horror enshrined in the imagery of the apocalyptic horseman, or the all-powerful Dark Destroyer, or the skeletal Grim Reaper who viciously scythed and harvested humanity, was tamed.[5] In

1898, in a series of cartoons for the *Western Mail*, later published as *Cartoons of the Welsh Coal Strike April 1st to September 1st, 1898*, J. M. Staniforth showed a skeletal death as a character of exquisite patience, gently gathering the children and mothers of south Wales into his embrace.[6] The poet Alun Lewis, in the early 1940s, a time when death appeared to be in the ascendant, noted: 'Death the wild beast is uncaught, untamed . . . but . . . our soul withstands the terror'.[7] Waldo Williams in 'Mewn Dau Gae' portrayed death as 'yr heliwr distaw yn bwrw ei rwyd amdanom' (the silent huntsman casting his net over us).[8] To Tom Parri Jones in his poem 'Angau' (Death), death's carriage still had about it 'aroglau'r oesau' (the scents of the ages), but it was now a Saturday night taxi, whose monosyllabic driver, quietly took his fares to 'Dim . . . Dim' (Nothing . . . Nothing).[9] R. Williams Parry also considered that death was a journey conducted by 'hen gychwr afon angau' (the old boatsman of death's river).[10] Edward Jones (1826–1891), Glasfryn, in 'Dyfodiad Angau', portrayed death as a stealthy, sudden, gentle killer – 'ni edwyn neb ei nodau na sŵn ei droed yn nesáu' (no one recognises his sound or his footstep as he nears).[11] Death might still be loathsome, his visage grim, his embrace terminal, but he now trod lightly.

Popular beliefs presented a plethora of portents of death that ranged from the relatively timid to the terrifying. 'Y Tolaeth' described both the plaintive wail that was heard before a child's death, and the knocking heard in a carpenter's shop before the commission was received to build a coffin. Across Wales, unctions of undertakers received such ghostly commissions. 'Canhwyllau Cyrff' were nightly, ghostly lights that preceded a funeral, marking out the route that a cortège would take in a few days. The 'Toili' were phantom funerals. 'Y Cyhyraeth' were an inhuman, chilling chorus that were encountered at crossroads. Beasts and birds were often death's messengers. The 'aderyn corff', an ashen coloured bird, with 'eyes like balls of fire' traumatised the tender souls of Llanddeiniol in Cardiganshire in 1911.[12] More terrifying were vicious spirit dogs that assumed many forms and answered to many names – 'Cŵn Bendith y Mamau', 'Helgŵn Cythreulig', 'Cŵn Annwn', 'Cŵn Cyrff', 'Cŵn Uffern', 'Y Gwyllgi', or 'Ci Mawr Du'.[13] These fearful hounds hunted the spirits of wicked people, dragging them to the infernal halls of the lower regions. Such curious incidents of dogs at night-time were relatively common, especially in the early part of our period down to the First World War. But in some places, somewhere around that time, many people's belief in such supernatural phenomena began to unravel.

The silent statistics tabulated in the annual report of the Registrar General of Births, Deaths and Marriages provide empirical evidence of the poetic domestication of death and the ebbing of belief in a supernatural fauna.[14] The 'crude death rate' (per 1,000 deaths) in Wales, in 1871, stood at 21.2. By 1914, it had declined to 14.5, and by 1948, it had fallen again to 11.8. There were years, such as 1915, during the Great War, and 1918, when the flu pandemic swept across the world, when the rates rose to 15.4 and 16.5.[15] In these grievous years, the Grim Reaper seemed to have resumed his conscientious harvesting, but over time, rates of mortality were reassuringly in decline.

The infant mortality rates, generally considered to be the most accurate reflection of the health of people and populations, were also improving.[16] In 1871, the rate of infant mortality in Wales stood at 126.2 per 1,000 births. By 1914 it had declined to 110. In 1948, the rate had fallen further to 39 per 1,000 births. Again there were individual years when, due to various diseases and epidemics, the rate jumped suddenly upwards against the general pattern of decline over time. In 1886–7 it increased to 131.7. In 1891 it suddenly, inexplicably leaped upwards to 150.1. In 1899, following 1898 – that year of depression, distress and discontent in the Welsh coalfields – the massacre of the innocents reassumed its early Victorian levels and reached 174 per 1,000 births.[17]

It should not be forgotten that the infant mortality rate refers to live births. No one knows the extent of stillbirths, or the horribly named and emotionally traumatic 'lifeless births', and the deaths of children in de facto marriages. The latter were, by definition, illegitimate and unregistered, beyond the reach of registrar or historian.[18] Illegitimate children were doomed.[19] The fate of such infants casts an unhappy light on 'the age of progress'. Death in childbirth was a pervasive fear, which shadowed a mother's joy at the possibility of bringing new life into the world and even darkened young women's prospective views of marriage. Many women never gave birth to a child, but died in the agony of the effort, perhaps the most aggravated of circumstances in which a woman can leave the world. In 1937 the government's report into the *Maternal Mortality in Wales* revealed levels of death that were a 'disgrace to a civilized society.'[20] In 1899, when giving birth to her third child, Margaret Lloyd of Llanddewi Brefi contracted septicaemia and died. Aged three weeks and named for her, Margaret Ann Davies was baptised on her mother Margaret's coffin on the day of her funeral in Bethesda Chapel.[21] The artist Christopher Williams was also baptised on his mother's coffin.

The Registrar General's tables of statistics reveal that one of the most fundamental transformations that has ever taken place in Welsh history occurred during the period 1870–1945. Over these years, despite all the sorrow and suffering, it is a salient fact that people's life expectancy almost doubled. In 1871, the average life expectancy for a male who had survived the Herodian years of youth was 39. By 1951, the average male, if there is such a person, now had a far better chance of surviving childhood and could expect to live to 69.5 years of age. Women, society's survivors, had the expectation of living for at least five years longer. For a significant proportion of the population, the Psalmist's promise that 'the days of our age are threescore years and ten' had at last been honoured.[22]

It is important to note that the rates of death and infant mortality in Wales continued to be far worse than they were across the border in England and even, on occasion, in the poorest parts of Ireland or Scotland.[23] Comparisons over time and across different geographic areas reveal profound differences and inequalities in the rates in Wales. There were generational and geographic, status and social factors that affected how individuals experienced these demographic changes. Food, space and time, the prerogatives of the rich, helped to keep death at bay. But for the poor, in their over-crowded, single-roomed rural cottages and sunless, stinking urban hovels, there was little defence from cold and hunger, those indefatigable generals in Death's dark armies. Death had a close alliance with poverty.

Different places had different experiences. The Gwyrfai area in north Wales had more than its fair share of death as consumption, diphtheria, scarlet fever and typhoid ravaged the community. In some families siblings disappeared into thin air or thick earth with distressing rapidity. In Builth, in 1871, the town's crude death rate stood at 17 per 1,000. Just thirty miles south at Merthyr Tydfil, in the same year, it was 29. In that same year, despite the improvements of the mid-nineteenth century, more than one third of all deaths in Wales were still those of children. And what can we say of those unfortunate people and places whose sombre ill-luck weights down the figures to these averages? Proverbs with an egalitarian cynicism warned 'Heddiw yn frenin, yfori yn farw' (today a king, tomorrow dead) and 'y tlawd a'r cyfoethog sydd gydradd yn y bedd' (rich and poor are equal in the grave).[24] But death's carriage, despite all the portrayals of the driver as even-handed, treating rich and poor alike, still gathered his fares more regularly from cottage than castle. Nevertheless, during the lifespan of a single individual, Wales experienced a profound demographic revolution.

Death remained inevitable, but it had shed the terrifying imminence that it carried in the mid-nineteenth century. Fictional encounters with death were frequent in crime novels and in cinematic detective films, but in real life death was more infrequently encountered. Death remained vigilant, ever-ready, but now, perhaps, appeared to be more patient, unhurried. This had far-reaching effects on the Welsh people and their cultural, emotional and spiritual lives. The fact that death's sting was softened, that the grave's victory was postponed, was a vital element in the ebbing of the sea of faith. With death less frequent and fearful, it became increasingly difficult for people to believe in the dire warnings of the fate of lost souls. Placards carried by 'Wil Salvation' around Caernarfon in the 1930s still drew their inspiration from Luke and warned 'Repent o ye sinners' and 'Prepare to meet thy doom'. But the sense of urgency was less intense than it had been before 1870.

The traditional Christian belief, that because mankind was sinful, then it followed that life had to be a vale of tears, lost much of its credibility. The fires of hell cooled without the stokers of old. Such changes concerned the more serious-minded. Gladstone, the

Flintshire-based Prime Minister, so beloved by the Welsh, worriedly asked, 'What would happen to morality if terror was removed?'[25] It is impossible to quantify spiritual fear, the registers in which the statistics are recorded are not accessible to the earthly historian, but all the qualitative evidence suggests that it declined over the period 1870–1945.[26] Satan's empire crumbled in a similar and simultaneous process to the collapse of the Ottoman Empire. Superstition also suffered, for without terror or fear, it was difficult for people to believe in supernatural phenomena, and, without belief, people no longer saw the ghostly legions. Demographic changes had a profound role in the disenchantment of the world, the dechristianisation and desacralisation of Wales.[27]

Behind the sensitivities of the poets and the statistics of the demographers, we can discern hints that people's life experiences were assuming new forms. In the mid-nineteenth century, emotional bonds within families, especially between parents and children, had strengthened, but they were reinforced in the years from 1870 to 1945.[28] The death of a child came now to be regarded as a relatively rare occurrence, one that cut across the grain of nature and humanity. Poets reflected the change in sensitivities and sensibilities. In the mid-nineteenth century, especially in the works of the 'graveyard poets', there was a stoical acceptance of death, even of the very, very young that is shocking to modern sensibilities. The denominational press, periodicals such as *Y Goleuad, Y Tyst, Seren Gomer, Y Wawrddydd* are brimful of obituaries of those who died in the spring of their lives with a precocious piety. In many of these tragic reports of truncated lives, death was not so much the end as the beginning. Christian belief as fostered by countless sermons and services indicated that death was to be welcomed as the gateway to eternal euphoria and ecstasy. Holy lives led to happy deaths.[29] Not only were such deaths less sorrowful, they were also less fearful. Blessed spirits, as the children's illustrated books and the stained-glass windows of Sir Edward Burne-Jones showed, had chubby, cherubic angels to gently lead them into eternity.[30]

Despite its morbid subject matter, Ellen Egryn's poem of 1855, 'Cwynfan Mam: Ar ôl ei dwy ferch a fuont farw yn ieuainc' (A mother's cry after her two daughters who died young), is joyous, for Ellen Egryn, the bereaved mother, decides to rejoice rather than indulge remorse or regret.[31] By 1941, Dylan Thomas in 'A refusal to mourn the death, by fire, of a child in London' provides an alternative view. To Dylan Thomas, youthful death was an obscenity, the cause of heartbreak not happiness.[32] The iconography of the age changed. The Victorians took not only their name from a death-obsessed sovereign in her widow's weeds, they also derived their image as a people locked in a bible-black, protracted mourning. Manufacturers of lace, silk and taffeta breathed a collective sigh of relief when the Edwardians and Georgians rediscovered fashion, fun and flash – colour was the new black.

A new attitude towards childhood took root in the period 1870–1945. The concept that childhood was a sheltered period of ten or twelve years developed.[33] The cult of childhood emerged almost simultaneously to the evolution of Christmas into a commercial festival. Children's literature developed. Moelona's *Teulu Bach Nantoer* (1913) was perhaps the most famous evocation of the Arcadian, rustic Welsh childhood. There is an additional poignancy in that so many of those authors who looked back on these years considered them to be an idyll, the lost paradise of their childhood – an idyllic, idealised illusion.

All experience, of course, is relative, but even the darkest historical periods were a golden age for some. Older writers like Gwyn Thomas and D. Gwenallt Jones remembered the 1930s as the grim time of economic depression, but for the younger Leslie Norris, they were simply the Edenic years of childhood. 'I'm glad I knew the world when it was innocent and golden' he later wrote.[34] In the early 1870s, children did not stay long at the parental hearth, for poverty forced children as young as seven or eight years of age to go out to work, often having lost either one or both parents.[35] By 1945, legislation on compulsory education necessitated that children did not, usually, go to work until at least fourteen or fifteen years of age. Following childhood, a new intermediate period of adolescence emerged, in which youth were given an additional opportunity to mould their persona and personality before entering the adult world with all its woes and worries.[36]

In the mid-nineteenth century, many marriage partners were relatively swiftly parted by death. By 1945, lower death rates for adults and improvements in maternal mortality meant that fewer marriages were broken by the premature demise of one partner. More grandparents, old, brown and wrinkled in the countryside, work-scarred in the coalfields, survived to assist with the care of children. The 'traditional' three-generation family had long been celebrated with saccharine clichés in Welsh prose and poetry as the ideal social unit, but in truth, it was a relatively recent phenomenon. Family affections were deepening. Lawrence Stone's concept of the rise of an 'affective individualism' was probably more relevant to the years 1870–1945 than the early-modern period.[37] Society became less crude, gradually even affording more rights, reason and responsibilities to women. The aged were being accorded some more respect, and for their part, were beginning to insist on living their lives right through, seeking enjoyment and trying to be useful to the end of their days.

Old-age pensions from 1911, paltry though they were, eased some financial pressures.[38] The proportion of the elderly in the population rose. The 1911 census indicated that under 7 per cent of the population were old (over sixty years of age). By 1931 this had risen to 9.6 per cent, and by 1951 rose again to 13.6 per cent. Such longevity was not without its problems as the young had to wait longer to inherit family fortunes or farms. Hence, perhaps, the explanation for all those funeral jokes about the quiet satisfaction of heirs and young widows who were not inconsolable.

More profoundly, perhaps, a new notion that a person could expect to live for a standard life span took root in this period. The old sense of continuous uncertainty and limited expectations of life were gradually eroded over the years from 1870 to 1945. People still had to harden themselves to sickness, pain, disability and premature aging. Even the rich were no strangers to tragedy. Gwendoline and Margaret Davies, undoubtedly the richest women in Wales, perhaps in Europe, lost their mother in their infancy and their father in their early teenage years.[39] Those living on the margins of society and survival, especially the illegitimate and the ill, were exceptionally vulnerable. Stoicism remained strong,

but from around the turn of the twentieth century, people abandoned the fatalism in the face of death that had been so characteristic of earlier generations. Senescence rather than sudden demise
became more common as the cause of death. This, of course, is
not to deny Death's power to disrupt and destroy. Some individuals, such as the writer Caradog Prichard, who had suffered
a traumatic childhood in the shadow of suicide, depression and
war, had a morbid obsession with death.[40] David Rees Griffiths
(Amanwy, 1882–1953), attained an astounding level of grandeur
in bereavement, having lost his brother, wife and son within a
brief period of time.[41] Disease, disasters and the destructive forces
of war could still wreak havoc on humanity, but many people
were aware that their odds of survival were higher than they had
been in their parents' youth.[42]

'The last dance': grief and ars moriendi (the art of dying)

Wedi'r chwarae daw'r gaeaf
(After play comes winter)

> Quoted in Alan Llwyd, *Bob: Cofiant R. Williams Parry*
> (Llandysul, 2013), p. 177.

'Grief', a statue by William Goscombe John (1860–1952), who
sculpted so many of the heroes and heroines of the Welsh past,
is located in the cemetery at St Brynach's, Llanboidy.[43] It com-
memorates the life of W. R. H. Powell (1819–89), that remarkable
bundle of sensations – an Anglican, a landowner, master of fox-
hounds, horse rider and racer, and one of the greatest of Welsh
radicals.[44] From the marble John released the angelic form of a
distraught young girl. Stricken by death's impact, by the shock
and the sorrow, the sylphean figure turns her back to the viewer
so she can indulge her tears. It is the silent language of grief.
Helpless and hopeless, she is caught in the eternal present – the
exact moment at which Miss Havisham touches all the clocks.
Grief, the figure in the rippling marble seems to suggest, is private.
It cannot be shared. Everyone carries it alone.

The long goodbye – the journey of an individual from life to death and of kith and kin from prescience to grief and grieving, was both intensely private and immediately public. Death, like birth, was an immensely important fact in the lives of communities and a whole range of behaviours and beliefs became associated with it. Only the abject and the abandoned went unaccompanied to 'death's great adventure'.[45] Members of the whole community would extend their support and sympathy to the bereft and bereaved, for although death is such a personal tragedy, it is also 'the sorrow of all people'.[46] At times of death community support was often at its strongest. People were at their most sympathetic and generous. There was gracious giving of money and clothes, cakes, advice, consolation and time. Time for people to sit with the dying, to sit all night with the dead and with the bereaved. Time to 'wylio' (watch over) the dead with dignity.

Grief unassuaged and unappeased was a powerful force within Welsh society. The deaths of siblings gave rise in some people to a survivor's guilt and a bitterness that curdled, becoming septic and painful, rather than universal and poetic. The novelist Kate Roberts began to write after the death of her youngest brother, David, in an army hospital in Malta, in 1917. A fickle fate is one of the strongest characters in her works, especially those set in childhood, such as *Deian a Loli* (1927) and *Laura Jones* (1930).[47] A sense of sibling loss permeates many of the writings of Dylan Thomas, for an unnamed stillborn male child had been born to his parents ten years before Dylan.[48] Caradog Prichard also suffered an element of 'survivor guilt' within his complex psychology. Before his birth, his parents lost the five-week old William, and three years later lost Howell, a stillborn child. Both haunt Caradog's autobiographical *Afal Drwg Adda* and his later writings.[49]

Parents were also exposed to tortuous grief. The novelist Jack Jones, of the Rhondda, lost his son, Lawrence, in action in 1942, his wife Laura in 1946 and his son David in 1948.[50] The Calvinistic Methodist minister John Thomas Job (1867–1938), lost his first wife Etta and three infant children. He married again in 1915 and had two children with Catherine Shaw of Denbigh, one of whom died. Moral evaluations of death did not help the guilt of siblings who survived. *The Goleuad* in January 1872 carried a spiteful obituary of the alcoholic Lord Brinckman of Llansantffraid who would go on week-long binges on brandy. Amy Dillwyn (1845–1935), the Swansea industrialist, suffered great mental trauma when her brother Henry, the possessor of 'a Rabelasian thirst' died drunk and dissipated in 1890.[51] Henry's death, or rather his suicide by drinking, was considered shameful, a 'bad death', a 'valueless death'. The costs and humiliations people suffered after the deaths of their loved ones influenced Amy to establish the Mourning Reform Society and to campaign for the ending of some burial customs.

The Welsh often had plenty of warning of impending death so that they could prepare their souls, for the journey from here to eternity. Corpse candles were ghostly nightly lights, widely believed to have been sent by St David. These followed the route a funeral cortège would take later. If the lights did not shine then 'y ci corff' (corpse dog), 'y cyhyraeth', 'y tolaeth', or the 'aderyn corff' (corpse bird) would warn of death's approach and where the Angel would blow the trumpet.[52] Miners at Llanbradach in 1901 recalled, after a disaster in their pit, that a robin had been seen underground a few days before and regretted that more workers should have heeded the omen and stayed at home.[53]

There were strict procedures to follow by the living to ensure that the dead's journey to the other world was trouble free. Crying too soon was problematic. Folk-belief warned that the Devil's dogs lay in wait for passing souls and might be roused from their sleep by premature wailing and weeping. Once the body was laid out then the mourning could become vocal. In south Cardiganshire, north Pembrokeshire and west Carmarthenshire it was said that a person who had died suddenly had gone 'rhwng llaw a llawes' (between hand and sleeve). It is difficult to imagine a more graphic presentation of the sharpness, the instantaneousness of the moment of death. And maybe the departed went on his way to 'seler rhosto' (the roasting cellar). To guard the soul, a 'gŵyl nos' (watch night), would be held that could range from the religious to the raucous. In Denbighshire they would be called 'cyfarfod galar' (mourning meeting), whilst the people of the Vale of Ceiriog went to 'coffa am y marw' – to remember the dead. At a Llandysul gwylnos in 1907, one informant felt that the thatched roof of the house itself was vibrating with the fervour of the praying and singing of the religious gathering. In contrast, at Margam mourners complained 'it wasn't much use as a wake – there wasn't anybody crying there'.[54]

The extent and elaboration of funerals had grown steadily since 1870. The family vigil over a corpse, in a bedroom transformed by candles and black drapes into a *chapelle ardente*; the coffin, in oak, sometimes in ebony or mahogany and ivory; the dark plumed horses and the hearse; the mourning clothes and the black shoes, everything new and stiff and creaking; but all expensive. It was an observation, often voiced in jest, but with a strong element of deeper truth, that Welsh funerals were more memorable for the food and the finery than for their words of spiritual fervour.

Departure from life was naturally described in the idioms of the departed's work. The quarryman would have 'rhoi'i gerrig i fyny' (given up the stone), a miner would have 'doti'i dŵls ar y bar' (put his tools on the bar), whilst a seaman would have 'wedi coelo'r rhaff' (had coiled the rope). These were not occasions for a stoic and silent response but for wholesale weeping and wailing. The doctor Francis Maylett Smith recalled the shrieks that greeted the death of a young man that filled the entire street in Aberffrwd.[55] At Senghennydd in 1901 and 1913 eye-witnesses of the aftermath of the disasters were struck by the noise from the women and children when the extent of the losses were realised.[56]

On occasions of mass public death, as Ken Etheridge (1911–81) noted in his 1940 poem 'Blades in the flag', 'the cross of custom held us'.[57] Customs, rites and rituals that gathered around funerals were the way the living learnt to cope with death. 'Cynhebrwng blêr, cynhebrwng buan' (an untidy funeral, another one soon) and the belief that if any person walked alone in funeral procession he or she would be the next to be buried, encouraged mourners to observe protocol and to walk in order. The order for the cortège of the Revd J. Jones Talsarn in 1877 was impressive:

Y meddygon – 8 mewn nifer
65 o Weinidogion a Phregethwyr – bob yn dri,
70 o flaenoriaid – bob yn bedwar,
200 o gantorion a chantoresau – bob yn chwech;
Oddeutu 4,000 o feibion ac o ferched – bob yn chwech.
Yna yr allorgerbyd
Y perthnasau mewn 40 o gerbydau, ac ar 15 o feirch.
Canwyd yr emynau canlynol ar y ffordd o Dalysarn i Lanllyfni:
    'Mae 'nghyfeillion wedi ngadael'
    'O ddydd i ddydd, o awr i awr'
    'Mae'r brawd wedi gorffen ei daith'
    'Yn y dyfroedd mawr a'r tonnau'
    'Ymado wnaf o'r babell'.[58]

(Doctors – 8 in number
65 ministers and preachers – 3 abreast,
70 deacons – 4 abreast;
200 singers – 6 abreast;
About 4,000 men and women – 6 abreast
Then the hearse
Relatives in 40 carriages and 15 on horseback.
The following hymns were sung between Talysarn and Llanllyfni:
    'My friends have gone . . .'
    'From day to day, from hour to hour'
    'Our brother has finished his journey'
    'In the deep waters and waves'
    'I now leave the tent'.)

The funeral of that rare combination of coal owner and eisteddfodwr David Williams (Alaw Goch, 1809–63), drew similar crowds who had to be ranked and regimented.[59] Tailors and milliners, shoe-makers and florists had a great time, even the undertaker was happy. At Rhyl in the 1870s, funeral processions were organised by J. B. Williams, draper, and T. Hughes, clothier.[60] To help boost attendance at his funeral, Solomon Andrews (1835–1908), the Cardiff and Pwllheli businessman, offered any of his employees who attended the tempting inducement of either a new suit, or an overcoat or a new pair of shoes. With slow solemn steps, funerals would inch ceremoniously to the cemetery, a crowd all-heads-bowed in creaking and crunching new shoes. Black shoes were perhaps more important than the suit, for they were all one saw with one's head down. Such dynamic performances with the plangent marching bands, all bugles and brass solemnly blowing, served a deeper function for they emphasised both the ritualistic and the imperialistic traits of the Welsh. One such remarkable event was the internment of Mr and Mrs Powell and their son John in the family vault at Bassaleg church near Newport. The three had been massacred in 1869 in Abyssinia and their remains had, eventually, been gathered together and placed in a single coffin. Though the funeral was strictly private, a large crowd gathered that was inevitable in Victorian Wales, for people were morbidly obsessed with death and incorrigibly inquisitive. The reporter in the *Western Mail* took comfort in the fact that the tribe who had perpetuated the 'barbarous outrage' had been 'annihilated'.[61]

The journey from the corpse's secular to sacred space, from deathbed to the dormitory of Christians, was often too long for the mourners to cover on foot. In 1876 the family and friends of Sir James Hills Johnes marched through the town of Pumsaint, but retired to carriages for the journey to the cemetery at Caio church. The fact that Sir John had been murdered by his butler, Henry Tremble, generated considerable interest and swelled the crowds so that the entire neighbourhood was represented.[62] Walking side-by-solemn-side with the coffin might have been wiser for mourners of John Batchelor ('the friend of freedom') for his motorised hearse crashed into a lamppost in Penarth on the way to his funeral. The saga of Jane Pysgotwr's funeral procession in 1876, over eighteen miles of barren land between Llanddewi Brefi and Llanddewi Abergwesyn with only thirty stalwart bearers, still lives on in local folk memory. The bearers carried her over moor and down and up mountain paths, through the two rivers Doethïe and the Towy, to the remote chapel at Soar-y-Mynydd.[63] On occasion women would act as bearers, as at the funeral of a young maiden in March 1914 and in parts of Carmarthenshire in 1898, when young women 'threw their shawls over their shoulders as a cushion under the bier'.[64] The labour involved in carrying the coffin meant that many journeys were often thirsty occasions. Whilst carrying Twm Sion Pritchard of Tal-y-Waun, Monmouth, the bearers stopped at the St Illtyd Inn, where, despite the protestations of the vicar, they stayed for the night.

These via dolorosa, the ways of sorrow of Welsh history, were legion for people made the greatest efforts to attend a funeral to show their sympathy, solidarity and support. Attendance meant everything. Perhaps the most remarkable journey to a funeral was that of Owen Lloyd George (1924–2010) to attend his grandfather David's wartime interment in March 1945. Churchill determined that all four of his old friend's grandsons in the services should be brought home to attend the funeral in north Wales. One was fighting near the Rhine, another was flying a bomber, a third was serving on the HMS *Enterprise* in the North Sea, and the fourth, Owen, was fighting in Italy. Owen was at once dispatched to Naples by fighter plane, given a bed in Field Marshall Alexander's villa, flown by bomber to England the next morning, whisked up to north Wales in a Spitfire (flown by a Polish pilot with only a schoolboy atlas to help) and arrived at Llanystumdwy one hour before the funeral.

Colliery disasters created a host of problems in dealing with the sheer volume of bodies. Management and men of the Albion Colliery, Cilfynydd were presented with a host of logistical problems following an explosion on 23 June 1894, which killed 290 miners.[65] There were not enough pall-bearers for the funerals. There was no room in the cemetery. A team of forty workmen from the Albion Colliery was sent to dig graves in the Llanfabon churchyard, in the section of the cemetery across the road from the church that was speedily and specially sanctified for burials. Seven bodies were sent from the village by train to north Wales for burial in their home villages and two were dispatched to Strata Florida in Cardiganshire. Another group of miners set to work burying the 118 horses that had died. Moriah Welsh Congregational Chapel had lost forty of its members. One hundred miles away the body of Richard Jones from Penparc, Cardigan, arrived for burial barely two weeks since he left home to commence work at the Albion Colliery. Insurance agents and representatives of the Miners' Provident Fund worked overtime to help the bereaved meet the costs of the funerals.

Inquests were urgently held, 242 bodies were relatively swiftly identified. The urgency was intensified by the fact that this was one of the hottest summers for several years. The heat accelerated the process of decomposition and the stench became unbearable. Thus eleven unidentified bodies were hastily buried in Llanfabon.[66] In addition, fifteen other victims were buried together in the church-yard, attended by a crowd of more than 500.

That final expression of camaraderie became a deeply emotional custom amongst Welsh workers. Those who were taken away by the continual 'drip, drip of death' were accompanied on their final journey by miners and iron workers and quarrymen. In the mines and quarries it became an established custom that workers would finish early and sacrifice a day's pay in order to attend the funeral of a colleague who had died at work. A bitter dispute took place in May 1937 when the Powell Duffryn Company went against protocol and common decency and fired seven men who, they claimed, had taken unauthorised leave of absence to attend the funeral of a fellow workman. When another collier died in the Bwllfa No. 1 Colliery, 600 men, in defiance of the owners, finished work early and attended the funeral.[67] In contrast to such solidarity of sympathy, there were cruel boycotts of the funerals of 'blacklegs' who had broken a strike.[68] This was even, on occasion, taken to the extreme of defacing the gravestone of a person who had returned to work. To paraphrase one of the slogans of the 1900–3 north Wales slate quarry strike, 'nid oes bradwr yn y fynwent hon' (there is no traitor in this cemetery).

Celebrity status served to swell the crowds at funerals. One of the largest gatherings in Welsh history was the funeral of the world-renowned boxer 'Peerless' James (Jim) Driscoll in 1925. At Aberdare, one of the largest funerals was that of the four-times world champion, the professional cyclist Arthur Linton in 1896. Those without such local or national celebrity could utilise other strategies to ensure a well-attended funeral. Even so, Ellis Pierce (Ellis o'r Nant, 1841–1912) chose a somewhat unusual practice of inviting people to his own funeral in 1912.[69]

The most famous or infamous act in Welsh death customs took place on 13 January 1884 at Llantrisant.[70] Two men walking home saw a fire in the fields owned by the eccentric medic Dr William Price. They went over to discover that Dr Price, clad in a white robe, his hair and beard streaming in the wind, arms outstretched as if on a crucifix, was chanting a lament in his version of druidic, ancient Welsh. Before him a cask of paraffin oil was on fire. Within it was a baby's corpse wrapped in napkins. News of the macabre events swept through the village swifter than a politician with good news. People streamed to the scene, many of whom shouted, 'Let us burn the old devil'.[71] The body in the burning barrel was that of Dr Price's son, provocatively and blasphemously named Iesu Grist (Jesus Christ) whom he claimed was the next Messiah. Price was arrested and charged at Cardiff at the winter assizes of 1884 for the crime of cremation. The jury found him not guilty. The trial and Judge Fitzjames Stephen's judgement effectively established the legality of cremation in Britain.

The judgement was hailed by promotors of cremation, but Price's actions were motivated not by concerns of hygienic disposal of a body, but by his druidic beliefs. Price was renowned both for his eccentricity and his originality. He believed that patients should only pay if one's health was restored. He rejected conventional medicines as poisons, and condemned vaccination. A nudist, a vegetarian, Price refused to treat smokers and had highly un-orthodox views on marriage and death.[72] In his late eighties he fathered three children with his young housekeeper in their 'druidic marriage'. After a glass of champagne, he died on 23 January 1893 in relative poverty, having made detailed arrangements for his body to be cremated in a brick kiln with cast-iron sheeting on Cae'r Lan fields where he had earlier burnt Iesu Grist. An estimated 4,000 people gathered to see the event that was undertaken under the supervision of the local police. Commemorative items, such as plates, ballads and handkerchiefs were sold.[73]

Cremation was promoted as a more hygienic and eco-friendly means of disposing of corpses. Yet the practice was slow to advance and be adopted. Even after the superstitious concerns as to how a cremated body would enter the afterworld were countered by ministers and preachers, cremation remained a relatively rare occurrence. One of the first instances in Wales took place in the late 1890s at the isolation hospital at Flat Holm island, when the body of a victim of bubonic plague was burnt. The first Welsh crematorium opened appropriately enough at Pontypridd but not until 1924.

'Y Tlawd a'r cyfoethog, sydd gydradd yn y bedd' (rich and poor people are equal in the grave) was the claim of the cautionary proverb, but one only needed to visit a Welsh graveyard to see the falsity of the claim.[74] Death was no leveller down in the catacombs and the cemeteries. Earthly power, wealth, religion, sex and professional status were even more rigidly distinguished in the realms of the dead than in the world of the living. The poor lay un-noted, unmarked in the overgrown corners of graveyards, many people rested under weathered plain grey slate gravestones, but a few lay under monuments reflecting a medley of architectural styles. Sir John Morris Jones (1864–1929), the grammarian, and Sir William T. Lewis (1837–1914), the imperious coal owner, both lie under towering Celtic crosses. Across Wales Roman sarcophagi, gothic shrines, Egyptian tombs hold the remains of the once famous or fabulously wealthy. Many are guarded by a legion of angels, muses and pretty neoclassical weepers wringing their hands and staring to heaven, their strong air of pathos only a little reduced by incontinent pigeons. Many individuals were and are, remembered in bas relief carvings of themselves on their graves. William Williams (Caledfryn, 1801–69) stares out from bas relief at Greenacre cemetery in Caerphilly. Griffith Rhys Jones (Caradog, 1834–97), the blacksmith, publican, businessman, conman and conductor who gave Wales the name 'Gwlad y Gân' (the Land of Song), stares out between two guardian angels at Aberdare cemetery. In Criccieth cemetery, Mair Lloyd George (1890–1907) stares out from pristine Portland stone. The death of his favourite child at a precociously young age deeply affected Lloyd George. His emotional outpourings of grief and deepest mourning seemed to question the supposed relationship of heroic, stoic, masculinity and death.[75] Other people lie under statues of themselves that tower over the other tenants of the cemetery – that of David James in Strata Florida seems to tower over the church and the ruins of the abbey as well.

Some graveyards resembled tawdry souvenir shops, redolent of Rome, with their pottery roses frozen under glass domes, paper lilies, gold-sprayed Christs, china bibles with gilt-edged pages, cherubs, angels and all the aristocracy of heaven and all the bric-à-brac of belief.[76] Women went to the cemetery not just to cry over the dead, but to reminisce, to remember, to pay respect. To the delight of local florists, Flowering Sunday, Easter, Christmas, the deceased's birthday were the occasions when they bought bunches of flowers to carry to the graves. If the doom-laden preachers were to be believed, then such women were risking their lives in the cemeteries, not just from coughs, cold and chills, but from the imminent earthquake that would shatter the graveyards of the Seions, the Bethels, the Elims. The theology of death was stark. The grave welcomed good souls. From here they patiently waited for their transfer to paradise. But for evil souls the grave, warned the theologians, was a dark, lonely place inhabited by maggots, beetles and worms. Fearful fallen angels and demons would sweep the wicked on their downward journey through the warming circles of hell.

Death certainly brought together some strange resting fellows. In the cemetery at Menai Bridge, the archdruid, the poet Cynan lies alongside John Evans, fondly known as 'Y Bardd Cocos', the author of doggerel.[77] It was intended that Cathays cemetery would be 'the principal walk of the inhabitants of Cardiff', a theatre not just for increasingly elaborate funerals but for new rituals of memorial visiting.[78] The great mining, shipbuilding, shipowning and business dynasties – the Corys, the Tatems, the Reardon Smiths – are all present, many under obelisks and statues of impressive grandeur. Sportsmen here are legion and legendary – the boxers James Driscoll and Jack Petersen, and the aeronaut Louisa Maud Evans, the fourteen-year-old servant with Hancock's circus who was blown out over the Britsol Channel and drowned. Here lies the novelist and hymnist Thomas Rowland Hughes (1903–49), whose great hymn 'Tydi a roddaist liw i'r wawr, a hud i'r machlud mwyn' (Thou gavest colour to the dawning and enchantment to the gentle setting sun) gave such plangency to so many Welsh funerals. Here too lies, under a formidable granite obelisk, the indomitable and incorrigible Jack Matthews, owner of a string of brothels.[79] The earth at Trealaw cemetery must be anything but quiet. For here lies the socialist, the fiercely anti-communist and much decorated war hero David Watts Morgan MC, DSO, CBE, MP, JP (1867–1933), cruelly caricatured as 'Dai Alphabet', and the communist agitator and novelist Lewis Jones (1897–1939). How appropriate, then, that here too rests James Kitchener Davies (1902–1952), author of one of the greatest Welsh poems of the twentieth century, 'Sŵn y gwynt sy'n chwythu' (the sound of the wind that's blowing).

Some chose to avoid the ecumenicalism of death and be buried with kindred souls and spirits, as are many of the Jews of Wales in a special cemetery at Cefn-coed-y-cymer. Ann Jones of Glandenys, Lampeter, lies not with her husband William in Lampeter churchyard, but on the mountainside above with Edward Hesketh Formby in 'The Lover's Grave', with spectacular views of the verdant countryside.[80] Auguste Guyard (1809–82), the French social reformer and friend of Lamartine, had to flee France after the Franco-Russian War. He found asylum at Barmouth and lies in a grave high on the surrounding hills, enjoying spectacular views of the coast. William Charles Wynn, 4th Baron Newborough (1873–1916), died as the result of wounds or a chill acquired in the trenches of France, but left instructions in his will that he be buried on a bluff at the top of the family's estate at Llanffestiniog, 'from which spot is my favourite view of the Vale of Ffestiniog.'[81]

Charles Wynn was invalided home where he died from injuries or an illness contracted in the First World War, but one of the greatest problems of the war was what to do with all the bodies. In the early months, debate centred on whether the bodies should be repatriated and buried at home, or whether they should be interred in communal burial grounds so that the band of brothers of battle remained united in death.[82] The exhumation, repatriation and reburial of William Glynne Charles Gladstone MP, the twenty-nine-year-old grandson of Prime Minister W. E. Gladstone, master of Hawarden Castle and Lord Lieutenant of Flintshire, was the case that hardened the resolve of the Imperial War Graves Commission that the bodies should remain together.[83] Gladstone was a lieutenant in the Royal Welch Fusiliers and was honest enough to admit that he had no talent for fighting – 'heaven knows, so far from having the least inclination for military drive, I dread it and dislike it intensely.'[84] Robert Graves claimed that Gladstone only volunteered because his tenants had threatened to throw him in the duck pond if he did not.[85] Once at the front, the story rapidly unfolded with a poignant inevitability that makes it a minor classic of its kind. William Gladstone inherited the very tall genes of his grandfather, but not his elasticity of conscience, for he went to war from a strong sense of duty, despite knowing that he was temperamentally unsuited for it. He was shot in the head by a German sniper.

In life, William Gladstone made little impact on the Army. His death, however, had a profound effect. The family used their considerable influence and appealed to the King to have the body exhumed from the mass grave into which it had been placed and brought home. 'With full military honours, Will was laid to rest by the side of his father in the quiet churchyard of Hawarden'.[86] This despite the fact that no other bodies were brought home, that a ban had been placed on battle-front exhumations and that the burial party who exhumed the body did so under enemy fire. Privilege and position it seemed, were more important than the democratic notion that the dead, officers and men, should lie together. Before the full impact of the mass mechanical slaughter of the trenches from mid-1915 onwards made it impractical to repatriate bodies, the death of William Gladstone, on 11 April 1915, made it impossible.

When the guns finally fell silent on the eleventh hour of the eleventh day of the eleventh month of 1918, those who had lost loved ones in the war were presented with the problem of having no visible, visitable memorial on home soil.[87] Thus communities began to establish communal war memorials to commemorate and ensure their heroes would not be forgotten. Sculptors, carvers and monumental masons had a busy and profitable time in the 1920s carving the memorials to the glorious dead. The war memorials are the most remarkable public artistic achievement of Wales. There is no music hall sentimentality, no hackneyed glory of the dead or histrionic sacrifice in these monuments. The statues, invariably of soldiers, are engaged in the business of soldiering as they were in life. In the freshness of a nation's sorrow, sculptors, architects and artists created works notable for their simplicity and honesty, timeless items that would not grow old as other art grows old. In most villages a lone soldier stands sentinel above a list of war dead carved in marble or white Portland stone, vigilantly awaiting the last trumpet. William Goscombe John, the sculptor, became the national remembrancer, creating a number of iconic statues.[88]

Probably the most remarkable war memorial in Wales, perhaps in western Europe, is the Aberystwyth town war memorial. On a perilous rock high above the wave-lashed and windswept promenade, two female figures are suspended. They are the work of the Italian sculptor Professor Mario Rutelli of Palermo (1859–1941). The pneumatic lower figure shows humanity emerging naked from the horrors of war, her modesty only slightly saved by a few fronds of seaweed. She faces the sea and every westerly gale that will blow onto this achingly beautiful spot. She is one of the most buxom statues in Wales, her exultant nipples indicate excitement at war's ending, or coldness, or embarrassment at being exposed in such an exposed spot. One wonders what the pious and 'parchus' Nonconformist leaders of the town made of her when she was unveiled in 1923. Rising behind her octagonal plinth is a tapered phallic shaft of stone. On top of it, laurel wreath outstretched, flies the feyly angelic form of Nike – the Goddess of Victories. The names of the 111 who died in the First World War, and the 78 who fell in the Second World War, are listed below her with the legend 'Dros Ryddid' (For Freedom). The normally sedate Pevsner guide notes with surprise 'unexpectedly sensual for a Nonconformist country'.

Death was the most productive muse for artists, musicians, painters, photographers and poets. Scenes of death and dying featured in many paintings done in the grave's shadow. One of the most notable being C. R. Leslie's *Sarah Dillwyn on her Deathbed*, which shows the family gathered around ten-year-old Sarah as she lay dying and they commenced grieving. The painting had to be staged later after the event.[89] By the end of the century, photographs of the dead acquired considerable popularity.[90] Local photographers recorded the deceased before the coffin lid was hammered down. This was especially true of dead celebrities such as the surgeons Sir John Williams and Dr William Price, and the poets Talhaiarn, Dylan Thomas and several others.[91] The death of children, especially of infants, was an emotionally traumatic time for parents and many sought to capture the child's final image within its coffin in a photograph. This ghoulish tradition was wholly understandable and is a graphic confirmation of how close the bonds were between parents and their children.[92]

Poets were much in demand at times of death. Study any nineteenth-century or early twentieth-century secular or religious newspaper and one cannot help but be struck at the sheer immensity of the poetry of grief and grieving. Elegies and eulogies ranging from the touching and tender, to the tortuous and terrible can be found in almost every single issue. In Welsh, those with the ability to craft an 'englyn' were frequently called upon to test their muse for this short poetical form was ideal for a gravestone.[93] However full the life, even Lloyd George's, it could still be compressed into four poetic lines carved into stone or slate. Talking stones in graveyards record the bare facts of a person's life and the dates of their birth and death, their family and emotional ties, their neighbourhood, sometimes adding a verse of scripture or an 'englyn coffa'.[94]

Despite all the controversies that he caused with his caustic literary portrayal of the Welsh in *My People* (1915), Caradoc Evans lies under this tender inscription of his own devising:

Bury me lightly so that the small rain
may reach my face, and the flutterings
of the butterfly shall not escape my ear.

Death lingered long in some areas. Ghosts, those images of absences, reveal how the living haunted themselves. During the First World War, Dunraven Castle became a convalescent home for wounded soldiers.[95] Staff and patients were often disturbed by the ghost of a young girl, known locally as the Blue Lady. Her chilling journey through the cold corridors could be followed for a considerable time after her departure as eyewitnesses stated that she left behind her a strong scent that resembled that of the yellow mimosa flower.[96] Those brave enough to venture outside the castle sometimes heard the terrifying sounds of the 'Cyhyraeth'.[97]

Spiritualism became increasingly popular from the mid-nineteenth century.[98] At several séances summoned by Madame Blavatsky, Captain Henry Morgan, the seventeenth-century Welsh buccaneer and pirate, was a regular visitor.[99] The torrents of grief unleashed by the First World War created a craze for the services of spiritualists to reconnect the living with their lost loved ones. The Welsh medium Evan Powell put Sir Arthur Conan Doyle in touch with his dead brother via the spirit of a Native American Indian named Black Hawk.[100] The politician Hugh Dalton, however, did not need the assistance of a medium to talk to the dead, for he clearly saw the ghost of his friend, Rupert Brooke, in 1921.[101]

Spirits and revenants were contacted in a range of séances in which the dearly departed rose to the occasion. Much of these activities appear to have a deep pathos in which the dead, rather than offering any deep insight into the afterlife, seemed to concentrate on the mundane aspects of earthly lives – the purchase and presence of new curtains, new kitchens – were often remarked on by the dead. The scientist and seer Alfred Russel Wallace accepted the underlying truth of spiritualism. So much so that his reputation as a scientist is still somewhat overshadowed. Winifred Coombe Tennant became the most celebrated spirit medium of the interwar years, recording her journeys between two worlds in her remarkable diaries. Her interest, indeed obsession, with the dead was sparked by the death of her daughter and especially that of her son Christopher who died in the First World War.[102] Winifred seemed to have lived in a house of the spirits, indeed she was concerned that her son had not passed on: 'my living son. It is not the past I must turn to, but the present'.[103] Her diaries provide a powerful example of how death and the dying abided with the living. The brothers John Morgan Pryse (1863–1952) and James Morgan Pryse (1859–1942), sons of a Monmouthshire Presbyterian minister who had a deep faith in druidism, established the Theosophical Society and the Gnostic Society, which enabled them to expand their eclectic ideological mixture of Buddhism, Brahmanism and Methodism.

Reincarnation and spiritual evolution formed the core of James's belief in the afterlife, as outlined in *The Apocalypse Unsealed* (New York, 1910).

The years 1870–1945 were probably the most traumatic ever experienced in Welsh history. Industrial disasters blighted the years, taking at best tens of lives, at worst hundreds.[104] The flu epidemic of 1918 tore through communities already shattered by the ordeal of war, cruelly taking the young, the vital and the virile. These truly were the war years in Wales, for virtually no year was untouched by some calamity of British foreign policy – Afghan Wars, Zulu Wars, Boer Wars, Anglo-Irish wars, wars against the Bolsheviks, and the First and Second World Wars. Death, anxiety, grief and trauma were widespread and penetrated deeply into Welsh communities. The Second World War was not a distant experience for death was on the doorstep.[105] Barry, Cardiff, Swansea and Pembroke Dock were cruelly bombed. On the night of 29 April 1941, German bombers overshot Cardiff, and, as was common, unloaded their bombs so they could get safely back to France. A mile in any direction would have meant just the death of a few sheep but the bombs landed on Cwmparc in the Rhondda. Twenty people were killed, including three children who in an obscene irony had been evacuated there for their safety. An eye-witness recalled death's visitation to the village:

> One of my school friends was found dead in an armchair with her baby ... and she was pregnant with another one ... a bomb landed near the cemetery and I was afraid that my mother had been blown out of her grave ... The effect of the bombing on Cwmparc people was shattering. The community was used to living with mining disasters and the hardship of the period but this was something different ... The funeral of all twenty was held on one warm sunny day. Thousands of people lined the streets ... there were not enough hearses to carry the coffins and people in the crowd were fainting with grief and the warm sunny weather.[106]

Art, literature and music were some of the vehicles through which people were able to release their feelings and emotions of heartache and heartbreak, loss and loneliness, and above all their grief. A study of mourning for the dying and the dead is not a morbid obsession with death, but reveals powerful expressions of hope.[107] In all humanity's dealings with death, the recurrent theme is hope.[108] Hope is not just the belief in the heavenly path of a stairway to heaven, but is deeply based on human reflections upon earthly relationships. In the obituary pages, the graveyard carvings, the eulogies and the elegies, the requiem masses, the folk beliefs and the folklore surrounding death, an element of hope shines through the lamentation. A history of death seems also to be a history of hope.[109]

2

The Citadel: Pain, Anxiety and Wellbeing

Bûm gall unwaith – hynny oedd llefain pan ym ganed.
(I was once wise, when I was born I cried.)
    H. H. Vaughan, *Welsh Proverbs with English Translations* (London, 1889).

Healthy or Hungry Wales?

Gwell penloyn yn llaw na hwyad yr awyr
('A tit at roast makes better fare than does a wild duck in the air');

Gloddest awr a newyn blwyddyn
(Feast an hour, starve a year)
                    Hen Ddiharebion (Old Proverbs)

Wales, during the period 1870–1945, has traditionally been portrayed as the sick man of Britain. The litterateur W. J. Gruffydd entitled his memoirs, which cover much of these years, *The Years of the Locust*, an evocation of almost biblical suffering and sorrow.[1] Even more dramatically another misery memorist remembered of the 1930s that 'the stench of death was everywhere'.[2] Disease, decline and death are the constant undertones in Ron Berry's memoir *History is What You Live*. His people, as he said of one local family, the Jopers, 'were strangers to paradise'.[3] Richard Vaughan, in his popular novel, indicated that conditions were little better in rural Wales, where people were *Moulded in Earth*.[4] A persistent, persuasive element in Welsh poetry and prose appears to have been a prostrate, vulnerable youth phlegmatically coughing blood and membrane into a handkerchief. Tender youths died a wheezing, spitting, aching, phlegmy death. Historians have shown that they had an even better bedside manner and have enthusiastically taken up such themes presenting these years as ones of poverty, passive starvation and premature death.[5] The great industrial disputes of the 1870s, 1893, 1898, 1900–3, 1911, 1921, 1925 and 1926, the Great War 1914–18, the economic collapse of 1929 and the depression of the 1930s, and the Second World War are the chronological markers of the via dolorosa of Welsh history.

As the twenty-first century dawned these pessimistic views of health, welfare, wellbeing and death in Wales were questioned by a revisionist school of historians who argued that, despite all the horrors and hardships, conditions actually improved over the period 1870–1945.[6] Previous historians, they argued, provided an awed impression, not an accurate account. Their bleak portrayal of Wales as a place of terrible hunger and things falling apart was the historical equivalent of a Van Gogh painting in which dark clouds provide the dramatic background for darker crows to prey. The new, more 'optimistic' view, questioning whether Wales was healthy or hungry, is reminiscent of the arguments of social historians of the 1970s who deigned and dared to ask, 'Were hunger rioters hungry?' and 'Did peasants really starve?' Their counter-intuitive arguments demand a leap of logic, or a willing suspension of belief, for sentiment is often more compelling than statistics. It makes it difficult to be subjective and to answer as to whether Wales was healthy or unhealthy.

Tempests in academic teacups are rarely satisfactorily resolved.[7] Despite the best efforts of demographers and historians of medicine and health, we still know relatively little about the interactions between death, disease, diet, hospitals, housing, medicine, sanitation, water supplies and so many other factors. The human body paradoxically remained a largely mysterious organism whose laws and inner dynamics were imperfectly understood, not just by laymen but by the medical and scientific elite. The debates initiated in the 1870s on evolution, inheritance, natural selection and much more are still in dispute. Thus it seems foolhardy to leap to conclusions that are too firm, for complexity and contradiction are powerful aspects in the history of health and death in Wales.

Across Wales in the 1870s living conditions appear to have been, as one social observer noted, 'a negation of civilised existence'.[8] People were, as they said in Cardiganshire, 'yn byw ar gefn whannen' (living on the back of a flea). Dr Hunter reported that:

> The farmer in Wales as well as the labourer, must be taken to mean a person generally badly lodged, and insufficiently fed and clothed ... The evil effects of poverty upon the health is rather increased by the frugal habits of the Welsh farmers ... In Cardiganshire district a medical practitioner described the children as 'pining for want of food as soon as weaned', and thought that if the climate were cold the whole race would perish.[9]

Some decades later and the living was still far from easy. The indefatigable D. Lleufer Thomas in the report on the conditions endured by *The Agricultural Labourer* (1892) noted a catalogue of insanitary buildings, harsh living conditions and low wages. People were still living in cottages that had been condemned in the 1810s. The labourers undoubtedly suffered, but Lleufer Thomas concluded that 'the wife and children are considerable losers . . . The wife makes shift with tea and other slops all through the day and every day.'[10] The evidence given to *The Royal Commission on Agriculture in Wales* (1894–6) similarly emphasised that the greatest frugality was exercised. W. O. Brigstocke of Newcastle Emlyn considered that 'the Welsh tenant farmer is most thrifty and frugal . . . his diet, is somewhat rough . . . consists of tea, bread, butter, cheese, milk, bacon and vegetables: fresh meat is rarely seen at table, and the diet of the ordinary farmer differs little from that of the labourer.'[11]

Many commentators noted that several farmers, smallholders and cottagers kept a pig – 'the patron saint of the countryside', as every piece of the pig was used, 'heb law am y gwich' (except the squeak). Even so, the best hams went to market. At Llandeilo, John Thomas told the commissioners of the cramped living conditions:

> In one farm where all the buildings are deplorably bad, the farmer and his wife slept downstairs, whilst the men and maid servants,

the carpenter, the tailor, the sons on their holidays, all sleeping in the same room upstairs . . . In another farm where the rent is £88, the son of the farmer who has a high social position has to sleep with the servant man over the cows, or in the loft where the servant girl sleeps, which is not partitioned.[12]

Such conditions were not conducive to health, but inevitably in Wales at the turn of the twentieth century, the commentator's concerns turned not to physical dangers, but to threats to chastity and morality.[13] John Rhŷs and David Brynmor Jones in *The Welsh People* (1906) expressed their concern that there had been little change.[14] It was a standing joke in Llanfihangel that Mary Jones cleaned the house by letting the chickens loose in the rooms – it fed the chickens and kept the vermin down. The odour was indescribable. Edgar Chappell in a series of articles in the *South Wales Daily News*, in 1911, drew attention to the cottages of south and west Wales that 'had pretty exteriors of crawling ivy and bushes but inwardly were veritable death traps.'[15] Such imagery abounds in the popular poetry of the period. In 'Cartref' (Home), 'Y Bwthyn ar y Bryn' (The Cottage on the Hillside), 'Bwthyn Bach fy Nain' (My Grandmother's Little Cottage), and 'Y Bwthyn Bach Tô Gwellt' (The Little Thatched Roof Cottage) – the cottages are cosy, white-washed, rose-covered, set in a green and pleasant land.[16] Yet, the poem 'Y Bwthyn Bach Tô Gwellt' points towards the grimmer realities, for in the opening stanza, the author has lost his mother, father and siblings to disease. It was such shocking realities that inspired one county councillor, 'normally', wrote Edgar Chappell, 'the most unsympathetic people to sanitary reform', to compose the following parody:

> The cottage homes of Gwalia,
> How dreadfully they smell,
> With phthisis in the thatched roof,
> And typhoid in the well.[17]

All the evil smells in the world seemed to be concentrated in some toilets to which only people with bursting bladders would go (or those with very poor olfactory powers). Observers of social conditions in north Wales revealed that, if anything, conditions were worse there than in the south. Amlwch acquired a reputation, against much competition, as the worst place in Anglesey. In 1893 the sanitary authorities in their report noted:

> The most usual method of excrement disposal . . . is by means of privies which are almost invariably in a filthy condition and often dilapidated, while their contents are often allowed to accumulate for a year or more before removal. For many of the smaller cottages there is not even an apology for a privy, and the male inhabitants have to resort to the fields while the excreta of the old and infirm, and of the women and children are passed into pails, and have to be thrown on the refuse heap or into the neighbouring brook.[18]

In such conditions the maintenance of cleanliness must have been a considerable challenge. Despite their criticisms of Welsh living conditions it is somewhat surprising that social observers rarely passed comment on the physical appearance of the Welsh people they observed. Others however had no such reticence. The photographer John Thomas, in a series of remarkable photographs, showed the layers of dirt that covered the residents of the alms houses of Ysbyty Ifan and Ruthin in 1875.[19] In the same year Thomas's camera captured the villages of Pendre and Caerwys in all their glorious squalor. In another iconic photograph he shows Harri Bach Clocsiau of Bodedern, who, remarkably for a disabled person, made his living carrying goods around the area on his donkey and trap. His damaged leg is wrapped around a wooden peg. Harri walked lopsidedly as if he had been punished in a fairy tale. Just as it is said that a person grows to look like one's dog, Harri looks like his donkey but, of the two, seems the dirtier.

It was dire social conditions such as these that prised people from the supposed paradise of rural Wales and drew them in droves towards the towns and urban areas. But their hopes evaporated upon arrival. Bangor, Cardiff, Caernarfon, Wrexham, Carmarthen, Llanelli, Newport and Swansea were all established towns where, despite new developments, much of the accommodation was in slum dwellings.[20] 'Go to the towns, go to the works' – the advice was an expression of hope, but also a gesture of despair.[21] At Carmarthen one medical officer reported that

> the poor of Carmarthen are housed in slums and hovels that were not fit for human habitation. I will go further – some of the houses are not fit to kennel a dog in. Some are veritable death traps . . . To provide new houses for the children would be like transporting them to paradise.[22]

There were attempts to clear some of the worst slums, but because of overcrowding and the demand, 'people had', as Dr Thomas James Dyke said of Merthyr Tydfil, 'refused to be cleared with the housing', creating the problem of declining provision of accommodation for the constantly increasing numbers of people. Perhaps the most remarkable transformation in the built environment of Wales took place in the coal-mining areas where thousands of houses were built for the 'condensations of people' gathering around the coal pits. Ribbons of terraced housing trudged up hills and tumbled down valleys without any regard to topography.

The housing that was built at the end of the nineteenth century, either by private individuals, landlords or housing clubs, was better than those that were scrambled together in the iron-making towns earlier in the century by a bodge of builders.[23] But immigration and the large families that still characterised mining communities, especially those of south Wales, created serious overcrowding. Most homes, designed for a family of four, had ten or more people living in them. It was also very common for lodgers to be taken in due to this shortage of housing and because their rent helped with family finances, which exacerbated the overcrowding. As the local police courts showed, the presence of a lodger created profound tensions within many marriages. The shift systems in the mines meant that beds rarely cooled, for no sooner had one person risen for work then another returned to rest.

The coal-mining towns of north and south Wales, and the slate-quarrying villages of north Wales had one thing in common. They lay under clouds of fine dust – gritty and grey in the north-west, black and oleaginous in the north-eastern and the southern mining communities – silicotic everywhere. It was the women of these communities who had the Sisyphean task of attempting to maintain cleanliness and a modicum of civilised conditions in this brutalising environment.[24] One campaigner for baths at the pithead that would reduce some of the burdens noted of the miner's wife:

> She gets up any time from 5 to 6am, prepares breakfast and sends off, maybe, her son, next comes in another son from the night shift. She then prepares a bath for him, which means the lifting of a heavy boiler on and off the fire. He goes off to bed. Then the younger children get up and get ready for school. When they are safely off, she tries to clean up and clear a little bit of the pit dust . . . Then dinner has to be cooked and her husband got ready for the afternoon shift. Then her son returns again from the morning shift bringing with him some more dust. The same process has to be gone through again. He then goes off and she again turns around to clean and tidy up before tea-time and the children return home from school . . . Just as she thinks she can have an hour or two to sew or read, she again has to be preparing water and supper for her husband returning from the afternoon shift and so it goes on day after day.[25]

It is little surprise therefore to learn that:

> Many deaths of children occur by their falling into tubs and being scalded while the mother is preparing for the worker's bath. One of the coroners in south Wales has said 'Every winter I hold more inquests on miners' children who die from scalds or burns than I do on miners who are killed underground.'[26]

The outside environment was little better. The Medical Officer of Health for the Rhondda Urban District Council in 1893 reported on the condition of one of the area's rivers:

> The river contains a large proportion of human excrement, stable and pigsty manure, congealed blood, offal and entrails from the slaughterhouses, and the rotten carcases of animals, cats and dogs . . . old cast-off articles of clothing and bedding, and boots, bottles, ashes, street refuse and a host of other articles . . . In dry weather the stench becomes unbearable.[27]

The malodorous Rhondda Fach had everything in it except fish. Other Welsh rivers were just as polluted. 'The streams around Dolgellau are choked with empty salmon tins', said one witness to a Royal Commission in 1938. But living fish were rarely seen in Swansea. The River Tawe was polluted, well before it flowed through the town, by a variety of alkali works, copper works, collieries, by the sulphuric acid liquid and sulphate of iron from tin-plate works, and by town sewage, slag, cinders, small coal and dead animals. Bridgend's Ogmore river was similarly polluted whilst Cardiff's Taff was dark with the town's sewage and the liquid refuse of iron, chemical, and other factories.

Living conditions, tenuous at best, became traumatic on some occasions. Periods of industrial dispute and depression for example gave rise to considerable social hardship. The industrial history of Wales is characterised by general brutal and brutalising strikes and stoppages – 1893, 1898, 1900–3, 1910, 1911, 1915, 1925, 1926 are deeply carved on the tombstone of Welsh industrial relations, whilst the economic depressions of the 1870s, 1890s, 1920s and 1930s still resonate in the psyche of several Welsh communities. Contemporary newspapers often printed a dark picture of living conditions on such occasions. Two months into the 1898 coal strike and the *Aberdare Times* announced that local people were 'practically on the borders of starvation', whilst the *Western Mail* claimed that the children of Merthyr Tydfil were 'on the verge of starvation'.[28] Similarly in the twentieth century, especially the 1920s and 1930s, as economic depression and decline set in across Wales, levels of suffering intensified. Dowlais, the citadel of the industrial revolution in Wales, featured in a series of investigations by both the *Western Mail* and *The Lancet*, in which the town was compared with Hamburg. Dowlais did not do well. The authors utilised their negative alliterative skills to christen the town 'Dismal Dowlais', 'Depressing Dowlais' and 'Difficult Dowlais'.[29] Hilda Jennings in an investigation into conditions in Brynmawr, a town where 70 per cent of the insured workforce was unemployed in 1933, recorded a local prayer:

Oh, Lord, have mercy on us
And keep us all alive;
There's round the table nine of us
And only food for five.[30]

Somewhere between the sensational and scandalous, the emotive and the emotional, the chaotic and the comic, lies the truth of the condition of the Welsh people. Very often many commentators sought to outdo each other in providing a multiplicity of depressing evidence. The only logical conclusion from such dark evidence must have been to point to the fact that it was miraculous that anyone managed to stay alive in Wales in the years 1870–1945. The medical officer's description of some people sounds like an anatomical manifest, a symptomologist's gift, impossible to think that people so affected would wish to survive. The annals of the poor were not short and simple, but long and complex. Poverty, health and wellbeing are protean problems. Unlike beauty, poverty is both in the guilty eye of the beholder and in the empty belly of the sufferer. Poverty, health and wellbeing are relative. Levels of each were probably worse in the countryside where, despite all the saccharine clichés of romantic poets, peasants toiled in a grim and unpleasant land. Professor Ashby of Aberystwyth and his students undertook a detailed study that showed that the employed in rural Wales earned less than the unemployed in urban Wales. Entire families, in their hardscrabble existence, could only produce a gross income from their farms that was lower than the sum paid to an unemployed individual by a Public Assistance Committee.[31]

Conditions, as the mortality statistics confirmed, had improved over the period 1870–1945. More support was provided to enable people to survive, whereas in previous generations, they would have perished. This is not to deny the horrific levels of suffering endured by the people especially in the 1870s, the 1920s and the 1930s. The ultimate indignity, or the confirmation of the depths of suffering was given in the 1930s when large parts of south Wales were ironically and obscenely designated as a 'special area'.

Historians have searched in vain for a single fact to explain this improvement for the reasons for the improvements are manifold and many.[32] Several factors combined in complex and contradictory ways to improve people's lives. One expectation, often voiced, is that increased economic prosperity would lead to an improvement in the general condition of workers, but workers often spent any additional resources on things that were bad for them. Alcohol, sugar and tobacco were consumed in increasing quantities in Wales down to 1945. Consumption of beer in 1895–1900 was 32.2 gallons and 1.03 gallons of spirits for every person in the country. The levels only gradually declined. The dangers of alcohol were severe. The mortality rate of publicans, many of whom were women, was nine times higher than that of any other profession including mining.[33] The mass production of cigarettes from the 1890s and the glamour of the stars of the silver screen who smoked incessantly created an insatiable demand for tobacco.[34] In some cinemas it must have been impossible to see a film so dense was the smoke from the audience busily and boldly puffing away. But smoke inhalation was not the only danger. Chewing tobacco was common and the masticators would often spit the nauseous, tubercular content onto pub and chapel floors. Some chapels had their 'poerlestri' (spittoons) to collect the offensive material. Elsewhere, as Archdeacon David Evans (1830–1910) of St Asaph and Edward Matthews of Ewenni noted with disgust, carcinogenic mouthfuls were just spat onto the floors of Tŷ Duw (God's House).[35]

The state intruded further and further into people's lives over the period 1870–1945 as a whole range of Acts attempted to improve living conditions.[36] Compulsory schooling was introduced in 1870 and several Acts on child health were enacted between 1907 and 1910. The Public Health Act of 1875 meant that every part of Wales had a local sanitary authority wielding mandatory and discretionary powers with which to regulate water supplies, sewage, overcrowding, slum clearance, food adulteration, and the notification and isolation of infections and diseases. Despite the battle between public and private providers of water, supplies to most Welsh towns improved. Port sanitary authorities had even stronger powers to enforce isolation of the sick, often in hospitals on small islands around the coast.[37] The level of activity varied enormously. Several bodies in north Wales, in Pembroke and especially at Merthyr Tydfil were condemned for their laziness and lassitude. Nevertheless, improvements were achieved.

To some commentators, the heroes of the story were those in the medical profession, especially doctors. The heroisation of the noble medic reached its peak in A. J. Cronin's portrayal of the south Wales doctor Dr Manson, in *The Citadel* (1938), and especially in King Vidor's cinematic presentation of the novel, with the angelic Robert Donat in the lead role. Both novel and film played an influential part in the eventual victory of the medical profession over its rivals.[38] The years down to 1945 saw homeopaths, hydropathists and practitioners of 'fringe' medicine lose out to their 'professional' rivals. Practitioners of folk medicine lost out to the purveyors of a more mysterious 'scientific' medicine.[39] Undoubtedly, much was gained in these years. Many people had access to the medical services of the Poor Laws. Others established friendly societies and insurance schemes for medical services such as the cottage hospital at Ebbw Vale that so inspired Aneurin Bevan in establishing the National Health Service. But to many people, right to the end of the Second World War, and the establishment of the National Health Service, personal medicine was either an object of stigma or an expensive and unaffordable luxury. For many people were outside the assistance of the health societies and voluntary provident schemes. In addition access to specialist treatments depended largely upon the geographical accident of their living within the catchment area of a hospital.

The relationship between health, sanitation, medicine and the wider society was increasingly complex, often contentious. As scientific knowledge advanced, fatalistic attitudes to sickness and mortality declined, popular expectations of medicine rose, and access to medical services and resources became increasingly entwined with political and economic power. The religious revivals that accompanied the cholera epidemics in the 1840s and 1850s were not experienced again irrespective of the virulence of an outbreak of disease.[40] Fear of a growing underclass of degenerates and the poor showing of the British Empire's soldiers in the Boer and other wars led to increasing demands that action be taken to improve the physical and mental condition of the people. As ever, warfare was the midwife of welfare.[41] People had to be fit to die for their King or Queen and country. Thus the National Insurance Act of 1911 provided sickness insurance and a rudimentary health care for all the employed working population, whilst the Old Age Pensions Act of the same year provided financial help to those in their twilight years.[42]

It was the confluence of these myriad changes that led to the improvements in the nation's health. Often it was the efforts of much derided and despised bureaucrats that led to the greatest improvements in water supplies, cleaner food and local areas that were free of noxious nuisances.[43] Mundane, seemingly inconsequential things led to significant transformations in people's lives.

'The Massacre of the Innocents': infant and maternal mortality

'Now, Gentlemen of the Jury', said
The coroner – 'this woman's child
By misadventure met its death'
'Aye, aye' said we. The mother smiled.

And I could see that child's eye
Which seemed to laugh, and say with glee
'What caused my death you'll never know –
Perhaps my mother murdered me.'

W. H. Davies, 'The inquest', in J. Barker (ed.),
W. H. Davies: Selected Poems (Oxford, 1985), p. 99.

Wales was a land long well acquainted with death. But despite all the perils of various occupations, it was a sober and salient fact that the most dangerous time was the first month of one's life, then the first year. In 1915, at a time of profligate waste of human life, the Bishop of London, a man who had thrown himself wholeheartedly into the First World War (or at least to recruiting for it) made an uncharacteristic startling revelation and remarked that 'while nine soldiers died every hour, twelve babies died every hour so that it is more dangerous to be a baby than a soldier.'[44] The infant and maternal mortality rates are emotive and emotionally charged barometers for measuring the health of an area. Wales, throughout the period from 1870 to 1945, endured rates of infant and maternal mortality that were much higher than was the case in England, and on occasion, worse even than the most insalubrious and unhealthy parts of Scotland and Ireland.[45] In the stark words of so many contemporary authors in contemporary newspapers, 'Wales massacred her innocents' with a profligacy that Herod would have envied. Biblical advice did not help for many pessimistically believed the divine instruction that 'in sorrow shalt thou bring forth children'.

In 1914 the Local Government Board undertook a detailed investigation into the levels of infant mortality across England and Wales. Durham topped this grim table with an infant mortality rate of 134 per 1,000 births. Then came Carmarthenshire (125), then Glamorgan (124), then Caernarfonshire (118). Seven of the ten worst counties for infant mortality were Welsh. A map was printed in the report that used a variety of shades of grey to indicate the level of infant deaths. Wales made a heavy demand on the printer's ink supplies for it is almost entirely coloured black.[46] The 'supertramp' W. H. Davies (1871–1940), a man well aware of the wrong side of the law, in his poem 'The Inquest', drew attention to one of the darker aspects of this dark tale.[47] The slaughter or massacre of the innocents was not just the result of an environmental or economic catastrophe, there was a wilful, intentional aspect within it. Abortion, however late, concealment of birth, infanticide or suicide were often the only choices that offered themselves to a girl often abandoned by her seducer, cast out by her family and condemned by society.[48] Across Wales the local press is littered with reports of the distressing discoveries of rotting infant corpses – in a bucket in Cilgerran (1887), in an old iron mine in Mumbles (1886), in a ditch in Gowerton (1907), in a pigsty in Bangor (1909), in a blocked drain at Caernarfon (1909).[49] Fishermen often caught the ghoulish catch of drowned baby, as did an angler in the Towy river (20 April 1877), and another at Swansea (5 December 1895), and another near Llanelli docks (3 January 1912).[50] Baby farmers took cash to dispose of infants.[51] Other people, such as Mary Ann Ledster of Llwynhendy, could not afford to pay and thus decided to dispose of her child's body by placing it in a parcel and disposing of it between two hayricks, where pigs found it and commenced to devour it, until they were prevented by the farmer.[52]

Abortion, even at the latest stages of pregnancy, was a frequent recourse. All the newspapers of Wales, even the Welsh-language denominational press, carried advertisements for products such as Towle's Pennyroyal and Steel, which were meant to induce abortion.[53] Court cases confirmed that such products were widely used. In December 1899, John Phillips, landlord of the Hope and Anchor Inn of Bridge Street, Cardiff, was accused of having purchased abortifacients and forcing his servant Alice Miller to take them.[54] David Jones, a chemist, of Adam Street, Cardiff, was charged with similar offences in 1873.[55] A Mrs Rees of Swansea and a Mrs Earle of Cathedral Road, Cardiff, were charged with using 'instruments' to try to get rid of the child of a Mrs Williams in 1888.[56] Ten years earlier, two ladies were charged with similar offences at Llantwit Vardre.[57] In 1899 the Revd Evan Jenkins, of Garnant, Carmarthenshire, was charged at the Bridgend Assizes of gross cruelty and abandonment of his wife Ellen 'and, when she became enceinte defendant bought some drugs in order to procure abortion.'[58] Abortion was clearly a practice that occurred at all levels of society, a fact confirmed by the *Report on Maternal Mortality in Wales* of 1937, which stated:

> the mortality rate from abortion per 1,000 births is much higher in Wales than in England, suggesting either a crass fatality or a greater incidence of abortion, or possibly a combination of both . . . The statistics of deaths from criminal abortion show that mortality from this cause is much higher in industrial Wales than in rural Wales and that the number of deaths increased between the two periods 1924–8 and 1929–33.[59]

Such measures were most often the resort of desperate people. It is vital to remember that the loss of a child through miscarriage or stillbirth was deeply traumatic. The poet Lynette Roberts in 'Lamentations' describes the results of a bombing raid in 1940 at the same time as evoking her miscarriage:

But my loss. My loss is deeper
Than Rose's of Chapel House Farm
For I met death before birth.[60]

For Lynette Roberts, like many other women, men and children
across Wales it was their environment that militated against the
creation of life and birth. In many of the Herodian areas of Wales,
getting into the world was an achievement, a stroke of luck, the
first, and, sadly for many, the last, success that they experienced.
In England and Wales between 1920 and 1924 and between 1925
and 1929, infant mortality fell from 76.8 per 1,000 live births to
55.4 in 1939. A few Welsh areas also experienced falls but those
were significantly lower than the combined rates. Newport county
borough saw an infant mortality rate of 70.8 per 1,000 live births
in 1920–4, which was better than the England and Wales rate; it
improved to 62.3 in 1935–9, which was also higher than the national
average. However, the town was almost unique in Wales. Cardiff,
Merthyr, Swansea, Glamorgan, Monmouthshire, Carmarthenshire,
Caernarfonshire, and Anglesey all had rates in excess of the combined England and Wales averages throughout the first forty-five
years of the twentieth century.[61] Economic distress and depression
created profound inequalities. The weather rarely helped. Cold
winters saw increases in deaths from respiratory diseases. Warm
summers were not always welcomed, for they resulted in an increase
in diarrhoeal deaths. As the heat rose, the piles of garbage warmed
and steamed, the butchers' premises stank and the maggots hatched.
Death rates in Monmouthshire rose from 6.7 to 17.3 per 1,000 live
births, in Swansea they rose from 9.8 to 14.2, and in the Rhondda
the rates rose from the already high 13.9 to 23.9.[62] Deaths from
respiratory diseases were similarly high in Wales. Damp, poorly
ventilated houses where a coal fire burned every day of the year
were lethal. People who opened windows let in not just fresh air
but atmospheric pollution caused by various metal industries,
mining and quarrying.

Nevertheless, the fact remains that despite the higher levels of
infant and maternal mortality in Wales relative to the England and
Wales averages there had been an improvement by 1945, compared

to the 1870s. Better water quality, sewerage systems, scavenging and the cleaner public environment had their impacts. Foods were less adulterated and milk was no longer 'poison delivered to the doorstep'. Nascent health services developed incrementally but influentially. Antenatal services, maternity and child welfare as a result of the Maternity and Child Welfare Act of 1918, and hospital provision for the more difficult pregnancies, helped to improve the general situation.[63] In these latter areas tensions arose between an increasingly professionalised medical and nursing profession and mothers. The Ministry of Health's *Report into Maternal Mortality* (1937) noted that women were often loath to accept the patronising advice on household management and childrearing of 'meddling officials'.[64] The professionals countered, condemning the fact that young girls and wives accepted the advice on childrearing given by their mothers, who had often lost two or three or more children – the 'infanticidal experts'.[65]

One factor of particular note is that in many parts of Wales neonatal mortality rates (the death of a child within its first thirty days of life) worsened during the 1920s and 1930s.[66] Across Wales, in countless cemeteries, talking stones tell tales that little children called Lyn, Mary and Myrddin 'Bach' died before they learnt their name. In Abertillery, Mountain Ash, Penybont, Merthyr, Newport, Bethesda, Bangor, Gwyrfai, Caernarfon, Llanelli and Cwmaman the rates worsened. The neonatal mortality rate is a particularly sensitive indicator of the nutritional status and health of expectant mothers, and it is significant that the neonatal mortality rates reflected the rates of unemployment and poverty. Stillbirths, notifiable from 1927, reveal a similar pattern, with the highest rates in England and Wales occurring in Merthyr Tydfil. Rates of death for children aged between a month and a year reveal a similar pattern. The Ministry of Health's investigation into *Maternal Mortality in Wales* (1937), revealed that puerperal mortality increased in the 'special areas' of Wales from 5.16 deaths per 1,000 live births in the period 1924–8 to 6.5 deaths in 1929–33.[67] Elsewhere across Wales rates remained stationary. Such losses had a profound impact on people and communities.

Older infants and their mothers benefitted from the general improvements in sanitation, sewerage and scavenging and greater welfare provision. But the physical demands of their environment struck women when they were most vulnerable, in the periods just before and after they gave birth. Thus levels of neonatal and maternal mortality and stillbirth were highest in those parts of Wales that suffered most during times of economic crisis. The materials and 'medicines' given to children left much to be desired. Most 'medicines' were opium-based, often, as at Llanelli in 1883, resulting in a child's death.[68] Alcohol was even more freely available and indiscriminately given to children. As the *Carmarthen Weekly Reporter* noted in 1909:

> The giving of alcohol to children is a common practice in the town of Carmarthen. In some localities mothers have great faith in a 'little drop of gin' for the baby. The baby cries and some experienced dame explains that it wants a little drop of gin to 'warm it up inside'. The baby gets the little drop of gin – sometimes in its feeding bottle. It soon stops crying and goes to sleep. The fact of the matter is that the poor baby has got 'blind drunk' and will be quiet enough until it has slept off the debauch. Then it wakes with a 'bad head' and is very cantankerous until it gets a 'pick me up'. Infant mortality will remain high so long as this idiotic practice prevails.[69]

Medical officers of health could always find evidence of abhorrent public behaviour that appalled them. Medics, midwives, nurses, public health officers and navvies working in the large sanitation projects all laboured hard in the herculean task of attempting to make Wales a healthier country. In the 1920s and 1930s the impact of economic depression and depravation, environmental privation and pollution created an emaciated people living on the edge of health in many parts of Wales. The outcome was often in fine balance. The duality of experience was perhaps best captured at two book launches in London in 1939. Jack Jones in promoting his novel *Bidden to the Feast* spoke movingly of the 2,000 children in his home town of Merthyr Tydfil who went to school without shoes. In contrast Edith Picton-Turberville, herself well familiar with the sufferings of south Wales, launched her book called, of all things in 1939, *Life is Good*.[70]

Endangered lives: disease and society

'Ein cymdogion, teulu o Ferthyr Tydfil oeddent hwy,
'Y Merthyron' oedd yr enw arnynt gennym ni,
Saethai peswch pump ohonynt, yn eu tro, dros berth yr ardd
I dorri ar ein hysgwrs ac i dywyllu ein sbri.'

(They were our neighbours, a family from Merthyr Tydfil,
'The Martyrs' was the name we gave them,
the coughs of five of them, in their turn, shot over the garden hedge
To cut across our talk and to darken our fun).

> D. Gwenallt Jones, 'Y Meirwon' (The Dead), in *Eples: Cyfrol o Farddoniaeth*
> (Llandysul, 1951), p. 9. (Lost in translation above, as is so much so often, is
> the fact that Merthyr is both a placename and the Welsh word for 'martyr').

Perhaps the most terrifying and troubling aspects of people's lives in late Victorian and Edwardian Wales was that the greatest dangers came from unseen and unknown agencies. Pathogenic micro-organisms and viruses, the causes of so many diseases, remained mysteries. Only gradually during the 'golden age of microbiology' did scientists begin to discover the microscopic killers that wreaked such havoc on society. As with the impact of new technologies that, over the period 1870–1945 enabled humanity to begin to make gains in the conquest of time and space, advances in medical knowledge and science were not universally or instantly adopted. Some historians, especially those who have had a medical training, have argued that health scientists were the true heroes in the decline of mortality. Medics portrayed themselves as white-coated saviours, but the lived reality was more prosaic and developments were more protracted and partial.[71]

In the heroic portrayal, figures such as Koch and Pasteur stand tall in the pantheon of medical heroes.[72] Their work was at the pinnacle of a process of considerable scientific endeavour in which a number of individuals were probably outpasteurising Pasteur. They were the wizards, but bacteriology's evolution into a scientific discipline was based on the efforts of countless sorcerer's apprentices whose painstaking microscopic work definitively established the germ theory of disease. Amongst them were a number of Welsh people, such as Timothy Richard Lewis (1841–86), the surgeon and pathologist of Llangwm. He worked in several London and Indian hospitals to unravel the mysteries of cholera. The flagellate that he discovered in 1877 bears his name, *Trypanosoma lewisi*. Sir Daniel Thomas Davies (1899–1966), of Pontycymer, worked in London hospitals to develop and refine a serum for the treatment of pneumonia. He joined a notable tradition of Welsh people who became physician to the Royal family, working for George VI and later Queen Elizabeth and the Duke of Windsor, to whom he remained a life-long friend.[73]

Typhoid was one of the diseases for which an effective therapy was developed in the period down to the First World War. Episodic outbreaks affected Welsh communities throughout the nineteenth century, either killing outright or severely debilitating its victims. People whose lives were blighted by typhoid include Henry Thomas Edwards (1837–84), dean of Bangor, the precocious MP Tom Ellis (1859–99) and the litterateur John Gwenogvryn Evans (1852–1930). At least they woke up after their sufferings with aches and pains. Many were less fortunate as typhoid tore through rural communities killing many people. At Bangor, in September 1882, there were several deaths that led Florence Nightingale to write to William Rathbone MP calling for action. Although she blamed 'local causes', her solutions were the sensible ones of clearing slums, enforcing cleanliness, and introducing the Welsh to carbolic soap.[74]

Although a cure for typhoid was available from 1897, its acceptance was delayed due to medico-political reasons. Thus only a few troops were immunised during the Boer War. In South Africa 13,000 men were lost to typhoid as against 8,000 deaths in battle. Even the British Army learnt from this experience. During the First World War widespread immunisation was instigated resulting in far fewer deaths from typhoid.[75] War, ironically, resulted in significant developments in British health.

Death was extremely active in 1918, but with pestilence, not just with shot, shell and shrapnel. Nature revealed that it was a far more grimly effective killer than mankind. An elegantly simple flu virus, by now identified as the H1N1 strain, was matched only by its lethality. Across the world, H1N1 was a far more complex and capable murder machine than the First World War. In all it killed over 50 million people worldwide (almost four times as many as the war). Some statisticians put deaths from flu at over 100 million. It was probably the most public and most lethal pandemic the world has ever seen.[76]

The Welsh experience reveals how ghastly efficient an agent of death influenza was. In the 51 months of war, 40,000 Welsh people died, averaging 784 deaths a month. In the four months of flu, over 9,190 died. Flu killed with a death rate of more than 2,297.5 each month. Within a few weeks of the first outbreak there had been 701 deaths from influenza in Cardiff, 253 in Merthyr Tydfil, 245 in Newport, 458 in Swansea, and more than 1,071 in various parts of Monmouthshire. In the smaller, primarily rural counties of Anglesey, Montgomeryshire, Pembrokeshire and Radnorshire death was busiest in the period between 2 and 16 November. The sixty-six deaths in these two weeks in the rural expanses of Montgomery must have been exceptionally traumatic.[77]

The circumstances of war aided the pandemic's spread. The movement of people required to wage war, the crowding of troops into camps, trains and transport ships created the perfect 'culture' for the virus to grow and flourish. Unlike most other epidemics, this contagion killed the young and the relatively healthy in a horrific 'cytokine storm' (overreactions in the body's immune system). Some turned black, others just bled to death. Uncertainty remains as to where the influenza started. It probably commenced in the military camp at Etaples and spread rapidly to most of France, Germany, Britain, the US and Spain. Spain was a neutral country with less government censorship and so more attention was given in the press to the flu's impact. Thus the illness was christened 'The Spanish Lady'. This señorita scattered disease, dismay and death wherever she went. Censorship and the fact the flu deaths followed so closely on the mass deaths of the First World War have resulted in the fact that, until relatively recently, little attention has been given to the influenza epidemic.

The newspapers of Wales, despite wartime censorship, with their wide-eyed immediacy, still reveal the impact of the flu across the nation's communities. Deaths litter the pages with distressing frequency. For the greatest horological collector of all time, the clock-maker Evan Roberts (1836–1918), time was finally up. Sir James Hills-Johnes, of Dolaucothi, Carmarthenshire, had survived the tumult of the Indian Mutiny where he won the Victoria Cross for his bravery, the Second Anglo-Afghan War, and the Boer War, but found the influenza virus an implacable foe. Richard Morris Lewis, the translator of Gray's 'Elegy in a County Churchyard', which many considered to be a great improvement on the original, entered the quiet earth of Brechfa churchyard. The Dean of Bangor, the Bishop of St Asaph and Lord Kenyon all suffered but survived, unlike many of the prisoners of war at the Frongoch camp in north Wales. Mrs D. Evans and her son David, of Mynyddbach, Swansea, were buried in the same grave within just two days of each other.[78] A week earlier, eighteen-year-old Private William Taylor, of Brynmill Avenue, Swansea, home on leave, brought with him an unwanted present. Father and son died of the flu and were buried together.[79] James Thomas, a Swansea boot-maker, lost three of his children, one of whom was a soldier.[80] At Port Talbot, two sisters, Mrs Hopkins and Mrs Dawkins of Scutari Row, died, both leaving two orphaned children.[81] The eminent Welsh soprano, Madame Edith Evans, sang her last notes, and died quickly of influenza.[82]

The Welsh had seen it coming. Newspaper reports in June and July 1918 spoke of a terrifying new disease that was sweeping around the world. Forewarned was not forearmed. There was little medical authorities or people could do to prevent influenza from sweeping through their communities. Influenza travelled the communication routes of war, tracing their human pathways with the finger of death. On 22 June 1918, the *Cambrian Daily Leader* reported that an 'unwelcome Spanish visitor reaches Swansea'. Its onset was swift and sudden: 'Ordinary influenza creeps up on you. The new kind comes with a jump. The one attacks you as a craven wolf might; the new one springs upon you like a lion. It has reached Swansea and other parts of Wales.'[83]

A few days later the paper reported that 'in one controlled works in the area over 40 girls are down with it . . . whole families in the Hafod are suffering . . . and everywhere one hears the same tale of woe.'[84] Many of the poorer parts of Cardiff, Llanelli and Swansea showed that they had no shortage of Good Samaritans who took over the care of abandoned and orphaned children whose parents had been infected. Little Louise Maunder, a fourteen-year-old of Burry Port, died with frightening suddenness: 'she was talking to her parents in the kitchen when she fell back on the couch and expired'.[85] At Graig colliery, Pontarddulais, on 20 July, it was reported that 270 were absent from work.[86] Swansea court lost the services of its Greek interpreter, George Nicolas, who had worked there for forty-five years. The 'well-known' comedian Little Titch also died.[87] D. P. Williams and other ministers now took their texts from Ecclesiastes and warned that the heart of the wise is in the house of mourning, but the heart of fools is in the house of mirth. The *Cambrian Daily Leader* published an apology to the Carl Rosa Company, for when they had published a scathing criticism of their recent performance, they were unaware of the fact that the choir had been devastated by influenza.[88]

In contrast to this last choir standing, local ministers were in constant demand. The Revd W. D. Thomas of Brynaman officiated at seven funerals within three days.[89] Doctors were even busier. Many found it impossible to visit all the patients and so they just issued death certificates, thereby saving some work for the coroner and sparing the family from the horror of attending an inquest. Chemists were busy selling quinine, cinnamon and even snuff as preventatives. It was the season to be sombre as bell ringers, grave diggers and funeral directors bustled about their business. Grave diggers were advised not to fill in some graves as the rest of the family would soon join the deceased. There were even rumours that some critically ill people were taken to their grave still alive alongside a dead relative.

Responses to the contagion varied from the psychological to the pragmatic to the practical. The churches and chapels of Skewen, Caernarfon, Bangor, St Asaph, St David's, Flint, Holywell, Rhyl and several other hamlets, towns and villages, held special prayer meetings to beseech God to restore his mercy.[90] The Llanelli and the Swansea hospitals announced in the press that visiting was suspended whilst the epidemic lasted.[91] At Ystradgynlais, a special plea was made for 'ladies with a knowledge of nursing' to volunteer their services.[92] At Swansea mourners were banned from several cemeteries, resulting in complaints from the town's branch of the National Federation of Discharged and Demobilised Sailors and Soldiers that they had been refused permission to get a firing party together to mark the deaths of two soldiers.[93] Labour activists in Neath complained that they had been denied access to several schoolrooms for campaign meetings for the election because the rooms had been fumigated.[94] Schools were closed in October in seventeen areas of Swansea and the Swansea Medical Officer of Health informed the town's people that 'in accordance with the Swansea Corporation Act (Section 77) it will be illegal for parents to permit any children to attend a Sunday School'.[95]

Into the vacuum created by the uncertainties of the medical professions stepped the purveyors of quack medicines. Welsh newspapers were packed with advertisements for potions and unctions that were claimed to be efficacious in every way against influenza. Clymol, Nostroline, Bovril, Oxo, Dr William's Pink Pills and Veno's Lightning Cough Cure, all claimed to cure influenza.[96] Local purveyors were not to be outdone. Formamint advertisements advised Swansea people to 'suck a few formamints every day, and you will be safe from Spanish Influenza and other epidemics.' Rich the Chemist of Surgical House, 50 High Street, Swansea, asked in bold headings 'HAVE YOU THE GERM? SWANSEA'S INFLUENZA EPIDEMIC' and answered the town's worries – 'to keep yourself free, take 'Flemeltis' in water three times a day'.[97] Much to the delight of Swansea's drinkers, *The Cambrian Daily Leader* announced that 'where medical opinion shows that the need exists, special supplies of spirits will be supplied to influenza patients'.[98] Perhaps the only service you could trust were those offered by Ben Evans and Co. Ltd, the 'Complete Funeral Furnishers. Cremations Arranged. Orders by phone received at any hour of the day or night. Telephone 1015 telegrams Swansea.'[99]

Then the outbreak seemed to dissipate and disappear with the rapidity with which it had appeared. It left a cruel but less lethal legacy, an epidemic of *encephalitis lethargica* (an inflammation of the brain and spinal cord), which affected people like the artist

Ernest David Bell, author of the *Nubian Madonna*. The flu was the most deadly pestilence since the Black Death.[100]

Infectious diseases such as diphtheria, measles, scarlet fever and smallpox were more inconspicuous and insidious killers than the malevolent influenza. Although smallpox could be effectively treated since the mid-nineteenth century, outbreaks still occurred. In the Grangetown area of Cardiff in 1908 an outbreak took four lives. It was a horrible way to die, in misery and disfigurement, nothing like the sentimental clichéd deaths of Welsh poetry of leaves gently falling.[101] Measles was a constant threat to the health of children and often took young lives. The diphtheria patient simply drowned in his, or her, own fluids. Popular attitudes did not help, for people often harboured the strangest and deepest superstitions. When an outbreak of measles occurred in Merthyr Tydfil in 1900, parents refused to send their children to a local school because they believed the illness had been caused by a pickled snake that the teachers used for science lessons.[102]

In comparison to the coalfields of south Wales, that of the Wrexham area in north-east Wales is either forgotten or, if it is remembered, is portrayed almost as an Elysium.[103] Yet here too communities fell victim to the ravages of diseases. In the Wrexham Rural District, deaths from diphtheria in 1934 had improved from 7.7 per 1,000 deaths a year earlier, but this was still nearly five times as high as the average figure of 1.6 per 1,000 for England and Wales.[104] The mining community of Rhos had 143 deaths due to diphtheria and scarlet fever in 1931.[105] By January 1933, the medical officer of health reported that deaths in Rhos were in excess of births during the previous three months. This prompted councillor J. W. Williams to describe the 'disease-breeding, death-spreading, insanitary conditions' of Rhos. He concluded 'talk about pilgrim's progress leaving the city of sin, it appears that we are living in the city of death at Rhos.'[106]

The disease most closely associated with the Welsh way of death by the twentieth century was tuberculosis.[107] Art, drama, music, poetry and prose of the 1910s, 1920s and 1930s have a scarlet stain running through them. It was the stain of arterial blood, the vivid fruit of tuberculosis, otherwise known as 'y dyciáu', 'y pla gwyn', 'consumption', or the 'wasting sickness', or more dramatically 'the white plague', or the 'white death'. The characters in the short stories and novels of Geraint Goodwin (1903–41), such as Evan in *The Heyday in the Blood* and Wyn in *Watch for the Morning*, are tubercular, which is not surprising for the author spent a long period of his sadly short life in the sanatorium at Talgarth, Brecknockshire. Tuberculosis was Goodwin's curse, too. It shackled him to the house as effectively as a ball and chain – a chain you could hear rattling inside him, forged from gaspings and wheezings, fighting for breath like a spent fish.[108] The author and playwright Alun Richards (1929–2004) spent two years in the same sanatorium amongst silicotic miners, which he recalled was a dreadful but enriching experience. The roll-call of the devoured and the dying is long. The heightened artistic sensitivity of the Llanelli painter J. D. Innes (1887–1914) was attributed to the fact that he suffered from tuberculosis for a long part of his brief life.[109] Timothy Evans (Telynog, 1840–65) was one of the most precocious poetical talents in Wales. The brevity and fragility of his life was encapsulated in his still-remembered poem 'Blodeuyn bach wyf fi mewn gardd' (I am a little flower in a garden). Its biblical connotation was clear, for Telynog insisted that humanity shared the fate of the flowers of the field. Nowhere perhaps was all the elemental, emotional power that tuberculosis could harness seen more clearly than in the funeral of Jim Driscoll in Cardiff in 1925. Driscoll, the bantam-weight boxing champion of Europe, had fought a close match for the world title in New York, for which he had been christened 'Peerless Jim' by none other than the legendary ex-sheriff Ben Masterson. Offered a rematch, Driscoll declined, because he had promised to fight in Wales to raise money for Nazareth House, the Cardiff orphanage. Driscoll was peerless within and without the ring. When he died of tuberculosis, more than 100,000 people followed his coffin to Cathays Cemetery. Death's magnet attracted the largest crowd that had ever gathered in Welsh history.[110]

Tuberculosis was everywhere. It was the major killer in the north-western highlands and in the north-eastern lowlands and the Clwydian hills. Tuberculosis killed just as efficiently in the confined industrial valleys of south Wales as it did in the agricultural west. It seemed to pay no heed to the bracing sea air of the western coasts. It struck agricultural workers, miners, colliers, ministers, midwives, maiden aunts, misers and quarrymen with equal finality. Tubercular disease took the young, it took the old, it took girls and boys, men and women. More perhaps than any other malady, it won death its reputation for even handedness – 'ni edrych marwolaeth pwy decaf ei dalcen' (death does not care for the fairest forehead). In the period 1930–6 mortality from tuberculosis in England and Wales was 724 per million people. As always the statisticians tabulated fear. The seven worst counties for tuberculosis deaths in the UK were Welsh – Caernarfonshire (1,283), Merioneth (1,196), Anglesey (1,153), Cardiganshire (1,104), Pembrokeshire (956), Glamorgan (938) and Carmarthenshire (918). The most unhealthy parts of that most unhealthy county Caernarfonshire were the rural districts of Gwyrfai (2,052), Glaslyn (1,810), Geironydd (1,675), and Nant Conwy (1,607). Names synonymous with rural beauty. Death traps. Only Llanwrtyd (1,813) and Machynlleth (1,708) had higher rates of tubercular death. By the late 1930s almost 10 per cent of the Welsh people were on the TB register.[111]

There is, as Clement Davies noted in his scathing *Report on the Anti-Tuberculosis Services in Wales* (1937), an obscene irony in the fact that Wales supplied seven of the ten worst counties in Britain for tuberculosis deaths. The cure offered to so many who suffered from the disease was fresh air, plenty of room, good nutritious food, and space between dwellings. These were resources that Wales seemed to possess in plenty, yet the contributors to the report revealed a land of object and abject deprivation.[112] Social behaviour, such as large turnouts at the funerals of tubercular people, were condemned. Dr Walter Davies of Llanidloes called for washbasins to be installed at schools and 'deprecated our habit of greeting one another with hand shaking, which undoubtedly may spread infection from one person to another.'[113]

There were a bewildering number of treatments, many of them injurious or even fatal to the patient – the various materials injected into the windpipe, for example, included olive oil, iodides, dyes, creosote, copper cyanvirate and pig-spleen extracts. Some advocated inhaling the breath of cattle, whose efficacy, given bovine tuberculosis, must have been questionable. Through it all the patient would, between hoarse, shallow breaths, cough blood and membrane, raving and twisting in the damp coils of bed linen. The truth is that for much of the period, down to the 1930s, many doctors simply did not know what they were doing: with all the false authority of an assertive manner, they misdiagnosed and mistreated many hundreds of consumptives.[114] Doctors seemed most capable of killing, rather than curing, their patients. There were some notable exceptions, particularly those doctors working within the King Edward VII Memorial Association. This had been established in 1910, by public subscriptions and the generosity of David Davies and the Llandinam family, to help to fight tuberculosis in Wales. In 1911 the National Insurance Act allowed local authorities to contribute financially to the association. From its centre at the Temple of Peace in Cardiff, the memorial association investigated the causes of the disease and attempted to effect cures. It also established chairs in public medicine at Cardiff university in 1921 and in the new medical school in 1931.[115]

The initiative that is most often associated with the memorial association was the establishment of sanatoria across Wales to isolate and treat patients. At Llanybydder, Talgarth and Craig-y-Nos, tubercular patients were housed in conditions that Thomas Mann depicted in *The Magic Mountain* – peace, pine trees and panoramic views. Even so, the local wiseacres at Llanybydder still noted the finality for the patients whose fate was 'coughing in and coffin out'.[116] A sense of enforcement, of entrapment, comes through very strongly from the experiences of many former inhabitants of the sanatoria. In the reminiscences of the former residents of Craig-y-Nos it is clear that many considered themselves to be more prisoners than patients. They hint at lack of liberty, of a conscious and unconscious cruelty, and at a darker culture of sexual abuse. Diet, nutrition, rest and cleanliness were the most efficacious treatments given to patients.[117] The introduction of mass radiography from 1943 meant that the disease could be tackled in its early stages.[118] In Wales mobile X-ray units reached some of the remoter rural areas. The same year, the first effective anti-tuberculosis drug – streptomycin – was discovered. By 1949, milk was categorised, with a programme of pasteurisation and testing for therulin, and, in 1953, vaccinations began in schools.

William Fisher contracted tuberculosis whilst working as a rescuer at the Senghenydd mining disaster in October 1913. In one of his letters he offers the sardonic optimism that was perhaps characteristic of many tubercular patients who always had to look on the bright side of life: 'this is an interesting (if a wicked) old world. I don't think I'll leave it yet awhile.'[119] He died just a few days later.

Dead Souls: disasters and misadventures

'O what is man that coal should be so careless of him,
And what is coal that so much blood be upon it?'

Idris Davies, *Gwalia Deserta*

'BANG'. The explosion always came without warning. The activities of mandrels, picks and shovels, miners and horses, trams and trucks, released forces that had been locked deep in the earth since its formation. Colourless and odourless, the gas built up in the mine with each blow of the pick, each scrape of the shovel, each load of coal. It only took a single spark – from a malfunctioning lamp, or a faulty electrical wire, or friction on the rails – to set it off. Sometimes water would rise, roar and rush into the workings, sweeping all before it, drowning the miners.

Thousands of lives were extinguished in a way that became sadly all too familiar. A flash of methane's distinctive blue flame began a chain reaction. The explosion sent a wall of pressure down the narrow workings strong enough to throw one-tonne trucks and men the length of the gallery and force them into cracks in the coalface. Veteran miners knew that when they heard a rush of gas they would have to throw themselves flat onto the floor, for it was followed instantly by a flame like a blowtorch – the flash at head height. But many were too slow, or unaware, or just unlucky. The wind sucked coal dust from every crevice and suspended it in the air and then the flash ignited it. Coal dust could turn even the smallest firedamp flash into a raging inferno as wind and then fire roared through the mine as if through the barrel of a gun. Hell hath no fury like firedamp. The fire raced through the tunnels, charring everything in its path – tools, horses, men, children – with the ferocity of a blast furnace.

The underground disaster announced itself to the world above when the wind and fire found the shaft and exploded out of the pithead with a stupendous roar – 'like the report of a gigantic cannon', according to one eyewitness at Senghenydd in 1901. Twelve years later, in 1913, in the same pit, the cage shot up the shaft with such force into the winding gear that the miner who operated the cages was killed instantly. Soon afterwards, a huge bubble of unignited gas rushed up the ventilation shaft and burst into a great ball of flame above the mine complex. People in the sorting sheds were battered and burnt. Dark, thick, acrid smoke hung heavy above the mine signalling to the surrounding villages and countryside the cataclysm underway deep in the earth.

Sirens wailed. Women and children streamed into the roads, hurrying, worrying, towards the spreading black stain in the sky. As they arrived, the mine still reverberated to aftershocks. Survivors would stumble out, or be carried by colleagues. Shouts of anger, screams and curses mixed with wails of grief as the magnitude of the tragedy became clear. Grey faces received grave news. Fatherless children, childless mothers and widows wept, whilst others waited in hope until it became clear that rescue missions had turned into ones of recovery. At Senghenydd in 1913 it took over three weeks to recover most of the bodies. Four months later eleven men were still missing.[120] Elsewhere, some bodies were never recovered, but lay entombed together in the camaraderie of death. The salt taste of sorrow soured several palates.

Then came the inquests. Then the recriminations. Then management would be absolved of all responsibility. Then the declarations of outrage in the press that proved that a journalist's and a politician's words were more transient than most of humanity's bumblings. Then the ballads.[121] Then the funeral processions. Part mourning, part protest, they wound through the shrouded landscape in black trains. That such events were endlessly clichéd and caricatured in a series of mining disaster movies does not diminish the human tragedy.[122] A woman from Llwynypia, born in 1904, recalled: 'We were more or less living with death everyday . . . There was always that tragedy hanging over . . . I felt that as a child. That there was something hanging over us all the time.'[123] One reason perhaps why Wales coped so stoically with the carnage of the First World War is that so many people were familiar with the spectacle of mass public death.

Which of these terrible disasters is representative, which in Michael Lieven's inspired title to his poignant book on Senghenydd, was the universal disaster in the universal pit village?[124] The answer is that each was representative, but that each was also deeply individual, particular and peculiar to its time and environment.

The Tynewydd pit, not surprisingly perhaps, if we remember that it was physically located in the 'V' where the rivers Rhondda Fawr and the Rhondda Fach meet, was flooded on 11 April 1877. Nine miners were drowned, five were trapped underground in a higher section.[125] Rescuers entered the mine and heard the miners tapping the walls with their picks and singing hymns. Water pumps were brought in but the volume of water meant that the entrapped men would have starved to death before they could be rescued. The only way to get to the men was to dig through 113 feet of coal. Rescuers worked non-stop in four-man teams. They had been briefed of the dangers from water, gas and compressed air. In all probability they, the rescuers, would either be drowned, crushed or suffocated. But they only had one choice, one chance. They started digging on Monday, 16 April. Britain's nations literally waited with baited breath for the daily updates in the newspapers. On Friday, 21 April, the rescuers succeeded. They saved the men.[126]

As the good news broke, newspaper reporters rushed to the scene to cover the story. Those from the London press seemed to have entered a foreign land for the mine was solidly Welsh speaking. The disaster was the making of the Welsh reporter Owen Morgan, Morien, (1836?–1921), who translated much of what was going on.[127] Throughout the period the entrapped miners had sung hymns, one of which was the great hymn by Dafydd Williams (1720–94) that was presciently appropriate:

Yn y dyfroedd mawr a'r tonnau
Nid oes neb a ddeil fy mhen,
Ond fy annwyl briod Iesu,
A fu farw ar y pren;
Cyfaill yw yn afon angau
Ddeil fy mhen yn uwch na'r don,
Golwg arno wna i mi ganu,
Yn yr afon ddofon hon.

(In the deep and mighty waters
There is no-one there to hold my head,
But my dear saviour Jesus,
Who died for me on the Cross;
He's the friend in death's river
He will hold my head above the wave,
Seeing him keeps me singing,
In this deep river.)

It had all the components of a great Victorian melodrama.[128] Bravery, belief, faith, valour, self-sacrifice, dedication, determination, but above all, deliverance – a happy-ever-after. Queen Victoria sent down her personal photographer to photograph the rescued heroes. Joseph Parry set the 'collier's hymn' 'Yn y dyfroedd mawr a'r tonnau' into the anthem 'Molwch yr Arglwydd' (Praise the Lord), which he composed to thank God for the rescue. At the Cymanfa Ganu in Carmel Chapel, Treherbert, held to mourn the dead and celebrate the living, they sang all the moon long, for the hymn was 'dwblyd' (repeated) over sixteen times. It was, as one survivor wrote, a tale of *Life from the Dead*.

Less dramatic, but no less tragic, were the incessant accidents that took a consistent toll of lives. Between 1874 and 1914 there were 9,294 deaths due to a plethora of accidents in Welsh mines. Not only was the pace of growth in Welsh mining reckless, it was accompanied by a profligate waste of life. Mine owners blamed men for their carelessness and cavalier attitudes towards health and safety, whilst the men blamed owners for lack of investment in the pits that would assist in making the hazardous workplace a little safer. Company officials appeared venal and villainous, their sole concern their mission to avoid a future of diminishing profits. In 1874, there were 173 deaths in Welsh mines. By 1914 the number had more than doubled to 376.[129]

Deaths at work, as the poet D. Gwenallt Jones recalled, were 'y llewpart diwydiannol a naid yn sydyn a slei / O ganol dŵr a thân, ar wŷr wrth eu gwaith' (the leopard of industry which pounces suddenly and silently / from the centre of water and fire attacking men at work).[130] Iron works, factories, mills and foundries took a persistent toll of between 100 to 200 lives each year. The frailty of human life in the claws of industry is witnessed in the death of Myrddin Morris, a 14-year-old cold-roll-boy at the Barry Tinplate Works. When his clothes became caught in the rolling gear, he was wheeled round by the machine with the result that 'fragments of the poor lad's remains were scattered around, and had to be collected in a sack for conveyance to his home.'[131] The remains of the poet Gwenallt's father, a metal worker, had similarly been carried home unceremoniously in a sack after an accident in a tin-plate mill. A crash on the Taff Vale railway on 23 January 1911 killed eleven people, including two women (Hannah Jenkins, Treherbert, and Elizabeth Davies, Pantygwaith) and three local councillors. A local balladeer told the dramatic story in *Cân am y Ddamwain Ddifrifol ar Rheilffordd y Taff Vale, D. C. Dydd Llun, 23 Ionawr, 1911* (A ballad about the fateful crash on the Taff Vale Railway, Monday, 23 January, 1911). The internal combustion engine began its devastating impact on human lives from 1907 in Wales and regularly took a fleet of victims. Authors of ballads would also find sensational material in the slate mines and quarries of north Wales.[132]

The most feared workplace was the sea. When clouds turned colour from a deep Episcopalian purple to a sinister bible black and winds of *Wuthering Heights* power blew, sailors were at the mercy of elemental forces. The sailor's plight was worse because ship owners, especially those based in Cardiff, over-insured their ships and deliberately set out to engineer a maritime casualty, often accompanied by loss of life, in order to collect inflated insurance claims.[133] The Welsh coastline had a justifiable reputation for savagery. The coast of Pembrokeshire was described as 'one of the most dangerous stretches of coastline in the world'. In the early hours of 27 January 1883 winds off Beaufort's scale hit the Gower coast.

As dawn broke at Port Eynon Bay, horrified spectators watched as the steamer *Agnes Jack* broke up. Men clinging to the masts were cast into the sea and the entire crew and the Llanelli pilot Phillip Beynon were drowned. It was months before some bodies were recovered. In all, the day saw an unlucky seven ships sunk or wrecked along the coast, with forty-eight deaths.[134]

Ships carrying emigrants to their new lives were usually buoyant with hope and optimism. But in a number of instances, all the hopes were dashed when the ship sank. In 1873, the *Northfleet* sank after being hit by an unidentified steamer, resulting in 293 deaths. It was as a result of this tragedy that it became a legal necessity for all British ships to have their names written on the stern and both sides of the bows. A year later, the White Star's *Atlantic* sank resulting in the deaths of 546 emigrants.[135] This already perilous workplace was even more lethal during the two World Wars. The Welsh coast saw horrific losses, especially in the unrestricted U-boat warfare after 1915.[136] In February that year, seven ships were sunk around the coast of Anglesey. During the Second World War more than 1,000 Welsh sailors were drowned as a result of enemy action. Wars, naturally, created enhanced awareness of the imminence of death, that the end was nigh.

Violent deaths were frequent and the press and popular memory seemed to pick out those years stained bright scarlet far more effectively than any political or religious events. In 1935, Gareth Jones, the precociously talented journalist, was found with a bullet in the back of his head in Manchuria.[137] Others did not need to travel far to meet their death by bullet or blade. Guns and knives were freely available and often used in murders across Wales. Frederick Kent, the landlord of The Gloucester Arms, Swansea, was murdered by Thomas Allen, a Zulu who had broken into the premises. Whilst Allen and Kent fought with a knife in the bedroom, Mrs Kent coolly shot the intruder. Wounded, Allen fled, but Mr Kent died of his wounds.[138] Edward Lewis George Bindon was hanged by hangman John Ellis at Cardiff in March 1914 for shooting his former lover, twenty-year-old Maud Mullholland of Cambridge Road, Cardiff.[139] David Roberts of Penrhosgarnedd, Bangor, was imprisoned for shooting his mother-in-law in December 1899.[140]

Some people were simply and sadly unlucky. In July 1878, William and Elizabeth Watkins and three of their four children, Charlotte, Alice and Frederick, were found brutally murdered in their cottage at Llangibby. Spanish sailor Joseph Garcia was hanged for the crimes.[141] Certain parts of Wales acquired a reputation for frequent violent deaths. The China area of Merthyr Tydfil continued its notoriety into the twentieth century as too did the districts around the docks in Cardiff, Newport and Swansea. Welsh ports were the venue for transients of all sorts, the human flotsam and jetsam that were washed in and out by various economic tides. Despite such dangerous places and people, the greatest risks a person faced were at home. Envy, malice and spite were the dark trinity that ruled on several hearths.

Survivors had to contend with the traumatic impact of sudden, terrifying and terrible death. The journalist Robert John Rowlands (Meuryn, 1880–1967) lost his father at the age of six. Louise Myfanwy Thomas (Jane Ann Jones, 1908–1968), the novelist of Holywell, was raised by her grandmother after her mother's death. When the grandmother died, she was then transferred to the 'care' of her parsimonious aunt and uncle, who suffered religious delusions and paranoia. Her bitter experiences as an orphan are set out in her novels Y Bryniau Pell (The Far Hills) (1949) and her study of transience Diwrnod yw Ein Bywyd (Our Life is Just a Day) (1954). The blind and deaf poet John Richard Williams (J. R. Tryfanwy, 1867–1924) lost his mother and father when very young and went to live with an aunt in Porthmadog. His life could serve as the tragic plot for a country and western or a jazz song, instead he put his angst into his poems Llofion yr Amddifad (1892) and Ar Fin y Traeth (1910), which reveal how resilient people can be even against the darkest and grimmest misfortune. David Richard Davies (1889–1958), Richard Thomas Evans (1892–1962) and Daniel John Davies (1885–1970) each lost his father in accidents in quarries or mines and entered the ministry. To such people there was little point wallowing in self-pity and self-sorrow. One had to get busy living rather than busy dying.

'In place of fear': defences against death and disease

'Mr Anaesthetist, if the patient can keep awake, surely you can?'

Dr Ernest Jones, quoted in Brenda Maddox, *Freud's Wizard:*
the Enigma of Ernest Jones (London, 2006), p. 29.

Ernest Jones's rebuke to the sleeping anaesthetist suggests that despite the advances medicine had made since the late nineteenth century, medics were still regarded with an element of suspicion in the 1950s. In the story 'The Madness of Winifred Owen' by Bertha Thomas (1845–1918), a young woman 'from the heart of south Wales' is treated by a Dr Dathan, a vivisecting scientist who is reported to practise black magic and raising the devil. She recalled 'in the long after-years I have been in lands where they still offer up human sacrifices to their gods. I thought once or twice then of Dr Dathan.'[142] Arthur Machen's classic gothic novel *The Great God Pan* has an amoral doctor who accepts no responsibility for the human lives he destroys. Perhaps the most famous portrayal of Welsh medicine came in 1938 in the film of A. J. Cronin's novel *The Citadel*. Though the hero of the story is a medic, Dr Manson, who goes to work in a doctor's surgery in a south Wales mining community, the portrait of the medical profession is far from flattering. Manson's colleagues are 'Mephistophelean', 'penny pinching', 'lazy, evasive, incompetent swine'. The hero himself makes a dash for easy cash in London away from the serious problems that beset Welsh communities.[143]

Doctors have been revered and reviled in almost equal measure. The portrayals of doctors by contemporaries veered from the hateful to the heroic extremes of the hagiographic. The miner-writer B. L. Coombes noted that 'for the most part no praise could be overdone' for the majority of doctors in mining regions were 'guardian angels'.[144] C. B. Edwards of Garndiffaith recalled that the local doctor was 'the king of life and death a God like man'.[145]

Some commentators have been sceptical of many of the claims made for the beneficial effects of medicine in improving mortality in the period 1870–1945, yet there were many significant advances.[146] Hospitals for the first time became major agencies for the cure and prevention of disease rather than mere prisons for the deviant and depositories for the dying. Established in 1921, the Welsh National School of Medicine provided medical training within Wales, so that standards and professionalism across the nation were enhanced. Medicine as a science advanced rapidly in status, as medical researchers and practitioners successfully extended treatments and cures.

Welsh people within and without Wales played a significant part in medical developments and advancements. Given the limited opportunities available within her borders, it is no surprise that so many eminent Welsh doctors worked in London, Cambridge, Manchester and Edinburgh. This was extensively a man's world, but it was not exclusively so, for women were active at all levels of medicine. Frances Elizabeth Hoggan (1843–1927) of Brecon became the first British woman to obtain a European MD degree at Zurich university in 1870. She worked as an 'unregistered' physician with her husband in a private practice in London, as the British medical authorities refused to accept women. Hoggan campaigned on a number of issues, especially the right of women to receive an education and for them to become doctors. Many of her ideas were set out in *Education for Girls in Wales* (1882). She also campaigned for women to be trained as doctors in India.[147]

Medical provision in Wales could be divided into two areas – the 'popular' and the 'professional'. It was not always clear which offered the best solution. In the world of 'popular' or 'folk' medicine local wisewomen and wisemen, herbalists, patent medicine manufacturers, quack doctors and spiritualists offered solutions that ranged from the bad, to the mad, to the occasional efficacious.[148] One of the greatest boundaries in life is that between wellness and illness. The journey of people across this Rubicon was closely watched within families and networks of friends. There were several aspects. Ailments such as skin eruptions, eczema, blood impurities and anaemia were more evident in early spring and late autumn, due, some said, to the influence of the astral planes and the vegetation they controlled. Certain hours of the day were more testing for the sick. To some, 11 p.m. was 'yr hen awr ddu' (the old black hour). Other people saw 2 a.m. as the longest hour or considered

4 a.m. to be the 'soul's darkest hour'. Inhabitants of Manafon in Montgomeryshire often said that this was the time when 'the hwnt [mole] winked on me'. Even in the twentieth century, people still consulted almanacs such as *Almanac Caergybi* to decide which were the most appropriate days to undertake various tasks or administer potions. They took careful note of the Egyptian or dismal days and the 'dog days' when the greater dog star (Sirius) or the lesser (Procyon) were in the ascendant.[149]

The natural pharmacopoeia of the countryside provided a bounty of medicinal herbs. Old wives scoured hedgerows for the cures that would be the foundations of their tales. In many parts of mid-Wales, even after the Second World War, an infusion of rue, made by pouring boiling water over the leaves, was administered as a drink to children suffering from worms. Rosemary was regarded as an excellent cure for chronic drunken habits, and an infusion of it would sometimes be put into beer casks. A poultice made from the leaves kept wounds from running. With honey, rosemary was used to sooth sore throats. In the Vale of Clwyd, Cardiganshire and Carmarthenshire, houseleek was used as an eye ointment. Ivy, pennywort, stonecrop, dandelion, dock and daisies, wood sage, buckbean, plantain, coltsfoot, cinquefoil and gorse were widely used. The use made of these herbs and flowers varied from area to area, and even from humans to beasts. In the Aberystwyth area an infusion of wood sage was used as a diuretic and stomachic, but in south Caernarfonshire its use was confined to sooth sore udders (in cattle). Holly was used to whip chilblains. Urine was even more efficacious, it eased chilblains, poured into the ear it cured earache, whilst washing one's face in one's own had cosmetic properties.[150]

The animal world also provided a bounteous benefit. Goose grease cured sore throats, eased swollen joints and, taken orally, cured croup. 'Glain nadredd' (adder beads) were good for all afflictions of the eyes. Honey was used by miners in south Wales to keep wounds and scars clean. Some believed it cured cancer in the mouth, typhoid and dysentery. In the Llanwrtyd area of Brecon-shire, it was customary for women, when they went to the seaside, to collect limpets and bring them home to be applied to the breasts of those having feeding troubles after childbirth. Hence the Welsh name for a limpet – 'cragen y fron' (breast shell).[151]

People's credulity in and the credibility of such cures continued into the twentieth century. Often such cures were administered by the women within the family. Many areas and neighbourhoods had a number of women who could perform such services. From a person's first to last breath it was women who were the attendants. Midwives were the guardians at the gates of life and death. They laid out the dead and let in the living. They were with people as they entered and exited the world, washing away the first day's blood and the last day's sick, sweat and tears. Childbirth, in particular, was often a female collective experience, with goodwives gathered together in a darkened room attending and watching the midwife.[152] Mrs Hopkins, Meifod, Mrs Evans, Viggin, Maesmawr, Gwen of Berth-lwyd in the Swansea Valley and Granny Marsh of Griffithstown, Pontypool, were all renowned for their skills and solutions. In a sense, it is no surprise that women played such a role in informal medicine, for they were scandalously barred from the medical profession.

Some people took piecemeal folk remedies across into a more professional basis.[153] Dr John Rees Yemn had an extensive herbal practice in the Ammanford area in the 1920s. He edited the journal *Medical Herbalist* and established the National Association of Medical Herbalists that aspired to official recognition from the government.[154] Robert Isaac Jones (Alltud Eifion, 1813–1905), pharmacist, litterateur and printer, established the Cambrian Pill Depot in Tremadog. From here he sold his Pelenau Jones Tremadog (Jones's Tremadoc Pills), 'sef yr hen feddyginiaeth Gymraeg Adnabyddus' (the famous old Welsh medicine), which was efficacious for a host of troubles. He also produced Balm Treiddiol Jones, his Nervous Tonic, his Warm Lozenges, his Piles Cream and his Enaint Euraidd Jones.[155] Robert Jones advertised extensively, both within his own publications, such as *Y Brython*, and in a host of newspapers across north Wales. The line between his professional pharmaceutical training and that of patent medicine was fine. Across Wales chemists presided behind their counters in front of a bank of dark brown bottles – compounds of arsenic and antimony, mercury and lead – the complete Crippen compendium.

In the Cardiff area in the early 1920s, some fifteen people earned a living as herbalists and listed themselves as such in local directories and in *Kelly's Directory of South Wales*. In Monmouth there were twelve herbalists listed in a local directory.[156] David and John Evans of Cardigan were part of a family that offered cancer cures by a secret herbal recipe. The Revd Thomas Gwernogle Evans of Neath was perhaps the most prominent medical herbalist in Wales. In *The Cup of Health* (1922) he argued that plants were heaven sent and could restore equilibrium to the sick because they were in harmony with nature. 'Along with the Bible', Evans suggested to his readers, 'keep my book of medical botany on your table . . . consult the both continually for the highest welfare of your body and soul.' Evans was obviously deeply resentful of the medical profession because like the medieval Guilds, it restricted practitioners only to those it recognised. He concluded with the thunderous declaration, 'Degrees and diplomas will not cure diseases.'[157]

The Revd Gwernogle Evans was not the only one who suggested that the best cure for such diseases was not the pharmacist's pills or potions, or the doctor's delusions, but faith and piety. Griffith Ifor Evans (1889–1966) was a surgeon who trained in Oxford and London, winning a number of prizes when qualifying in 1916. But despite his promise, Evans worked, not in the London hospitals, but in general practice in Caernarfon. In 1931 he published the influential *Essays on Familial Syphilis*, which showed the extent of that affliction across society in north Wales. Evans became increasingly interested in the borderlands between medicine, philosophy, theology and belief. Mind and emotion were powerful forces to secure the 'complete health' of an individual. He established the Centre of Spiritual Healing at Caernarfon and later at London.[158] Others who caught up with the craze for spiritualism, that began in Victorian Wales and gathered pace after the First World War, argued that it was not from Christian faith that salvation would come but from the spiritual. Talking with the dead could save the living.[159] Spiritualism and spiritual healers were common across Wales in the 1920s and 1930s. In an inquest into the death of a woman from Llantwit Major in 1927, it was revealed that when the doctor had failed to cure her, she had turned to a spiritual healer.[160]

Broken limbs and other deformities were often treated by a bonesetter. The Lloyds who lived in Llanbadarn Fynydd in Radnorshire enjoyed widespread fame as bonesetters in the 1930s. People from as far away as Llanfair Caereinion would travel there by car to seek healing. Many mining and quarrying communities in north Wales had individuals, usually men, to whom people would turn when limbs were injured. A family in Pwllheli had considerable renown for their manipulative healing powers. In a photograph taken in 1875, by John Thomas, that remarkable chronicler of rural life, Mr H. Davies, the bone doctor of Cynwyd, sits rather awkwardly for the photographer. He looks as if he could do with his own services. He stares nervously and rather apprehensively at the camera; perhaps he thought that the act of taking the photograph would steal away his gift of healing.[161]

The most famous dynasties of Welsh bonesetters were undoubtedly the Thomases and Joneses of Anglesey and Liverpool. Sir Robert Jones (1857–1933) was perhaps the most distinguished. When war broke out in 1914, Robert Jones joined the army as a captain and discovered not only a military, but a medical disaster.[162] Surgeons stood helpless before men shattered by shell and shrapnel. Refusing to be overwhelmed by the catastrophe, Robert Jones urged that the Thomas splint, which had been used with such success to help crippled children in Liverpool, should be used to help injured soldiers. The Thomas splint could be put on in a few minutes, usually without an anaesthetic. Its use resulted in mortality from fractures dropping from 80 per cent in 1915 (before its widespread introduction) to 20 per cent in 1918. Robert Jones also pioneered specialist hospital treatment for soldiers. He became the Army's director of orthopaedics in 1916 organising more than twenty orthopaedic centres. The flagship of orthopaedic centres was that established in May 1916 at Shepherd's Bush, London, where no fewer than 1,000 of the first 1,300 disabled soldiers were rehabilitated to active military duty.[163]

Sir David Thomas Rocyn-Jones (1862–1953) is another figure whose career spans the worlds of popular and professional medicine. Rocyn-Jones was a member of a famous family of bonesetters from Maenordeifi, who became the medical officer of health of

Monmouthshire, where he established an impressive service of preventative medicine, particularly in relation to tuberculosis.[164] It was in administrative positions that many people with a medical training made their greatest contributions. David Llewelyn Williams (1870–1949) of the Vale of Conwy, a surgeon who won the Military Cross at Mametz in 1917 and the Médaille des Epidemics and the Médaille de la Reconnaissance Française, made a special contribution to the success of the 1911 health insurance scheme. He travelled widely in Wales to promote the scheme and to address meetings on health problems, temperance and morality, and wrote extensively in Welsh on these subjects. Dame Juliet Evangeline Rhys-Williams (née Glyn) was made a Dame Commander of the Order of the British Empire in recognition of her part in drafting the Midwives Act 1936.[165] Sir Thomas William Phillips (1883–1966) of Cemaes, Montgomeryshire, was instrumental in implementing many of the reforms outlined in Beveridge's plans to reform national insurance and the welfare state.[166] Gwendoline Joyce Trubshaw (1887–1954), Ada Marian Vachell (1866–1923), and Dame Agnes Gwendoline Hunt (1866–1948) worked in administrative capacities with blind and disabled people.[167] In the battles of medicine and public health against disease, depression, decline and death, the foot soldiers often had to undertake a slow bureaucratic march to establish systems and structures of care.

Doctors, as Dylan Thomas advised, were best avoided for the emotional and economic costs involved. It was desperation that drove many to the doctor. In rural Wales, as the 1913 House of Lords investigation into the operation of the 1911 National Insurance Act discovered, distance prevented people from being able to consult a doctor.[168] Even when they had to attend, labourers could not afford the fees, which created additional tensions between healer and patient. Despite the stigma and shame associated with poverty, many people turned to the Poor Law authorities for medical care and attention. In 1931, a survey of Welsh Poor Law authorities revealed that there were 5,170 beds available, of which 4,138 were occupied by people receiving treatment. The statistics remained relatively stable until the establishment of the National Health Service in 1948.[169] It was not only the most disadvantaged – the lunatics, the lost and the lonely – who turned to the Poor Law authorities, for desperation forced many people to seek care.

In several parts of Wales, communities of workers would co-operate to establish clubs and medical societies to ensure that workers in need would receive the appropriate service. These organisations provided sick benefits and, more importantly, medical attendance and drugs for the workmen and their dependants in return for a payment of about 2d or 3d in each pound of a worker's wage.[170] In the north, Cymdeithas Llesgarol Ffestiniog (Festiniog Benevolent Society) and the Dinorwig Quarries Benefit Club were established in the 1860s.[171] The most celebrated example in Wales was the Tredegar Medical Aid Society. Established in 1874, the society by the 1920s offered its members the services of five doctors, one surgeon, two pharmacists, a physiotherapist, a dentist and a district nurse. Glasses could be obtained for 2s. 6d, whilst false teeth were sold at less than cost price. Wigs, artificial limbs, patent foods, drugs, X-rays, injections and much more were free to members.[172] The Tredegar society was the model upon which Aneurin Bevan built his idea of a national health service.[173] The medical societies often contributed to the costs that their members would accrue if they needed to attend hospital.

A network of hospitals had developed in Wales since the mid-nineteenth century. The majority were relatively small cottage hospitals such as Ebbw Vale Workmen's Cottage Hospital with sixteen beds ranging to Merthyr Tydfil General Hospital with 115 beds.[174] Many institutions, such as the Cardiff Infirmary, were created through private and philanthropic support.[175] As Martin Powell has shown, the level of hospital provision in Wales was seriously disadvantaged in comparison to that in England. Even allowing for the existence of large metropolitan hospitals in London and Manchester in particular, where economies of scale could achieve a comprehensive service, Welsh hospitals compared un-favourably with hospitals in the south-west and north-east of England. Whilst there was a provision of 6.58 hospital beds for every 1,000 people in England, in Wales there was 4.65. Institutions in Wales were also unsatisfactory in terms of their small size, their age and their structural condition.[176]

As with the hospital provision, there were relatively few doctors in general practice in Wales. In 1949, there were 1,092 doctors and 519 dentists practising in Wales.[177] Isolation was a constant problem, particularly for doctors working in rural areas. Doctors had to serve a taciturn people who were reluctant to pay any fees and still deeply superstitious, for medical enlightenment reached no further than the light of the lamp on the front of the surgery porch. Francis Maylett Smith, in his partly factual, partly fictional, auto-biographical portrait of *The Surgery at Aberffrwd*, captured something of the isolation and fear that confronted young doctors.[178] A doctor never knew what was coming next, day or night, through the surgery door – a breach birth, an amputation, a tracheotomy, an obstructed labour, a dental extraction, a horrifying disease. Medical practices were located in places of great beauty but greater isolation.[179] Sir William Pratt (1831–82) a Montgomeryshire doctor, in an article on 'Cases in County Practice' in *The Lancet* in 1881, recalled:

> the county medical man ought to be the most accomplished of all practitioners, in as much as to him it falls at one time to tie an artery, at another to manage a complication of childbirth and at a third to treat pneumonia . . . Metropolitan practitioners, accustomed to easy consultation and to the frequent aid of specialists, cannot understand the anxieties and responsibilities of their provincial brethren, who often times unaided, and uncounselled, must grapple with the most formidable accidents and the most unmanageable diseases.[180]

In such conditions honouring the Hippocratic oath must have been a profound achievement.

3

Going Gently into that Good Night: Desolation, Dispiritedness and Melancholy

Fuom ni yn unlla ond cerdded o gwmpas a doeddwn i ddim yn gwybod tan bora ma, ar ôl imi fynd i Cwt Ned Crudd i gael hoelan yn fy nghlem, fod Yncl Now Moi wedi crogi'i hun yn y tŷ bach, a bod nhw wedi mynd â Jini Bach Pen Cae a Catrin Jên Lôn Isa i'r Seilam. Mae na leuad llawn heno. Pam na newch chi adael i Huw ddwad allan i chwarae, O Frenhines y Llyn Du?

(We went nowhere much, just wandered around and I did not know until this morning, after I went to Ned the Cobbler's shed for a nail in my shoe, that Now Moi's uncle had hanged himself in the toilet, and that Little Jane Pen Cae and Catrin Jane Lower Lane had been taken to the Asylum. There is a full moon tonight. Why won't you let Huw come out to play, oh Queen of the Black Lake?)

Caradog Prichard, Un Nos Ola Leuad (Dinbych, 1963), p. 8.

'Un Nos Ola Leuad' (One Moonlit Night): suicide

Dim ond nyni a ddianc o wledd y bleiddiaid, nyni, ddiderfysg dyrfa'r hunanleiddiaid'.

(Only we escape from the feast of the wolves, we, the peaceful crowd of suicidees).

Caradog Prichard, 'Terfysgoedd Daear', quoted in Alan Llwyd, Rhyfel a Gwrthryfel: Brwydr Moderniaeth a Beirdd Modern (Llandybïe, 2003), p. 288.

Suicide, even when committed in public, is the most private and personal of human acts.[1] The historian is presented with the insurmountable problem that the participants usually leave behind them no written records, only a rippling pool of regrets. The great value of suicide to the historian is that it shines a harsh light onto the problems that tormented and tore apart individuals in Wales. As through a glass darkly we see social realities. Like crime and sex, there was an alleged absence of suicide in Wales.[2] The statistics available in the Registrar General's reports indicate that the standard mortality figures for suicides for Wales were below those for England and Wales, but the number of deaths from suicide increased over the period 1861–1910. In north Wales, the suicidal mortality rate for males increased from thirty-nine in 1861–70, to fifty-nine in 1901–10, whilst the ratio of female suicide deaths increased from twenty-two to sixty-two over the same period; suicide deaths of males in south Wales increased from forty-nine to fifty-nine, and that of females increased from seventy-four to eighty-one. In contrast suicidal deaths of men in Glamorgan increased from fifty-three to fifty-five, but those of females declined from eighty-six to sixty-nine.[3]

The reasons for the lower rates of suicide in Wales are complex and contradictory. Local government machinery for most of the period was weak and fragmentary, as were the forces of law and order. Many of the representatives of these forces were Anglicans and Anglicised, who were often regarded with suspicion by the bulk of Nonconformist and Welsh-speaking people.[4] To attempt suicide, an offence against God, was also a crime against humanity and, until 1961, punishable by the law.[5] There was stigma and shame attached to suicide. Within living memory in the 1880s people recalled that individuals who had committed suicide were buried at crossroads.[6] In a land, anxious to prove its high moral values, in the years following the debacle of the education reports of 1847, there was a distinct reluctance in Wales to accept that such things happened. There is a general sense that attitudes towards suicide in Wales became more tender and tolerant over the course of the nineteenth century. Some ministers noted that Christian martyrs had courted death and refused to save themselves and resolved that the same right, perhaps, should be accorded to other people. Certainly stigma seemed to linger less in Wales than in England. When Robert Jones of Raglan, the hero of Rorke's Drift where he won a Victoria Cross defending the hospital, died from self-inflicted gunshot wounds in 1898, he was initially refused permission to be buried in St Peter's Church in Herefordshire. Eventually, after some remonstrations, the church authorities consented to Robert being buried in consecrated ground. There were, however, conditions. Unlike other gravestones, Robert's had to face away from the church and his coffin was carried into the churchyard over the wall, rather than through the lychgate.

Welsh juries at coroner's courts were often reluctant to pass verdicts of deaths by suicide.[7] Such verdicts often gave rise to endless and disputatious legal cases, in which there were no real beneficiaries, apart, of course, from the legal profession. A better course of action was to speed and ease the journey of property to its inheritors. We should perhaps therefore treat the apparently low levels of suicide mortality with the same scepticism and suspicion with which the criminal and sexual statistics of Wales are greeted.

Suicide, like madness, is often portrayed as a female malady.[8] Several artistic, dramatic, literary and musical sources portray the Welsh Ophelia in her watery grave. Picturesque and poetic images show white-nightgowned women floating, face-up in the water. Shoeless, barefooted, wide-eyed in the reeds and rushes. The plangent song by 'Llew o'r Wern', 'Yr Eneth Gadd ei Gwrthod' (The girl who was spurned), is a mournful, reflective song recounting the sad life of a young girl who had been rejected by her lover and family. The final verse reveals the melodramatic melancholy:

A bore drannoeth cafwyd hi
Yn nyfroedd oer yr afon,
A darn o bapur yn ei llaw
Ac arno'r ymadroddion:
'Gwnewch imi fedd mewn unig fan,
Na chodwch faen na chofnod
I nodi'r fan lle gorwedd llwch
Yr eneth gadd ei gwrthod.

(The following morning she was found
In the cold waters of the river,
With a piece of paper in her hand,
And on it the instruction:
'Make me a grave in a lonely place,
Raise no headstone or inscription,
To mark the place where lies the dust
Of the girl who was spurned'.)[9]

Only a crass cynic would question the legibility and longevity of the poor girl's suicide note after a night immersed in the river. Other tales from the riverbank show that death by drowning was not an exclusive female preserve.[10]

The Registrar General's statistics provide some support for the view that suicide was a female, rather than a male activity. In north Wales the standardised rates in 1901–10 were relatively close – 59 male:62 female per 1,000 people – but in the south and Glamorgan, females predominated, 59:81 and 55:69 respectively. However, care needs to be taken in reaching any firm conclusions on the basis of these general statistics. Similarly, the explanation for the remarkable transformation in the respective levels of the mortality of females between north Wales and Glamorgan needs considerable further study. In north Wales, mortality rates from suicide of females increased from twenty-two in 1861–70 to sixty-nine in 1901–10. This was due to a combination of forces – the secularisation of society, the impact of industrialisation, the effects of a market economy, the retail revolution and the emergence of a consumer society, coupled with the breakdown of rural society and economy over the same period. Contemporaries were conscious of how life had speeded up over the period before the First World War and devised a host of pseudo-medical conditions to describe those people who were unsettled by the process.

If we look at one county then some interesting trends within the overall Welsh patterns emerge. In Carmarthenshire, over the period 1900–19, suicide was primarily a rural phenomenon, for the highest rates occurred in the rural parishes. The person most likely to take his or her life was a farmer. Those aged between forty-five and sixty-five years of age in both rural districts (48.5 per cent of deaths by suicide) and the urban districts (47.2 per cent) were the most suicidal age group. Further more detailed work is needed before firm conclusions can be reached. Studies of court transcripts, coroner's inquests and newspaper reports indicate that death by suicide was a multifaceted phenomenon with almost as many motives for, as there were means of, committing suicide.

'Le mal d'amour', 'tor calon', heartbreak – love, rebuffed or scorned, the classic suicide motive of the girl in contemporary literature, had parallels in real life. In 1917, Maggie Morgan threw herself under a Great Western Railway express train after her boyfriend 'finished with her'.[11] Margaret Williams, a cook, poisoned herself, whilst Muriel Morgan drowned herself in the Tywi river following similar experiences.[12] Catherine Jones of Stanley Street, Senghenydd, killed herself in 1906. The coroner's inquest reveals something of the emotional ice-house in which she had lived with her father after her lover deserted her.[13] Other fathers were more considerate and compassionate. David Davies, a farmer, found his daughter and her baby poisoned in their bedroom in November 1916. At the inquest he poignantly and painfully recalled that she normally spoke in her sleep, but that night she had been quiet and his suspicions had therefore been aroused. She had twice attempted to take out an affiliation order for the child's paternity at the Llanelli Police Court. Twice she failed. Strychnine ended her fears. At the inquest, the coroner, Dr Thomas Walters, remarked: 'Whoever the man is who led her astray, I doubt if he will have comfortable feelings hereafter.'[14] Men also felt the wounds of love. James Evans, a farm servant, 'worried over a girl', hanged himself at Caer-bryn, Pen-y-groes in January 1905. Henry Thomas, a collier, drowned himself in Pwll Du in the river Marlais, Llandybïe, when a paternity order was awarded against him.[15]

Those who survived the trials and tribulations of courtship found life no easier when married. Love was a temporary insanity cured by marriage. Mary Lewis of Llanelli took carbolic poison when her husband left her.[16] Mary Davies, a farmer's wife of Carmarthenshire, committed suicide when she and her husband separated in March 1906. Thomas Rees Richards committed suicide rather than appear in court for arrears of £30 on a separation order awarded to his wife.[17] Having just lost a child, Mary Ellen Davies of Penclawdd murdered her three daughters, aged between two and four, and then committed suicide in an upstairs bedroom.[18] Ann Joseph drowned herself and her infant daughter at Porth in the Rhondda in September 1878.[19]

A profound sense of melancholic loneliness permeated many people's lives. Henry Watkins, a Cardiff businessman, shot himself on his wife's grave. With great deliberation he put the gun into his mouth and pulled the trigger. On his body police found a valuable gold chain and watch, a gold ring, a photograph of himself, deeds of his wife's grave, two letters and notes in which he said that he had no friends and that the workhouse awaited.[20] At Canton, Cardiff, in 1878, Miss Williams, 'a single woman somewhat passed the prime of life', as she was rather cruelly described in the *Western Mail*, attempted to hang herself. She was upset at the loss of her sister. On the railway line between Cardiff and Newport, workmen found a severed head – how much unhappiness was compressed in that small head we will never know.[21]

A *cri de cœur* based on a sense of personal worthlessness and failure permeates the lives of many suicide victims. The poet Talhaiarn, John Jones (1810–70), caught between the pressures of ideological Victorian Utilitarianism and Benthamism, felt increasingly disenchanted and became obsessed that his life and his poetry were meaningless and worthless. He shot himself. Typically he did not do a good job of it, for he died days later after a period of protracted agony.[22] Edward Thomas John (1857–1931), an MP, an ironmaster and a Welsh nationalist, of Pontypridd, looked back over a parliamentary and political career that he felt was a complete failure and committed suicide.[23] Pryce Lewis (1832–1911) left the grinding poverty of Newtown for a better life in Chicago. There he joined Allan Pinkerton's detective agency. Disguised as an English aristocrat, Lewis toured the American south, gathering intelligence for the northern armies. The years of failure, penury, loneliness and possible madness had shown him a different face of death. Terrified and traumatised that he was returning to the poverty of his youth, he committed suicide by throwing himself off the Pulitzer Building in New York in 1911. A more dramatic attempt to obtain press attention is hard to imagine.[24]

The inability to cope with adverse economic fortunes also features prominently in the reasons witnesses gave to inquests for the suicide of a friend or acquaintance. Charles Griffiths cut his throat with a razor because of his worries about his unemployment.[25] Arthur Williams, a bookmaker, committed suicide in July 1907 because of his financial problems.[26] George Blake, agent to the Stradey Estate, cut his throat in a greenhouse when his employer told him that his services were no longer required as the son would manage the estate.[27] David Bowen, a publican and timber merchant, a man, according to witnesses, with few problems, hanged himself with a horse's harness after he failed to sell the animal.[28] John Jones of Llangynnwr, a coachman, committed suicide when he was sacked by his employer as the result of the purchase of a car.[29] When he became unemployed, Evan Williams of Hirwaun murdered his wife by strangling her and hanged himself in their bedroom, leaving their little daughter to witness the carnage.[30] The story was virtually repeated in 1876, when nine-year-old Cecilia Tree woke to find that her stepfather Charles had murdered her mother and slashed his own throat.[31]

The rise in unemployment in Wales in the 1920s and 1930s saw an increase in suicides amongst the unemployed. The press often offered little sympathy. After John Pember of Senghenydd, who had been unemployed for nine months, hanged himself from his bedstead in May 1923, a local newspaper reported, 'A Coward's Suicide'.[32] Considerably more consideration and compassion was shown to William Felton, the stationmaster for the Taff Vale Railway at Pontypridd. In a 'terrible tragedy', Felton shot himself due to concerns that he would not be repaid for a loan he had made to a friend. Additionally Felton 'had given way to the betting craze, and one or two disappointments on the turf on Thursday brought things to a crisis'.[33]

Catastrophic events had a profound impact on those who either survived, or had lost loved ones. Further tragedies were added to that capital of death in Wales, Senghenydd, after the pit explosion of 1913. Mary Saunders, who had lost her son in the disaster, committed suicide by drinking carbolic acid a week later. Annie Gay cut her throat in May 1914, in her parents' kitchen. She was much agitated after the disaster in which her sister's young man was killed, telling her parents, 'Oh dear, all those souls have gone home and I have suffered terribly.'[34] Her own grief grieved her. Her sister's devastated her.

The First World War had a profound psychological impact on the home front as well as on soldiers, and this is reflected in suicide cases. Soldiers suffering from 'shell-shock'[35] and hysteria, a condition that had previously been considered peculiar to women, committed suicide with distressing regularity between August 1914 and November 1918.[36] Receipt of a letter confirming that the King required a person's service in the trenches was a frequent trigger to self-harm and suicide. Henry Ridgen attempted to commit suicide at Llanarthne on receipt of such an invitation in August 1915.[37] Ernest Lloyd Morgan, a court registrar and nephew of the aspirant Poet Laureate, Sir Lewis Morris, was more successful. He 'shot his face off' after being passed fit to serve his King and Country.[38] But it was not only those directly involved in the fighting who found the pressures of the war too great to bear. Ruth Williams, worried about her sons in the colours, hanged herself in an outhouse, whilst Ann Williams, who had two sons on the Western Front, cut her throat.[39] When Elizabeth Mundy's husband Frank returned to the war in August 1917, she drowned her youngest son and attempted to drown herself.[40]

World events pressed hard on some individuals. David Richard Davies (1889–1958), the theologian and journalist, was deeply troubled by the course of the Spanish Civil War and the threatening shadow of Nazism darkening across Europe. He attempted suicide by drowning at Southerndown, but had a vision of his mother reading from the children's catechism *Rhodd Mam* and asking him 'Who is Jesus Christ?', to which he answered, 'Jesus Christ is my saviour'. He left the sea and gave his attention to the theology of Niebuhr.[41]

The author and pacifist George Maitland Lloyd Davies (1880–1949), a Christian Pacifist MP in 1923, a minister with the Calvinistic

Methodists, an anti-fascist and a peace campaigner, was another for whom the world and its woes became unbearable. Whilst people questioned his sanity, few questioned his sanctity for Davies was widely considered as a 'saint', a somewhat incongruous description for a Nonconformist. Burdened by the legacy of the horrors of Auschwitz and Belsen, Changi and Kinkaseki, the devastation of the atomic bomb on Hiroshima and Nagasaki, he obsessed that humanity's capacity for evil would outweigh its ability for goodness. His messianic forebodings presented the world poised on the brink of another Apocalypse more terrifying than those he had lived through. Davies believed that there are no absolutes in human misery and things can always get worse. Darkness had fallen over the face of the world, and the only escape was not an optimistic dawn, but death. Davies took his own life when enrolled as a voluntary patient at the North Wales Mental Hospital, Denbigh.[42]

Religion, as the life of George Maitland Lloyd Davies showed, sometimes intensified mental instability. Christianity, with its own savage death at its core, proved problematic for some people. In 1919, the Revd John Crwys Evans committed suicide after prolonged depression following the death of his son.[43] The Revd John Thomas of Capel Isaac, suffering from indigestion but apparently no other problems, hanged himself in the garden shed.[44] But religion itself not only coloured the problems of an individual, it created new fears. Fears of God's revenge, of the fallen nature of man, or of Hell, were real anxieties for a number of individuals. William Morgan, a forty-year-old collier from Llanarthne, advised to take a change of air by his doctor, walked to Dryslwyn Castle, where he jumped into the River Tywi. Dragged out 500 yards downstream, he insisted that his sins were unpardonable. He was admitted to the asylum in Carmarthen.[45]

Religion coloured the delusions of Sarah Jacob, the famous or infamous fasting girl. Her protracted suicide by starvation is one of the most remarkable and reprehensible stories in Welsh history.[46] But it is not unique. Others were similarly mentally torn and tortured by their religious anxieties and obsessions. Martha Davies of Aberdare in 1870, Elizabeth Davies of Aberavon in 1876, and

Emily Rees of Cardiff took their own lives through poison because 'their sins were too great a burden to bear'.[47] The note left by Thomas Hambury Powell tells us much about the motives that drove him to his death in Llanelli Dock and the forces that operated in his society:

> I did this rash thing because of drink. It forced me to do it, and I must make an end to myself in this way. The snares of death compressed me round about, and the pains of hell got hold upon me. O Thou Great and Merciful God, wilt thou forgive and pardon my sins that I have sinned against Thee, and for this wicked thing that I have done. – Dear Father, Mother and Sister, will you forgive me for this wicked thing I have done. Do not let it trouble you for I shall have forgiveness in the Lord. I hope all the young men of Llanelli will give up the evil drinking, and take a warning from me, dear friends.[48]

Such notes from beyond the grave are, despite the plots of melo-dramatic novels, relatively rare. Those that do exist often show how hard an individual person grappled with the 'Savage God', before deciding to 'go gently into that good night'.[49] The writer Dorothy Edwards (1903–34) left perhaps the bleakest suicide note after she threw herself under a train on a Cardiff railway line in 1934: 'I am killing myself because I have never sincerely loved any human being all my life. I have accepted kindness and friendship, and even love without gratitude, and given nothing in return.'[50]

The blue-eyed blonde Peg Entwhistle left Port Talbot to become an actress in Hollywood in the 1920s. Despite starring in films with Humphrey Bogart, her latest and last film *13 Women* proved to be unlucky and received hostile reviews. Reading the reviews, emotionally she shattered like glass. Peg became the misbegotten heroine of her own demise. On Saturday afternoon, 18 September 1932, she climbed to the top of the 'H' of the Hollywood sign, and jumped off. A note found on her battered body read, 'I am afraid I am a coward. I am sorry for everything. If I had done this a long time ago, it would have saved a lot of pain. P.E.' Her uncle, with whom she was lodging, read a notice in the *Los Angeles Times* that a body had been found and went to identify her. Two days later he received a letter addressed to Peg Entwhistle from the Beverly Hills Playhouse. It was offering her a lead role in a play about a woman who committed suicide.[51]

The caves of alienation: worry, boredom and hysteria

I have begun to die.
For now at last I know
That there is no escape
From night.

Alun Lewis, 'The Sentry', in Meic Stephens (ed.),
Poetry 1900–2000 (Cardigan, 2007), p. 177.

Madness, like beauty, is in the eye of the beholder and the mind of the afflicted.[52] The line between sanity and madness was often just the thickness of an asylum patient's uniform. The medical officer at Carmarthen's Joint Counties Hospital in 1885 was concerned at the experience of one of his patients who had been discovered in the hospital grounds in a state of uncontrollable and unstoppable laughter. Laughter often has a darker association with the crueller and callous aspects of the damaged mind for, as Dryden said, 'there is a pleasure fair in being mad, that none but man men know'. But this was different. The patient, it seems, had been the recipient of verbal abuse from Llanelli people visiting Carmarthen to drink on a Sunday, circumventing the Welsh Sunday Closing Act of 1881 as they had travelled over three miles. When restrained and rested, the patient explained that he had 'been laughing at the likes of them behaving like that and being outside and free. Yet I behave well, and I am locked up in here.'[53]

Mad people have illuminating things to say because madness presents a world through the looking-glass, or indeed holds up the mirror to the logic (and pseudo-logic) of so-called sane society.[54] It focuses and points to truths that test the nature and limits of the rationality, humanity and 'understanding' of the normal. The history of unreason, as Michel Foucault and others have argued, is coterminous with the history of reason.[55]

The years 1870–1945 represent probably the golden age of the asylum, if such an enlightened metaphor can be applied to an institution that is usually disparaged and portrayed as depressing and dark.[56] The number of asylums and their inmates increased significantly over the course of the nineteenth century.[57] When Cardiff City Lunatic Asylum opened in April 1908, it joined the institutions in Carmarthen, Denbigh, Pen-y-Fal, Abergavenny, Cefn Coed (Swansea) and Vernon House (Bridgend), which together housed more than 7,000 people.[58] As the doors swung open to receive Cardiff's mentally ill, the prospectus for the pristine institution spoke of the superb facilities of a hospital, not an asylum. The journalists covering the event for both the *Western Mail* and the *South Wales Daily News* gave themselves over to a Gradgrindian surfeit of factoids – 10,000,000 bricks, 30,000 tonnes of concrete, 980 yards of corridors, 58 miles of electric wiring.[59]

In time, it was discovered that the electricity could do little to enlighten the people who wandered the corridors, for despite the high hopes and the noble aspirations, Cardiff City Lunatic Asylum soon became, like the other Welsh mental hospitals, a custodial rather than a curative centre, devoted to constraint and control rather than cure, another museum of madness. The transformation from care to custody was captured in the victorious sonnet at the National Eisteddfod of 1944. Set in the Cefn Coed psychiatric hospital, Swansea, it was given the title 'Carcharorion' (Prisoners). The metaphors are those of a locked fortress, 'mae cadarn glo ar ddrysau'r gaer'n gaeëdig fore a hwyr' (there are stout locks on the doors of this locked fortress, morning and night). Dante's advice might well have been carved on the gates – 'All hope abandon ye who enter here'.[60]

This is not to minimise the attempts of Welsh doctors to improve the lives of their patients. At Cardiff, the medical officer Dr Edwin Goodall was one of the leaders of his profession and president of the neurology and psychiatry section of the Royal Society of Medicine. He was also author of the standard textbook in the field – *Insanity and Allied Neuroses: a Practical and Clinical Manual* (Chicago, Ill., 1907). He had previously been head of the Joint Counties Lunatic Asylum in Carmarthen, where amongst other achievements he had learned to speak Welsh within six months.[61] The psychiatrists Sir Robert Armstrong-Jones (1857–1943), Linford Rees, J. R. Rees and T. P. Rees also did pioneering work to unravel some of the afflictions of the mentally ill. Thomas Parry Rees (1899–1963), in a number of roles in Welsh and English asylums, inaugurated 'the open door policy' that brought welcome elements of freedom, dignified work, a general enthusiasm, activism, fresh-mindedness and general friendliness to his patients.[62] Those attempts to gain understanding by doctors working within the public asylum system were complemented by the efforts of doctors working within private care. One of the most notable was Dr Ernest Jones (1879–1958), the biographer of Freud, who became known as 'Freud's Welsh Wizard'. He, perhaps more than any other figure in the early twentieth century, was responsible for the popularisation of Freud's ideas and the establishment of psychoanalysis and 'the talking cure'.[63]

Yet despite their finest and firmest efforts, for most patients within the asylum system there was little real sense of optimism, and the future for the majority was bleak. At the north Wales asylum in Denbigh in 1927, the medical superintendent reported that, out of a total of 1,359 patients he regarded 1,308 as incurable. Only ten men and eleven women were likely to be cured, whilst a further fifteen of each sex might have some chance of recovery.[64] The day books of the medical superintendent at the Carmarthen asylum reveal the tragic lives and the intractable nature of insanity within west Wales. On 8 April 1881, Margaret Jones, aged thirteen, of Llandovery Union, was admitted to the asylum after continuous night wanderings, during which she tore her clothes and was 'dirty in her habits'. She was described as suffering from 'nervous debility', which was probably congenital. Margaret joined her three brothers in the asylum.[65] On 25 November 1882, James Davies, aged thirty-six from Lampeter, an 'imbecile' from birth who had two illegitimate children, and whose father and sister were 'imbeciles', was admitted and described as being violent and suicidal.[66] In the medical officer's annual report of 1889, Dr Goodall remarked that a male 'idiot' admitted was one of thirteen illegitimate children by the same mother. The mother and grandmother, he said, were both 'peculiar'.[67]

The medical officers of health in the asylums within rural Wales frequently noted the high incidence of intractable hereditary cases. At Carmarthen more than 80 per cent of patients suffered from 'hereditary disposition' or 'congenital defects', many of whom were dangerous and suicidal. Despite all their portrayals as an Elysium of health and a stronghold of family values, several parts of rural Wales had been torn asunder by serious social problems. Migration had taken away the youngest and fittest, leaving a rural population that was aged or helpless or hapless. As society broke down, more and more people would be transferred to the care of the asylum. D. J. Williams, usually such a tender chronicler of rural Wales, in his short story 'Pwll yr Onnen' highlights the brooding and brutal tensions that existed even in this bucolic paradise.[68]

Several of the melancholic suicide victims, whose tragic stories litter the pages of local newspapers, had at one time or another been patients at Welsh asylums. Some form of custodial care was clearly needed, not just to protect the insane and their families from their unpredictable and violent behaviour, but also to protect the mentally ill from the public's treatment of them. In his *Chapters in the History of the Insane in the British Isles* (1882), D. H. Tuke refers to the case of a female, 'AB', from near Brecon:

> She had been chained in a crouching position, her knees forced up to her chin, and she sat wholly upon her heels and her hips, and considerable excoriation had taken place where her knees pressed upon her stomach . . . When she died it required very considerable dissection to get her pressed into her coffin. This might be taken as a sample of Welsh Lunatics.[69]

In 1873, Dr Hearder, medical superintendent at Carmarthen, complained that the local populace were slow to send their patients to the asylum for 'treatment', and that the general belief that they were treated kindly at home was false. He wrote:

> The bodily condition of the patients admitted in very many cases gives evidence to the lamentable neglect and cruel treatment to which they had been subjected . . . Two cases suffering from acute

mania had been tied down to their beds, and their excretions allowed to remain until extensive sores had formed on their backs ... whilst a twenty-seven year-old man was a mass of sores from the soles of his feet unto his mouth, he had been certified as insane for years ... Now here is a picture of scenes which are to be found in a land proud of its Christianity and civilisation. Do they not fasten a stigma on both, and cry out for reform?[70]

In 1907 the head attendant at the Carmarthen asylum complained to the medical superintendent that he was continually being disturbed late at night by people bringing in their uncertified lunatic relatives.[71]

Attendance at church was frequently praised and urged by the lunacy commissioners, but its value in the recovery of patients is doubtful.[72] In 1884, in his twentieth annual report to the committee of visitors, the medical superintendent declared that 'the prevailing feature of insanity in this area as in the other asylums of Wales seems to be morbid depression of spirits connected with religious views.'[73] Kate Roberts's novella *Tywyll Heno* (*Dark Tonight*, 1962) shows how religious belief could be the source of prolonged mania and depression. This first-person narration by the madwoman herself is a searing indictment of both religion and the prison that was the asylum.

Ministers of religion provide a frequent occupational group of patients housed at the Welsh asylums and their suicides dot the pages of the newspapers of Wales.[74] Throughout the night of 22 December 1883, David Williams, a patient in the Carmarthen asylum, was much depressed, sleepless and tearful as the result of his religious insecurities.[75] Alfred C., a patient at Pen-y-Fal, Bridgend, claimed that going down Chapel Street he saw the Almighty who told him to go and have a gin and water, which he did. Renewal of religious allegiance and the intensification of religious beliefs in revivals were reflected in the issues that troubled patients in asylums. Following 1904–6, those remarkable years of religious revival, the medical superintendent at Carmarthen Joint Counties Lunatic Asylum noted, in his *Forty-first Annual Report* of 8 January 1906:

Sixteen cases were admitted as a result of emotional influences of, in this instance, a religious kind which their hereditary unstable natures were unable to withstand. Religious emotion, being more massive and more intense, and having so to say a wider striking area than other causes of emotion, is more apt to cause mental breakdown, and more apt to tinge mental disorder than other factors.[76]

But despite these views, religion continued to be viewed as a beneficial influence on the insane. Charles Williams, in his *Religion and Insanity* (1908), argued that religion is 'seldom a cause of insanity, but rather it is a preventative, its absence or loss is often a direct cause, while its restoration is sometimes the only cure.'[77] In a similar way, the effects of venereal disease, in particular the role of syphilis in the production of congenital defects, were not acknowledged, often for moral rather than medical reasons. But such causes must have been more widespread than the one or two cases given official recognition annually as suffering from general paralysis of the insane. In 1898 the coroner for West Carmarthenshire noted that in examining the bodies of persons dying in asylums:

one observes the comparative frequency of degeneration of the blood vessels (arteries) of the brain, and I quite subscribe to the view expressed by eminent authorities, that syphilis is the most frequent cause of organic brain disease in persons not much past middle life . . . A careful inquiry into the history of these cases often discloses the existence of hereditary or acquired syphilis to a surprising degree.[78]

The tension between those who argued for and against the asylum system intensified after the First World War. An anonymous author in *Baner ac Amserau Cymru* in January 1925, writing on 'Gwallgofdai' (mad houses), condemned the institutions for the harm they inflicted on those who were not completely mad.[79] The poet Ivor Gurney, himself a long-term inmate, condemned the 'Strange Hells' of the mental hospitals.[80] Caradog Prichard, who never recovered from the guilt of seeing his mother committed to the asylum in Denbigh, where she was incarcerated from 1923 until her death in 1954, was often physically ill after visiting her.[81] The asylum's regime was often one of chastisement and punishment, rather than care and protection. It is important to remember that the medical staff of these institutions had the unenviable tasks of trying to piece together the nightmare worlds of the broken dreams of very brittle people, but some appear to have been more cruel than caring.

The world they tried to control was a savage, vicious one. It is a world in which jealousy, spite, envy, hatred, fear, resentment and malice were the main operating emotions – a world of forks being driven through eyeballs, of noses and ears bitten off. It is a savage, vicious world, a world in which fear ruled. But it is a world above all of the individual – the starting point of all histories. Ann Praws, from the Cardigan Union, admitted to the Joint Counties Asylum on 23 July 1881, imagined that she was 'to be boiled alive because of the enormity of my sins'.[82] Margaret Morrels, a thirty-four-year-old from Carmarthen, admitted to the asylum in February 1882, had been a gibbering wreck ever since her husband had deserted her two years previously.[83] Mary Rogers, aged thirty-six, admitted from Llanelli Union on 15 January 1884, was said to have been insane for six years as a result of injuries inflicted by a threshing machine.[84] The unsavoury atmosphere of jealous gossip and spite that permeated some neighbourhoods, which spilt over from the street corner into the police court, is also seen in the asylum. Fanny Thomas, a fifty-four-year-old woman from the Llanelli Union, was convinced on 27 April 1887 that her neighbour had sent two men and a woman with loaded pistols and other weapons to 'destroy' her. She joined her husband in the asylum. In another case, Mary Ann Jones, aged twenty-one from Carmarthen, certified as insane for a month, was admitted following accusations of immorality.[85] On 12 October 1881, John James, a blind man, was described as being very dangerous to those near him, as a result of his 'imagining that he can see his wife misbehaving herself.'[86] Henry Heeson was one of the many who chose escape from the pressures of nineteenth-century life through creating a dream world of his own. Henry's was the world of a seventeenth-century Tsar of Russia.[87]

The most, perhaps, that the medical staff could achieve for such sufferers, was to turn some of their neuroses and psychoses into common unhappiness. For psychiatry and psychoanalysis, as Ernest Jones once said, like politics and pedagogy 'were the impossible professions'.[88]

4

Where, When, What Was Wales and who were the Welsh? Contentment, Disappointment and Embarrassment

'A man is greater than his country. Therefore, I do not exist for Wales, but Wales exists for me'.

Rhys Davies, Wales, 2 (October 1943).

'Gwlad, Gwlad: Wales! Wales?'

Ond yma ym mro'r cysgodion y mae hil
Gondemniwyd i boen Sisiffos yn y byd,
I wthio o oes i oes drwy flynyddoedd fil
Genedl garreg i ben bryn Rhyddid, a'r pryd –
O linach chwerw Cunedda –
Y gwelir copa'r bryn, drwy frad neu drais
Teflir y graig i'r pant a methu'r cais,
A chwardd Adar y Pwll ar eu hing diwedda.

(But here in the land of the shadows is a race
Condemned to the pains of Sisyphus in the world,
To push from age to age through millennia
The stone of nationhood up Freedom's hill, and when –
From Cunedda's bitter lineage –
We see the hilltop, through betrayal or crime
The stone is cast into the ditch and the effort fails
To the plaintive cry of the Birds of the Pit.)

Saunders Lewis, 'Marwnad Syr John Edward Lloyd', in Bethan Mair
and Elinor Wyn Reynolds, Hoff Gerddi Coffa Cymru
(Llandysul, 2014), pp. 30–2.

When, where, what was Wales, and who were the Welsh? These are questions that have been often posed and pondered.[1] As the twenty-first century turned, the greater devolution of powers of governance to Wales intensified debates and discussions over the characteristics of the Welsh national identity. Historians delineated the economic, cultural, social and political forces that interacted in the imagining of the nation.[2] Some writers considered complex conceptualisations such as whether Wales was post-colonial or postcolonial or post-nationalist, or postnationalist. Not since the days of Salesbury has a simple punctuation mark conveyed so much.[3] With or without a hyphen, whichever concept was discussed, the complex and contradictory nature of the people's lived reality meant that even at best it was a partial explanation. In the previous volume *People, Places and Passions* it was shown how in an age of British imperial expansion, the Welsh too eagerly shouldered the white man's burden and sought dominion over palm and pine. Wales and the Welsh were conquered and conquerors, oppressed and oppressors.

In this process of national reimaging some of the most per-ceptive work was produced by literary critics especially in the University of Wales Press's series *Writing Wales in English*. Writers such as Katie Gramich, Simon Brooks, Kirsti Bohata, Jane Aaron, M. Wynn Thomas and Daniel G. Williams have teased out the 'hybridity, diversity and ambivalence' of personal and national identities. Fiction, they showed, was a vital force in the forging of the nation.[4]

When, and if, they considered such questions, contemporaries often provided negative answers, evidence that in the 1870s, Wales remained much of a *terra incognita* and Welshness a vague con-cept that was often denied or derided.[5] On St David's Day 1879, at the Castle Hotel, Merthyr Tydfil, Welsh national sentiment ap-peared confused, perhaps understandably so given the venue, as Mr T. Edwards proposed a toast to 'Old England – including Wales'.[6] *The Encyclopaedia Britannica* infamously echoed Mr Edwards's view in 1881, with its lazy instruction 'for Wales, see England.' Five years later in 1886, Bishop Basil Jones of St David's, who, characteristically for a bishop, had recently made a diagonal move back to Wales, declared that 'Wales is at present nothing more than the Highlands of England without a Highland Line: it is a geographical expression.'[7] On the matter of Wales, Anglicans and Catholics were obviously in accord for a Papal encyclical of 1916 declared, 'Wales is such a peculiar part of England.' Even at the turn of the twentieth century Wales had no parliament, government, bureaucracy, or state structure around which a 'traditional' sense of identity, nationality or statehood could form. This situation led Gwilym Davies to lament in *The Welsh Review*, in 1939, 'To say Wales is a nation and not a state is to emphasise that it remains a soul without a body.'[8] Wales had survived, artificially in some respects, as an entity, its administrative cohesion was more apparent than real, but in cultural terms, perhaps, it was more real than apparent. Unlike the nations that Benedict Anderson considered were 'insufficiently imagined', Wales existed in a virtual rather than a veritable reality.[9] It had an anthem, a flag, founding myths and founding fathers, all of which were being celebrated in new statues and new national histories.

The situation was not helped by the fact that Wales was divided into distinct regions of north and south, which appeared to have little contact or little in common. Communication, transport and logistical networks ran east to west across the country into England or out into the 'Atlantic economy' so that there was little national integration. Bristol, Chester, Shrewsbury, Kington and Liverpool were more familiar to many people than any Welsh town. Indeed, the Merseyside city had strong claims to being the capital of north Wales. In the 1890s there were an estimated 90,000 Welsh speakers living in Liverpool, making it, many claimed, 'y lle Cymreiga yn y byd' (the most Welsh-speaking place in the world). To confirm this the National Eisteddfod was held there in 1917 and 1927. The local council in Bootle even issued rate demands in Welsh. In his memoir, the photographer John Thomas claimed that there were at least fifty-nine Welsh chapels in the city by 1895.[10] Shrewsbury had 1,378 Welsh-born people living with the Shropshire lads and lasses in 1871. Bristol, in the 1880s, was gradually losing its reputation as 'the metropolis of Wales' but people still referred to the city's docks as 'the Welsh back'.

The north-south divide was not just geographical, but cultural, temperamental and linguistic, for the Welsh, too, were a people separated by a common language. Language is the signature of both individual and collective identity, and even small differences of accent identify speakers of a particular community or a county. Language is thus a perennial contradiction. It is supposed to nourish communication, yet it often achieves the opposite. It is meant to sustain communities, but it also breaks them apart. Geographers have identified no fewer than twenty-eight distinct linguistic areas in Wales. 'Cardis' would have difficulties comprehending 'Cofis', 'Moniars' would struggle to understand Monmouthshire Welsh or 'Gwenhwyseg'.[11] Thus some resorted to English as a lingua franca. It was no surprise perhaps that the late nineteenth century saw a concerted campaign to standardise the Welsh language and to create a common pattern of standard usage. Sir John Morris-Jones, and many grammarians and philologists, were busy trying to create an argot for their imagined community.

To many southern commentators, northerners were dour and melancholic, existing in a state of perpetual depression the same colour and quality as the slate they sliced. To northerners, people in south Wales were irresponsible, rootless hedonists. J. Hugh Edwards, on his journey of discovery through north Wales in 1907, remarked, 'I have again and again been exceedingly amazed at the suspicion and distrust with which North Walians and South Walians, among the lower classes, regard each other.' O. M. Edwards was even clearer about the distinction between northerners and southerners: 'dydi chwarelwyr ddim fel coliars; mae nhw yn fwy gwareddiedig, yn fwy efengylaidd; ac mae'n well gennyn nhw ddiodde na gwneud dim o'i le' (Quarrymen are not like miners; they are more cultured; more evangelical; and they would rather suffer than do anything wrong). A man who left the depressed slate industry of the north in 1912, for the Eldorado of south Wales, noted simply, 'Ni ellid dweud fod yr Hwntw a'r Northman yn orhoff o'u gilydd' (You cannot claim that south Walians and northerners are fond of each other).[12]

Yet, despite its apparent absorption into her more powerful neighbour, Wales and the Welsh had sufficient individuality and idiosyncrasies as to be deemed different to England and the English. 'According to all accounts', an English commentator observed in 1912, 'it was Offa who built a dyke to separate Wales from England, and we are all inclined to think that Offa was a man of sense and discernment.'[13] Of great influence in the foundation of the Welsh identity was the development of the English national character. For some people the form that the resurgence or reawakening of the nation took was largely that of stark opposition in which what was validly and properly Welsh was whatever was furthest from English culture. If England was urban, Wales had to be rural. If England was secular, Wales had to be devout.[14] This was the process that Freud's backer and biographer Dr Ernest Jones described in 'the narcissism of minor differences'. Instead of looking clearly at Welsh life in all its diversity, the new cultural movements tended to provide simplistic definitions of Welshness, which excluded much of the reality. Though the characteristics that distinguished Wales and the Welsh were often complex and contradictory, contemporaries and subsequent commentators have simplified reality into a series of clichés or stereotypes. The complex, unsettling, real course of things was reduced to a clear, satisfying, and, above all, simple story. Hence Jan Morris's complaint that 'Wales is a land of stereotypes, often self-inflicted.'[15]

'Yr hen ffordd Gymreig o fyw': rural idylls

'Nid dinesydd yw'r Cymro, ond gwladwr'
(The Welshman is not a citizen, but a countryman).

Ambrose Bebb, Calendar Coch (1946).

In Welsh society down to 1945 there emerged two views of Wales based on characterisations of rural or urban society. The pastoral tradition of Welsh prose and poetry eulogised rural society as the source of traditional values and virtues. Rural Wales was a society where Welsh was the most commonly spoken language, Nonconformity the most important religion and Liberalism the dominant political creed. In pen portraits, character sketches, polemics, poems and hymns the villages and hamlets of rural Wales were portrayed as the natural home of the Welsh people. Between 1870 and 1945 authors were surprisingly consistent in their presentation of life in rural Wales. Bundle the clichés together and the story is clear: in the countryside in a dazzlingly whitewashed cottage lived the noble rustic, existing in peaceful contentment with his sweet wife – the good, moralistic Mam. The moral Welsh matriarch was a total contrast to her presumptuous English cousin who strutted as debutante, Suffragette or Flapper. Around the contented couple, their child – half angel, half Bambi – frolicked innocently in the fresh air. The only serpent in this prelapsarian paradise was the cruel English 'schoolin' (schoolmaster). The only cloud on their mental horizon was that their son, when grown, would be exiled from this bucolic idyll. Like all the other sad, uprooted, ungodly souls, he would be drawn to the town by the excitements and dangers of football, the theatre, the cinema, newspapers, penny-dreadfuls, gambling and, even worse, the most dangerous temptation of all – the demon drink.

The idea that the nation's spirit burned most brightly in the common people, 'y werin', was an attractive one for the kind of romantic who found technological and social change confusing. The nation's ancient airs were transcribed by the Welsh Folk Song Society and later recorded on hissing phonographs. Peasant sayings were treasured as if they were keys to a secret world, a disappearing wisdom that literate men and women, deprived of daily contact with the earth, could only enviously glimpse. Hence the vogue at the turn of the twentieth century for works such as Henry Halford Vaughan's *Welsh Proverbs* (1889), T. O. 'Tryfan' Jones's *Diarhebion y Cymry* (1891), and Sir O. M. Edwards's *Diarhebion* (1912). The idea was given academic credibility in the geographical and anthropological work of Herbert John Fleure (1877–1969) and Emrys George Bowen (1900–83). They attempted in the 1910s and 1920s to classify and uncover the geography of Welsh physical type, through measuring the head shape and facial characteristics of approximately 2,500 people. One notable type was a Palaeolithic survival found in upland Wales. Local legend in Cardiganshire has it that Fleure persuaded one of these, the elder of two farming brothers, to sell him his head – for which the farmer, naturally being a 'Cardi', demanded payment in advance. Fleure's later work with Elwyn Davies, on the distribution of blood groups, served to further strengthen the perception of the antiquity of Welsh peasant society. So too did the work in social anthropology of Professor Daryll Forde and Fitzroy Richard Somerset (1885–1964), Fourth Baron Raglan.[16]

The tales the academics, poets and novelists told to eulogise rural Wales was, basically, one of fear – the fear of change. Many of these writers yearned for stability in an ever-changing world. The most notable symbols of rural Wales, the mountains, sacred as Islwyn envisaged them, unchanging as Ceiriog thought them, remained, but their contours had been transformed by quarrying and they were tunnelled into. Nothing lasts for ever, even cold November rain on Cadair Idris.

The landscape, such a vital component in the geography of place, was being transformed. Much to the chagrin of poets such as Gwenallt in 'Rhydcymerau' (1951) the Forestry Commission had carpeted hillsides with conifers, displacing people – 'coed lle bu cymdogaeth' (trees where once were communities).[17] Pristine valleys that had about them an air of Genesis's first morning were entombed beneath reservoirs whose waters were pumped east into English cities. The Ministry of Defence closed off extensive areas of Wales so that the army and air force could practice mass destruction. In the late 1930s Epynt became the 'lost lands', the inhabitants who had trodden local pathways since prehistory were cast out in what one elderly lady described as 'diwedd y byd' (the end of the world).[18] A cartography of control was enforced as the names of farms that had an age-old intimacy with their landscape were lost in the encroaching darkness of 'Brechfa Forest'. Waldo Williams concludes his poem 'Preseli' (1946) with the terribly prophetic vision:

Mae rhu, mae rhaib drwy'r fforest ddiffenestr
Cadwn y mur rhag y bwystfil, cadwn y ffynnon rhag y baw.[19]

(There is a roar, there is a ravening through the windowless forest
Keep the wall from the brute, keep the spring clear of the filth.)

The twentieth century saw a battle between two rival concepts of land and people, space and place. Government, with the imperiousness with which it treated its overseas colonies, regarded Welsh lands empty, underoccupied and unproductive. In contrast, Welsh writers emphasised the almost sacred bonds that existed between the land, language, race and place.[20] Many authors stressed the merits of 'yr hen ffordd Gymreig o fyw' – the traditional Welsh way of life. In 1911, a writer, probably O. M. Edwards, in the magazine *Cymru* noted:

'I harddwch ei wlad mae y Cymro yn ddyledus am ei feddwl naturiol farddonol. I symlrwydd y wlad y mae yn ddyledus am yr ysbryd caredig, gwerinol, sydd ynddo ar ei orau. I gyfrinion ac arucheledd ei môr a'i mynydd mae yn ddyledus am grefyddolder ei ysbryd a'i gariad tuag at ryddid. Y mae ei wlad, fel ei iaith, yn anadl einioes i'r Cymro. Ofnaf mai dirywio wna mewn trefi os na bydd yn medru cadw y cysylltiad yn fyw rhyngddo ef a bywyd y wlad'.[21]

(The beauty of his country gives the Welshman his naturally poetic mind. To the simplicities of the countryside he owes his unpretentious kindness which is one of his best characteristics. To the secrets and majesty of sea and mountain he is indebted for his religious spirit and his love of liberty. His country, like his language, is the breath of eternity to the Welshman. I fear that spirit will wither in the towns unless there is some way to preserve the Welshman's link with life in the countryside.)

Beautiful places made beautiful people.[22] In 1915, T. H. Parry-Williams wrote a pioneering poem 'Y Ddinas' (The City), which set a new tone and timbre for Welsh poetry. Less romantic than his predecessors, Parry-Williams gave a more 'realistic' portrayal of the city, yet his work also served to accentuate the contrasts between rural and urban societies, in ways that were unflattering to the latter.[23] There was still a nostalgia, an elegiac hint of 'hiraeth' for an escape to the slower pace of life of the countryside, geared either to the gambol of a horse or the glide of a coracle. A few years later, Cynan in 'Mab y Bwthyn', his evocative recreation and recollection of the First World War, presented the same value-laden stereotypes, writing of 'y dref a'i brad' (the town and its treason) and 'Nef y grug' (the heaven of the heather).[24] In 1933, David Evans published a book titled *Y Wlad: ei Bywyd, ei Haddysg, a'i Chrefydd*, which emphasised that down the ages, religion and morality, as much as the economy, were the foundations of life in the countryside: 'Ni sylweddolir hanfod bywyd drwy wneud busnes da, hel arian lawer, cael swyddi di-rif eto, eithr drwy geisio'r gorau ym myd moesoldeb a chrefydd' (You will not find life's secrets through good business, making a lot of money, or having several jobs, but through seeking the best in morality and religion).[25]

Ironically, David Evans's book appeared when rural Wales was being increasingly rediscovered by the motoring pastoralism of the Shell county guides and the observations of travel writers such as H. V. Morton, who went *In Search of Wales* (1932). Even so, the émigré James Hanley still thought that the mountains of Wales were the home of true Welshness, a notion summarised in the poet Islwyn's simple description that Wales was 'Gwlad y bryniau' (the land of the hills).[26] Many authors sought escape to real places – Eifion Wyn to 'llechweddai . . . annwyl' (sweet slopes) of Cwm Pennant, T. Gwynn Jones to 'noddfa dlos' (beautiful sanctuary) Rhos y Pererinion, and R. Williams Parry to 'llonydd gorffenedig' (perfect peace) Y Lôn Goed. But others yearned for sanctuary in places of their imaginations, as did Gwilym R. Jones in his fruitless search for Cwm Tawelwch (silent valley).

Rural life was portrayed as simple, natural, innocent and pure, a mirror image to urban areas where life was complicated, unnatural, vicious and polluted. Such presentations, personified in Crwys's pryddest 'Gwerin Cymru', were myth functioning as memory.[27] For, despite the ideals, rural Wales was no idyll. In this peasant land realities were far from green and far from pleasant. Only in rural nostalgia was the countryside settled and placid. In reality it was the scene of conflict involving class, power and money. There was hardly a feature of the rural landscape that did not represent somebody's triumph or tragedy. Power was enshrined in the law, in the wills, entitlements and codicils, which were such an obsession of rural people. Class tensions were tense, particularly between tenants and landlords, farmers and labourers, as the tithe riots of the 1880s and 1890s and the growth of agricultural trade unions showed.[28] Co-operation in agricultural work between different farmers and between the landed and the unlanded were not the quaint customs of folk tradition or folklore. They were debts of honour, part of a deeply felt and tightly controlled system of obligation in the exchange of services and implements. Labour conditions on the land were more penal than pleasant. Many authors who wrote in the pastoral tradition ignored a modern Wales of planes, trains, tractors, telegraphs, the penny post, mowing and reaping machines, Lucifer matches, and labourers who could read and write. Such writers preferred rural Wales to be picturesque, poor and peasant. Rural Wales was their timeless refuge, the riverbank on which they withdrew from the rapidly rushing stream of life.

A few prescient authors had different tales from the riverbank and presented rural Wales not as a utopia, but as a dystopia. The 'gwerinwr', especially the hill farmer and shepherd, were often portrayed as saintly, simple figures. But these gnarled men's struggle with the landscape left many people physically and psychologically maimed. A sense of decline was clear in the work of many poets, even those who eulogised rural society. Crwys's elegiac sonnet 'Melin Trefin' is often considered the epitome of the virtues of country living. But read the poem carefully. Surely the central themes are transience, the brevity of man's days and the folly of his works? This is a lament for a decaying community. Decay sets in from the sonorous opening line, 'Nid yw'r felin heddiw'n malu' (the mill does not grind today).[29] The sisters Mallt and Gwenffreda Williams, writing under the pseudonym, 'The Dau Wynne', penned a novel, *A Maid of Cymru* (1901), which was serialised in the magazine *Young Wales*. This sets out the tragic lives of the rural poor in 'the cloud country'. From dawn to dusk they endured sad lives of ceaseless drudgery, deprivation and desperation.[30] The people's struggle to wrest an existence from inscrutable nature was a Sisyphean fight with no respite until the end of their indomitable days. In a cruel economic survival of the fittest, the old, the infirm and the disabled were abandoned in rural communities as the young fled to far-flung foreign parts. This was the stark, dark reality underlying Kitchener Davies's play *Meini Gwagedd*. Set on All Soul's Night, in idyllic but not idealised Cors Caron, the ghosts of three generations who have farmed Glangors-fach are doomed to return to the scene of their eternal angst.[31]

Rather than steadfast continuity, rural Wales was transformed by emigration and depopulation. Caradoc Evans was one of the many escapees. Having been raised in great poverty in Rhydlewis, Caradoc left at fourteen years of age to work as a draper's assistant in Carmarthen and then London. His creative work has none of the sentimentality of the emigrant exiled from his home writing to salve the personal pains of 'hiraeth'. In *My People* (1915), Evans parodied the prose style of the Old Testament and portrayed west Wales society as avaricious, vicious and malicious – 'a mean and peasant land'. 'Rural Wales was a Boschian landscape of iniquity, Cardiganshire its sewer'. The press response to Caradoc's work was 'an anguished howl of protest'. His books were banned and burnt. When his portrait by Evan Walters was displayed in public, a zealot knife slashed it across the throat.[32] But his nightmare was not unique. In the greatest Welsh-language novel of the twentieth century, *Un Nos Ola Leuad* (One Moonlit Night, 1961), Caradog Prichard relived the agonies of his tortured childhood in Bethesda. Writing with terrible honesty, Caradog described and detailed the doings and misdoings of a savage, ravaged community. Incest, indecent assault on women and children, insanity and idiocy stalked the village of his childhood innocence. This was purgatory, not paradise.

Despite such dissonant voices, the associations of rural Wales as the source of 'true Welshness' – 'the Pura Walia' – continued to have their advocates throughout the years down to 1945. In *The Culture and Civilisation of Wales* (1927), T. Gwynn Jones contrasted asinine English culture with the accomplished civility of Wales in which even labourers could converse authoritatively on the mysteries of 'y gynghanedd'. Often the views of virtuous villages and harmonious hamlets were linked with the Welsh language. This was intended to give the portrayals a heritage, but it often served to make them more divisive and exclusive definitions of Welshness. The museum curator, poet and scholar Iorwerth Cyfeiliog Peate

(1901–82) penned some of his most elegiac and elegant verses in praise of the radical folk culture he called 'the Llanbrynmair tradition'. Peate's work contrasts what he saw as the barbarism of urban, English-speaking Wales with the stability of the culturally rich, monoglot, Welsh-speaking, rural society of his youth. From his study in the 'garden village of Rhiwbeina', he thundered against 'this Age of Trash'. Peate's most practical attempt to preserve the glories of pastoral Wales was the Welsh Folk Museum at St Fagans, which he founded.[33] Wyn Griffith in *The Welsh* (1950), for all his fastidiousness in presenting the culture and history of Wales, still concluded that the real Wales was where the Welsh language was spoken. The Welsh-American newspaper *Y Drych* confidently declared in an editorial in 1935, 'You are not a Welshman without the Welsh language.'[34] *Y Drych's* definition excluded the majority of the Welsh people. The 1931 population census revealed that only 36.8 per cent of the people of Wales could meet the exclusive definition of *Y Drych* of Welsh manhood. In many communities, especially in 'y fro Gymraeg' (the Welsh heartland) Welsh was the robust living language of popular culture, politics and personal lives. But due to the influence of schools, the telephone, the wireless, television and the mass media, bilingualism became increasingly the norm. Lovers of the language, such as Waldo Williams in 'Yr Heniaith', would lament the loss:

> Hyn yw gaeaf cenedl, y galon oer
> Heb wybod colli ei phum llawenydd.[35]
>
> (This is a nation's winter, the cold heart
> Not aware of her five joys lost.)

The late nineteenth century was a time of national awakening across Europe. The effects of the emergent national movements – the Risorgimento in Italy, the reunification of Germany, the crusade for Hungarian independence and the campaign for Home Rule in Ireland – were followed and felt in Wales. In the years before the First World War, Wales experienced 'a Rebirth of the Nation', an increase in national self-awareness and self-expression.[36] But despite the cries of some that Wales should rule herself, politicians such as Tom Ellis and E. T. John were convinced that politically Wales belonged within, not without, the British Empire. In 1892, at the British Empire Club in London, Tom Ellis replied to the toast 'The Principality of Wales' with the observation: 'the more Wales has the power of initiative and decision in her own affairs, the more closely will she be bound to the very texture of the imperial fabric'.[37]

Two common themes in Welsh poetry and prose from the mid-nineteenth century were mawkish religious sentiment and intense, high-flown patriotism detached from terrestrial realities. The poet John Ceiriog Hughes, Ceiriog (1832–87), one of the most popular of all Welsh poets, composed several poems that strengthened the pastoral tradition. Ceiriog's Wales was essentially that of the farmer and the shepherd and their valour amongst nature's splendour. Stoic and silent like Fenimore Cooper Indians, they were lonely figures lost in immense landscapes, clinging to their identity in the midst of nothingness. Within that identity, the national heroes – Arthur, the Llywelyns (the Great and the Last) and Glyndŵr – were such distant memories that Ceiriog could emphasise that the future for Wales was not as a separate nation, but as part of Britain. The ale-house-boasting of his poem 'John Jones and John Bull' indicated that the Johns were contented drinking partners:

> Britannia fawr a Gwalia fach,
> Gymrodwyd yn y fangre hon.[38]
>
> (Great Britain and little Gwalia,
> Are united in this place.)

In the age of Empire, when Britain ruled the waves, Wales eagerly sought her place in the global institution upon which the sun would never set. In countless cartoons published in the newspapers, portly Dame Wales sought to claim her place instead of the pretentious Britannia as pugnacious John Bull's perfect partner. Within the Empire, Welsh and British identities were intertwined and inter-related in subtle ways. Welsh societies were established around the world, and identified and differentiated by a host of clichéd icons – roaring red dragons, harps and leeks.[39] In February 1891,

New York fruiterers had such a demand for the vegetable from the immigrant Welsh that the price rose by 400 per cent. People have often assumed that because Lloyd George opposed the Boer War, he was not an imperialist. On the contrary, he always took great pride in the British Empire, but never thought it was being run properly – presumably, that is, until he became Prime Minister. When the Great War broke out in 1914, Lloyd George famously claimed that this was to be the crusade of the 'little five-foot-five nations'. Yet at the peace conferences 'the man who won the war' ensured that his vertically challenged nation did not join the 'overnight nationalities' of 1919. The cultural and linguistic distinctiveness of Wales need not be a divisive but a strengthening force within the Empire. To Lloyd George, like Tom Ellis, home rule for Wales, Scotland and Ireland did not mean imperial disintegration, but integration. The alliance of nations would be strengthened as each country would assume greater responsibility for its affairs. 'Home Rule for Hell' cried a heckler during one of his speeches. 'Quite right', retorted Lloyd George, 'let every man speak up for his own country.[40]

Legislatively the major achievements of 'Liberal Wales' were the 1881 Welsh Sunday Closing Act ('the first distinctly Welsh Act of Parliament') and the radical Act to disestablish the Church in Wales of 1920.[41] In many respects these were the results of the hellfire politics of the late nineteenth century. But perhaps the most significant achievements, in the long term, were the establishment of national institutions, which would further extend and enhance the ideas of nationhood – the University of Wales in 1892, the national library in 1907, and the national museum in 1909. This was a cultural nationalism as opposed to a stridently separatist movement. The ambitious ceremonies of the Pageant of Wales in 1909, and the investiture of Edward as Prince of Wales at Caernarfon in 1911 provided almost cartoonic confirmation.[42] Those who gathered together at these pageants reveal a remarkable diversity of support for the events from all social strata of Wales. Proud of her Welsh heritage, Edith Ruth Mansell Moullin (1858–1941), led the Welsh contingent in the 'suffrage' contingent in the investiture in 1911. From this she founded a unique organisation, the Cymric Suffrage

Union, dedicated to uniting Welsh people of differing viewpoints to work for women's enfranchisement. Walter Fitzuryan Rhys, 7th Baron Dynevor (1873–1956), carried the ring when Edward was invested Prince of Wales. So inspired was Walter that he promptly used his royal contacts to decree that his name now reverted to the Welsh style of Rhys, rather than Rice. The splendour of the events gratified Welsh national pride, whilst at the same time reassuring traditionalists in every part of the UK.

The experiences of the terrible World Wars in 1914–19 and 1939–45 had a contradictory effect.[43] They undoubtedly further tied Wales into a British identity. Through releasing and realising pent-up patriotic passion, war enhanced some embattled connectivities of a British identity. 'Taffs' fought alongside 'Jocks', and 'Micks' and 'Paddys', in groupings where perhaps the focus of loyalty was to a particular regiment, as much as a national one. Other soldiers had an even broader fellowship, for they fought alongside Americans, Belgians, Frenchmen, Norwegians, Russians, Poles and Ukrainians. The reports of VE Day 1945 in the *Western Mail* showed the duality of Welsh identity. There was an emphasis on how 'we British had saved the world from German brutality' but also a feature on the special contribution of the Welsh.[44] In contrast, for some people the experience of war heightened their perceptions of the nation's crisis and their determination to work for Wales. Many resented the fact that England was unwilling to accept the Welsh as equal citizens, but anxious to have them as cannon fodder. The nationalist and republican Clifford Ifan Bere (1915–97) became deeply engaged with the nationalist cause during his war-time service in North Africa. In 1940, Professor J. E. Daniel described the conflict as 'England's imperialist war' and explained that it was 'a clash of rival imperialisms from which Wales, like the other small nations of Europe, has nothing to gain but everything to lose. It does not accept the popular English view that this war is a crusade of light against darkness. It does not accept the right of England to conscript Welshmen into her army!'[45] Saunders Lewis, a combatant in the First World War, poured his disenchantment with Britishness into the evocative verses of his poem 'Canlyn Arthur', in which Wales was the precious vineyard.[46]

To many observers the eternal inheritance of the vineyard was religious. Religion was the rock upon which the nation was founded. To such authors, Wales was a holy place that possessed a deep-dwelling spiritual presence that seemed to emanate from the earth itself. The Welsh were the people of the Book. The poet D. Gwenallt Jones, whose furrowed face suggested a lifetime spent 'agonising over immensities', begins one of his many poems to 'Cymru' confidently, 'Gwlad grefyddol gysurus oedd hi' (She was a comfortable, religious country) – gently washed by 'gwlith a glaw Rhagluniaeth' (the dew and rain of Providence). In his great poem 'Y Sant' (The Saint) Gwenallt noted in 1928, 'Bu saint drwy hedd defosiwn gweddi / Yn gweld y Nef yn ein gwlad ni' (Saints through peaceful pious prayer / Saw Heaven in our country). Gwenallt's vision is the prophet Zachariah's version of Jerusalem.[47]

When contemporaries asked 'Who made Wales?', the answer, obviously, was 'God', but it was clear that he subcontracted much of the work to the Nonconformists. The politician Henry Richard claimed that the Welsh were a Nonconformist nation.[48] Gladstone, whose photograph decorated thousands of Welsh hearths, confirmed this when he declared 'the Nonconformists of Wales, are the people of Wales'.[49] It appeared easier for a rich Anglican landowner or industrialist to pass through the eye of a needle and enter heaven than it would be for such a person to be accepted into the Welsh nation. The association of Wales and Nonconformity intended to bolster the campaign for the disestablishment of the Anglican Church in Wales served to exclude the contribution of the Church to the nation's history and also the 195,004 people who, in 1905, were adherents of the Anglican faith. It also excluded the 90,000 or so Catholics, as well as adherents of other faiths who lived in Wales. Ironically, in that history it could be argued that Catholicism was a more established and deeply rooted tradition in the religious life of Wales, for there was little specifically Welsh in Nonconformity.[50] This lack of a 'historical tradition' in Nonconformity was the reason John Owen (1854–1926), later 'the battling' Bishop of St David's, and Timothy Rees (1874–1939) turned their backs on their respective Calvinistic Methodist and Independent upbringing and entered the church.[51]

Nonconformity was not uniformity. Nonconformity was split into three major groups, and several subgroups, who had their own beliefs and organisations. Baptists, Independents and Methodists (Calvinistic and Wesleyan) were separate entities. Some commentators considered the Sabbath in Wales to be a 'shouting competition about who could shout to God the loudest – a conflicting babble of faiths'. None of them could find any room for doubt, and with nothing else to unite them (apart from enmity to the church), they were divided by their convictions. Even within denominations differences and disputes often dominated. Samuel Roberts, the famous 'S.R.', dissipated much of the energy of his final years in a disputatious dispute with Michael D. Jones over definitions of the Independents's faith. Debates on metaphysics between the minister and his flock resulted in physical fighting in Bethlehem Welsh Independent Chapel in Blaenavon in January 1888. To quell the enraged congregation the police had to be summoned on several occasions. At the opening of the twentieth century, the Baptists of Cardiff showed themselves to be interested in social issues such as poverty, prostitution, public drunkenness and the general moral collapse of society. These top-hatted theologians had little in common with their cloth-capped fellows in the baptismal faith from rural areas who prayed for fair weather and fertile harvests.[52] Cardiff city Baptists would have little sympathy with the notion that the soul of Wales resided in a damp country chapel.

Prometheus unbound: urban and industrial Wales

> Mae'r tramwe'n dringo o Ferthyr i Ddowlais,
> Llysnafedd malwoden ar domen slag.
> Yma bu unwaith Gymru, ac yn awr
> Adfeilion sinemâu a glaw ar dipiau di-dwf.
>
> (From Merthyr to Dowlais the tramway climbs,
> A slug's slime-trail over the slag heaps.
> What's nowadays a desert of cinemas,
> Rain over disused tips, this once was Wales).

Saunders Lewis, 'Y Dilyw, 1939', in Gwynn ap Gwilym and Alan Llwyd (eds), *Blodeugerdd o Farddoniaeth Gymraeg yr Ugeinfed Ganrif* (Llandysul, 1987), pp. 3–6.

In stark contrast to the rural idyll was the society of urban and industrial Wales, principally that of the south (the coal mining and slate quarrying communities of the north barely seem to have registered in this presentation). The stereotypes dealt in opposites – the one was rustic, rural and religious, the other urbanised, industrialised and secularised. Rural Wales suffered social stasis and claustrophobia – it was haunted by memory. Urban Wales was exciting, characterised by novelty, impermanence and anonymity. These dynamic representations of Wales centred on an industrial economy, especially the coalfield, which to many commentators represented all of south Wales, if not the whole of Wales.[53] By the late 1890s these communities were becoming largely (though not exclusively) English speaking, lacking in faith and strongly supportive of the Labour Party. Narrow nationalistic viewpoints were supposedly eschewed for the broader horizons of British and international socialism in which the identity of class outweighed that of nation. Aneurin Bevan was the articulation and embodiment of this Wales. Professor Dai Smith, Bevan's most astute biographer, explained his appeal: 'Aneurin attended two chapels as a boy; he left both after too close a disquisition of Darwinian evolutionism for the taste of the ministers. He was never baptised. He spoke no Welsh. And in all this he was typifying individually the self confident and progressive world of South Wales'.[54]

Some of the same clichés that were used to describe the ideal rustic were also employed to portray the industrious urbanite. Above or below ground, the Welsh 'gwerinwr' was dedicated to his work, devoted to his religion, and decent in his morals. He also had an unquenchable thirst for knowledge and learning.[55] The miner, brave at times of danger and disaster, was basically a noble figure, a hard worker, married to a decent woman – the Angel at the hearth – who, despite all the deprivation and disadvantages of life, managed to raise the children devotedly and devoutly.[56] The heroic exploits of the miners at Tynewydd colliery in April 1877, in rescuing their hymn-singing colleagues from a watery death in their flooded mine, caught the attention of the press in England and Wales, and established the role model of noble collier hero. These folk tales reached their zenith, or depending on your cultural standards, their nadir, with Richard Llewellyn's novel *How Green Was My Valley* (1939), and especially in John Ford's 1941 cinematic presentation of the book.

In reality there was far more in common between rural and urban, agricultural and industrial societies than some have been willing to accept. These were not polarised places and states of mind in perpetual opposition. Language, religion, folk traditions, customs, cultural and sporting pursuits crossed artificial boundaries. Though substantial numbers of English, Greek, Irish, Italian, Jewish, Scottish, Somalian, Spanish, Trinidadian and other nationalities had been drawn into Wales, the majority of the people who moved into industrial and mining communities were Welsh. Even after that Klondike decade of reckless population growth between 1901 and 1911, two thirds of the population of Glamorgan, the most populous and industrialised county, had been born in Wales. People carried with them into this strange new world ideas and concepts that had served them well in the countryside. The miner responded to the same portents of ill luck as did the peasant. Nor was there a deep cultural chasm between town and country in Wales that may have been the case for other nations. In the short stories of the great Rhondda writers, Rhys Davies and Gwyn Thomas, the adventures of the urbanites are often enacted in the countryside. Town and country were also inextricably linked in the fine mesh of commercial transactions, further interlinked by kinship contacts. Mining towns felt like rural villages not only because of the animals that grazed gardens and allotments, but also because they were places where everyone appeared to know everyone else, where people seemed to live out their lives in tight-knit communities, where they relied on the mutual support of their family and friends. The intimacy of country living was also found in the towns.

To some people, their journey to manufacturing and mining towns or ports might as well have been journeys to another country. They were strangers in a strange land, awkwardly suspended between the world they had left behind and a world where they were not yet, perhaps never would be, fully at home. Gwyn Thomas's description of two Rhondda bachelor brothers is an eloquent evocation of how the old co-existed with the new, of *rus in urbe*:

They spoke a soft purring kind of Welsh, designed not to upset coracles or alert water bailiffs. They never ceased to yearn for the safe tranquillity of Cenarth. The Rhondda they regarded as a catalogue of rate paying outrages. The sounding cinema, as the Spaniards called it, struck them as just another antic of industrial man at his vilest.[57]

W. J. Gruffydd conveys this feeling of alienation in his evocative, if slightly sentimentalised, *Hen Atgofion*:

> a gresyn o beth yw i Gymro fod yn alltud yng Nghymru, ac alltud heddiw yw pob Cymro sy'n byw yng Nghaerdydd a'i maes trefi . . . Trigo yr ydwyf yma – cysgu, gweithio, a bwyta – ac nid byw . . . Nid oes neb o'm cwmpas yn siarad yr un iaith â mi, nac yn meddwl yr un pethau; pobl heb wreiddiau ydynt i gyd, ac ni chleddir yr un ohonynt gyda'i dad.

(It is a shame that so many Welsh people are exiles in Wales, and the Welsh who live in Cardiff and its satellites are exiles . . . I exist here – I sleep, I work and I eat – but I do not live here . . . No one around me speaks the same language as I, nor thinks the same things; they are all people without roots, and no one is buried with his forefathers).[58]

Nothing is more fixed than graves, and there is no more visceral attachment to a place than the pull that people feel towards the spot where their ancestors are buried. Gruffydd felt this acutely for his greatest poem is to the yew tree in the cemetery of his home village, 'Ywen Llanddeiniolen'. He was an exile in his own country, a sense of feeling that intensified for his kind as Wales became increasingly English speaking.

Such alienation, however, was not universal. Many Welsh-language writers wrote directly and powerfully of their lives in urban and industrial Wales. The industrial and urban experience of Wales was chronicled and captured in the works of authors and poets like Amanwy, Tilsli, D. T. Davies, Islwyn Williams, Alun Llewelyn Williams, Gwenallt, T. E. Nicholas (Niclas y Glais), Pennar Davies, T. Rowland Hughes, Kitchener Davies, Euros Bowen, Caradog

Prichard and Kate Roberts. The literature of industrial Wales, says its most astute analyst, Professor Wynn Thomas, is 'rich, complex and bicultural'.[59]

A few contemporary commentators were conscious of the differences that existed within the portrayals of Wales. In a much-quoted lecture to the Cambrian Society at the University of Oxford in 1921, Sir Alfred Zimmern, holder of the world's first academic chair in international politics at the University College of Wales, Aberystwyth, shared his impressions of Wales with the audience and posterity:

> The Wales of today is not a unity. There is not one Wales, there are three . . . there is Welsh Wales, there is industrial or, as I sometimes think of it, American Wales, and there is upper class or English Wales. These three represent different types and different traditions. They are moving in different directions and, if they all three survive, they are not likely to re-unite.[60]

Obviously worried at the imminent disintegration of the nation, Professor Zimmern fled Aberystwyth for London, taking with him, for safety or succour, Madam Barbier, the wife of a fellow academic.[61] Had he stayed in Aberystwyth, he would probably have realised that Wales had more than three representations. To some it was a 'thousand countries with a single name.' A later historian perceptively noted: 'Wales is a singular noun, but a plural experience.'[62]

Rural, agricultural, urban and industrial Wales were not monolithic structures. Hamlets, villages and towns added character and colour to a region. These settlements responded in various ways to varied foci and stimuli, which depended upon the peculiarities of their own characters. They were all unique and different places. Some pen portraits or caricatures of these settlements although generalisations can, perhaps, serve to give a flavour of their diverse nature. The power of place provides not only a portal into the past, but a glimpse of differing public, social, cultural and psychological realities that made for broad-ranging communal identities.

South Wales is often portrayed as being simply a tale of coal, colliers and the coalfield. Menna Gallie was unapologetic and unequivocal in declaring that 'a mining village is a very special kind of village for the *raison d'être* of the place is the mine . . . all those who are not miners are mere hangers on, not important.'[63] However, coal-mining communities were not carbon copies of each other in which the demands and the devastation of an extractive industry had brutalised mankind. A rich diversity of experience could be found in the coal-mining towns of north and south Wales. Coastal communities were radically different to those inland. Nowhere was this more apparent than in the largest towns in Wales – Cardiff, Newport and Swansea. These ports into which the valleys poured their coal had already by the 1890s become irritatingly different to the 'traditional' Welsh way of life. William Llewelyn Williams (1867–1922), politician and author, in a letter to T. E. Ellis on 19 February 1892, complained of the 'howling wilderness of Swansea philistinism', that Barry was 'intent on nothing but money-making', whilst Cardiff 'was lost to Welsh nationalism'.[64]

By 1911, more than 160,000 people lived within the newly anointed Cardiff city boundaries. Amongst them, especially around the dock area, there gathered a remarkable cosmopolitan community, 4,768 of whom were foreign-born. Chileans, Chinese, English, Greeks, Irish, Italians, Jews, Poles, Somalis, Trinidadians, Yemenis, and other nationalities dwelled cheek by jowl in this 'Babel of a Bedlam'.[65] The same sea lanes that carried silk, tea and porcelain brought traders and transient sailors. But Tiger Bay also had a strong Welsh contingent. Within sight and sound of the sea, the exotic was domesticated, as Madras merged into Mount Stuart Square, Bangladesh blossomed in Butetown, the Pearl of the East rubbed columns with Bowen's Emporium and The Zanzibar stood shoulder-to-shoulder with Ebenezer. This community attracted the artist Henri Gaudier-Brzeska in the 1900s and attracted the young Polish novelist Joseph Conrad in the 1890s. The tall tales told in the town's pubs were probably the factual foundations for his greatest fictional work – *Nostromo*.[66] It was also into this community that the novelist Bernice Rubens (1923–2004) was born, the third of the four children of Eli Rubens, a travelling tallyman, and his wife, Dorothy, née Cohen. Bernice's maternal grandfather, Wolf Cohen, a master tailor, had left Poland with only his sewing machine. Whilst her paternal grandfather, Eli Rubens, fled from Latvia carrying only two violins, one full-sized and one half-sized. He arrived in Cardiff thinking it was New York, for which he had bought a ticket in Hungary. He spent two weeks in the bustling Welsh seaport before he discovered the deception.[67] The town also had a floating population of Chinese mariners and merchants, who ran the 'Washie, Washie Laundries'. Though ancient prejudices disappeared in the play of children, they were still powerful enough for racial tensions to burst in vicious and violent anti-Chinese and anti-Negro riots in 1911 and in 1919.

Further west, the coal-mining, tinplate producing port of Llanelli appeared to be solidly Welsh, but it too had a hint of eastern exotica. These exotics included Donald Ibrahim Swann (1923–1994), composer and pianist who achieved fame as half of the 'Flanders and Swann duo', the elder of two children of Herbert William Swann, a medical practitioner and his wife, Naguimé Sultán née Piszóva, a nurse. His forebears had emigrated to Russia in 1840. Donald's father, having surmounted many difficulties to marry Naguimé, a Muslim of Azerbaijani parentage, in 1917, escaped to Wales with her in 1919. Swann grew up in a house as much Russian and Transcaucasian as Welsh, and the influences went deep into the music he composed.[68]

In the west, coastal villages such as Cardigan, New Quay, Aberaeron, Aberdyfi, Tywyn, Porthmadog, Pwllheli and Porth Dinllaen drew their livings and identities from the sea.[69] These seaside towns looked outwards to the world of 'the Atlantic economy' as much as they did to Wales. Culture and identities on both sides of the Atlantic, the Welsh and the American (north and south), were joined as strongly as the ports and their home hinterland. Messages in bottles united communities across the waves. In the north-east, the coastal communities of Llandudno and Rhyl took on a seedier, slightly down-market, character of fairs, candy floss and the puerile fun of kiss-me-quick-hats and what-the-butler-saw machines. Their location drew in countless visitors and settlers from England, which led to a transformation in their linguistic character. In his poem

'The Sea and the Skylark' of 1877, Gerard Manley Hopkins sadly notes that Rhyl was 'this shallow and frail town symbol of our sordid turbid time.'[70] Wrexham also appeared to be a town of contradictions. A citadel of Nonconformity and Anglicanism, it was also home to a military establishment and one of the biggest breweries in Wales. The presence of both in the town perhaps helped to explain the significant numbers of Irish who had been attracted to Wrexham.[71] The search for respectability and religiosity clashed with the pursuit and practise of pleasure on the town's streets. Much to the townsfolk's disgust, the garrisoned soldiers often displayed qualities that should ideally have been confined to enemy territory.

The towns and villages of Wales became the foci for strong feelings of loyalty and identity. People's attachment to a place was often profoundly personal, the result of deep emotional experiences and a bundle of sensations.

Weird Wales

'Lightning is different in Wales'.

Keidrych Rhys, 'Tragic Guilt', *The Van Pool* (London, 1942), p. 21.

The appeal and attraction of a Welsh identity for many was linked not to the modern country, but to the myths and mysteries of ancient, once-upon-a-time, long, long ago Wales. Historians, with a Gradgrindian dedication, have warned against the dangers of accepting a nation's founding myths. Such tales, they say, are composed of fantasies and fables and have little grounding in fact. The imagined past of Wales, they warn, was allowed to balloon into the stuff of myth not truth. Compared to Welsh tales about their Middle Ages, all knights in shining armour and prancing princes rescuing virtuous maidens, the romances of Walter Scott or Tennyson's *Idyll of the King* were social realism.[72] These stories quite literally were 'forged', an appropriate word to catch the fundamental contradiction, for this process was both a forging and a forgery. Yet these invented traditions and manufactured myths have a strong basis in human experience and are what a people rely on when rationality seems exhausted. Stories held and hold people together. In ways that are imperceptible to people, they bent their lives to the templates that myths and archetypes provide. These are the sacred and secular foundations of the national identity, the mythic, magic realism that helps to anchor people in the face of so many different levels of experience.[73] Did the Welsh believe in their myths? Yes and no. Were they true? Absolutely – yes and no.

To a large number of people the ancient tales of Wales had extraordinary energy and attraction. Many, such as Richard Williams Morgan (c.1815–89), a clergyman and author, worked tirelessly in the Gorsedd of Bards to inspire a Celtic revival linked with the resurrection of the ancient British Church. Perhaps the most iconic presentation of the crisply starched, white-gowned druids was Christopher Williams's painting of 1905 of the Revd Rowland Williams (1823–1905) – Hwfa Môn, Archdruid of Wales from 1895 to 1905. Hwfa Môn was the leader of the Welsh 'Gorsedd' and 'Eisteddfod', those egalitarian cultural phenomena that had been conjured into life by the fertile imagination of Iolo Morganwg, the inventor and forger of traditions par excellence. The robes, ranks and rituals of the Gorsedd set the hierarchy of the creative life of Wales. Not all, however, subscribed freely to the myths. The poet D. Gwenallt Jones, who won the chair at the National Eisteddfod, remarked 'y mae llef y corn gwlad fel rhech hynafieithol o'r cynfyd' (the sound of the proclamation horn is like an ancient fart from the past).[74]

Eisteddfodau were popular across Wales and were transported wherever the Welsh went – Liverpool, London, Chicago – and even injected culture into Australia. Celticism, or the Cambro-British revival, was not the sole preserve of Welsh speakers. The aristocratic Frederick George Robertson Williams ('Jim'), like his sister Mallt, was conspicuous at Welsh gatherings on account of his dress modelled on the conjectured style of a Welsh lord of the thirteenth century. He was a generous patron of many Welsh artistic literary and musical endeavours. Occasionally, his enthusiasm veered into the eccentric. At his funeral a gaucho led the cortège and a simple epitaph was carved on his gravestone 'Hollgelt' (a complete Celt).

David Jones (1895–1974), the artist and author, was profoundly attracted to and influenced by *The Mabinogion*, 'that Old Testament of national myth', and other ancient tales and fables.[75] So, too, was the dramatist Howard de Walden who wrote the libretto for three operas based on the tales, a kind of Welsh Wagnerian fantasy of hero-gods and Valhallas called 'The Cauldron of Annwn'. In 1912, the painter Augustus John was commissioned to paint a portrait of Lady and Lord Howard de Walden (T. E. Scott-Ellis) at Chirk castle. Of Welsh extraction, de Walden had a romantic attachment to the ancient history of Wales that was unusually intense. He often gave people the impression that to him, the twelfth century was just an 'afternoon ago' and that he himself had come clanking out of the Middle Ages. An inveterate gossip, Augustus John could not resist confiding in his diary that de Walden took him 'deer stalking with bows and arrows', and 'goes in for falconry and now and then dons a suit of armour'.[76] Howard de Walden's life was more Le Morte d'Arthur than twentieth-century Wales.

Perhaps the most remarkable visual expression of Welsh fables and fantasies were in the work of Edward Burne-Jones and his Pre-Raphaelite Brotherhood. Burne-Jones's fascination, indeed obsession, with Celtic art and legend, gave rise to a series of paintings of wounded, armoured Arthurian warriors swooned over by vulnerable, scantily clad, dark-eyed, russet-haired stunners. His belief in his own Welsh and Celtic identity was ever present. He was often to acknowledge 'whatever I do in art, even if I deal with Greek or Norse legends, I want it in the spirit of a Celt'.[77]

The novelist, the 'obstinate Cymric' John Cowper Powys (1872–1963) was also strongly influenced by ancient Welsh tales and mysteries. His *Autobiography* reveals his 'addiction' to ancient Wales, his frustrated attempts to learn Welsh and his experience of life in Blaenau Ffestiniog. 'I soon gave up trying to learn Welsh', he recalled, 'But the idea of Wales and the idea of Welsh mythology went drumming on like an incantation through my tantalised soul'.[78]

Other people rooted their Welshness, not in the myths of the nation, but in the land's ancient mysticism. Margiad Evans (1909–58) was born in Uxbridge, Middlesex, as Peggy Eileen Whistler.

Aged only nine, she underwent some kind of extraordinary, mystical experience on the banks of the river Wye. She stayed in Ross-on-Wye for a year soon afterwards on her uncle's farm, and she and her sister took their grandmother's surname and used the Welsh forms of their first names (Margiad and Sian). Her works, especially *A Ray of Darkness* (1952) and *Autobiography* (1943), are mystical evocations of life on the Welsh borders and the border condition of epilepsy.[79]

Wales inspired not only romantic yearnings after the green and pleasant, long-forgotten land of bards, druids and mystics, but a whole range of exotic and extraordinary stories of the Welsh gothic. In the 1932 film classic, *The Old Dark House*, Charles Laughton and Boris Karloff take sanctuary in an eccentric, haunted Welsh household. In *The Wolf Man* (1940), 'the best werewolf film ever produced in Hollywood', Lawrence Talbot returns to his ancestral home in Llanwelly, Wales, where he is bitten by a werewolf. The sequel *Frankenstein Meets the Wolf Man* (1943) starts in Cardiff, for 'werewolves are often found in Wales'.[80] Welsh werewolves provided thrilling entertainment on screen, stage and page as they got their teeth into their victims.

The sub-humanising of indigenous populations is, of course, a classic tactic of the coloniser. These filmic portraits presented the Welsh as animalistic, even monstrous, their language the babble of beasts. Wales was the Annwn of legend, an underworld, its people, in the words of the hated education commissioner of 1847, 'seething under the hatches'. But Welsh authors also presented Wales as a startlingly occult land.[81] Wales was the Celtic Transylvania in which the natural and the supernatural were intertwined. Richard Hughes in *A Moment in Time* has goblins enlighten the main character as to a range of human truths. Arthur Machen (1863–1947), born in Caerleon, Gwent, despite his career as a Fleet Street journalist, wrote mystical tales such as *The Great God Pan* (1894), *The White People and Other Weird Stories*, and *The Hill of Dreams* (1907). Machen made the stories live, not by reporting the facts, but by manufacturing the fiction. In his most famous story, 'The Bowmen', which gave rise to the fable of the 'Angel of Mons', a ghostly army of archers fought alongside British troops at Mons in 1915, Machen notes that 'the bowmen were mostly mercenaries from Gwent'. He joined the Hermetic Order of the Golden Dawn and was heavily influenced by the occult and spiritualism. Even that most gifted of writers of tales of the supernatural, M. R. James, found something unsettling in Machen's dark tales that mixed natural and supernatural in a complex world of human sacrifice, dark sexual desires, fantasies and frustrations. A careful reading of the tales reveals the strong influence of mystical Wales.[82]

Gentler tales of the unexpected were also inspired by Wales. After the death of her fiancé, Norman Wane, in September 1905, Beatrix Potter escaped to Gwaenynog Hall, Denbigh. Beatrix liked to paint, and the house had 'the prettiest kind of garden where bright old-fashioned flowers grow amongst the currant bushes'. In watercolour and pencil the magic garden appears in *The Tale of the Flopsy Bunnies* (1909). Between 1935 and 1965, the scenery of Beddgelert and Nantgwynant provided the inspiration for Alfred Bestall (1892–1986) in creating the landscape for the adventures of Rupert the Bear.[83]

In 1916, a son was born 'in a fine house in the village of Llandaff', to a prosperous Norwegian ship-broker and his wife who had settled in Cardiff in the 1880s. They had a theory that 'if a pregnant woman constantly looked at beautiful things then her baby would grow up to be a lover of beautiful things'. On that basis, and judging by the gruesome characters 'the Boy' Roald loved to create for children, and the spooky events in *Tales of the Unexpected*, then Mrs Harold Dahl must have had a horrific time in Cardiff in 1916.[84]

Curiouser and curiouser, Wales, perhaps, was the inspiration for *Alice's Adventures in Wonderland*. Certainly the links were strong enough for the ageing Lloyd George to unveil a memorial to the book's author, Lewis Carol, on the seafront at Llandudno in 1933. Several decades later, in the National Screen and Sound Archive of Wales, you can still watch through the looking glass newsreel footage of the grand ceremony of David in Wonderland.[85] This Wales was so odd that the time-obsessed White Rabbit himself would be baffled here.

The dramatic Welsh landscape of quarry, mine and mountain provide the inspiration for the geology of bare slate and stone of

Mordor and Moria in Tolkien's Middle Earth. The Mountains of Iron, belching forth 'stinking fumes and rivers of flame', were probably modelled on the burning slag heaps Tolkien visited above the Neath valley. From his childhood, he had been enchanted by the Welsh language. He remembered reading the names of Welsh mines painted on the coal trucks that clattered and clunked past his home village – Nantyglo, Blaenserchan, Bargoed, Brithdir, Cwmtillery, Werntarw. The syntax and structure of Elvish was probably modelled on Welsh.[86] Tolkien's friend C. S. Lewis, the great Christian author, used the name of his family's home in Caergwrle near Wrexham – Cair Paravel – as the name of the castle in *The Chronicles of Narnia*. Lewis was brought up in Ireland but valued his Welsh ancestry, believing himself to be more Welsh than Irish, and often sprinkled Welsh words into his work. Narnia, the land of perpetual winter, was not a wardrobe, but a train-ride away.[87]

'Cry the beloved country': national character and identity

'Wil Rogers, the American comedian who claimed Red Indian descent, used to say 'My family didn't come over with the *Mayflower*. They met it.' My family were in a similar sort of situation.'

Glyn Jones, *The Dragon Has Two Tongues* (London, 1968), p. 17.

One of the major advantages of placing the emphasis on the experiences and emotions of individuals is that eccentricities and oddities of people and the true colours of the national identity can be glimpsed. Some of the characters in this study appear to have been as exotic and as un-Welsh as a unicorn, but their lives indicate how rich, varied and vibrant the experiences of Wales and the Welsh were. A common birthplace does not guarantee that individuals will follow the same paths of ambition and aspiration. Cecil Blanche Woodham-Smith (1896–1977), biographer and historian, was born in Tenby. Though her mother, Blanche Elizabeth Phillips, was Welsh, she felt Irish, since her father, Colonel James Fitzgerald, an Indian army officer who served in the mutiny, belonged to the family of Lord Edward Fitzgerald, hero of the Irish rising of 1798. Her feelings can be read in her superlative study of the Irish Famine, *The Great Hunger* (1962).[88] Also born into a similar social background in the seaside town was Augustus John, who gave such chiaroscuro, character and colour to early twentieth-century Welsh art.[89] Edward Hugh Neale Dalton (1887–1962) and Sir Arthur Sackville Trevor Griffith-Boscawen (1865–1946) were born, not so much with silver spoons, rather with whole canteens of gilded cutlery in their mouths, however their careers were vastly different. Griffith-Boscawen followed a natural path to the extreme right of the Tory party, whilst Dalton, 'the gilded shit', despite his descent from significant Welsh landowning stock, served in the post-war Labour government.[90]

Ancestry was a source of pride for many, but despite their attachment by name and title to Wales, many were deemed to be amongst the Anglo-Saxon exploiters. In 1901, Lord Penrhyn claimed a pedigree that could be traced back to the age of the Welsh princes, yet his indifference to the plight of his quarrymen was a source of considerable tension that led many, then and since, to question his Welshness.[91] H. A. Bruce, MP for Merthyr Tydfil, was castigated as an employer with a dubious record in Welsh industrial disputes, a churchgoer and an Englishman. Yet in 1889, the selfsame H. A. Bruce, as Lord Aberdare, was lionised after he proposed and headed a landmark inquiry into Welsh intermediate and higher education. Perhaps one of the most remarkable occupants of a Welsh parliamentary constituency was Stuart Rendel. He was idealised as a Liberal friend of freedom. But in actual fact, he was an Englishman, an Anglican, and an arms manufacturer.[92] His career contrasts strongly with that of his Liberal colleague Henry Richard, the world leader of the peace movement. Richard possessed all the personal characteristics of the very model of a late-Victorian Welsh liberal – a statue-in-waiting. But despite his sitting as an MP for Cardiganshire, he spent far more time in Manchester than in Tregaron.[93] Neither Aneurin Bevan nor J. H. Thomas as Members of Parliament, or as government ministers, displayed much sympathy for any specific Welsh political causes. In contrast, Sir Alfred Mond, the son of a German Jew, as Liberal MP for Swansea and later Carmarthen, displayed considerable commitment to Welsh issues. Despite his devotion and dedication to his adopted country, Mond's guttural accent was cruelly mocked. Hecklers disrupted several of his meetings, chanting 'Vales for the Velsh' and 'Home Vule for Vales'.[94]

It is almost impossible to identify the standard bearers of a uniquely Welsh consciousness, for whichever test of belonging is applied creates as many problems as solutions. To have been born in Wales was obviously an important part of an individual's national identity. But such a criteria would exclude Lloyd George (born in Manchester), and Saunders Lewis (born in Liverpool). Another trio who would be discarded from the Welsh nation on the criteria of birthplace were men who did so much for the writing of Welsh history, the 'Merseysiders' R. T. Jenkins, Sir John Edward Lloyd, and Captain Arthur Owen Vaughan (Owen Rhoscomyl). Their work gave pride and importance to dates and events that had been forgotten like dropped stitches in the ornate tapestry of English history, but were significant for Wales. Sir Idris Bell (1879–1967), one of the foremost authorities on early Welsh manuscripts, also failed to be born in Wales. Though Bell came from generations of yeomen farmers in the north of England, the Welsh inheritance from his mother meant more to him and was the determining factor in his life. Sir John Lias Cecil Cecil-Williams (1892–1964) did a remarkable amount of work for the Cymmrodorion Society and secured the funds to publish the monumental and magisterial *Y Bywgraffiadur Cymreig* in the austere 1950s. He spoke Welsh with the soft cadences of Uwchaled, but had been born, bred and lived throughout his life in London. For these people, and many others, Wales had resonance because it was the home of their hearts.

Sport nurtured and nourished national identities as people played for and supported their countries. Rugby in particular became the avatar of the nation. The Welsh way to play was a unique blend of the athletic and the aesthetic with its brilliance, its magic, its style and its dash. The fabulous myths and stories that developed around the game ignored the fact that it was a regional pastime confined to the south. The creativity of the players and the conviviality of it supporters, belied the introspection and inequalities. To some commentators, the foundation of the Welsh Rugby Union in

1881 was the very first example of a national institution in Wales. It was tangible evidence of the Welsh nation's existence. James Bevan became, in 1881, the first man to captain what soon became regarded as the defining characteristic of Welshness, the Welsh international rugby team. But sporting heroics was, and is, no guarantee of nationality. Bevan had been born in Brisbane. Frank Hancock, born in Wiveliscombe, Somerset, into the brewing dynasty, the 'inventor' in the 1880s of the 'four three-quarter' system of rugby back play, captained Wales on several occasions. Had he not been injured before the match against England in 1886, then he would have played against his brother, P. T. Hancock. Dick Halling, who did play for Wales against England in 1900, and despite a broken arm scored a try, was from Tiverton. Erith Gwynne (Gwyn) Nicholls (1874–1939) led Wales when they achieved the legendary 3–0 victory over the otherwise unbeaten New Zealand rugby tourists in 1905. To many this heroic, iconic victory was *the* defining moment of Welsh nationhood. Nicholls was 'one of a number of Cardiff rugby players who were West Countrymen by birth, but Welsh by location, adoption and inclination'.[95]

Wales-born people appeared to be as confused about their allegiances as their England-born compatriots. W. J. A. (Dave) Davies was one of the most graceful and gifted rugby outside halves of the interwar years. In 1923, his retirement season, he even arranged for his honeymoon to be spent in Paris, so that he could lead his side to the fourth Grand Slam of his career with a victory over France at the Stade Colombes. Welsh-born Dave captained England. In June 1934, C. F. Walters, the Neath-born amateur, made sporting history in the 'quintessentially English sport' of cricket when he captained the England XI against Australia. The highly talented all-round sportsman Maurice Turnbull (1906–44), could be forgiven for any confusion in his national identity. Turnbull represented Wales in hockey and rugby, and England in cricket, the only person ever to do so.[96]

In cultural spheres distinctions are especially difficult to draw, for so many who were generous in patronage and patriotism to the Welsh national revival were 'English'. Welsh art benefited greatly from the bequests of Sir Frank William Brangwyn (1867–1956).

Brangwyn had been born at 24 rue du Vieux Bourg, Bruges, and christened Guillaume Francoise, yet his strongest emotional link was with his mother's Brecon origins.[97] Born in Langland into a wealthy Anglicised background, Winifred Coombe Tennant had a peripatetic upbringing around western Europe that would have bewildered a Bedouin. She used her wealth to serve as a sponsor for many Welsh artists, especially Evan Walters and John Elwyn and the National Eisteddfod, where she, under her bardic name 'Mam o Nedd', became Mistress of the Wardrobe.[98]

The Welsh, as Dylan Thomas noted, were forever praising their maker that they were a musical nation. But Welsh music was often conducted by outsiders. Despite his name, Sir Walford Davies had only a tenuous claim to be Welsh by blood, but he was instrumental in promoting Welsh musical education and performance. In 1919 he embarked on his 'Welsh mission' to resuscitate and revive the nation's music after centuries of alleged neglect. The musicologist and composer Peter Charles Crossley-Holland (1916–2001) published the innovative multi-authored study *Music in Wales* (1948). The composer Edward German showed the complexities and contradiction of identity in his work. Best known for his 'Welsh Rhapsody' (1904), he also sang the praises of the 'Yeomen of England' in his hit musical *Merrie England* (1902).

Welsh theatre was supported by the generosity and benefaction of people with titles and pedigrees as exotic as Lord Howard de Walden. Ostensibly, Sir Eric Ommanney Skaife (1884–1956) was everything the Welsh detested: an Anglican, a conservative and a former soldier. But he proved himself a remarkable supporter of all aspects of Welsh culture, from the National Eisteddfod to Urdd Gobaith Cymru, and was a generous patron to Welsh writers and musicians. Lady Mallt Williams (1867–1950) was another whose aristocratic and privileged background was no deterrent to her love and promotion of Welsh and Celtic culture. Mallt was the second person to join 'Urdd y Delyn' in 1896. She was the founder of 'Ysbïwyr y Frenhines' (The Queen's Spies) in Byddin Cymru (Welsh Army) under the auspices of *Cymru'r Plant* from 1911 to 1916. The members of this organisation took an oath to serve Wales with heart, mind, tongue and hand. Evan Frederick Morgan (1893–1949), second Earl Tredegar, established the Celtic Society at Oxford. It is an ironic fact that the three greatest achievements of 'liberal' and 'imperial' Wales of the years before 1914 – the university, library and museum – were run by the very Anglican and anglicised authority figures who had previously been castigated as the people's enemies. The generosity of these people greatly endowed and enhanced the institutions – indeed not one of this cultural trinity would have survived without aristocratic support. The emotive support of the poor and their pennies was important, but the economic security of the pounds of the rich were needed for national library, museum and university to survive and succeed.[99]

Issues of identity and belonging provided fertile fields for novelists, poets and writers of all backgrounds. The twentieth century witnessed a damaging and disputatious confrontation between those who wrote in Welsh and those who wrote about Wales in English for 'the dragon had two tongues'.[100] Though these were, in many respects, 'corresponding cultures', some argued that the authors defined by Sir Idris Bell in 1922 as 'Anglo-Welsh' were nothing but English writers.[101] On this issue, Saunders Lewis and W. J. Gruffydd found themselves, for one of the very few times in their lives, in agreement. 'And as for Anglo-Welsh literature, I blush for my country at seeing any of it in print', thundered Gruffydd.[102] 'Mr Dylan Thomas is obviously an equipped writer, but there is nothing hyphenated about him. He belongs to the English', was Lewis's harsh verdict.[103] In contrast, Keidrych Rhys noted in his editorial encyclical in the magazine *Wales*, in the apocalyptic summer of 1939, 'Though we write in English, we are rooted in Wales.'[104] Rhys and several others were adamant that to be anglicised was not at all the same thing as to be English.

The novelist Berta Ruck, of Aberdovey, was bewildered by the complexities of her identity:

Why, with only one quarter Meirionethshire blood in my veins, why with a Kentish grandfather and an Irish-named mother who was proud of her Norman-French descent, why do I call myself *Welsh*? A mongrel has the right to choose which breed it prefers of a mixture . . . Further, my father used to say that his family of eight divided themselves on sight into Welsh and English members . . . I went to school in Wales. I am Welsh in temperament. I have an unreasoning, instant sympathy with nearly all people of the Welsh race. My vividest hours as a small child were lived in this richly picturesque, hospitable, unreliable, beloved country. Continentals have spotted me at once as being not typically English.[105]

The poet Edward Thomas (1878–1917) noted 'an ambivalence' towards his 'Englishness . . . I am 5/8 Welsh . . . I have some Spanish blood and some from Wiltshire in my veins'. At ten, he would sing the Irish nationalist song 'The Minstrel Boy', believing it to be about Wales, 'and as I sang the song I melted and trembled with a kind of gloomy pleasure in being about to die for Wales'. Eleven years later he wrote of the country as a calling: 'it is like a homesickness, but stronger than any homesickness I ever felt – stronger than any passion'.[106]

Allen Raine (1836–1908) was well aware of the 'gloomy pleasure' of Welshness and the pains of a fractured consciousness. In *By Berwen's Banks* (1899), one character, the daughter of Welsh Patagonian missionaries, later an orphan in Wales, has multiple identities and reflects: 'Well, indeed, I don't know what I have grown up! Welsh, or English, or Spanish, or Patagonian! I am mixed of them all, I think'.[107] The novelist and adventurer Eluned Morgan lived with these pains of identity and belonging and never really resolved her inner tensions. In a sense, it was no surprise, for Eluned had been born on a journey between two worlds, the old and the new, on the ship *Myfanwy*, sailing from Wales to Patagonia in 1870. One of her biographers simply noted 'broc môr oedd Eluned' (Eluned was flotsam).[108]

Those who lived on the border between Wales and England also suffered a fractured sense of identity. Much to the relief of the county's tipplers, Monmouthshire was excluded from the Sunday Closing Act of 1881, the first specific Welsh legislation, which closed pubs on the Sabbath. Regardless of the Lord or the licensing laws, they, unlike their neighbours, could drink on Sunday. They tasted bitter disappointment, when the Attorney-General reversed the ruling in 1921. This was a double blow for some, not only were they not allowed to drink on Sunday, but the ruling confirmed that

Monmouthshire was part of Wales. Problems of identity were compounded by administrative decisions, in which the boundaries between Wales and England were regularly redefined and redrawn. Between 1871 and 1881, Radnorshire lost 1,262 people to England and another twenty-six between 1881 and 1891. During 1891–1901, Montgomery and Denbighshire lost 1,595 people. The losses were reversed in 1901–11, when Flintshire's boundaries were revised, resulting in a gain of 18,275 persons for Wales.[109] The stroke of a census enumerator's pen had more effect on people than the slash of a medieval prince's sword.

Borders, those no-man's-land are not only zones of conflict but regions of cultural exchange and interchange. People were perhaps especially culturally and socially fluid in these areas. The effects on people's awareness and consciousness were noted by the novelist and Shropshire lass Mary Webb who claimed that the population she drew upon was Welsh in almost everything but language – and the language, she noted, 'died hard in some of the outlying districts . . . a submerged part of Wales – a kind of Cantref-y-Gwaelod lost to its own people in the rising tide of Anglo invasion.' Like many of her characters, Mary continually criss-crossed, country-dance-like, between England and Wales, English and Welsh. In a letter to Gwyn Jones in 1946 she stressed, 'I'm very glad of my drop of Welsh blood and I'd never want to move out of range of the Welsh voice'.[110] Nigel Heseltine is another author who articulated the angst of a border condition of fluidity and uncertainty. The 'scarred background' Heseltine referred to in his first travel book, *Scarred Background* (1938), was perhaps not Albania, but his home on the English-Welsh borders.[111]

Welsh identities were thus fragmented, complicated and contradictory, elusive and enigmatic. A detailed examination of any general characteristic that is deemed an appropriate definition of national identity reveals many exceptions and exclusions.[112] Just when you think that you have the defining feature, you find that the opposite is true in other places. Wales, and the Welsh identity, are full of surprises, of enigmatic variations. Nations are the products of many things – of birth, of culture, of history, of inheritance, of politics, of race, of religion, of sport. Individuals are influenced by a single or several of these forces. Thus it is that the great athlete Harold Maurice Abrahams (1899–1978) is seen as the epitome of the English sportsman, but was in actual fact half Lutherian Jew on his father Isaac's side, and half Welsh on his mother Esther's side.[113] Although it is difficult to define a national character or identity that does not mean that one does not exist. The poet Waldo Williams in his poem 'Pa Beth yw Dyn' (What is a man) explained the feeling of belonging thus:

> Beth yw bod yn genedl? Dawn
> Yn nwfn y galon.
> Beth yw gwladgarwch? Cadw tŷ
> Mewn cwmwl tystion.
>
> (What is being a nation? A talent
> Springing from the heart.
> And love of country? Keeping house
> Among a cloud of witnesses.)[114]

'To me', said the poet and novelist Glyn Jones, 'anyone can be a Welshman who chooses to be so, and is prepared to take the consequences.'[115] Presumably, the same choice was available to women who wanted to be Welsh. The challenge to the historian is to provide a pluralist and multicultural interpretation of the national character, which avoids the divisiveness of narrow-gage nationalism, without sacrificing the core concept of a common Welsh experience. Wales, with its manifold nuances, is as constant as a chameleon. Given the diversity of experience, it appears presumptuous for a historian to determine which experiences were authentic and to decide who spoke for Wales. In view of the pitfalls, this study thus attempts to avoid exclusive definitions and opts instead for a more inclusive interpretation of national identity.

In another of Waldo Williams's poems, 'Cymru'n Un' (Wales is One), he says simply, 'Ynof mae Cymru'n un. Y modd nis gwn' (Within me Wales is one. The manner, I know not).[116] Deep down, national identity was bred in the bone. To many people, such things do not need explanations. They are there because they are there.

5

'The Way of all Flesh': Prudery, Passion and Perversion

Nid rhyfedd fod yr hen gân adnabyddus 'Hen Wlad y Menig Gwynion' mor boblogaidd, nid yn unig ar gyfrif ei cherddoriaeth uchelryw, ond hefyd ar gyfrif y ffaith gysurus a ddyg i'r cof, sef gloewder ein hannwyl wlad oddi wrth droseddau ac anfoesoldeb.

(It is not surprising that the familiar song 'Old Land of the White Gloves' is so popular, not only because the music is outstanding, but also because of the comfortable fact that it brings to mind the freedom of our dear land from crime and immorality').

Seren Cymru (22 July 1887).

'Yes Mog, Yes Mog, Yes, Yes, Yes': popular sexuality

It is the Protestant Nonconformity of the Welsh people, as lived and taught by their religious teachers during the last two centuries, that has preserved them from ignorance, lawlessness and irreligion, and made of them one of the most scripturally enlightened, loyal, moral and religious nations upon the face of the earth.

David Davies, Echoes from the Welsh Hills (London, 1908) p. 171.

Sexual abstinence and abnegation were regarded amongst the strongest characteristics of the Welsh people by the 1870s. Sacred and secular journals, magazines and newspapers presented a tableau of passionless men and platonic, passive females – citizens of a solemn, glandless utopia in which duty had defeated desire.[1] Courtships were chaste, marriages continent, conceptions immaculate. Sex, if it happened, must always have been an anti-climax.

It is hard to penetrate the silences and to discover the sexual lives of people, to recover their passions, peccadillos and perversions. Many writers seem to have assumed that an apparent absence of evidence equals evidence of absence and have accepted contemporary insistence that Wales was morally pure. But the stringent denials of any moral incontinence in Wales often brings to mind Queen Gertrude's quip in Shakespeare's *Hamlet* that 'the lady doth protest too much, methinks'. Caradoc Evans, that acerbic critic of his people, put it succinctly. 'Wales', he wrote, was 'a land of secret sins'.[2] The moral leaders of Wales might have been preoccupied with sex, but the Welsh were fully occupied with all sorts of sexual behaviour, in all sorts of places with all sorts of people. Like Saint Augustine many Welsh people prayed 'Dear Lord, give me Chastity, but not yet'.

In the 1970s an American social historian could lament, with obvious innuendo, that the history of sex was a 'virgin field'.[3] By the second decade of the twenty-first century it is obvious that the field is now well furrowed. Even Clio, it seems, has discovered the clitoris.[4] In the Welsh context, the years 1870–1945 saw alongside the 'second industrial revolution' and the 'consumer revolution', a related revolution in popular morality and sexuality.[5] Many of the features of the sexual revolution at the turn of the twentieth century had a strong Welsh dimension to them. The terms of the Freudian revolution in popular sexuality, concepts such as the Id, the super ego, the Oedipal complex, the counter-wish, the Dreamwork, the Ego, the Electra Complex, and Penis Envy, were slipped into the attention of English-speaking audiences through the work of Gowerton-born psychoanalyst Dr Ernest Jones, the president of both the British Psychoanalytical Society and the International Psychoanalytical Association in the 1920s and 1930s. Thanks to Jones, people who have never read the works of Freud are familiar with such concepts.

How widespread such ideas were accepted is difficult to establish. In Wales greater sexual freedom was welcomed by progressive opinion and absorbed into modernist literature, but the emphasis in psychoanalysis on sexuality was also perceived to be socially dangerous as much as psychologically liberating. Even the medical establishment was reticent to adopt the new concepts. There were many ill-tempered arguments within the British Medical Association's ethical committee over some of Ernest Jones's contentions, such as that Napoleon had been an anal-erotic. When Jones was cross-examined by a BMA committee in June 1928, the discussion, or rather argument, centred almost entirely on sex. Jones provided examples of a patient who constantly imagined a greenish snake, which he insisted 'undoubtedly was a phallic symbol', but he seemed to stretch belief too far when he also insisted that a flea was a 'penis symbol' (size was, perhaps, not important). Jones insisted that 'unconscious sexual impulses operated in all kinds of acts that were not conventionally regarded as anything to do with sex at all'. When asked to name one he suggested 'thumb sucking'.[6]

Jones was not the only Welsh thinker to be influenced by Freud. Stanley Price Morgan Bligh (1870–1949) of Brecon, whose ancestor had made a somewhat poor impression on the ship *The Bounty*, also proved himself to be equally at variance with his times. He learnt German in order to attend Freud's first psychoanalytic convention in Vienna in 1908. Bligh, in *The Direction of Desire* (Oxford, 1910), *The Desire for Qualities* (Oxford, 1911) and *The Art of Conversation* (Oxford, 1912), provided a Freudian interpretation of life and love. Freud's ideas also influenced Mervyn Montague Levy (1914–66) in his *The Moons of Paradise: Some Reflections on the Appearance of the Female Breast in Art* (1962). Saunders Lewis in his biographical study *William Williams Pantycelyn* (1927) drew heavily on Freud's work to clarify the sexual and spiritual tensions of Wales's greatest hymnist. Lewis argued that Williams's work, especially *Ductor Nuptiarum neu Gyfarwyddwr Priodas* (1777), and his poem 'Bywyd a Marwolaeth Theomemphus', were suffused with the sexual tensions of one who was simultaneously a saint and a sinner. In *Psychoanalysis and Morality* (1923) and *In Defence of Sensuality* (1930), John Cowper Powys drew heavily on psychoanalytical knowledge to reveal how 'sex invades every thought we have' and that 'the secret of life and the purpose of life' was happiness.

Fact and fiction were merged in the sexual lives of Wales. Radclyffe Hall's 'lesbian' novel *The Well of Loneliness* (1928), which was prosecuted for obscenity, was based on the real-life relationships of Carmarthen-born suffragette and women's rights campaigner Rachel Barrett and her lover Ida Wylie.[7] Barrett's 'sexual inversion', a crude term for lesbianism, taken from Havelock Ellis's *Sexual Inversion* (1897), had been apparent from an early age.[8] The availability of such publications in Wales was assisted by the Cavendish-Bentinck library as a subscription library for suffragists. Established in 1909, it was from here that the future Lord Rhondda, unable because of censorship to buy a copy of Havelock Ellis's *Studies in the Psychology of Sex*, asked his daughter, a member of the library, to borrow a copy for him.

As always, the writers of fiction showed that they were in tune with the spirit of their age. A constant theme in the novels of the 1920s and 1930s is an awareness by the authors of the ways of all flesh. Lewis Jones, the communist agitator, in his novels *Cwmardy* (1937) and *We Live* (1939), revealed the sexual tensions and inequalities of his people in the coal-mining communities of south Wales.[9] Though he was an avowed communist, Jones revealed little sympathy with the sexual equality being promoted by the Bolshevik revolution.[10] His literary work is strongly patriarchal. In his private life, he revealed a libido that was positively feudal, and seemed more concerned with his erection than insurrection.[11]

D. Gwenallt Jones, in his fictional autobiography, *Ffwrneisiau*, which was finally published in 1982 when concerns both for his reputation and his reader's morality had subsided, lamented the high moral tone of the eisteddfodic adjudicators of the 1920s and complained, 'mae'n hen bryd i feirniaid gofio fod gan bardd goc' (it is about time that adjudicators realised that a poet has a cock).[12] Yet the tendency for the penis to rule the poet was in ample evidence in the years from 1915 to 1930. In 1915, T. H. Parry-Williams's 'Y Ddinas' (The City) showed familiarity with the night-time activities of London and especially Paris. In 1924, Gwenallt himself received the ire of the eisteddfodic judges for his poem 'Y Sant' (The Saint), a character whose morality was anything but saintly.[13] Prosser Rhys in 'Atgof' (Memory), a homoerotic epic of 'the love' that even then 'still did not dare to speak its name', encountered even greater opprobrium.[14] A few years later Kitchener Davies's play *Cwm Glo*

(The Coal Valley) enraged critics and audiences for his exposé of the sexual dynamics of macho-domination and female exploitation of industrial Wales. The play was banned in Wales, but even so, critics pondered where in Wales could a girl be found to play the part of Marged, the young whore, who leaves the valley to earn a living on the streets of Cardiff.

Art, even that executed in the best possible taste, had a strong sexual aspect. The painting 'DD' (1924) of a ginger-haired nude by the Royal Academician Sir Gerald Kelly was purchased for £250 by Newport council in 1947. Confidently, some said brazenly, 'DD' stares at the viewer in a pose that confirms that she was a natural redhead. It proved too much for a local bishop who campaigned to have the painting of the pubicly hirsute 'DD' removed from public display. When 'DD' returned to the gallery in 2007, she once more encountered a storm of controversy, not because of her brazen nudity, but because she held a cigarette in her hand. Few noticed the cigarette in 1947.[15]

For those, especially women, who preferred to take their entertainment from the silver screens of the cinema rather than the silk screens of art, sexuality was a constant theme. The Welsh-descended director D. W. Griffith provided one of the first scenes of cinematic high sexuality when the vulnerable Lilian Gish is almost raped by a German officer in *Heart of the World* (1917). Men sat agog, open-mouthed as the joke-cracking, fast-talking, pneumatic May West, all lashes and lips, tits and hips, undulated across the screen in perpetual motion. The censors cut Miriam Hopkins's time on screen to five minutes in *Dr Jekyll and Mr Hyde* (1931) because of their explicit nature, but even so her character still had enough time for some 'sexually-decadent and sadistic sexual encounters with Mr Hyde.' Freud famously pondered 'what women want' but the cinema answered a different question as to 'who women want'. The choice of heartthrob screen idol ranged from the sensitive Brontë and Byronic hero, to the swashbuckling pirate, to the sensual Arab sheikh. In the 1920s Ivor Novello was invested as the Prince of Wails such was his reception by female Welsh cinema audiences. Moralists were horrified for 'good girls' should not publicly express their sexuality. As the Second World War wore interminably on,

Prince Charmings became all the rage with women who were bored with make do and mend and longed to be fairy-godmothered into a better life. The reception such films received seems to have veered between those daydream believers who loved the 'shop-girl romance movies', to realists who warned that a girl began by sinking into the hero's arms only to end up with her arms in his sink.[16]

Sexual terms permeated the lore and the language of several areas. In Cardiganshire's rich dialect, a lady like May West would have been referred to as 'Ffrwlen o groten' ('happy-go-lucky' is the closest translation), even perhaps a 'Hen Hwdwch' (an immoral woman).[17] She certainly would have attracted the attention of every 'tipyn o geiliog' (a randy man) in the area from his favourite activity of 'sbaddu malwod' (castrating snails, that is doing nothing). A few miles over the border in Pembrokeshire, and the locals would probably have agreed that she was 'cocwyllt' (a nymphomaniac). Certainly, she would never be considered a 'shabwchen' (a disagreeable lady). Such choice phrases reveal that even in the remoter outposts of rural Wales, the worm was in the bud.[18]

Folk songs echo this obsession with the carnal. The song 'Hiraeth am Feirion' (Longing for Meirion) is narrated by a female emigrant forlorn on a foreign seashore beneath the wailing gulls, who yearns for her Merionethshire home. But it soon becomes apparent that her 'hiraeth' is not for her homeland, rather her heart aches for her lover, as Meirion is both a personal and a placename. Hugh Evans in *Cwm Eithin* (1931), relates the folk song regarding the marriage of the sixty-five-year-old spinster Miss Morgans and the lusty youth Siôn, whose physique she had admired whilst she voyeuristically watched him churning.[19] Unsurprisingly the wedding was brief, for Siôn's physicality wore Miss Morgans out:

> Roedd Siôn ar ôl priodi
> Yn corddi fel y cawr,
> Nes daeth yr angau'n ddistaw bach
> I nôl Miss Morgans fawr;
> Cadd Siôn yn wir y tai a'r tir,
> Ac ail briododd Cadi Dafydd,
> A chorddi fyth o hyd mae Siôn
> Ac yn ei fuddai newydd.[20]

(After marrying Siôn
Churned like a giant,
Until death silently descended
To gather large Miss Morgans;
Husband Siôn got the house and the land
Then remarried Cadi Dafydd,
And he's still busy churning
In his new homestead.)

The wages of sin it seems was a happy death for the elderly spinster, but the spice of vice gave riches to the lusty youth. The song 'Oes yn y tŷ 'ma win i werthu?' (Does this house have wine for sale?) has a series of innuendoes in verses that question the purpose of the house and concludes with:

Swllt yw pris y gwin i werthu,
Swllt yw pris y brandi,
A rhyngoch chi a'r lodes lân
Sy'n swit fel siwgwr candi.

(A shilling is the price of wine for sale,
And a shilling is the price for brandy,
But agree your own price with the girl
Who is as sweet as sugar candy.)

In 1909, in a series of articles in *Y Geninen*, the indefatigable social reformer Gwilym Davies discussed 'Cyflwr Moesol Cymru' (The Condition of Welsh Morality) and complained that evidence of the people's base, elemental sexual nature could be found everywhere:

Nawr onid yw yr ysgrifen ar furiau ein urinals cyhoeddus yn ein lleoedd poblog, yn fynegiant o feddwl digon o'n pobl ieuangc yng Nghymru? Lle bynnag yr ewch fe ganfyddwch y geiriau Saesneg am noethni y ddau ryw wedi eu hysgrifennu mewn sialc. Yr wyf, cyn hyn, wedi gweld darluniau o ddyn a dynes noeth ar lyfr emynau mewn capel yng Nghymru, ac ar Destamentau a ddefnyddir yn yr Ysgol Sul! Y mae yn ymddangos fod yna nifer – pa wŷr fawr y nifer, nis gwyddom – o'n bechgyn a'n merched ieuengc sydd â'u meddyliau wedi eu mwydro mewn syniadau o'r fath fwyaf cnawdol. Y mae ein heglwysi yn fud, y mae tadau a mamau yn rhy aml yn fud: goddefir i'r plant dyfu i fyny yn ysglyfaeth rhwydd i'r blys sydd yn dueddol i fod yn un o bechodau etifeddol y Cymro.[21]

(Now is not the writing on the walls of public toilets evidence of the low moral standard of many young people in Wales? Wherever you go you will see the English words for the nudity of both sexes written in chalk. I have before now seen drawings of naked men and women on a hymn book in a Welsh chapel, and on a Testament used in Sunday School! It appears that there is a large number – how many I do not know – of our young men and women whose minds are corrupted by ideas of a carnal nature. Our Chapels are silent, too often fathers and mothers are also silent: they allow their children to grow up enslaved to one of the inherited sins of the Welshman.)

It was no revelation that *Caniadau Solomon* (*The Song of Songs*) was the most well-thumbed section of many chapel Bibles. The next most thumbed section was Ezekiel 23:20 in which 'she lusted after her lovers, whose genitals were like those of donkeys and whose emission was like that of horses'. In 1898, Elwyn Thomas also complained at the ubiquitousness of sexual imagery:

The unscrupulous fortune-hunters of every description [who] know in these days that, after failing in every attempt to make money, they can always succeed by devising some way to insert the semi-nude figure of a woman in their advertisements . . . the impetus to evil given by the too suggestive and unspeakably vulgar female sketches which accompany present day advertisements . . . are enough to weigh down the heart of the most cheerful optimist alive. Think again of the guilty silence of the pulpit in regard to this terrible sin.[22]

Antiquity, like the Bible, provided a wealth of terms to describe sexual behaviour – Satyr, Sapphists, Lesbian and the practise of 'gamahuche' (oral sex). Boys in public schools, according to *The Lascivious Hypocrite* (*c.*1891) reported 'plenty of details concerning mutual friggings, and pointed out pretty boys who could be found in each other's beds, and had been detected in gamahuching and every kind of excess'.[23] Christ College Brecon and Llandovery

College were each the scenes of 'delicate' sexual scandals in the late nineteenth century.[24] In later life Ernest Jones declared that in his long career in psychiatry he had failed to find any sexual practice or perversion that his schoolmates had not heard of. He should have known. In *Free Associations*, written at the end of his life, he claims that he first experienced sexual intercourse 'at the ages of six and seven'. The plural seems deliberately chosen.[25]

The rise of a consumer society, which intensified in the period down to the First World War, had far-reaching influences into people's emotional lives. By the turn of the twentieth century there was a greater awareness that pleasure should be assuaged in this world as well as the next and some people sought greater physical gratification.[26] The gradual loosening of the moral and religious sanctions against consumerism had their impact in people's daily lives.

Many of the inventions of the second industrial revolution had unexpected sexual value. Rail carriages provided ample opportunities for situational sex. Many trains by the 1880s had female-only carriages to try to protect vulnerable women from predatory males. The development of the internal combustion engine similarly provided ample opportunities for the sexual predator. Ladies on the upper levels of double-decker omnibuses were frequently subjected to suggestive behaviour and lusty or lewd offers.[27] The development of the car provided greater privacy and one of the most popular locations for sexual intercourse – the back seat. Some of the richer people in Wales acquired that ultimate status symbol and aphrodisiac – the Rolls-Royce Silver Ghost. New technological advances assisted pornographers. Printing presses produced not just the classics of the Victorian literary canon but also an enormous amount of pornographic work – the sort of book that Rousseau described as being written to be read single-handed. It catered for all tastes – incest, flagellation, lesbianism, communal sex, sadomasochism, homosexuality, paedophilia. It was from such works published in the 1890s that John Cowper Powys acquired a life-long penchant for lesbianism. As he admitted with characteristic candour 'nothing excites my amorous nerves more than the sight of two young girls twining and twisting round each other in excited desire'.[28]

Pornographers also benefitted greatly from the development of better and lighter cameras. In Margiad Evans's novel *The Wooden Doctor* (1933) seventeen-year-old Arabella becomes aware of her awakening sexuality when she discovers some photographs of Beardsley prints. She develops an admiration for powerful women, is uninhibited about her nakedness, while the bath of flowers she takes implies something other than a concern for cleanliness.[29]

Picture postcards ranging from the suggestive, to the saucy, to the salacious were widely sold in coastal resorts across Wales. The cartoonist Herbert Samuel (Bert) Thomas (1883–1966) proved that he could outdo Donald McGill in sauciness with a series of cartoons for the newly established men's magazine *Men Only*.[30] Pembrokeshire was well versed in seaside salaciousness. The coastal resort of Saundersfoot published a series of postcards in which a rather coy and demure lady is advised, 'it is no crime to kiss in Saundersfoot'.[31] Whilst the third Marquess of Milford Haven collected a substantial number of scatological and obscene postcards that are today housed in the Victoria and Albert Museum.[32] Those who visited the piers and promenades could pop a penny in a slot machine to discover 'what the Butler Saw' and view 'Milady in her Bath'.

Technological developments appeared in many aspects of sexual life. Doctors treating 'hysterical' female patients had to spend considerable periods of time massaging ladies until they reached a 'hysterical paroxysm' (the lady, not the doctor). Much to the medic's relief, the process was accelerated by the application of the novel new source of power – electricity. Electric 'lady massagers' were eagerly obtained by medical doctors such as Ernest Jones in their treatment of female patients. But gradually, such massage devices became more widely available so that women could 'cure' themselves of any hysterical tendencies. 'Electromagnetic massagers' were widely advertised in general magazines such as *Women's Home Companion*, beneath slogans describing them as 'such delightful companions' and promising 'all the pleasure of youth . . . will throb within you'. In 1909, *Good Housekeeping* published a 'tried and tested' review of different models, whilst an advert in a 1906 issue of *Women's Own* assured readers 'it can be applied more rapidly, uniformly and deeply than by hand and for as long a period as may be desired.' The *Western Mail*, 'the voice of the nation', published such advertisements, so too did *the South Wales Daily News*, and *the Carmarthen Journal*. Did women really not know what they were buying? Despite all the medical decorum, the innuendo of the advertisements make it unlikely, for with its purchase a woman was guaranteed 'thrilling, invigorating, penetrating, revitalising vibrations'. That the 'hysterical paroxysms' they gave rise to were never referred to as an 'orgasm' was in keeping with an age that believed that, in the absence of penetration, nothing sexual could possibly be taking place.[33] Use-centred history reminds us of the fact that although an invention becomes available at a particular time it does not mean that it is immediately, universally utilised. Some devices take time to become widely used. Not all Welsh women buzzed away contentedly by the First World War, but a few undoubtedly did.

The telephone was another device that liberated people's emotional lives in ways that its inventors had not intended or anticipated. Men flirted with female telephonists in a manner that they would never have dared in person. Some even proposed marriage. Party lines (the sharing of phone lines) also resulted in greater intimacy between individuals who were outside a recognised relationship. After his engagement to Eric Gill's daughter Petra ended in 1927, the painter and poet David Jones (1895–1974) had several *amitiés amoureuses*, mostly conducted on the telephone.[34] The telephone was also crucial to the relationship between the beautiful socialite and antiquarian Gladys Ashton of Yelston Court, Pembrokeshire, and the elderly Matthew Lewis Vaughan Davies of Tan-y-bwlch, later Lord Ystwyth.[35] The poet and litterateur W. J. Gruffydd also used the telephone to assist in the arrangements for his long-standing affair with a local schoolmistress whilst he was a school inspector.[36]

Popular sexuality in rural Wales clearly ran contrary to the morality that was often promoted from pulpit and the press. There were several affairs, clandestine and public, between masters and maids, and between head carters, ploughmen, 'y gwas mawr' and maids and mistresses on their own or neighbouring farms. James Williams recalled that:

Girls were 'dated' at chapel concerts, eisteddfodau, singing festivals, and at harvest time. There were some who believed that no maid was more easily seduced than she who had been to an emotional prayer meeting, or a sermon with *hwyl*, or above all a singing festival. A good intake of Handel or Bach would apparently lower the lady's defences sufficiently for her to stoop to folly. Tutors at theological colleges would advise their students not to go a-courting on Sunday, an emotional day, when *les girls* were most inclined to be permissive.[37]

Mothers in Carmarthen were well aware that the apprentices to the Word in the town's religious seminaries were not without sin. Daughters were warned not to go with ministerials on a Sunday for they were too excited.[38] Certainly this was advice Emily Maria Richards should probably have taken greater heed of. In October 1918, she took an affiliation order in the local police court against the Revd Gwilym Nicholas, a Congregational minister of Carmarthen, for the paternity of her child. Their courtship had flourished whilst he lodged with Emily's mother when a student at the Carmarthen theological college. Despite his claim that 'I cannot think how it happened', he was ordered to pay 5s. a week plus costs.[39]

Ministers, newspaper editors and other commentators inferred that affiliation order proceedings were the consequences of the behaviour of intemperate, wasteful people who submerged themselves in the impure and immoral atmosphere of public house and street-corner gangs. But temptation existed even in the most exalted places. In January 1906, two months before the religious revival abated, David Henry Thomas, a draper of Capel Hendre, who had provided a Bible, a £5 donation and the carpet for the stairs and the pulpit of Moriah Chapel, found his respectability and his character trodden upon as well as his gifts when he was summoned by Mary Williams for the paternity of her child. He was ordered to pay 3s. 6d until the child was fourteen, together with the costs of obtaining the order and the costs of the midwife.[40] In June 1905, Elizabeth Ann Rees, aged nineteen, of Pwll, Llanelli, summoned Joseph Morse, a tinplate worker at the Old Castle Tinplate Works, to answer charges of fathering her illegitimate son. The authorities at Bethlehem Chapel, the place where the relationship germinated and grew, responded in a manner sadly too common amongst Nonconformist chapels by expelling him.[41] Lydia Lewis, of Llangennech, was seduced by Morlais Harry, a fellow member at Saron Chapel, on a Sunday School trip in August 1907.[42] Such episodes show that no matter how stern the sermon, the twinkling, inviting eyes in a young face could conjure away the wages of sin.

The majority of the girls involved in affiliation order transactions claimed that they had been seduced by the promise of marriage. This is understandable and natural when we remember that the girls had been raised in a society that placed great emphasis on the values and virtues of purity, self-restraint, chastity and marriage (especially for women). In order to win a case, society demanded that the girl prove she was the innocent victim of a calculating seducer. In court the majority of affiliation order applicants stressed that it was the promise of marriage that led to their fall from virtue. It was as if the promise pulled back a curtain in the girl's mind and led to thoughts of marriage, of homes, of a family, above all to thoughts of happiness and an end to loneliness.

For many girls the attempt to portray themselves as innocents corrupted by the man's deftness in covering his foul intentions could fail in a torrent of character assassination from the defendant, the defence lawyer and witnesses. In May 1907 the case of Rachel Jenkins, of Vauxhall, Llanelli, against Samuel Jones, a servant at the Cleveland Hotel, was rejected when he and his witnesses claimed that she had kept frequent company with local soldiers and that she had been seen by one voyeuristic witness having intercourse with a soldier in Stradey Woods.[43] From the beginning of her affiliation order proceeding against David Thomas, Maria Bowen of Bryn Terrace, Llanelli, was put on the defensive. It was no great shock, for it was her second appearance.[44] She had to strenuously deny that her mother kept an immoral house, and that on the weekend of Buffalo Bill's Wild West Circus's visit to the town, she proved to be more of an attraction with the cast than the preparations for the show. Esther Davies was rumoured to have had so many suitors that in court she had to deny that she had to consult a fortune-teller to help her identify the father of her child.[45] It was cases such as these that drew crowds of people to the police court. Often the atmosphere in the courthouse resembled that of a burlesque comedy in the music hall.

One aspect of the affiliation order cases that were presented to the courts in Wales which has been forgotten is that many men and women seemed to have enjoyed their lovemaking. In March 1902, Hannah Prosser summoned Frank Gray, a Senghenydd collier, for financial contributions towards the upkeep of her child. They had made love on the second time they walked out together. And the third time. And the fourth. And the fifth time. And so on. Annie Harper and Alexander Davies were even more eager, for they made love on their first date on Good Friday 1914. Beatrice Elias was equally eager for she too made love on her first date with William Webb in the somewhat unromantic setting of Penyrheol cemetery. The following Sunday, they made love near the hospital. In the following months in between quarrels and reconciliations, the couple made love in their 'old spot' near the cemetery, as well as beside the old mill and in a local plantation. On several of these occasions, they were accompanied by some of Beatrice's friends[46] – the Mercutios who pandered to the peccadillos of Rhondda's star-crossed Romeos and Juliets. Court papers and newspapers from all over Wales reveal the myriad melodramas of teenage soap operas: the fighting and coupling and betrayals and heartbreaks and tears – always tears, drawn from the pain only a youth who has mislaid a first love can feel.

It is one of the great ironies of the history of love in Wales that so many courtships in industrial areas were conducted alfresco, whereas those of rural areas were often conducted behind closed doors.[47] The inhabitants of rural Wales, because of the long hours of work involved in farming, developed the habit of courting late at night in the kitchen or bedroom of the girl's house or lodgings. The agreement to meet would be made during working hours, perhaps by an intermediary, for the suitor to call at the girl's lodgings at night.[48] To attract her attention it was customary for the young man to throw sand or light gravel at her window – called 'cnoco lan' – and he would then be allowed into the kitchen – 'noswylio' (nighting) – or into her bedroom for 'caru yn y gwely' (courting in bed). That the practice continued into the twentieth century and did not end in the 1890s, as David Jenkins suggested in his study of rural society in west Wales,[49] and that it might entail pitfalls other than that suggested by the Registrar General is shown in some criminal cases that were brought before courts. Daniel Rees and Evan Jones, farm servants from the Pembrokeshire borders district, were both fined for criminal damage to farmhouse windows in 1905 and 1906. Having failed to attract the attention of the servant girls through throwing sand and gravel, in their frustration they threw cockles and half a brick.[50]

If sex was an obsession that the Victorians sought to keep quiet, their obsession with statistics was made public. Following the 1847 education report, many writers raided the reports of the Registrar General of Births, Deaths and Marriages to prove indisputably that Wales was more pure and moral than England. In his defence of the Welsh against their alleged unchastity, Thomas Rees produced figures for 1861 that proved that both south and north Wales were more sexually moral than 'those English counties whose inhabitants most resemble the Welsh in social position and occupations', in terms of illegitimate births per 100 births.[51] Yet, in 1909, when Gwilym Davies compared the immorality of the Welsh with a different set of English counties, he discovered a rather different picture.[52] There had not been a revolution in Welsh morals between 1861 and 1909. The different conclusions arise from the fact that Thomas Rees measured the illegitimacy of all sections of society, while Gwilym Davies used a more scientific measurement of illegitimate births against the number of women aged between fifteen and forty-five. But the Victorian proclivity to throw the first stone obscures one important fact that is apparent in the statistics of both Thomas Rees and Gwilym Davies. It was the rural areas of Wales that experienced the highest levels of illegitimacy.

This fact is graphically illustrated if we examine the illegitimacy rates of Carmarthenshire parishes and registration districts. Llanelli was the most heavily industrialised parish in the county. In the decennial periods of 1885–94 and 1895–1904, the illegitimacy rates for Llanelli averaged at 3.37 and 2.91 per 1,000 births respectively.[53] In the same periods the rates for Llan-non, which was predominantly a mining parish, were 3.50 and 3.21. Those registration districts that were purely agricultural had higher illegitimacy ratios. Llanddeusant had a rate of 8.13 in 1885–94, 7.53 in 1895–1904 and 7.15 in 1905–9; Talyllychau had rates of 7.61 in 1885–94 and 5.48 in 1894–1904, whilst Cynwyl Gaeo had rates of 10.12 in 1885–94, 8.60 in 1894–1904 and 6.68 in 1905–9. If we pick out individual years, the rural-urban disparities become greater. In 1885, for example, the illegitimacy rate of Llanddeusant stood at 25.00, while that of Llanelli was 3.38. Clearly each village had its idiosyncrasies, and often its own code of morality. This pattern of higher rural illegitimacy is not a Welsh peculiarity. T. C. Smout and others have shown that it was a common feature of many British rural communities.[54]

The major point to note with regard to the illegitimacy ratios of Wales over the period 1870–1945 was that they were in decline. In 1874 the rate stood at 37.1 per 100 births. By 1900 it had declined to 31 and continued to fall to 27 in 1914, to 20.7 in 1919 and to 17.1 in 1945. Despite the hopes of pious moralists, this is not to suggest that the Welsh were sinning less in 1945 than they had in 1870.[55] The greater availability of birth control mechanisms and contraceptives, more sexual knowledge, and a general change in mentalities are probably the most likely causes of this decline rather than an increase in moral scruples. The years of the World Wars 1914–19 and 1939–45 stand out against the periods of general decline in the rate of illegitimate births. These years of terror, of the imminence of death, saw not so much a loosening of morals as a rush to experience sex, probably for the first and perhaps the last time. The same phenomenon can be seen in the marriage rate that reached peaks of 16.7 in 1914 and 20.8 in 1940.[56] This rush of the senses was commented upon by contemporaries. *The Carmarthen Weekly Reporter* wrote in April 1915:

> A proportion of our girls have simply flung themselves at the soldiers and many of them will be called upon to pay the bitter price. Such warnings as were given have been in certain cases, of no avail, and now we have to face the grim question of the sad, undesirable harvest. We shall be hearing of the slaughtered innocents and the unwanted baby will be the subject of many an inquest.[57]

It was feared that a large army would encourage an 'amateur draft' of otherwise decent women into prostitution. Munitionettes with spare cash were often cruelly assumed to be making money on the side by immoral means. For this reason in Cardiff, women were banned from pubs between 7 p.m. and 8 a.m. The result was to force genuine prostitutes to entertain 'men in their homes instead of being out on the streets which did more harm than if the women had actually been in the public houses and in the streets where people would see them'.[58]

Fears of an epidemic of immorality prompted the foundation of the Women Patrols Committee and the Women Police Service. These were voluntary groups that patrolled cinemas, ports, camps, parks and any areas where soldiers congregated, aiming to 'save girls from their own folly'.[59] The Women's patrols and police sought to prevent girls from 'sinking so low in their sin that they can never rise again, rather they sink lower and lower until they die a lonely and terrible death'.[60] Undoubtedly they were well meaning but the power to pry into other people's behaviour was often abused. Perfectly innocent behaviour, such as a married couple fondling in a park, could attract the officious attention of prudish police-women. For the real concern was the welfare of men:

> There is a great danger of the men being damaged and made unfit for the hard and awful work in front of them unless parents and employers try to prevent the girls from getting excited, running wild in the evenings and forgetting their honour, their purity, their self-respect . . . It is terrible to think that the folly and sin of many of these women and girls should make these men less fit to die and send them away with a guilty conscience.[61]

War was undoubtedly erotic.[62] Take a man in uniform often of leather, throw into the mix the machismo of fighting and guns, add a woman susceptible to romance and excitement, bring them together in the urgency of a forty-eight-hour leave, and the result can be explosive, if highly enjoyable. The posting of American troops in Wales in 1918 and again from 1941 added an additional dimension to the romance. Ribald comments in the 1940s compared a Welsh woman's knickers with Italian troops – 'one Yank and they're off'.[63] As always, it was the woman who had most to lose and had to live longest with the consequences.

The wars revealed that venereal disease was a serious problem for both partners. In 1917, thirty-two out of every 100 enlisted soldiers was afflicted. The Royal Commission on Venereal Diseases reporting in 1916 estimated that in many working-class areas 8–12 per cent of men and 3–7 per cent of women suffered from syphilis, with the figures higher for gonorrhoea. The 1916 Public Health (Venereal Diseases) Regulation Act established a network of clinics offering free confidential diagnosis and treatment. Attitudes were transformed within just a few years. Whereas the Edwardians had viewed VD as something that men gave to helpless women, now the disease was seen as a scourge inflicted upon innocent soldiers by lascivious women. Regulation 40D of the Defence of the Realm Act, passed in March 1918, made it illegal for a woman afflicted with VD to have intercourse with a serviceman. After March 1918, a woman suffering from VD could be arrested for having sex with her husband, even if he had infected her in the first place.[64] Movies such as *Damaged Goods* and *The Dangers of Ignorance* informed cinema audiences of the dangers of VD.

Fear of venereal diseases had been the cause of lurid headlines in 1928 of 'The Devil in Caernarfonshire', whilst the magazine *John Bull* claimed that 'the county of Caernarvon is in the fearful grip of an age of terror that strikes at the future of the Welsh race.' In that year, 101 people were treated for venereal disease at a Bangor clinic.[65] A similar number had been treated at Pembroke in 1871, because the town, being a naval base, was included under the strict terms of the Contagious Diseases Acts.[66] Concerns at the impact of venereal disease continued at the start of the Second World War. The charismatic historian Gwyn Alfred Williams was as concerned with the possibility that he had acquired VD at the Urdd camp in Llangrannog as he was with the onset of war: 'I had VD! . . . I never slept all night . . . How was I going to tell mam? Tell her I had VD . . . But in the morning, a Friday, Hitler did indeed march into Poland . . . and I forgot about my VD.'[67]

The Harlot's Progress: pimps, prostitutes and professionals

A place where methylated-spirit drinkers danced into policemen's
arms and women like lumps of clothes in a pool waited, in doorways
and holes in the soaking wall for vampires and firemen . . . These
were bad, ragged women who'd pretend against the museum wall
for a cup of tea.

Dylan Thomas, 'Just Like Little Dogs', quoted in Jeff Townes,
Dylan Thomas: the Pubs (Talybont, 2013), p. 59.

Nothing risqué, nothing gained seemed to have been the attitude
of so many of Gwyn A. Williams's compatriots at the Urdd camps
in the 1930s and 1940s. The young lady who had caused him such
concern was probably a talented amateur. But a history of the
pleasures of the flesh is often a history of prostitution, for sex and
commerce have long been intertwined. Two themes were consistent,
the exploitation of women by men, but also of men by women.[68]
The harlot's progress of the Moll Hackabouts of Wales reveal considerable variety in the range of prostitution. Some women, the
pavement labourers of radiant charm, were forced into prostitution
by poverty, or pleasure. Some reached the heights of the demi-
monde and near respectability. For the majority, however, it was
the shady world of shabby one-night hotels, the passive providers
of that delicious anonymity of transience. Many of them were very
young and well dressed and looked demure, even sweet until they
hissed their offers like a cat – 'want a nice time?', 'want a fuck?'
There was no mystery about their hang-outs for the prostitutes
followed the money. They had the lingering look and the familiar
smile that is common to car salesmen, politicians and prostitutes.
Girls went into prostitution for a host of reasons. The cycle of
poverty, pregnancy and survival by theft or prostitution featured
as the plot of a thousand melodramas and ballads because it was
one of the most common things that could happen to a girl. Poverty,
abandonment by a lover or family were powerful factors that could
push a girl into prostitution. Others sought to feed their dependency
on alcohol, or drugs or mind-altering substances – many of the
heroines of the whorehouses of Wales were hooked on heroin.

Many girls discovered that they could earn more in twenty minutes on their back than in a week in one of the sweated trades. As prostitutes paraded in fine clothes and fripperies, local girls could only conclude that the wages of sin were higher than those based on sweat.

Prostitution was fraught with dangers. If a girl worked the streets, she would find herself progressively devalued, carrion to vultures who would pimp her and beat her, a prey to the police, who would rob her and demand favours, and periodically arrest her in any case, a slave to bad liquor, drugs, disease, malnutrition and the elements. Very soon, she became tarnished and backdated merchandise. Twenty-year-old Elizabeth Lee of Rodney Street, Swansea, was murdered by two militia men, John Elias and Richard Walters, in 1891.[69] She was one of several whose lives ended violently.

Another who died violently was Mary Ann Rees.[70] At Merthyr Tydfil in 1909, William Joseph Foy gave himself up to police because, 'I have murdered Sloppy. I have thrown Sloppy down a hole in the old works. She told me she was going to give me away for living on her prostitution and I done for the bugger. If you come with me, I will show you where she is.' Police did, and saw. The places where Sloppy and the girls plied their trade in the sub-economy of survival and sordid sex, were half-spun out of fairy tales and were often scenes of vicious violence. The unfortunate nickname 'Sloppy' suggests that her face was no lure to lust. Both face and nickname belonged to Mary Ann Rees, a thirty-three-year-old, who worked at the lowest rung of the netherworld that existed beneath the sexual underworld of Merthyr Tydfil. The trial revealed a world of casual sex in the open air where warmth was provided both from the female bodies and the coke ovens. On 8 May 1909, William Joseph Foy was hanged at Swansea prison for Mary Ann Rees's murder.[71]

The lives of ladies such as Elizabeth Lee and Mary Ann Rees reveal much about the dark underside of Welsh society. Over the course of the period 1870–1945 the routes into prostitution were often hidden by a thin veneer of pretence. In an editorial in 1894, the *Western Mail* warned about the dangers of the increase in the number of massage parlours:

We understand that a good many 'massage shops' the advertisements of which are frequently inserted in the newspapers, are very little more than houses of accommodation. A very common plan, we are informed, is for some man with a little capital to open an establishment of this kind, and then to advertise for half-a-dozen young lady assistants to do the work. Their remuneration is minimal but they are at liberty to accept presents from the customers, who pay the principal from half-a-guinea to two guineas for each visit. If the young lady is willing to make herself 'agreeable' she is retained on the staff, but if she has conscientious scruples she is discharged and someone is found to take her place . . . We are given to understand that the subject has attracted the attention of the local police, and that quite recently one of the best known of these places has been raided and stopped. Certificates in 'massage' are given, even by qualified medical men, after the most perfunctory course of instruction.[72]

'We understand', 'we are informed', 'we are given to understand' – the author of this article is trying too hard to retain his or her respectability. Presumably the courses of instruction were 'perfunctory' because the girls only needed a scant anatomical knowledge to get their clients to a happy ending. The ending was far from happy for some clients. Judge Sir Charles James Watkin of Llansannan died in such an establishment in Nottingham on 17 July 1884, 'in disreputable circumstances'.[73]

One of the most sensitive portrayals of a man's relationship with prostitutes is provided in the poet and supertramp W. H. Davies's *The True Traveller* (1912), which recounts his relationships with prostitutes when he was on the road and his posthumously published *Young Emma* (1980). Although the events happened in the 1920s and 1930s, it was not published until after Emma's death because the reader at Jonathan Cape publishers to whom W. H. Davies submitted his manuscript thought it too revealing. His relationships with Bella and then Young Emma are frank portrayals of a man who had been crippled as the result of losing his leg when jumping trains when tramping in America but who still had physical needs. Davies provides an eloquent reminder that one of the prostitute's greatest services was to provide companionship and comfort, to give succour as much as sex. Clients bared their souls as much as their bodies for sometimes they just wanted someone to listen to their woebegotten tales of woe.[74]

The numbers of girls and ladies involved in prostitution is impossible to establish for contemporary estimates varied enormously and only a very few people would admit on a census that she, or he, was involved in 'immoral earnings'. Bangor in the 1860s and 1870s, Caernarfon in the 1870s, Swansea in the 1890s, 1900s and 1920s, Merthyr in the period 1860–72 were each the venue of sensational moral outbursts against prostitution. And then there was Cardiff. Say what you want, and the morally outraged said an awful lot of awful things about the town and then the city, Cardiff was consistent in being the Welsh capital of 'the great social problem'. Estimates varied, but it is probably safe to conclude that in the 1890s there were some 229 brothels and more than 3,000 prostitutes in Cardiff.[75] The number of both rose and fell, not always in tandem with the fluctuations in the local economy, for this great industry operated even, perhaps especially, during times of economic depression. In the 1890s the *Western Mail* had a habit of running a series of headlines above each other on the same story, which presumably saved one the bother of reading the copy. On 15 September 1894, the paper published the following headlines:

CARDIFF'S IMMORALITY

ARE THERE 3,000 FALLEN WOMEN IN THE TOWN?

COUNCILLOR ANDREWS WILL GO ON A TOUR OF INSPECTION[76]

Lucky, or unlucky, Councillor Andrews. But the Sisyphean task of counting proved beyond his calculus. The Solomonic job of deciding who was a prostitute was too complex for in a world of one-off, part-time, or 'just-as-a-favour-for-an-old-friend', and professional sex, morality had to deal in more than fifty shades of grey.[77] The difficulties of drawing distinctions was revealed in the case of David Davies of Pontypridd in 1916. David went with a woman who claimed that her husband was dead to have sex in her home. Soon there was a knock upon the door. David was unwise enough to open it on the husband, who fought amazingly well, for a dead man. The husband was back on leave from France, back from the dead.[78]

The milk of human kindness might have soured for finger-wagging moralists, but not everyone within Welsh society condemned and censured the prostitute. Undeb Dirwestol Merched Gogledd Cymru (The North Wales Women's Temperance Union) gave practical advice and help to girls on the dangers of prostitution. They and several temperance and suffrage groups established houses of refuge to rescue prostitutes.[79] The Prime Minister, William Gladstone, often left his Hawarden home to 'rescue' prostitutes. Yet, his diaries reveal that his motives were not always as high-minded as they seemed, for Gladstone had an almost sado-masochistic urge to punish himself for each time he was 'tempted' during his dealings with the 'women of the pave'. His wife, Catherine Gladstone (née Glynne), the heiress to the Hawarden fortune, was also much involved in 'rescuing' prostitutes; she sometimes sought to restore their sense of self-respect by entertaining them to tea at 10 Downing Street.[80] The Cory brothers of Cardiff, John Cory (1828–1910) and Richard Cory II (1830–1914), gave substantial sums every year to rescue missions, the Young Women's Christian Association and Magdalen houses.

At Swansea, the Cwmdonkin Shelter was run on interdenominational lines to provide a temporary shelter for 'Friendless Women and Girls and to give protection to those in danger'.[81] The shelter, established in 1887, moved to Clifton Hill in 1921 but retained the name. The shelter's ladies committee did not confine themselves to pious platitudes but strived practically to save girls from the workhouse, prison and 'the low parts of town'. In 1895 Mrs Roberts James had been employed as a 'mission worker' and within the first four months she had visited the police court ninety-three times, 'where she had been the means of helping many women with a kind word.' Mrs Roberts James also persuaded the magistrates not to impose custodial sentences, to give the girls more time to pay fines, to look for employment and opportunities to emigrate.[82] 'Llety Cranogwen' did similar work in the Rhondda from 1922.

Individuals also undertook brave work. Pamela Shepherd (née Morgan), 'Mother Shepherd' (1836–1930), worked for the Salvation

Army in their rescue homes in Cardiff (from 1891) and at Paentwyn Bach at Trecynon (from 1908 to 1925).[83] The infamous world of China,[84] that rowdy and raucous area of Merthyr Tydfil where prostitution by the 1870s had declined from its mid-Victorian glory, is revealed in a remarkable document, 'A Journal Kept by a Scripture Reader', deposited in the National Library of Wales.[85] The journal was written by a young Anglican who had the courage to turn his creed into deed and embark on a mission to China to rescue the 'nymphs of the pave' from the 'dens of misery', to escape the 'clutches of vice' and lead them to decency and respect.

Prostitutes paraded in all parts of Wales. Charles Ashton in *Ffeiriau Cymru* (1881) complained at the female 'crwydriaid carpiog ac annuwiol, anfoesol a masweddol' (wanderers in rags, ungodly, immoral and obscene) who could be found in each of the fairs of the citadels of rural Wales at market time.[86] In 1882 the *Western Mail* revealed the 'disgraceful revelations' of the 'amours of an Aberaeron solicitor' Thomas Pugh. One of his sexual partners gave a different meaning to the word soliciting, for Margaret Davies was allegedly a prostitute who worked the rural fairs.[87] Minnie Price (alias Doyle), 'a woman of evil repute', was convicted of keeping a 'disorderly house' at 50 The Street, Abergavenny, in 1894. In order to provide an example to others, Minnie was imprisoned for three months hard labour.[88]

The number of prostitutes in Carmarthen increased every time there was a fair or a mart in town and when the local militia were on manoeuvres.[89] In June 1907, the editor of *The Carmarthen Weekly Reporter* reported that 'the Carmarthen Police have been greatly troubled by a number of undesirable females who have come to Carmarthen since the militia training started.'[90] The ability of some of these ladies to entertain the militia men is questionable. Mary Ann Davies, from Cardiff, meaty, beaty, big and usually bouncy, was so drunk that she had to be taken to the police station in a wheelbarrow.[91] Alfresco lust was the order of the day for those sexual visitors of no fixed abodes. In July 1884, Thomas Thomas (Twm Twice) was fined for having intercourse with a 'woman of low character' in the Carmarthen churchyard. One of the most famous girls to have walked and worked the streets of Carmarthen was the unfortunate Marie Jane Kelly (*c*.1863–9 November 1888), alias Marie Kelly, alias 'Fair Emma', alias 'Ginger', alias 'Black Mary'. Mary was the final victim of the notorious unidentified killer Jack the Ripper.

Yet some people in the bucolic citadel attempted to establish the business of prostitution on more profitable and comfortable lines.[92] In February 1913, the police raided the premises of Bird in Hand in Carmarthen, having received complaints from a mother that her teenage daughter and her friends were entertaining men in the upstairs rooms. The police found a couple in one bed and two men and a woman in another bed. Following an admission by one of the girls that 'there were tremendous numbers of fellows who went upstairs at a fee of 1 shilling each time', the Carmarthen Borough Police Court fined the publican Williams Evans £20 and sentenced him to two months' hard labour.[93] At the time of the First World War it was a popular saying in the town that 'a Bird in Hand is worth two in the Ivy Bush'.

An element of acute desperation underpins much of the history of prostitution in north-east Wales. Denbighshire Quarter Sessions were horrified to hear the sordid details of the case against the parents for prostituting their daughter Mary Jones, a deaf and dumb girl.[94] Unsurprisingly, perhaps, police had great difficulty in obtaining evidence. Wrexham County Court heard the remarkable case of Mary Williams in 1878. In return for supplies of beef from Ingman the butcher in Wrexham, Mrs Williams provided sexual services until she fell and broke her leg whilst drunk and was unable to continue payments.[95] As in Carmarthen, when the militia were on duty in Mold, Wrexham and Denbigh, herds of harlots would descend on the towns. Elizabeth Lewis, 'a prostitute', was charged with 'sleeping in a large barrel in the yard at the rear of the Rainbow Vaults' in Wrexham. Her naked lover ran away just as the police arrived.[96] The barrel must have been a firkin.

In north-west Wales, prostitutes had similar problems of obtaining appropriate places to entertain their clients. Local authorities closed down many 'houses of ill fame' in Mill Lane, Caernarfon, in a concerted campaign to eradicate prostitution between 1870 and 1872. A woman charged with soliciting explained why she had sex on the castle green – 'houses where girls assembled had been done away with but prostitution must be carried on somewhere.'[97]

The development of the docks in Llanelli, Swansea and Newport saw a professionalisation of sex in the three coastal towns. In 1897 at Llanelli, several local ministers and Mr G. Pike of the National Vigilance Association opposed the granting of dancing licences to the White Heart Inn, the Swan Inn, the Square and Compass, the Cambrian Hotel and the York Hotel for they all doubled as brothels.[98] To the prurient dancing was vertical expression of a horizontal desire, just one step away from sex. Local moralists were consumed with the fear that someone, somewhere might be having a good time. Their fears seemed justified in the 1930s when Llanelli's Flappers whirled in the latest dance craze, 'the shag'.

At Swansea the 'ladies of the pave' would frequent one of the many pubs down in the dock and museum area such as The Bugle, The Jew's Harp, The Fishguard Arms, The Heart's Delight, The Lord Nelson, The Cuba or the Queens. These premises doubled as brothels. The Queens served 'the better class of girl and a better class of customer', the officers and captains. Regular seamen had to make do with a dark and dank area just along from the pub, in front of the oldest museum in Wales, the Royal Institution of South Wales – 'The Museum' that Dylan Thomas considered 'belonged in a museum'. The rougher girls would just do it on the steps. The girls and 'shilling women' in The Queens would sit at the bar, their feet on the footrest, with the price-list/menu chalked on the soles of their vampy shoes.[99]

As the navvies arrived in November 1884 to dig the docks at Barry and to build the fast-growing town that coalesced around it, so too did the prostitutes. Thompson Street, which linked Barry docks with the town centre, was as notorious and famous amongst seamen as Cardiff's Tiger Bay. In 1891, anyone walking along the street would be 'accosted by at least a dozen prostitutes of the most ungainly, the filthiest and the most abandoned type that could be found in the foul vomiting dens of Babylonian Cardiff'. Houses in Thompson Street and Gueret Street were 'the most unhallowed haunts of vice and degradation of every conceivable type'. A resident complained:

Rowdiness of some kind or another is daily, almost hourly, occurring
... it is well known that brothels exist ... under our very eyes without
the slightest restraint ... men cannot go outdoors at night without
being molested and solicited by immoral women living in several
of these small streets.'[100]

'Liverpool Jennie', 'Black Annie', and their pimps 'James Bond
and 'Lord Wellington' ruled. The collective efforts of the police,
fires and floods failed to end the area's notoriety. Meetings of
the National Vigilance Association and the Cadoxton and Barry
Temperance Crusade Council heard details of 'deplorable immorality'. Married women, it was claimed, sent their nine or twelve-
year-old daughters out to the streets to pursue 'by means of their
shame' the money to pay for their mother's drinking.

Cardiff's infamous Tiger Bay 'out-soddomed' everywhere else
in Wales. Most of the dancing houses and drinking dens of the
lanes leading off Bute Street – Whitmore Lane, Charlotte Street,
Adam Street – doubled as brothels. Places of swindles and scandals,
of bugs in bed and bedlam in the bordello. Their fetid bars were
the working premises of local prostitutes. In the 1880s Amelia
Stephens aged twenty-three and Phoebe Davies aged twenty-one
were representative of the girls who worked here. They were a
good team. Amelia was a pert little lady with a notable mammary
endowment that made her an object of lust amongst all the male
staff at the pubs she worked in. Trouble, like the male staff, followed
Amelia around. Phoebe was larger, louder. A human Old Faithful
who could be relied upon to fling noise and vapours into the air
wherever she went. Both were Welsh girls who had moved into
the booming coal port in the 1880s. In 1890, they were charged
with assaulting and theft from Erik Danielson, a Swedish seaman.
In addition to clothing and cash, Danielson lost papers and love
letters from his girl in Copenhagen.[101] He was not alone. Crews of
Austrian, Chilean, Chinese, Dutch, English, French, Greek, Lascar,
Malayan, Portuguese, Scottish, Spanish and Welsh ships cavorted
with the local prostitutes every evening.

The streets were full of transients, passing through and passing
on, washed in with the tides that moralists wished would wash

them straight back out to sea. Bute Street was the 'street of a thousand whores'. Do-gooders and 'God-botherers' failed to do good in this area, but were sent on their well-wishing way with excrement on their shoes and execrations in their ears.[102] The case of twenty-eight-year-old Sarah Roberts of No. 7 Harvery Street, Canton, in November 1870 revealed that in addition to piston rods for legs, pneumatic Cardiff prostitutes needed a good right hook.[103] Her beauty in the chaotic and cramped wasteland was like a metaphor for Tiger Bay: lovely people, awful place; or was it the other way around?

Brothel owners were the entrepreneurs of vice. They certainly started young in Cardiff. In 1885, 'a prepossessing young woman named Margaret Robinson, only eighteen years of age, was charged with keeping a brothel at No.21 Nelson Street'. According to the report in the *Western Mail*, 'the case disclosed a state of things as grossly immoral as it is almost impossible to imagine'. Margaret, all silks and satins, worked with six other girls, all under twenty years of age, in what she claimed was a communal enterprise. Their speciality was apparently a two-girl and one-man special deal, which Inspector Harris witnessed in an upstairs bedroom.[104] The owner of the house was traced to the ironically named Temperance Town. Such owners controlled their vicious empires with a savage severity. Edward Llewelyn was the notorious owner of a beer shop and brothel in Charlotte Street, famous for its bosomy serving women in their frilly finery, and the rubato hurly-burly of the piano.[105] One of the most infamous brothel-keepers in Cardiff's history was Jack Matthews, owner of the appropriately named Spread Eagle.[106]

In the 1930s and 1940s, according to the novelist, short-story writer and playwright Gwyn Thomas, Cardiff brothels morphed into clubs. He recalled that 'chauvinism, sex and race are the dark trinity that head the curriculum of the idiot. You can find traces of all three in Tiger Bay'.[107] Characteristic of the area was:

> the bullying pimp fixing boxing bouts and promoting his whores
> ... His club is thronged with girls from the Afro-Arabian quarter,
> deep-voiced, self-defensively insolent, diluted by girls who have
> drifted down from the mining places, unable to endure one more

gulp of the gruesome cocktail of coal and Calvin. The club swings between poles of lechery and sport. Even the copulation is tempered by the simpler rules of Queensberry.[108]

The relationship between the Welsh and prostitution was not confined within Welsh borders. The rambunctious and randy professional soldier Frank Richards, in *Old Soldier Sahib*, recalled that he and his fellow soldiers of the Royal Welch Fusiliers had no concerns about visiting brothels to satiate their lusts. Indeed, these institutions were an organised part of the British soldier's life in India. But most people would probably insist that the only time they paid for sex was emotionally. Elizabeth Preece and Mary Ann Cooper, who usually worked in the Newport area, were arrested in Hereford in 1869.[109] It was Mary Ann's seventeenth court appearance on charges associated with prostitution. The Revd W. O. Jones was alleged to have more than a pastoral interest in local girls who worked as prostitutes in Liverpool. He was also claimed to have had sex with a prostitute in the back streets of Marseilles. Young Welsh girls venturing to work in the 'modern Babylon' of Liverpool, such as Elizabeth Jones, found themselves, despite the best efforts of the Young Wales Society, working as prostitutes. Elizabeth, understandably, but unwisely, had placed her trust in the nearest policeman on her bewildered disembarkation from the Llandudno steamer.[110] Many Welsh girls followed Mary Kelly's example and worked in the world of gaslight and garters amongst the London prostitutes who dropped their drawers faster than their vowels. Good time girls with their surrendering flesh. When the Welsh Gorsedd visited Chicago for the 1893 international eisteddfod, many were enticed into the 'best little whorehouse in America', at 441 South Clark Street, by a parrot that squawked the greeting 'Carrie Watson: come on in gentlemen'.[111] Mary Williams was a Welsh-speaking girl who worked there. Perhaps the girls who ventured furthest to ply their trade were Billie Thomas, Siân Griffiths and Lily Davies, who worked as good-time girls during the Alaska-Yukon gold rush.[112]

It is important to remember that it was not only women who worked as prostitutes. Ivor Novello both in life and on stage played it both ways.[113] In his play and film *Down Hill* (1927), which he authored, he acts the role of a man who worked as a gigolo in Paris. Ivor Novello's own 50/50 club in London provided opportunities for elite Metropolitan bohemia and elite queer circles to intermingle and integrate.[114] Amongst the habitués were Rhys Davies and Emlyn Williams who were predatory in their encounters with homosexual sex-for-sale in London in the 1930s.[115] Amongst their most frequent providers were men of the Welsh Guards Regiment, who subsidised their soldierly earnings working in the 'rough trade'. Closer to home, the genteel town of Abergavenny was rocked by a homosexual sex scandal in 1942 in which twenty-four men were imprisoned for periods ranging from three months to ten years for their parts in a sex-for-cash scandal.[116]

Brief Encounters: alternative sexualities

Na thwyller chwi; ni chaiff na godinebwyr, nac eilyn-addolwyr, na thorwyr priodas, na masweddwyr, na gwrw-gydwyr, na lladron, na chybyddion, na meddwon . . . etifeddu teyrnas Duw . . . bydd eu rhan yn y llyn sydd yn llosgi a thân a brwmstan . . . Yn ddiau os na chaiff y bygythion sobr a dychrynllyd hyn o lyfr Duw effaith arnot, dos rhagot, ddyn aflan. Dos rhagot yn dy lwybrau aflan . . . Croesawa Uffern! Croesawa fflamiau! Croesawa gythreiliaid.

(Do not be deceived; neither adulterers, nor the worshippers of false gods, nor marriage-breakers, nor homosexuals, nor thieves, nor misers, nor drunkards will inherit God's kingdom . . . Their place will be in the lake which is consumed by fire and brimstone . . . undoubtedly if these frightening warnings from the word of God have no effect on you then go away, vile man . . . Go away along your vile roadway and prepare to Welcome Hell! Welcome flames! Welcome devils!)

'Ewyllyswyr Da' (E. Edwards and W. Pryse), *Y Sefyllfa Briodasol: Neu Cyfarwyddiadau a Chynghorion i Wŷr a Gwragedd Er Meithrin a Chynnal Heddwch Teuluaidd* (Newport, 1871), p. 19.

E. Edwards and W. Pryse, 'Ewyllyswyr Da' (Well-wishers), must have chosen their nom-de-plume with considerable irony for those people, like homosexuals, graphically described in their hellfire Welsh as 'gwrw-gydwyr' (literally male-grabbers), could look forward to a fate worse than a fate worse than death. Many people who did not consign homosexuals to immolation in fiery subterranean bitumen lakes were far from supportive. Lloyd George allowed his distaste for the alleged homosexuality of the Turks and their 'unnatural sexual habits' to influence his policy in the Near East with disastrous results after 1919. Even the masters of sexual psychology, Siegmund Freud and Ernest Jones, regarded homosexuality as a problem, best avoided. In 1932, Jones had repeated his concern that Freud's ideas on human sexuality were too phallocentric. However, Jones agreed with Freud that homosexuality was a developmental phenomenon, caused by young children's fantasies about their own and their parents' sexual organs.[117] In females, Jones told Freud (after analysing many homosexual women), 'the fantasy of the father (especially of his penis in her womb)' played a part of some importance. Bertrand Russell in his *Marriage and Morals* (1929) also took his cue from Freud and saw homosexuality as one of the outcomes of the sexual frustrations that parents could inflict on their children.[118] This was especially the case for boys, for the origins of female homosexual tendencies did not often trouble Russell.

Russell, Freud, Jones and Ellis did at least have an element of sympathy with homosexuality. The law was less tolerant.[119] Sections of the Offences Against the Person Act 1861, dealing with buggery and indecent assault, were followed by the notorious section 11 of the Criminal Law Amendment Act 1885, defining any act of 'gross indecency' between men in 'public' or 'private' as an offence. Statute law was complemented by the offence of 'indecency' legislated against under many local by-laws.[120]

Uncovering the vanished world of the homosexual past is challenging. Not everyone who lived a single life was homosexual or lesbian. Not everyone who lived as a 'couple' were practising homosexuals or lesbians. Those single uncles who slumbered in their chairs, watching the child's Christmas in Wales, were not all homosexual.[121] Terms such as 'lavender aunts', 'musical young men', 'dainty boys', 'delicate boys', suggest much but hide more.

As ever popular sayings were colourful – 'milfyr-mihafar dim buwch na gafr' (a milfyr-mihafar neither a cow or a goat).[122] Newspapers would refer to homosexual scandals with the faintest of allusions. Words, gestures and symbols (crooked fingers, green carnations, yellow books) suggest that, perhaps, homosexuality was far more prevalent in Welsh society than it seems.

Certain trades and occupations acquired a reputation for their links with homosexuality. The armed forces with their strong tradition of male bonding, as we have already noted, acquired a reputation for same-sex friendships that took on a physical as well as an emotional dimension. The Navy was traditionally considered to be about 'rum, the lash and sodomy'. By the First World War, all had become optional, but many still chose the final option. The career of Violet Douglas-Pennant as head of the Women's Royal Air Force was seriously undermined by a series of rumours, unfounded and unjustified she argued, of 'Sapphic orgies' within the service. At Aberystwyth the establishment of Alexandra Hall in 1904 was meant to provide a haven for young lady students to shelter from the unwelcome attention of predatory male students. Yet it also, ironically, provided the ideal environment for many Sapphic romances.[123]

Boarding colleges such as Llandovery and Brecon were schools for scandal – the venues where many developed their sexual identities as homosexuals. It was here also that many acquired their penchant and predilection for flogging – 'Le Vice Anglais'. Even after forty years, Sir Charles Bruce, son of Lord Aberdare, still 'trembled' when he recalled his headmaster's castigation, 'Cast forth that evil person from among you', swiftly followed by the swish of his cane.[124] The castigating headmaster, Dr Vaughan, knew what he was whipping, for he had been dismissed because of his affair with one of his pupils at Harrow.

Many of the economic and social developments that swept through Wales in the years 1870–1945 provided opportunities for predatory homosexuals. The growth of retail, in particular the development of gentlemen's outfitters, was one such area. 'Which side does sir wear himself?', 'Are you being served?' carried additional connotations.[125] The development of the cinema, the bathhouse and the swimming pool similarly provided ample opportunities for male and female same-sex love.[126] The Turkish baths in Merthyr Tydfil acquired somewhat of an unsavoury reputation in the 1900s for the activities of 'deprived moral decadents'. Long-term relationships also developed amongst members of the tramping fraternity, for the open road proved to be as straight as the yellow brick road. W. H. Davies recalled that most homosexual relationships were carnal and incidental, but that a few were longer-term partnerships.[127]

Religion, despite the warnings of the hellfire preachers such as 'Ewyllyswyr Da', was not immune from homosexual relationships. Indeed the Anglican and Catholic churches seemed particularly prone. Gerard Manley Hopkins (1844–89), poet, painter and priest, during his time at St Beuno's, near St, Asaph in north Wales, had 'evil thoughts' while sketching a crucified arm. A crucifix had stimulated him 'in the wrong way'. In one sermon he notes that Christ 'in his body was most beautiful'.

> I leave it to you, brethren, then to picture him, in whom the fullness of the godhead dwelt bodily, in his bearing now majestic, how strong and how lovely and lissom in his limbs . . . and for myself I make no secret I look forward with eager desire to seeing the matchless beauty of Christ's body in the heavenly light.[128]

Homoeroticism seemed quite compatible with religious fervour. Along with David and Jonathan and their 'wonderful' love 'passing the love of women' (2 Samuel 1:26), the 'soft' apostle was a focus for homosexual attention. The New Testament was even more problematic, for John is described (in John's Gospel) as 'the disciple whom Jesus loved'. At the Last Supper, he talks to Jesus whilst 'leaning on his bosom' or 'lying on his breast'.[129] Those who scoured the Bible, such as W. C. Fields, 'looking for a loophole' were not surprised to find that Jesus never condemned homosexuality or sodomy. Those who took refuge in the church, or who mistook their lack of sexual interest in women for a vocation, often found themselves in what must have been a painfully hypocritical position. Robert Owen (1820–1902), of Dolgellau and Barmouth, author of *Sanctorale Catholicum, or, Book of Saints* (1880), and *A Pilgrimage to*

Rome (1883), must have debated these issues intensely having been deprived of his Fellowship at Jesus College, Oxford.[130]

Sporting endeavours also provided agonising internal tensions for many. Rugby and football were the very epitome of heroic masculinity in the imperial age of Empire. Climbing called for co-operation, co-ordination and strength of its participants that, often, in the locale of a small, intimate tent resulted in a physical relationship. One who was so tortured by his suppression of such tendencies was John Menlove Edwards (1910–57), one of the greatest of all Snowdonian and Alpine climbers. After years of mental anguish over his sexuality and periods in the north Wales mental hospital, Denbigh, Edwards committed suicide taking potassium cyanide.[131]

Particular professions soon acquired a penchant for men and women of an 'artistic disposition'. The precociously gifted artist J. D. Innes (1887–1914), who died tragically young of tuberculosis, had several affairs with both men and women in his brief life. Obeying what he called the 'stern call of dissipation', Innes had liaisons with Trelawny Dayrell Reed, John Fothergill and a Moroccan carpet-seller in Tenerife.[132] The theatre manager Hughes Griffiths Beaumont, ('Binkie', 1908–73), had several affairs with leading homosexuals in the theatre, including John Gielgud and Noel Coward, and his fellow Cardiffian, Ivor Novello.[133]

What is quite remarkable in the homosexuals and lesbians who worked in the artistic world is the love and loyalty many showed to their partners during exceptionally long-lasting relationships. Not all homosexuals lived a furtive existence of episodic, knee-trembling, guilt-ridden brief encounters. The actress Dame Gwen Lucy Ffrangcon-Davies (1891–1992) first played Juliet to John Gielgud's Romeo in 1924, thereby starting a stage partnership that was to last for almost half a century. During that time she was to be the Queen to his Richard of Bordeaux (1932) and Gwendolen in his classic 1940 revival of *The Importance of Being Earnest*. Her acting as a wife on stage was obviously of the highest quality, for Dame Ffrangcon-Davies lived with the actress Marda Vanne.[134] The artist Sir Cedric Lockwood Morris (1889–1982), the painter and plantsman of Swansea, worked hard to foster Welsh self-confidence in the arts. His first one-man exhibition in Rome, in 1922, was closed by the fascists. Amongst his pupils were Lucien Freud, Maggi Rambling and several inhabitants of Dowlais, where he taught art in an educational settlement during the economic depression. Morris lived for more than sixty years with the painter Arthur Lett-Haines (1894–1978).[135] The sculptor Betty Marion Rea (1904–65) lived with her life-long companion Nancy Mayhew (Nan) Youngman (1906–95).[136] Margaret Haig Thomas lived with Helen Archdale until they split up and thereafter cohabited with Theodora Bosanquet.[137] The Welsh sculptor Mary Lloyd lived with Frances Power Cobbe. Both found the company of men 'tedious'. When Cobbe died in 1904 she was buried alongside her beloved companion who had preceded her by eight years. What the gravedigger thought of the unusual arrangements is not recorded but it does perhaps point to the possibility that people's attitude to lesbianism was a little more tolerant than it is traditionally considered. Such relationships between artists gave rise to the idea that a 'Homintern' – a clique of gay men and lesbian women – controlled the art world from behind the scenes.[138]

Edith Picton-Turbervill (1872–1960) lived the life of a well-to-do country squire's daughter at Ewenni Priory until, in June 1895, in the unlikely venue of an express train from London to Bridgend, she had a conversion experience, and from that date entered on a life of religious activism. She contributed extensively to political, religious and social reform movements both in the UK and in India. In the 1930s she lived with Emily Kinnaird. Distressed by the propensity in the 1920s and 1930s of some who called such relationships 'unwholesome' or 'perverse', in *Life is Good: An Autobiography* (1939) she insisted, 'with a ring of challenge', that 'women's loving friendships could be as deep, beautiful and as exhilarating as any human relationship'.[139]

It is important to remember that popular attitudes to homosexuality continued to be more complex and contradictory throughout the period down to 1945. The treatment given to those men who were 'delicate' and women who were 'Sapphic' varied enormously. Some were tolerated by kith and kin, others were emotionally tortured. The surrealist photographer Angus McBean (1904–90) left his Newbridge home for the supposed greater enlightenment of England. He worked at London's Liberty store and commenced his interests in photography and theatrical mask-making. He gained a commission in 1936 for masks for Ivor Novello's play *The Happy Hypocrite* and took the production photographs. The photographs he took of the young actress Vivian Leigh established his position as one of the most significant portrait photographers of the twentieth century. In 1941 he moved to Bath. Here he allowed various male evacuees of different ages to move in with him in his flat. Neighbours complained about 'decadent' goings on and the 'perversion of minors'. In the spring of 1942 he was arrested on charges of undertaking criminal acts of homosexuality. McBean was sentenced to four years in prison but released after two years in 1944.[140]

The fear that exercising one's sexuality could lead to imprisonment was an ever present one for many homosexuals. The obvious solution to many was a marriage of convenience. Henry Cyril Paget (1875–1905), the 5th Marquess of Anglesey, married his cousin Lily in what was probably a ploy to unlock the restrictions on the family wealth. It was well worth the effort. The inheritance was more than £110,000 a year. Lily, with her golden hair and pale green eyes, was a Pre-Raphaelite stunner. She may have been everything Paget wanted to be himself. Powdered, peroxided and pomaded, Paget indulged his taste for outlandish costumes and diamonds. On their honeymoon, when Lily stopped and window-shopped at a jeweller's display in Paris, Paget went inside and bought the whole lot for her, much to her public embarrassment. In private her embarrassment continued. Paget liked to view his emeralds, rubies and diamonds displayed on her naked body. Diamonds might have been a girl's best friend, but they did not serve as a conduit to sex, for the wedding was unconsummated.

In the decadent 1890s, a German sex almanac named Paget as a homosexual, and rumours abounded about his liaisons in Paris and in British theatrical circles. Paget converted the family chapel at Plas Newydd into his very own theatre, the Gaiety, with seats for 150. He hired his own cast of leading actors at extravagant salaries to star in his productions. Most of them featured Paget who would be required to change his jewellery-encrusted satin costumes several times in each production. Irrespective of the production he would have an opportunity to flit and fly in his 'Butterfly Dance'. They even went on a world tour for three years producing Shakespearean tragedies, and, daringly, Oscar Wilde's *The Importance of Being Earnest*. Paget was anything but. Inevitably, tragically, the stars lost their twinkle, debts rose and the diamonds had to be sold in 1904. The sale lasted forty days with 17,000 lots going under the hammer. Paget's end had an echo of Oscar Wilde's death. He died alone at the Hotel Royale in Monte Carlo. The family tried to obliterate him from their archive, his theatre was torn down. The obituarists cruelly compared this effete, effeminate descendant with his heroic grandfather, whose military deeds at Waterloo were legendary.[141]

It was not only the flash and the flamboyant who resorted to a marriage of convenience to cover their sexuality. Alan Llwyd, in *Kate: Cofiant Kate Roberts, 1891–1985*, suggests that Kate Roberts's marriage to Morris T. Williams was a cover for her lesbianism and his homosexuality. He quotes one letter from Kate Roberts to Williams in which she describes kissing a butcher's wife from Pontardawe and coded references lesbianism in her novels as evidence that she was sexually attracted to women. Morris T. Williams (with whom Roberts ran the Denbigh press Gwasg Gee) was most likely in a relationship with their mutual friend, the poet E. Prosser Rhys (an author published by Gee).[142] Prosser Rhys won the crown at the National Eisteddfod in Pontypool in 1924 for his searing pryddest 'Atgof' (Memory).[143] The poem was judged to be immoral by some adjudicators, for not only did it describe sexual activity outside marriage, but with agonising honesty it described the physical lovemaking of two men. For once in its history, the Eisteddfod allowed literary merit to triumph over moral concerns. The young Caradog Prichard, a colleague and close friend of both Williams and Rees, noted that the poem was based on real life and derived from the bard's heart, and a 'love that transcended the erotic'.[144]

Another who poured his sexual tensions and traumas into his writings was the prolific novelist and short-story writer Rhys Davies

(1901–78) of Blaenclydach. The son of shop-keeping parents, Davies is often portrayed as an outsider within the mining communities of the early twentieth-century. Those writers who discuss Davies and his characters as not being a real part of their community because they were not miners, or involved in mining, are guilty of a gross misreading of social reality. What sort of community has no women, or commercial activity within it? It was in the shop that Davies encountered local people, particularly the womenfolk, for whom he developed a deep sympathy. In his fiction many of the characters are women of Lawrentian heroism who can perhaps achieve redemption through their sexuality. The story 'Nightgown' is one of the most remarkable stories ever written by a Welshman about women. A faded woman, fated to be drudge to her domineering husband and their five baleful sons, scrimps and saves her pennies to buy, by instalments, a beautiful silk nightgown, which she hides and keeps for her shroud. Dead, she lies before the startled eyes of her husband, attired in a parody of a wedding dress, a testament to her previously obscured and oppressed femininity. It is a scene of sacrifice that echoes Caradoc Evans's story 'Be This Her Memorial'. One did not need to be a code-breaker in Bletchley Park to crack the link to Davies. Aware as Davies was of his own homosexuality, life in the homophobic but male-dominated world of the Rhondda Valley became unbearable and he fled to Cardiff, then London.[145]

Rhys Davies, who in many respects resembles the torments suffered by the Welsh-descended author Tennessee Williams, set out his inner demons in the remarkable autobiography *Print of a Hare's Foot* (1969) as a form of literary puzzle. Literary critics have been busily 'decoding the hare' ever since.[146] The book is not so much a whodunnit, but an exposition of what he might have done to whom and when, as he groped from youthful heterosexual encounters towards his homosexual identity. In the London of the 1920s and 1930s, Rhys Davies was fully immersed in the homosexual subculture. He had brief orgiastic sexual encounters with artists, actors, soldiers (especially Welsh Guardsmen) and manual workers. Much of it was clandestine, most of it was cathartic, a lot of it was paid for. Covert pick-ups seemed to suggest that when a particular form of behaviour is absolutely forbidden, it becomes unbearably exciting – ever since the Garden of Eden, forbidden fruit was sweetest.

Sharing that metropolitan milieu of homosexuality, but at a somewhat more rarefied level, was Ivor Novello (1893–1951), the composer, actor and playwright of Cardiff. Novello had grown up alongside his accountant father in the shadows of his larger-than-life mother, Clara Novello Davies (1861–1943), the musical impresario with her audacious personality and ample bosom. Novello, it seems, had the classic background ingredients beloved of amateur psychological profilers of homosexuality – a strong-willed mother and a subservient father. At fifteen, Novello won a choral scholarship to Magdalen College choir school, Oxford, and hit the jackpot at twenty-two when his stirring ballad, 'Keep the Home Fires Burning', became a great morale-boosting anthem of the First World War. He then entered the movies and the musical theatre where he authored, produced and performed in some of the greatest musicals of the twentieth century.[147]

Novello's Latin good looks, soulful eyes and Byronic profile enabled him to conduct a series of passionate and promiscuous sexual liaisons with other men. His lovers included a handsome young Bristol actor called Archie Leach, later to win worldwide fame after changing his name to Cary Grant. Novello also bedded Hollywood idol Tyrone Power. The actor Robert 'Bobbie' Andrews was Novello's partner for thirty-four years but that did not stop him sharing Andrews with another of his famous lovers, Noel Coward. Siegfried Sassoon was deeply embittered by the callous treatment he received from Novello. Sassoon recalled that Novello pitched him into an 'unblinking little hell', an 'inferno'. Novello's cultivated charm concealed his fundamental egotism and did not prevent him from satisfying his own sexual appetite with very little concern for the other person involved. One of Siegfried Sassoon's biographers complained that Novello was 'a consummate flirt who gathered lovers as others gathered lilacs in the spring'.[148] It is even alleged that the youthful Novello seduced the happily married, supposedly firmly heterosexual and middle-aged Winston Churchill. Asked, by Somerset Maughan, one of Churchill's closest friends, whether the rumour was true, and if it was, then what sleeping with Novello was like, Churchill puffed on his cigar and responded with a smile 'magical'.[149] Despite his brief fall from grace after being imprisoned for petrol offences against the Second World War rationing restrictions, Novello's funeral brought London to a standstill as thousands lined the cortège's route.

Actor and playwright Emlyn Williams (1905–87) soon immersed himself in the homosexual culture of London, when he moved there after Oxford in the 1920s.[150] His first acting role was in 1927, at the Savoy, with a small part in the appropriately titled *And So to Bed*. And how. Considering his promiscuity, perhaps he didn't need to act. He found 'pick-ups' in the Fitzroy Tavern, the Trocadero's Long Bar, the Teakettle and the Charlie Bar and 'dined' with Charles Laughton in Perroquet. His longest relationship was with the actor Bill Cronin-Wilson. Disturbingly, as his endearingly honest memoir, *Emlyn*, reveals, he was still attracted to women – 'I was stock still in the middle of the road, and that's as good a way of getting run over as any.'[151] After Bill's death in 1934, this conflict came to a head. After a long holiday, Emlyn returned to London, fell in love with a girl named Molly and proposed to her:

> I faced the final hurdle, the high one I had been skirting, my attitude towards my own sex . . . though I had never been a slave to pursuit, however undemanding my sudden sallies I had always been free to indulge in them. The idea that I should be cut off from that freedom was alarming.[152]

Emlyn's 'alarm' at meeting the standards of fidelity and commitment marriage demanded was compounded by his developing relationship with Fess, a young workingman. At one point, real-life resembled a theatrical farce, as Emlyn, Fess and Molly were holidaying in the same house:

> I looked at the door. If it opened which of the two would I hope to see? . . . I was waiting for him now in a torment I had not expected and if he entered now I would feel tormented relief. If she appeared I would be delighted by the sight of the person I loved.[153]

Such tensions threatened to tear Emlyn apart, as he agonisingly pondered, 'Is everyone two people constantly?' When he discovered that Fess had been stealing from him, Emlyn finally discarded him and married Molly. Emlyn had oscillated uneasily between the two lives of 'normal' and homosexual until he finally resolved it by forging that loving, intimate relationship so cherished by society – heterosexual marriage.

Queen Victoria allegedly refused to believe that lesbianism existed, so too many Welsh moralists refused to accept that homosexuality could exist in Wales. Yet a series of cases reveal that arcadian Wales, like metropolitan London, had a diverse range of sexual experiences. Prim and pious Aberystwyth was rocked by a homosexual scandal in 1941 and again in 1944 when ten men were imprisoned on charges of gross indecency.[154] The most notable scandal, however, took place in Abergavenny in 1942. In all, twenty-four men were charged with 192 offences against section 11 of the Criminal Law Amendment Act 1885. They were imprisoned for periods of a few months to, in the cases of William Neville Holly and Frederick Percival Turner, ten years each. The cases revolved around the local cinema, The Coliseum, and the home of its owner George Rowe. Those arrested revealed that a broad cross-section of the townspeople were involved in the homosexual culture of south-east Wales. The village people involved included a cinema manager, two farmers, an airman, a hairdresser, a clerk, a hotel porter, an actor, an electrical powerhouse worker, a worker in a paper mill, a miner, two chefs, a rail worker, a cafe assistant, a factory worker, a manager of a grocery store, a bank clerk, a fireman, two shop assistants, a hotel worker, a warehouseman and a window dresser. Two men involved attempted to commit suicide but survived, whilst nineteen-year-old Lewis Reginald Thomas Matthews killed himself under a Great Western Railway train.

Despite the sensation caused in the local press the case was not unique in Abergavenny's history.[155] In a separate case in 1942, William Henry Anderson Edwards, the manager of the local YMCA was charged with eighteen offences of indecent assault against ten teenage boys and youths. The youngest boy was twelve years of age, the eldest fifteen. Edwards had previously been imprisoned for nine months in 1939 on two charges of gross indecency with another male. He had links with a number of the twenty-four involved in the later case and was almost certainly given a lighter sentence because he acted with police as a foil to capture George Rowe and his homosexual circle. There were a further two cases in 1943.[156] The Abergavenny case reveals the extent of homophobia in Welsh communities. The press, as ever, had a field day, with the *News of the World*, as always, providing lurid eyecatching headlines such as 'An orgy of perversion'.[157] More surprising comments came from the magistrates who initially heard the cases and the judges who tried them at the Monmouthshire Assizes. Mr Justice Singleton ordered women to be cleared from the court to 'preserve their moral welfare'. Mr Justice Raglan Somerset reflected that 'if they are all from the same neighbourhood it strikes me that there must be a remarkable number of men there suffering from arrested development'. Sentencing Norman Roberts to fifteen months in jail, Mr Justice Singleton explained that he was doing so because his 'character needed stiffening'. The irony that so many men were sent to prison, a hotbed of homosexual behaviour was probably lost on the judges. The people involved were invariably treated at best with condescension, at worst the authorities treated them with contempt.

There are some areas of the human psyche where we cannot penetrate, except to record without comprehension areas opaque to our understanding, where sympathy dies. Diarists such as Francis Kilvert reveal an unhealthy obsession with prepubescent girls.[158] Richard Hughes's *High Wind in Jamaica* derived much insight from the author's easy intimacy with prepubescent girls.[159] As in *Hamlet* the heyday was in the blood of the old. Authors such as John Cowper Powys recorded their sado-masochistic frustrations and fantasies. Lavish, luscious prose described the darkest, dirtiest things.[160] The Revd Robet Jones (Trebor Aled, 1866–1917), the poet and Baptist minister, revealed that pleasure and pain were intertwined. In his relatively brief poem 'Pleser' (Pleasure) the word 'pleser' is repeated an almost masturbatory sixty-four times:

Pleser isel darfodedig
Pleser afiach, pleser tlawd,
Pleser calon halogedig
Foddi nwydau gwyllt y cnawd.[161]

(A low corrupt pleasure
An obscene pleasure, a poor pleasure
The pleasure of a corrupt heart
Fulfills the body's wild urges.)

People might not have been able to pronounce it, but the practices of sado-masochism were not unknown in Wales. In 1883, Pontypridd and Aberdare were shocked at the sadistic treatment given to a farmer, Mr Jenkin Morgan, by two 'gentlemen' John and Thomas Harries. The Harrieses branded Morgan with irons, 'scalped' his genitals and sexually abused their tenant. Scandalously they almost managed to get the local authorities to cover up their crimes.[162]

The murder of Gwen Ellis Jones, by William Murphy at Holyhead in 1910, had several of the characteristics of a classic Welsh murder – police incompetence, a murderer who turned himself in, casual sex, careless violence, all set against the Dickensian pathos of Christmas. When an eyewitness to the murder was telling a beat policeman what he had seen, William Murphy walked up and announced, 'Are you looking for me? Here I am.' At the guardhouse he declared, 'I have come here to give myself up as I have killed a woman not very far from Captain Tanner's house, by cutting her throat with a knife, and chucked her body into a sewerage drain.' Police listened and pondered. Eventually, they decided they had better investigate. They went to the place Murphy described and found the dead body of Gwen Ellen Jones with its throat cut. In the cells on 26 December, Murphy told a police officer, 'I have made a happy Christmas for myself, haven't I?' Sergeant Roberts replied, 'Yes it seems. I'm sorry for you Murphy.' To which Murphy replied, 'I'm not sorry for it. I'm damned glad I've done it.' In his confession Murphy confirmed that he had been in a relationship with Jones for a few months and that, on the day of the murder, they had arranged to meet:

We went to look for a certain place to have connection. So, I took her right across the field from Captain Tanner's house. She told me that she was going to Bethesda tomorrow and said 'I like you and we will have a bit before we go.' I said 'What road?' (meaning by what method), and she said 'Any road you like.' I said 'We'll have a bit back' (meaning rear entry) I had connection and had a bit back. I said to her, 'Turn around and we'll have a bit front', so we had a bit front. While we were having a bit front I said 'Why don't you pull this off?' meaning the ruff around her neck. She said 'It's hooked underneath.' I then caught hold of her with my left thumb and began to strangle her . . . I then drew my knife from my pocket and commenced to use it by cutting her throat. When I cut her throat I dragged her into the drain. She was still alive, gurgling, when I got her into the drain . . . I commenced cutting her throat further, from ear to ear. Then I got my fingers into her throat and opened the wound more . . . Then I turned her belly downwards and shoved her beneath the water to smother and drown her.

The jury needed just three minutes to decide guilt. Murphy was hanged at Caernarfon on 15 February 1910.[163]

The press in reporting cases of bestiality often hid the gravity of the case in the term 'unnatural offence', as did the *Western Mail* on 1 April 1874. But this was no April Fool's story. George Bassal of Grosmont was imprisoned for ten years for an 'unnatural offence'. A previous conviction was also proved.[164] Carmarthen Jail's Register of Felons records four such cases, one of which was against Daniel Griffiths of 'healthy complexion' from Laugharne, who was charged with having 'committed buggery with an ass'.[165] Eric Gill, a talented artist but a monster of a man, indulged in a number of sexual deviancies, including bestiality and incest at his artistic retreat at Capel-y-Ffin.[166] David Harsent, a Swansea sailor, shot his landlord and landlady, Ann and Antonio Roderick, when she accused him of committing acts of bestiality with the family's dog and cat.[167] Darkest and most inexplicable of all was the behaviour of Thomas 'Tom' Caller of Cardiff[168] and John 'Jack' Edmunds of Abersychan.[169] Having murdered their victims both had intercourse with the corpse. The press reports described evil men and monstrous acts. But these murderers were not monsters. They were men. And that was the most frightening thing about them.

6

Love in a Cold Climate: Fidelity, Friendship and Fellowship

In the Terraces, we never opposed love. The way we viewed this question was that love must be pretty deep rooted to have gone on for so long. One would have to be very deep to tinker with so deep a root, deeper than we were. Also, love passes on the time that is a prime feature in any place where there is a scarcity of work for the local men and women to do, a state which prevailed on a high plane indeed during the dark years now being spoken of. Also, love, properly used, keeps people warm.

Gwyn Thomas, The Alone to the Alone (London, 1947), p. 71.

'The Alone to the Alone': the power of love and the battle to avoid loneliness

> Cyfoeth, nid yw ond oferedd
> Glendid, nid yw yn parhau
> Ond cariad pur sydd fel y dur,
> Yn para, tra bo dau.
>
> (Wealth, it is just vanity
> Cleanliness, it does not last
> But pure love is like steel,
> Lasting, as long as two).

Traditional, quoted in Bethan Mair (ed.), Hoff Gerddi
Serch Cymru (Llandysul, 2002), p. 59

Love, people knew, was the most powerful emotion, for the Bible told them so, time after time after time. Love was what gave meaning and measure to life. Christian love took many forms for in their father's house there were many mansions. In a simple couplet, under the title 'Duw Cariad Yw' (God is Love), Richard Griffiths noted:

> Awdur pob cariad ydyw
> Duw y cariad: ei Dad yw.
>
> (The author of all love
> God of love; its father is He).

Even that most acerbic of atheists, Bertrand Russell, considered that 'to fear love is to fear life, and those who fear life are already three parts dead.[1] He further considered: 'the root of the matter ... the thing I mean ... is love, Christian love, or compassion. If you feel this you have a motive for existence, a guide for action, a reason for living, an imperative necessity for intellectual honesty'.[2] Russell, who practised what he preached, much to the shock of many of the women he encountered, warned that 'of all forms of caution, caution in love is perhaps the most fatal to true happiness'. After an intensely lonely childhood in 'an emotional icehouse', Russell explained the importance of love in modern society: 'Love is something far more than the desire for sexual intercourse; it is the principal means of escape from the loneliness which afflicts most men and women throughout the greater part of their lives.'[3]

The young certainly approached every opportunity to taste love with zing and zest.[4] In rural Wales the fairs and markets were celebrated, infamous social occasions, drawing the youths from miles around. At Sardis, Llandysul, the annual Ffair Cileth was famous as the starting place for the courtship of local couples. One of the few to observe the rowdy romping of Welsh fairs without a veneer of moral worry was the American consul in Wales in the 1880s, the rumbustious Wirt Sikes. In his *Rambles and Studies in Old South Wales*, he recounted with obvious delight the fair in Llandaff:

> By nightfall, the scene becomes a sort of pandemonium ... Deep darkness falls; but the diversions of the pleasure-fair abate no jot. On the contrary, they increase; for all the young folks of the village being now assembled on the green, they not only dance, but play kissing-games full of romping and boisterous merriment. A great

circle is gathered in one part of the field, lads and lasses to the number of fifty joining hands in the fitful light of the torches, and amid much slapping of backs and frantic scampering, playing *cusan-yn-y-cylch*, or kiss-in-the-ring. They . . . are as full of fun as young colts; and the air echoes with shrieks of laughter mingling with the music of the band, and the rousing smack of rustic lips on rustic red cheeks rivals the popping of the air-guns, where the gaudy shooting-gallery glitters in the light of a dozen flaring flambeaux.[5]

Sikes added that the hiring fairs, horse shows, flower shows, Christmas shows, fat-cattle shows and poultry shows were also occasions for merriment and mirth. The joyful carousing and court-ing of the fairs was captured and chronicled in tuneful and mirthful folk songs and ballads.

Chapels and churches, especially on occasions of singing festivals, were not just centres for moralistic condemnation of the young. Cymanfaoedd Canu (Singing Festivals) were often occasions of conviviality and courtship as young people sought earthly as well as ethereal love. In urban areas across Wales there developed the remarkable institution of the Sunday 'monkey parades' when boys and girls would parade in rows before pairing off with their chosen paramours. When the university colleges of Wales accepted women students in the 1890s there began one of the most effective marital agencies in Welsh history. Against the principles of the Lady Principal, male and female students transferred the concept of the monkey parade to the architectural splendour of the quad-rangle in Old College, Aberystwyth.

Despite the impacts of dechristianisation and desacralisation, of globalism and consumerism, of technology and change, the power of love did not diminish. The cinema extolled the virtues of romantic love with relentless persistence and passion. On the silver screen the promoters of the love laws, the producers, scriptwriters and actors laid down who should be loved. And how. And how much. Some loved a lot, some a little, some a little less. But films extolled the virtues of love in all its various guises – love at first sight, young (and older) love, unrequited love, obsessive love, sentimental love, spiritual love, forbidden love, sexual and passionate love, sacrificial love, explosive and destructive love, and tragic love. The late 1920s and the 1930s were the golden era of that much disparaged phenomenon, the 'romance film' or 'girlie movie'. But as Elinor Glyn noted, 'romance is the glamour which turns the dust of every-day life into a golden haze.'[6] It was also good box office. Eyes watered, breasts heaved and pulses quickened at the romantic exploits of Greta Garbo and John Gilbert, Clark Gable and Joan Crawford, and Clark Gable and Jean Harlow.

Musicals further emphasised both the importance of love and romance and the profits that could be obtained from films that had plenty of both. *Casablanca* (1942) featured some of the most memorable songs such as 'As Time Goes By'. Members of the audience could also buy the sheet music. People who had never been out of Port Talbot could sing at home that 'We'll always have Paris'. In the music halls and theatres, high-romance and Ruritanian weepies were all the rage in the interwar years as Cole Porter, Rogers and Hammerstein, and Irving Berlin penned some of the greatest of all love songs – 'How Deep is the Ocean' (1932), 'Smoke Gets in Your Eyes' (1933), 'Cheek to Cheek' (1935) and 'I've Got You Under My Skin' (1936). Cardiff's very own stars were at the height of their powers. Ivor Novello created the world of Ruritania in musicals such as *Glamorous Night*, *Careless Rapture* and *The Dancing Years*. Few in the audience were untouched by songs such as 'Waltz of My Heart', 'Shine Through My Dreams', 'I Can Give You the Starlight' and 'We'll Gather Lilacs'.[7] Novello's near Cardiff contemporary, Teresa Mary (Tessie) O'Shea (1913–95), as suggested by her sobriquet 'Two Ton Tessie', added a note of realism when she sang 'Nobody Loves a Fat Girl When She's Forty' and 'I Fell in Love with an Airman but I'm Nobody's Sweetheart Now'. In the era of the silent movies, live music accompanied the film and added melodrama. G. W. Robinson at Porth believed that his musicians were at least partly responsible for the success of *Madame X* in 1921:

> Never in my experience have I known a picture with such universal appeal as *'Madame X'*. To see hundreds of people leaving a hall some openly crying, and the majority of men and women dabbing their

eyes (in the case of the ladies) very red ones at that, is a most remarkable sight. I have had showers of personal congratulations and thanks for having screened such a picture.[8]

Those who failed to obtain love or a lover through the routes of chapel, church, cinema or fair, sought comfort and companionship through the 'personal advertisements' in the newspapers and magazines. 'Lonely hearts' placed advertisements in newspapers in which they sought love as did the correspondents to Thomas Owen's magazine *The Matchmaker*, who were often in search of 'platonic friendship'. One letter came from a south Wales 'businessman' seeking 'a young lady who would teach me dances'. Another advertisement was from a 'Lady . . . stylish in dress' who wanted 'a real good pal' to 'come and have a cup of tea'. The First World War intensified such feelings of loss and loneliness and people soon grew familiar with the piteous and pitiful advertisements from 'lonely soldiers'.[9] When the authorities clamped down on such advertisements, the Swansea newspaper *The Cambria Daily Leader* was instructed to wind up the correspondence club. Nevertheless, at the time of the Second World War, one gentleman of Monmouthshire continued to advertise himself as a 'clean, good looking man, 44, prepared to satisfy any lady's wishes, completely safe'.[10]

Correspondence clubs and the personal columns provided services that drew the attention of the police. One man the police spoke to, a Cardiff steelworker, had used the columns for lonely hearts clubs in the local newspaper to acquire a series of French and American magazines featuring naked women, and books such as *Amour de Paris, Free For All, Piccadilly Eyeful*, and 'anthropological' works such as *Far Eastern Sex Life*, instruction in sex technique in the form of *Life Long Sex Harmony, Sex Instruction* and *Life Long Love*, and *The Truth About Nudism*.[11] Bernice Rubens in her disturbing and dark novel *I Sent a Letter to My Love* warned of another danger of the personal column as two frustrated, loveless middle-aged siblings unknowingly correspond with each other.[12]

Love, like Christmas, became secularised and commercialised over the period 1870–1945. Lovers corresponded through letters

and cards. With the development of the penny post and the commercial cards, pre-printed valentines became increasingly popular.
That astute observer of Welsh life, Wirt Sikes, noted of Valentine's
Day: 'In Cardiff the postmaster thinks himself lucky if he gets off
with 15,000 letters in excess of the ordinary mail. Nineteen extra
sorters and carriers were employed for the work on February 14th,
1878, and the regular force was heavily worked beyond its usual
hours.'[13] To help her with her love letters a Montgomeryshire
woman turned to the essential guide for the pen-tied lover, *On the
Art of Writing Love Letters*.

Those who preferred their prose longer than a letter could enjoy
the romantic novels of Mills and Boon, which published hundreds
of books for the lonely from the early 1930s. Mary Edith Nepean
(née Bellis) (1876–1960) of Llandudno ran them close. She wrote
one book based on her extensive and exotic travels, *Romance and
Realism in the Near East* (1934), but her real forte was the 'light
romantic novel'. She produced her first offering in *Gwyneth of the
Welsh Hills* (1917), which was then followed by thirty-four novels
all of which had Welsh settings or characters.[14] Mary's near contemporary, Amy Roberta (Berta) Ruck (née Oliver) (1878–1978), of
Machynlleth, produced a series of novels of scant literary value but
'strong on love interest'. From *The Girls at His Billet* (1916), to *The
Unkissed Bride* (1929), to *He Learnt about Women* (1940), to *Shopping
for a Husband* (1967), her books had a common Cinderella motif,
whereby, after many vicissitudes, a neglected or impoverished
heroine gained a rich and loving husband. What more could a girl
want?[15]

Poets were even more prone than prose writers to ponder the
power and persistence of love. Into the strict meters of traditional
Welsh verse and the freer *vers libre*, poets poured out their pain
and passions, endlessly, often badly. It is a great irony that a man
usually considered to be curmudgeonly and crusty produced some
of the most sensitive love poetry. Sir John Morris-Jones (1864–1929),
might have been seen as stern in laying down linguistic laws, but
in matters of love poetry he was in a league of his own:

Dau lygad disglair fel dwy em
Sydd i'm hanwylyd i, . . .

Mae holl dyneraf liwiau'r rhos
Yn hofran ar ei grudd;
Mae'i gwefus fel pe cawsa'i lliw
O waed y grawnwin rhudd.[16]

(Two bright eyes like two gems
Has my dearest, . . .

All the tender colours of the moor
Hover in her complexion;
Her lips seem to have the
Colour of red wine.)

What an exquisite creature she must have been. But his chat-up lines must have been irresistible.

Young men would often carve their feelings out of wood into complex love spoons. These highly ritualised and symbolic love and fertility tokens had a range of specific meanings: a horseshoe for luck, a cross for faith, bells for marriage, hearts for love, anchors for a sailor, a lock for security. Caged balls indicated the number of children hoped for. The love spoon was a tangible evidence to a girl of her suitor's love and to her father that the lad could provide a living through his skill.[17]

Of all the artistic material created by love, unrequited love has produced the most poignant and popular. The anonymous authors of 'Torri Calon', 'Beth yw'r Haf i Mi?' and 'Paid â Deud' poured out their sorrow into songs lamenting love's labour lost.[18] In 1875 composer Joseph Parry (1841–1903) put the lament for lost love written by Richard Davies (Mynyddog, 1833–77) to music in 'Myfanwy'. With clawing sentimentality, the song features in John Ford's film *How Green Was My Valley* (1941) and remains a staple of male-voice choir repertoire in the twenty-first century. When it is sung people are often in tears – sometimes because of the words, often because of the quality of singing.

Perhaps the largest and most impressive confirmation of unrewarded love are the murals that the artist Rex Whistler (1905–44) painted at Plas Newydd, Anglesey. The sixty foot-long mural in the dining room, depicts a broad seascape, and even contains Neptune's wet footprints, as if the god has just left the scene. Whilst painting it, Whistler fell in love with and was spurned by Lord Anglesey's daughter Caroline. The rejection is the clue to unlock the painting's haunting quality. Whistler painted himself as Romeo, languishing beneath the balcony of a Juliet who is unmistakably Lady Caroline. He also appears as a gardener, which implies that he felt he was rejected as a suitor because of his social status. The painting is a poignant confirmation that the hardest thing to do is to watch the one you love, love someone else. Caroline married Sir Michael Duff, grandson of the fourth earl of Lonsdale and godson of Queen Mary, wife of King George V. Duff owned the Faenol estate, on the opposite side of the Menai from Plas Newydd. Whistler spent his last Christmas alone at Pickering, north Yorkshire, where he organised a party for local children in the memorial hall. On 18 July 1944, Whistler was killed by a German machine gunner in Normandy as the Allied invasion force fought to break out of the salient east of Caen. As he parted from a friend on the night before, Whistler had remarked that 'he hoped he would see you tomorrow'. Real life could be far more cruel than the melodramatic plots of a thousand love stories.[19] Love could be magical, but magic can just be an illusion and so the scars of love can be deep.

'Till death do us part': marriage, femininity and masculinity

Cyn mynd i ryfel, gweddia unwaith; cyn mynd i'r môr, gweddia ddwy-waith; ond cyn mynd i dy briodi, gweddia dair gwaith.

(Before going to war, pray once; before going to the sea, pray twice; but before going to your wedding, pray three times).

Y Ffraethebydd (quoted in Russell Davies, *Hope and Heartbreak: a Social History of Wales and the Welsh, 1776–1870* (Cardiff, 2005), p. 430.

Y Punch Cymraeg's advice to men about to marry was even briefer than the *Ffraethebydd's* – 'paid' (don't). But, despite the warnings of the satirists, marriage grew in popularity over the period 1870–1945. People followed the advice and warnings of the poets and proverbs. As usual the proverb was direct: 'Hir yw'r nos i gobban unig' (the night is long for the lonely negligée).

The Registrar General of Births, Deaths and Marriages enable us to ascertain the ebbs and flows in the marriage rates in Wales. In 1870 across Wales 10,953 people, or 15.7 for each 1,000 persons in Wales married. The rates stayed at this level until the 1890s experienced an increase in marriages to 14,457, or 16.4 per 1,000 Welsh people. In the twentieth century the number of marriages rose to 16,214 in 1900 (16.2 per 1,000), 17,062 in 1910 (14.2 per 1,000), 25,667 in 1920 (19.4 per 1,000) and 26,291 in 1940 (20.8 per 1,000). The social and economic traumas that Wales experienced were reflected in the marriage rate. The angry summer of industrial discontent and disquiet of 1926 saw a fall in the numbers getting married to 16,320 or just twelve people in every 1,000, one of the lowest figures ever recorded. The economic depression of the late 1920s, the collapse of the banks in 1929, and the 'economic Armageddon' of the 1930s, were also reflected in slumps in the numbers getting married.[20]

The events that had the biggest impacts, however, were the two World Wars. Thousands of Welsh people were not all swept away to graveyards and flowers in 1914–18 and 1939–45, but to girls and bouquets. In 1914 amongst the euphoria and pain, 20,052 (15.8 per 1,000) of the Welsh people married, followed by 21,479 in 1915 (16.7 per 1,000). The onset of peace saw no let-up in the numbers who married. The 24,397 (18.3 per 1,000) marriages of 1919 were eclipsed by the 25,667 (19.4 per 1,000) of 1920. The Second World War saw an even greater rush to the altar. In 1939, 23,401 (19 per 1,000) married, whilst in 1940 the number marrying was 26,291 (20.8 per 1,000). Marriage was at its most popular during the Second World War. Four of the five years that recorded the highest rates of marriage in Wales, 1940, 1945, 1939 and 1941 were during the conflict. Amongst the chaos and catastrophe, people sought security and succour and married at haste to, perhaps, repent later at leisure.[21]

The Registrar General's statistics reveal one surprising development in marriage in Wales. In the 1880s down to the early twentieth century Wales had some of the highest civil marriage rates in England and Wales. In the nineteenth century Wales found secular, civil marriages more congenial than a religious marriage ceremony. But in the twentieth century civil marriage became less common in Wales than it was in England for the first time since the early 1860s. The Welsh now preferred a religious marriage service. Olive Anderson, the historian of marriage, concludes:

> the upshot has thus been a paradoxical one, for as Welsh rhetoric and culture have become more and more secular, the Welsh way of marrying has become more and more religious – a warning, surely, against too readily interpreting social habits associated with religious institutions in specifically religious terms, and one which is particularly salutary for the Victorian period.[22]

Perhaps the answer to the perplexing conundrum as to how the dechristianisation of Wales led to an increase in the frequency of Christian marriage ceremonies is to be found in some of the changes that swept over Wales in the period 1870–1945. Commercialisation, globalisation and the retail revolution, together with the public presentation of marriage as the gateway to romantic love, which Wales experienced, coupled with the public perception of the wedding as the gateway to the romanticised happy-ever-after, had a profound influence on the marriage ceremony. It became increasingly an occasion for conspicuous consumption as much as a religious rite of passage. By the First World War chapels and churches were chosen as venues because they provided, not only the religious rites for a marriage ceremony, but also the best venue for public parading and photographs.[23]

Marriage was 'for better or worse', not always happily ever after. The wedding that committed a couple to domestic duties could also set them on the path to household horrors.[24] Courtship was meant to have been the opportunity to avoid a bad marriage, but popular proverbs and aphorisms, heavily freighted with misogyny, warned against wilful, wanton wives and rakish, wastrel husbands. Wives were warned to be wary of a 'mochyn dou dwlc' (a pig of two sties), whilst husbands were warned:

Mae gen Marged fwynach Ifan
Glocsen fawr a chlocsen fechan
Un i gicio'r cŵn o'r gornel
A'r llall i gicio'r gŵr i gythrel.[25]

(Marged of Ifan's tender lineage
Has a large and a small boot
One to kick the dogs from the corner
And one to kick her husband to hell.

Like Rhett Butler and Scarlet O'Hara in *Gone With The Wind* (1939) many couples quarrelled incessantly and skirmished enjoyably, for as the proverb insisted 'trwy gicio a brathu mae cariad yn magu' (through kicking and biting love grows). The tension was vital to the prolongation of the relationship. Many were familiar with the story of the married couple who only ever had one argument. It lasted forty-one years. For others, two sets of furious spites clashed in indeterminate violence that inevitably featured in the courtroom and the 'police intelligence' columns of the newspapers. It was for this reason that separation orders and maintenance orders were introduced in the 1860s as a result of Dolgellau-based Frances Power Cobbe's campaigning article, 'Wife Torture in England'. The so-called 'divorce of the poor' could separate warring partners and provide financial support for dependents.[26]

The authors of the prose and poems that extolled family life offered little practical advice as to how this ideal domestic happiness was to be achieved. They were reluctant to discuss aspects of domestic relations and especially the relationship between husband and wife. As late as 1900, in advising young girls, a writer under the pen name 'Chwaer' advised thus:

Y mae rhyw bethau y dylai y rhyw fenywaidd eu dysgu, ac nid oes dim galw am i'r rhyw arall fod yn hysbys iddynt, ac yn wir byddai eu bod yn gwybod rhywbeth yn eu cylch nid yn ychwanegiad at eu gwybodaeth ond yn arwydd o wendid ynddynt. Dylai pob rhyw rhagori yn y wybodaeth fwyaf buddiol i'w sefyllfa.[27]

(There are some things the female sex should learn, but there is no need for men to be knowledgeable in them, indeed familiarity with these topics would not add to one's knowledge but be a sign of weakness. Each sex should excel in the knowledge which is most useful to its own situation.)

Similar attitudes hampered Rhys Gwesyn Jones during his lecture tour on the subject of 'Caru, Priodi a Byw' ('Love, Marriage and Life').[28] One deacon refused to announce the title of the lecture from the pulpit because it was Sunday. The lecture, which was delivered frequently from the late 1870s, was a reasoned attempt to provide sensible and practical advice to young couples on how to live contentedly together.[29] That there was a demand for the advice is shown by the fact that the lecture was reprinted five times before 1904. The Revd M. Hopkins of Pen-bre was another minister who sought to provide advice on marriage in *Cyn, ac ar ôl Priodi; a'r Fodrwy Briodasol* ('Before and after marriage, and the Wedding Ring').[30] Though he ignored physical relationships, his criteria of the characteristics for a good wife – purity, sobriety, honesty, faithfulness, cleanliness, and thrift – were sensible.

A whole range of conceptualisations of society operated in the area of marriage, morals and manners. Two of the most influential were the idealisation of 'separate spheres' for men and women and the operation of a 'double standard'. The Victorian marriage was based upon a clear understanding that there were separate spheres for wife and husband. Hers was the private world of her family; his the public world of work. The home was the seat of Welsh conservatism, an 'island' or a 'castle', often deeply resistant to change. Its running was delegated to the wife in her sacred function as mother, nurse and God's policewoman, moving within cultural confines that approached a condition of purdah, with her horizons limited to the home, the children, the chapel or church, and the little theatre of formal society. In this conception the house for some people was more a prison than a palace. It was the husband's duty to provide an income for his family and the wife's role to ensure that it was employed efficiently in providing a morally inspiring home for their children. Within the family unit the children, and in particular the daughters, were insulated from the dangers of the outside world. The virtues to cherish and aspire to were godliness, honesty, self-restraint, thrift and chastity. A contributor to *Y Gymraes* expressed this view succinctly in 1909: 'Angen ein gwlad yw merched ieuainc a nôd uchel i'w bywyd sef cael cartrefi Cymru, a chartrefi y Deyrnas, yn esiampl i bob gwlad mewn trefnusrwydd, purdeb, a pharch i Dduw a dynion'[31] (The requirement of our country is young girls devoted to the high ideals of making the homes of Wales an example to the world for their good housekeeping, purity and respect for God and man).

Women who transgressed this ideal especially in its moral dimensions were criticised. Those ladies who were as obsessed with sex as the average man, were condemned as 'nymphomaniacs' or 'prostitutes' (presumably on the basis that sex was the great amateur art, in which the professional was frowned upon). Thus the double standard provided men with ample opportunities to satiate their lusts, but damned wanton wenches and wayward wives. This is shown at its highest level in the fact that Lloyd George retained his public reputation despite a reprehensible private life.[32]

Both the notions of separate spheres and the double standard came under increasing pressure from around the time of the First World War onwards. These beliefs, which seemed to be so powerful in nineteenth century Wales were challenged and changed by a plethora of economic and occupational, industrial and psychological, social and cultural developments. The commercialisation and commodification of culture, the revolution in time, the acceleration of the pace of life, the professionalisation of the occupational profile that provided more opportunities for women to work, the greater opportunities to travel, the notions of heroism at times of empire and war, the dechristianisation and desacralisation of Wales, and many other factors had an impact on how the Welsh people constructed their femininity and masculinity.[33] Femininity and female identities, and masculinity and male identities were protean phenomena that had a range of complex and contradictory features. The roles and relationships ascribed to manly or to good womanly behaviour overlapped. The defining character traits for manhood were often found amongst women, whilst, worryingly for many moralists and social modellers, feminine traits could be found amongst males.[34]

One of the defining features of masculinity was man's role as a provider. Man's labour and honest toil were supposed to provide the hearth from which the wife could create the home and the sanctuary in which to raise the family. Yet the castle of the home was increasingly intruded into by the state. Almost all aspects of daily life became subject to some legal dictate or diktat. Paternalism, in its sternest Victorian portrayal, was undermined by legislation such as the Children's Act 1908 and legislation against assaulting and the abuse of women. With characteristic pessimism the proverb warned of 'angel penffordd, diawl y pentan' (angel on the roadways, a devil at home) but in the early twentieth century many men had to reappraise such roles. The introduction of bank holidays in the 1870s and 'holidays with pay' meant that many men had to impersonate erring politicians and spend more time with their families. There was fluidity in the notion of fatherhood as the 'fun dad' came home to play, indicating that duty and discipline could be instilled in the young without inflicting pain.[35]

Men and women's place in the workplace also experienced changes over the period 1870–1951. The fact that the total number of women in paid employment rose from 152,880 in 1871 to 259,361 in 1951 had profound implications for the notion of separate spheres. By 1951 there were 166,997 men and 185,005 women working as colleagues in a range of clerical, professional, recreational trades and in retail.[36] The rise of new opportunities as clerical and secretarial workers, administrators, health professionals, teachers, sport and recreational workers provided increased opportunities for men and women to work together and to work out new ways to work, if not always with full equality.

Masculinity suffered considerable blows in the twentieth century. Many men, in the new trades, amid the pressures of modern mobile society felt pressures as never before and suffered from new diseases and conditions such as 'neurasthenia' and neuralgia.[37] That man was the 'stronger' sex was seriously questioned by the experience of war, when many (from 1915) were found to be anguished by a 'feminine' malady – hysteria. Men, those Homeric heroes, were found to be suffering from intense post-traumatic stress disorders. The collapse of the stock market in 1929, and the prolonged and profound depression of the 1930s, robbed many men of their work and their capacity to serve as the provider.

Many men had to assume new roles within the domestic sphere by assuming new 'masculine' roles within the home that were as close to their 'traditional' role as provider as possible.[38] They worked on allotments where they raised crops to feed their families. Breeding chickens, rabbits and pigs became increasingly common. William Rosser Jones remembered 'that the few eggs we had I would give to the daughter, whose husband was unemployed, and then we would kill an occasional chicken as required.'[39] Another unemployed miner, Mr Hughes, would illegally catch rabbits and take them home for his family to eat. Men also scavenged for fuel, especially wood and coal. Scavenging on coal tips was common. In the Ogmore Valley, Clive Menadue's father would sit contentedly and watch his wife and daughter sitting in front of the fire he had made from coal scavenged from the tip.[40] Some men made 'pele mond' a mix of either cement and fire coal or clay and coal dust from a disused coal seam that they illegally reopened. Throughout the period of high unemployment thefts of coal increased dramatically but within a moral code: stealing from ordinary people was abhorrent; sealing from mine owners and others considered to be 'wealthy outsiders' was acceptable. Sometimes a group of men would target coal trains and railway sidings. As one unemployed miner in the Rhondda explained: 'men worked in groups, two or three would get in the truck, and their pals would gather what was thrown out.'[41] Many men, however, also undertook domestic roles that had previously been the duty of wives and daughters.

Manliness, by the turn of the twentieth century, had become a composite of several factors, many of which were contradictory: spiritual qualities, hard labour, Christian values and virtues, but also values of ethnicity and race. In the age of Empire, the Welsh also scrambled for their place in the sun and shouldered their share of the 'white man's burden'.[42] Darwinism, in its crudest social dimension, and the Smilsean self-help philosophy together with the nascent racism of Empire helped to form a new definition of masculinity at the turn of the twentieth century. Most notably it was portrayed in Sir Henry Newbolt's poem 'Vitai Lampada' (1897) in which the brave former schoolboy reinvigorates the soldiers edging towards defeat with his defiant, echoing cry 'Play up! Play up! And play the game!' The Welsh people had their own equivalent, in the spectacular and successful defence of Rorke's Drift by 150 soldiers, mostly Welsh, against 3,000–4,000 Zulu warriors on 22–3 January 1879 during the Anglo-Zulu War. Yet, when the dust settled on the South African hillfort station, some realised that the battle was as much cause for concern as celebration. The Zulu, 'an inferior race', were far 'fleeter of foot' and more 'physically impressive' than their British opponents. Concerns at the fitness of the race were further intensified by the poor performances in the Boer War, when the military might of the 'world's greatest nation' was out-thought, out-fought, and out-foxed by the 'amateur army' of the Boers.[43]

A whole plethora of phobias seemed to torment men at the turn of the twentieth century. Military incompetence tarnished the empire, the dilettantism of the decadents at the *fin de siècle*, the panic that the nation's youth was taking its sexual life too much into its own hands, the masturbation panics of the 1880s and 1890s, and the trials of famous homosexuals in the 1890s all seemed to imply that there was a crisis in masculinity.

Christian manliness, the source of inspiration in the mid-nine-teenth century in determining what made a man a man, became less influential at the century's close. In the 1850s and 1860s, the manly boy, as portrayed in the denominational journals and news-papers, was often brought to spiritual perfection through illness, humiliation or powerlessness. Thus the manly boy of the 1860s may well reach his greatest heights from a sickbed, almost indistinguish-able from the experience of a fasting girl, such as Sarah Jacob. Longer life expectancy from the 1900s onwards further undermined the credibility of such ideals.[44] Christian strength, as exemplified perhaps in the lives of men such as the saintly George Maitland Lloyd Davies, took on a more nuanced character of dignity, defiance and deity.

Male friendship was problematic.[45] Military leaders emphasised the importance of the creation of a band of brothers who could be bold in deed and duty. The much-vaunted pals battalions of the

First World War were perhaps the best example of such simple human friendships. Male bonding in the wars was essential but it worryingly could lead into homoeroticism and homosexuality. The most famous literary meeting of the war, between Robert Graves and Siegfried Sassoon, was tinged with the frisson of sexual attraction that transcended friendship. As Sassoon later recalled, 'there was some vague sexual element lurking in our war-harnessed relationship. There was always some restless passionate nerve-wracked quality in my friendship with R.G., although he has been one of my most stimulating companions'. An even more stimulating companion was David Cuthbert Thomas of Llanelli whose death devastated Sassoon. In his diary and his portrait of Thomas as 'Dick Tiltwood' in *Fox-Hunting Man*, Sassoon makes it clear that he was deeply in love with the young Welsh subaltern, whom he nicknamed 'Tommy'.[46]

Humphrey Ellis Evans, Hedd Wyn, famously outlined the characteristics of the Welsh warrior hero in his epic poem 'Yr Arwr'.[47] Charismatic, heroic leaders sometimes accentuated these tendencies. Most notable, in this respect, perhaps, is the figure of Tremadoc-born T. E. Lawrence, 'Lawrence of Arabia', the 'Sodomonic Saint', who strutted so wonderfully in Arabic drag across the world stage in 1917–19.[48] Sporting heroics also provided opportunities for homoerotic admiration. Men-only environments, such as sailing and steam ships and lodging houses were problematic.

Though men have always been regarded as having been on top in the history of sex, the period from 1870 saw a number of developments that threatened such dominance.[49] A number of theorists in the last quarter of the nineteenth century criticised the equation of virtue and the repression of 'animal instincts'. The historian Stephen Kern proposes 1870 as the year writers on sex began to feel a benevolent interest in the female orgasm and an increasing concern about 'male psychic impotence'.[50] Havelock Ellis in his study of 'Auto-Eroticism' (1900) warned that, for men and women, 'whilst excessive masturbation was bad, not to masturbate at all may be worse.'[51] Taking oneself in hand, on occasion, did one good. To Ellis, the danger of not doing so, was degeneration. Edwardian and later writers such as Ernest Jones and Bertrand Russell pointed to sexual repression as the cause of an assortment of physical and psychological woes; and while mid-Victorian thinkers had recognised and applauded the idea that piety might sublimate the sex urge, their heirs condemned piety for precisely that reason. Not to do what came naturally had struck mid-Victorians as admirable self-control. By the early twentieth century, it now seemed merely sick. Men were not always the victims in the transformation, but they had the perplexing problem of what women wanted and how, and how often. In 1927, a new aspect came into consideration – the clitoris. Was it an inferior penis, a sign to the female of her innate castration? Or was it an equivalent organ, playing the same part in a girl's emotional growth as the penis did in a boy's? One man knew where to find it, and perhaps the answers. Ernest Jones in his paper on 'The Early Development of Female Sexuality' berated male psychoanalysts for underestimating the importance of female organs and scalded Freud for his phallocentric view of woman as a disappointed man. Concerns over castration, Jones argued, could affect both sexes and obscure the deeper and more common fear – 'the permanent extinction of the capacity (including opportunity) for sexual enjoyment'.[52]

How widespread and influential such ideas were in society it is difficult to assess. Even before Victoria's reign was over, both men and women were writing voluminous treatises, fictional and non-fictional, in medical tomes and family magazines and sixpenny pamphlets, on prostitution and venereal disease, birth control and masturbation, until the discourse itself became a subject for discourse. Emily Davies asked plaintively in *Reynold's News* on 21 April 1895: 'What does all this perpetual discussion of sex mean? Wherefore this constrained analysis of the passions? How comes it that the novels of today are filled with nothing but sex, sex, sex?'[53]

That a far more 'modern' attitude towards sex and sexuality existed within Wales by the time of the First World War is seen in the fact that many couples considered that birth control was an issue of importance for both partners. This was not, of course, universally adopted across Wales. Moral and religious leaders still intensely condemned birth control as ungodly and unchristian.

In a sense this was inevitable in the period 1870–1914, for contraceptives had about them a hint of 'French folly and frolic' and a hint of a guilty secret.[54] The immodestly, but probably spuriously, titled 'Professor Deakin', a herbalist of Alexandra Road, Swansea, advertised in several newspapers in south Wales: 'French Novelties: 6d each, 3 for 1s, or a dozen for 3s 6d; postage extra. For sale weekly at the Saddler's Shop at the back of Llanelly market every Thursday . . . Also available confidential cures by Herbal Treatment'.[55] The advertisements ran from 1901 to 1907, providing sufficient motives for the parsimonious and the promiscuous to buy in bulk. The other venue for the sale of contraceptives were the barber's shops, when after the haircutting was done the customer would almost inevitably be offered 'Something for the weekend, sir?' So common were contraceptives that Dylan Thomas recalled New Quay, Cardiganshire, as 'the wild umbrella'd and French lettered beach'.[56] The locations of the sale of contraceptives seemed to ensure that the majority of the clientele would have been male. A fact that was confirmed in Mass Observation's 'Little Kinsey' survey into sexual habits in the 1940s, which concluded that 'women are worse informed than men about birth control'.[57] Women's lack of knowledge of physical and barrier methods of contraception was the overwhelming message given to Dr Kate Fisher by witnesses who had been sexually active from the 1930s.[58] Men and women, unusually for sexual matters, were in agreement that it was the man's task to obtain contraceptives. Ernest, born in 1915, a fishmonger from Pontypridd, recalled:

> Oh, well we used, we used to use the, err French letters we used to call 'em, I don't know, what's the official thing called, what was the expression? Sheaths. The sheath, that's right. Yes it was the man's option to prevent the children but err . . . we were responsible, we took the responsibility . . . It was the man, it was the man's job.[59]

Ernest might not have been very efficient at this job, for he and his wife had five children. Edith of Penarth, born in 1908, left not only the sourcing of condoms to her husband, but also the initiation of sexual encounters, as she explained: 'I just laid back and thought of England, like as they call it.[60]

The establishment of birth-control clinics across Wales increased in the late 1920s. After the short-lived clinic at Abertillery in 1925, clinics were established in Butetown, Cardiff, Swansea, Llanelli, Wrexham, Colwyn Bay, Denbigh, Llangollen and Llanrwst.[61] Marie Stopes's travelling birth-control caravan toured south Wales from 1929, whilst the feminist Stella Browne lectured at several venues on birth control.[62] One of her listeners greeted her after a lecture with the claim, 'You've come too late to help me comrade, but give me some papers for my girls. I don't want them to have the life I've had.'[63]

The 1930s saw a bitter battle between people of a religious and moralistic background and those with a medical training and humane ideals over the establishment of birth control clinics. The experiment to establish the clinic at Abertillery proved to be short-lived due to the opposition of religious leaders who seemed to have regarded the Pope's Evangelical 'Casti Connubii' of 1930 against birth control as too moderate.[64] The parlous state of women's health attracted attention. The *Report on Maternal Mortality in Wales* (1937) published by the Ministry of Health revealed horrific evidence, which intensified the determination and demand that greater methods of birth control be introduced.[65]

One of the most outspoken, perhaps outrageous, supporters of birth control was Dr Herbert, a county councillor for Denbighshire. His professional expertise served him well as chairman of the Denbighshire County Council 'Committee for the Care of Mental Defectives'. In 1930 he proposed a motion that the council adopted that 'the multiplication of the unfit should be limited'. His views were reported in the *Birth Control News* in July 1930:

> The better classes are sterilising themselves, the disease ridden are breeding copiously and the result is the country is not getting the children it ought to have. Vast numbers of wives suffered insanity due to pregnancy. Most of them would recover, but they would return again and again and the children they bore would themselves create further children in their own mental image ... Married women should be taught birth control and mental visitors should, for this

purpose, be linked up with maternity homes and clinics. The amount of insanity amongst unmarried mothers is terrible, and in large industrial areas there is a large amount of abortion. Quacks flourish apace. Already we are a C3 nation. What we shall be in fifty years time I dare not contemplate.[66]

Dr Herbert's support for the sterilisation of the 'mentally unfit' was not particularly unusual or surprising in the 1930s. Lord Dawson of Penn (1864–1945), who accompanied Lloyd George on his visit to Hitler at Berchtesgaden in 1936, was one of several who argued for the compulsory sterilisation of Welsh miners in the 1930s to prevent the breeding of 'morons . . . that is, of mental defection of a comparatively high grade.'[67]

Dr Herbert drew attention to the danger, which was also pointed to in the *Report on Maternal Mortality in Wales*, that the fact that the medical profession shied away from birth control allowed quacks to operate and to profit. These interlopers were not only the disreputable English, who, local moralists would claim, could be expected to be 'dabbling in Satan's evil works', but also several Welsh quacks. Local newspapers revealed that 'Baron Watkin' (Glancothi), Mrs Steward the 'Lady Specialist' (9 Grove Place, Swansea), Mrs Huxley (57 St Helen's Road, Swansea), John Gower MPS (14 Vaughan Street, Llanelli) and the infamous Professor T. W. Price, MH, FFBIMS (Medical) Phrenologist (50 Station Road, Llanelli), made decent livings from the sale of noxious products to procure abortion. The local newspapers, even the denominational papers, such as the Independents' *Y Tyst*, the Baptists' *Seren Cymru* and the Methodists' *Goleuad*, carried the advertisements for abortifacients. Whether the product's advertisements were in Welsh or in English, their purpose was clear:

Pelenau Penny Royal a Steel i Fenywod
Cywira yn gyflym pob afreolrwydd. Symuda bob rhwystr, a lliniara yr arwyddion poenus sydd mor gyffredin i'r rhyw.

(Towle's Penny Royal and Steel Tablets
Woman's Unfailing Friend – guaranteed to correct all irregularities,

remove all obstructions, and relieve the distressing symptoms so prevalent with the sex.)[68]

When the quacks' potions proved to be ineffective, then people sought other means to get rid of unwanted pregnancies. In 1941, Phillip Rees Thomas, a seventy-two-year old herbalist of Caerbryn, Llandybïe, was sentenced to nine months imprisonment 'for performing an illegal operation on Margaret Haulwen Jones, 32, the wife of the Rev John Thomas Jones, minister of Tabor Baptist Church, Cross Hands'.[69]

In the columns of the influential women's magazines *Y Fythones* and *Y Gymraes* though women authors waxed lyrical that a woman's place was in the home, some also suggested that they should play a greater role in the world outside. Many men, perhaps naturally, echoed the domestic ideology. The Revd William Williams, Beaumaris, confirmed the home-based doctrine – 'gartref, yn ddiau, y trefnwyd fod cylch gwasanaethgarwch a llywodraeth y wraig, mewn ymddarostyngiad i ewyllys y gŵr'[70] (At home, without doubt, it has been decreed is the wife's circle of work and rule, and that in subservience to her husband's wishes). The wife was thus, in this conception, mastered for life in a far harsher regime than that of even a servant's.[71] Yet, real life was never as simple as this ideology implied. Welsh women had many roles from angel on the hearth to agent provocateur, from worshipper to wanton, from economic organiser to evil temptress. Women could simultaneously be home maker and home breaker.

Bohemian Rhapsodies: Bohemian Wales and Welsh Bohemians

Sin openly and scandalise the world.

Augustus John, quoted in Michael Holroyd, *Augustus John: the New Biography* (London, 1997), p. 547.

Wales, in the first half of the twentieth century, had a King and a Queen. They reigned, not over the Welsh nation, but over another 'imagined community', another 'country of the heart' – Bohemia.

Both were artists. Both had been born in the coastal town of Tenby, clinging to the clifftop above its 'fishing-boat-bobbing-sea'. The Queen of Bohemia was the one, the only Nina Hamnett (1890–1956), who danced naked on the table-tops of cafes from Fitzrovia to Montmartre to Montparnasse. In the 1920s and 1930s, Nina, the 'laughing torso', was 'on everything and everyone'. The King, appropriately, was called Augustus – the imperious Augustus John (1878–1961). 'A great man of action', as Wyndham Lewis described him, 'into whose hands the fairies had placed a paintbrush instead of a sword'. John lived and worked with a feverish speed and his creations marked what Virginia Woolf called 'the Age of Augustus John'.[72]

Hamnett and John's Bohemia had a mythical geography. One visitor considered that 'it was a sad country. It is bordered on the north by need, on the south by poverty, on the east by illusion and on the west by the infirmary'. Another writer considered that the four compass points delineated an even sadder country, for 'Bohemia is bordered on the north by cold, on the west by hunger, on the south by love and on the east by hope'.[73] The personnel of Bohemia was amorphous as different relationships merged and melded and then diverged and devolved. The poet Dylan Thomas, one of Augustus John and Nina Hamnett's most loyal subjects, complained that 'this bloody land is full of Welshmen'.[74] The natural habitat that the Bohemian evolved into was the bar room, the bedroom and the brothel. The Bohemian's personality was alternative, artistic, amoral and anarchic. Like Nonconformity, Bohemianism was a counter-culture that gradually evolved its own code of conformity. Bohemians were creative and carefree, devil-may-care and debonair, ingenious and innovative, fun-loving and free-loving people.

Wales had a number of characters whose free and easy sex lives were the precursors of a Bohemian lifestyle. Dr William Price (1800–93), the physician, self-proclaimed archdruid, proponent of nudism and free-love, and advocate of cremation was familiar with Bohemian circles having fled to France in the 1830s. The elderly Price 'lived in sin' in Llantrisant with a number of young 'housekeepers' with whom he had 3 children. In terms of free love, Price obviously practised what he preached. On 14 June 1868, he received this letter from Vanessa, one of his many lovers:

> My dearest, most extraordinary, most loveable Welshman . . . I still tingle to the memory of your hands caressing my body, of the thrill of your possessing me, so different from the clumsy attentions of my husband, a man whose emotions are in a permanent ice age. He knows little of the needs of a woman. But you, my Druid lover, you do not just use a woman, you seem to know my needs. You make love so I share your pleasure.[75]

The *Welsh Dictionary of National Biography* described Price as 'an odd man'. One suspects a note of jealousy.

Like William Price, Ruabon-raised Frank Harris (1856–1913) had insatiable sexual appetites. After a time as a cowboy, he became a writer and was a pugnacious, precocious editor of periodicals on both sides of the Atlantic, counting people like Oscar Wilde, H. G. Wells, James Thurber, Bram Stoker and George Bernard Shaw among his circle of friends. In the 1920s Harris shared a house with the occultist Aleister Crowley. From the time of his second marriage in 1892 he maintained an American mistress, and after that arrangement broke up he was so flagrant in his infidelities that his wife separated from him in 1894. In 1898 Harris was maintaining a *ménage* at St Cloud with an actress named Mary Congden, with whom he had a daughter, as well as a house at Roehampton containing Nellie O'Hara, his helpmate and *âme damnée*, with whom he probably also had a daughter (who died young). His life-long friend Oscar Wilde recalled that 'Frank Harris is invited to all the great houses in England – once'. 'He blazed through London like a comet, leaving a trail of deeply annoyed persons behind him', said Bernard Shaw.[76] His sexual conquests he related in his unreliable memoirs *My Life and Loves* (1922). No mere rake admits to anything but progress but an analysis of the nationalities of those seduced reveals him sowing the seeds of a European union of love. Italian women said 'si'. French ladies said 'oui'. Whilst a Swiss lady said 'si', 'oui' or 'ja' – or all three at once. He also included several photographs of nude women, supposedly his conquests, but possibly just published in the book to help boost sales. The tactic worked. The book became a *succès de scandale*, achieving the rare distinction of being banned even in Paris. With modesty he detailed his sexual conquests – 'Casanova! My dear man, Casanova is not worthy to untie my boot strings.'[77]

One who might have felt entitled to untie the great philanderer's boot strings was Lloyd George, the British Prime Minister. Even his son Richard in his biography depicted his father as an over-sexed philanderer. Perhaps this was little surprise, for Lloyd George contrived to have an affair with his own daughter-in-law, Richard's wife, Roberta.[78] He was insatiably attracted to pretty young women, he never felt shackled by the marital vows and admitted as much to his wife Margaret when they were courting. He demanded unswerving loyalty from his women, but was unfaithful himself within months of his marriage. During the First World War, Kitchener declined to share military secrets with the Cabinet for fear members would share those secrets with their wives in bed, except, of course for Lloyd George, whom he feared would share them in bed with other men's wives. Lloyd George certainly had affairs with the wives of three Liberal MPs, Timothy Davies, Sir Charles Henry and Sir Arthur Crosfield. There were rumours of many others. Other Welsh-descended MPs were less fortunate. Eliot Crawshay-Williams had to resign in 1913 following his being named as co-respondent in a divorce case brought by fellow Liberal Hubert Carr-Gomm.

At the Paris Peace Conference Lloyd George allowed the glamorous red-haired writer Elinor Glyn, the author of the *It Girl*, to seduce him into allowing her to attend the final ceremony as a 'reporter'[79] Lloyd George was probably saved from scandal by his links to the newspapers and the honours he had sold to the magnates – quite literally making the owners of newspapers press barons. Even in old age, Lloyd George continued to pester the female house and farm servants for sexual favours, who found it hard to resist the attentions of a former prime minister.[80] Alongside his marriage to Margaret, Lloyd George conducted a far-from-secret affair with his secretary, Frances Stevenson, for thirty years. It was a strange, and, despite all their voluminous outpourings of epistolary gush to each other, unequal relationship.

Lloyd George was immensely attractive to women, with his beguiling charm, bright blue eyes, fashionably long hair, sartorial elegance and, in his glory days, the ultimate aphrodisiac – power. His personality was hypnotic, it was said that 'he could charm a bird off a bough' or seduce an angel. But perhaps the secret was more prosaic – the size of his penis. 'The biggest I have ever seen . . . it resembles a donkey's more than anything else', said an admiring male secretary. Another complained that Lloyd George's indiscriminate search for sexual gratification, the quest for 'cunt, cunt, cunt', diverted attention from more important affairs of state.[81] The prime minister had the prime member and morality of a feudal lord insisting on his *droit du seigneur* coupled with the self-control of a school disco. Lloyd George was forever poised between the immoral and the immortal.

Celebrity status and high public profile also gave opportunities for promiscuity. The legendary Welsh goalkeeper Leigh Richmond Roose (1877–1916) had a flamboyant style both on and off the pitch. When he was a student at Aberystwyth, groups of gaggling girls would gather around his goal to admire the giant. One of football's first superstars, Roose was listed by the *Daily Mail* as one of the UK's most eligible bachelors. He was immensely popular with women. Rumours abound that he could count the queen of the innuendo and double entendre, the risqué music hall superstar Marie Lloyd amongst his many conquests. As she would advise in one of her songs, 'A little of what you fancy does you good'. Roose showed equal bravery at war. Awarded the Military Medal for his heroism on the first occasion he saw action, Roose was killed at the Battle of the Somme in October 1916.[82] One who preceded Roose at the university in Aberystwyth was the litterateur and educationalist Sir Owen Morgan Edwards (1848–1920).[83] His herculean work ethic was not without opportunities for romance. In 1896 his wife Ellen wrote to him:

Fy Annwyl Owen,
Dydw i ddim yn gweld fod achos am wneyd cymaint o Eluned Morgan. Ydych chi yn cael rhywbeth oddiar ei llaw heblaw ei bod yn prynnu rhai o'ch llyfrau? . . . Gan fod gennych chwi gymaint o

ffansi ati, cymerwch hi atoch i Oxford a chysgwch hefo hi os leiciwch chi.

Cofion cynnes oddiwrthym,
Ellen[84]

(My Dear Owen,
I do not see the case to make so much of Eluned Morgan. Are you getting something from her apart from her buying your books? . . . As you have taken such a fancy to her, take her to you in Oxford and sleep with her if you wish.

Warmest regards from us all,
Ellen)

The anger in Ellen's letter is palpable.

Mimi's operatic tiny frozen hand symbolised one of the strongest defining factors of many Bohemians – their poverty. For some this was part of the core of their rebellion against convention. Bohemia on the whole displayed a psychic distaste for Mammon. Despite his wife and family, Dylan Thomas took such attitudes to their extreme form and vaunted his poverty as an indispensable ingredient in his art. His close friend and biographer, Constantine Fitzgibbon, who accompanied Dylan on many a pub crawl, best described Dylan's attitude:

Just as at school he had to be thirty-third in trigonometry, just as in America he had to be the drunkest man in the world, so in London in 1937 he could not simply be a poor poet: he had to be the most penniless of them all ever. Therefore such money as he might make or be given had to be spent, given away, even lost immediately. Money had become only another skin to be removed as quickly as possible in the revelation of the absolute Dylan. Like so many, perhaps like all, his attitudes, this one never really changed. It was one of the causes of his ruin.[85]

Dylan's wife Caitlin found herself almost dazzled by 'the romance of poverty' – the inspiring squalor of the artistic works in which the two of them lived. Yet the romance of poverty soon wore thin against the stresses of a young family's survival. In her later memoir

Double Drink Story: My Life with Dylan Thomas, Caitlin bitterly castigated Dylan's renunciation of money as it entailed an enthusiastic advocacy of the poetic Chatterton life-and-early-death-style: 'Poverty and preferably for the perfectionist, an early agonising death thrown in too. Dylan scrupulously fulfilled both these romantic conditions'.[86]

For many Bohemians, the distinction between borrowing and downright dishonesty became blurred. Cheques bounced, shops were lifted, hotel bills left unpaid by fleeing guests, or in the case of Dylan and Caitlin, put down to Augustus John's account. When Dylan stayed as a guest at someone's house, he invariably stole one of his host's shirts.

One of the characteristics of the Bohemian lifestyle was the social network that could be a lifeline for those who were desperate. Somebody usually knew somebody who could help, rally others, organise a temporary whip-round – even if they themselves were little better off. Nina Hamnett was saved from complete destitution by the compassion and generosity of Vira King. Nina Hamnett's life was a parable for all that was good and bad about Bohemia and the Bohemian lifestyle. When she arrived in London in 1911, her exuberance and spontaneity won her a wide circle of friends at the Café Royal, including Augustus John, Walter Sickert, Roger Fry and Henry Gaudier-Brzeska. Nina soon conquered Paris, where she became a habitué of the left-bank cafes, a friend of Modigliani, Picasso and Cocteau. She was a lover to several and modelled for more artists. Much to the surprise of other cafe customers she would often reveal her breasts and claim, loudly, that 'Modigliani says that these are the best tits in Europe'.[87] Herself a talented and much-admired painter, her real gift was for living life to the full. Whenever she had anything, Nina would unselfishly share with those around her in the Fitzroy or a Parisian cafe, often staying out half the night – or indeed all the night – with any man who took her fancy. Nina was famous for discovering beautiful young men whose charms were not so immediately apparent to other eyes. In the 1930s her tastes turned to the 'rougher trade' of boxers and sailors. Homosexuality was very prevalent amongst Nina's circle of friends, and it was probable that she and Nancy Cunard were lovers. To Nina, sex was as much a companionable gesture as a pleasure. One of her friends recalled:

> Nina had affairs with all sorts of awful people but didn't appreciate anybody . . . Nina slept with more or less anyone who was of any apparent interest at all but just like having a glass of wine with a friend – I mean she was apparently completely frigid – she told me that she had never felt anything.[88]

Asked once why she liked sailors so much, Nina responded 'because they go away'. She was highly promiscuous, with the receptiveness of a letter box. Sexual liberation was merely one aspect of her rebellion against convention and her quest for personal independence. There was nothing romantic or idealistic about her approach to sex and she once remarked to her friend Gladys Hynes: '(So and So) said the other day, "You love me with your body, I wish I could think that you loved me with your soul" . . . What the hell do you suppose he meant?'[89] In 1931 the novelist Ethel Mannin published *Ragged Banners*. In the scene set in the Fitzroy Tavern, Nina is portrayed as Laura, an ageing, drunken sculptress. One of the novel's central characters watches her and reflects: 'there was something dreadful about that middle-aged, passée woman who had once been attractive, and her passion for the completely selfish and unscrupulous young man . . . She was dreadful, too, with her glazed eyes, and her tawdry clothes, a ruin of a woman.'[90]

Nina's ruin was that she never managed to keep her head above whiskey – water only rarely entered into her lifestyle. Neither her artistic potential, nor talent was fully realised for Nina's art was always in her life. Her life reveals that the road of excess does not always lead to the palace of wisdom. Nina's death, impaling herself on railings forty feet below her apartment's window from which she fell, may have been a suicide, or a tragic accident. As her body convulsed on the railings on which it was impaled some observers noted the irony of the title of her autobiography – *Laughing Torso*.

The Queen of Bohemia was not the only woman to suffer, for Bohemia could be a terribly challenging place for people whichever of its tenets they followed. In *Pererinion* and in *Storïau Hen Ferch*,

Jane Ann Jones sets out the relationship between Myfanwy and a married man, the mysterious 'G', who was an influential figure in literary Wales. As the famous song would ask – 'Paham mae dicter, o Myfanwy?' (Why is there anger, oh Myfanwy?). The answer, because during their long love affair, Myfanwy gradually becomes aware of the fact that, even though she has had a child by him (who died soon after birth), the married 'G' will never leave his wife.[91] The literary affair was based on Jane Ann Jones's own affair with a married man from 1929 to 1944. The life of novelist Jean Rhys (1890–1979) has several curious echoes of that of Nina Hamnett. Rhys called herself 'a doormat in a world of boots'.[92] Her life was one of much hardship and more heartache. Rhys became a chorus girl, the first in a series of bad career choices including work in Madame Fabre's massage service.

Despite the glorification of poverty, the possession of riches did not exclude a person from being considered Bohemian. Even the most dissolute appreciated that someone, somewhere, sometime, would have to pick up the party's tab. The King of Bohemia, Augustus John, the son of a Tenby solicitor, was not averse to profit from his fellow Bohemians. He established a number of drinking clubs, including the Toucan and the Bar 22, which became popular haunts for London Bohemians and profitable for John: he was also one of the highest-paid living artists in Britain, painting several world leaders in 1919 and millionaires (one such portrait sold in 1923 for 3,000 guineas). Yet still Augustus encapsulated the very image of the Bohemian in his manners and appearance.[93] The aristocracy, especially in the 1920s and 1930s, the days of the Flappers and the 'Bright Young Things', jigged and jazzed their way around the depression.[94] Bohemia always had a hint of champagne and Chanel about it.

One such well-to-do Welsh Bohemian was Wogan Phillips, 2nd Baron Milford (1902–1993), the son of a shipping and insurance magnate,[95] who could afford to indulge his senses and artistic sensibilities. His father agreed to pay for him to pursue a career as a painter, but was enraged when he arrived unannounced at Wogan's studio to find a painting of a nude woman. His father's concerns continued as Wogan embarked on a painting tour of

Wales with Augustus John. Wogan Phillips's first wife was the novelist Rosamond Lehmann, whom he met when she was married to his friend Leslie Runciman. Despite the birth of a daughter, Sally, the embers of their passion soon turned to grey, for Rosamond was far too big a character to fit into the glass slipper of traditional femininity. She entered into intensely physical relationships with the poet Cecil Day-Lewis, and the 'cad' and dilettante Goronwy Rees. The affair between Rees and Rosamond Phillips began during a weekend staying with Elizabeth Bowen at Bowen's court in Ireland, when Goronwy was ostensibly in love with Elizabeth herself.[96] Elizabeth was deeply hurt by the behaviour of both guests, complaining to her friend, the philosopher Isiah Berlin, that Goronwy had visited Rosamond's bedroom in the night and upset Elizabeth's innocent niece, who was forced to listen through the thin partition wall as the earth moved.[97] Wogan also took his passion into the arms of others, in his case those of Cristina, wife of the Earl of Huntingdon, daughter of the Marchese di Roma and his eccentric wife Luisa, both leading Spanish Communists. Infuriated that his son had joined the Communist Party, had married and remarried, Sir Lawrence, now Lord Milford, disinherited Wogan.

Amongst the brightest of the Bright Young People in the 1930s was Alan Pryce-Jones, heir of the fortune made by his grandfather at the Royal Welsh Warehouse in Newtown. He remembered his echt-Victorian father warning him that he was 'old enough to know that there exists a man named Evan Morgan. If you find yourself in the same room as Evan Morgan you must leave it immediately'.[98] That reprehensible character was Evan Morgan, 2nd Viscount Tredegar (1893–1949), son of the great Monmouthshire landowning family. Evan had the wealth and privilege to indulge many of the core aspects of Bohemianism – a little painting and poetry, but a lot of partying. Morgan came from what the Duke of Bedford, an expert in such things, described as the 'oddest family I have ever met'. His mother was rumoured to have built bird nests large enough to sit in. His father, Courtenay, like his father Freddie, provided love nests for a succession of mistresses. Freddie settled his mistress Ella K. Millar in the splendid Ruperra Castle, whilst

Courtenay took as his mistress Lady Corisande Rodney (née Guest), whose own marriage, like Courtenay's, was ultimately loveless. Another of his mistresses was Alys Bray, who was involved with Maud Allen in the infamous 'Cult of the Clitoris'. Evan Morgan's ancestral home, Tredegar Park, teemed with ghosts. It was perhaps these surroundings that encouraged his later fascination with the occult. It was certainly not a house conducive to 'normality'. Evan Morgan himself kept a menagerie of animals including a boxing kangaroo, a honey bear, a troop of baboons and flock of macaws. One of his party pieces was to have a parrot crawl up his trousers and peep out from his flies announcing 'pretty polly'.[99]

Evan Morgan was a bundle of contradictions. He was an occultist, a close acquaintance of Aleister Crowley, 'the most evil man in Britain', yet he was also a chamberlain to two popes. He was an open, promiscuous, predatory homosexual yet he married twice, firstly to the actress Lois Ina Sturt (1900–37) in 1928, and then in 1939 to Princess Olga Sergeivna Dolgorouky (1915–98). He mixed freely with royalty and rabble. His close friend, the nymphomaniac Nancy Cunard, was alert to his Janus-like nature, calling him 'a fantasy who could be most charming and most bitchy'.[100] In 1932 he infamously dined with Rudolph Hess, Ernst Röhm and other leading Nazis at Bad Wiessee, Munich. Alan Pryce-Jones's father was not the only person to warn of the dangers of Evan Morgan. The authorities initially refused to allow him to play any part in the Second World War but were eventually persuaded by the persistence of his friends. Evan Morgan was charged with monitoring carrier pigeons, just in case the Germans resorted to them for espionage purposes. In one of his schemes, thousands of pigeons were shredded in the engines of the jet plane they were being released from. In 1943 he was court-martialled for offences against the Official Secrets Act when he let slip war secrets to a pair of Girl Guides. Despite his two marriages, Morgan's longest and strongest lifelong attraction was to the novelist Ronald Firbank, who introduced himself to Morgan in London's Eiffel Tower restaurant with the novel chat-up line, 'Your name is Rameses'. Firbank soon, however, preferred to refer to him as 'Heavenly Organ'. One of their friends famously would blow cigar smoke onto his pubic hair and declare 'Abracadabra' as his hardening penis emerged from the cloud.[101]

Evan Morgan's social and sexual world took in a plethora of places, mostly the venues for an alternative, Bohemian lifestyle: brawling with sailors in Paris in the early 1920s, saying 'hello' to Berlin in the 1930s, and roughing it in Monte Carlo with the bisexual Somerset Maughan for Christmas 1933. The places he frequented were degenerate just as the people he mixed with were the usual dissipated crowd – Augustus John, Nina Hamnett, Peter Warlock, Lady Ottoline Morrell. The most revealing insights into Evan Morgan's predilections came from Richard Rumbold, author of the homosexual novel the *Little Victims* (1933).[102] Morgan sourced and accepted invitations to the sex parties with indulgent themes where drugs and sexual prancing with young men and boys and girls were de rigueur. To the party held by the disgraced Infante of Spain, Don Luis, Prince of Orleans, in which naked Negro boys served cocaine on silver trays, Morgan wore clerical dress. His repertoire of sexual pleasures took in the rites of 'symbolic magic' including fellatio, sodomy and mutual masturbation. His sex games, including his stay-overs at Rosa Lewis's Cavendish Hotel, involved 'instruments of the most blood-curdling nature . . . sadistic gear, whips and handcuffs.' Robin Bryans recalled a Black Magic Mass at the deserted Baile Glas church (near Dinas Powys) in which 'young men followed Evan . . . for flagellation as live tableaux of Christ-at-the-pillar'.[103]

Wales had long been an ideal location for a Bohemian lifestyle. At Ruthin Castle, Mary Cornwallis-West, 'Patsy', proved a vivacious hostess who was visited at the castle by one of her more well-known lovers, Edward Prince of Wales. Together with her friends Lilli Langtry and Jenny Jerome (later Lady Randolph Churchill and mother of Winston), Patsy entertained a host of notables and politicians.[104] At Harlech, George Davison, chief executive of Kodak, enjoyed a lavish Bohemian lifestyle. At Craig-y-nos, Glyn-neath, the famous Spanish opera star Adelina Patti (1843–1919) entertained a series of lovers before marrying one, a Swedish baron, twenty-seven years her junior.[105] Surprisingly for a nation burdened with a Nonconformist religious identity, local people often proved themselves to be as at ease with an unconventional lifestyle as their exotic visitors. At Laugharne and New Quay, Dylan and Caitlin Thomas discovered an easy-going amiability and a relatively free-and-easy attitude towards sex. At Plas Llanina near New Quay, Lord Howard de Walden's parties often slipped over into orgies.[106] At Aberystwyth, Sir Alfred Zimmern (1879–1957) discovered musical and then romantic interludes with Madam Barbier.[107] Kingsley Amis enjoyed a similar milieu at Swansea, where the 'very lecherous' lecturer made passes at all suitable females.[108]

Gwen John, John Innes, Caradoc Evans, Georgina Wheldon and several others were prolific in their private lives as they were in their cultural and literary pursuits. William Emrys Williams (1896–1977), the founder of Penguin Books, had a complicated private life. Williams had a lifelong marriage with the distinguished economist Gertrude Rosenblum, but also had a passionate relationship with Estrid Bannister – once identified in the *Sunday Telegraph Magazine* as 'the naughtiest girl of the century'. She was Williams's mistress for twenty years.[109] His wife tolerated this affair, but was far less complacent about her husband's relationship with his secretary, Joy Lyons, to whom he insensitively dedicated his selections from Hardy's poems. In a dramatic gesture, Lyons destroyed the text of his autobiography on the night of Williams's death, before killing herself. The great travel writer Norman Lewis, 'the matinee idol of the travel book', was just as restless in personal life as in his wanderings and writing. Lewis, who married twice, had several affairs, fathered five children with three women, and had a dubious record as a family man. When he visited the maternity hospital to see one baby for the first time, his wife looked out of the window to spot the proud father in a sports car with a blonde. His wife recognised Lewis's two favourite things – fast cars and faster women.[110] The architect Frank Lloyd Wright, at his spectacular creation of an American home, Taliesin, proved himself a philandering sociopath who abused the trust of the three women who married him and several mistresses.

Roald Dahl was one of the few who was actually ordered by the military authorities to serve his country in the bedroom. Having been wounded as an RAF pilot in 1942 he was transferred to the USA as an envoy. The tall, debonair Dahl was meant to influence people expressing anti-British sentiments to change their mind by seducing their wives. He soon became acknowledged as 'one of the biggest cocksmen in America'. Having served his country with distinction with Millicent Rogers, the oil heiress, he was ordered to seduce Clare Booth Luce. She, however, proved to be such a tigress in bed that he begged his superiors to take him off the assignment – 'I'm all fucked out'. But he was ordered back to the bedroom, told to close his eyes and think of England.[111]

Welsh speakers were no strangers to the ways of all flesh. The acerbic critic W. J. Gruffydd (1881–1954), editor of the influential *Y Llenor*, had a long-lasting affair at the end of the 1920s and the 1930s with Mary Davies, a fellow member of the schools inspectorate. Their liaison was a regular on-expenses fling of booking into hotels under the names 'Mr and Mrs John Morris' – perhaps a sly kick at the Victorian moralist and man of letters Sir John Morris-Jones. As the output of one of Welsh literature's greatest figures, Gruffydd's letters of supposed love to Davies are remarkably poor fare, with several classic clichéd lines about his wife's lack of understanding.[112]

Eluned Phillips (1914–2009), who won the crown twice at the National Eisteddfod, participated in the Bohemia of the 1920s and 1930s. This 'reluctant redhead' became an established habituée of Bohemia and friends with Pablo Picasso, Edith Piaf, Dylan Thomas and Augustus John. On one occasion, she comforted Augustus John after he discovered his wife Ida and his mistress Dorelia in a lesbian tryst in their Parisian flat.[113]

One of Eluned Phillips's closest friends was the highly talented preacher, poet and performer, Dewi Emrys (1881–1952). Before abandoning family and formal religion in 1917 when he enlisted in the army, Dewi Emrys was a minister in Dowlais, Buckley and Pontypridd. Between 1921 and 1942 he lived the life of a wanderer around London and Wales, often begging for board and lodging. Had Dewi a door then the wolf would have been camped at it. Despite his charisma he had a callous and cruel aspect to his character that could deeply wound those who cared for him. This was no Restoration drama in which many ladies went from being miscast to being cast off, the women involved were real and really suffered. But he was one of those rare free spirits who could not abide authority or false respectability, whether in religion or culture. He was forever the outsider, forever taunting those in power or positions of privilege. He annoyed the Nonconformists for singing outside their chapels to beg for money. Hymns, they thought, were not suitable for busking. He won the crown at the National Eisteddfod and then to fund a spree he pawned it at a Swansea pawn shop. When he won a chair at the National Eisteddfod he gave it to a local pub. When he won his fourth chair, the eisteddfod 'Sanhedrin' had enough and brought in the rule restricting bards to just two victories. He had a convivial, charismatic vulnerability that women found irresistible. Asked late in life about his womanising, he admitted that he found it hard to resist when so many were throwing themselves at him. In a letter to his friend Oliver Stephens, Dewi Emrys explained his life view:

Melltith Methodistiaeth i mi ydyw ei bod yn lladd y Duw a chwardd y blodau, gan gyfrif digrifwch yn faswedd a'r nwydau mwyaf naturiol yn bethau trythyll ynddynt eu hunain: ie a chyfrif byw'n wastadol yng nglyn cysgod angau yn rhinvedd ac yn iechydwriaeth! . . . Ymwrthodaf yn bendant â'r 'grefydd' honno nad yw'n gyson a'r Fohemiaith iach a beir i ddyn ymddiddori'n llawen yn ei gyd-ddyn a chydfwynhau ag ef beth hyfryd a phrydferthwch bywyd.'[114]

(The curse of Methodism to me is that it kills the God who created the flowers, counting fun a sin, and the most natural urges as obscenities in themselves: yes, and it considers living grimly in the valley of the shadow of death a virtue and a redemption . . . I definitely refuse that 'religion' which is not consistent with the joyful Bohemianism that promotes a man's interest in his fellows so that together they enjoy the beautiful and wondrous things of life.)

Eluned Phillips found one of her sweetest and simplest metaphors to note his death: 'When Dewi Emrys died in 1952 rainbows faded.'[115]

The silver threads linking many of these disparate, desperate lives were the King of Bohemia, Augustus John, and his heir apparent, alternatively the crown prince or court jester, Dylan Thomas. This Dionysian, dynamic duo put the Bohemian into Bohemia. The lives of the inebriate, intoxicate poet and the insatiable, intense artist were like Thomas's tragically comic creation Captain Cat 'sardined with women'. Biographers still vie with each other to compile their respective romantic scorecards. Augustus was probably the most promiscuously prolific. Max Beerbohm, with a suspicious exactitude claimed that Augustus fathered ninety-nine illegitimate children. Others suggest that he was a centurion. For some families, like the Macnamaras, Augustus satisfied (or slept with) mother, two daughters, and an aunt. It was said that if he walked down a street in Chelsea, he would pat the head of any child he saw in case it was one of his offspring. During his wanderings with the Romany gypsies, his philandering with their womenfolk resulted in an ear being sent to Augustus as a warning as to what would be cut off next. But old habits died hard. On his eighty-first birthday he was found in bed with a girl sixty years his junior[116] – the cold comforts of old age.

Dylan too had a romantic incontinence that would enable him to get into bed with a series of women. Within just a few days of his arrival in New York, he boasted to his tour guide, the poet John Malcolm Brinnin, of his affairs with three women, including a boyish poet. It was the shock value of the encounter that often motivated Dylan. Asked by the actress Shelley Winters why he had come to Hollywood, Dylan replied, 'To touch the titties of a beautiful blonde starlet and to meet Charlie Chaplin'. Shelley Winters granted both his wishes, allowing him to sterilise one finger in champagne and brush each of her breasts with its tip, and then taking him and her flatmate Marilyn Monroe to dinner with Chaplin where Dylan promptly, typically disgraced himself.[117]

Death and sex are the two great themes that permeate Dylan Thomas's work. His contemporary and one of his finest biographers Constantine Fitzgibbon testified to the poet's masturbation throughout his life, and his early poems certainly revealed that tendency:

Now that drugged youth is waking from its stupor,
The nervous hand rehearsing on the thigh
Acts with a woman . . . [118]

Another friend noted Dylan's fear of death and his need for physical release. In this case with the friend's brother's girlfriend, a 'lank, red-mouth girl with a reputation like hell', who then babysat for Dylan whilst he and his wife Caitlin went to the pub.[119] He also noted Dylan's lifelong fascination with pornography, particularly periodicals dealing with rubber fetishism.[120]

Dylan and Augustus had many things in common, one of them was the ravishing Caitlin Macnamara, Augustus's mistress, then Dylan's wife. Whilst she was still with John, Thomas slept with her in London's Eiffel Tower Hotel, and charged the bill to Augustus's account. Later, at Laugharne, they fought over Caitlin's honour, which was perhaps more than she ever did.

In his wit and humour Dylan had a gift capable of arousing a woman's most sensitive organ – her brain. He could convince a lady that he was a great lover because he would love her greatly and that he cherished her individuality even though he loved women holus-bolus. Yet over time the flummery and mummery became as obvious as a flim-flam man's tent show on tour. Over time the magic faded. 'O God', Dylan once told Rayner Heppenstall one night as he sidled along to Bloomsbury and his probable fate, 'I'm so tired of sleeping with women I don't even like'. Yet he never found the balance or the moderation to resist temptation. Very soon both Augustus and Dylan had to live up to their public persona. As Dylan once said when asked why he drank too much, 'Because they expect it of me.'[121]

There was something profoundly egotistic about the lives of Augustus John and Dylan Thomas. The mundane things of life, the practicalities and punctualities of family life and the bringing up of children were left to the wife, or in the case of Augustus his wife, Ida, and his live-in-lover, Dorelia. It was the wives who suffered as Augustus and Dylan pursued their 'sullen art and crafts' of painting and poetry or just chased the pleasures of the flesh. Caitlin was borne along in the wake of Dylan's drunken disorderliness, gasping to keep her head above water, cook, wash up and raise the children.[122] As Augustus John once honestly admitted, 'though I admire children, I wouldn't care to take charge of a nursery'.[123] Such reticence did not stop him from populating one. When his wife Ida died of puerperal fever in 1907 in Paris at the birth of their fifth child, Henry, Augustus's mistress Dorelia was looking after six other children. Ida, once a promising art student, saw her life wholly submerged in the children's needs. The day began at 5.30 or 6.30 a.m., and she was unceasingly on the go until the infants could be put to bed at 7.30 in the evening. A blissful 'three hours' of relative calm preceded the night session, for Caspar was a wakeful baby. Many commentators noted the innocence of the John, or Thomas, children frolicking in the fields, often naked. Yet the children, in later life, remembered not an idyll but a yearning for the reassurance of discipline, order and structure. Caspar rebelled into respectability, becoming an admiral of the fleet.[124]

The Bohemian notion of free love, often, applied only to the male. The women who loved freely were often castigated. The Rabelaisian principle of *fais ce que voudras* (do what thou wilt) was usually a male preserve. Caitlin's many affairs with locals, in Laugharne and New Quay, deeply wounded Dylan (even one of the bearers at his funeral was one of her ex-lovers). Augustus similarly pouted when Dorelia left him for a while to pursue an affair with a young artist. In his fury and frustration he wrote:

> You sit in the nude for those devilish foreign people, but you do not want to sit for me when I asked you, wicked little bloody harlot ('lubni') that you are. You exhibit your naked fat body for money, not for love. So much for you! How much do you show them for a franc? I am sorry that I never offered to give you a shilling or two for a look at your minj. That was all you were waiting for. The devil knows I might have bought the minj and love together. I am sorry that I was so foolish to love you. Well if you are not a whore, truly tell me why not. Gustavus.[125]

It took all his sister Gwen's diplomatic skill to get Dorelia home.[126] In the emotional oceans of flirtation and affairs, it was the women of Bohemia who had to navigate marriages back to the shoals of their ideals. Bertrand Russell, perhaps the high priest, certainly the philosopher of the Bohemian lifestyle, was also emotionally traumatised when his wife Dora entered into an affair. This irrespective of the fact that he had a series of liaisons with students and a thrashingly carnal affair with one of Augustus John's conquests, Lady Ottoline Morrel. Despite the fact that he offered practical advice to others in his *Marriage and Morals* (1929), Russell never managed to put the theory into practice in his own life. D. H. Lawrence cruelly pointed out the irreconcilable discrepancy between Russell's ideal of universal love and his alienation from humanity.

Was Bohemia a happy place?[127] On the surface the hedonistic parties, the devil-take-the-hindmost insouciance of the Bohemians would seem to suggest that it was. Their philosophy 'digon i'r diwrnod ei ddrwg ei hun' (enough for the day its own darkness) or *carpe diem* was one of the instantaneous gratification of the senses. Alan Pryce-Jones entitled his bittersweet memoir of growing up as one of the most luminescent of the bright young things *The Bonus of Laughter*. Laughter was perhaps the natural reaction of people who lived in the shadows of war. Dylan Thomas, born in 1914, was quite literally a war baby, but each year of his brief life was marked by a conflict in some corner of a not too distant field. Laughter, music, dancing, partying were perhaps the only ways to protect oneself from the horrors of life and the agonies of the creative process.

Liberated sex was perhaps the most celebrated, certainly the most controversial, aspect of the Bohemian world, but it was not their greatest revolutionary experiment. The Bohemians' greatest revolutionary experiment was friendship, for they seemed to value personal relationships above all others. Alfred Janes, Dylan Thomas, Mervyn Levy and Daniel Jones became friends as 'young dogs' in and around Swansea and then in London. Their early friendships endured into later life. Levy in *Reflections in a Broken Mirror* (1962) and Daniel Jones in *My Friend Dylan Thomas* (1977) revealed how youthful friendship endured into old age. Significantly, Gwen Watkins named the study of her husband Vernon's friendship with Dylan Thomas simply *Portrait of a Friend* (1983). Camaraderie and comradeship were what characterised the Bohemians. The true Bohemian did not come from crossing the frontiers of monogamy and sexual freedom, but from reinventing and protecting the personal relationship when they reached the other side. Few people subsequently have been so brave.

If history is a form of time travel, then perhaps the best place to return to in order to sample the Bohemian milieu at its truest is to one of Augustus John's riotous Mallord Street (No. 28) parties. These gatherings were populated by barmaids, painters, poets, pimps, policemen and prostitutes and anyone who could be fished out of the pub to join in. Caspar John, on shore-leave from the navy, felt like an alien confronted by his father's cohorts of remarkable friends: 'I suppose they were Bohemians', he conjectured.[128] Augustus and Dylan are paralytically drunk; there have been brawls, gropings, attempts at the guests' virginity, music, dancing, singing and sinning. What once were the 'best tits in Europe' are on display as Nina Hamnett, four sheets to the wind, jitterbugs topless on the table-tops – for girls too just want to have fun. These hedonists, the heroes of bars and beds, are outside time, oblivious, ecstatic, with the future as unimaginable as the sorrows that would come with it.

7

Religion and Superstition: Fear, Foreboding and Faith

Wales is a bit crazed on the subject of religion.

George Borrow, Wild Wales: its People, Language and Scenery
(London, 1862), p. 77.

'Some trust in chariots': religion and Welsh society

Pan dynnwn oddi arnom bob rhyw wisg,
Mantell parchusrwydd a gwybodaeth ddoeth,
Lliain diwylliant a sidanau dysg;
Mor llwm yw'r enaid, yr aflendid noeth:
Mae'r llaid cyntefig yn ein deunydd tlawd,
Llysnafedd bwystfil yn ein mêr a'n gwaed,
Mae saeth y bwa rhwng ein bys a'n bawd
A'r ddawns anwareiddiedig yn ein traed.

(When we cast off all clothes,
The shrouds of respectability and wise knowledge,
Culture's fabrics and the silks of learning;
How poor is the soul, the naked impurity:
The primeval dirt is in our poor material,
The lusts of beasts in our blood and bone,
The bow and arrow between our finger and thumb
And the uncivilised dance controls our feet).

D. Gwenallt Jones, 'Pechod', Ysgubau'r Awen
(Llandysul, n.d.), p. 80.

'WELE' (BEHOLD), the manic street preacher Richard Owen's opening declaration held the Penmaenmawr audience spellbound in 1873, for they knew that it would be swiftly followed by an apocalyptic warning from some of Scripture's sterner pages. Ecclesiastes, Ezekiel, Isiah, Jeremiah, Joshua, Job, Ruth or Zachariah would provide him with his theme of lamentations. Richard Owen (1839–87), 'Y Diwygiwr' (The Revivalist), and his enraptured audience were a people who walked in darkness, eagerly anticipating the great light that would save the enlightened and cast sinners into 'pydew o dân a brwmstan' (a pit of fire and brimstone). These eagerly anticipated services were public celebrations of the spirit, but they were composed of hundreds of private cleansings of souls. The power of the gatherings came from the breadth of emotions displayed in these 'orgies of emotion', these outpourings of angst, anguish, fear, faith, hope and love. But the greatest of these was fear. A person's awareness of being nearer my God to thee engendered fear. The revival associated with Richard Owen's ministries in Rhos-cefn-hir and Pen-y-sychnant, north Wales, in the early 1870s revealed one of the underlying truths of the growth of Welsh religion – it was driven by fear.[1]

Love was all people needed, faith could move mountains, but it was fear that motivated the revivals that renewed and reinvigorated the religious life of Wales.[2] People seemed to believe that they were living in Revelations rather than in Rhos-cefn-hir. The years 1870–1945 saw a series of revivals that were local, national and international in their impact. Ministers frequently invited the Holy Ghost to leave the Trinity, rent the heavens and be active in Wales. The solid battalions of the theologians, the irresponsible cavalry of hellfire preachers and the menacing Robspierres of the deaconate constantly craved a revival. 'Angen Mawr Cymru' (Wales's Great Need), wrote R. P. Williams of Holyhead in 1890, 'ydyw tywalltiad o'r Ysbryd Glân i beri adfywiad ysbrydol' (is an injection of the Holy Spirit to create a spiritual revival).[3] The Holy Ghost proved to be accommodating. There were notable revivals in 1873 in Anglesey and across north-west Wales, in 1887 at Llandeilofawr, in 1890–1 at Dowlais, in 1891 in Cardiff, in 1892 across Monmouthshire and east Glamorgan, in 1894 at Merthyr and Aberfan, again in 1896 at Aberfan, once more at Llandeilo-fawr in 1897, and in 1899 at Llanelli. The Holy Ghost was even more obliging to Anglicans who wished for revivals. On the back wall of St David's

Cathedral is a tablet commemorating Dean David Howell (1831–1903), 'Llawdden'. In the year of his death he wrote the prophetic lines inscribed thereon –

> Take note, if I knew that this was to be my last statement to my fellow countrymen the length and breadth of Wales, before my summons to judgement and the light of eternity breaks over me, this is it – that the main need of my land and my dear nation at this time is – spiritual revival through a special outpouring of the Holy Spirit.

A few months after Dean Howell saw the light of eternity, Wales and 107 countries around the world witnessed scenes of orgiastic religious revival.

Church and chapel membership and attendance ebbed and flowed according to the lunar pull of religious revivals.[4] The denominational yearbooks and the *Report into the Condition of the Church of England in Wales* (1911) enable one to trace the level of religious affiliation in Wales.[5] For Nonconformity the climacteric years were those of the 1904–6 revival. Each of the denominations had their highest levels of membership in those years when, in D. J. Williams's evocative phrase, 'y mae Duw yn gwneud pethau mawr yn ein plith' (God is working wonders in our midst).[6] The Baptists increased in membership from 64,255 in 1871 to 106,566 in 1900 and 143,584 in 1906. This despite the fact that theirs was a hard salvation for even in the depths of winter they baptised outdoors in cold, cold water. Membership of the Calvinistic Methodists followed a similar pattern, increasing from 92,735 in 1870 to 158,114 in 1900 and a peak of 189,164 members in 1905. The Congregationalists, like their baptismal and methodistical brethren, also went forth and multiplied, increasing from 86,718 members in 1870, to 144,918 in 1900, and 174,313 in 1905. The Union of Independents united with their Nonconformist brethren and conformed with their pattern of growth – from 125,418 members in 1877, to 127,865 in 1900, to 152,165 members in 1905. Thereafter, all the denominations witnessed an ebbing of the sea of faith. By 1939 the Baptists had 116,813 members, falling to 110,328 in 1945; the Calvinistic Methodists had declined to 177,448 members in 1939 and 172,954 in 1945, Congregationalists fell to 162,691 in 1939 and 160,519 in 1945; whilst the Union of Independents declined to 133,235.[7]

In contrast, the numbers of members, or 'Easter Communicants' as the Church of Wales termed her faithful, followed a somewhat different pattern. In 1885 there were 74,778 members, increasing to 105,449 in 1891, to 141,008 in 1900, to 160,291 in 1904, 159,957 in 1920, rising again to 193,668 in 1939 and then declining to 155,911 in 1945. Disestablishment of the Church in Wales when it finally, at long-long-last after a Jarndycean journey through the courts, became law in 1920, seemed to have confounded the critics. The new Church of Wales in the 1920s and 1930s appeared to have been reinvigorated rather than ravaged by disestablishment. It was the Second World War that proved to be catastrophic for the church.[8]

In addition to the larger denominations there was a smorgasbord, a glorious gallimaufry of more than thirty other religious sects and denominations in the eclectic spirituality of Wales. There were many Christian sects, even if, as Voltaire's quip went, there was only one sauce. Amongst them were 44,991 members of the Wesleyan Methodists and 8,308 Primitive Methodists. Certain denominations were concentrated in certain areas. The 1,898 Unitarians were mostly located on the Carmarthenshire–Cardiganshire borderlands. The area became known as 'Y Smotyn Du' (the Black Spot), which was not a reference to a paucity of laundries, but to the concentric concentration of Unitarian chapels marked in black on a map.[9] The onward marching Christian soldiers of the Salvation Army took their war cries onto the streets with their militarism and marching brass bands as they harried and hounded the souls of the godless. Theirs was not a hidden-away religion as they stood up, stood up for Jesus. They created so much noise that it belied the fact that they only numbered 1,266 in 1905.

There were also sixty-nine priests serving 123 Roman Catholic churches and 105,500 members. Catholics were suspect in Wales for despite its Welsh heritage, Catholicism was seen as the idolatrous faith of the low Irish immigrants. Anti-Catholicism in press and on platform was consistent down to the 1960s. Attempts to establish Catholic schools in Colwyn Bay in the 1930s and Flint in the 1950s were greeted with hostility. One councillor even warned local Catholics that he intended to make 'the Reformation itself pale into insignificance compared to this religious war'. Immigration into Wales in search of work, from Spain, Italy and Poland, but especially Ireland, as the Y *Cymro* newspaper noted in 1933, strengthened the Catholic faith whilst Calvinism was in decline.[10] Nevertheless, despite the open hostility, Catholicism in Wales attracted some creative and colourful characters. The historian and judge Thomas Peter Ellis, the writer and MP William Llewelyn Williams, and the debauched Evan Frederick Morgan were all accepted into the faith, showing how catholic it was in its appeal. The conversion of Saunders Lewis to Catholicism in the 1920s resulted in a corpus of great Christian poetry, *Byd a Betws* (1942), in which what is evident to the rational eye is contrasted to that viewed by the eye of faith. In 'Y Lleidr Da' (The Good Thief), Jesus, 'a sack of bones . . . nailed on a pole . . . like a scarecrow', is both a flea-bitten robber and a God. 'Y Saer' (the Carpenter) outlines the agonising doubts that Joseph must have suffered concerning the paternity of Mary's child.[11]

Exodus might have dictated that people should only have one God, but the Christian deity had rivals in Wales. Allah, Brahman, Elohim (Jehova), and Waheguru also had their devotees who tried valiantly to interpret the actions of these omnipotent and omniscient immortal forces. The sea lanes and trade winds had carried and blown around 7,000 Islamic, Buddhist, Hindu and Sikh people to the ports of Newport, Cardiff and Swansea. The largest non-Christian community was the Jewish. By 1910, around 10,000 Jews were scattered around Wales with the major concentrations in Glamorgan and Monmouthshire. The anti-Jewish riots of 1911, although triggered by socioeconomic tensions, also had an element of anti-Semitism that poisoned relationships between the Welsh and Jewish settlers.

In addition to their formal members, all denominations claimed to have high levels of 'adherents' or 'listeners' who, whilst not actual members, frequently attended services. The short-story writer Gwyn Thomas noted the case of an inveterate 'sermon taster' who toured the valley chapels in search of the spirit's most powerful draughts. Denominations also claimed high levels of 'Sunday Scholars' who attended the Sunday schools and Bible classes. Their numbers were certainly impressive – 197,129 in the Sunday schools of the Church in 1910; 143,037 at those of the Baptists in 1906; 195,227 with the Calvinistic Methodists in 1905; 165,918 at the Congregationalists in 1905; and 133,834 at the Independents in 1905. But many people who attended these Sunday schools were also members of the denominations and so there is a risk of double-counting. Just like the Jesuits, Welsh sects took the child so that they could produce the adult. In 1912, there were 15,436 pupils at sixty elementary day schools and 453 pupils at thirteen secondary schools under the auspices of religious denominations. Thus the influence of religion reached far into a person's life.

The statistics of religious membership reveal that both the apologists and the abusers of Welsh religion have overemphasised the condition of faith. Religion was not as sickly, certainly not in such a terminal condition, as its opponents insisted, but neither was its health as robust as its adherents claimed. Like the smile on the face of the Cheshire Cat it lingered long. In 1905, the year that probably saw the highest level of religious affiliation in Welsh history, 909,517 of the people of Wales were members of a Christian denomination or sect. The estimated annual population of Wales in 1905 was 2,148,827. Thus well under half of the Welsh people were formally attached to a religious order. It was an uncomfortable fact for those who sought to present Wales as a religious, indeed as a 'Nonconformist Nation', that the bulk of the people were without the fold.

These years, especially the decade before the First World War, were perhaps *the* golden age, the finest hour of Welsh religion in terms of participation. Whatever the challenges that lay ahead, at the end of the nineteenth century, it seemed clear that Welsh religion would emerge into the new century victorious, happy and glorious. Wales had a special relationship with God; she was 'Erw'r Sant' (God's Acre), her people, his chosen elect. The future seemed as firmly fixed on earth as the signs of the Zodiac in the sky. 'Criticus', writing in *Seren Gomer* in 1899, proved that he had little of his (or her) nom-de-plume's critical faculties declaring that 'tybed nad y gwir yw fod Cymru yn well, ac yn burach ei chyflwr, nag y bu erioed o'r blaen?' (I wonder if the truth is rather that Wales is better, and purer her condition, than she has ever been?).[12] Lewis Jones, of Ty'n-y-coed, insisted in 1901 in *Y Diwygiwr*: 'Ni bu un ganrif er dyddiau yr Apostolion ag yr oedd crefydd yn cael lle mor amlwg ynddi â'r ganrif hon' (There has not been a century since the days of the Apostles that has given so much attention to religion as the present one).[13]

Other voices, however, were doubtful. This was just as much the epoch of incredulity as the epoch of belief, the season of Darkness as much as the season of Light. To paraphrase the Welsh-born Australian Prime Minister William Hughes's comment on the British Empire in the early twentieth century, 'the splendid glow', which Welsh religion, 'cast over the country reflected not its noon-day greatness, but the fading hues of sunset'.[14] Dusk was settling on the eternally sunlit world of religion in Wales. Thomas Charles Edwards (1837–1900), principal, preacher and perceptive exegete, discerned a sense of apprehension and anxiety in the religious life of Wales. In 1899 he warned: 'Nid yw yn amhosibl i Gymru eto droi yn ddigrefydd ac yn anffyddiol . . . Ac os cyll Cymru ei chrediniaeth o'r efengyl . . . y mae yn sicr y bydd ein gwlad yn fwy anghrefyddol, ac yn fwy annuwiol, nag y bu erioed o'r blaen' (It is not impossible for Wales to turn irreligious and unbelieving. And if Wales loses her belief in the scriptures . . . it is certain that our land will be more ungodly and irreligious than she has ever been before).[15]

Whether Wales would remain godly and goodly, as Thomas Charles Edwards so fervently hoped, depended on what religion offered to the people of Wales. Why, three-times a Sunday, Sunday after Sunday, and often on weekdays, did people enter chapel and church? Why did so many profess belief? Christian religion and its inheritance in Wales has suffered in recent years. A few people still believe, others labour under a residue of a little guilt at 'the immensities that will not return', but others have discarded, disparaged and disobeyed the beliefs that seemed once to be so certain and so confident.[16] In twenty-first century Wales we seem to be living through the morning after the divine din of a spiritual night before that still echoes across the centuries. Despite its apparent familiarity, for so many of its structures and symbols, its buildings and beliefs still stand, like stage props for Miss Havisham's feast, religious Wales is now almost a closed book. Yet at the turn of the twentieth century it is clear that, at its peak, religion in Wales was a protean phenomenon that touched and tinged the entire fibre and fabric of people's lives.

Religion educated the people of Wales. The Sunday schools, since the circulatory schools of Griffith Jones had come to rest, made people literate long before the state reluctantly intervened in 1870. Thereafter, the religious sects continued to instruct and inspire generations. The debates and discussions articulated in the pulpit were affirmed in print. *Y Diwygiwr, Y Drysorfa, Y Dysgedydd, Yr Eurgrawn Wesleyaidd, Yr Haul, Seren Gomer, Y Gad Llef* and *The War Cry* provided articles and ample poems and prose pieces to enhance the listener's experience. Such mental fodder provided food for thought for generations of political and social, as well as religious leaders. The academies of Anglicans and Nonconformists equipped an elite to perform with intellectual confidence. The *cofiannau*, hagiographic though many of them were, presented heroic role models for aspirational individuals. Biblical commentaries, denominational yearbooks, theological treatises, provided a wealth of reading material, whilst the Bible itself proffered role models and a model of morality for people to follow. The Bible was both the opium and the idiom of the Welsh. The rich metaphors of biblical language coloured local dialects and patois and gave inspired reading material – moral fables, travel narratives, adventure stories, fairy tales, everything from two naked people in a garden to revelations.

Despite its presentation as dour and dismal, doggedly pursuing redemption frown by frown, Welsh religion was capable of penetrating and humorous works of self-criticism. *Y Punch Cymraeg* and *Y Ffraethebydd* were largely the work of preachers and pastors who were willing to look on the bright side of life. In three brilliant novels – *Rhys Lewis* (1885), *Enoc Huws* (1891) and *Gwen Tomos* (1894) – the Mold novelist Daniel Owen (1836–95) praised and parodied his society with a scabrous pen that revealed both the positive and the negative aspects of religion.[17] Religion certainly provided some of the most inventive nicknames to the Welsh. A minister obsessed with John 18:36 'my kingdom is not of this world', became 'Dai Otherworldly'. He was joined by 'Dai Hallelujah' and 'Dai Jehova', whilst the miserable and morose north Walian Glyn was fondly known as 'Glyn Cysgod Angau' ([Glyn of the] Valley of the Shadow of Death).

Religion also provided an outlet for the artistic talent of Welsh people.[18] Though many artists strove hard to visualise the invisible, the drawings and paintings reproduced in denominational magazines and illustrated Bibles were often reminiscent of the artist's own world rather than ancient Palestine or Egypt or a celestial paradise. The art of piety was sometimes piteous. Edward Burne-Jones belittled much of his own work as 'Christmas Card Christianity', but in a number of stained-glass windows, his angels are transcendent. 'I must by now have designed enough to fill Europe', he claimed as he designed his final host of angels, for Gladstone's memorial in the church at Hawarden, Flintshire, in 1898.[19] A claim that might well have been true, for Burne-Jones and William Morris, through their company Morris and Co., provided window glass for countless chapels and churches. His angels are Botticellian, girlish, golden Primaveras of extraordinary sweetness, piety and promise. They are perhaps the one area in which the art of Wales comes close to the Italianate tradition of devotional art. Yet there was still something profoundly worldly about the images. These were angels of his own desires. Like Caravaggio, that other great painter of the divine, the angels in these chorus lines of beauty on their stairways to heaven are the beauties who so obsessed the faithless Burne-Jones.

Once gathered into the fold, the faithful were provided with a bewildering variety of entertainment. Chapels and churches were cultural, social and spiritual centres that provided theologically sound, occasionally suspect, services. Prayer meetings, Sunday schools, Bands of Hope, temperance societies, gospel missions, sisterhoods were all highly regarded. So too were 'y cyrddau diwylliannol' (cultural meetings), 'y cyrddau mawr' (great meetings), 'cyrddau gweddi' (prayer meetings) and the 'penny readings' and the 'pwnc' readings, for they enhanced the didactic functions of the chapel. But the churches and chapels also proved that they were people of the world, as well as of the word. There were ambulance clubs, cycling and walking tours, trips to the seaside, cricket, rugby and football teams and a myriad other activities. From the 1910s, some opponents when losing to the football teams of Ammanford's 'Cymry'r Groes' would complain that they had the unfair advantage of divine intervention. On the coast there were ship regattas against other denominations. There were pageants and parades in which people marched behind the rip-roaring bands and rippling banners of their chapels and churches in public affirm-ation of their faith. There were even, surprisingly given religion's sanctions against gambling, horse races. Denominations and sects also established their own welfare system. Closely associated with some churches and chapels were savings banks, building societies, friendly societies, and fundraising ventures. At times of economic distress, chapels and churches put their creed into deed and pro-vided for the bodily as well as the spiritual needs of people with their religion of the soup kitchen.[20]

To accommodate such activities churches and chapels sprouted vestries, sometimes threatening to rival the main building in size and structure.[21] These were the visible confirmation of how chapels and churches provided a comprehensive range of services to their members. Their architecture reflected the style of the mother build-ing, in a bewildering array of architectural styles – everything from startling Rococo and Art Deco beauties, to elephantine Classical edifices. As John Angell James put it in 1856: 'Dissent, once the religion of barns' was being 'infected with the ambition of becoming the religion of cathedrals'.[22]

Vestries, especially in their early days, were vibrant social centres. But buildings needed money. God might have been omnipotent, Jesus might have cast out the moneylenders from the temple, but their worshippers needed cash. The Anglican Churches had learnt early that they had to have the support of the rich in order to survive. Thus they were often criticised for being in an ungodly alliance with industrialists, coal owners and landlords – 'the Tory Party at prayer'. But the Nonconformists also found that buildings, even the humblest erected from the stones of the fields, required cash in order to continue. Thus many chapels were funded by the larger owner-occupier farmers or coal owners. The Calvinistic Methodists benefitted greatly from the generosity of coal magnate David Davies (1818–90), that embodiment of the link between religion and the rise of capitalism and of the archetypal Smilesean self-made man – whom Disraeli had so cruelly mocked for 'worshipping his own creator'.[23] Many people in rural and urban Wales found that attendance at a particular church or chapel would secure employment at a particular mine, quarry, farm or agricultural estate. Though the churches and chapels were seen as 'models of self-governing republics' that served as an engine of social reform and political democratisation, such influence and preferment was also significant.

Religious revivals made good business sense for the chapels and churches. Denominations and sects were soon in fervent competition with each other to renew, not just the spiritual condition of their enlarged congregations, but the silver collection. As the faithful prepared to mark Christmas 1902 with hosannas and hallelujahs, the gossip columnist Alethea in the *Carmarthen Weekly Reporter* warned that 'monetary success was the measure of local religion which is ruled by class and cash'.[24] A few months later and Alethea gave her Easter message pointing to the hypocrisy of some men 'praying on their knees in church on Sunday and then preying on their neighbours for the rest of the week'.[25] Despite the anarchic release of the revival meetings of 1904–6, few forgot the collection. As Rhys Davies noted in *The Withered Root*, 'silver tinkled into pewter plates' as the organisers revealed a banker's faith in sterling. Welsh sects accepted notes of all denominations.

The novelist, playwright and raconteur Gwyn Thomas recalled the cultural effervescence that accompanied the credo and creed:

> the brittle spiritual body of a place like Wales is a thing to wonder at . . . The chapels filled our early lives. Culturally and educationally they competed with the state schools . . . And within the chapels themselves there was endless ferment. Fundamentalism and a neurotic unease about the desires and antics of the flesh had made any sort of suavity impossible. In the average congregation the local pit owner or manager was the king. His deacons would normally be the deputies or overmen and firemen who ran his pit. The preachers he would expect to be servile to his own little quirks of doctrine

in religion and politics. If the preacher turned out to be a run-away independent with enough power of intrigue or eloquence to turn the larger part of the congregation against their master, then the latter would stamp out, followed by his little court, and found a new conventicle nearby. New chapels flew through the air like shrapnel. In the street where I grew up there were dozens. There were two of the same denomination frowning at each other across a narrow street.[26]

Gwyn Thomas pointed to one of the fundamental truths in the history of religion in Wales in the years 1870–1945, the provision of the means of grace was far greater than its practice. The church building programme of the late nineteenth century so dedicatedly chronicled by Professor Ieuan Gwynedd Jones, and the remarkable chapels erected by the Nonconformists, were premised on the basis of 'if you build it, they will come.'[27] But they did not. Churches and chapels were only rarely full. A 'gymanfa' (singing festival), a musical performance, or a funeral could fill these impressive edifices, but often ministers were preaching to empty pews of pitch pine. In a rare instance of jocularity, the historian R. T. Jenkins expressed this well:

> Rh'w ffeirad yn Aberdaugleddau
> A'th mas i bregethu i'r beddau
> Meddai ef: 'Nid yw'n syn
> 'Mod i'n gwneuthur fel hyn
> Ma' nhw'n llawer mwy effro na'r seddau'.[28]

> (A vicar from Milford Haven
> Went out to preach to the graves
> Said he: 'Tis no surprise
> That I behave like this
> They are more awake than the pews.)

Unlike mercy, the quality of such preaching was sometimes strained. The cult of the preacher 'aflame with the fire of God', the rabble-rousing, roustabout preaching of rednecks such as Matthews Ewenny, John Elias, Christmas Evans, John Jones (Talysarn), Henry Rees and Williams o'r Wern was in decline from the late nineteenth century. There was a little less of the hellfire, as those educated in the theological academies headed by luminaries such as Lewis Edwards or Thomas Charles Edwards tended to preach more intellectually searching sermons.[29]

A transfer market operated for ministers as the most gifted and eloquent were 'called' to the larger chapels where the remuneration was highest. Silver-tongued ministers were rewarded with silver. Many received a 'galwad' (a call) to move from their rural Nazareth to an urban Bethel where the road to the New Jerusalem would be paved with a little more gold. The crass realities of capitalism penetrated into the deepest areas of Welsh religion. Ministers learned that man does not live by bread alone for variety is the spice of life in this world. The minister John Hughes (1842–1902), 'Glanystwyth', had either the migratory instincts of a Bedouin or an inability to produce more than a few years' worth of sermons. In 1866–7 he was at Aberystwyth but soon moved to Treherbert (1867), Mountain Ash (1868), Cardiff (1869), Tre'r-ddôl (1872), Trefeglwys (1873), Machynlleth (1876), Coed-poeth (1878), Caer-narfon (1881), Llanrhaeadr-ym-Mochnant (1884), London (1886), Rhyl (1889), Manchester (1891) and Liverpool (1894–7). Many of the most talented ministers, such as Hugh Price Hughes (1847–1902), eventually made their livings in England. Hughes, a Wesleyan Methodist minister, was descended from two of the 'mastadons' of the Welsh pulpit, David Charles I and David Charles II. He established a mission in London in 1886, became editor of the *Methodist Times*, and was one of the strongest upholders of the 'Nonconformist conscience'. Hughes contributed something unique to English culture – scruple.

For many people the power in the glory of Welsh religion was in its music. Church and chapel choirs and orchestras regularly established a repertoire of musical works in a soundscape of belief. Tabernacle, Morriston, 'the cathedral of Welsh Nonconformity', with its 1,080 members and 550 'listeners', produced 'Stabat Mater', 'Hymn of Praise', 'Hiawatha', 'Messiah' and 'Galatea' in 1905. Chapels and churches soon sought to outdo each other with their harmoniums, organs and pianos. Organists began and ended services with voluntaries. Anglican churches in north-east Wales had established a strong tradition of choral festivals by the 1880s. Trinity Church, Rhyl, had seven choirs and 2,000 voices primed for the baton in 1885.[30] The chorales, cantatas and compositions of Handel, Haydn and Vivaldi soon became staple fare as ordinary people displayed extraordinary talent. The choir was a crucible of religious alchemy. Singers in the children's choirs were transformed from urchins into angels. Behind the neat and nervous children their booming guardians sang out all those divine and distinctively Welsh feelings about religion and the cycle of life: the innocence of childhood, the pastoral idyll, the victory of the underdog against unsurmountable odds, the building of the New Jerusalem, the guilt (always guilt). In 1872 and 1873, the tradition of Wales as 'Gwlad y Gân' (the land of song) was confirmed when choristers from several chapels in south Wales joined together into 'Côr Mawr Caradog' (Caradog's Great Choir) and were victorious in the Crystal Palace competitions.[31] Complete bliss for the Welsh was that Heaven would surely be a place of recitals and recitations, an eternal eisteddfod. A feeling given confirmation in the great hymn of David Evans (1879–1965), the chief inspector of the Welsh Board of Health, 'Yng Nghôr Caersalem Lân' (In Pure Caersalem's Choir).[32]

The hills of Wales were alive to the sounds of hymns for it was in the perfect marriage of tune and words that many could express their beliefs, confess their sins, pray for forgiveness and enjoy cathartic, orgiastic release.[33] Hark the herald angels of Wales sang their songs of praise with power and passion. Simple people – shepherds, tinplate workers, blacksmiths, miners, station masters, farmers, shopkeepers – wrote memorable hymns that perfectly paired theology and tone. They were supplemented by the catchy English and American hymns, especially the immensely popular outpourings of Moody and Sankey.[34] When it was discovered that the latter's wife was Welsh, their hymns acquired even greater appeal. John Roberts (1822–77), 'Ieuan Gwyllt', established the first 'Gymanfa' (singing festival) in 1859 in Aberdare, and published a hymn-book so that the people could have something to sing along to. Both proved to be immensely popular. The hymn-book Sŵn y Jiwbili sold 17,000 copies in a little over a year and an estimated quarter of the Welsh population attended a Gymanfa Ganu in

1900.[35] Denominational and sectarian rivalry was soon displayed in the hymn-books of Wales.

Even more popular was the English inspired and imported tonic sol-fa. Night classes in sol-fa made ordinary people musically literate and laid the basis for the 'muscular four-part congregational singing' that so characterised the Welsh.[36] Hymns deepened people's sense of place and belonging for many of the greatest and most popular were named after Welsh places. 'Cwm Rhondda', 'Bryntirion', 'Llwynbedw', 'Meirionydd', 'Penmachno', 'Rhosymedre, 'Saron' and many, many more. The toponomy of hymnody mirrored the topography of Wales reinforcing the sense that she was 'God's Acre'.

Even in their darkest hours, especially in their darkest hours, the Welsh turned to their hymns for comfort and joy. To maintain their spirits as they awaited rescue the miners entombed in their flooded pit at the Tynewydd mine in 1877 sang the hymn 'Yn y dyfroedd mawr a'r tonnau' (In the deep and mighty waters).[37] At Ammanford during the tense strike of the anthracite miners in the summer of 1925, a nervy face-off between strikers and police seemed to be edging towards violence. The miners sang 'Aberystwyth'. The police were 'terrified'. Visiting rugby teams to Cardiff Arms Park were often intimidated by hymn-singing Welsh supporters. During the First World War there is a heart-stopping account of a Welsh battalion moving up in the dark singing 'Aberystwyth', a battle cry as much as a hymn, until the voices were lost in the sound of shellfire.[38] The Welsh Guards choir came second in the male voice competition at the Welsh National Eisteddfod in 1918, but its finest hour had probably come earlier, as the regiment's historian, an eyewitness, remembered:

> The really effective singing did not come from the choir standing in a body on a rough platform, but from the heart of the battalion when going into battle or after the fight. 'In the sweet bye and bye we shall meet on the beautiful shore,' after the engagement at Gouzeaucourt when the shattered battalion was withdrawn to a wood behind the village, brought a hush over the camp. The hymn singers were hidden amongst the trees in the moonlight and the air was frosty and still. This was not a concert, but a message, a song of hope and faith.[39]

The Revd Harold Davies was struck by the paradox in the behaviour of a Welsh battery he visited:

> The most foul-mouthed lot that I have struck since I came to France. Yet after nauseating me for an hour this afternoon with their 'poisoned gas' they suddenly began to sing hymns with real feeling and piety. There is some real religion deep down in the hearts of these lads – one cannot call them godless because no sooner has one come to this conclusion than some spark of the Divine flashes out of them. The difficulty is to seize it and kindle a real fire within them.[40]

Apocalyptic power and erotic yearnings characterise many of the great Welsh hymns. Hymns harmonised the feelings and yearnings of the congregation. They provided release and relief for individuals. They were public expressions of the most private and personal emotions. Daniel James (1847–1920), Gwyrosydd, a Swansea tinplate worker, wrote one of the hymns that has been sung most often.[41] A simple, sacred hymn that has become a secular sporting anthem:

> Nid wy'n gofyn bywyd moethus,
> Aur y byd na'i berlau mân;
> Gofyn wyf am galon hapus,
> Calon onest, calon lân.
>
> Calon lân yn llawn daioni,
> Tecach yw na'r lili dlos
> Dim ond calon lân all ganu –
> Canu'r dydd a chanu'r nos.[42]
>
> (I seek not life's ease and pleasures,
> Earthly riches, pearls or gold;
> Give to me a heart made happy,
> Clean and honest to unfold.
>
> A clean heart o'erflowed with goodness,
> Fairer than the purest lily
> A clean heart forever singing,
> Singing through the day and night.)

Despite the collective groups in which the great hymns were sung, or the social gospel that developed in Wales, much religious outpourings were intensely egotistic. Individuals had a profound fear of cosmic isolation. The hymns of Wales are perhaps the nation's greatest contribution to religion, but they also serve to emphasise that salvation is a lonely experience. At the heart of many of the greatest hymns is a timorous thing – the soul and its search for a saviour. People gathered, sang and prayed in public groups, but their motives were private and personal. This is why the great rites and rituals of the churches and chapels were tied to the great events of individual lives – birth, marriage and death. As the poet Gwenallt said of the chapel in Carmarthenshire:

Y capel a roddai yn ddi-wahaniaeth,
Yn y glesni a'r glaw gwledig, ac yn y mwstwr a'r mwrllwch,
Y dŵr ar dalcen, y fodrwy ar fys a'r atgyfodiad
                            uwch yr arch.

(The chapel gave without prejudice,
In the rural greenery and rain, and in the noise and dirt,
The water on forehead, the ring on finger, and the resurrection
                            above the coffin).[43]

It is in its capacity to call down divine blessings on the arrivals, unions and departures of people that religion came closest to providing something profoundly important to the Welsh people. It is this perhaps that explains the fact that despite the increasing secularisation and dechristianisation of Welsh society, the number of people who opted for a religious wedding service increased over the period 1870–1945, whilst the number of those who opted for a secular service decreased. It is also this that probably explains why people were so reluctant to be cremated but opted for a formal funeral.

The galleries of the chapels and the transepts of the churches were often packed with ladies, some scented with lavender, others smelling of sweat, all twittering like a cage of linnets. More superficial than supernatural, some women attended the services more for the fashion than the passion, as they sought to outdo each other in the one-upwomanship of the front-of-the-gallery posturing. Their presence indicated an idea central to Welsh religion, that suffering would flower into purity. Their presence indicated one of the greatest strengths of Welsh religion, for without the women-folk it would have little power or purpose. Their presence indicated the greatest weakness in Welsh religion, in that the potential of its greatest asset, its womenfolk, was never effectively harnessed.[44]

Women were involved within Welsh religion in informal religious organisations, in the temperance and anti-white slavery campaigns, and in rescue work. They were the organisers of charitable fund-raising and social activities. In the missionary field they were domin-ant. Gwenfron Moss (1898–1981), Jane Helen Rowlands (Helen o Fôn; 1891–1955), Susannah Jane Rankin (1897–1989) and Mary Myfanwy Wood (1882–1967) served with distinction in foreign lands. In 1924, of fifty-six Welsh missionaries in the field in India, thirty-six (66 per cent) were women, twenty-one of whom were unmarried.[45] During the 1904–6 religious revival, the stars of the services were Evan Roberts's 'lady friends'. Yet there was never a feminine theology. The priesthood remained solidly patriarchal. Rachel Davies (1846–1915), 'Rahel o Fôn', was something of a rare figure. Rahel o Fôn was born-again in the USA, and returned to Wales as a lecturer and preacher with the Calvinistic Methodists in north Wales. Rosina Davies encountered 'persecution, zealous prejudice and selfish unwillingness that a Girl Evangelist should come into the arena and fight the Good Fight in public' but she persevered with her preaching.[46] So too did Edith Picton-Tubervill. She became a suffragist, later an MP, because 'my religious experi-ence inspired me to attempt achievements I could never have other-wise have dreamed of.'[47] With typical contradictory complexity, Christianity could both be a source of an oppressive domestic ideology and a starting point for feminist activism.[48] Nevertheless, women's role in Welsh religion, despite their immense potential, was often just to provide the counterpoint and counterpart to tenor, bass and baritone, or just to make, and, of course, clear the tea.

The ladies in lavender were present because of their fears and hopes. Their gnarled hands could barely close over hymn-book or prayer book. They were slow, breathless, cancerous, old and cold. Belief warmed the tundra of their days and even seemed to heal the hurt of time. These were society's survivors. Disease, disasters and deaths of loved ones they had encountered and endured. Their entire lives had been a vigil, a long waiting for the last trumpet to sound, when, as the preachers promised them, in a moment, in the twinkling of an eye, they would be changed and carried heavenwards on the wings of angels. Their earthly torments would be transformed into ethereal titillation.

The re-enchantment of the world: the 1904–6 religious revival

> It was the whole tormenting storm of sin, despair, God's angels opting for cloth-capped squalor . . . A large, hastily assembled and vigorously abused world was lifting its sad sails to catch the wind of a little restitution.
> Evan Roberts was the wind that came, and like the wind he went.
>
> Gwyn Thomas, *High on Hope* (Bridgend, 1985), pp. 47–8.

To be born again, first you have to die. Spiritually your world has to turn upside down. These were the traumatic and transformative experiences of people such as Rosina Davies, Maggie Davies, Anne Davies, Sarah Jones, Alice Uray, Catherine Roberts, Mary Evans, Maud Davies, Sidney Evans, Seth Joshua, Frank Joshua, Joseph Jenkins, Nantlais Williams, and, of course, Evan Roberts, and many, many more in the 'spiritual earthquake' of 1904–6.[49] How many more – 100,000? Probably, for many insist that the number of people 'saved' in Wales far exceeded this number, which, Evan Roberts claimed, God had challenged him in a dream to save – an entire nation on the road to Damascus. Or 500,000? Possibly, for many people who were already chapel and church members were also traumatised in those 'years of the spirit'. Or 1,000,000? Potentially, for the revival was a trans-oceanic phenomenon that affected people from Bangor to Bangalore, Colwyn Bay to the Congo, Rhyl to Rio, Ynys-hir to Yokohama.[50] The actual number? God knows. There was one born-again every minute in 1904–6.[51]

In the beginning, as the Bible insists, it is always worthwhile and wise to set down some basics. Though the revival is often referred to as the Evan Roberts revival of 1905, there was far more to this remarkable phenomenon. The revival was like a contagion that affected separate parts of Wales simultaneously.[52] Whilst Evan Roberts concentrated his efforts on missions in Loughor in late October/early November 1904, there were also independent outbreaks of religious fervour in Blaenannerch, Cardigan and Llangrannog in Cardiganshire, Llandudno and Rhosllanerchrugog in north Wales, and Ammanford and Pen-y-groes in Carmarthenshire.[53] Sidney Evans, Joseph Jenkins, W. Nantlais Williams, R. B. Jones and those brotherly fishers of men, Seth and Frank Joshua, were also working to convert Wales. Rosina Davies led a mission to Colwyn Bay. The revival lasted longer than 1905. Its origins were in one of the innumerable lantern-lit meetings that characterised 1903 and 1904. God knows which or when. In some areas the spirit of revival lasted long into 1906. In the Mynydd Mawr (the Great Mountain) area of Carmarthenshire and the Bryncrug area in Merioneth and Harlech, people jumped and jehova'd well into 1906, even until 1912 they prayed and praised, for these people of the spirit had stamina. At Maesteg in Glamorgan, the brothers George and Stephen Jeffreys channelled the enthusiasm of 1904–6 into the establishment of the Elim Pentecostal Church in 1915, one of the world's largest Christian groups.

Welsh religion is often portrayed as a masculine prerogative, but the moving forces in the Welsh revival were girls and young women. With their pointer-pigeon bodices, some looked like men playing women in a play by Oscar Wilde, but many sinners were often delivered to salvation by nubile, pneumatic angels of redemption who sang as they turned Wales into a land of hope and glory. Of the ten leading vessels or ventriloquisers of the Holy Ghost in 1904–6, eight were women. There is as much reason to name this the Jessie Penn-Lewis revival as the Evan Roberts revival, for when his flame flickered, hers burned bright. For a period in 1905 he seemed to follow her as faithfully as a shadow. Theologically, she was sounder than the theistic Roberts.[54] The righteous fervour and fertile, febrile carousel that swept across Wales in the revival had a feminine aegis.

Reader, there are two other basic facts to grasp. If you do not believe, you will never understand the forces at work in '1905 and all that'. The emotions and experiences of the saved are supposedly beyond the ken of the unbeliever (that is, if you are an unbeliever). As one interviewee told 'Awstin', the *Western Mail's* special correspondent at the revival, 'you have sense, we have faith. There is no thinking, only belief.'[55] Subsequent historians have been equally abrupt. R. Tudur Jones insisted that unbelievers could never understand 'cymhellion yr etholedig rai' (spiritual motives of the saved elect).[56] It was a question the structuralist anthropologist E. E. Evans-Pritchard also pondered – did understanding follow belief? 'God works in mysterious ways his wonders to perform.' Such abstractness is apparently beyond the apperception of faithless historians. The second factor to grasp is that the years 1904–6 saw one of the most spontaneous outbreaks of felicity and happiness in Welsh history. In Victorian and Edwardian Wales, those who served God reputedly did so with a fierce solemnity, only occasionally consenting to a saintly smile. Laughter within the gloomy aisles of Welsh chapels and churches was about as welcome as breaking wind. But the 1904–6 revival services had a heady, happy-go-lucky character, for joy and jubilation were, temporarily, put into worship.

The story of Evan Roberts is one of the saddest in Welsh history.[57] For all the angst and agonies he suffered in the spotlight of the 1904–6 revival, today his inheritance is suspect, his reputation tarnished. Nothing succeeds like excess and Roberts seemed to have provided so much enthusiasm that his name is forever tainted. 'A prophet', it seems, 'has no honour in his own country'. When the fires of the revival cooled to clinker, Wales reacted like the woman who had yearned for years for an orgasm, only to complain, after finally experiencing one, that it was the wrong type. The transcendent, the heavens-storming, the world-changing aspects of the revival that Roberts did so much to foster was treated with the scepticism with which Holy Roman Emperor Joseph II greeted *The Marriage of Figaro* – 'too many notes'. The Welsh people created Evan Roberts as the idol and then turned on him with devastating force in what his near contemporary and fellow Llwchwr inhabitant Dr Ernest Jones would characterise as the 'ambivalence of emotion'. Roberts is the Dresden china doll of evangelists.[58] In a sense this is due to Evan Roberts's behaviour. Roberts wrestled with the tensions and travails of the revival and his only response was sometimes to escape the limelight into his 'silent retreats'. His hallucinatory visions grew stronger and stranger, the demons that haunted him would not release their hold. He sat in his room seized with a paralysing fear and hallucinating fevers. Wave after wave of despair washed over him. In that fateful, fantastic time, his waking hours were suffused with the supernatural, his haunted dreams had conquered his conscious life. On occasion, his condition resembled that of the people who had been confined to the asylums suffering from 'religious excitement'.

Posterity in both factual and fictional work has not been kind to the prophet.[59] Daniel Mydrim Phillips (1863–1944), author of the first Welsh book on the psychology of religion *Athrawiaeth y Meddwl* (1901), wrote fairly objectively about Roberts in *Evan Roberts the Great Revivalist and His Work* (1906), yet he tempered this with some sarcasm in *Athroniaeth Anfarwoldeb* (1908). Monsignor Robert Hugh Benson, a Roman Catholic priest, in his dystopian novel *Lord of the World* (1907), is astoundingly hostile. Benson presents Evan Roberts and his acolytes in the 1904–6 revival as the models for the Antichrist. Rhys Davies in *The Withered Root* (1927) provides a Freudian interpretation of the revivalist. Although the revivalist set out on a path 'to lessen the sorrows of the world', the journey proved to be more problematic.[60] As so often is the case in the work of Rhys Davies, the consummate voyeur of south Wales society, the strongest characters are the women, especially Eirwen Vaughan after whom the revivalist Reuben Daniel alternatively lusts and loathes. Her first name meant 'snow-white' but this fallen angel had clearly drifted. It was a saga typical to Wales, the revivalist's tortured sexuality and fractured personality was all Mam's fault for she 'did not believe in surrounding a child with a sickly heat of pronounced affection.' Starting a revival was as good a way as any to get Mam's attention.[61]

The reputation of Evan Roberts, Welsh religion's sacred cow, was soon made into mincemeat. This seems unfair to the revival in general and particularly unfair to Evan Roberts. The over-association with one person distorts much of the complexity of the revival. 'Un wennol, ni wna wanwyn' (a single swallow does not make a spring), neither does a lone evangelist make a revival. The origins of 1904–6 lie not with one person, but in the Welsh historical revivalist tradition. From 1897 through to 1904, there were several groups, independent and interdependent, around Wales who were working towards a revival.[62] At Llandrindod Wells, Dr F. B. Meyer undertook a month-long mission in early 1903. A group from Carmarthen attending one meeting felt that a new world had opened to them and they could not but lead others in. As a result evangelistic meetings were held in Carmarthen under the leadership of the Pentecostal League and Reader Harris, QC, the Revds R. B. Jones and W. S. Jones and Mrs Penn-Lewis. Similar experiences occurred at Rhosllanerchrugog and Rhyl in the north. Anglesey was soon claimed to be 'Christ's Island'. The Revd W. W. Lewis of Carmarthen addressed the Cardiganshire Methodist 'seiat' in October, convincing two local religious leaders, John Thickens and Joseph Jenkins, that they too should intensify their efforts to lead others into this 'new world'. At Ammanford several individuals influenced by the Keswick mission were also active.[63]

In October 1904 the excitement seemed to reach a crescendo. At Blaenannerch in Cardiganshire, as Seth Joshua led the congregation into worship, a twenty-year-old collier fell poleaxed to his knees, his face streaming with sweat, with great difficulty he uttered the words that hundreds of tortured souls would subsequently utter: 'Plyg fi o Arglwydd' (Bend me o Lord).[64] The collier, a student at the Revd John Phillips's private grammar school in Newcastle Emlyn, was Evan Roberts. Almost simultaneously at a meeting on 30 October 1904, at Bethany Calvanistic Methodist Chapel in Ammanford, as Joseph Jenkins led the prayers, the minister W. Nantlais Williams noted 'torodd yr argae' (the dam burst). From then on meetings lasted for hours. Cockerels crowed breakfast, but still they prayed. Meetings were characterised by public confession of sin, intense and impromptu praying and singing, and weeping. All the moon long the faithful hymned and rumpussed. There must have been a deep reservoir of sin in Wales for no prayer seemed long enough to express all the congregation would like to say about the need for mercy on their souls. Like the Corinthian in the wake of St Paul's mission, they would 'jabber and quake' when the spirit rushed in. The revival turned the traditional order of the world of chapel and church upside down. The young people commonly took over the meetings, and women became extremely prominent. Revival meetings were notable for their spontaneity and lack of formal procedures, and the preaching itself was the work of laymen and women rather than the ministers.

'Bands of angels' travelled around Wales to spread the word and share the joy. Those of Tabernacle Calvinistic Methodist Chapel, New Quay, visited other chapels at Blaenannerch, Penmorfa, Cardigan, Cilgerran, Twrgwyn, Capel Drindod, Newcastle Emlyn and Aberystwyth. Those from Tywyn Congregational Church, New Quay, visited Capel Crugiau, Gwernllwyn, and Pisgah. In these bands, the young were prominent. It was at a young people's meeting that the revival started in Caerfarchell, Pembrokeshire, and at a Band of Hope meeting that it began in Cilgerran, also in Pembrokeshire. At Caerfarchell and Cardigan women 'gospel singers' were to the fore. At Abermeurig, female hot-gospellers were also active.[65] An eyewitness told a newspaper reporter that 'the revival has taken the form common in this Revival – the young women and older women have taken to praying, as well as the young men'.[66] Often this was in a formless anarchic release. Some speakers sought to outdo each other in outlandish public confessions of sin committed and lusts assuaged. Ministers found themselves unable to address the congregation. This undoubtedly created tensions. As one minister recalled:

> As the Revival proceeded, Joseph Jenkins and the other brethren who had been involved with the conventions, became worried because they thought that the Word was being dethroned, and that men were readier to speak to God rather than listen to what God had to say to them through the preaching of the Word . . . The leadership passed into young men's hands, hands less suitable.[67]

In 1905, Seth Joshua, Joseph Jenkins, Evan Roberts, Jessie Penn-Lewis, R. B. Jones, Nantlais Williams and several others undertook missions that criss-crossed Wales from Tonypandy to Trelawnyd, from Pembroke to Penmaenmawr. The collective effervescence and excitement of these revival meetings were exacerbated by the reports in the press. The *South Wales Daily News*, the *Western Mail* and denominational papers such as *Y Goleuad* and *Seren Gomer* and the journal *Y Geninen* carried stories of the remarkable goings-on in Wales. Uncontrolled exuberance was a marked characteristic of the meetings. As one person spoke, others would weep, collapse, beseech salvation, confess their sins, or pray. The mention of a line in a hymn could bring forth an immediate rendition. Even Evan Roberts found it hard to lead such anarchic meetings. Often he would remain quiet in the pulpit for extensive periods – 'y canol llonydd distaw' – the eye of the storm. On occasion Evan was a man of few words, but they were enough to express his range of ideas. Some people were concerned at the unregulated enthusiasm of the revival meetings:

> At one revival meeting, there was a great noise and commotion, when the leader of the meeting . . . asked all those to stand up who were 'on their way to Glory' or wished to go. Up stood all the congregation, consisting of all types of people, who had been swept in from the public houses and the streets. There was one exception. An old deacon in the corner of a big pew, sat down persistently . . . At last the leader of the meeting, looking at him, asked 'Don't you want to go to Glory, John Thomas?' The old man looked up and replied, while he remained seated 'Oh yes, I want to go to Glory, but not with this excursion, thank you!'[68]

Many ministers found it intolerable that those who were supposed to follow were at the forefront of the revival.[69] The most famous clash occurred between Evan Roberts and the Revd Peter Price of Dowlais. In a letter to the *Western Mail* on 31 January 1905, Price, at one time of Aberystwyth where they took a stern view of religious enthusiasm, later of Dowlais, condemned:

> A sham Revival, a mockery, a blasphemous travesty of the real thing . . . There is a true and a false revival – the heavenly fire and the ignis fatuus . . . The chief figure in this mock revival is Evan Roberts, whose language is inconsistent with the character of anyone except that of a person endowed with the attributes of a Divine Being . . . Are there four persons in the Godhead, and is Evan Roberts the fourth?[70]

To emphasise his educated enlightenment and scriptural superiority, he signed the letter 'Peter Price (B.A. Hons), Mental and Moral Sciences Tripos, Cambridge (late of Queen's College, Cambridge)'. A similar clash took place at Cardigan between the Revd Seth Joshua and the Revd Dr Moelwyn Hughes. Seth Joshua, one of the Forward Movement's leaders, had received little formal education and had commenced work driving a donkey: 'I had more out of that donkey than I would get out of any College in the land . . . I maintain that if a man knows how to handle a donkey for three-and-a-half years he is qualified to handle anything awkward'.[71] Seth Joshua was clear that it was inspiration and not academic qualifications that would lead to salvation.

Others were more kindly disposed towards the chiliastic and anarchic enthusiasm of the new-found converts. The Revd Elvet Lewis, for example, considered that

> We need scarcely refer to some of the extravagancies of excitement which have spasmodically broken out here and there; they are local, they are temporary, they are confined to the few. They are part of any great movement; perhaps Flagellants and White Hoods in one age and country, Pentecostal Dancers and miracle-mongers in another age and country.[72]

It is possible to sense a feeling of jealousy in the attitude of ministers like Hughes and Price who came to oppose the revival. Yes they wanted a revival. They prayed to God, Jesus and the Holy Ghost to deliver one to Wales. Yes they rejoiced when the revival began. But did the Trinity really have to choose the vessels they did to deliver it? Like the devout Salieri who saw the divine in the music of the debauched Mozart they felt somewhat betrayed. They wanted to have their communion wafer and eat it. They wanted to shower their people with God's grace, to inundate their barren hearts with love and faith. It would only take a sign from their crucified Lord, or the flutter of a wing from one of his angels, but they wanted to lead, to control, to harness the power of the glory. But, as the Revd Eliseus Howells, a revivalist in 1904 and 1905, recalled: 'The Revival took a very different path from the one that they wished it to take, "for your ways are not my ways" sayeth the Lord.'[73]

As the outsiders rushed in, the insiders sought to rush out. One area where there was universal agreement was that the revival had a beneficial influence on popular morality. The revival was a powerful force for social control and the reformation of manners. In the services people attested how their lives had been transformed. With a touching colloquialism individuals explained that once they had played football for Satan but were now on the side of the Lord, or how they had once been in a tug-of-war team but were now 'pulling for Jesus'. Activities that had previously been considered harmless and recreational were now suspect. Rugby was viewed as 'kicking the head of John the Baptist'. Eisteddfodau and concerts ceased, or took on a religious flavour. Mines, mills and slate quarries now commenced with morning prayers that were repeated at the lunch break. Conversation at 'Y Caban', the slate quarrymen's lunchtime discussion forum, took a sacred rather than a secular flavour. Some pit ponies no longer understood the ostler's commands for there were no swear words. Drunkards became devout. Solicitors at Rhos, Caernarfon and on Anglesey complained that they had no representational work, for there were no miscreants to defend.

Fields of praise, snugs, bars and courtrooms might have been silent, but the astral planes of Wales were in uproar during 1904–6. Angelic voices and visions were heard and seen across south Wales in 1904–6 as were ghosts and ghouls and things that went bump in the night. In the hills around Aberdare, gypsies spoke in tongues and strange 'heavenly' languages. Above the same town people heard the sound of 'angelic voices singing in the air', a phenomenon that had previously been experienced during the 1859 revival above the Hiraethog Hills, and in Snowdonia during the 1817 revival.[74]

Such visions from beyond and behind the clouds were a marked feature of the ministry of Evan Roberts in 1904 and 1905, who clearly sought to present himself as a visionary. Roberts had weirder visions than the prophets Ezekiel or Zachariah put together. At Swansea in 1905, he saw a large column of candles in union with each other but without light. This he interpreted as the converts yet to be lit and to give light to others, the believers were Matthew's 'the light of the world', a unique image he insisted that prophesised the revival's success.[75]

The forces of Light and Darkness appeared to be having a rare old battle in Wales between 1904 and 1906. The *South Wales Daily News* reported in November 1904 that a boy and a woman had seen both Christ and the Devil.[76] At Neath in Glamorgan, Jesus Christ was seen with his arms outstretched in a gesture of benefaction.[77] He was also seen in a vision of dazzling glory in the gallery of Ainon Baptist Chapel at Ystradgynlais, Breconshire.[78] In February 1905, several students simultaneously saw a dazzling light incorporating a scene of the crucifixion, and a farmer received a vision calling him to preach.[79]

The Prince of Darkness made several visits to Evan Roberts. He saw Satan on his left side once whilst he was leading a prayer meeting. On another occasion he saw his mocking face in a hedge at Newcastle Emlyn. Satan obviously liked gardening, for Roberts also saw him taunting him from a bush in his back garden in Loughor. On a Sunday in October or November 1904, the chronology is hazy, but the vision was clear, Satan was once more in the garden:

> In the hedge on his left he saw a face full of scorn, hatred and derision, and heard a laugh as of defiance. It was the Prince of this world who exulted in his despondency. Then there suddenly appeared another figure, gloriously arrayed in white bearing in hand a flaming sword borne aloft. The sword fell athwart the first figure and it instantly disappeared. He could not see the face of the sword bearer.[80]

Nevertheless, Roberts recognised Christ by his brilliant white raiment. In another vision, Roberts saw endless fields of heavenly corn being harvested by happy celestial harvesters. More terrifyingly, and perhaps inevitably, Roberts saw Revelation's fiery pit of the Apocalypse. Biblical events, belonging to remote times, were given a contemporary immediate, telling impact of prophecy in revivalist preaching. Evan Roberts could evoke great visions of judgement with almost a documentary wealth of description outlining the geology and geography of Hell, which, startlingly was full of Welsh people.

Christ also spent a considerable amount of time in Wales in 1904. The Revd J. T. Job, the highly talented minister of Bethesda, Caernarfonshire, in December 1904, reported excitedly:

Dyma noson fawr yr ystorm. Pan edrychwyf yn ôl at y noson hon, nis gallaf lai na'i disgrifio fel hurricane yr Ysbryd Glân! . . . Teimlais yr Ysbryd Glân fel cenllif o oleuni yn peri i'm natur siglo drwyddi; gwelais Iesu Grist – aeth fy natur yn llymaid wrth ei draed; a gwelais fy hunain – a mi a ffieiddiais . . . Bellach, yr oedd yr holl le wedi myn'd i ddawnsio – y pregethwyr a'i merched bach yn y pulpud – Welsoch chwi'r fath gynnwrf yn eich bywyd?

(This was the night of the great storm. When I look back at that night, I cannot less than describe it as the hurricane of the Holy Spirit . . . I felt the Holy Spirit like a flood of light that forced my nature to quake throughout; I saw Jesus Christ – my nature weakened at his feet; and I saw myself and I was ashamed . . . By now the entire place was dancing – the preachers and their little girls in the pulpit – Have you ever seen such ferment in your life?)[81]

The Revd E. Isfryn Williams, Ponciau, saw Jesus at a meeting in Rhosllanerchrugog at almost the same time.[82] Jesus also appeared to Daniel P. Williams (1882–1947), a collier and the founder of the Apostolic Church in Wales. The conduit for his vision was Evan Roberts who 'laid hands' upon him. Williams blacked out and upon gaining consciousness he heard:

a woman singing a hymn. 'The gates of heaven opened wide. I see a sea of blood.' It was then that Daniel had a vision of Jesus on the cross. His body streaming with blood, and underneath it a sinner's head, and as the blood of Jesus fell on the parts of the sinner's head, it became white – like snow. The sinner, Daniel realised, was none other than himself.[83]

Another who saw the holy dandruff as the result of Evan Robert's ministrations was Sarah Jones, 'The Wonderful Woman of Carmel' in Carmarthenshire, who led what was described as the 'New Revival' of 1906. For two weeks in April 1906, Sarah Jones's husband, Daniel, had been unable to attend his work as a collier in Cross Hands colliery because she was, in the words of one follower, 'living almost completely in the spiritual world' in a perpetual state of ecstasy. A reporter noted:

Though she was illiterate and could not even read her Bible, 'There are scores of good Christians in the District who thoroughly believe in her. They say that she has been born again and is with Christ.'[84] Her services, which commenced at 7.30 p.m., often did not finish until 11 a.m. the following day and were characterised by frenzied, uncontrollable worship. At Cross Hands 'men and women tore their hair, threw themselves on the floor and prayed with intense fervour.'[85] One observer in the congregation noted: 'When she speaks there is a strange light in her eyes, her countenance beams, and she is as one transfigured.'[86] During the mission organised by the Revd William Bowen at Pen-y-groes, in a packed afternoon session, she seized the seat in front 'without word and swayed to and fro in great agony of soul'.[87]

This was faith with the flim-flam of a fairground, people were amazed and aghast in the services. Amidst the singing Sarah claimed:

I have been speaking with Jesus himself. He is coming to the world again shortly. You don't think that I can cast out Devils but I can [cries of 'Yes, you can']. There are wonderful things at hand. Christ is coming to the world. He is going to do wonderful things through me. Do not fear me but fear the Lord . . . You must believe in Jesus . . . If you only have faith in Him, He will receive you . . . The second coming of Christ is coming near . . . [88]

Sarah then collapsed. The preacher, on his knees with his head in his hands, commanded the congregation to sing 'A welsoch Chwi Ef?' ('Did you see Him?'). Several people publicly confessed their sins while others saw the presence of Christ.[89] At Maesypica Farm, Cwm-twrch, when Sarah Jones saw 'a thousand angels', it was claimed that several people 'spoke in tongues', that a portrait of Christ appeared on the ceiling and that the Devil had been cast out of a man.[90]

One newspaper caused great offence to her followers by claiming that in a spate of spiritual excitement she had climbed the garden hedge to levitate to heaven, only to fall prostrate in the onion patch.[91] The Revd Evan R. Hughes of Taff's Well was also scathing in his condemnation of Mrs Jones. But Seth Joshua, speaking at

Swansea's Central Hall, stated: 'I believe in the depths of my heart this woman is blessed by the Spirit of God. So you will kindly pass it on to our friends. Don't ask them to see Mrs Sarah Jones. Ask them to come and meet the Lord.'[92]

Given the intensity of millenarian belief in 1904–6, it is not surprising that some people became mentally unstable. A man from Llanelli was confined to the lunatic asylum in December 1904. At Capel Mair Baptist Chapel he prayed for the minister and the deacons who, he insisted, were 'addicted to drink'. He refused to work at the tinplate mill and, on God's instructions, prayed for the manager, the company and 'the spiritual welfare of the clerical staff'. He then prayed until 4 a.m. for his wife to be saved. In all, sixteen people were confined in the Joint Counties Lunatic Asylum in Carmarthen by the early part of 1905 because of religious delusions and thirty people were confined in the North Wales Asylum at Denbigh.[93] Owen Jones, a twenty-year-old from Egryn, was confined in the North Wales Asylum on 7 March 1905 because of 'religious excitement'. He had seen the Holy Ghost in the form of smoke, changing 'into the shape of a dog'. His neurosis did not seem out of place in the area in 1905, but his behaviour did, for like the dog, he bit people. William Jones, a nineteen-year-old Calvinistic Methodist from Porthmadog, joined him in the asylum because of 'the Religious Revival and too much reading'. William saw visions of doves and devils, and heard the voices of heavenly choirs that sang to him and urged him to be born-again. As he was not, he could not get himself into the proper spiritual state, and in his anger he became a danger to all around him.[94]

When wonders did take place their credibility depended on the authority and conviction of those who reported them. Whether it was a magical issue or a mental illness was a matter of judgement. It was a fine line between sanity and insanity. When people talked to God, they were praying, but when God talked to them they might be schizophrenic. This was the tragic tale of Caradog Prichard's mother who was confined in the mental hospital in Denbigh. The revival was one of the forces that unhinged her. Yet the voices that spoke to her, not just 'Un Nos Ola Leuad' (One Moonlit Night), but incessantly, insistently, also speak in Caradog's work. 'Yr

Anwylyd', 'Arglwyddes Hardd', 'Yr Hendduw', and 'Brenhines y Llyn Du' all spoke in the mental torture chamber of Caradog's head – just because he was not paranoid, it did not mean they were not out to get him as well.[95]

Many visions were internalised, highly personal experiences. But Mary Jones, a thirty-five-year-old smallholder at a bleak farmhouse at Islawrffordd, Egryn, between Barmouth and Harlech in Merionethshire, was different. Mary actually inspired paranormal phenomena to be visible to others. The name of the farmhouse where Mary eked out a hardscrabble existence with her husband is appropriate – 'Islawrffordd' (beneath the road). Mary was representative of all the groups who would come to prominence in the millenarian world turned upside down of 1904–6 – the poorest, the disadvantaged, the forgotten, the overlooked, the lonely and the forsaken. Even more relevant and obviously, she was a woman. It was appropriate that the Man of Sorrows appeared to console her, for Mary was no stranger to hard times and bereavement. Within a few weeks of each other her young son, her sister, her father and mother had died. For solace she turned to God. Scripture had healing words but the minister's sermons did not always provide her with the balm to soothe and so to release some of the tension from the tempest in her head, she began to preach.[96]

Whenever she preached, strange lights appeared nearby. Sometimes, too, mysterious stars could be seen in the vicinity of her chapel at Egryn. At Christmas 1904, the area around Egryn resembled Bethlehem at Christ's birth, for a star seemed to be permanently hovering above. People sighted it on 5, 8, 15 and 22 December 1904, on 2, 5, 13, 16 and 31 January, on 9, 10, 11, 12, 13, 14, 20 and 21 February, on 4, 5, 10, 13, 15 and 25 March, on 13, 15 and 20 April, and 25 and 27 May 1905. Eyewitnesses described it as like an 'Auroral Arch', a 'Black Bottle', 'the Prince of Wales feathers', a 'Shooting Cap', the 'Chapel Roof Arcs', the 'Northern Flashes', 'the Rainbow Bottle'. The lights of these stars were 'gleaming and scintillating'. Neighbouring villages were not be outdone by the seers of Egryn. People in Tywyn, Bryncrug, Ty'n-y-Drain, Pwllheli and Llanfair also claimed to see lights in the skies at night. Stars even appeared in the eyes of people as far east as Wrexham.

When Mary Jones went to preach at Ystrad in the Rhondda on 25 May 1905, the Revd E. W. Evans confirmed seeing lights towards Penrhys Hill. So too did Dr R. J. Morgan when Mary held a meeting at Libanus in the Rhondda on 27 May.

As in biblical Bethlehem, in Egryn local shepherds followed the star and wise men came on pilgrimage (but probably not on camel-back). The wise men had been sent by the *Daily Mirror* to investigate the 'Welsh Seer and Her Star', the 'Woman with a Halo', and the 'Welsh Miracle'.[97] Letters about the lights flowed into the *Mirror's* post box, as they also did to local papers the *Caernarfon and Denbigh Herald*, *Yr Herald Cymraeg* and appropriately, remembering the star, people wrote on their enlightenment to *Seren Gomer* and *Y Goleuad*. Questions raged about the star's origins:

Is it supernatural?
Is it a sign from Heaven?
Is it marsh gas or 'will-o'-the-wisp?
Is it electric or St Elmo's light?
Is it an astral body attempting to materialise?
Is it due to radium?
Is it 'imagined' by Mrs Jones and 'induced' in others by hypnotism?
Is it the planet Venus?
Is it the Aurora Borealis?
Is it the Fata Morgana?

The sceptics, of course, immediately asked, 'Is it a trick?' Whatever it was, as religious fervour declined sightings became fewer. In heavens below, all paradises are lost. Just as Evan Roberts had gone with the wind and 1905 drew to a close, the lights all went out in Merionethshire.

Christians were relatively united in explaining the cause of the enlightenment of places such as Egryn. R. B. Jones in *Rent Heavens* (1931) put some of the causes down to the La Niña's effect on the weather, but the real cause he insisted was that 'the sense of the Lord's presence was everywhere. It pervaded, nay it created the spiritual atmosphere'. Gwili Jenkins, in his sermon 'Y Sŵn o'r Nef' (the Sound from Heaven), commented 'wedi blynyddoedd o sŵn y ddaear, y mae'r sŵn o'r nef yn ein tir drachefn. Nid rhaid mwy ofyn ystyr y sŵn seraffaidd nefol . . . canys ni a'i clywsom ef ein hunain . . . Yr Arglwydd a wnaeth i ni bethau mawrion, am hynny yr ydym yn llawen' (after years of the sounds of the earth, the sounds of Heaven have returned to our lands. There is no need to ask the meaning of 'the heavenly seraphical sounds' . . . for we have heard it ourselves . . . the Lord has done great things to us, and we are joyful).[98] D. P. Williams, of Pen-y-groes, one of the founders of the worldwide Apostolic church remembered:

> During 1904–05, God's visitation to our village was like unto a moral earthquake shaking the neighbourhood to its foundation. Sinners trembled with fear at God's justice . . . We witnessed the sublimest manifestations of the Holy Ghost with tongues of fire. They were days of wonderment and amazement, bearing as they did, the impress of His Divinity.[99]

Blithe spirits: ghosts, ghouls and Gothic Wales

9pm, 30 September, Sunday 1917

I went and sat on the step of the garden door – a still, autumnal evening, all so lovely and peaceful, and there I wept. And when I came in I sat down and prayed and then I decided to try for a script. Instantly it came – Fred Myers, a message from Christopher and oh! so convincing to me, so suiting himself. It brought such a vivid feeling of his personality and outlook, of a 'not-me' youth and gaiety, so that at the end I could with a laughing face fling, as it were, my arms around him and say 'Yes, yes, of course, oh darling how glorious to see you.'

It lifted me out of all the incongruous atmosphere of sadness. There was my radiant boy beside me, full of life and spirits and pleasure and love and determination to cheer me up! This he has completely succeeded in doing, God bless him, and I still feel 'all joyful within'.

Quoted in Peter Lord (ed.), *Between Two Worlds: the Diary of Winifred Coombe Tenant 1909–1924* (Aberystwyth, 2011), p. 233. Under the name Mrs Willet, Winifred Coombe Tenant was one of the most prolific spirit mediums of the 1920s and 1930s. Fred Myers was one of the spirit conduits for her son Christopher.

This is the saddest story I have ever read. The 'radiant boy', Christopher Tennant had died in action in France on 3 September, more than three weeks before his mother Winifred Coombe Tenant recorded this meeting with her son in her remarkable diaries. Winifred was no stranger to sorrow. Her infant daughter, Daphne, had also died. From this experience began periods of deep depression and a life-long interest in the spirit world. She became one of the most successful spirit mediums in British history. She literally, in Peter Lord's evocative phrase, lived 'between two worlds'. She was not the only one.

'Is there anyone there?' The question, more anticipatory than interrogatory, was invariably followed by a 'knock, knock' or a loud 'thump'. It is the quintessentially English farcical parlour scene of the late Victorian Pooters vainly trying to summon the spirits of their dearly departed. But such scenes were also common in Wales as the cloth-capped Fausts in their kitchens, 'valiantly', as Percy Bysshe Shelley wrote, were 'pursuing hopes of high-talk with the departed dead.'[100]

Opprobrium and oppression have characterised the history of spiritualism from the mid-nineteenth century. Rationalists and religious leaders criticised what they insisted was neither a religion nor a rational pastime. Developments in geology, evolution, historical dating techniques, biblical criticism, chemistry, biology and a host of 'ologies' seemed to have undermined the capacity of people to believe in the world of the spirits. Christians condemned what they considered to be the base superstitious practice of Spiritualism. Yet, for many people, scientific developments resulted in a deep-seated feeling of unease. God had been dismissed from his universe, but his absence had left a yawning chasm.[101]

Spiritualism offered comfort to those people who feared such cosmic loneliness. The most famous widow of the Victorian era, Queen Victoria herself practised 'table-turning' to see if she could recontact and reconnect with her beloved Albert.[102] More profoundly perhaps, spiritualism seemed to provide a focal point, for all those folklore and folk beliefs in the supernatural that had survived for centuries despite religious reformations and industrial revolutions. Spiritualism was also championed by a number of people who provided it with the most valuable thing for a belief – credibility. The socialist pioneer Robert Owen (1771–1858) played a crucial role in the dissemination of millenarian-tinted spiritualism to the labour movement.[103] Few of his followers would have expected their venerable leader to proclaim: 'I am not only convinced that there is no deception with truthful mediums, in these proceedings, but that they are destined to effect, at this period, the greatest moral revolution in the character and condition of the human race.'[104]

Mesmerism, phrenology and spiritualism were just as intriguing to Alfred Russel Wallace, one of the greatest scientists raised in Wales, as they were to Robert Owen. Wallace believed that evolution suggested that the universe had a higher purpose, for natural selection could not explain intelligence or morality. In his *The World of Life* (1911) he proposed that the spiritual realm of humanity could not have come about by natural selection alone, and that the origins of the spiritual nature must originate 'in the unseen universe of spirit'. Whilst his advocacy undoubtedly assisted spiritualism, it proved to the detriment of Wallace's scientific reputation. Few scientists, it seems, at the turn of the twentieth century had his curiosity to capture the natural history of the paranormal.[105]

After detailed investigations, Wallace became convinced that some phenomena at séances were genuine. For Wallace, Spiritualism provided a scientific challenge, the possibility to discover other dimensions, the desire to explain the material and non-material, the natural and the supernatural worlds.[106] In 1874, he visited the spirit photographer Frederik Hudson, who produced a photograph of Wallace with the spirit of his deceased mother. Despite the fact that Hudson's other photographs were exposed as fakes, Wallace declared: 'I see no escape from the conclusion that some spiritual being, acquainted with my mother's various aspects during life, produced these recognisable impressions on the plate.'[107]

It is an ironic fact that those technologies of modernism that were meant to discredit spiritualism, themselves became haunted.[108] There were ghost trains, photographs froze ghostly images, whilst phonographs captured the spirit voices in darkened rooms.[109] The magic lantern and the cinema screen presented images of ghosts that flickered and fluttered, creating the illusion that they possessed that quality of conscious life – animation. Visually, if not literally, they could raise the dead. Spirits and science seemed to be in accord. The wireless, the telegraph, the telephone, the pictures (when they talked) could move voices and images through the air and displace them in time as well as place. One star of the silver screen actually became a famous ghost. Port Talbot-born Peg Entwhistle committed suicide by jumping from the letter 'H' in the Hollywood sign in Los Angeles. Thereafter, many people claim to have seen a worried looking lady wandering underneath whilst the scent of gardenia, Peg's favourite perfume, pervaded the area.

Not all people with a religious training were antagonistic to spiritualism. Several sought to answer Jeremiah's question, 'Is there balm in Gilead?' The Unitarian minister and school teacher Rees Cribyn Jones (1841–1927) had a profound interest in spirits that did not have a biblical provenance. 'Busloads of people' reportedly attended the Congregational chapel of David William Richards (1893–1949) at Porthcawl. He won a prize at the National Eisteddfod for an essay speculating on *The Philosophy of Immortality in Light of Recent Spiritualist Theories*. The congregation tolerated his speculations on immortal matters, but cast him and his family out of the manse when he stood as a Labour candidate in the University of Wales constituency in 1929. His speculations ended when he took his own life after the suicide of one, possibly two, of his sons. The much-travelled and many-named Windham Thomas Wyndham-Quin (1841–1926), 4th Earl of Dunraven and Mount-Earl in the Irish Peerage and 2nd Baron Kenny of the United Kingdom, also speculated on the survival of the soul after the body's death in *Experiences in Spiritualism* (1871). So too did the judge and MP for Denbighshire Sir Charles James Watkin Williams (1828–84) in *An Essay on the Philosophy of Evidence* (1855). Williams had the perspicacity and perception to suggest that life after death was a more complicated matter than some suggested. The richest man in Wales, John Patrick Crichton Stuart, third marques of Bute (1847–1900), was also attracted to spiritualism as well as Judaism, Islam and Buddhism.

The death of a loved one, and the wish to recover the lost companionship were often the trigger that resulted in the career of a number of remarkable mediums. After the death of his sister Connie, Alec

Harris (1897–1974), who had been brought up in the Nonconformist traditions of the Rhondda, entered a career as a brilliant physical medium in the Whitchurch area of Cardiff. One astonished sitter at one of Harris's meetings remarked: 'The materialised people came out of the cabinet sometimes two or three at a time. On that amazing night, about twenty fully-materialised forms greeted us and spoke with us, quite naturally. After a while you forgot you were conversing with so-called "dead" people.' The editor of the *Psychic News*, Maurice Barbanell, said of Harris's mediumship that the 'spirit forms not only show themselves in good red light, but they also hold sustained conversations, after having walked about ten feet from the cabinet.' The spirits conjured forth by Harris were undoubtedly a cosmopolitan group for they included ancient Romans, Greeks, Tibetans and, inevitably perhaps, his sister Connie. His wife Louie captured some of the goings-on in the remarkable memoir *They Walked Among Us* (1980).[110]

The mediumship of the Loughor ex-miner Jack Webber (1907–40) was even more remarkable.[111] Before audiences of up to 500 people he levitated objects, moved tables and trumpets, produced ectoplasm and spirit voices, transmitted spiritual healing and spirit gifts or 'apports'. In a credible series of photographs he is seen covered in foul-looking ectoplasm. He had a host of ghostly spirit guides that included Malodar (a healer), Talgar, the Revd John Boarden (his great uncle), a Dr Millar and a Professor Dale. For the sake of posterity, the record company Decca recorded the bump and thump and ghostly goings-on at a Webber séance. His activities operated in that curious area where rationalism, displaced religious sensibility, and the circus act were uncomfortably conjoined. Another celebrated Welsh medium was Evan Powell, who got Arthur Conan Doyle in touch with his deceased brother via the spirit of a Native American Indian, Black Hawk. Mediumship could be as much a bane as a blessing. Both nice and nasty spirits had their faults. Those who had a banal self-absorption in real life relayed boring and bland news from the afterlife. Whilst those bullies and bruisers in their daily lives appeared to threaten dark forces and danger from the great beyond. Which character appeared, friendly or foul, was beyond the medium's control.

Women too could summon spirits and speak to and have the dead speak through them. Winifred Coombe Tenant, through the nom de plume Mrs Willet, created a remarkable series of spirit scripts from a host of different people.[112] So, too, for a period in the 1870s, did Georgina Wildon (1837–1914), the campaigner against the lunacy laws and celebrated litigant, the daughter of another Welsh landed gentry family. Doris May Fisher Stokes (1920–87), a member of the Women's Royal Air Force in Port Talbot during the Second World War, as a jest attended the local spiritual church. Grief at the death of her five-month-old son, and the lack of consolation in the Church of England faith in which she had been raised, seemed to awaken her innate talents as a medium. In 1949 she was officially recognised as a practising clairaudient medium by the Spiritualists' National Union. She toured Britain, Australia and conducted ceremonies on three occasions to capacity audiences at the Sydney Opera House. She related the experience in her first volume of autobiography, *Voices in My Ear*, appropriately written with the help of a ghost writer.[113] The great travel writer Norman Lewis did not need such help for he related the ghostly presences attracted to their house by his spiritualist parents in his autobiography *Jackdaw Cake*.[114]

Certain places at certain times saw a fracture in psychic dimension that strengthened the appeal of spiritualism. Spiritual churches were established at the turn of the twentieth century in Bangor, Wrexham, Prestatyn, Llandysul, Cardiff and Newport. In the 1890s Llanelli was reported to have been a veritable hotbed of spiritualism. But the Welsh capital of spiritualism was probably Merthyr Tydfil. Harry Edwards in *The Mediumship of Jack Webber* (1940?) noted that 'almost every other person one came across in south Wales was hot on the subject of Spiritualism'.[115] For Jessie Penn-Lewis the defining year was 1906. That year, when the fires of the religious revival had begun to cool, marked 'the beginning of the reign of the beast' when Satan was working in retaliation against the events of the 1904–6 revival.[116] The influential Welsh Baptist minister R. B. Jones (1869–1933) also warned of the dangers of 1906: 'In these days we need to be very wary, for there will be increasingly days of supernaturalism; much of the divine restraint upon Satan will be withdrawn, and he, knowing that his time is short, will redouble his efforts to deceive and destroy.'[117]

The First World War was another period of heightened sensitivity, loss, loneliness and bereavement as death took the youthful, the virile and the valiant. Trade boomed for clairvoyants, palmists, teacup-readers and anyone who could foresee and foretell the future. Robert Graves in *Goodbye to All That* (1929) noted how the people of Harlech were susceptible to spiritualism in the war years.[118] In south Wales Drusilla Markham, Alice 'Gipsy' Smith and Professor and Madame Virago were busy throughout the war.[119] In 1917 Rose Barnes of Swansea was imprisoned for 'making statements likely to interfere with the success of His Majesty's Forces'. She had predicted an explosion at the west Wales munitions factory.[120] Like Madame St Leonard, of Coldstream Street, Llanelli, such people took over some of the functions that had previously been performed by the wise man and the white witch. In the cracks between religion and rationalism people chose to place their faith in the paranormal. The Second World War saw a re-emergence of such tensions. The witch Doreen Edith Smith (1922–99) was working as a clairvoyant in Cardiff in 1941. She later became a high priestess of a coven and produced some major works of a Wicca religion, including the enduring version of the most important *The Charge of the Goddess*.[121] Dylan Thomas had an affair with Ruth Wynn Owen in 1942. Part of her charm for Dylan was her fey north Welsh mysticism that later became more marked as she developed into one of Britain's leading 'white' witches, heading the Plant y Fran branch of the Wicca.[122]

Blithe spirits conjured forth by the mediumships of Evan Powell, Jack Webber and Alec Harris were relatively benign and beneficent. But other spirits uninvited and unheralded by a medium were positively baneful and baleful. Poltergeists, those psychopaths of the psychic world, often created havoc around Wales.[123] Clerics, especially those within the Church, were often called upon to rid people of these troublesome and terrifying presences. So troublesome was the poltergeistic presence in Mrs Edwards's house in Campbell Road, Llandybïe, that the attendance of three clerics, the Revd Phylip Evans, Revd D. Davies and Revd Canon D. W. Thomas, was needed to exorcise it. Even so, the outnumbered spirit, still put up a stern fight throwing chairs, tables and clothing. The local holy trinity were reported to be 'terrified' when the spirit added kleptomania to its capabilities and stole the vicar's hat and gloves.[124] Throughout January and March 1917, the *Western Mail* and local newspapers related the activities of the Kidwelly ghost. J. Arthur Hill, author of *Religion and Modern Psychology* and *New Evidence in Psychical Research*, visited the house on behalf of the Society for Psychical Research and declared that the ghost was genuine. A week later, the ghost was either annoyed with Hill, or in a celebratory mood, for it threw a chair.[125] Non Davies, a soloist at a concert in Craig-y-nos in the winter of 1928–9, met the ghost of the former owner, the world-famous opera singer Adelina Patti.[126]

Those spirits who made their appearance in the years 1870–1945 were certainly a diverse and disorderly lot.[127] There were at least thirty-one poltergeists who made their demented presence felt as they proved determined to display their powers of telekinesis. There were sightings of White Ladies (thirty-two), Grey Ladies (eight), Green Ladies (six), and Ladies in Black (nine). When, in 1902, the ghostly shape of a Lady in White appeared at the Glyncorrwg mine, Glamorgan, more than 300 miners refused to work. Hugh Dalton saw the ghost of his friend Rupert Brooke in 1921. There were headless ghosts, spirits of monks, nuns and other clergy, ghostly apparitions of people who had once lived (privateer Harry Morgan frequented many séances in Wales and the USA), there were phantom armies and soldiers, ghostly outlines that resembled humanoid shapes, and headless horsemen and horses and carriages. The ghost of the local vicar, Revd John Ponsonby Lucas, who served at Rhosilly from 1855–1898, is still said to race on horseback along the beach. Occasionally, he races against the ghost of a local squire, Mansell, who thunders along the sands on stormy nights, in his coach and horses, in search of his lost fortune. The equestrian skills of Welsh ghosts was legendary. There were more ambulating ghosts and a range of anthropomorphic spirits who took the form of 'y gwyllgi' (Dogs of Darkness), cats, horses, bulls, cows, calves, pigs, birds, mice and a host of other fauna. One of the hounds of hell was seen at Colwinston in 1938. Parishioners in Disserth church in Breconshire were terrified when a spirit in the form of 'a raving mad bull with bloodshot eyes and clouds of breath coming out of his nostrils' thundered down the aisles in the 1890s.

There were amorous ghosts (wicked Lady Jeffrey who haunted Llandrindod in the 1910s), drunken ghosts (the ghost of 'Tom the Lund' haunted an Abergavenny cider still), and there were helpful ghosts (a woman from Llanfair in Cardiganshire claimed that she had received £500 from a ghost in the 1930s). The morality of spirits was often higher than that of earthly people. At Broughton in Flintshire in the 1930s, several courting couples who dared to venture into the local lover's lane, a tree-lined avenue known as the 'Old Warren', reported that they had been chased back out by the apparition of a disapproving clergyman. At Northop near Mold in the 1930s, the Revd J. J. Morgan saw a ghost about to attack a courting couple with a knife. When the voyeuristic vicar cried out in warning, the ghostly apparition disappeared. Without the excuse of the ghostly tales, one wonders how he would have explained his presence. There were even musical ghosts. The spirit of Jenny Jones, who had won a prize at the Cardiff National Eisteddfod in 1883, was reputed to return to her home in Tonna to play her harp late at night.

Some places acquired more than their share of ghosts. When Dunraven Castle was converted into a military hospital there were reports in 1917 and 1918 of a lady in blue who walked the corridors. St Donat's, further along the coast, had four ghostly presences. Yet the place that could lay claim to being the most haunted in Wales was probably Llanwddyn. When workmen arrived there in the early 1890s to begin work on the dam that would flood the valley and deliver water to the Liverpool City Corporation, there were no fewer than thirteen (unlucky for some) ghosts in the valley. Ysbryd Cynon had been trapped in a bottle in a large stone by a conjurer in the eighteenth century, and had remained entrapped until the navvies arrived to commence work. When they blew up the stone, a live frog emerged. The frog apparently left the navvies bewitched, bothered and bewildered for the locals insisted it was the previously imprisoned spirit intent on revenge.

Ghosts of the period 1870–1945 were a curious mix. There were the long-deceased, often anonymous, sometimes celebrities, who still clanked their chains, carried their heads and charged aimlessly around on horseback. But there were also the recently dead, clearly remembered in the communities that they had inhabited in life, and which they now traumatised in death. In the 1880s Harry Parry of much haunted Llanwddyn was dragged through the local mill-pond by the ghost of his former drinking partner John Kynaston and then dumped in the churchyard at a particular grave. Here the spirit's 'last mission' was performed and the terrified Harry returned home. His wife accepted his story because on his arrival home 'he smelt strongly of some sulphurous matter'.[128] Ghosts were problematic. Scientifically and theologically they did not seem to fit and yet, as so many witnesses insist, they existed. The ghosts of loved ones who died far away from home would call by just to say goodbye; sailors were seen before the news of their drowning was received by relatives; soldiers were spotted before the post office boy read out the telegram that told monolingual Welsh mothers in cold English of their son's death.

Angels had a biblical pedigree that gave them a credibility denied to ghosts. In literature and art they abounded. William Jones of Dolwyddelan noted that these angels were ever present on earth:

Y mae angylion yn yr oedfa yma heddyw, a phe byddai i bechadur ddechreu edifarhâu a galaru am ei bechod, a gofyn pa beth i'w wneud er bod yn gadwedig, brysiant am y cyntaf i gario y newydd da i'r nefoedd.

(There are angels present in this congregation today, and if a sinner begins to repent and grieve for his sins, and asks what to do to be saved, they will rush to carry the good news to heaven.)[129]

When Morris Hughes of Cwm Corryn, Llanaelhaearn, died in 1875 two yellow birds that he had hand-reared came to flap at his window to aid his soul's passing. Sir John Rhŷs related that 'the little birds are believed to have been angels'. In the Carmarthenshire village of Pen-y-groes in 1912 a statistically minded observer saw 'a thousand angels'. The credulous people of London were traumatised when angels appeared on the clouds above the city. The angels were an astral projection produced by the Clydach-based inventor Harry

Grindell-Matthews, the creator of the 'death-ray'. These winged, haloed 'oll yn eu gynnau gwynion' (all in their white gowns) angels were obviously more suited to the prim late Victorians than were the naked, cheerful cherubs of medieval art. The functions of angels had also changed. They were now less the fallen angels, or guardian angels, as angelic go-betweens between heaven and earth.

The most remarkable angelic sighting took place in 1914, at the battle of Mons when, against all the odds, the heavily outnumbered, retreating Allied forces, stopped the German advance. Many eye-witnesses claimed that supernatural forces assisted the British troops. One soldier saw 'a long line of shapes, with a shining about them'. Others saw a line of 'shining beings between the two armies'. The redoubtable Frank Richards who was present in the action recalled in his *Old Soldiers Never Die* (1964):

> We retired all night with fixed bayonets, many sleeping as they were marching along. If any angels were seen on the retirement, as the newspaper accounts said they were, they were seen that night. March, march for hour after hour, without no halt: we were now breaking into the fifth day of continuous marching with practically no sleep in between . . . Stevens said 'There's a fine castle there, see?' pointing to one side of the road. But there was nothing there. Very nearly everyone was seeing things, we were all so dead beat.[130]

Moving lights, imaginary arches and fine castles were soon joined in the retelling by visions of angels, which appeared in the sky to hold back the advancing Germans. It was, of course, an enormous boost to the morale of the troops. Here was visual and visceral confirmation of what many ministers of religion had insisted.[131] God was on the side of the British.

The story of the Angel of Mons, as do all stories, had its origins in the particular confluence of circumstances that came together in the heady atmosphere of 1914. At a time of profound anxiety and terror, outlandish stories were common.[132] There were spy scares, Russian troops were seen in Cardiff, there were stories that German troops committed horrific brutalities against children and women civilians, they were even reportedly burning corpses to obtain oil.[133] In the general atmosphere of paranoia and panic, the mystical and horror writer 'the sinister genius' Arthur Machen published a short story entitled 'The Bowmen' in the London newspaper *The Evening News* on 29 September 1914.[134] In the story, phantom Welsh bowmen who had fought at the battle of Agincourt return to assist British troops in the First World War. Many troops also felt this sense of following a militaristic tradition – that they were part of history. Both David Jones and Robert Graves noted how they had a visceral feeling that they were accompanied by long-dead soldiers who also fought in France.[135] David Jones in *In Parenthesis* (1937) recalled the continuity of soldiers in battle and their reincarnations:

> I built a shit-house for Artaxerxes,
> I was a spear in Bolin's hand
> That made waste King Pellam's Land.[136]

Through a complex process of transference, Machen's ghostly soldiers had become the angel of Mons. Panic and paranoia partly explain the process, but the role of the intelligence services cannot be underplayed. Here, for once, the conspiracy theory of history is more credible than the cock-up explanation. In May 1915, Arthur Machen tried to set the record straight, but any attempt to lessen the impact of such an inspiring story was considered treasonable. The propaganda value of angelic assistance was far greater than anything that ghostly bowmen could offer. As the *Lusitania* went down, and the zeppelins began their attacks on the Western Front and the south-east of England, people wanted to believe that super-natural forces were on their side. One soldier who undoubtedly believed in the angels was Private Robert Cleaver, of the First Cheshire Regiment, who signed this affidavit for George Hazelhurst, a Justice of the Peace in Flint:

> I, Robert Cleaver (No. 10515), a private in the 1st Cheshire Regiment of His Majesty's Army, make an oath and say as follows: – That I personally was at Mons and saw the vision of Angels with my own eyes.

Sworn at Kinmel Park, in the County of Flint, this 20th day of August, 1915. Before me, George S. Hazelhurst, one of his Majesty's Justices of the Peace acting for the County of Flint.[137]

When you believe, you can see angels. When you believe enough, you can even see higher-ranking members of the Christian celestial hierarchy. At Capel-y-Ffin in the Llanthony valley in Monmouthshire, the Virgin Mary was seen on four occasions between August and September 1880. The place she chose to materialise was a field beside the monastery belonging to Father Ignatius. Ignatius, whose real name was Joseph Lester Lyne, was an eccentric clergyman with extreme views on monasticism. His followers were regularly flogged, spat upon and had to beg for their food which they had to grow. Ignatius had ambitions to restore spiritualism into the Church of England.

The Virgin first appeared on 30 August to a group of choirboys and then disappeared into a bush. On 4 September the bush was 'aglow with a mysterious light' in which the form of a woman and a man in a loincloth could be seen. As the figures met, they vanished. Daniel Maguire said that an angel touched him and cured his headache. On 5 September, Mary returned in a 'flickering light'. On 15 September, the Octave of her Nativity, the Virgin made a dramatic visitation that was witnessed by Ignatius himself during a severe rainstorm that swept over the valley:

> The whole heavens and mountains broke forth in bulging circles of light, circles pushing out from circles – the light poured upon our faces and the buildings where we stood and in the centre circle stood a most Majestic Heavenly Form, robed in flowing drapery. The Form was gigantic, but seemed to be reduced to human size as it approached. The Figure stood sideways, facing the Holy Bush. The Vision was most distinct and the details were very clear: but it was in the 'twinkling of an eye'.[138]

Despite the reputed healing powers of the 'Holy Bush' and attempts of some enterprising hoteliers to exploit them, the area never became a site of pilgrimage as did Lourdes in France or Knock in Ireland where the Holy Mother was also seen in the mid-nineteenth century.

By the 1920s the buildings that had been built by the faith of Ignatius and his followers, but with little practical building skill, were almost derelict.[139]

Fairies, like ghosts, were agencies that could work for both good and evil purposes. Some people refused to believe in the fairies, even if they existed.[140] But others obviously fervently believed in the presence of fairies amongst them. That remarkable chronicler of Wales and the weird, the wonderfully named Wirt Sikes, the American consul, considered that 'among the vulgar in Wales, the belief in fairies is less nearly extinct than casual observers would be likely to suppose.'[141] Thirty years later 'the loneliest man in Wales', Jonathan Ceredig Davies, discovered that the 'vulgar' were still away with the fairies.[142] The author Byron Rogers, recalled of his childhood in mid-twentieth century Carmarthen: 'our neighbour each night put out a saucer of milk to appease the fairies – just as her mother had done before her and her mother before her. And each morning the milk had been drunk.'[143] But then they did live in the shadow 'of the old oak': 'a long finger of deadwood, that stood in concrete and the council routed the road around it, because of a prophecy, associated with the magician Merlin, that when the old oak fell so would the town supposedly by flood.'[144]

The photographer John Thomas (1838–1905) included a number of photographs of fairies or sprites in his remarkable collection assembled over a lifetime snapping in north Wales. In one photograph above a sick person's bed, the fairies seem to play, or taunt the bedridden figure.[145] Fairies not only lured the elderly into their dancing circles, they also stole 'lovely children', away from their parents, often leaving cantankerous 'changelings' in their place to terrorise the traumatised parents. Sir John Rhŷs in *Celtic Folklore* (1901) recalled that the physically deformed dwarf Elis Bach of Nant Gwrtheyrn, with his piercing squeaky voice, was widely believed to have been a changeling. When no child was substituted it is possible that the fairies became a convenient excuse for infanticide. An old woman living in a small house near Ynys Geinon, in the Ystradfellte area, in the 1870s was rumoured to spend seven days, seven hours, and seven minutes with the fairies every year and was paid in gold for every child she could steal for them. Wirt

Sikes considered that such reports of infant abductions by fairies around Wales were 'innumerable'. John Rhŷs refers to traditions, which he said were still current in the 1880s amongst sailors on the western and northern coasts of offshore fairy islands that would disappear when a sailor attempted to land. The inhabitants of these lands were said to frequent markets at Laugharne, Milford Haven and Pwllheli.[146] Fairies were blamed for the price inflation experienced at the market at Cardigan in 1868 (an explanation of inflation more credible than that proposed by some economists).[147]

Of all the supernatural beings in Wales, the ones most feared were the fairies. There is something almost comedic about the headless ghost clanking its chains – until, presumably, one met one on a dark winter's night. But there was malice and malevolence about the fairies. 'Y Tylwyth Teg' (the fair relatives) were anything but. They were evil. Occasionally they would bless a favoured person with a gift of gold, but more often they would blight humanity.[148] Historians have shown that the persecution of witches in Wales was relatively rare, a practice imported from England in the seventeenth century.[149] But fairy faith, however, ran deeper back into the nation's formative myths. In this it was similar to other Celtic societies, particularly the Gaelic-speaking communities in Scotland and Ireland.[150] Under a variety of different names, 'Y Tylwyth Teg', 'Gwyn ap Nudd', 'Plant Rhys Ddwfn', Welsh fairies were particularly perilous to lone travellers, beautiful people, and the family home. The remedies believed to be efficacious against them were as many and various as in the Gaelic lands, ranging from special prayers to the cementing of scythe blades point-up into chimneys in order to prevent fairies from entering by that route.[151]

This mystical and magical Wales proved inspirational for a number of people. It was to the myths that many such as William Morris, Edward Burne-Jones, David Jones, Lord Howard de Walden and Philip Arnold Heseltine (Peter Warlock) turned for their national identity.[152] The writers Mary Gladys Webb (1881–1927), especially in *The Sprig of Joy* (1917) and *Precious Bane* (1924), and Hilda Campbell Vaughan (1892–1985), in *The Battle to the Weak* (1925) and *Harvest Home* (1936), revealed the strength of magical and mystical beliefs in Wales 'far away: not long ago'.[153] Dylan Thomas in a series of short stories such as 'The Burning Baby' and 'The School for Witches' revealed a dark, grim, bestial, elemental underworld in Wales where the supernatural was more potent than the natural world. As he explained to his friend Trevor Hughes: 'I wished I loved the human race, but ghouls, vampires, women-rippers . . . pass by the window, going God knows where or why, in a dream up and down the hill.'

The undoubted master of the gothic and the ghoulish in Wales was Arthur Machen (1863–1947). In *The Great God Pan* (1894) and *The Hill of Dreams* (1907) the earth's most horrid progeny, creatures of darkness, emerge into everyday life. The real explanation for the darkness in his tales is the sinister and brooding Welsh landscape in which he spent his formative years. In *The Great God Pan*, *The Three Imposters* (1895) and *The Hill of Dreams* (1907) Wales is the locale for the pagan darkness, with something evil in every wood-pile. An underworld of insatiable sexuality, satyrs, nymphs and 'a tribe of little people four foot in height, accustomed to live in darkness, who inhabited the area before the Celt set foot in Britain and who flourish in it still . . . This folk . . . dwells in remote and secret places, and celebrates foul mysteries on savage hills.[154] As one of his characters once noted: 'There are sacraments of evil as well as of good about us . . . it is possible that man may sometimes return on the track of evolution, and it is my belief that an awful lore is not yet dead.'[155]

'Some enchanted evening': magic and the pursuit of happiness

'Wel', meddai Tom yn barod,
'Mi gefais wersi hynod,
Pan ar fy nhaith i Ben-y-bryn
Daeth ebol gwyn yr Hafod,
Ebolyn cynta'r flwyddyn,
I'm golwg, do mor sydyn,
A'i ben-ôl welwn, er fy mraw,
Wel drwg a ddaw i ddilyn.'

('Wel, said Tom readily,
I had a remarkable lesson,
When on my journey to Pen-y-bryn
The white foal of the Hafod,
The first foal of the year,
Suddenly came into my view,
And his behind I saw, for all my fears,
Evil will follow me now).

Anon. in 'Ofergoelion' [Superstitions],
Cymru, XII (68) (1898).

In the early twentieth century, just as the 'mastodons', the great preachers of the Welsh pulpit 'had gone the way of the dinosaurs' so too did belief begin to wane in the power of the wizards, warlocks and witches of Wales.[156] Thaumatomanes were few and far between after the Harries's of Cwrt y Cadno, John Savidge of Llangurig and Mary Berllan Biter of Pennant had gone wherever magicians used to go.[157] Behind the sky. On the other side of the rain. Infrequent fires were burning, cauldrons bubbling and the incantations were silenced as fewer went about their dark materials and business. Double, double, toil and trouble no more. Although Jessi Penn-Lewis in *The War on the Saints* (1912) had declared that 1906 would be 'the year of the beast', the Devil's legions appeared to be much depleted in Wales.[158] Many of the duties and functions of wizards and witches were now being undertaken by other agencies. Doctors, nurses and midwives could cure, or at least ease, many of life's illnesses and inconveniences.[159] The police would (occasionally) find lost people and stolen property. There was also perhaps less need for an intermediary to serve between the supernatural and the physical world, for there had been a notable democratisation of access to the gods in Wales at the turn of the twentieth century. People of all walks of life saw Jesus, Mary, the Holy Ghost and Satan. Cottagers such as Mary Jones of Egryn, and Sarah Jones of Carmel, and colliers like Evan Roberts and Daniel Williams saw all four at some point in the century's opening decade. Unremarkable people saw remarkable things.

This is not to say that belief in the power of the maleficent people had entirely disappeared. L. Winstanley and H. J. Rose, both based in the University College of Wales, Aberystwyth, uncovered a rich tradition of living superstitious belief in 1926.[160] They based their findings on research undertaken with fellow members of staff and students at the university – was Aberystwyth ever a rational institution? The investigators discovered that there were witches at Aberystwyth and a 'powerful wizard' at Llangurig who could cure 'mental cases', whilst another at Pwllheli cured 'what he calls are wild warts'. The researchers retold the tale of an instructress from the dairy department who was once asked to go to give assistance at a farm where for many weeks they had been unable to make the butter come. She discovered what was wrong with the milk, and her instructions being obeyed, the butter soon came. The farmer's wife however explained matters by saying that some-one had laid a spell upon her churn, but that the witch from the college, being the more powerful sorceress of the two, had been able to take it away.[161]

Most remarkably of all, Winstanley and Rose were informed by one informant that 'dragon's blood is used in this neighbourhood (Aberystwyth) as a love philtre'. One wonders that there was any love in Aberystwyth at all, if the ingredient required to induce it was so rare. It also points perhaps to the nature of many of the cunning folk of Wales. They were not the benign, altruistic figures that the modern witchcraft movements often portray white witches as. Cunning folk lived up to their name. They were opportunistic entrepreneurs, whose basic motivation was usually to squeeze as much money out of a client as possible, whenever possible, whether it involved deception or not.

Superstitious beliefs were most powerful where mankind was most powerless. Farmers, who worked closely with the elemental forces of nature, and sailors in peril on the sea, developed a wealth of beliefs based on acute observations that foretold future weather. Sailors learnt the hard, horrible way where the love of God goes when the waves turned the minutes to hours. Many had a profound pessimism, for like the proverbs of the Welsh, the weather predictors of Wales were based on cold November rains. If the new moon rose on a Saturday or a Sunday it foretold bad weather. If it rained as the tide ebbed, then bad weather would follow. Each month it seemed had its share of pessimism – 'Os y borfa dyf yn Ionawr / Gwaeth y tyf trwy'r flwyddyn rhagor' (if the grass grows in January / it will grow badly the rest of the year). 'Mawrth a ladd, Ebrill a fling' (March kills, April flays). Of all the months February appeared to be the most dangerous – 'Byr yw Chwefror ond hir ei anghysuron' (February is short but long is its suffering).[162] God tried to signpost bad weather through nature, the only problem was that people needed to learn to read the runes. In Llanuwchllyn people warned 'Gwylanod yn dod i'r mynydd / Dyma'n sicr arwydd stormydd' (Seagulls coming to the mountain / Here's a sure sign of storms) and 'Pan ddaw Brain Bach y Bala dros Fwlch y Groes am Fawddwy, maent yn dŵad o flaen strellach' (When the black-headed gulls fly over Bwlch-y-groes for Mawddach they fly ahead of a tempest). Cuckoos, crows, gulls and guillemots and all kinds of fauna of Wales had idiosyncrasies that could reveal future foul weather. Knowing them was vital to people dependent upon the harvest or on their safe return to harbour.[163]

Given their image in many works of history as atheistic, rationalistic, socialist or communist people, it is perhaps surprising that miners were probably the most superstitious of all Welsh workers.[164] The journey to work was perilous. If they met a redheaded woman, a cross-eyed woman, a rag-and-bone merchant, or a gypsy, then many would return home rather than risk their fate at the pit. Animals were equally unlucky. Meeting a black cat or a black bird would result in many refusing to work. Miners in Flintshire and the Swansea valley believed that seeing a single crow or a lone magpie on the way to work augured badly.[165] D. Rhys Phillips in *The History of the Vale of Neath* (1925) attested that in the Neath district seeing a pigeon at the pithead was considered to be a forewarning of death.[166] On 14 September 1901, the *South Wales Weekly News* carried a report that a robin redbreast had been seen in the Llanbradach pit before an explosion that killed twelve miners.[167] A robin had also been seen before the explosion at the ill-fated Senghenydd pit in 1901, and again in 1913. On 4 October 1901, the *Westminster Gazette* related how miners in the Bridgend district were disturbed by 'the bird of death omen'.[168] The following year ornithologically aware miners saw more birds blown in on ill winds. The *South*

Wales Echo on 15 July 1902 told of a similar disturbing occurrence at Glyncorrwg pit, which caused 300 men to refuse to work:

> The men have been whispering their fears to each other for some time past, but the drastic action of Monday was probably the outcome of so called evil omens which are said to have been heard in the mine. About two months ago the night men began to tell creepy tales of strange supernatural happenings which took place in the colliery every night . . . Now and then a piercing cry for help would startle the men and during the night shift, horrid shrieks rang through the black darkness of the headings and frightened the men nearly out of their wits. There is, of course, the usual tale of the dove hovering over the mouth of the level.[169]

As at sea, whistling underground was considered to be unlucky, the sign of a false bravado and a fake bravery. As at sea, the presence of a woman anywhere underground in many mines was considered to be particularly unlucky. The spot at which a miner had been killed was often considered to be haunted. In the Afan district if a collier who had met with a fatal accident had left behind any of his tools it was believed that that part of the mine would be ghost-haunted until the equipment was found and removed. This echoed the tales around Wales of ghosts appearing to help people unearth buried or hidden treasure. It also indicates the importance of a miner's tools for they were his own personal property. Many strikes in south and north Wales commenced with the symbolic removal of the miner's tools. Portraits of death such as 'Y Tolaeth', 'Corpse Candles', y 'Lledrith' were all seen in Welsh mines at the turn of the twentieth century.[170] They were as reliable as the tooth fairy.

Such spirits were not all bad. In the 1890s there was a belief in Rhosllanerchrugog, Denbighshire, that a collier named Dic Humphreys, who always worked alone and at night, succeeded in cutting such a phenomenal amount of coal because he received the help of fairies and the spirit of the mine to undercut the coalface. This Celtic Stakhanov was given the nickname of 'Y Safiwr Mawr' (the Great Undercutter).[171]

In a report on 'Superstition Among Miners', an anonymous writer in the *Western Mail* on 11 March 1871 recounted with a supercilious tone that already characterised Wales's 'national news-paper' the fact that hundreds of miners in Tredegar, Cwm Nantddu and Pontypool refused to go to work because of ghostly knockings, and a gypsy woman's prediction that an explosion was imminent. The author noted that:

> one man is said to have seen something covered in a white sheet and to have hit a hole right through it with his fist! The tom-foolery of this is too obvious, one would think, to need comment, and yet such ridiculous stuff is actually believed! . . . In the noises that are heard in mines, we believe that in one sense, they are 'warnings', warnings of the possible proximity of noxious gases or accumulation of water, forced near by the down-settling of the strata, and calling for extra care and precautions in working the mines where such noises are heard. But there is certainly nothing supernatural in them.[172]

But then, of course, the writer was not the one working in the damp and dark mine when the 'Cyhyraeth' roared.

The natural world signposted various plants that would benefit mankind, for God was considered to have been both inventive and practical. Kidney-shaped leaves were considered to offer certain cures for kidney complaints. Herbs such as rosemary, groundsell, rue, parsley, wormwood and tansy were the basis for many cures. Animals were also useful. In Caernarfonshire and Merionethshire, eels were pushed down the throat of cattle suffering from grass disease. In Anglesey a chicken was forced down a horse's throat to cure worms: the worms would loosen their grip on the lining of the stomach and feed on the chicken, which would eventually pass out of the horse.[173] The water of the holy wells of Wales were still believed to offer cures for a host of ailments. During the 1914–18 war people visited Ffynnon Deilo (Pembrokeshire) to drink water from the skull of a saint, hoping thereby to secure a speedy end to hostilities. In 1911, a crippled girl from Glamorgan visited the well at the eastern wall of the churchyard of Llanfihangel Genau'r-glyn, Cardiganshire. She drank the water and was able to walk away without her crutches.[174] Desperation was the mother of desperate solutions.

'The Disenchantment of the World': the ebbing of religion and magic

Gwae fi fy myw mewn oes mor ddreng
A Duw ar drai ar orwel pell.

(Woe am I to live in such a cursed age
As God ebbs on a far horizon.)

Hedd Wyn, 'Rhyfel', *Cerddi'r Bugail* (Wrexham, 1931), p. 1.

Welsh Christian religion had as much of the characteristics of a Methuselah as a Lazarus. Even in 1945 the levels of church and chapel attendance were still significantly high for a modern industrialised and commercialised society and probably far higher than the levels of religious attendance in England or Scotland. In that hopeful year there were 155, 911 members of the Church in Wales, 110,328 Baptists, 172,954 Calvinistic Methodists, 160,519 Congregationalists, 133,335 Welsh Independents and 105,775 Catholics.[175] Not all members, however, attended regularly. This in many respects was an age-old problem, the nunc dimittis of Welsh religion – worship had diminished, but ought to be increasing, devotion withered. Yet, beneath all the rationalism, worldliness and indifference, religious urges remained deep and strong as many people were terrified of damnation. Even in the twilight of the gods people were still afraid of them – deisidaimonia, the fear of the gods, was still present and powerful. Many retained their own version of a 'Creator', of a place in Heaven, and had concepts of good and evil, crime and punishment, goodness and reward. Belief was a matter of private judgement. Not all accepted the rigidity of formal religion as a system of commandments, given in stone, dispersed through scripture, and accepted on faith. Belief was often more complex as a fig leaf of Christianity covered a body of inherited magic and superstition.[176]

Magic and religion were far closer than many people were willing to accept. The supernatural and the spiritual were intertwined in complex and contradictory ways. While the pleasures of the next life would compensate for earthly pains, few people could hold their focus indefinitely on the world to come. People needed resolution of the pains and problems, the woes and worries of this world and so they turned to the agencies that promised that they had efficacious solutions.

The supernatural fauna of Wales had a mix of creatures that had both a biblical pedigree and secular origins. Indeed, it was not often clear whether the source of some phenomena were spiritual or superstitious. The tradition of the 'Cannwyll Corff', those ghostly ambulating nocturnal lights that marked out the route that a funeral would subsequently take, had a Christian origin.[177] In order that his people would be ready for death, God had agreed to St David's request that they be forewarned and so the 'corpse candle' came into being. The scientist Alfred Russel Wallace accepted corpse candles as 'facts'.[178] In 1940, air-raid officers in Pembrokeshire complained that it was impossible to enforce a blackout as 'death and the cannwyll corff were so active that night was as day'.[179] In the spellbinding world of the hocus-pocus and abracadabra of the witches and wizards of Wales, many spells were based on biblical texts. Ministers, of all denominations, were called upon to conduct exorcisms to cast out devils and demons. Each denomination and sect contained a core of magical and mystical beliefs in the transformation of bread into flesh and wine into blood. Their buildings were the gateways to the grace of God, the venue where the eternal met the everyday. Despite the puritan reformation within Nonconformity, trinkets and treasures, much polished, returned in some services, confirmation of Oscar Wilde's observation that in spiritual matters, style was often more important than substance. Religion and magic were symbiotic, interdependent and declined together.[180]

Considering the earthly powers aligned against them it was surprising that spirituality and superstition survived in the twentieth century. Demographic, economic and social changes, and the emergence of anglicised, commercialised and industrialised communities battled both for and against Welsh religion, as they had over the survival of the Welsh language. It was not simply the case that an urban Wales equated to a Godless Wales. Just like Welsh speakers, Welsh believers were also drawn into the industrial areas. Many of the larger chapels were built in urban areas where, initially at least, the congregations and the collections flourished. The influence of immigrants from England and around the world, especially in that decade of the 'black gold rush' 1901–11, presented a serious challenge to Welsh religion. The 'English cause' chapels, where the services were in English, were one contentious attempt to assimilate the incomers. Yet, eventually, such sandcastles of hope were swept away with the incoming, anglicised, secularised tides.

Theologically, as the Revd Dr R. Tudur Jones showed so eloquently, Welsh religion was in crisis in the late nineteenth century.[181] There were crises of leadership, of belief, of faith and of feeling. Decades of theological controversies weakened Christianity from within. Doubt became more normal than conviction in the face of an empirical historical approach to Christian evidence. Biblical criticism, spiritual and scientific discoveries produced a transformation in the cosmologies and world views of people across Wales. Though such issues barely register in the religious poetry of the period, Islwyn's great poem 'Y Storm' reveals that the more perceptive writers were aware of the threats to religion. By the 1870s, no 'man of sense' believed in the 'creation of the world within six days of twenty-four hours'. Yet many ministers and poets, virtually the same people, were in denial.[182] Although they sought to portray themselves as a unified force, especially during the campaign against disestablishment of the established church, Welsh Nonconformists were deeply divided. Denominational rivalry extended into all sorts of areas. In Carmarthenshire, the local authority failed to appoint a Christian missionary to work amongst vagrants because they could not agree which denomination he should belong to.[183]

The crisis in faith was seen in the uncertainty that seems to characterise so much of the years leading to the religious revival of 1904–6. In 1888, Thomas Charles Edwards could not quite explain the reasons why but noted 'wrth hir graffu, cydnabod raid mai pryder sydd yn meddiannu meddyliau y dynion mwyaf ysytriol a dwys, a threiddgar eu golygon'[184] (Through long consideration, one has to admit that worry seizes the minds of the most considered and serious, far-seeing men). In 1890 Dr John Thomas of Liverpool coined the phrase 'seciwlareiddio' (secularisation) to describe one aspect of this malaise.[185] The ways of the world were reaching into the chapels and churches. All seemed to be more concerned with music, literature, social engagement, public affairs and temperance than the scriptures. In 1906 prayer meetings were cancelled for political election rallies. Again, during both general elections in 1910 politics took precedence over praise and chapel vestries became Liberal campaign centres. The closeness of the links between Liberalism and Nonconformity and Anglican and the Conservatives would become problematic as Wales increasingly moved into the politics of socialism.[186] One author in *Y Drysorfa* outlined the history of religion in Wales as a tale of decline: 'O'r holl gyfnodau y presennol yw y mwyaf difrifol. Ie yn wir, a bron na allaf ddweyd fod fy nghalon yn crynu wrth sylwi arno' (Of all periods the present is the most serious. Yes indeed, and I can almost say that my heart shakes whilst looking at it). Faith had faltered, which was perhaps not so surprising for leaders such as Robert Ambrose Jones (Emrys ap Iwan; 1851–1906), who set an impossible standard for the faithful:

A oes arnoch ofn y nos? Ofn y dydd sydd arnaf i. A oes arnoch ofn mynd i'r bedd? Ofn codi ohono sydd arnaf i. Mi wn, pe byddai brycheuyn arnaf i, y gwelid Ef yn fwy amlwg o lawer yng ngholau'r Oen nag wrth olau pŵl Gehenna.

(Are you afraid of the night? I fear the day. Are you afraid of going to the grave? I fear rising from it. I know, that if I have the slightest blemish, He will see it far clearer in the light of the Lamb than in the light of the pool in Gehenna)

Emrys ap Iwan further warned: 'Nid y pechod mwyaf amlwg yw'r pechod mwyaf damniol' (It is not the most obvious sin which is the most damning). Woe, he warned, is the nation that is full of religion but empty of faith.[187]

Sacred festivals became secular festivities as Welsh society became increasingly commercialised. Easter was not so much a Christian event as an opportunity for calorific overindulgence. With the advent of Cadbury's Dairy Milk from 1905 the moulded chocolate Easter egg became increasingly popular. The symbolism of eggs at Easter still awaits serious consideration by a historical anthropologist. Giving eggs was a pagan fertility ritual that was usurped by the church in the Middle Ages. At the turn of the twentieth century, as society secularised, chocolate eggs became even more potently symbolic of Easter, for they were hollow. At the same time, the central Christian message of Christmas was reshaped, reordered and repackaged into a secular festival. Advent became a blessed time for advertisers. It was no longer a period of liturgical expectation, but a time for limitless expenditure. Father Christmas, the portly patron saint of the season, presided over the celebrations from his winter fairyland grotto. Christmas was not about sharing or giving, in reality it was a time for buying. The rise of 'rational recreation' also affected religion. This is not to say that all religious people were against sport and the more sedentary pleasures such as reading for enjoyment as much as enlightenment. Yet, by the turn of the twentieth century the emphasis had moved from holiness to happiness in this world. Scorning gravity and the grave, Bertrand Russell's *The Pursuit of Happiness* (1930) championed the virtues of pleasure rather than the pleasures of virtue.

Agnosticism and atheism became far more common in Wales as the twentieth century progressed. One man who proudly proclaimed that he was unsure as to whether God existed or not acquired the sobriquet 'Dai Agnostic'. But others were more articulate in their unbelief. Bertrand Russell in his immensely influential *Why I am Not a Christian* (1927) emphasised the truth of Darwinian evolutionary theories, expressed doubts about the historical existence of Jesus and questioned the morality of religion:

> I say quite deliberately that the Christian religion, as organised in its churches, has been and still is the principal enemy of moral progress in the world. Religion is based, I think, primarily and mainly upon fear . . . the terror of the unknown . . . A good world needs knowledge, kindliness, and courage, it does not need a regretful hankering after the past or a fettering of the free intelligence by the words uttered long ago by ignorant men.[188]

Some aspects of Christian beliefs made it easy to ridicule Belief. Many people pondered the physics and geography of the afterlife, the precise location of heaven and hell. Were they allegorical or did they have a physical reality? Others considered the biology and physiology of angels. How big was a soul? Did angels have sex? Did angels eat food? Were there toilets in heaven? Did amputees regrow their limbs in heaven? What about the victims of cannibals? Such questions might appear facile, but if the reality of the Christian afterlife was accepted, then such questions were vital as part of the attempt to describe the eternal destiny of the human species. Such metaphysical conjectures reflect the great seriousness with which religious matters were addressed in Wales.[189]

One of the great problems for Welsh religion was that too often it was seen to have been against fun. Rather than spread joy wherever they went, some Welsh religious leaders spread joy whenever they went. Those prudes on the prowl saw evil everywhere. Pubs with their allure of hops and hope had long been a target for the ire of the godly. The 1881 Welsh Sunday Closing Act was the high watermark of the 'hellfire' politics of the 1870s and 1880s. The Sabbath was sacrosanct, on this day God's people, the Welsh, like their maker would enjoy (or suffer) a day's rest. A wag pointed to the illogical length that some people took sabbatarianism with the anecdote about a constipated deacon who refused to take laxatives on a Saturday night because they would work on a Sunday. The Revd W. Cynog Williams complained in 1912 that the streets of Aberdare 'teemed with moral consumptives' and that magistrates had been bribed by the entertainer and entrepreneur William Haggar into allowing his cinema to open on a Sunday.[190]

The argument about Sunday openings for cinemas resurfaced time and again. During the First World War magistrates in Bangor, Caernarfon, Barry and Llanelli refused cinemas permission to open on a Sunday, despite the complaints that shift workers in the munitions factories had nowhere else to go.[191] In 1934, the newly formed, 12,000 strong Cardiff Board of Catholic Action declared 'war on immoral films', threatening to advise parishioners to boycott films for they were unwholesome. Archbishop Mostyn, after a visit to Rome, reported excitedly that the Pope approved of the proposed ban and warned that 'unless there is an improvement in the standard of films shown the 90,000 adherents of the Catholic faith in south Wales may be forbidden to attend cinemas'.[192] The Bishop of Swansea and Brecon warned against 'immoral plays, films and books'. The report of the bishop's views in the *South Wales Daily Post* further condemned the cinema for the presentation 'of a civilization that is hectic, violent, undisciplined and semi-pagan'[193]

Yet not all the cinema's offerings were 'semi-pagan' for scriptural swords and sandals epics were screened as well. The screening of *From the Manger to the Cross* (1912) at Cardigan in 1914, two years after its original release (the town was behind the times then as well), gave rise to a bitter and very Welsh debate about belief and public morality. Worse of all perhaps, as the attendances of local chapels dwindled, the film played each night to capacity crowds of 500.[194] At Llanelli in 1913, when *Dante's Inferno* played at the local cinema, crowds of several hundred flocked to see the flickering images of the torments of the damned. The posters, in lurid colour, spoke of 'the realistic breathing effects, and the agonies of the Lost Souls'. The fact that admission was restricted to those over sixteen years of age, guaranteed full houses for each performance.[195] Rather than see it as a means of communicating its messages, Welsh religion viewed the cinema, as it did the theatre and the circus, as morally corrupt.

The functions that religion and superstition had undertaken for people were undertaken by other agencies from the 1870s. Chemists took the place of, or competed with, herbalists; midwives replaced wise women; doctors were consulted instead of conjurors. The police searched for stolen or missing property or people. Secular schools from the 1870s taught English and the wonders of new scientific discoveries – the world of the child was disenchanted long before that of their parents or grandparents. The schools taught far more in their extensive extra-curricular roles. The master at Cwmcothi school in Carmarthenshire in 1877 noted: 'The children in order to conduct and behave themselves properly were this afternoon duly cautioned in habits of punctuality, of good manners and language and cleanliness, of obedience to duty, of consideration and respect for others, and of honour and truthfulness in word and act.'[196]

The rise of empirical science, the development of distinct scientific disciplines and their teaching in schools was a crucial force in the disenchantment of the world. When Bertrand Russell wrote a short and polemical pamphlet on *Icarus: Or the Future of Science* (1925), one reviewer described it as 'utter pessimism', a reaction that is understandable if we note the scientific advances and their challenges to religion.[197] In Russell's view, physicists had explored the balanced Newtonian universe; biologists exposed the power of genetic inheritance and the possibility of degeneration; psychologists suggested that rational modern man was a chaos of instincts and urges within; chemists and engineers promised a new material environment, but also produced modern weapons of terrible destructive power; whilst social scientists argued that the existing capitalist social system was corrupt and insupportable. In so many fields discoveries seemed to question the very basis of faith. The author Richard Hughes claimed that he lost his faith in God after reading Freud. 'God and his sin' became meaningless to him because 'Freudian analysis had explained how such notions arose historically'.[198]

The machines and inventions of the early twentieth century offered profound challenges to an enchanted world. When man flew into the skies, where had God and heaven disappeared to? On the land the development of steam power, then the internal combustion engine and the arrival of the petrol engine had profound effects. Reaping and mowing machines, tractors, motor cars and omnibuses impacted on the land and its spirituality. The introduction of electricity had even greater impact for previously troublesome spirits would just disappear at the flick of a switch. The social historian Professor Gareth Williams has noted:

> On the land and on the road, people were coming to see that they lived their lives within a world that was increasingly subject to mechanical processes and scientific laws rather than to supernatural forces . . . Near-veneration for the land as a living partner must diminish for the farmer who inflicts fertilisers and machines upon it. As the twentieth century dawned, his social cosmology was becoming more rational, less mystical. The earth was becoming desanctified, harvest rituals and age-old wedding and other customs defunctionalised.[199]

The impact of machines was seen at its strongest in the First World War in which the real steam and petrol-powered Apocalypse dwarfed anything in the imaginary pages of Revelations. The Second World War inaugurated a new dimension of horror as bombs fell and Cardiff, Swansea and Pembroke burned, for the terror was both local and global. The war ended with the obscenity of the atom bombs at Hiroshima and Nagasaki in August 1945. Many people would ask why God had allowed such devastation to take place in his creation. Had God deserted mankind? In 1905 John Cowper Powys, somewhat prematurely considering it was at the height of the religious revival, announced the demise of God in a poem entitled 'The Death of God'. Powys outlined a psycho-sensuous philosophy as an alternative to Christian religion.[200] The poet with the most inappropriate name for a warrior, Hedd Wyn, spotted God in 1917 'ar drau ar orwel pell' (ebbing on a far horizon).[201] Another poet, Gwenallt, took a bleaker view:

Nid oes na diafol nac uffern dan loriau papur ein byd,
Diffoddwyd canhwyllau'r nefoedd a
thagwyd yr angylion i gyd.

(There is no devil or hell beneath our world's paper floors,
Heaven's candles are extinguished and
all the angels have been strangled.)[202]

8

The Pursuit of Pleasure: Enthrallment, Happiness and Imagination

'Cultural history must be more than the sum of particular histories, for it is with the relations between them, the particular forms of the whole organisation, that it is especially concerned. I would then define the theory of culture as the study of relationships between elements in a whole way of life'.

> Raymond Williams, 'The Analysis of Culture', quoted in John Storey, *Cultural Theory and Popular Culture: A Reader* (Athens, Ga., 1998), p. 52.

'It's in the Air'[1]: *culture, technology and time in the first multimedia age*

'Are you ready?'

> Message received at Lavernock Point, Penarth 13 May 1897 from Guglielmo Marconi. Quoted in Hugh G. J. Aitken, *Syntony and Spark: the Origins of Radio* (New York, NY, 1976), p. 77.

Tommy Cooper (1921–84), the Caerphilly-born comic who conjured cash out of the comedic value of his apparent ineptitude as a magician, once tried to nail a custard pie to a wall.[2] Whatever this act was – popular culture (?) – it certainly was not magic. The curdled custard cascaded down the wall. 'Just like that'. People laughed. That's entertainment. Never underestimate public taste. The historian of culture, as opposed to the cultured historian, is in a predicament similar to Cooper's. Hammering down culture is a messy business. Culture grows from the world and the cultural world is incorrigibly plural, protean and pliable.[3]

In a series of influential works, Raymond Williams (1921–88), especially in *Culture and Society: 1780–1950* (1960), showed how 'culture . . . came to mean a whole way of life material, intellectual and spiritual'.[4] 'It could also', Williams added, 'be a word which often provoked either hostility or embarrassment'.[5] Hostility and embarrassment were evidenced throughout the cultural life of Wales in the period 1870–1945, for cultures not only co-existed but sometimes clashed. Culture, like class, had a hierarchy which could be divided into three or more groups – highbrow to middle-brow to lowbrow, or should it be listed in the opposite order? The boundaries between the groups were fluid and never fixed, for taste was infinitely subjective and selective. Plebeian culture rivalled patrician. The former were allegedly tasteless and retrograde whilst the latter were tasteful and avant-garde. Plebeians had bad tastes and base arts, patricians possessed good taste and refined art. Spiritual cultures rivalled secular. Urban and industrial contrasted with rural and agricultural. Oral folk tales and folklore seemed to be rivalled by literate fiction and factual reporting. The Welsh people were supposedly locked by their language behind the door that separated the medieval from the modern age. Matthew Arnold and a host of contemporary cultural critics castigated the barbarity of the Welsh language.[6] This of course was the colonialist's classic tactic, of belittling the aboriginal culture. But ironically in a process of reverse colonialism and cultural supremacy, this was a role the Welsh themselves played in India and in several outposts of the Empire.[7]

Welsh culture in the period 1870–1945, and especially at the turn of the twentieth century, has been presented as the product of a spiritual people. T. J. Morgan, Huw Walters and Hywel Teifi Edwards dedicatedly and diligently recreated the rich cultural milieu of this world. Their 'thick descriptions', to use the term popularised by cultural anthropologists, have uncovered the core characteristics of this culture – dramatic, musical, poetic, prosaic, autodidactic.[8] Given that the built environment in Wales was so poor, it was natural that churches and chapels doubled as concert halls. This was the feature of industrial and urban as much as rural Wales. Bangor, Caernarfon, Cardiff, Llanelli, Neath, Wrexham were urban areas where this quintessentially 'Welsh culture' flourished. In print the magazine *Y Geninen* testified to the extent of the culture's poetic endeavours, whilst *Y Cerddor* amplified the claim that the Welsh were a musical nation. The secular merged with the spiritual. In 1903, the choir at Morriston's Tabernacle produced Dvorák's *Sabat Mater* in Latin, whilst Siloh Newydd Glandŵr had Creole composer Samuel Coleridge-Taylor to adjudicate in their eisteddfod, and to conduct the evening concert of his composition, *Hiawatha*.

Culture, in its original nineteenth-century sense of cultivation, undoubtedly, had a strong affinity to traditions that were linked to the land. Perhaps the most remarkable expressions of these links are to be found in the work of Iorwerth C. Peate (1901–82). In his *Cymru a'i Phobl* (1931), *Diwylliant Gwerin Cymru* (1942) and his volumes of poetry *Y Cawg Aur a Cherddi Eraill* (1928) and *Plu'r Gweunydd* (1933), Peate walked again with those enlightened and enlightening people of Llanbrynmair that had made his youthful years so culturally rich. In article after article in *Y Llenor* in the 1930s he thundered against the present as 'The Dirt Age', 'This Age of Trash', and implored his readers to help him to restore reason and tolerance to a deranged world. Above all, Peate's greatest legacy to Wales is the folk museum at St Fagans, which opened in 1948 under his curatorship.[9] This cultural richness was the pattern under the plough that George Ewart Evans also tried to uncover.

Yet Welsh culture was not ossified in a bucolic backwater. Change and continuity were the perennial features of the cultural life of rural Wales, as well as urban. Ceiriog's popular poem 'Alun Mabon XXVI' is often seen as the epitome of cultural permanence, yet it has an acute perception of change:

> Eto tyf y llygad dydd
> O gylch traed y graig a'r bryn
> Ond bugeiliaid newydd sydd
> Ar yr hen fynyddoedd hyn.
>
> Ar arferion Cymru gynt
> Newid ddaeth o rod i rod.
> Mae cenhedlaeth wedi mynd
> A chenhedlaeth wedi dod.'

(The daisies still grow
Around the feet of rock and hill
But there are new shepherds
On these old mountains.

Upon the customs of the former Wales
Change came with the Earth's turn,
A generation has gone
And a new generation has come.)[10]

The cultural wealth that Peate and his colleagues in St Fagans uncovered revealed that rural Wales saw as much change as continuity. Situated on the outskirts of the industrial port city of Cardiff, St Fagans itself was culturally diverse for it was located in the grounds of a former castle gifted to the nation by the Earl of Plymouth. Its collections and buildings, crafts and artefacts demonstrated that traditional rural tradesmen and craftsmen adapted existing technologies and tools to suit local environments and circumstances. Craftsmen, farmers and tradesmen based close to or in hamlets, villages and towns were exposed to new equipment and ideas that they refined to their work places.[11] Such changes were gradual, almost glacial, but the years 1870–1945 saw cultural changes that revolutionised Welsh and world culture.

The list of superlatives to describe these changes is legion and long. The period 1870–1945 was the first multi-media age. It was the age of the mass media and the age of 'electric culture'. This was the time when the workshop of the world turned into a dream factory. This was the age of technological entertainment – the cinema, the radiogram, the wireless, the radio, the bicycle and the motor car, and many, many more devices came into being. This was the period when the 'Carboniferous Age' of coal power began to give way to the world of oil, electricity and technology. This was the age when the 'leisure industry' and the 'creative industries' came into existence, when sport became as much a force in the economy as a feature in entertainment. These years saw the feminisation of leisure, as in the cinema, music hall and theatre, women dominated as actors and in audiences. The communications revolution took humanity from the dot-dot-dash of the telegraph to radio, radar and television.[12]

Communication and cultural changes were accompanied by social and economic changes that enabled people to benefit. The rise of real wages by one third in the final two decades of the nineteenth century allowed all but the very poor to do more with their lives than struggle for survival. Household expenditure on recreation increased from 7.8 per cent in 1931 to 15.6 per cent in 1951.[13] But the increase in 'disposable' income would have been of limited benefit had it not been accompanied by an expansion of time available for what contemporary moralists often referred to, rather disapprovingly, as 'play'. The Factory Acts of 1874 and 1894 and the rather unimaginatively titled Coal Mines Regulation Act (1908) set the working day at eight hours. What this legislation created was not simply a total reduction in the length of the working week, but rather a changed attitude to time itself. A sharp differentiation was drawn between the hours employees owed to their employer and the hours that could be devoted to their private affairs. Bank holidays, dating from new laws in 1871 and 1875, denoted another new development: the creation of secular days of leisure. Miners during the period 1888–1898 enjoyed their very own day of holiday – 'Mabon's Day', named after trade union leader William Abraham's bardic name of 'Mabon'.

Timekeeping now had to be both accurate and absolute. This did not mean that those worshippers of 'Saint Monday' had deserted their deity. Some miners and dockers still worshipped at the altar, with a few of the more devout, or debauched, also honouring 'Saint Tuesday'. Seasonal demands and weather determined that agriculture had to be flexible rather than fixed in its time, as too did many casual labour tasks. But such irregular work patterns were now portrayed as pathological. Work was no longer the main or the only signifier of personal identity and psychic satisfaction.[14] People had to be educated to cope with their leisure. William Morris and the Edwardian Arts and Crafts Movement, for example, provided practical examples of how people could enjoy their freedom away from the drudgery of work.

The Education Act of 1870 was also crucial in the transformation of Welsh culture. A much broader constituency of the literate lived in Wales by 1900.[15] Although the Sunday schools had laboured hard to create a scripturally enlightened and literate people, the new schools as envisioned by Lord Aberdare greatly extended the numbers of people who could read.[16] There was considerable demand for reading material of all types. Newspaper circulation doubled between 1896 and 1906 and then doubled again by 1914. Indeed, publishers of all kinds flourished in response to a popular interest in books and their authors, which may have been proportionally greater in late Victorian and Edwardian Britain than at any time before or since. Investment in new web-based printing presses and in linotype typesetting machines and competition between publishers lowered prices.[17] Technological change was reflected in art. T. H. Parry-Williams 'unashamedly' wrote a poem in praise of his greatest love – 'KC13' – his motorbike.

Of all the technological changes that affected culture, it was perhaps music that experienced the greatest transformation. In 1877, Sir William Henry Preece (1834–1913), the head of the Post Office's telegraph section, during a visit to his American friend, the inventor Edison, suggested a method through which the human voice could not only be broadcast, but recorded.[18] As a reward for his insights, Edison sent Preece the first phonograph to be made. One of its earliest uses was to record Welsh folk songs, for Preece was the active president of the Welsh Folk Song Society.[19] The recording of the ancient airs of Wales reveals one of the truths of the history of technology – the old co-existed with the new.[20] Use-centred history is not simply a matter of moving technological time forward, for time is always jumbled up: people worked with new things but continued their old interests.[21] Timelines of progress are not as tidy as many historians imagine. Preece also pioneered an early method of wireless telegraphy using induced currents and in 1896 gave an enthusiastic welcome and financial backing to Guglielmo Marconi's new system using Hertizan waves. Despite the claims of Edison, the microphone was invented by Corwen-born David Edward Hughes (1831–1900). Hughes was a remarkable combination of inventor, practical experimenter and professor of music. He was one of the most creative inventors for he also pioneered a printing telegraph (the forerunner of a fax machine) and methods for radio wave transmission and detection. Hughes was elected a Fellow of the Royal Society in 1880 and won the society's Royal Medal in 1885.[22]

The musician in David Hughes might have realised that his own and Preece's inventions made possible the soundtrack of the twentieth and twenty-first centuries. The birth of recorded sound represented a profound shift in the nature of human existence. It ranks with the representation of human speech and thought on papyrus, parchment or paper. No matter how crude its early manifestation, it provided people with the tunes of their years, the tracks of their tears. The invention of recorded sound transformed music from an experience into an artefact, with wide-ranging physical and psychological consequences. Irrespective of when music was made, it could still be heard. Performances were no longer unique, but could be repeated endlessly. There would be no more lost chords. An entire industry devoted to the making, selling and disseminating of recordings came into being. The revolution in sensibility left its mark on whole areas of people's lives. Recordings have altered the way people speak to and deal with each other, they have changed the language of love and the rhetoric of hate.[23] They have enabled races to integrate and even influenced people's underwear, or so the horrified commentators complained in 1925 as the young ladies of Cardigan unfastened their corsets to dance the Charleston.[24] Far more people were made aware of their freedom by blues and jazz music than were driven to the streets by the Communist manifesto: 'No one knows the troubles I've seen'.

Music created the urge for motion and clothing, and much else in life, had to adapt. Dance halls suddenly sprang up around Wales as the young, and some not so young, sought to jive and jig the nights away.[25] Recorded music also featured on the two most iconic features of Welsh parlours – the radiogram and the wireless. The advent of the radio and radiogram would anchor people to their parlours for decades. Despite the dour and stern Scottish Presbyterianism of its first director general, the BBC soon realised that music was what their audience really wanted.[26] As well as the confrontational music of the young, there was the comforting and classical music of the old and the songs of praise of the devout. The early BBC, a single radio station, had the impossible task of attempting to appeal to all tastes, regions and ages. Above all, perhaps, musical recordings saw the expansion of the role of women within the leisure industry both as creators and consumers. It also saw the Americanisation of Welsh cultural life.[27]

The increasing visibility of women in the world of technological entertainment was also experienced in the growth of the cinema in Wales. By the 1930s the cinema had moved from its disreputable origins in the fairground shows of pioneers like William Haggar and the salacious what-the-butler-saw machines of the piers, to palatial palladiums and palaces.[28] Inevitably some contemporaries detected a moral downslide in the popularity of the cinema among the young. During the First World War critics complained that 'the darkness encourages indecency'.[29] But such fears were soon swept aside. Cinema offered a far more rational form of recreation than heavy drinking, rowdyism and violence. The backbone of the cinema audience in the 1930s was female. Jack Jones in his 1934 novel *Rhondda Roundabout* wrote of the 'thousands of women that pack the Rhondda cinemas night after night', whilst James Hanley recorded that 'the crowds for the 4d cinema seats consisted largely of women'.[30]

This represented a novel development because up to this time the very concept of women's leisure had scarcely been recognised. Cinemas were more enticing and entertaining than pubs. Whilst the dance hall provided the best way of meeting boyfriends, when people began courting an evening at the cinema offered an ideal means of developing intimacy in the dark. The subject matter of the movies soon descended into gender stereotypes – longing, leg-overs, and loving for women, hardship, humour and heroes for men. Girls and women would go together and swoon over matinee idols such as Rudolph Valentino, Ivor Novello or Gareth Hughes. Costume dramas such as *Madonna of the Seven Moons* (1944) and *The Wicked Lady* (1947), described as 'women's pictures', were often top of the bill at Welsh cinemas. As in a morality play such films had a traditional set of characters – the golden-haired and hearted saloon girl (the tart with a heart), the stern ranch owner, the gambler, the idler, the widow. The flickering images on the screen brought magic and mystery into many otherwise miserable lives. Cinema captured people's imaginations. Men (the Lotharios of the Lyrics), lusted open-mouthed as Mae West drifted across the screen, her body in perpetual motion and Jean Harlow, Carole Lombard and Greta Garbo vamped. Women aped the mannerisms and manners, the styles and hairstyles of the stars. In anger they were Bette Davis, when contrite they were Joan Fontaine.

The development of cinema affected people's perception of time, speed and space. The very name of the new medium confirmed this impact – 'moving pictures'. Action could be frozen, or with creative editing could move as fast as it did in one of D. W. Griffiths's last-minute rescues. Cinematic news coverage was greatly accelerated in 1911 when a special express train outfitted with a dark room was used to develop and transport a film of the investiture of the Prince of Wales at Caernarfon at 4 o'clock in the afternoon and have it ready for public viewing in London at 10 o'clock that night.[31]

The early pioneers of the cinema were fascinated by any moving object, however simple – Niagara Falls, horses jumping over hurdles, workers emerging from a factory. At Bangor in 1898 viewers stampeded for the exits at the on-screen image of an approaching train. This culture of accelerating time and constricting space was further amplified with the discovery of the internal combustion engine. Cars were not just a method of transport but a sporting and cultural phenomenon. At Pendine sands, Carmarthenshire, several land-speed records were broken in the 1920s. On 27 and 28 April 1926, John Godfrey Parry Thomas (1884–1927) became the first person to break two world speed records during two consecutive days. A few months later, trying to recapture his record, he was decapitated when the gear chain broke.[32] Speed also enchanted Mildred Mary Bruce (1895–1990), wife of Victor Austin Bruce (1897–1978), youngest son of Hugh Campbell Bruce, second Baron Aberdare. Mildred, with a characteristic string of pearls swinging around her neck, won the *Coupe des Dames* at the Monte Carlo rally, covering 1,700 miles in seventy-two hours. She also set the fastest ever time for a Dover–Calais crossing by motor boat and flew 20,000 miles around the world in 1930. Mildred drove like a get-away driver. She was the first woman to be fined for speeding in Britain, and the first to ride a motorcycle. Mildred published *The Woman Owner-Driver* (1928), as a response to 'the growing tendency for women to drive and look after their own cars'. She also contributed a series of articles to *The Sketch*, which were later collected in a book, *The Peregrinations of Penelope* (1930).[33]

The mass production of fantasy and fun became lucrative businesses, as the cultural industries were born. In what Raymond Williams has described as 'the greatest change ever in the history of cultural production', culture was for the most part no longer a critique of modern manufacture but a highly profitable part of it. Creativity was incorporated into capitalism for the pursuit of pleasure could yield cash. In the 1911 census, 127,112 Welsh people were recorded as employed in the occupational categories of 'Services, Sport and Recreation' (including 'Personal Services'), the majority of whom, 106,719, were women. The need to raise spirits during the economic depression ensured that these occupations still employed 124,111 in 1931.[34]

'The Battle to the Weak': sedentary pleasures

I know this life more intimately than any other and I am anxious to record the old ways and types which are fast vanishing before the levelling influences of universal education, early transportation, and wireless.

Hilda Vaughan (1892–1985), quoted in John Harris, 'Anglo-Welsh Literature', in Philip Henry Jones and Eiluned Rees (eds), *A Nation and its Books: a History of the Book in Wales* (Aberystwyth, 1998), p. 357.

Welsh national identity is often presented as being defined either by the energetic posturings of men on the fields of praise, or people emphatically praising their maker that they were a musical nation.

Both football and rugby claim, with considerable bitchiness and bitterness, to be the national game, and are yet, even after over a century of rivalry, to call half-time on the argument. But the true national obsession, the activity that was participated in most widely by the Welsh people over the years 1870–1945, was far more sedate and sedentary. The Welsh people read.

By the 1870s the printed word became increasingly dominant in work, worship and play. As with so many aspects of life, the impact of literature varied from person to person, from group to group. Literacy was not a prerequisite for the enjoyment of leisure. But as the twentieth century turned, new leisure activities were shaped, directed and elevated to the level of mass consumption by the deployment of the printed word. Travelling circuses, cinemas, freak shows and music halls depended for their growing custom on both word of mouth and on handbills, advertisements and press reports, excursions to seaside towns were advertised on billboards and hoardings, and football and rugby matches were announced and reported on in local newspapers. Literature itself was dependent upon heavy commercial advertising. A plethora of cultural and entertainment activities jostled for space in newspapers and on walls, along with millions of other goods and services anxious to catch the public eye and people's purses. The back pages of every daily newspaper circulating in Wales had its sports pages providing reports on local and national matches. It is evident that the leisure industries aimed themselves at a literate market. Literacy and literature were both the functions and cause of a growing preoccupation with pleasurable (occasionally useful) use of a person's free time.[35]

Publishing in Wales, in Welsh and in English, increased substantially in the period down to the First World War. In the 'golden age' of Welsh-language publishing, from the 1870s to the late 1890s, a number of companies came to dominance such as Gee a'i Fab of Denbigh and Hughes a'i Fab of Wrexham. Although their efforts were hampered by a primitive distribution system – itinerant booksellers were still influential even in 1914 – sales of some volumes were impressive. Hughes published a penny almanac, *Almanac y Miloedd* (The Almanac of the Thousands), which had a print run of 60,000 a year during the 1870s. Sales of shilling volumes of verse could be high: between 1866 and 1914 more than 17,500 copies were printed of the first volume of verse by Richard Davies 'Mynyddog' (1833–77), at least 13,500 copies of the second volume, and 19,500 of the third. Cheap popular handbooks also sold well. Hughes printed 36,000 copies of a shilling English–Welsh letter-writer between 1870 and 1912. Spurrells of Carmarthen published more than 100,000 copies of their dictionary.

Secular works became more important than spiritual works. As early as 1887 Charles Tudor Hughes warned Owen Evans (1829–1920), author of religious bestsellers such as *Oriau Gyda'r Iesu* (Hours with Jesus), 'that the sale of volumes of sermons (be they ever so good) is at a minimum' and complained at the financial losses the firm had incurred by publishing such books.[36] The crisis of confidence in Welsh religion had an impact on Welsh book sales at the close of the nineteenth century.

Other publishers tried more innovative titles and tactics. Isaac Foulkes of Liverpool launched a shilling series of 'Cyfres y Ceinion' (The Series of Fine Works) titles and in 1898 a threepenny series of Welsh classics, 'Y Clasuron Cymreig' (The Welsh Classics). O. M. Edwards published books and periodicals designed to appeal to his idealised vision of the knowledgeable and cultured Welsh people – 'y werin'.[37] Yet despite the innovations in marketing and promotion, by 1914 sales of Welsh books were flagging. Both Gee and Hughes regularly advertised special offers, cut-price parcels of remainders and clearance sales.[38] It was one of the greatest ironies in Welsh cultural history that the growth of education resulted in a decline in Welsh-language publishing. The development of a national system of schools from 1870 resulted in an increasing demand for English and American books and journals.

The needs of children were not ignored, for they were often seen as a profitable market. O. M. Edwards's *Cymru'r Plant* (1892) was the latest in a number of magazines intended for children. The Nonconformists of Wales had shown that they had a Jesuistic awareness and appreciation that if they could capture and control young minds then they would have the adult. The Wesleyan Methodists published *Y Winllan* (The Vineyard) from 1848 to 1965, the Independents produced *Dysgedydd y Plant* (The Children's Instructor) from 1871 to 1933, and the Calvinistic Methodists printed the most successful of all children's papers, *Trysorfa y Plant* (The Children's Treasury), which ran from 1862 to 1965. Under the editorship of Thomas Levi (1825–1916), *Trysorfa y Plant* had a circulation of 40,000 copies a month.[39] Thomas Levi also produced more than forty books for children.[40] Faced with a declining market for adult books in Welsh, publishers such as Hughes a'i Fab turned to the safer and stronger market of Welsh schools. In the 1920s teachers replaced preachers as authors of books for children. New genres such as the historical novel, the mystery novel, the adventure story and science fiction all proved popular, but it is worth noting that no writer of fiction for children ventured to address contemporary life in industrial Wales. The adventure stories of R. Lloyd Jones (1878–1959), such as *Ynys y Trysor* (Treasure Island) and *Mêt y Mona* (1929), were gripping adventures set in exotic faraway places.[41] Although the 1920s and 1930s were the 'years of the locusts' for Welsh-language publishing, nevertheless the quality of Welsh writing was not compromised by the lack of quantity. This was a – if not *the* – golden age of Welsh writing. In this sense 1936 was an *annus mirabilis* – the year when so many of the creative fires of writers were sparked by the arson attack on the bombing school near Pwllheli – the 'Tân yn Llŷn' (The Fire in Llŷn). The 1930s saw Kate Roberts, T. H. Parry-Williams, Saunders Lewis, Waldo Williams, R. Williams Parry, Thomas Parry and so many of the greats of Welsh literature in full creative flow.[42]

Welsh-language newspapers flourished in the period from 1890 to 1919. Indeed, the First World War could well have been the golden age of the newspaper in Welsh. Despite shortages of paper and printing workers, *Baner ac Amserau Cymru* (1857–1910; 1914–19), *Y Drych* (The Mirror) (1875–1919), *Y Dydd* (The Day) (1868–1919), *Y Genedl* (The Nation) (1914–17), *Yr Herald Cymraeg* (1901–10; 1914–19), *Udgorn* (Cornet) (1913–18) and the Liverpool-based *Brython* (Briton) (1914–19), were in circulation. Expatriates in London published a number of Welsh-language and bilingual titles in the early decades of the twentieth century, such as the London-based *Celt – Celt Llundain* (1895–1904), *London Welshmen – Cymru Llundain*

(1904–6), *Y Cymro a'r Celt* (1907–10), and *Y Dinesydd Cymreig* (Welsh Citizen, 1914–19). Nevertheless, no single Welsh-language journal, magazine or newspaper could be really regarded as the 'voice of the nation'. Challenges of distribution, secular and spiritual outlooks and taste proved insurmountable.

Similar problems beset the English-language newspapers of Wales. The commercial pressures that saw a growth in the monopolistic practices of large corporations and companies in the coal and steel industries were also experienced in Welsh newspaper publishing. With typical entrepreneurial flair and flourish, the Welsh coalowner D. A. Thomas, enobled as Viscount Rhondda in 1915, acquired the controlling interest in papers as different in their styles and situations as the *Western Mail*, *The South Wales Journal of Commerce*, *Y Faner*, *The North Wales Times*, *Y Tyst*, *Y Darian*, *The Cambrian News*, *The Merthyr Express* and *The Pontypridd Observer*.[43] The titles were then transferred into the control of the Merthyr Tydfil-born Henry Seymour Berry, created Baron Buckland of Bwlch in 1926, the first true Welsh press baron. In the 1920s and 1930s, Seymour Berry and his two brothers, William Berry, enobled as Lord Camrose in 1929, and Gomer Berry, enobled as Viscount Kemsley, created the greatest newspaper dynasty in Britain. The titles they owned included *The Sunday Times*, *The Financial Times*, *The Daily Graphic*, *The Sporting and Evening Chronicle* and *The Empire News*. In 1928 William and Gomer Berry revisited their south Wales origins and acquired the *South Wales Daily News*, *The South Wales Echo* and *The Cardiff Times* and incorporated them into the *Western Mail*. After a bitter circulation battle with Lord Rothersmere's papers *The Cambrian Daily Leader* and *The South Wales Daily Post*, the Berry brothers acquired these titles in 1932. By 1936 the Berry Group owned four British national newspapers and forty-nine provincial newspapers. In January 1937, the newspaper empire was divided into Camrose's Amalgamated Press and Kemley's Allied Newspapers, both with capital of more than £6 million.[44]

Rationalisation of ownership was reflected in the reduction of titles. By 1945, the number of newspapers in Wales had fallen from 152 titles in 1920 to 114 and the ratio of the Welsh-language titles was halved from 17 per cent in 1914 to 8 per cent in 1945. Yet the strongest competition that Welsh-based newspapers faced came from those titles published in Manchester and London. *The Daily Herald, The Telegraph, The Times,* the *Daily Mail* and *The Manchester Guardian* sold significant numbers across Wales, thus drawing the Welsh into a British, even an 'English', sphere of cultural influence.

If the paternity of the Welsh novel is usually accorded to Daniel Owen, that of English-language writing in Wales is often ascribed to the publication of Caradoc Evans's psychologically perverse *My People* (1915).[45] Such a view, however, ignores the claims, equally valid, of other writers who were publishing a range of literature at the close of the nineteenth century. Arthur Machen (1863–1947) produced a number of innovative works in the supernatural, horror and fantasy genres. Well before Caradoc put pen to paper, Arthur Machen published *The Great God Pan* (1894). It is still widely regarded as the best horror story in the English language. Complaints at the sexual and horrific content of the book ensured that sales would be buoyant. Machen also integrated the lore and legends of Celtic Christianity, the Holy Grail and King Arthur in works such as *The Secret Glory* (1922). Most famous of all was his story 'The Bowmen' (1914), which laid the basis for the actual sightings of 'The Angel of Mons'.[46]

The *Daily Mail*, somewhat uncharacteristically, showed an interest in Wales when it joined the attempt to identify both the date of birth and the paternity of the great Welsh novel. 'Wales', noted the *Daily Mail* in 1897, 'has waited long for her novelist but he seems to have arrived in the person of Mr Allen Raine and his novel *A Welsh Singer*'.[47] More characteristically the *Daily Mail* got it wrong, for the author was a woman – Mrs Anne Adaliza Beynon Puddicombe, the sixty-six-year-old wife of a London banker. The couple returned each year to her Newcastle Emlyn birthplace, and to nearby Tresaith, the seaside village where the Puddicombes had built their summer residence and later retired to when the husband had a mental breakdown.

Raine's stories were comforting moral fables in which the good end happily, the bad end badly. Raine's age-old romantic concerns had captured a significant readership. Cinematic productions helped sales as too did the pricing policies of her publisher Hutchison.

By 1911, sales of Allen Raine's ten novels, all set in west Wales, had reached over 2,500,000. Individual titles sold unprecedented numbers – *A Welsh Singer* (1869) sold 378,000 copies, *Torn Sails* (1897) sold 287,000 copies, whilst *A Welsh Witch* (1902) sold 281,000 volumes. Allen Raine was truly novel – one of the first worldwide bestsellers. She commanded a global readership. *The Bookman* noted that Raine ranked amongst the four most popular authors of the day, together with Marie Corelli, Hall Caine and Silas Hocking, and that 'tributes to Raine flow in from all quarters of the world – from Jamaica to the Yukon territory'.[48]

The dark, dishonest decade of the 1930s proved to be an inspirational period – 'the golden age of Anglo-Welsh writing'. First books were published by Dylan Thomas (1934), Jack Jones (1934), Gwyn Jones (1935), Glyn, David and Lewis Jones (all in 1937), Idris Davies (1938), and Richard Llewellyn (1939). The works of these writers rubbed covers with those of published authors such as Caradoc Evans, W. H. and Rhys Davies, Hilda Vaughan, Richard Hughes, Geraint Goodwin and many others. As with Allen Raine's work, Richard Llewellyn's *How Green Was My Valley* has not been kindly received by literary critics. Yet it appealed to a significant audience with its elemental tale of a family struggling against the odds, of childhood as Eden and a lost golden age. At a time when first novels did well to sell 2,000 copies, and despite being launched three weeks after the outbreak of war, Llewellyn's novel sold 1,000 copies a week to the end of 1941, and went through twenty-eight impressions in five years. In contrast, David Jones's classic *In Parenthesis* (1937), 'dripping with critical praise', sold just 1,500 copies. Llewellyn's success is still a sore point with literary critics who display enormous delight in disparaging his novel. It seems perverse that a literary lightweight has outsold the more realistic and grittier work of writers such as darkly humorous Gwyn Thomas and the dementedly hyperactive Jack Jones. Jack Jones's *Some Trust in Chariots* (1948), *Off to Philadelphia in the Morning* (1947) and *River Out of Eden* (1951) were not bidden to the feast, whilst Gwyn Thomas's *The Alone to the Alone* (1947) suffered the fate suggested in the title. Yet *How Green Was My Valley*, despite its many faults, sold on and on and on. Llewellyn must have laughed all the way to the bank.[49]

Public libraries further illustrated the gap between literary praise and popular taste. Two paths divergent. Welsh readers chose to follow the one more travelled. As in England only a few Welsh local authorities had taken out library powers in the 1880s. Only six – Aberystwyth, Bangor, Cardiff, Newport, Swansea and Wrexham – had done so by 1886. But by 1913, this number had increased to fifty-nine authorities in Wales.[50] This provision was supplemented by that of miners' institutes and welfare hall libraries, which reportedly numbered 253 by 1946.[51]

Analysis of the titles stocked by the libraries revealed that Dickens, Scott, Jack London ('easily the most popular story teller of today'), Rider Haggard and Hall Caine were the most popular titles. Welsh-language books varied considerably between 15.3 per cent of stock at Abercynon to only 5.7 per cent at Gwauncaegurwen. Thomas Jones detected a change in his local library from theology to history and fiction.[52] Female authors of romantic and moralistic novels, such as Mrs Henry Wood and Marie Corelli, were also well to the fore in miners' institute libraries. Catalogues confirmed what books were held by a library, but not what was actually read. Issue statistics were dominated by fiction. At five Rhondda libraries more than 90 per cent of the books borrowed in 1926 were fiction titles. Romances and thrillers were always on loan whilst works of Marxist dialectics were left on the shelf.

The oral testimonies gathered by the South Wales Miners' Library in the 1970s reveals the impact and true significance of the public libraries in Wales. An army of the culturally deprived – housewives, housemaids, servants, miners, labourers – rapturously acclaimed the moment when they first picked up a book and commenced on their journey to self-discovery and self-education. Agnes Jones, of the mining village of Tumble, recalled her attempts to read in the 1900s and 1910s as a secret adventure.[53] Agnes had been taken out of school early so that she could help at home and become a maid. Yet she yearned for the better, brighter things in life, and so she secretly borrowed books from the library, which she then hid in the toilet at the bottom of the garden. Only through reading did many come to think of themselves as individuals. The Everyman's Library's cheap classics edited by Ernest Rhys (1859–1946) brought further self-realisation for many people. Penny dreadfuls and sensation fiction were relished alongside the classics, and the Bible was valued as a secular anthology of adventure stories, bloody battles and a spiritual guide.[54]

'Perchance to Dream': producers, players and performers

> Somewhere there's another land,
> Different from this world we know;
> Far more mercifully planned,
> Than the cruel place we know:
> Innocence and Peace are there,
> All is good that is desired;
> Faces there are always fair,
> Love grows never old nor tired.
>
> Ivor Novello, 'The Land of Might-Have-Been',
> from the musical *Perchance to Dream* (1945).

Performance, the urge to stand up and speak or sing and inflict the result on an audience, became a marked characteristic of the Welsh people by the turn of the twentieth century. J. M. Keynes, that acute observer of the Paris peace conferences of 1919, noted that Lloyd George's greatest gift was that he was the 'consummate actor'.[55] His dramatic charisma was seen to its best effect in his visits to the National Eisteddfod. In the 1920s and the 1930s the most important day of the week-long cultural festival was Thursday, 'Lloyd George's Day', when the political royalty, if not the deity, of Wales blessed the cultural endeavours of his people.[56] Welsh culture could be found in some strange places. Eddie Gurmin of Tredegar spent the winter of 1941–2, the coldest on record, in Stalag III E. In April 1942, fifty-two men escaped from a tunnel under his bed. He was then transferred to Stalag Luft III, the camp made famous by the film *The Great Escape*. Not involved in the escape, Gurmin recalled that 'to keep ourselves entertained, we built a theatre and we would hold shows and concerts. We men held an Eisteddfod to show people what it was like'.[57] Was there no end to their suffering?

Eisteddfodau took many forms. Chapels, churches, hamlets, villages and towns organised an annual eisteddfod to display the abundance or absence of local artistic, dramatic, literary and musical talents. The miners of Wales also had their own annual eisteddfod. Some of these acquired a reputation both for the excellence of the performers and the value of the prizes. Others had pretentions beyond their locality with their claims of being 'semi-national' festivals. The National Eisteddfod, reorganised by the organisational obsession of Hugh Owen from 1880, provided a small nation with a stage on which she could prove her value and display her talents to the world.[58] The eisteddfod was also carried by Welsh emigrants in their cultural baggage. Many expatriate Welsh communities in America, Argentina, Africa, Asia and Australia established an eisteddfod. Indeed, the concept of the eisteddfod as a diverse cultural festival proved to be highly popular and became a noted feature of the wider life of Australia and South Africa. At the opening of the nineteenth century, Wales provided convicts to populate Australia, at its close the Welsh provided it with a feature not often associated with the continent – culture.[59]

As with so much in Welsh cultural life there was as much conflict as concord, as much tension as talent in the eisteddfod. Critics invariably decried the standards displayed in the competitions. Literary standards were often woeful, musical ability painful. Despite the attempts of archdruids such as Hwfa Môn (1823–1905), who was immortalised in paint by Christopher Williams, to provide gravitas to the goings-on of the Gorsedd, there seems something inescapably pantomimic about the eisteddfod as it migrated annually from north to south Wales with the robed bards marching in hierarchical union. In a competitive environment clashes were inevitable. 'Cythraul y Canu' (The Singing Devil) sowed discord. Bards, soloists and choristers in the massed choirs sought to win centre stage for their events. The language was often a bone of contention. In the 1860s and 1870s, the Welsh language was sidelined by the ambition of Hugh Owen and his supporters in the 'social science section' of the National Eisteddfod anxious to prove that the Welsh were a modern people.[60] It was not until 1937, with the establishment of the Welsh language rule, that the dispute was finally settled in favour of the language. The adoption of the Welsh language rule in National Eisteddfod competitions reflects a deep-seated challenge that was a perennial problem in the cultural life of Wales. The Welsh lived in the cultural shadows of two of the most aggressively imperialistic and influential cultural powers of the world – England and the English-speaking world, and America and the American-speaking world.

Amateur dramatics through the aegis of 'Y Mudiad Drama' (The Dramatic Movement) flourished in the years from 1900 to 1924.[61] Theatrical companies were set up in hundreds of hamlets, villages and towns across Wales. Church and chapel vestries and school-rooms provided the venues for practice and performance. By 1931 there was an estimated 500 dramatic companies active and at least 300 Welsh plays in print. Over the course of the period 1890–1914, there was an increasing shift away from the religious drama to those of a more secular nature. There were many notable successes such as the appearance of *Beddau'r Proffwydi* by W. J. Gruffydd, and works by J. O. Francis, D. T. Davies and R. G. Berry. Classics of world drama were also translated into Welsh, including works by Ibsen, for example when Ifor Williams translated *Tŷ Dol* and Thomas Parry *Hedda Gabler*.

After the First World War the National Eisteddfod sought to promote drama through commissions and competitions. This initiative saw success for new Welsh-language material by J. Ellis Williams and Idwal Jones. As so often with cultural endeavours, tender sensitivities resulted in the best drama submitted to the Eisteddfod, Kitchener Davies's *Cwm Glo* (1934), being banned for its alleged immorality.[62] Notable individuals also sought to provide funds to promote drama. The Wynne family of Garthewin provided financial support to Saunders Lewis to write and to have his dramatic works performed.[63] Saunders Lewis's *Buchedd Garmon* was probably the pinnacle of the creative work of Welsh dramatists in the period 1870–1945. The play was broadcast in 1937, when the author was in prison for his role in the arson attack on the bombing school in Penyberth. Though it is set in the Dark Ages, with the ancient Britons being confronted with potent threats to their survival, *Buchedd Garmon* has contemporary resonance. The words uttered by Emrys

Wledig became a rallying cry for subsequent generations of lovers
of the Welsh language:

Gwinllan a roddwyd i'm gofal yw Cymru fy ngwlad,
I'w thraddodi i'm plant, ac i blant fy mhlant,
Yn dreftadaeth dragwyddol.
Ac wele'r moch yn rhuthro arni, i'w baeddu.
Minnau yn awr, galwaf ar fy nghyfeillion,
Y cyffredin a'r ysgolhaig.
Deuwch ataf i'r adwy: sefwch gyda mi yn y bwlch,
Fel y cedwir i'r oesoedd a ddêl y glendid a fu.[64]

(Wales, my country, is a vineyard entrusted into my care
To be passed on to my children and my children's children
An eternal heritage.
But the swine rush over her and despoil her.
Now I call upon my friends,
Commoners and scholars.
Come with me into the breach; stand with me in the gap
To keep for the ages to come the purity which was.)

Welsh dramatists made a notable contribution to English-language
theatre both in America and in Britain. Thomas Job, the Carmarthen-
born lecturer in English at Yale and Columbia, wrote one of the
most successful plays of the Second World War. Job's *Uncle Harry*
tells the story of illicit, incestuous love that ends in poisoning. It
is a dark, claustrophobic drama that ends brutally, unlike the film
that was made of it (*The Strange Affair of Uncle Harry*, 1945) which
was sanitised for American tastes. An even more dysfunctional family
features in the dramas penned by Tennessee Williams (1911–83),
who won the Pulitzer Price for *A Streetcar Named Desire* in 1948,
and again in 1955 for *Cat on a Hot Tin Roof*. His father Cornelius
was an abusive alcoholic. His mother, Edwina, a hysteric. His sister,
Rose, a slim beauty of a girl, was schizophrenic. Tennessee himself
was effeminate and a guilt-wracked homosexual. Towering over
them all was the tormented psychological figure of his Welsh-
speaking maternal grandfather, an episcopal priest. In the London

theatre world Emlyn Williams (1905–87) a Welsh speaker from
Mostyn, Flintshire, came to prominence in the 1920s and 1930s
with *Full Moon* (1927), *A Murder Has Been Arranged* (1930), and *The
Late Christopher Bean* (1931). He became an overnight star, however,
with his thriller *Night Must Fall* (1935), in which he also played the
role of a psychopathic murderer (a subject he returned to in his
non-fiction work *Beyond Belief*).

A significant English-language theatre was also active across
Wales. At Carmarthen, Bangor, Cardiff, Llanelli, Newport, Swansea
and Wrexham, well-equipped theatres offered an extensive repertoire of classic dramas, comedies and Christmas pantomimes.[65]
Conditions were far from palatial, as Arthur Mee recalled of the
theatre in Llanelli:

> Years later, when there was a theatre in Cowell Street – Noakes' or
> Rainbows' or somebody else's – there was good acting to be seen,
> that is to say, when the stage could be seen at all, which was seldom
> on account of the tobacco smoked. Everybody smoked and perspired
> and was happy and so were the fleas.[66]

The Star Theatre chain of theatres had branches at Carmarthen and
Neath. The repertoire was tailored to the venue. At Carmarthen's
Star Theatre in 1883, Gardiner Koyne, the Dublin comedian, at-
tracted large audiences to hear his variant of the Irish joke. But at
Neath, audiences preferred more esoteric fare such as *Harlequin
Fairy Kindheart*, *The Pigey King* (*sic*) and 'erotic' material like *The
Wicked Squire Who Had His Fling*. Down to the First World War,
touring companies traversed Wales with their portable theatres.
Edward Ebley's 'Theatre of Varieties' performed at Wem, Wrexham,
Hay, Buckley, and then went south to Dowlais.[67] The youthful
Thomas Jones recalled his curiosity to see a travelling theatre:

> Near the Castle Hotel periodically appeared Noake's Theatre, a
> wooden structure, which I was not allowed to enter on religious
> grounds, but I sometimes peeped through the joints and got a glimpse
> of the stage. Among the plays whose names I recall from the hand
> bills were *The Maid of Cefn Ydfa*, *The Murder at The Red Barn*, *The Silver
> King*, *East Lynne* and *Maria Martin*.[68]

Other shows rumbled and rumpussed through Wales. Between 1897 and 1905, Buffalo Bill's Wild West Show, the simulacrum of manifest destiny, came a-whooping and a-heehawing into many Welsh towns.

Welsh music and the musical life of Wales experienced a similar series of tensions as did drama and dramatic activities. Sacred songs of praise sought to drown out secular arias. Yet, despite the strictures of the devout who insisted that music should have a scriptural basis, folk traditions continued. The Welsh Folk Song Society at the turn of the twentieth century sought to reveal the extent of these traditional songs. In 1928, the American collector James Madison Carpenter gathered more than fifty sea shanties from sailors in Barry, Cardiff and Swansea from singers such as Rees Baldwin, William Fender and others. J. Glyn Davies (1870–1953) gathered even more songs in Welsh and in English from the sailors of the Cambrian Line and the Welsh shipping companies on Merseyside. Davies, after a stormy period as Librarian in the university in Aberystwyth, published his findings in *Cerddi Huw Puw* (1923), which further popularised the song 'Fflat Huw Puw'.[69]

Communal hymn singing, which added such power and passion to the religious life of Wales, was one realm where Welsh music aspired to and sometimes achieved transcendence: to outlive the time and place of their creation. The terrifying tensions in their theology tinged Welsh sacred music towards the grave, the impetuous, the wrathful, even the anarchic – 'A'r maglau wedi torri a'r holl yn gwbl rhydd' (The chains are broken the masses are freed).[70] But the choral repertoire was greatly extended from the 1870s. Though the works of composers such as Gwilym Gwent (William Aubrey Williams; 1838–1891) were tailored to a Victorian taste, those of his close contemporary Joseph Parry (1841–1903) have a more lasting appeal.[71] The duet 'Hywel a Blodwen' from his opera *Blodwen* (1878) remains popular, whilst his part-song of unrequited love 'Myfanwy' attained legendary status. Other composers sought to take Welsh music further into the Wagnerian worlds of ancient battling princes and princely battles. Amongst the bruising songs composed were 'Charge of the Light Brigade' by D. C. Williams (1871–1926), 'Fallen Heroes' by Cyril Williams, 'The War Horse' by David Jenkins and the cataclysmic 'Battle of the Baltic' by D. Afan Thomas (1881–1928).[72]

The ancient tales of Wales were the inspiration for many, such as David Vaughan Thomas (1873–1934) in his 'Llyn y Fan'. Thomas, along with the precociously gifted David de Lloyd (1883–1948) and the operatically attractive yet sensitive to the point of being saintly Morfydd Llwyn Owen (1891–1918), revealed the musical potential of early Welsh poetry.[73] Morfydd's brief life was one of the true sadnesses of Welsh history (there was much that was tragic in Welsh music). She died of a botched appendicitis operation performed at home by her husband, the psychoanalyst Dr Ernest Jones. Morfydd's tragic death ranks with that of the poet Hedd Wyn. A precocious talent and its unfathomable potential was lost. The compositions that survive her merge traditional Welsh melodies with a discordant modernism – the harmonies have an apparent folkish familiarity, but there is still the hint of the modernistic, mechanistic broken fan belt.[74] Those who heard her sing recalled an 'eos' (a nightingale) or 'angel' (an angel) – an angel that looked as if she had emerged from a seashell by Botticelli.

The continual battle to raise musical standards in Wales was aided by the establishment of music departments in the constituent colleges of the University of Wales. Aberystwyth opened the score with its new department of music in 1873 under the baton of Joseph Parry and in 1903 Cardiff joined in, as then did Bangor in 1923. Joseph Parry's need for female voices in his performances greatly enhanced the demand for women to be admitted to the university as students. His successor as Professor of Music, Walford Davies (1869–1941), further improved standards not just in the seafront town, but across Wales. Davies was instrumental in establishing the Cyngor Cerddoriaeth Cenedlaethol (National Music Council). Under his leadership Welsh musical tradition moved from an overemphasis on the choral and the competitive to the instrumental and the classics of European music. Although it is often condemned for its parochialism and petty standards, the National Eisteddfod did give opportunities for the musical avant-garde. At Barry in 1921, Stravinsky's *Firebird* was sung in Welsh as *Aderyn Tân*, whilst a year later at Ammanford, Bach's *Requiem in B Minor* was performed. Other musical festivals also provided opportunities for wider musical genres to be performed. The annual festivals at Harlech (1869–1934), Cardiff (1892–1910), and the 'Three Valleys Festival' in Mountain Ash (1930–9) provided opportunities for classical and instrumental performances. Most remarkable of all was the patronage provided to musicians by the sisters Gwendoline and Margaret Davies in their annual festival at Gregynog. Conductors and composers of true international stature such as Gustav Holst were attracted to the cultural hothouse that was their mock-Tudor mansion at Gregynog between the wars.[75]

The BBC, like the University of Wales, was influential in fostering and furthering Welsh music. The corporation's attempt to serve the nation meant that its musical provision had to be eclectic – everything from the classical to the commonplace. The BBC acted with the largesse of the medieval gentry in its patronage of musicians. The composer Grace Williams (1906–77), who had studied composition in London and Vienna, just about kept the wolf from her door with commissions for film scores such as *Blue Scar* (1949) and radio performances of plays including those of Saunders Lewis. Her lyrical, symphonic compositions merged the intricacies of Welsh *penillion* with the darker tones of a world cast into the shadow of nuclear war. The BBC series 'Noson Lawen', the brainchild of Bangor's producer of genius, Sam Jones, propelled local singers such as Robert Roberts ('Bob Tai'r Felin'; 1870–1951) to national acclaim.[76] The pianist, composer, and producer of light entertainment programmes, Gladys May [Mai] Jones (1899–1960), created an English-language equivalent, 'Welsh Rarebit', from 1941, which featured many of her own compositions. Arwel Hughes (1909–98) and Mansell Treharne Thomas (1909–86) also served as directors of music at the BBC. During the Second World War there were three BBC orchestras stationed at Bangor – the BBC Dance Orchestra, the BBC Revue Orchestra and the BBC Variety Orchestra. So important was music in the repertoire of the BBC's provision, that the National Eisteddfod of 1940 was a 'Radio Eisteddfod' in order to overcome wartime restrictions.[77]

The much-vaunted claim that Wales was 'Gwlad y Gân' (The Land of Song) was primarily based on the choral tradition. In 1891, when a rugby international could attract a crowd of 10,000, very often 15,000 or more would cram in to listen to the chief choir competition at the National Eisteddfod. There were legendary victories, such as Côr Mawr Caradog's triumph at Crystal Palace in 1871 – a victory given an encore in 1872. Even more remarkable were the victories of Madam Clara Novello Davies's Welsh Ladies Choir at Chicago in 1893, and at the Paris Exhibition in 1900. Welsh music was cosmopolitan and international in its ambition and outlook.[78] Choral competitions at the Eisteddfod often resembled the combativeness of some of the test pieces. 'The Martyrs of the Arena', 'The Destruction of Gaza', 'Comrades in Arms', 'The Destruction of Pompeii', 'The War Horse', 'The Assyrians Came Down', 'The Glories of Our Blood and State' and the bloodcurdling choruses of David Jenkins's 'Vengeance Arise' were all test pieces at the National Eisteddfod between 1890 and 1914.

Though the emphasis is placed on male voice choirs, it is important to note that women were an important force in the musical life of Wales. At the National Eisteddfod of 1926 there were eighteen 'ladies choirs' in fierce competition. The term 'ladies' might not always have been appropriate. At an eisteddfod in Treharris in 1891, the female members of the characteristically combative Dowlais choir were well to the fore in the barracking of other choirs in a manner that even abashed their male companions. A reporter from *The Merthyr Express* described them as 'quite an army of Amazons'. Their coarse language caused them to be expelled from the eisteddfod and they kept it up even at the train station. At Newport in 1897, it was the power dressing of the female members of the choirs that caught the eye of the special correspondent of the *Western Mail*: 'the Merthyr choir seemed to have come to a wedding feast. All the girls wore white blouses and jubilee bonnets . . . and to heighten the effect the sopranos had blue sashes around their waists and the contraltos red ones.' The adjudicator was excused for ostentatiously turning his back on them as they formed up for 'no one could pay attention to the music with eyes on that dream of dressed bliss on the platform'.[79] They dressed to impress, they sang to escape the tedium of their lives of unremitting toil. Thirty years later the music critic of *The South Wales Daily Post* was even more critical of Welsh lady songsters carping that 'leading ladies sometimes have the countenance of a seraph and the voice of a seagull'.[80]

Conductors such as Dan Davies (1859–1930) who conducted the Dowlais and Merthyr choirs and Walter Protheroe of the Abersychan and Pontypool United choirs, developed what came to be regarded as the 'Welsh choral tradition'. It was deeply emotional, occasionally sentimental, almost ecstatic, always powerful. English or Scottish adjudicators, brought in to provide a much-needed independence of judgement and an enhancement of standards, often suggested the need for more refined singing and a more secure intonation. The comments in 1897 of Sir Alexander Mackenzie, principal of the Royal Academy of Music and an experienced choral conductor whose composition 'Rose of Sharon' was popular with Welsh chapel choirs, enraged the editor of the *Western Mail*. It was wrong, the editor argued, to judge Welsh singing by external standards. 'If the Cymry', the editor pontificated, 'should ever permit their choral singing to descend to the lifeless level it occupied in England and elsewhere, they would lose that which made their country the land of song'. A correspondent, a Mr Angry from Abertillery, argued the true character of Welsh singing was 'passion and emotion . . . It is as wrong to place English and Scottish adjudicators to judge Welsh music as it would be to hand over the essentially English offices, the Board of Trade and the management of our Colonial Empire to the druids.'[81]

Bands, all bugles blowing and cymbals crashing, were another element in communal music making in Wales. At the turn of the twentieth century it was estimated that there were more than 200 bands in Wales. Many, such as the Cyfarthfa, the Deiniolen and the Penrhyn, were closely linked to the workplace. Others that won considerable renown, such as the Dowlais, the Merthyr and the Llanelli, served the needs of wider communities. In 1892, the Llanelli band was victorious in a brass-band competition in that stronghold of brass-band music – the north-east of England. As a participant recalled: 'They expected to see a mountain pony sort of people, each munching a leek, and were disappointed to find that we were, at least in appearance, no different to other people.

When we won they gave us a right hearty reception and at once we became prime favourites.'[82]

The Llanelli band were not always prime favourites at the town's famous rugby ground, Stradey Park, for when the home team lost, they invariably ended proceedings with the march in Act Three of Handel's *Saul*. The Rechabites and the Salvation Army made their performance known to sinners through the portentous marching music of their bands. Less pugnacious perhaps than the onward marching Christian soldiers were the bands that accompanied the dogs of war. Bands were a vital aspect of the military in Wales. They boosted morale (especially when in tune), marked the point-of-no-retreat at which the troop's colours stood, and strengthened resolve. Joining the band might have seemed to be a safer option than enlisting as a soldier. But in countless bloody battles the bandsmen's fate was terrifying. As 9,000 chanting Zulu warriors, 'black as hell and thick as grass', came swarming towards him at Isandlwana on 22 January 1879, all Sergeant David Gamble of Brecon had to defend himself with was his Irish-made cello. It was a bad gamble. Gamble died a painful death.

Though the English adjudicators at the choral and band competitions in Wales often behaved with a condescending cultural imperialism, the real cultural power by the 1880s was America. Over the period 1870–1945, a bewildering range of musical genres swept across the Atlantic into Wales – spiritual, blackface minstrelsy, Appalachian folk songs and fiddle music, ragtime, blues and jazz. The Welsh lent an ear to them all. An independent declaration of American cultural superiority was given in 1880 with the tour of the blackface minstrels, the Fisk Jubilee Singers, on a fundraising tour for the new campus buildings at Fisk University in Nashville, which had been inaugurated 'for the education of freed slaves and their children'.[83] There was an immediate resonance for at the same time the 'pennies of the poor' of Wales were being cadged to support the fledgling University College in Aberystwyth. The New Theatre, Wind Street, Swansea, in 1888 hosted the fabulous Bohee Brothers from the United States performing popular ballads and comic songs, clog dances and soft shoe shuffles, all to the accompaniment of their duelling banjos. Sensationally, some of the 'brothers' were black women performers – Josie Rivers, Amy Height and Carlene Cushman. They were followed by the American-European Coloured Operatic Kentucky Minstrels, who were obviously playing safe and catering to all tastes. Welsh people also sought to get into the act. In 1890 Swansea formed its own Black Snowdrop Minstrels who performed at Craig-y-nos castle for the opera star Madame Adelina Patti. It seemed to have been more cultural chaos than concord, as the Swansea black-faced minstrels were accompanied in the 'Plantation Scenes' by the Penwyllt Black Hussars.[84]

The burdens of supporting the traditions of a musical nation were not only shouldered by the collective efforts of bands and choirs but rested on individual shoulders. For a small nation on the periphery of Europe, Wales produced a remarkable diversity of musicians who contributed to a plethora of musical genres. Instrumentalists such as the harpists John Roberts ('Telynor Cymru'; 1816–94), John Thomas ('Pencerdd Gwalia'; 1826–1913), the jazz pianist Dillwyn Owen Jones (1923–84), and the guitarists the three brothers from Tiger Bay, Frank Deniz (1912–2005), José William Deniz (1913–94) and Lawrence Richard Deniz (1924–96), and Henry Victor Parker (1910–78) strummed and scratched a living from their strings from St Davids Cathedral to Soho cheap joints.

Singing provided not just the imaginary impermanent release from poverty during the performance, but for some provided a permanent escape. Orphaned at seven years of age, Benjamin Grey (Ben) Davies (1858–1943) of Pontardawe won a prize at the 1877 Swansea Eisteddfod that enabled him to study at the Royal Academy of Music with Fiori and Randeggar (1878–80), where he won the Evill Prize and became one of 'the rising stars among English (sic) tenors'. [85] He graced opera houses from Chicago to Berlin to London. His fine natural gifts, which included an attractive timbre and clear enunciation, disciplined by an excellent technique, enabled him to continue his career well into his sixties. His broad experience he gave of freely in his role as president of the Society of English Singers. Leila Megáne (Margaret Hughes, née Jones; 1891–1961), from a similar background, became one of the legendary opera singers performing at Monte Carlo, Moscow, Milan, New York and Paris. Her first husband, the composer and pianist Thomas

Osborne Roberts, was so inspired by Leila that he poured his feelings into solos – 'Y Nefoedd', 'Y Gwanwyn Du' and 'Cymru Annwyl' ('Heaven', 'The Black Spring' and 'Dear Wales').[86] At a less elevated level, 'Smiling' Donald Peers (1909–73) who had escaped the poverty and piety of his Plymouth Brethren parents in Ammanford, thanks to the support of his English-language teacher at Amman Valley Grammar School, grinned all the way to the bank after his 1928 hit, 'In a Shady Nook by a Babbling Brook', topped the charts.[87] Teresa (Tessie) Mary O'Shea (1913–95) similarly escaped the poverty of Plantagenet Street, Cardiff, thanks to her voice. The sylph like eight-year-old, who had tied for first place in a talent competition with an entire Welsh choir, soon ballooned out to resemble one. Weighing more than eighteen stones at the height of her career, she seemed more like a female wrestler than a musician. But while the songs of 'Two Ton Tessie' alluded to her lack of sexual success – 'Nobody Loves a Fat Girl When She's Forty', 'I met him by the withered weeping willows', 'I fell in love with an airman but I'm nobody's sweetheart now' – their tone was one of self-celebration, reinforced by high kicks and a brisk banjolele self-accompaniment. From the 1940s she moved into a new career as a film and television actress and made one of her best remembered cinematic appearances in the Disney fantasy *Bedknobs and Broomsticks* (1971).[88]

Some of the most iconic songs of the twentieth century were composed by Welshmen. That anthem for doomed youth 'Keep the Home Fires Burning' (1915) was penned by Ivor Novello (1893–1951), Felix Powell of St Asaph wrote the music to 'Pack up Your Troubles in Your Old Kit Bag' in 1915, whilst Harry Parr Davies (1914–55), of Briton Ferry, wrote the even more popular hit for Gracie Fields, 'Wish me luck as you wave me goodbye'.[89]

It is impossible for one person to represent the vitality and the vibrancy, the confidence and the charisma of the cultural life of Wales, but Daniel Ivor Davies, who won fame and fortune under the nom-de-plume Ivor Novello, comes close. Despite his consummate achievements as a singer, actor, playwright and dramatist, it was in the field of musical theatre that Ivor Novello achieved legendary status. *Glamorous Night* (1935), *The Dancing Years* (1939) and *Perchance to Dream* (1947) dominated the musical theatre from the 1930s to the 1950s. *Perchance to Dream* ran for a record 1,022 performances and went on a world tour. In a world of rationing and shortages, war and outrages, Novello provided a self-consciously romantic counterblast of decency, romance and escapism. 'Some Day My Heart Will Awake', 'Rose of England', 'My Dearest Dear', 'My Heart Belongs to You', 'We'll Gather Lilacs', 'Shine Through My Dreams', 'The Land of Might-Have-Been' – who could resist such a mix of rousing opera choruses, jazz-age numbers, patriotism and sentiment?[90]

Ivor Novello was not the only character who could cross the boundaries and contribute to a broad range of cultural endeavours. The pioneer of the cinema in Wales, William Haggar (1851–1925), similarly made a contribution as a singer, a player in the perambulating theatre, a musical impresario, an actor, and a film producer, a distributer and a promoter. Haggar was one of the thousands of English-born people drawn into Wales in those Klondyke decades of the black-gold rush of the late 1890s and 1900s. He worked as a singer and stage carpenter with a group of travelling players around the south Wales coalfield communities. South Wales had the perfect environment for entertainment for there was an ample supply of young people with a surplus income who yearned for excitement and escape. Having seen the potential of the early cinema, Haggar decided to gamble on the new media and bought a bioscope machine for £80. His first showing of two films, *Turn Out the London Fire Brigade* and *Train Emerging From a Tunnel*, at Aberavon in April 1898 augured well. Despite the calamitous coal strike of 1898, Haggar's enterprise survived, returning a profit that paid for the equipment.[91]

William Haggar was soon making his own films, such as *Desperate Poaching Affray* (1903), *The Salmon Poachers – A Midnight Melee* (1905), *The Sheepstealer* (1908) and *The Life of Charles Peace* (1905). These subjects would obviously appeal to Welsh audiences who were still experiencing the poaching wars across Wales and involved the depravity of a notorious English murderer. But his films also sold exceptionally well across England and in America. The films realised the potential of the medium to create excitement and vicarious thrills. There were chase scenes when gamekeepers and police pursued poachers. There were panning shots, actors ran past the camera creating a sense of urgency and speed. The films were shot outside, often close to a river, and usually wrapped up within two hours. As with the greatest sportsmen, Haggar had an awareness of space and timing that helped to enhance the visual experience. In all, Haggar made more than thirty films. He pioneered moonlight filming, the use of guns in movies, whilst in films such as *The Tramp and the Washerwoman* (1903) and *The Tramp and the Baby's Bottle* (1903) he introduced a character that would later be made famous by Charlie Chaplin. The films were shown in steam-powered circus and portable theatre-style caravans that trundled around south Wales.

It is hard to imagine the remarkable impact of the early cinema. To a twenty-first century eye the special effects now appear to be neither special nor effective, but for audiences in the early decades of the twentieth century the early cinema was a revelation. For us, the parade's long gone by, but those people who watched their approach were struck with wonder.[92] The challenge to the cinema entrepreneur was to ensure an endless supply of material. Thus cinema pioneers such as William Haggar soon realised that they had to obtain films from other suppliers rather than just produce their own. Movies produced in England became increasingly common, but by the First World War, America had risen to prominence in the cinematic world.

Amongst the films that presaged the American dominance was *The Birth of a Nation*, an epic, blockbusting reinterpretation of the Civil War and subsequent history of the United States of America produced by the Welsh-descended D. W. Griffith, whose grand-father, 'Roaring Jack Griffith', had been a Confederate colonel. Griffith made *The Birth of a Nation* because he believed it. It was one of the most innovative and immoral films, uniquely both the best and the worst movie ever made. It was a racist rant that resulted in the glorification and reinvigoration of the Ku Klux Klan. Yet Woodrow Wilson, who watched it in the White House, considered 'that it was like writing history with lightning'. The technical innovations were endless: the use of a specially scored musical accompaniment, rather than a pianist making it up as the film went on. Griffith invented the fade and the panorama. The acting was more naturalist, and less histrionic. He had a filmic rather than a static approach that ensured a flow of action and pioneered the close-up to underline emotion and details and to move the plot. Storylines were woven together to give a sense of unfolding, complementary dramas. Griffith was clear in both his ambition and achievement: 'The task I am trying to achieve, above all, is to make you see. Remember how small the world was before I came along? I brought it all to life: I moved the whole world into a twenty-foot screen.'[93]

Despite its suspect moral legacy, *The Birth of a Nation* established America as the home of movies – it was the cinema's *Iliad*, the movie that made film an American dream. With the proceeds, D. W. Griffith set up United Artists with Mary Pickford, Douglas Fairbanks and Charlie Chaplin, the beginning of the studio system of film making and the ongoing battle between talent and technology.

By the 1920s and 1930s people appreciated the cinema's power to influence audience opinion, tastes and outlook. The sweeping cultural annexation by America was clearly perceived. The 1920s were clearly the golden age of the cinema, as the media turned from silence to sound. By 1934 there were 321 cinemas in Wales. Though there were Welsh movies such as *Y Chwarelwr* and films based in Wales such as *Proud Valley* and *The Citadel*, overwhelmingly the movies shown were those produced in Hollywood.

Their impact and influence were matters of cultural and moral concern. In March 1941, Abercynon magistrates refused a licence to an Ynysybwl cinema to show the film *Million Dollar Legs*. Despite the film's star Betty Grable proving that she had a pair, after scrutinising the synopsis, magistrate Mr J. Bowen Davies was horrified: 'Is this the sort of thing you are going to show?', he asked, ' . . . something to make your hair stand on end. No, I do not like the look of it.'[94] His was not a lone voice. Thomas Jones, the highly influential Cabinet Secretary of the 1920s and 1930s, lamented in 1934 how 'today a number of our institutes are dormant . . . cinema and billboards going strong and education going weak . . . I cannot imagine that this was the dream of the pioneers fifty years ago.'[95]

James Griffiths, in his opening address at the Ystradgynlais Miner's Hall and Institute, urged that:

> We should strive to make the institute the centre of our social and cultural life – a centre from which will radiate fellowship and will enrich the community . . . It is time we created our own culture. We are now importing culture from other countries which is infinitely worse than our own.[96]

In the 1930s the cinema became increasingly referred to as 'dream palaces', from which the 'dream factory' of Hollywood 'entertained' a pliant, plastic, day-dreaming people. For Iris Barry, this dream-like quality was what made the cinema so much more popular than the theatre:

> To go to the pictures is to purchase a dream. To go to the theatre is to buy an experience, and between experience and dream there is a vast difference . . . we come out of the pictures soothed and drugged like sleepers awakened having half forgotten our own existence, hardly knowing our names.[97]

'Fields of praise': sport and society

It was a wonderful cosmopolitan train that started the first Welsh Cup Final invasion of Wembley. There were professional men and ladies of leisure, shop girls, clerks, miners, artisans, seafarers and labourers, all equal and all happy on the common level of patriotism for the city and its association football team. Just the same equality of sport and of enthusiasm that carried Britain shoulder to shoulder through the nasty patches of the Great War.

All through the Friday night and the early hours of Saturday morning the streets of London were musical with Welsh hymns and songs. The leek and the daffodil were almost as abundant, worn as favours, as the City's colours. It was not merely a Cardiff City occasion, it was an all Wales occasion for national pride.

(*Western Mail*, 25 April 1927.)

Sport offered (and offers), a great deal to society. It tells us much about what it is to be human – co-operation, endeavour, escapism, futility, physicality, tribalism. Sport is the cliché of hope, an act of exuberance amongst hardship and squalor. The period 1870–1945 saw a remarkable transformation in Welsh sport, as the rough-and-tumble games of village yokels became the national soap operas and philosophies for life. Leisure life would become a glissando of air-punching triumph or knuckle-gnawing disappointment, an oscillating circle of emotion, a lifelong tease of little false endings in a drama without a plot, a national obsession, a people's identity.

As with the Greek and Roman empires, the sun would never set on the British Empire because sport had hardened the physicality and honed the pertinacity of her people. Games were a way of quickly and enjoyably working out leadership material, extolling and teaching all those things that the imperial administrative class so admired. Games, particularly team games, fostered clannish bonding and homoerotic hierarchy and hero-worship, all of which were considered to be good things when dealing with lesser people.[98] Games gave one a sense of honour and justice and were, especially when codified and structured, implicitly the gift and birthright of evolved societies. The captain of the First XI or the First XV was invariably regarded as the ideal candidate to run some lost corner of the Empire. Teams appeared to be selfless, highly industrious, all-for-one-and-one-for-all, collectively willing to battle to the final whistle, the Puritan virtues in play. Those who could survive the binding and bonding of rugby forward play and the brutal foot-rushes were deemed ideal for the frontal infantry charges of Spion Kop or the Somme. Though the scrum often proved to be too simple to produce anything but simpletons, people still argued that the playing fields provided the perfect preparation for the killing fields. The deaths of sporting stars such as the superlatively talented rugby international Norman Biggs (1870–1908) by a poisoned arrow in Nigeria, and that of the first football superstar, goalkeeper Leigh Roose (1877–1916) on the Somme, and countless others, revealed the tragic futility of the view.

Some corners of foreign fields further testified to the intimate and inextricable relationship between sport and Empire. When they were not fighting in battle, Welsh soldiers were often engaged in sporting conquest. The 1st Brecknockshire Battalion of the South Wales Borderers won the Calcutta Cup in 1917.[99] The press reports of their victory indicate that the qualities of discipline, team-spirit, endurance and fair-play were important in maintaining the imperial idea. Sports were also valuable in showing the native communities that the white settlers were superior. 'A test match today is an imperial event' pontificated William George Arthur Ormsby-Gore, fourth Baron Harlech (1885–1964) in the 1920s. One of the few successes of the period of the inimitable James ('Jimmy' or 'Jim') Henry Thomas (1874–1949) in the Colonial Office was the foundation of the British Empire Games that further symbolised the importance attached to the connections between sport and empire.[100]

Such imperial and imperious themes also played themselves out in the development of sport in Wales.[101] Fishing, hunting and horse riding were closely linked to the squirarchy.[102] Landowners and clubs who bought fishing rights on the rivers Wye, Severn, Teifi and Towy clashed with locals who regarded it as their natural right to poach the fish. There was conflict between those who fished for sport and those who did so for survival as salmon and sewin often supplemented family budgets.[103] Such tensions survived throughout the period 1870–1945. Fishing clubs, many of which had extensive working-class memberships, became increasingly popular at the turn of the twentieth century. But in the 1920s and 1930s economic depression saw an increase in the number of poachers intent on harvesting the natural bounty of the rivers. Fishing saw a remarkable creativity as people crafted flies that were carefully created for their location. Fishing, the activity in which a jerk on one end of a rod waited for a jerk on the other, probably had a greater participation across Wales than any other sport.[104]

Hunting was another area where there was tension between those who pursued fox or hare for pleasure and those who did so to protect their livelihoods. The game laws were a perpetual bone of contention between landlords and locals who hunted with snare and trap, dog and ferret. As large estates sought to safeguard their partridges and pheasants, the tensions between poacher and game-keeper often descended into open warfare. For two decades in the

1880s and 1890s, mid Wales was traumatised by the violence and open lawlessness of the 'Second Rebecca Riots'.

At the opening of the twentieth century, Welsh landlords seemed to revel in the Edwardian mania for avian holocausts. The hunting of foxes however saw a far stronger accord across social groups. In Wales the unmentionable of all classes enthusiastically pursued the inedible. Owner occupiers, tenant farmers, labourers and landlords were united in engaging the chase. Hunts were notable social occasions that drew large crowds.[105] Women also participated and had an opportunity to display themselves in the saddle. It was natural, perhaps, that Godfrey Charles Morgan, Viscount Tredegar (1831–1913), would gain renown as a huntsman and that his Tredegar Hunt was widely admired. During the Crimean War, Morgan had ridden 'into the valley of death' with 'the brave 500' and had survived unscathed. Due to his wit and wisdom he was known as 'the Mark Twain of Wales'. From his family's fortune he funded schools, hospitals, libraries, parks and eisteddfodau and still had enough spare cash to fund one of Britain's most well-provided hunts. For twenty years he was master of the Tredegar Hunt and he also took a strong interest in bowls, fishing, grouse shooting, hockey, 'and any and every manly sport'. In a portrait in oils by J. Charlton, he sits on his charger surrounded by his hunting dogs, refined, reposed, the perfect model of the sporting squire. Tally-ho, Tally-ho, a-hunting he did go.

Horse-racing had even greater concord across the classes. Ivor Churchill Guest, first Viscount Wimborne (1873–1939), Lloyd George's 'evil genius' who always had a hint of the night about him, won the Grand National as an owner in 1939, when Fancy Free flew to victory in his colours. Guest also found time in his busy political life for his diverse sporting talents. He captained the Quidnuncs, the trophy-winning polo team, was a good tennis player, golfer, fencer and rode to hounds. Fulke Thomas Tyndall Walwyn (1910–91) of Wrexham also won the Grand National, but as a rider, even though he lost both his whip and an iron. As a horse trainer he trained the winners of 2,188 races over jumps and hurdles.

On 4 April 1887, a crowd of 50,000, one of the largest crowds ever assembled in nineteenth-century Wales, gathered at the new Manselton Racecourse, Swansea.[106] The grandstand could accommodate 2,500 people and had dining and gambling facilities as well as its own telegraph office from which the eagerly awaited results were sent around Britain. Steeplechasing had become a significant business at the turn of the twentieth century, with notable competitions at Tenby, Carmarthen, Cardiff, Chepstow and Wrexham as well as Swansea. The attraction was not just the chase. The races at Llangyfelach fair in March 1891 had spacious drinking booths, which were

> filled with men and women, young and old, whose features are almost blackened with the smoke that fills the place. A glance at the faces of some present tell a tale of reckless dissipation . . . Here are town women and men, fairly well dressed, but who lead what is termed a 'loose life'. They are red with port, and redolent of slang. Close by sit three or four young fellows drinking and smoking, and their talk is of drink, women and betting . . . [107]

Betting and gambling took place not just on the horses. Gaming tables were in evidence and 'professors of the three-card trick and other species of social larceny worked themselves into proper business condition'.[108] In April 1887, George Thompson of Cardiff was caught playing a game of tombola with the crowd. As he stood upon a stool with a table in front of him, a monkey sitting on his shoulder would watch him deal out the tin tickets and, on cue from his master, pull one of the numbered balls out of the container. William Steward was arrested for playing a game of chance called 'over and under the seven' with a box and dice. Despite his defence that he had played the game before the Prince of Wales, and that it was therefore legal, Steward was fined £1.[109]

Doris Magness of Swansea recalled that her mother and her friend 'loved a gamble on the horses laying out 3d wins or 3d each ways'. This latter bet meant that they had a return on their money if the horse lost but came second or third, depending on the number of runners in the race. Superstitions grew. This feminine syndicate once bet on a horse called Lucky Seven in the seventh race at seven o'clock at Sandown Park. It came in seventh.[110]

Men 'studied the form' in the racing columns of the daily news-papers and invested their money with the large national betting companies such as Ladbrokes, William Hill and Coral. Runners were employed to collect bets and debts. By the 1920s organised criminal gangs controlled the betting at races in Cardiff, Newport and Chepstow. Gambling took other forms as well as betting on the outcome of horse races. Arab, Chinese, Irish and West Indian immigrants in Cardiff's Tiger Bay wagered on cards, dice and domino games as too did Welsh people in clubs, dives, dumps and pubs. The development of the football pools further extended the opportunities available to people to gamble. By 1953, an average Welsh family spent 5–7 per cent of their recreation expenditure on betting.[111]

As well as horse-racing the great outdoors of Wales provided a wealth of opportunities to those who wished to climb, walk or 'perambulate' in the fresh air. By the 1920s the ornithological riches of Wales was being enjoyed by a number of people inspired by works such as those by Richard Morgan (1854–1939): *Tro Trwy'r Wig, Llyfr Blodau, Llyfr Adar, Rhamant y Grug Lwydlas* (all *c*.1920). The teacher and naturalist Robert Ellis Vaughan Roberts (1888–1962) encouraged generations of people to enjoy outdoor life through his roles in the classroom, as president of the Chester and North Wales Natural Society and in articles in *Y Cymro, Yr Herald Gymreig, Llafar, Y Gymdogaeth, Countryside* and *Country Quest*. Local crags and cliffs in north Wales provided stern challenges to climbers. In the opening decades of the twentieth century, many of the most adventurous and astute Welsh climbers were female. Mary Ann Williams (1873–1942), Muriel Gwendoline Jones (née Edwards), Emmeline Lewis Lloyd (1827–1913) and her sister Isabella trained in Snowdonia and then adapted their techniques to climb in the Alps.[112] At the Pen-y-Gwryd Hotel, Snowdonia, in March 1921, the Women's Rock Climbing Club (later the Pinnacle Club) was estab-lished to elevate women climbers.

An obsession with the highest mountain on earth was perhaps understandable for it had been named after a Welshman. Everest drew one of the most colourful and charismatic characters in Welsh climbing history. After periods of training in Snowdonia, Charles

Bruce (1866–1939), the youngest of the fourteen children of Henry Austin Bruce, first Baron Aberdare, acquired extensive climbing experience during his soldiering in the Himalayas in the 1890s at the peak of 'The Great Game'. In 1894 he climbed Nanga Parbat and in 1907 Trisul, a 23,600 feet peak revered by the Hindus as the trident of Shiva, the god of destruction and procreation. For more than two decades this would be the highest mountain ever climbed.

In 1914, Bruce went to Gallipoli, in command of the 107 Battalion of the 6th Gurkha Rifles, a band he had created and trained. After two months on the front line he was 'cut down with machine-gun fire that nearly severed both his legs'. Advised by the medical board to retire to a quiet life and to be careful never to walk strenuously uphill, Bruce responded with typical aplomb leading the 1922 and 1924 expeditions to Everest. The 1924 group might well have achieved the first successful ascent of the mountain by George Mallory and Andrew Irvine. Romantics insist that they 'conquered' Everest, rationalists suggest that they got tantalisingly close. Certainly, during the expedition, Charles Bruce's nephew, Geoffrey Bruce, used oxygen to set a new height record of 27,300 on Everest via the North Col.

Climbing and mountaineering retained a reputation for being the preserve of the 'idle rich'. But several other sports acquired a reputation for exclusivity. Despite the renown of Welsh archers at the Battle of Crécy when they flashed their famous 'V sign' at the enemy, archery never became universally popular in Wales.[113] Nevertheless, one of Britain's most prestigious archery clubs was the Royal British Bowmen of Denbighshire whose patrons included the Prince of Wales. Sycophancy and snobbery rather than sportsmanship marked the club: 'members marched two and two to the shooting ground, the music playing a new march composed for the occasion, and colours flying. On their arrival at the ground, a royal salute of 21 guns was fired'.[114] One of the great attractions of archery for the paedophile and priest Francis Kilvert was not the pageantry, but the opportunity to view 'fine feminine forms' (the younger the better), such as 'Lovely little May Oliver with her bewitching face, beautiful eyes and golden curls. She was shooting and had no quiver, so I acted as quiver for her, loading her arrows, picking them up, and being her slave generally.'[115] Freud must have had a field day. Oh! What a perfect day it must have been with the enslaved priest all a quiver.

Croquet matches on the manicured lawns of Radnorshire's gentry also gave Kilvert the chance to indulge his favourite pastime – the pursuit of young girls. The North Cardiganshire Archery and Croquet Club similarly provided ample opportunities for the pervert for some unlucky soul had to ensure that the lady members were attired in the regulation red and cream striped petticoats.[116] One of the greatest croquet players of all time was Lilias Mary (Lily) Gower (1877–1959) of the Castle Malgwyn estate in Pembrokeshire. She won titles against both men and women, including the ladies championship of England in 1899, 1900 and 1901. In 1904 she won the Open Championship Cup and in 1904 the Open Championship.[117] The sports paper *Ladies Field* considered her success 'epoch-making . . . proof that a woman, if armed with up-to-date implements, can compete with success in the several and prolonged conflict of nerve, endurance and hard work which a croquet match requires'.[118]

The moral police were also active in the Penarth Yacht Club, ensuring that there was no Sunday drinking, or that any ladies were on the balcony unaccompanied by a 'gentleman' (although finding one was challenging for there were several complaints about obscene language). The Glamorgan landowner and politician Windham Thomas Wyndham-Quin (1841–1926) was best known as a yachtsman who spent a fortune on two gallant but unsuccessful attempts to bring the America's Cup back to Britain with Valkyrie II and III in 1893 and 1895.

Golf was another sport that was regarded as an activity of relatively well-to-do people. It was the upwardly mobile who would spoil their walk on the golf links. By the 1890s, Wales had a series of golf clubs, many of which, at Aberdyfi, Abersoch, Penarth and Ynys Las, were located amongst spectacular scenery that must have compensated for a poor lie. The tiniest thing could upset some golfers on these greens, even the uproar of the butterflies in the adjoining meadows. Golfers kept it in the family. Both mother and father of the champion Welsh golfer David James (Dai) Rees

(1913–83) were golf professionals at the Leys and Brynkill golf clubs in south Wales.

Another game suitable for ladies of both sexes and an ideal pastime for the rich was lawn tennis. More so perhaps than any other sporting pastime, lawn tennis has a claim to being 'the national sport', for at least the game was invented in Wales. Major Walter Clopton Wingfield (1833–1912), a soldier and inventor from Ruabon, gave the first demonstration of the new game at a party in the Nantclwyd Hall in Denbighshire in 1868.[119] To popularise his new game Wingfield authored two tennis books, *The Book of the Game* (1873) and *The Major's Game of Lawn Tennis* (1874). The game's popularity was not helped by the Major christening the game by the tongue-tying name of Sphairistikè (Greek for 'ball games'). He also patented a *New and Improved Court for Playing the Ancient Game of Tennis* and began marketing his game in the spring of 1874, selling boxed sets that included rubber balls imported from Germany as well as a net, poles, court markers, rackets and an instruction manual.

Some Welsh people proved to be remarkably good at Wingfield's new game. Clarence Napier Bruce, third Baron Aberdare (1885–1957), was the British rackets champion in 1922 and 1931, the British tennis champion in 1932, Canadian tennis champion in 1928 and 1930, the USA tennis champion in 1930, real tennis champion of the USA in 1930, and of England in 1932 and 1938. Bruce also won several tennis doubles championships and also played first-class cricket for Middlesex. His partner in the 1939 amateur racquets final was his son Morys, who became 4th Baron Aberdare. Morys placed much of his father's efforts with a racket on the record in *The Story of Tennis* (1959) and *The Willis Faber Book of Tennis and Rackets* (1980).

Vulcanised rubber balls were the key to the increasing popularity of tennis but technological change could not only improve pastimes and sports but also invent new ones. Despite its frightening appearance and bone-cracking ride, the high-wheeled 'penny farthing' bicycle of the 1870s had an immediate success noted in the much-sung folk song 'Hen Feic penny farthing Fy Nhaid'. By 1879, some sixty firms produced more than 300 different kinds of bicycles according to Henry Stormey's *Indispensable Bicyclist's Handbook* (1879). By 1880 there were more than fifty cycling clubs in Wales and cycling became ever more popular as the price of cycles fell from £20 in 1878, to 9 guineas in the mid-1880s. The invention of 'safety bicycles' and the development of pneumatic tyres created a safer, smoother ride.

Cycling was both a sport and an essential method of travel. By the 1930s, more than 40 per cent of Welsh miners travelled more than five-miles to work, whilst the long legs of the law, especially in rural Wales, pursued miscreants on their police-issue bicycles. An industry appeared almost overnight to provide the cyclist's needs. The Stepney Spare Wheel Co. of Llanelli and Tom Norton (1870–1955) of Llandrindod Wells sold wheels, bells, brushes, carriers, lamps, polish, pumps, repair outfits, spanners and stands. Cycling widened the circles of courtship of the Welsh people as men and women pedalled beyond their parish boundaries in search of love. Cycling also revolutionised women's fashion as some women, scandalously, would wear trousers to ride, whilst others, even more scandalously, would wear a shorter skirt that would not be entangled in the chain. As ever the puritan complained, the prurient celebrated.

The 1890s were probably the peak decade for the sport of cycling in Wales. Professional cyclists such as brothers Tom, Sam and Arthur Linton from Aberaman in south Wales came to national and international prominence. Arthur Linton virtually unbeatable in south Wales and London moved to Paris where he raced against the world's best cyclists before crowds of more than 20,000 at the Vélodrome d'Hiver, the Vélodrome Buffalo and the Vélodrome de la Seine. Another south Wales cyclist, Jimmy Michael, travelled to America where, in a series of high-profile victories in alleycat races, his *à bloc* earned him 'dazzling stacks of American dollars'.[120] In one memorable series of races, Michael competed against another Aberamanite, Sam Linton, in front of massive crowds and a band that heralded the two gladiators into the arena with a rendition of 'Men of Harlech'. The Welsh contribution to cycle racing was recognised in 1896 when Newport hosted the world championships.

Technology was also vital in the development of greyhound racing (the dogs raced each other, usually). At Cardiff and Newport, dog-race tracks offered anorexic-looking speedsters the opportunity to chase after an electric hare. Local dogs also chased gold on the London circuit. Modern sports co-existed with more primitive endeavours. Dog fights and cock-fighting (using cockerels) was still popular in the 1920s and brutal, bareknuckle boxing bouts that sometimes resulted in death took place in public houses such as the Iron Bridge in Aberdare. Arthur Vaughan of Penrhiwceiber lost his life in 1894 after a quarrel that resulted in a bareknuckle fight on Llanwonno mountain on a Sunday morning for a paltry £1 a round.[121] Boxing booths toured Wales alongside travelling fairs and circuses, where the brave, or the brainless, could challenge the champion over three rounds in the ring. Gloves on such occasions were often paper-thin stinging strips of flexible leather.[122] At Aberdare on 17 May 1894, in the Old Slaughter House, David Rees was killed when he was knocked out of the ring and landed on his head. His opponent, Thomas Edwards, was acquitted of a manslaughter charge.

Despite the dangers, boxing remained popular amongst an element of the Welsh people. Self-defence through 'the noble art' was a valued virtue. The poet Cynan when a soldier in the First World War watched in awe as a delicate-looking Welsh curate beat the brains out of a bullying gigantic sergeant from the north of England. The capacity to use one's fists was obviously a virtue.[123] Frank Richards, who escaped south Wales for the army after the intimidation of the coal strike of 1898, recalled his military career as one of perpetual fighting, not with enemy forces, but with rival regiments. The Welsh Regiment had a long-running feud with the Royal Marines that went back to Napoleonic times, but its memory was kept alive in many a beery den.[124]

In the early twentieth century, Wales produced three world-class fighters of fearless courage – 'Peerless' Jim Driscoll (1880–1925), Freddie Welsh (1886–1927) and Jimmy Wilde of Tylorstown (1892–1969).[125] Like Welsh and Driscoll, boxing success made Wilde a celebrity. The 'fistic marvel' lost in only four of his 864 bouts. He made guest appearances in music hall shows and comedy fights in England and even starred in his own film, *From Pit-Boy to World's Champion*.[126] Fred Dyer took national stereotypes to their illogical conclusion when he toured Britain as 'the renowned Welsh singing boxer . . . the most refined and only act of its kind'. Tommy Farr (1913–86) of Clydach Vale was another lone act in 1937 when he fought the legendary American Joe Louis in New York for the world heavyweight title. The fight, broadcast live on the radio, held the nation spellbound. Farr entered the ring wearing a cape emblazoned with the Welsh dragon. The fight was close, very, very close. But, as in so many of the great Welsh sporting events, Farr lost. For his valour he received £36,000, a sizeable fortune, and thereafter lived a champagne and celebrity lifestyle far-removed from his Rhondda roots.[127]

The cult of the gallant losers was integral to the amateur ethos that permeated team games in Wales. The debate over the respective merits of amateur versus professional sport played itself out in baseball, cricket, football, hockey, rugby and even water polo. The Welsh seemed to revel in the role of underdog, the Dafydd that defeats Goliath. Amateurism was deemed to be closer to the true ethos and the actual ideal of the game.[128] Professionalism prostituted the pastime. In a sense the support of the amateur ideal was natural in a country with so few financial resources as Wales. But twentieth-century sport learned to grapple with the harsh reality of capitalism. Cash is a magnate for talent. Those high priests of the fields of praise were attracted away across the border to play in the English leagues. William Henry 'Billy' Meredith (1874–1958) was transferred from Manchester City to Manchester United and back to City in a twenty-eight-year career (1892–1924) that would have been longer were it not for football being suspended during the First World War. Even so, he scored 470 goals in 2,000 matches. Leigh Roose, 'Yr Ercwlff synfawr hwn' (the wondrous Hercules), left his first team 'The Druids' (presumably they recited poems and played in flowing white gowns) to play for a series of professional teams in the north of England. The Welsh international Dai Astley cost Blackpool £10,000 in 1939. Cardiff City and 'ugly, lovely' Swansea Town, established relatively late in 1910 and 1912 respectively, soon found that remuneration and reward were better in the English leagues.[129] Newport County and Wrexham soon followed. Cardiff won the Football Association Cup in 1927, one of the pinnacles of Welsh sporting achievement between the wars. Swansea's victory in the League West Cup 1942–3 was less notable. Yet success in the English league was fleeting. In 1936, Cardiff played so badly that between their first victory and their next there had been three kings. Poet and doctor Dannie Abse recalled that the 'true tragedy' in the *South Wales Echo* in 1936 was not the headlines 'NAZIS ENTER RHINELAND' but the performances of his beloved Bluebirds. At one stage the team's top scorer was one of the defenders with own goals.[130]

Rugby players, like footballers, chased cash. Although Wales won the rugby championship in 1922, the national team was ravaged by defections to England to play rugby union and rugby league. More than 1,000 players deserted Gwalia and moved east of Eden to play in both rugby codes. Consequently Wales won only nine of thirty-two international games between 1923 and 1930 and failed to beat England once in this period. In 1928 even France beat Wales for the first time. Six of the English rugby XV who won four grand slams in the 1920s were born in Wales. Despite an offer to play football for Tottenham Hotspur, Augustus John Ferdinand (Gus) Risman (1911–94) signed, for £1 a week plus a £25 signing-on fee, for Salford rugby league club.

Sport achieved the remarkable feat of complicating even further the fractured national identity. Football supporters chanted, cheered and clanked their rattles for their local Welsh village teams, but also for Liverpool, or a Manchester team (usually United), or the Arsenal whose phalanx of Wales-born players in the 1930s made them a natural choice for Welsh people to follow. Welsh cricketers, 'those organised loafers', played for England. Despite all the talk about the 'England and Wales Cricket Board' the team was stubbornly always referred to in the singular – England.[131] Welsh Olympians such as Cardiff-born Paolo Radmilovic competed in five Olympic games, the last in 1928 when he was in his forties, winning four gold medals, all for Britain. Rugby player Gus Risman won eleven rugby league caps with Wales, one with England, and seventeen for Great Britain (including five Ashes series wins against Australia).

The tiresome dispute between football and rugby as to which was the national sport still drones on in the twenty-first century with the tenacity of bareknuckle boxers on Llanwonno mountain. Football, 'the beautiful game', was probably played and supported by a broader cross-section of the Welsh people – they were stronger together. A matter of greater importance than life or death, certainly more important than a game, football was a simple act that transcended borders and language – everybody spoke football from north to south, east to west. When the Royal Welch Fusiliers set out for their Christmas truce with the Germans in 1914, one of the first things they did was to kick a football around. Even in the most brutal of environments the Welsh played football. There was a Welsh football team in the Auschwitz Prisoner of War camp.[132] The advent of the football pools in the 1920s meant that the audience the sport reached was even greater as thousands of people around Wales were enslaved, week in week out listening to the results.

Rugby, despite attempts to broaden its geographical range, was very much the preserve of south and west Wales.[133] There was a 'tribal mystery' about Welsh rugby. But the much-vaunted Welsh way of playing the game was undoubtedly a reality, for in the 1880s Wales pioneered the use of four three quarters. The Welsh were mercurial, magical – invariably capable of producing the unexpected. In March 1934, in a match against Ireland, Bridgend's Vivian Jenkins defied convention by running the ball back from close to his own try line, kicking ahead, gathering and scoring at the opposite end. Jenkins was castigated by rugby purists for not kicking into touch in defence when he first received the ball.

Welsh rugby was characterised by the fluidity, stealth and speed of the backs.[134] Yet the grand slams and triple crowns of the first 'golden age' of Welsh rugby 1900–14 would not have been won without the steel and strength of the Welsh forwards. There was graft as well as glamour. Shady men were needed who could conduct dark deeds on the blind side of the scrum. The Welsh pack in 1914 under the leadership of the Revd Alban Davies, later an army chaplain and vicar of Hook in Pembrokeshire, came to be known as 'the Terrible Eight', not because they were bad players, but because of the terror they instilled in opponents. Imagine being told by Davies to repent. Some purists of the game insisted that Welsh rugby was at its best in those dour rain-drenched 0–0 or 1–0 encounters when the game only occasionally broke out around the fighting and the ball rarely emerged from powerful forearms. Taking apart was more important than taking part. After the 1925 strike in the anthracite coalfield and the 1926 general strike, scores were settled between strikers and policemen on lawless rugby pitches. To be on the safe side, one referee in Glyncorrwg took to the field with a revolver.[135]

It was not so much on the fields of praise that rugby's claim to be the national game lay, but around them. The hymn singing of the crowd touched a chord of the national psyche. A perceptive observer from England noted:

> Rugby football in South Wales produces an almost religious enthusiasm, and the Welshman has a wonderful power of giving vent to his religion in song. Certainly I have never witnessed anything comparable in emotional excitement as the scene before an international match in Cardiff . . . That famous song (Hen Wlad Fy Nhadau) is not so much a challenge to the enemy as a universal and tremendous prayer for their overthrow.[136]

The hymns and arias followed the Welsh team wherever they played. At Murrayfield in 1938, an estimated 20,000 Welsh people had saved their weekly shillings and undertaken the trip. More than thirty trains had carried them northwards in a major logistical challenge for the Great Western Railway that they had not faced since August 1914. One rail company 'drafted in Welsh-speaking staff who . . . through microphones and loudspeakers guided and directed passengers at Princes Street Station and acted as interpreters when necessary'.[137] Rugby internationals had become profitable business for cafes, hotels, pubs and travel companies.

The development of archery, cycling, tennis and other sports served to broaden the opportunities available to Welsh women to participate in a healthier lifestyle.[138] So too did some government legislation such as the Baths and Washhouses Act 1846. The Act encouraged local authorities to build covered swimming pools and open air lidos with the aim of helping working people to stay clean and healthy. The Welsh Amateur Swimming Association was formed in 1897, while south Wales was one of the earliest venues for water polo, especially for women. In 1899, the Swansea Ladies Water Polo Club was founded and it was soon competing nationally. In 1900 the club beat Jersey Ladies to win the Ravensbourne Shield, and did not lose again until 1907, surely one of the longest winning streaks in Welsh sporting history.[139]

Team sports nurtured that much-vaunted and valued virtue – 'team spirit'. Playing up, and playing the game in union were the characteristics that would create a national spirit fit for an imperial age. When Wales defeated New Zealand 3–0 in 1905, that home of good sports reporting, the *South Wales Daily News*, in the years before the cliché-ridden sports commentaries, excitedly declared:

> The men – these heroes of many victories that represented Wales embodied the best manhood of the race . . . We all know the racial qualities that made Welsh supreme on Saturday . . . It is admitted she is the most poetic of nations. It is amazing that in the greatest of all popular pastimes she should be equally distinguished . . . the great quality of defence and attack in the Welsh race is to be traced to the training of the early period when powerful enemies drove them to their mountain fortresses. There was developed, then, those traits of character that find fruition today. 'Gallant Little Wales' has produced sons of strong determination, invincible stamina, resolute, mentally keen, physically sound.[140]

Presumably the same could be said for the best womanhood of the race.

Yet for all the verve and vitality of the playing fields, for all those who worshipped the goddess of victories and just did it, there were many who considered how wonderful it was to do nothing, and then to rest afterwards. Like W. H. Davies, for many Welsh people exercise enough was just to go out to the garden:

> Where bumble-bees, for hours and hours
> Sit on their soft, fat, velvet bums
> To wriggle out of hollow flowers.[141]

'The Trip to Echo Spring': drink and dissolution

Up the street in the Sailor's Arms, Sinbad Sailors, grandson of Mary
Ann the Sailors, draws a pint in the sun-lit bar. The ship's clock in
the bar says half past eleven. Half past eleven is opening time. The
hands of the clock have stayed at half past eleven for fifty years. It
is always opening time in the Sailor's Arms.

Dylan Thomas, *Under Milk Wood: A Play for Voices*,
edited by Walford Davies and Ralph Maud
(London, 1995), p. 28.

In the period down to the First World War there was a transfer
from those who brewed beers and distilled spirits on a 'cottage'
basis into significant industrial enterprises. It is difficult to time
the transformation with any precision, for small-scale producers
could still be found across Wales. An old woman who kept a little
inn on the Gower still gathered her hops in the 1870s, as she had
in the 1850s, from the hedges, drying them in bags from the kitchen
ceiling, and 'from this economy she was able to brew an 18 gallon
cask of beer for one shilling and sixpence.'[142] Her home-brewed
rot-gut was deadly – drinking four pints resulted in oblivion. The
local ales of Llangollen, which had so impressed George Borrow
on his pub crawl around Wild Wales in the 1850s, still captivated
visitors with their potency on the palate. *Haywood's Guide to Llangollen* (1906) declared that 'the local beer is highly extolled for its
many excellent qualities and produced here in large quantities for
the supply of Llangollen and the neighbourhood and for foreign
demand'.

Cider of ferocious strength was produced in the Severn valley
and the river's tributaries such as the Bann extending as far north
as Llanfair Caereinion, the Vale of Lugg around Presteigne, the
Wye valley as far north as Builth Wells and the Usk valley and
parts of the Vale of Glamorgan. In all, some 6,000 acres of land in
this area were devoted to apple orchards. Periods of intense agricultural activity such as shearing, threshing, and the hay and corn
harvests were powered by the prodigious quantities of cider consumed. The inevitable results were drunkenness, accidents and
frequent brawls. Some farmers had to stop harvests because the

338

workers were too inebriated to work. Cider was liberally dispersed at farm sales, to get people to spend their money more freely. Auctioneers became adept at starting the sale as the level of noise and merriment reached a crescendo.[143]

Brewing became big business in some Welsh towns. Cardiff had several factory-scale breweries by the late 1870s. They included the 'Welsh Giant' Hancocks Brewery whose network spread from Swansea to Newport, and the much-loved Brains Brewery. Neath had the well-known Vale of Neath Brewery, which 'despite being a notoriously rotten concern eventually acquired a reputation for respectability'.[144] The company's managing director David Bevan, a major coal owner, became a town councillor in 1869, an Alderman in 1871 and mayor of Neath in 1872 and 1873, when he bought his own mayoral regalia. But civic duties did not curtail his commercial interests. Bevan bought and built pubs at such a rapid rate that by 1919 the company owned 148 public houses, most of which were in the industrial valleys around Neath. Carmarthen in the 1900s had four large breweries, one of which, Merlin's Brewery, reputedly produced magical brews.

The Llanelli district had two large factory enterprises, Buckleys and Felinfoel, which produced superb brews. When John Lewis shot himself in Felinfoel Brewery's office in 1920, his wife, Mary Anne, took over the running of the brewery. She proved to be a feisty woman and formidable business lady. She carried a big stick with her to work and if she was unimpressed with her workers she would beat them with it. Felinfoel's great innovation was pioneering a successful method of producing beer in cans in 1935.[145] In that year, every alcoholic on every park bench in Wales must have celebrated. Cans proved lighter and more disposable than bottles and so Felinfoel soon developed a worldwide clientele. During the Second World War the armed forces ordered substantial quantities of Felinfoel canned beer. One of the few cargoes that managed to break the German siege of Malta included cans of Felinfoel ale for the parched Llanelli Territorials manning the Mediterranean island's anti-aircraft guns. Thirsty 'desert rats' in North Africa also had good reason to thank the brewers for a little canned laughter.

At the turn of the twentieth century, the capital of brewing in Wales was Wrexham. By 1870, the town that had established the UK's first industrial-scale brewery had nineteen breweries busily brewing. Like Felinfoel, Wrexham also saw notable innovations. Perhaps the most significant was the establishment of Wrexham Lager Beer Company in 1882 by two German immigrants from Saxony, Otto Isler and Ivan Levinstein. As did Felinfoel's ales, Wrexham Lager followed the brave. The troops besieged with General Gordon in Khartoum, Sudan, sought refreshment by drinking bottles of Wrexham Lager. During the First World War, when anti-German hysteria in Wrexham led to stones being thrown through a shop window that was displaying a German sausage, the company followed the example of the Saxe-Coburg and Gotha family and emphasised its British origins. During the First World War the *Mauritania* carried 1,800 small casks of Wrexham Lager on every journey. In a later conflict, Churchill and Roosevelt sealed their agreement over a pint.

Stronger spirits were shaken and stirred. In 1889 The Welsh Whisky Co. Ltd began production at Fron-goch near Bala, where the purity of the waters of Nant Tai'r Felin promised a high-quality product. Richard John Lloyd-Price of Rhiwlas backed the venture with capital of £100,000. One of the first casks produced was sent to Queen Victoria, which, to boost the company's marketing, merited a name change to the Royal Welsh Whisky Co. The royal family obviously had a taste for the product, or a drink problem, for a barrel was also sent to the Prince of Wales in 1894.[146] The whisky had a much promoted potency, as an advertising slogan announced:

Bydd i un llwnc demtio dyn i ladrata ei ddillad ei hun; dau lwnc a wna iddo frathu ei glust ei hun, tra y bydd i dri llwnc ei demptio i achub ei fam-yng-nghyfraith rhag boddi.

(One sip will make a man steal his own clothes; two sips will make him bite his own ear; whilst three sips will tempt him to rescue his mother-in-law from drowning).[147]

'Tempt him' – the advertisers did not stretch belief too far. Despite winning a prize for the best whisky at the World Fair in Chicago in

1893, the venture folded and the site eventually became a prisoner-of-war camp in which the Irish Republican Army practised for the 1916 Easter Rising. Some of its produce was washed ashore at Llangwnadl beach on Easter Sunday morning, 5 April 1907, when the *Stewart* sank. Locals scrambled to the scene, including an entire Sunday school and its teacher, to save the delicate cargo from a watery grave, and the excise man. In December 1907, the local Sunday School Association suspended discussion of 'The Sunday Schools and Temperance' because 'fate recently sent a whisky ship onto the rocks in the neighbourhood and it would be hypocritical to discuss the temperance work of the Sunday School movement while the homes of so many members, including teachers, were storehouses of intoxicating liquor removed from the wreck.'[148]

Whisky drinking might have been a 'secret sin' for the Sunday schools of Pen Llŷn, but public houses lived up to their names. Every town, village, hamlet and several crossroads in the most far-flung outpost of rural Wales had a pub or inn to serve its clientele. Pubs were crammed hugger-mugger into streets. Llandovery had twenty-six in 1914, Llangadog twelve, Carmarthen about eighty with a licence and some thirty unlicensed premises. Sam Allen in his *Cardiff Reminiscences* (1918) recalled the growth of what he termed 'the central area' of the town that had ninety-three licensed premises and around fifty 'shebeens'. The development of international ruby matches in the area further intensified the provision of pubs, as too did St Helen's ground in Swansea and the Racecourse football pitch in Wrexham. Yet the town that wobbled with the greatest provision of pubs was Monmouth, with one for every eighty-three man, woman and child in the town.

To differentiate themselves from their competitors, pubs provided a host of cultural, recreational and sporting functions as well as drinking. Cricket, football and rugby teams met at pubs where often they changed into their kit. The victory in cricket of a Chepstow XI against the England XI under the captaincy of W. G. Grace in a three-day match on 15–17 May 1882 is still celebrated in the town's pubs and clubs.[149] The Pontarddulais Amateur Operatic Society before their production of the Mikado at Haggar's Pontardawe in 1921 met at the Dulais Arms. So too did the town's wonderfully named Royal Antediluvian Order of Buffaloes.[150] Brass bands and choirs were good for business as thirsty players and singers wanted refreshment before and after a performance.

Pubs were one area where women were often in prominence in running the venture.[151] When William Timothy died in 1880, his widow Sarah, aged sixty-six, served on as keeper of the Red Lion, Pontarddulais, until 1890. The three daughters and son of publican John Davies of Pontarddulais inherited two pubs each and a share of the profits of the Dulas Glen on his death in 1913.[152] The legends of some landladies lived on after their deaths when pubs were renamed – Tafarn Jem, Tafarn Molly. A good barperson had to be something of a lawyer, a bit of a sportsman, but be without opinion on politics, religion, or any controversial subject. Landlord and landlady had to be able to deal with drunks, bullies and bores, eccentrics and extroverts of all kinds and be aware of the ever present con artist.

Temperance hotels, despite the best efforts of their owners, never captured the fun and the frolic of the public houses. Offering coffee or tea or other soft non-alcoholic drinks seldom proved to be popular. At Chepstow, the Bell Inn was converted from 1876 to 1883 into the British Workman Coffee Place, the Hotel de Chili became a teetotal establishment, and the Bath Salvation Army Blue Ribbon Chapter 'invaded' the town. The debate between the town's tipplers and the temperance campaigners descended into a pitched battle outside the Hotel de Chili on Friday, 30 March 1883. Both sides disgraced themselves. Ladies, and horses, were frightened. The Blue Ribbon captain left town owing his rent and prophesying that the world would come to an end within ten years.[153]

Other temperance campaigners were less prophetic and more practical in their approach. The remarkable campaign for the reformation of manners through enforced temperance saw its greatest achievement on Sunday, 28 August 1881, when the Sunday Closing (Wales) Act came into operation. The Act was the first legislative recognition of Wales since the Acts of Union and had been achieved through the tireless campaigning of a disparate group. Prominent amongst them were several women temperance campaigners such as Sarah Matthews and Sarah Jane Rees and the Undeb Dirwestol i Ferched y De (The South Wales Women's Temperance Union) and Undeb Dirwestol Merched Gogledd Cymru (The North Wales Women's Temperance Union). The temperance movement provided valuable training for Welsh women in political campaigning that would later be utilised in the votes for women campaign. The fact that thousands of women across Wales were involved confirmed the social importance of alcohol both as a pastime and as a problem.[154]

Even before the ink had dried on the Queen's signature on the Sunday closing Bill, the wrath of grapes and the ire of barley broke out into a war of words and statistics. The brewing industry, a large business in Wales with significant enterprises at Felinfoel, Llanelli (Buckley), Cardiff (Brains and Hancocks), and Wrexham, and a major landowner across the country, was naturally outraged.[155] It used its considerable resources to campaign against the Act in public meetings, political canvassing and especially in the press in newspapers such as the *Western Mail*.[156]

Undoubtedly there was a need for legislation to control the drink trade and public drinking of alcoholic beverages. Many Welsh communities endured exceptionally high levels of drunkenness. Such statistics as are available point to the period between the late 1860s and early 1880s as being the high-water mark for arrests and convictions for drunkenness in Wales. The 'rubber-legged brigade' at Pwllheli were busy for convictions for drunkenness in the northwest Wales town, more than trebled between 1869 and 1870, and the average number of convictions for each year of the 1870s was twice that of every year of the 1860s.[157] In 1877, so the statistics show, the greatest number of apprehensions for drunkenness were made in Caernarfonshire (100 per 10,000 head of population), closely followed by Glamorgan (94 per 10,000) and Flintshire (84 per 10,000). In 1881, in south Wales the most drunken places were Pontypridd, with a proportion of 9.1 convictions for drunkenness per 100 population, and Cardiff with 8.9 per 100.[158]

The social class of the tipplers is problematic, but the evidence suggests, perhaps unsurprisingly, that all social groups were included in the statistics. Some people had a predilection towards drink, suggesting that habitual drunkenness was a disease as much as a deviance. Proverbs explained that such people had been 'wedi ei eni ar haf sych' (born in a dry summer). In Carmarthenshire by 1906 there seemed to be a competition amongst the local drinkers as to whom could acquire the most convictions for drunkenness – Francis Donnio (twenty-six convictions), Daniel Price (thirty-three convictions), James Davies (seventy-three convictions) and the Rae family of Carmarthen, of whom David had twenty-two convictions, brother William twelve convictions, whilst father George led the way with ninety convictions.[159] Women were not to be outdrunk by their male rivals. At Pontypridd in April 1905, Mary Northy, a 'celebrated Pontypridd blacklister, made her 79th appearance in the police courts after it had taken the combined efforts of 2 police-men to convey her to the station'.[160] At Tonpentre police court in May 1902, Ann Roberts, 'an old woman, respectably dressed', made her 189th appearance for being drunk and disorderly. She had just been released from prison so naturally Ann went on a spree to cele-brate. When the magistrate declared that 'they [habitual drunkards] always do get drunk when they come out', the courtroom erupted into open laughter.[161] Drinking everyone under the table was Ellen Sweeney, who, by the early 1890s, had amassed 255 convictions for drunken and disorderly behaviour.[162]

The Sunday Closing (Wales) Act had a series of consequences, few of which its promoters had previously envisaged. Despite the extent of the apparent support for the Act, in practice, once it had been passed, thousands of individuals around Wales found ingeni-ous strategies to circumvent it. Many publicans, especially those tied to the breweries, risked little apart from a fine, and so stayed open each Sunday. At Aberystwyth, that cosy Nonconformist and temperance stronghold, several pubs such as the Black Lion and the Skinners Arms ran their own 'Sunday school' on a semi 'official' basis for their regulars. In order to capture the miscreants, police had to resort to clandestine methods of surveillance that were highly labour-intensive and demoralising for both the observers and the observed. Chief Constable William Phillips of Carmarthen told the Royal Commission into the Sunday Closing (Wales) Act in 1889 that his officers had to hide themselves each Sunday morning to spy on pubs in the Llandeilo area. Despite the welcome overtime payment, officers felt that they were acting in a 'dishonourable' fashion.[163]

Brewers, especially in Wrexham, Bangor, Merthyr Tydfil, Cardiff and Swansea, provided publicans with nine-gallon casks (firkins) and four-and-a-half gallon casks (pins) of beer in order 'to meet the requirements of working men on Sunday', the casks were sold on Saturday night to customers for their Sunday consumption.[164] At Cardiff's Hancock's brewery the production of firkins increased from 738 in 1881–2 to 12,475 in 1888–9, that of pins from 72 in 1881–2 to 26,580 in 1888–9.[165] According to the *Western Mail*, a publican at Aberdare could sell sixty pins every Saturday. Grocers and publicans also did a brisk business selling 'belly cans' – saddle-shaped tin vessels that held four quarts of beer, designed to be carried under the clothes.[166] The effect of all of this was to transfer drinking from the public sphere of the pub, where most often the atmosphere was regulated, to the unregulated private world of the home and the attendant problem of overindulgence by women and children.

The clause in the Act that a person who had travelled three miles could claim a drink at a public house, the so-called *bona fide traveller* clause, gave rise to most problems. Very soon drinking trips were organised from places just over three miles away to obtain a drink on a Sunday: from Cardiff to Penarth and Barry, from Swansea to the Mumbles, from Trealaw to Treforest, from Bethesda to Bangor, and from Bangor to Beaumaris, and vice versa. Police in Carmarthen and Llanelli complained that they could cope well throughout the week with local drinking habits, but that on Sunday 'all hell's let loose' when strangers descended on the town. *The Carmarthen Weekly Reporter* recounted: 'It is called the Lord's Day, but in Carmarthen it is par excellence the Devil's Day. Not only the Law of the Land, but the Ten Commandments are regarded as suspended for the time being by a very large proportion of the population.'[167]

Police in Bangor, Caernarfon, Carmarthen and several towns complained to the Royal Commission in 1889 that when drink had been easily available on a Sunday, one or two drinks would probably suffice for the average drinker, but after 1881, when people had to travel more than three miles, one drink became a debauch.

The old anarchic tradition of the unlicensed 'cwrw bach' (shebeen or bogus club) re-emerged as a result of the Sunday Closing (Wales) Act. Their purpose – oblivion. Beer was sold in a turbulent, un-regulated environment that probably resulted in much greater drunkenness. Clubs were excluded from the act. At Ammanford, the local 'Conservative Club' only opened on a Sunday, and the debauches of its members appeared frequently in police court proceedings. The handful of respectable conservatives in the rip-roaring mining town were the keenest to have the institution closed. Police officers at Llanelli, Llandeilo, Bangor and Caernarfon all complained bitterly at the behaviour of people in Sunday drinking clubs. Between June 1882 and June 1883, more than 3,000 men joined clubs in Cardiff – an increase of more than 900 per cent over the previous year. A census undertaken by David Davies, assistant editor of the *Western Mail*, in the summer of 1889, revealed that the total number of shebeens in Cardiff was in excess of 480. These were concentrated in Grangetown (forty), Cathays (seventy-nine), Newtown (forty-five), Canton (thirty-eight), Roath (ninety-one), Dockland (fifty-seven), and in the central part of the town, including, ironically, Temperance Town (137). Their beer was often potent, always adulterated, described by one customer as 'a cross between senna and vinegar'.[168] The Hotel de Marl in Cardiff had a grandiloquent name but it quite literally was a hole – a hole in the ground on industrial wasteland.

The argument as to whether the 1881 Sunday Closing (Wales) Act was successful or not became increasingly intemperate. In 1889, in order to resolve the dispute, the government appointed a Royal Commission to inquire into the situation. The commission's report indicated levels of Sunday drunkenness had increased in several districts since the passing of the Act. Between 1877 and 1881 and 1884 and 1888, convictions for Sunday drunkenness had increased from 379 to 643 in Glamorgan, from eleven to seventeen in Pembroke, nine to eleven in Carmarthen town, thirty-two to ninety in Cardiff, and from eight to eighteen in Neath.[169] Yet this might well have just been as a result of the increased vigilance of the police who had to enforce the new legislation, rather than an increase in the numbers of people drinking to excess. Policies of policing differed across Wales. Some forces were vigilant. Others, especially in the rural areas and those areas where local police had a strong drink culture, were more relaxed in enforcing the Act. Despite the Royal Commission's best efforts, they could not conclude whether the Act had been a success or a total failure. Overall, the debate on the effects of the Act seems to have reached a rather unsatisfying stalemate. Nevertheless, Lord Aberdare, the Home Secretary when the Act was passed, felt himself obliged to admit that the Act was a failure.[170]

The commissioners recommended some amendments to the Act, but it was upheld and remained on the statute book until 1961. The debates between the temperate and the intemperate continued down to 1945, and beyond. Despite the adhesion to the concept of personal liberty, this did not mean an unlicensed freedom for people to behave in ways that were both harmful to themselves in particular and to society in general. The temperance cause continued to be a strong force in Welsh society and politics. Frequent calls were made to bring in local veto and legislation to control the drink trade in several parts of Wales in the period leading to the First World War. In 1915, Monmouthshire, much to the disappointment of local drinkers, was included in the terms of the Sunday Closing (Wales) Act. Initially, this was intended as a wartime measure, but in 1921 it was made permanent.

The First World War saw probably the greatest intrusion by the state into the drinking habits of the Welsh people. The Intoxicating Liquor (Temporary Restriction) Act, passed on 31 August 1914, gave local authorities the right to restrict pub opening hours.[171] Taps now stopped at 9 p.m. initially in the munitions areas such as Pembrey, Pembroke and Rhydymwyn, but soon an early close extended to all areas. The sale of alcohol, both for on- and off-premises consumption was restricted to four and a half hours a day. Other regulations included the banning of spirit bottles smaller than quarts (less easy to consume quickly and less transportable), restrictions upon the simultaneous purchase of spirits and a beer 'chaser', and the prohibitions of spirit sales (by the bottle) on Saturday and Sunday. One of the most unpopular measures was the banning of 'treating' (buying a drink for another individual, especially a soldier), a habit that was a particular characteristic of a gregarious and generous people like the Welsh.[172] This was designed to cut down on drunkenness among soldiers, who found that wearing a uniform in a pub virtually guaranteed a night of free drinking. The government lowered alcohol content and raised prices and taxes on alcoholic beverages. The price of a pint of beer rose from 3d in 1914 to as high as 10d by the end of the war, due mostly to taxation. But people accepted that desperate times needed desperate remedies. Even the *Western Mail*, which had served for so long as the mouthpiece of Welsh brewers, saw it as a munition-ette's and a warrior's duty to be sober to produce or perish.

One of the unintended consequences of the restriction of opening hours was the concentration of drinking. At open tap, pub doors would fly open and a fast stream of silent, intent drinkers rapidly moved into their positions around the bar. The air was immediately machine-gunned with a rapid series of orders – 'rum', 'whiskey', 'gin', 'rotgut', 'beer', 'stout', 'beer', 'pint-of-best', 'beer', 'stout'. There followed a slurping silence as the day's troubles and travails were washed down with liver-crippling draughts of alcohol. The pace of drinking would slow, until it accelerated again as stop-tap approached.

In the 1920s and 1930s, drink as a social problem began to decline in Wales. Levels of prosecutions decreased due to a plethora of reasons – economic slump, greater opportunities for entertainment in other venues such as dancing halls, cinemas and nightclubs, and the growth of popular sports. But the tension between the temperate and the intemperate continued. On those occasions of moral panics when the newspapers revealed levels of high drink-ing, voices would again be raised calling for complete prohibition. A number of Welsh people in the 1920s had first-hand experience of total prohibition. These people lived not in Wales, but in America. Margaret E. Roberts, who had emigrated from Hirwaun to Iowa, was one of the leading campaigners in favour of prohibition, a force that was becoming increasingly popular in the 1920s.[173] Charles Evans Hughes, the Welsh descended Republican presidential can-didate, probably lost in 1916 because of his equivocal attitude to prohibition. Margaret Roberts had some embarrassing allies – the

Ku Klux Klan, led from 1922–39 by Hiram W. Evans,[174] and gangsters like Llewelyn Morris Humphreys, son of a Carno family, who could see that prohibition would provide rich opportunities for bootleggers such as himself and his friend Al Capone.[175] In passing the Prohibition Act in 1922, the government effectively passed over control of America's fourth biggest industry to the criminal underworld and instigated the development of the gangster and gang culture of the 1930s.

For others all the harm of alcohol was self-inflicted. There is a tendency to celebrate drink and drinkers and perhaps to forget the darker legacies of alcohol.[176] Abuse, assault and aggression were powered by alcohol. Children and wives were abandoned and abused, families split asunder under horrific violence. Such tragic tales were the staple fodder in the newspapers of the temperance press. Victorian songs are often castigated for their gross sentimentality, yet such reports from the abyss were based on real life. Welsh writers in their lives and their literature lay out in the clearest way their rake's progress into alcoholic dependence. These were people who would get so drunk that they quite literally had to hold on to the floorboards.[177] Caradog Prichard, Dylan Thomas and Tennessee Williams were drinkers with a writing problem and writers with a drinking problem, as both aspects of their lives became entwined. There was a fine line between the conviviality and companionship of the public bar and the private hell of an alcoholic's life. These are the derelict characters we meet in the journals of the medical superintendents of the mental hospitals in Bridgend, Carmarthen and Denbigh as they shook and sweated in their delirium tremens.[178] Alcohol was a powerful solvent, dissolving marriages, families, careers and lives.

'Make Room for the Jester': happiness and humour

A minister had lost his prize possession – his umbrella. Having searched high and low he reached the somewhat startling conclusion that someone in the congregation must have stolen his umbrella. To uncover the thief, the stratagem he developed was to deliver a sermon on Sunday on the Ten Commandments. When he would reach the seventh commandment – 'thou shalt not steal', he would pause and scan the faces of the congregation. Whoever looked most shifty, then he or she (well, the minister was desperate), would undoubtedly be the thief.

Come Sunday, come sermon. But when the minister delivered the sixth commandment – 'na wna odineb', 'though shalt not commit adultery' – he remembered where he had left his umbrella.

Oral evidence from a twenty-first century minister.

The story of the minister and his lost umbrella is the quintessential Welsh joke.[179] It concerns those great Welsh obsessions – religion, snobbery and vengeance. It is imbued with a concern for social justice and equality that had become a notable characteristic of Welsh humour by the 1870s. Ambitious people were welcomed, their success celebrated by those whose feet were in the gutter but were looking at the stars. But successful people had to remember 'y graig y'm naddwyd ohono' (the rock from which one was hewn). Those who forgot were reminded that pride precedes a fall. Proverbs distilled such wisdom into an epigram of warning: 'A elo yn hwch i Rydychen, yn hwch daw yn ôl' (If as a pig you go to Oxford, as a pig you return); 'bach pawb o'i dybio yn fawr' (small everyone who think themselves big); 'gwell synnwyr na chyfoeth' (sense is better than wealth); and 'gwybedyn y dom a gwyd uchaf' (the dungheap's fly flies highest). Wit was a weapon to puncture pomp and pomposity.

Jokes have a wonderful potential to create moments of social informality, a sort of levelling out of the teller's and hearer's very unequal roles.[180] Despite their topicality, jokes often have an easy familiarity that aids laughter. Jokes are tiny folk tales, wonderful lies that reveal social truths. The psychoanalyst Dr Ernest Jones was struck by the similarities between the topsy-turvy logic of the dream world and the joke world. He argued that a joke, like a dream, comes from beyond or beneath the conscious mind and that the jokes people tell reveal hidden nervous tensions even as they release them in their laughter. Laughter, that comic relief, fulfilled an important psychological and physiological function.[181]

Trivial as they are often claimed to be (it's just a joke) people treasure jokes.

Humour was one of the most powerful defence mechanisms that people had available in their lives of quiet desperation. However dark or threatening a situation, Welsh people resorted to sarcasm and satire to save themselves from despair. Welsh people told jokes because they realised that human existence was an unforgiving slog. They told jokes in the face of overwhelming odds and despite the ravages of time and fate. In February 1916, whilst foraging for props to shore up the British trenches in Ypres, the charismatic London-Welshman Captain Fred Roberts and his men came across an old printing press in the basement of a convent. They decided to set up a newspaper. And what a paper it was. Named for the British soldiers' pronunciation of Ypres, *The Wipers Times* was an inventive mixture of fake articles, jokes, songs and even the odd poem (there was a standing joke against the surfeit of poetry in the war). It set out to find humour in the hell of war and despite the best attempts of higher-ups to close it down, it continued to print until the Armistice of 1918. Hard times in bad places are invariably where you will find good men. Roberts and his fellow writers used their gallows humour to make a series of barbed comments from behind the barbed wire. Along the way there were some lovely digs at grandiose newspaper columnists and hard-drinking, war-avoiding foreign correspondents and at those who cheered for war without actually having to take part. They lampooned officers who were so incompetent that they ordered a firing squad to assume formation in a circle. A fake review, for a spoof show called 'Over The Top', simply said, 'It's a gas.' This at a time of the worst poisonous gas attacks, and in which Roberts was himself gassed and hospitalised. There was a real and righteous strain of anger: at the waste of a generation, at the cavalier way these men were treated, and at the futility and stupidity of war.[182] During the Second World War, Chief Engine Room Artificer Trevor Lewis saw his ship the *Sikh* torpedoed and sunk. He recalled:

> The survivors now gathered together in small groups . . . some cry
> – usually the result of shock, not weakness; some curse with a long

tirade of abuse against everyone else; some laugh and crack jokes – 'Where's that bloody taxi I ordered' – or the most standard naval joke, 'If only my mother could see me now she'd buy me out'.[183]

Even in politics the Welsh looked on the bright side of life and took the political insult into new heights, or, depending on your taste, depths. Lloyd George described Irish leader Eamon de Valera as 'trying to pick up mercury with a fork'. His bitterest spleen, however, he reserved for his fellow liberals. Of Sir Herbert Samuel he quipped – 'when they circumcised Sir Herbert Samuel, they threw away the wrong bit'. Aneurin Bevan castigated both opponent and supporter. The Tories he famously condemned as being 'lower than vermin'. He had a series of bitter exchanges with Churchill: 'I welcome this opportunity of pricking his [Churchill's] bloated bladder of lies with the poniard of truth'. Refusing to direct his questions to the Foreign Secretary, Anthony Eden, Bevan questioned the Prime Minister, Churchill explaining, 'Why should I question the monkey when I can question the organ grinder?' 'Churchill', Bevan once memorably said, 'uses the majesty of his language to conceal the mediocrity of his thinking'. Bevan was equally sarcastic to his fellow socialists. 'Please don't be deterred in the fanatic application of your sterile logic', he once told a gathering. Hugh Gaitstell he considered 'a desiccated calculating machine', whilst Herbert Morrison was 'a squalid, backstairs, third-rate Tammany Hall politician.'[184]

Politicians used their wit, or what they regarded as wit, to disparage their opponents and cheer their supporters. For others it was the sole purpose of their lives. The role of the clown, the court jester, and stand-up comedian has a long tradition in Welsh history. The Lords of Misrule, of the world turned upside-down, were often a focus of attention. As stand-up comedians, actors in dramatic and cinematic comedies and as contributors to the 'Noson Lawen' (happy night) many Welsh people won fame and fortune. From the age of fourteen, comedian Arthur Lucan (1885–1954) served a seven-year apprenticeship with the Musical Cliftons at Colwyn Bay and Llandudno. In America, Welsh-descended comedians rose to prominence in the silent cinema years. Harold Lloyd (1893–1971) starred in a series of frantic slapstick comedies where jokes were drawn from the very real dangers he placed himself in, once losing two fingers when a stunt misfired. How else do you get audiences to laugh when the movie is silent? *Safety Last* (1923), a romantic silent comedy, summed up his film career as in an iconic movie moment he hangs from a clock face high above the morning traffic.[185] From the 1930s, Leslie Townes 'Bob' Hope (1903–2003), the son of Iris Townes, a light-comic opera singer from Barry, starred with Bing Crosby and Dorothy Lamour in a series of the 'Road to . . . ' comedy films. Bob Hope received more honorary degrees than any other person, played golf with five US Presidents and became the consummate master of the one-line gag – 'she said she was approaching forty, and I couldn't help wondering from what direction'; 'culture is the ability to describe Jane Russell without moving your hands'.[186] With the rise of cinema and radio, comedians were provided with audiences of a size previously undreamed of.

The life of Sir Harry Donald Secombe (1921–2001) from the beginning to end seemed to have been a 'loud raspberry blown at convention'. When called up for military service in the Second World War, he was driven in a friend's car through Swansea, standing up in it giving an impersonation of Hitler, with a black comb as the moustache. His war continued throughout to be one of absurdity, comedy and the surreal. The authorities soon realised that Secombe represented too much of a threat to friend rather than foe and so he was transferred from the artillery into the entertainments section in North Africa. Here he met Spike Milligan and so began one of the great comedy partnerships. In *Where Have All The Bullets Gone?* Milligan describes in detail the blunderings of the anarchic duo, especially those of 'the singer and lunatic, a little myopic blubber of fat from Wales'.[187] Upon demobilisation, Secombe got a job as a comedian at the risqué Windmill Club where the girls danced naked or in close-fitting skin-coloured costumes. Thereafter he entered the world of light comedic entertainment on radio and television and was one of the stars of the iconic *Goon Show*.[188]

Tommy Cooper (1921–1984) from Caerphilly proved to be even more successful in the worlds of live theatre and broadcasting. He exploited the comedy of failure and nervousness. Although he was a member of the select group of magicians, The Magic Circle, audiences were spellbound by his apparent utter incompetence. He was a child in the body of a giant, an amateur with the sparkle of a professional, an Easter Island statue with the light-footedness of Fred Astaire. His signature costume of a black full-dress suit topped off by a red Moroccan fez added to the incongruity.[189] People jested that Cooper got his looks from his mother Gertrude and his sense of fun from his father, Thomas Samuel Cooper, of Llwyn Onn Street, Caerphilly. Together with his brother Jimmy, Tommy Cooper senior used to sing at concerts and have crowds in stitches at legion halls and miners institutes as he enacted a sketch depicting a sentry on duty wanting to spend a penny. It was this legacy of comedic chaos that the son took to its illogical extremes. His jokes were silly, stupid, simple:

> My wife came in the other day and she asked, 'What's different about me?' And I said, 'I don't know. What is different about you? Have you had your hair done?' She said, 'No'. I said, 'Have you got a new dress on?' She said, 'No'. 'Have you got a new pair of shoes?' She said, 'No'. I said 'Well, I don't know. What is different about you?' She said, 'I'm wearing a gas mask'.[190]

The joke was topical when he first told it to wartime audiences, but people were still convulsed with laughter when he told it thirty years later.

By the 1870s, the major patterns of Welsh humour were well established. At the butt of many of the jibes were some familiar figures of fun: the poor, alcohol-loving Irishman, the talkative woman, the humbled Englishman, the sermonising minister and the master outwitted by a sharp servant, the precocious wit of children. This cast of characters were joined by others over the period 1870–1945. In north Wales 'Y Cofi', as the inhabitants of Caernarfon were known, became renowned for possessing a sharp wit and a sarcastic turn of phrase. As the newly established county councils acquired new powers for road maintenance in the 1920s, 'Bois yr Hewl' became legendary for their laziness. On one occasion when a gang of road workers in Montgomeryshire discovered that they had forgotten their tools, one borrowed a telephone and called the depot to ask their foreman, 'Boss what shall we do? We've forgotten our tools'. The boss answered: 'Don't panic boys. I'll get some tools out to you as soon as I can. Until they arrive, you will just have to lean on each other'. In the west, 'Y Cardi' acquired a reputation for such financial stringency that they could buy a product from a Jew and sell it at a profit to a Scot. Caradoc Evans took great delight recounting the dilemmas faced by a wife who had travelled in from Capel Seion to Aberstwyth by bus with her husband. He died in the seaside town, leaving her with the dilemma of what to do with their return bus tickets. For a true Cardi there could only be one solution and so she took the cadaver home on the bus.[191]

Even in death the Cardi's true character would shine through: A Cardi on his death bed asked:

'Are you here Mari my wife?'
'Yes I'm here'.
'Are you here Cati my daughter?'
'Yes I'm here father'.
'Are you here Siôn my son?'
'Yes I'm here father.'
'Then who the hell is looking after the shop?'

Another dying Cardi was reputed to have sold his watch to his son.[192] Students in the new colleges at Aberystwyth, Bangor and Carmarthen soon acquired much-deserved reputations for lethargy and uncleanliness. One student at Carmarthen decided that in order to save his father a journey into the mart in the town from Llanboidy, he would buy a pig for him, and take it home at the end of term. He told his friend about his plan, who promptly asked, 'Where will it be kept?' 'In my room'. 'But what about the smell?' the friend asked. 'Oh, don't worry about the pig, he'll soon get used to the smell'.[193]

The anti-mother-in-law and the anti-wife joke acquired great popularity in the period 1870–1945, evidence perhaps of how the downtrodden husband tried to fight back in the unequal battle of the sexes. The First World War saw a series of jokes told against women who were working in occupations that had previously been regarded as the privilege and preserve of men. Women tram and bus conductors and drivers were much criticised for becoming power crazed. Jokes were told against women who were intelligent, clever and funny.

Welsh literature abounds with almost endless examples of light-hearted and humorous prose and poems. The main *raison d'être* of the limerick was to make people smile or break out into laughter. Idwal Jones, D. Jacob Davies, Waldo Williams and the historian and litterateur R. T. Jenkins proved themselves masters at the art form. Obscene limericks were recited with glee in the bars of Welsh clubs and pubs. 'Yr englyn', that uniquely Welsh verse form similar to the Japanese haiku, was an ideal forum for humour. It was surprising how much spleen and spite could be squeezed into four lines. Englynion were penned on all of life's great tensions – that between men and women, miser and spendthrift, pompous politicians and people, preacher and worshippers. The englynwr was the chronicler of everyday life. In 'Yr Awen Lawen' you can find poetic responses to all of life from politics to prayer:

Tŷ'r Cyffredin 1911
Tŷ i hyrddod diurddas – guro cyrn,
   Agor ceg ddibwrpas;
  Tŷ cnoi a thrin cethin, cas,
  A llawr dyrnu lloi'r deyrnas.[194]

(House of Commons 1911
A house for clumsy rams – to knock horns.
Open their mouths without purpose;
A house for biting and nasty argument,
The threshing floor of the nation's calves.)

It throws a whole new light on the reforming parliament of the Edwardian-Georgian years.

Englynion had a familiar group of characters – the cheeky lawyer, the subtle poacher, the mother-in-law, the verbose wife:

Iaith fy Mam
'Cymraeg yw'ch iaith chi, ond, Dadi, pam
  'Rŷch chi yn ei galw yn Iaith fy Mam?'
'Am fod dy fam, mae'n debyg, Johnny,
Yn siarad llawer mwy ohoni'.[195]

(My Mother's Language
'Welsh is your language, father, but why
Do you call it my mother's tongue?'
'Because your mother, it appears, Johnny,
Speaks far more of it'.)

Mock epitaphs became a highly popular variant of the englyn in the period 1870–1945, but few, one hopes, would wish to have some of these missives carved in stone above their grave. Saddest of all were the englynion penned to spinsters and bachelors:

Beddargraff Hen Lanc
Ei anwylyd ni welodd – atyniad
  At eneth ni theimlodd,
  Efo'i hun byw a fynnodd,
  A heno mae yr un modd.[196]

(A Bachelor's Epitaph
His sweetheart he never saw – attraction
To a girl he never felt
On his own he wished to live
And so too alone he dies).

Beddargraff Hen Ferch
Er oes faith o obeithio, – digariad
  Ac oer oedd ei huno:
  Mwy unig yma heno
  Nag erioed o dan y gro.[197]

(A Spinster's Epitaph
Despite a lifetime hoping – unloved
And cold she died:
Lonelier here tonight
Than ever beneath the earth.)

Parodies of famous poems were given a topicality through telling the contemporary tales such as the wartime sagas of farmers and smallholders killing their pigs without permission in Carmarthen in 1939 and Corwen in 1943. D. Jacob Davies proved to be a master of the parody, providing a modern twist to an old favourite:

>*Nant y Mynydd*
>Nant y mynydd gromium plated
>Yn chwyrnellu tua'r tap,
>Rhwng y peips yn sisial ganu,
>Byddaf draw yn Lloegr chwap![198]
>
>*(The Mountain Brook*
>Mountain brook chromium plated
>Bubbling towards the tap,
>Between the pipes sweetly singing
>I'll be in England soon!)

D. Jacob Davies had a compatriot in the dramatist and humourist Idwal Jones (1895–1937) of Lampeter. In poems and plays Jones unleashed a torrent of gentle humour that was performed on stages and broadcast around Wales. His *Cerddi Digri: A Rhai Pethau Eraill* (1936) and *Cerddi Digri Newydd a Phethau o'r Fath* (1937) showed the wealth of talent in his tragically brief life.[199] Newspapers such as *The Carmarthen Weekly Reporter* and *The North Wales Chronicle* had a weekly column on 'Wit and Wisdom' and 'Jokes and Jokers' in the 1880s.[200] Joke books were surprisingly common in the period 1870–1900, especially when we consider the traditional view of the Victorians as stern and sullen. Their queen might not have been amused, but Welsh Victorians laughed all the way home from the bookshop. *Casgliad o Ffraethebion Cymreig* (c.1870); *Y Ffraethebydd neu Gymhorth i Chwerthin* (1875?), *Hynodion Hen Bregethwyr gyda Hanes Difyrus am Danynt* (1876), *Cymhorth i Chwerthin, sef Ystraeon Ysmala a Difyrus* (1876) by D. L. Jones (Cynalaw), and the Revd J. R. Hughes's *Humour Sanctified: the Memoir of Stephen Jenkins The Quaint Preacher of Pembrokeshire* (1902), T. Mardy Rees's *Hiwmor y Cymro: Sef Hiwmor Mewn Llenyddiaeth Cymraeg* (1922), *Ffraethebion y Glowr Cymraeg* (1928), and Thomas Phillips's *Humours of the Iron Road: Stories From the Train in Welsh and English* (third edition, c.1920), are just a selection of joke books published in the period 1870–1945 that undoubtedly achieved the founding objective of *Punch* of 'collapse of stout party'.[201]

In English, the writer and raconteur Gwyn Thomas (1913–1981) mined a deep seam of sarcasm from the brutalising effects of capitalism on the coalfield communities. The economic devastation and the consequent social dislocation were laid out with brutal honesty in profoundly humorous works such as *The Dark Philosophers* (1946), *The Alone to the Alone* (1947) and *All Things Betray Thee* (1949). 'Meadow Prospect', the fictional recreation of his Rhondda birthplace, comes close to being factual reporting. An otherwise bleak scenario of mankind, unemployment, poverty, ill health and bleak expectations is transformed by Thomas into a series of compassionate and often hilarious tales. Rather than mere darkness and depression the stories vibrate with the energy, humour and resilience of the 'voters' and the 'elements' coping with hard times.[202] Satiric, sarcastic, searingly honest, his tales earned Thomas the sobriquet 'Checkov with chips'.

Nicknames were another area where the Welsh showed their natural wit. The novelist James Hanley in his fictional recreation of a north Wales village had a remarkable character called 'Cadwalader Back-to-Front-Odd-Job', the chapel caretaker, so called because he buried someone upside down.[203] Yet, fact was more fertile than fiction in producing remarkable nicknames. An insurance agent in the Rhondda valley was known as 'Dai Death Club' whilst an undertaker in west Wales was known as 'Evans the Death'. In Machynlleth, undertaker Percy Edwards was known as 'Perce the Hearse'. 'Dai Loco' was an Abersychan engine driver, whilst 'Eric the Click' was a Kenfig Hill photographer. A surgeon in north Wales had the wonderful nickname Owen Lawgoch (Owen Redhand), whilst an orthopaedic surgeon became 'Jones the Bones'. A gaslamp lighter in Anglesey became 'Margiad, Gola Lamp', whilst two fishwives in Pwllheli were 'Catrin Pennog' and 'Nans Pennog Coch'. Most unfortunate of all was the sewerage worker who was named after his work 'Twm Cachu'.[204]

Those unduly touched by religion found their obsession with the next world reflected in their nickname. 'John English Cause' went to the English chapel, 'Jimmy Glory' went to the Gospel Hall, whilst 'Will Salvation' carried the banner in the Salvation Army parade. 'Iesu Grist Bach' and 'Plentyn Duw' both resembled Jesus, whilst 'Sbarcyn Bach Uffern' sounded like a remarkable character. Some nicknames were inherited. 'Tommy Onetune' was a pianist who accompanied the silent films in the local cinema. His repertoire was severely limited, but his son, a fine pianist, unfairly inherited the nickname and became 'Billy Onetune'.

A person's physical characteristics were cruelly played upon. After losing half an ear in an accident one man was christened 'Dai Eighteen Months'. 'Bob Un Glust' was born with just one ear. 'Tommy Titanic' weighed 20 stones, whilst 'Twm Nothing Straight' had a deformed arm, leg and nose. More cruelly, 'Georgie One Ball' of Llanelli was wounded in the First World War. In the Second World War a Carmarthenshire man who hid a pig in his bed during a raid by the Ministry of Food became 'Bili Mochyn yn y Gwely'. 'Lisa Lastig' was a flexible, fun-filled girl from Ynys-y-bŵl. 'Shillin Dadi' was so called because he had to pay for the maintenance of an illegitimate child. He obviously should have taken advice from 'Twm Cwrcyn Carcus' of Caernarfon. 'Cwrcyn' (male cat), 'Carcus' (careful), the first but not the second word could have been used for the father of thirteen children fondly known as 'Will Population'. 'Dai Agnostic' was uncertain about the existence of God. 'Elfed Ooh, There's Lovely' used the phrase once too often as did 'Dai Bugger' and 'Twm Bloody'.

It is not usually the purpose of a history book to make you laugh. For nothing kills laughter quicker than to explain a joke. Yet clowns and comedians fulfilled such important social and cultural roles that the historian must at least attempt to recapture some of the laughs of old. For the Welsh showed their true colours in the mirth of a nation.

Conclusion:
A Few Selected Exits

I learnt at Aberystwyth that it is not life that matters. It is the way
you get out of it.

Howell Davies in The College by the Sea (Aberystwyth, 1928).

'Once upon a time' is the familiar preamble to a fairy tale, a fiction
or a fable. But the author writing in the journal *Bye-Gones* in September 1897 was exact for she, or he, was recording fact not fantasy.
'Beware', the writer warned, 'there are fairy rings at Pantybeudy
and most beautiful music is heard on moonlit nights. People are
drawn into the rings by the music.'[1] If they were lucky these people
would re-emerge, Rip-Van-Winkle-like, from the fairy circles generations later. A person drawn into such a spritely gathering in 1870
to re-emerge in 1945 would have entered a brave new world.

The person who had been away with the fairies would soon
discover that it was not just Y Tylwyth Teg who flew around Wales
for mankind had also taken to the skies. Ghostly disembodied
voices were not just heard in enchanted places like Pantybeudy, but
in Welsh parlours, palladiums, plazas and playhouses. Electricity
brought enlightenment to every aspect of daily life over the period
1870–1945, in a revolution in sensibilities and survival that had not
been experienced since the domestication of fire. Mankind in 1945
had the power to create an apocalypse that the Book of Revelations
had never imagined. Humanity had to now live in the darkness
of the realisation that it had the power to destroy the world.

Though it had devised fiendish technology that could extinguish
life, mankind had also extended the life expectancy of people.
Between 1870 and 1945 life expectancy had almost exactly doubled.

In 1945 an average person could realistically hope to live for a lifespan of seventy years. At last the biblical promise that one's life was 'three score years and ten' had become a reality for the majority of the Welsh people. This demographic transformation had profound implications for people's belief in the supernatural and in superstitions. The years 1870–1945 saw a dechristianisation and a desacralisasion of Wales and a disenchantment of the Welsh world. Religion became increasingly the itch after the amputation. The peccatogenic outlook, which attributed all life's misfortunes to God's displeasure at mankind's sinfulness, began to lose its credibility as other explanations were given for misadventure. Fewer believed that God and his legions were as malicious, psychopathic and vindictive as the thundering priests who invoked them. Faith and fear declined over the period 1870–1945, but they did not completely disappear. A belief in heaven or a parallel spiritual world continued. It was to this world that people hoped to travel when they died, or in the words of the physical medium Jack Webber 'passed over'. The presence of this other world was confirmed by unwanted visitors and revenants who returned occasionally from eternity to here to disturb the Welsh people.

There was an increasing emphasis that happiness should be sought in this world as well as the next. The pursuit of pleasure became a marked feature of Wales in the period 1870–1945. One of the greatest developments in these years was the emergence of the cultural industries. Radio broadcasts and cinematic presentations changed the way all people spent their leisure time. Sporting and cultural activities had become profitable businesses as much as profligate pastimes. As the elderly Llanelli minister knew when he advised his young colleague to mention the living legend that was rugby star Albert Jenkins in his maiden sermon, and all would be fine, sport had taken over some of the functions that had previously been religion's preserves. Sport involved tribal loyalties and rivalries, symbolic rituals, fabulous legends, iconic heroes, epic battles, aesthetic beauty, physical fulfilment, sublime spectaculars, and a profound sense of belonging. Sport, not religion, would become the opium of the people. The idols of the field of praise were increasingly worshipped by people across Wales. At the turn of the twentieth century sport had its first celebrities who were idolised by the Welsh. For the first time they had stars in their eyes. Women gravitated towards Leigh Roose, the first football superstar, from all directions like a planetary orbit.

As the emphasis turned from ethereal titillation to earthly delights, some thinkers sought out and suggested that there could be other meanings to life. To some people such concerns were much ado about nothing, but many were intent in their pursuit of such mysteries. Stanley Bligh and several authors concurred with Havelock Ellis arguing that 'sex lies at the root of life, and we can never learn to reverence life until we know how to understand sex'.[2] Ernest Jones argued that sexual satisfaction for women was just as important as that for men. The prudes who patrolled the morals of their neighbourhoods argued that birth control was unnecessary, as they had their personality, but there was an increase in the number of clinics in Wales in the 1930s. There is considerable evidence that Wales experienced a revolution in sexuality over the period 1870–1945. In the 1920s in particular, sex, an activity that often takes up the least amount of time, seemed to cause the most amount of trouble. Sex was an issue that was raised time and again in art, cinema, literature and the performing arts. In *Under Milk Wood*, his fictional recreation of Wales, the poet and playwright Dylan Thomas drew on factual experiences, as he has Captain Cat instruct Rosie Probert: 'Lie down, lie easy. Let me shipwreck in your thighs'.[3]

The years 1870–1945 saw a remarkable series of experiments in living. Not the least of these was the attempt of Welsh Bohemians to create a lifestyle beyond the bounds of conventional morality and religion. Despite all the attention paid to their sexual frolicking and public folly, the Bohemians, with their emphasis on friendship and fellowship, their capacity to forgive and forget in their social relationships, provided an alternative lifestyle. The rediscovery of the 'lost art' of friendship was emphasised by the great Christian and fantasy writer C. S. Lewis in *The Four Loves* (London, 1960). Lewis, whose ancestral roots were in Caergwrle, emphasised that 'friendship is the happiest and most fully human of all loves: the crown of life and the school of virtue'. 'Aspects', Lewis lamented, 'which sadly, are ignored in modern society'. His frankness in the book about sexual aspects upset that allegedly most 'modern' of societies, America.[4]

As well as friendship, people emphasised that fun was essential to lighten people's lives. Gab-gifted comedians helped the Welsh to look on the bright side of life. Jokes often within a specific Welsh context proliferated in the years 1870–1945 and were a people's unique response to the darkness and terror of the early twentieth century. It is a truism, but nevertheless true, that much humour derives from pain. Jesters were the anthropologists of daily life, busily noting people's follies and foibles. Many were the unknown comics of the cheaper bars from Caernarfon to Cardiff, or the local heroes of the noson lawen. A few achieved comedic and financial riches. Tommy Cooper, who began his comedy career with the Navy, Army and Air Force Institutes in 1940, could easily mix the trivial and the tragic. He once shed genuine tears as he retold the story that he had 'backed a horse at twenty to one – it came in at twenty past four.'[5]

The responses of writers such as John Cowper Powys, Kate Roberts, Jean Rhys, Arthur Machen, Dewi Emrys, Rhys Davies, Kitchener Davies, Caradoc Evans, Gwyn Thomas, R. Williams Parry and so many others have been useful in revealing the ways in which the Welsh people coped in their ever-changing and complex worlds. Writers do not escape into other worlds, they go deeper into this one. They also reveal that because depths are often terrifying, then the creative writer has a price to pay, as Dylan Thomas, 'the druid of the broken body', so poignantly revealed in his own life. What such people had to say regarding the human condition in general and about what it meant to be Welsh have been the concern of these two volumes under the collective title *Pain and Pleasure*. The most prolific consideration of the meaning and purpose of life came from the pen of Bertrand Russell. The pursuit of happiness, the scramble for love, the procurement of wealth, and the cerebral hedonism of the mind's pleasures were just a few of life's purposes that he considered. Yet, according to T. S. Eliot, when Russell was asked by a taxi driver, 'Well, Lord Russell, what's it all about?', he was speechless.[6] His silence echoes the eclipse of meaning that was such a feature of modernist writing in the twentieth century as shown in works such as Joseph Conrad's *Heart of Darkness* or Howell Davies's *Congratulate the Devil* (1939). Creating a present was often problematic, especially when we remember the adolescent's illusion that the future is going to be great, whilst the adult believes that the past was. Such bleakness runs like quartz through stone in the work of T. H. Parry-Williams. He offers the deepest, darkest and bravest 'truth' about life in his bleak poem 'Dychwelyd' (Returning):

> Ac am nad ydyw'n byw ar hyd y daith,
> O gri ein geni hyd ein holaf gŵyn,
> Yn ddim ond crych dros dro neu gysgod craith
> Ar lyfnder esmwyth y mudandod mwyn,
> Ni wnawn, wrth ffoi am byth o'n ffwdan ffôl,
> Ond llithro i'r llonyddwch mawr yn ôl.

> (And because our life throughout our journey,
> From our birth to our last complaint,
> Is just a temporary crease or a scar's shadow
> On the smooth surface of time's immensities,
> We do nothing, as we escape forever our troublesome foolishness,
> But slip back into the great silence.)[7]

Historians historicise. They take acts, facts, figures, words and place them in context, or try their best to. Max Beerbohm once said, or is said to have said, that history does not repeat itself: it is historians who repeat one another. This is perhaps why histories often acquire the features of a fairy tale, a familiar order in which events are neatly set out with a comforting familiarity. In order to provide a hint of the complexity of the lived reality, this study has broadened the criteria for admission into the categories 'Wales' and 'the Welsh'. *Pain and Pleasure* has tried to incorporate evidence that encompasses the personal, the emotional, the exceptional, the contingent and the human into the narrative in order to provide a different portrait to the traditional picture. Such testimony is often dismissed as being digressive, disjointed and discursive. Anecdotes, say the purists, do not a country make, let alone history.

But anecdotes suggest colour, better still nuance, which mark local character, specificity, particularity. Therein lies the infinite aggregation of detail that, once elicited and ordered, can proffer an alternative version of history. Like Taliesin, poet, shaman and shape-shifter, the experiences of Wales and the Welsh were always evolving and elusive. Within a context of cultural unity, the Welsh as Welsh and as individuals are utterly different from each other, vastly varied, and unexpectedly sui generis. Yet there patently is a Wales, there palpably is Welsh history – aggregations of variants and of infinite detail, creations of imagination, of faith, of hope, of infinite effort and of love.

Notes

Introduction: 'To Begin at the Beginning'

1   On the film *A Run for Your Money* see David Berry, *Wales and the Cinema: The First Hundred Years* (Cardiff, 1994), pp. 10, 213–18, 224, 230, 236, 256.
2   On Dame Wales see Cartooning the First World War at *www.cartoonww1. org* (accessed 12 January 2017).
3   Declan Kiberd, *Inventing Ireland: The Literature of the Modern Nation* (London, 2009), p. 17.
4   Ernest Jones, 'The Welsh Inferiority Complex', *The Welsh Outlook*, March 1929.
5   David Cannadine, *The Undivided Past: History Beyond Our Differences* (London, 2013), pp. 92, 149, 259.
6   On Emma Goldman and Wales see Huw Walters, 'Emma Goldman: the Most Dangerous Woman in the World, the Amman Valley Connection', *The Carmarthenshrie Antiquary*, XXXIX (2003), 114–21. Also available at *www.users.ic24.net/~terrynorm/emma%20goldman.htm* (accessed 12 January 2017).
7   Virginia Nicholson, *Among the Bohemians: Experiments in Living 1900–1939* (London, 2003).
8   For an initial assessment of Welsh humour see Russell Davies, *Hope and Heartbreak: a Social History of Wales and the Welsh, 1776–1871* (Cardiff, 2005), pp. 324–75.
9   On Tommy Cooper's forerunners see John Fisher, *Tommy Cooper: Always Leave them Laughing* (London, 2006), pp. 19–25.
10 *Trysorfa y Plant*, June 1874.

1 'Dygwyl y Meirwon' (Festival of the Dead)

1   Arthur Cotterell and Rachel Storm, *The Ultimate Encyclopaedia of Mythology* (London, 2003), pp. 106–16.

2   Miranda Seymour, *Robert Graves: Life on the Edge* (London, 2003), pp. 21–39; Robert Graves, *Goodbye to All That* (London, 1960), pp. 39–59. See also John Grey, *The Immortalization Commission: the Strange Quest to Cheat Death* (Harmondsworth, 2011).

3   Olwen and Raymond Daniel, *Llyfr Mawr Llanddewi Brefi* (Aberystwyth, 2011), p. 60. For further consideration of life-after-death revisited see Carl Watkins, *The Undiscovered Country: Journeys Among the Dead* (London, 2013).

4   On Winifred Coombe Tennant see Peter Lord's detailed study *Between Two Worlds: The Diary of Winifred Coombe Tennant 1909–1924* (Aberystwyth, 2011). On spiritualism in the period 1870–1945 see Ronald Pearsall, *The Table-Rappers: the Victorians and the Occult* (Stroud, 2004); Antonio Melechi, *Servants of the Supernatural: The Night Side of The Victorian Mind* (London, 2009); Logie Barrow, *Independent Spirits: Spiritualism and the English Plebeians* (Manchester, 1986); Janet Oppenheim, *The Other World: Spiritualism and Psychical Research in England* (Cambridge, 1985); Alex Owen, *The Darkened Room* (Chicago, 1989); Alison Winter, *Mesmerised: Powers of Mind in Victorian Britain* (Chicago, 1998). See also Roy Porter et al. (eds), *Women, Madness and Spiritualism* (London, 2003).

5   On the imagery of death there is still much of value in Robert Hughes, *Heaven and Hell in Western Art* (London, 1968). See also Kate Forde, *Death: a Picture Album* (London, 2012). The book was the catalogue for a major exhibition on death that was held at the Wellcome Museum in 2012.

6   See *www.booksfromthepast.org/gsdl/cgi-bin/library.exe?e=d-000-00---osta%5fy%5f* (accessed 7 July 2014).

7   Alun Lewis, *In the Green Tree* (Cardigan, 2006); idem, *The Sentry: Poems and Stories* (Llanrwst, 2003), p. 39.

8   Waldo Williams, 'Rhwng dau gae', in *Dail Pren: Cerddi gan Waldo Williams* (Aberystwyth, 1971), p. 34.

9   *Cyfansoddiadau a Beirniadaethau Eisteddfod Genedlaethol Maldwyn 1965* (Llandybïe, 1965), p. 29.

10 R. Williams Parry, 'Hen gychwr afon angau', in Alan Llwyd (ed.), *Cerddi R. Williams Parry: y Casgliad Cyflawn, 1905–1950* (Dinbych, 1998); for a superb biography see the indefatigable Alan Llwyd's *Bob: Cofiant R. Williams Parry* (Llandysul, 2013).

11 John Thomas (ed.), *Pigion Englynion fy Ngwlad* (Caernarfon, 1881), p. 117.

12 Jonathan Ceredig Davies, *Folk-lore of West and Mid-Wales* (Felinfach, 1993), pp. 39–58.

[13] W. Howells, *Cambrian Superstitions* (Felinfach, 1991), pp. 51–61; Robin Gwyndaf, *Straeon Gwerin Cymru* (Llanrwst, 1988), pp. 30–4.

[14] HMSO, *Guide to Census Reports, Great Britain, 1801–1966* (London, 1977). See also the reports for each individual year 1870–1945.

[15] On the general trends see M. Anderson, 'The Emergence of the Modern Life Cycle', *Social History*, 10 (1985), 71–111; T. McKeown, *The Modern Rise of Population* (London, 1976); idem with R. G. Record, 'Reasons for the Decline of Mortality in England and Wales During the Nineteenth Century', *Population Studies*, 16 (1962), 139–51; R. Millward and F. N. Bell, 'Economic Factors in the Decline of Mortality in Late Nineteenth Century Britain', *European Review of Economic History*, 2 (1988), 263–88; S. Szreter, 'The Importance of Social Intervention in Britain's Mortality Decline c.1850–1914: a Reinterpretation of the Role of Public Health', *Social History of Medicine*, 1 (1988), 1–37; J. Winter, 'The Decline of Mortality in Britain, 1870–1950', in T. C. Barker and M. Drake (eds), *Population and Society in Britain, 1850–1980* (Oxford, 1982), pp. 99–119.

[16] D. Dwork, *War is Good For Babies and Other Young Children: a History of the Infant and Child Welfare Movement in England* (London, 1987); C. Dyehouse, 'Working Class Mothers and Infant Mortality in England, 1895–1914', *Journal of Social History*, 12 (1978–9), 117–29; E. M. Garrett, 'Was Women's Work Bad for Babies? A View from the 1911 Census of England and Wales', *Continuity and Change*, 13 (1998), 39–49; D. Graham, 'Female Unemployment and Infant Mortality: Some Evidence from British Towns, 1911, 1931 and 1951', *Continuity and Change*, 9 (1994), 21–39; P. Huck, 'Infant Mortality and Living Standards of English Workers During the Industrial Revolution', *Journal of Economic History*, 55 (1995), 29–49; N. Morgan, 'Infant Mortality, Flies and Horses in the Later Nineteenth Century: a Case Study of Preston', *Continuity and Change*, 17 (2002), 31–9; E. P. Peretz, 'Regional Variations in Maternal and Child Welfare Between The Wars: Merthyr Tydfil, Oxfordshire and Tottenham', in D. Foster and P. Swan (eds), *Essays in Regional Local History* (Hull, 1992), pp. 119–39; N. Williams, 'Death in its Season: Class, Environment and the Mortality of Infants in Nineteenth-century Sheffield', *Social History of Medicine*, 5 (1992), 118–29; idem with G. Mooney, 'Infant Mortality in an "Age of Great Cities": London and the English Provincial Cities Compared, c.1940–1910', *Continuity and Change*, 9 (1994), 49–61; J. Winter, 'Infant Mortality, Maternal Mortality and Public Health in Britain in the 1930s', *Journal of European Economic History*, 13 (2) (1979), 439–62.

[17] The Welsh figures are available in L. J. Williams, *Digest of Welsh Historical Statistics*, vol. 1 (Cardiff, 1985), and idem, *Digest of Welsh Historical Statistics*, vol. 2 (Cardiff, 1985).

18 See J. A. Priest, *Families Outside Marriage* (Bristol, 1993).
19 Winter, 'The Decline of Mortality in Britain', pp. 101–3.
20 Ministry of Health, *Report on Maternal Mortality in Wales* (Cmd 5432) (HMSO, 1937), pp. 12–14.
21 Olwen and Raymond Daniel, *Llyfr Mawr Llanddewi Brefi*, p. 276.
22 Winter, 'The Decline of Mortality in Britain', pp. 104–6; Anderson, 'The Emergence of the Modern Life Cycle'.
23 See also Martin Daunton, *Wealth and Welfare: an Economic and Social History of Britain 1851–1951* (Oxford, 2007), pp. 349–75.
24 J. J. Evans, *Diarhebion Cymraeg* (Llandysul, 1965), passim.
25 Quoted in M. Wheeler, *Heaven, Hell and The Victorians* (Cambridge, 1994), p. 28.
26 Karl S. Guthke, *The Gender of Death: A Cultural History in Art and Literature* (Cambridge, 1999); J. S. Curl, *The Victorian Celebration of Death* (Newton Abbott, 1971); G. Rowell, *Hell and the Victorians* (London, 1974). In the Welsh context see R. Tudur Jones, 'Daearu'r Angylion', in J. Caerwyn Williams (ed.), *Ysgrifau Beirniadol XI* (Dinbych, n.d.), pp. 71–119.
27 On these themes see John McManners, *Death and the Enlightenment: Changing Attitudes to Death in Eighteenth-Century France* (Oxford, 1985), pp. 438–66.
28 On the Welsh context see Russell Davies, *Hope and Heartbreak: A Social History of Wales and the Welsh, 1776–1870* (Cardiff, 2005), pp. 208–62.
29 R. Tudur Jones, 'Darganfod Plant Bach', in J. E. Caerwyn Williams (ed.), *Ysgrifau Beirniadol VIII* (Dinbych, 1974), pp. 192–5. For some contemporary views see the ballads *Gweddi Merch Ieuanc ar ei Gwely Angau* and *Ystyriaethau Difrifol ar Weithredoedd Angau, er Annogaeth i Bawb Ystyried eu Diwedd* (both D. Jones, Aberdare, 1882).
30 Fiona MacCarthy, *The Last Pre-Raphaelite: Edward Burne-Jones and the Victorian Imagination* (London, 2011).
31 Kathryn Hughes and Ceridwen Lloyd-Morgan (eds), *Telyn Egryn* (Dinas Powys, 1998), pp. 69–70.
32 For an explanation of the poem see Ralph Maud, *Where Have the Old Words Got Me? Explications of Dylan Thomas's Collected Poems* (Trowbrige, 2003), pp. 41–3.
33 Jon Savage, *Teenage: the Creation of Youth, 1875–1945* (London, 2007); Giovanni Levi and Jean-Claude Schmitt, *A History of Young People in the West* (Boston, Mass., 1997).
34 James A. Davies, *Leslie Norris* (Cardiff, 1991), p. 31.
35 Davies, *Hope and Heartbreak*, pp. 208–62.
36 See for example the definition of adolescence in G. Stanley Hall, *Adolescence* (London, 1920), pp. 11–18.

37   Lawrence Stone, *The Family, Sex and Marriage in England* (London, 1976).

38   Daunton, *Wealth and Welfare*, pp. 370–2.

39   Ian Parrott, *The Spiritual Pilgrims* (Llandybïe, 1969); Eirene White, *The Ladies of Gregynog* (Cardiff, 1985).

40   Menna Baines, *Yng Ngolau'r Lleuad: Ffaith a Dychymyg Yng Ngwaith Caradog Prichard* (Llandysul, 2005), pp. 17, 23.

41   David Rees Griffiths, *Caneuon Amanwy* (Llandysul, 1956); Huw Walters, 'Amanwy', in Hywel Teifi Edwards (ed.), *Cwm Aman* (Llandysul, 1996), pp. 71–85; and idem, *Cynnwrf Canrif: Agweddau ar Ddiwylliant Gwerin* (Llandybïe, 2004), pp. 318–71.

42   Winter, 'The Decline of Mortality in Britain'.

43   For a photograph of the statue see *victorianweb.org* (accessed 11 November 2014). See also the *Western Mail*, 29 September 1891.

44   W. H. R. Powell MP (1819–1889), despite being a rich Anglican, landowner at the Maesgwynne estate in Llanboidy, Carmarthenshire, was a supporter of the Rebecca rioters and tenant rights. As a Member of Parliament he was in early at his office at 5 a.m. and often worked through until midnight. He was a notable benefactor who took a paternalistic care of his people. See William Denby Owen, *Powell Maesgwynne: Philanthropist, Sporting Great and Radical Hero: an Account of the Life and Times of W. R. H. Powell Carmarthenshire, 1819–1889* (Carmarthen, 2012); see also Matthew Cragoe, *An Anglican Aristocracy: the Moral Economy of the Landed Estate in Carmarthenshire 1832–1895* (Oxford, 1996), passim.

45   The quotation is from J. M. Barrie's *Peter Pan, or the Boy Who Wouldn't Grow Up* (1904), based on the lives of the Llewelyn Davies brothers who experienced more than their share of death – their parents died of cancer (their father in 1907, mother in 1910); George was killed in the First World War, Michael drowned aged twenty at Oxford in 1921, whilst Peter committed suicide in 1960 by throwing himself under a train. See David Edwards, *The Tragic True Story Behind Peter Pan* (London, 2004); Piers Dudgeon, *Captivated: J. M. Barrie, the Du Mauriers and the Dark Side of Peter Pan* (London, 2009); and Lisa Chaney, *Hide and Seek with Angels: a Life of J. M. Barrie* (London, 2005).

46   Quoted in Robin Gwyndaf, 'The Sorrow of All People: Death, Grief and Comfort in a Welsh Rural Community', *Folk Life*, 36 (1997–8), 84–105; see also Elisabeth Kubler-Ross, *On Grief and Grieving* (London, 2005), and Kenneth J. Doka, *Grieving Beyond Gender: Understanding the Ways Men and Women Mourn* (Hoe, 2010).

47   Alan Llwyd, *Kate – Cofiant Kate Roberts 1891–1985* (Talybont, 2011), pp. 71–93.

48 Maud, *Where Have the Old Words Got Me?*, p. 37; see also Paul Ferris, *Dylan Thomas 1914–1953* (Harmondsworth, 1978), p. 17.

49 See Menna Baines, *Yng Ngolau'r Lleuad: Ffaith a Dychymyg yng Ngwaith Caradog Prichard* (Llandysul, 2005), pp. 7–8, 72; see *Yr Herald Cymraeg*, 19 September 1972.

50 Keri Edwards, *Jack Jones* (Cardiff, 1974), pp. 21–7.

51 David Painting, *Amy Dillwyn* (Cardiff, 1987), passim. Amy Dillwyn was familiar with death – in 1864 her fiancé, Llewelyn Thomas, died shortly before their planned wedding. In 1866 her mother died. In 1890 her brother died, followed by her father in 1892.

52 J. Towyn Jones, *Rhag Ofn Ysbrydion: Chwilio am y Gwir am Straeon Ysbryd* (Aberystwyth, 2008), pp. 9–24.

53 Catrin Stevens, *Cligieth, C'nebrwn ac Angladd* (Llanrwst, 1987), p. 10.

54 Quoted in Catrin Stevens, 'The Funeral Wake in Wales', *Folk Life*, 14 (1976), 39. For a Celtic comparison see Seán O'Súillebháin *Irish Wake Amusements* (Cork, 1967).

55 Dr Smith recalled: 'When I was called in to investigate the cause of his death, I found the house where he lived packed with scared and hysterical neighbours. There were some among them who refused to believe he was dead, though rigor mortis was plain to see; and suspended judgement until a doctor had confirmed their fears. When I announced the obvious truth, they began to wail, and the wailing was taken up by the people in the street outside, spreading from door to door'. Denis Hayes Corfton (ed.), *The Surgery at Aberffrwd: Some Encounters of a Colliery Doctor Seventy Years Ago by Francis Mylett Smith* (Hythe, 1981), p. 35.

56 Michael Lieven, *Senghennydd: the Universal Pit Village* (Llandysul, 1994), pp. 70, 218–31.

57 Ken Etheridge, *Songs for Courage* (Llandysul, 1940), p. 32.

58 *Baner Cymru*, 26 August 1877.

59 *Baner ac Amserau Cymru*, 11 March 1863.

60 Catrin Stevens, 'The Funeral Made the Attraction: the Social and Economic Functions of Funerals in Nineteenth-Century Wales', in Katie Gramich and Andrew Hiscock (eds), *Dangerous Diversity: the Changing Faces of Wales, Essays in Honour of Tudor Bevan* (Cardiff, 1998), p. 88.

61 *Western Mail*, 30 October 1869.

62 *Baner ac Amserau Cymru*, 9 September 1876. The reporter blamed the sale of alcohol for the death for this had turned Tremble from 'a man into a devil'. The fact that he was Irish was also a cause for concern.

63 Evan Jones, *Cymdogaeth Soar-y-Mynydd* (Llandybïe, 1978), p. 78.

64 Stevens, *Cligieth, C'nebrwn ac Angladd*, p. 95.

[65] R. Meurig Evans, *One Saturday Afternoon: the Albion Colliery, Cilfynydd Explosion of 1894* (Cardiff, 1984), pp. 33–40.

[66] Richard Griffiths, *The Entrepreneurial Society of the Rhondda Valleys, 1870–1920: Power and Influence in the Porth – Pontypridd Region* (Cardiff, 2010), pp. 150–5, 179–207.

[67] The dispute over attendance at funerals at Bwllfa Colliery is discussed in Kim Howells, 'Victimisation, Accidents and Disease', in David Smith (ed.), *A People and a Proletariat: Essays in the History of Wales 1780–1980* (London, 1980), pp. 181–98.

[68] See for example T. Rowland Hughes's novel *Chwalfa* (Aberystwyth, 1957), and Emyr Hywel Owen, 'Rhagor o Gefndir "Chwalfa"', *Lleufer*, XIV (1958), 124.

[69] *Baner ac Amserau Cymru*, 7 August 1912. Ellis had to be careful, not just to secure an attendance through the invitation, but to ensure that some of his many enemies attended. Between 1870 and 1874 he had to emigrate to Utica to avoid several threatened cases of slander and libel against him.

[70] The story has been well told in Dean Powell's excellent *Dr William Price: Wales's First Radical* (Stroud, 2012); see also J. Cule, 'The Eccentric Dr William Price of Llantrisant, 1800–1893', *Morgannwg*, 7 (1963), 98–120, and B. Davies, 'Empire and Identity, the "case" of Doctor William Price', in David Smith (ed.), *A People and a Proletariat: Essays in the History of Wales, 1780–1980* (London, 1980), pp. 72–93.

[71] Powell, *Dr William Price*, p. 256. See also Carl Watkins, *The Undiscovered Country: Journeys Among the Dead* (London, 2013), pp. 173–85.

[72] For contemporary views of Dr Price's eccentricities see *Cardiff Times and South Wales Weekly News*, 19 May and 23 June 1888.

[73] *South Wales Weekly News*, 23 June 1888.

[74] The late, great historian Richard Cobb, in *Second Identity: Essays on France and French History* (Oxford, 1969), advised aspirant historians to walk the area they were writing about. The next few paragraphs follow his sage advice.

[75] On the impact of excessive mourning on masculinity see Stephen Garton, 'The Scales of Suffering: Loss, Death and Victorian Masculinity', *Social History*, 27, 1 (2002), 40–58.

[76] There is an excellent guide to Welsh graveyards in Alun Roberts, *Discovering Welsh Graves: a Pocket Guide* (Cardiff, 2002).

[77] Roberts, *Discovering Welsh Graves*, pp. 4–5.

[78] Roberts, *Discovering Welsh Graves*, pp. 12–15.

[79] Davies, *Hope and Heartbreak*, pp. 16, 303–4.

[80] Bethan Phillips, *The Lover's Graves: Six True Tales That Shocked Wales* (Llandysul, 2007).

[81]   Roberts, *Discovering Welsh Graves*, pp. 61, 65. See also Richard Pawelco and Lionel Fanthorpe, *Talking Stones: Grave Stories and Unusual Epitaphs in Wales* (Llandysul, 2003).

[82]   On the impact of the war dead see David Crane, *Empires of the Dead: How One Man's Vision Led to the Creation of WWI's War Graves* (London, 2014), pp. 67–96.

[83]   Viscount Gladstone, *W. G. C. Gladstone: A Memoir* (London, 1918).

[84]   Viscount Gladstone, *W. G. C. Gladstone: A Memoir*, p. 107.

[85]   Graves, *Goodbye to All That*, p. 170.

[86]   Crane, *Empires of the Dead*, pp. 69–74.

[87]   Bush Way, 'Name upon Name: the Great War and Remembrance', in Roy Porter (ed.), *Myths of the English* (Cambridge, 1992), pp. 136–67; David Cannadine, 'War and Death, Grief and Mourning in Modern Britain', in J. Whaley (ed.), *Mirrors of Mortality: Studies in the Social History of Death* (London, 1981), pp. 187–242; Jay Winter, *Sites of Memory, Sites of Mourning: the Great War in European Cultural History* (Cambridge, 1995).

[88]   Angela Gaffney, *Aftermath: Remembering the Great War in Wales* (Cardiff, 1998); Ray Westlake, *First World War Graves and Memorials in Gwent* (Barnsley, 2001); Lester Mason, 'Is it Nothing to You, all ye who pass by?: Commemorating the Great War in Ammanford 1920–1937', *Llafur*, 11 (1) (2012), 49–62.

[89]   Richard Morris, 'The death of Sarah Dillwyn', *Minerva*, 13 (2005), 5–15. The most famous death painting is Herkomer's of Queen Victoria on her deathbed in 1901. On death in art in Wales see Martin O'Kane and John Morgan-Guy, *Biblical Art from Wales* (Sheffield, 2010).

[90]   The most evocative study of the power of the photographs of the dead is Michael Lesy, *Wisconsin Death Trip* (London, 1973).

[91]   For Dylan Thomas on his deathbed see James Nashol and George Tremlett, *The Death of Dylan Thomas* (Edinburgh, 1997), and David N. Thomas, *Fatal Neglect: Who Killed Dylan Thomas?* (Bridgend, 2008). See also Ruthven Todd, *The Ghost of Dylan Thomas* (Glenrother, Fife, 2014), and Robert Minhinnick, *The Mythic Death of Dylan Thomas* (Glenrother, Fife, 2014).

[92]   See for example the photograph in Stevens, *Cligieth, C'nebrwn ac Angladd*, p. 15.

[93]   On graveyard eulogies, elegies, and 'englyion' see M. Euronwy James, *Englynion Beddau Ceredigion* (Llandysul, 1983); H. Mytum, 'Welsh Cultural Identity in Nineteenth-century Pembrokeshire: The Pedimented Headstone as a Graveyard Monument', in S. Tarlow and S. West (eds), *The Familiar Past: Archaeologies of Later Historical Britain* (London, 1999), pp. 215–30; idem, 'The Language of Death in a Bilingual Community:

Nineteenth-Century Memorials in Newport, Pembrokeshire', in R. Blanch and M. Sprigger (eds), *Language and Archaeology III* (London, 1999), pp. 252–67. For a prolific eulogist of his people see Robin Gwyndaf *Taliesin o Eifion a'i Oes: Bardd y Gadair Ddu Gyntaf Eisteddfod Wrecsam, 1876* (Talybont, 2012).

[94] On the written context of the information recorded on gravestones and the sense of belonging to an area see K. D. M. Snell, 'Gravestones, Belonging and Local Attachment in England 1700–2000', *Past and Present*, 179 (2003), 97–134. There is a useful collection of remembrance poems in Bethan Mair and Elinor Wyn Reynolds (eds), *Hoff Gerddi Coffa Cymru* (Llandysul, 2014).

[95] Richard Holland, *Haunted Wales: a Survey of Welsh Ghostlore* (Ashbourne, 2005), p. 112.

[96] Peter Underwood, *Ghosts of Wales* (Llandybïe, 1978), p. 111.

[97] On the Cyhyraeth see Jones, *Rhag Ofn Ysbrydion*, pp. 9–19, 177–232.

[98] On spiritualism in the Welsh context see Jane R. Camerini (ed.), *The Alfred Russel Wallace Reader* (Baltimore, Md., 2002), pp. 163–87. Lord, *Between Two Worlds*; Signe Toksvig, *Swan on a Black Sea: a Study in Automatic Writing: the Cummins-Willett Scripts* (London, 1965).

[99] For Captain Henry Morgan's visitations see Marina Warner, *Phantasmagoria: Spirit Visions, Metaphors, and Media in the Twenty-First Century* (Oxford, 2006), p. 227.

[100] Arthur Conan Doyle, *The History of Spiritualism* (London, 1926), p. 170.

[101] Ben Pimlott, *Hugh Dalton* (London, 1985), pp. 126–9.

[102] Oliver Lodge, *Christopher: A Study in Human Personality* (London, 1918).

[103] Quoted in Lord, *Between Two Worlds*, p. 246.

[104] For 1870–1945 as an age of anxiety and traumatic death see Mark S. Micale and Paul Rerner (eds), *Traumatic Pasts: History, Psychiatry and Trauma in the Modern Age, 1870–1930* (Cambridge, 2001). See also Hans Pols, 'Shock and Horror', *History Workshop Journal*, 54 (2002), 261–4.

[105] Juliet Gardiner, *Wartime Britain: 1939–45* (London, 2005).

[106] Quoted in Philip Tapper and Susan Hawthorne, *Wales and the Second World War* (Cardiff, 1991), p. 40. The Cwmparc 'Bombed Areas' Distress Fund Committee produced a leaflet '*In Memorium*' as a 'tribute to our fellow villagers who fell victims to the murderous fury of Nazi war-planes on the night and morning of April 29/30th, 1941'. The actor and singer Ivor Emmanuel (1927–2007) lost his father, mother, sister and grandfather when their village, Pontrhydyfen, was hit by a stray German bomb.

[107] On these themes see Philip Ariès, *The Hour Of Our Death* (Oxford, 1991); Douglas J. Davies, *A Brief History of Death* (Oxford, 2005), pp. 110–11; Peter C. Lipp and Claire Gittings (eds), *Death in England:*

an *Illustrated History* (Manchester, 1999); Julie-Marie Strange, *Death, Grief and Poverty in Britain, 1870–1914* (Cambridge, 2005); Richard Huntington and Peter Metcalf, *Celebrations of Death, the Anthropology of Mortuary and Ritual* (Cambridge, 1979); and Antonius C. G. M. Robben (ed.), *Death, Mourning and Burial: a Cross-Cultural Reader* (London, 2004).

[108] Joanna Bourke, *What it Means to be Human: Reflections From 1791 to the Present* (London, 2001).

[109] On the theme of hope surviving even the most brutal and bloody trauma see Catherine Merridale, 'Death and Memory in Modern Russia', *History Workshop Journal*, 42 (1996), 1–18.

2 The Citadel: Pain, Anxiety and Wellbeing

[1] W. J. Gruffydd, *The Years of The Locust* (Llandysul, 1976).

[2] In Carol White and Sian Rhiannon Williams, *Struggle or Starve: Women's Lives in the South Wales Valleys between the Two World Wars* (Dinas Powys, 1998), pp. 129–30.

[3] Ron Berry, *History is what you Live* (Llandysul, 1998), pp. 81, 87.

[4] Richard Vaughan, *Moulded in Earth* (London, 1951). He also produced *There is a River* (London, 1945?), which is a fictional rendering of his childhood in Llanddeusant, Carmarthenshire. *Moulded in Earth* has all the depth of character and depression of circumstances of Zola's *La Terre* (The Earth).

[5] See for example Gwyn A. Williams, *When was Wales?* (London, 1985), pp. 253–5; John Davies, *A History of Wales* (Harmondsworth, 1994), pp. 509–96; D. Gareth Evans, *A History of Wales, 1906–1980* (Cardiff, 2000); and K. O. Morgan, *Rebirth of a Nation: Wales 1880–1980* (Cardiff and Oxford, 1981), pp. 210–40.

[6] See most notably the detailed study by Steven Thompson, *Unemployment, Poverty and Health in Inter-War South Wales* (Cardiff, 2006); and idem, 'That Beautiful Summer of Severe Austerity: Health, Diet and the Working Class Domestic Economy in South Wales in 1926', *Welsh History Review*, 21 (3) (2003), 552–74. See also Andy Croll, 'A Famished Coalfield or a "Healthy Strike?" Assessing Evidence of Hunger in the South Wales "Coal War of 1898"', *Welsh History Review*, 26 (1) (2012), 58–80.

[7] On these themes see William Lamont (ed.), *Historical Controversies and Historians* (London, 1998), and David Cannadine, *The Pleasures of the Past* (London, 1990), pp. 230–46.

8   Quoted in Russell Davies, *Hope and Heartbreak: A Social History of Wales and the Welsh 1776–1870* (Cardiff, 2005), pp. 164–5.

9   *Report on the Death Rate of the Population in Parts of South Wales*, Seventh A.R.M.D.P.C (1864), pp. 1865, XXVI, 498.

10   D. Lleufer Thomas, *The Agricultural Labourer: Wales Report: Poor Law Unions of Pembroke, Haverfordwest, Cardigan and Newcastle Emlyn*, HC 1893–4 (C6894–XN), XXVI, p. 63.

11   *Report of the Inspectors into the Condition of Agriculture (1894–6) Volume 3* (London, 1896), p. 553.

12   *Report of the Inspectors into the Condition of Agriculture*, p. 543.

13   On morality and housing see Revd Herbert Morgan, *Housing and Public Welfare: Some Economic and Moral Considerations* (n.d.), passim.

14   John Rhys and David Brynmor Jones, *The Welsh People* (London, 1906), pp. 540–56.

15   Edgar Chappell published articles on living conditions in the *South Wales Daily News*, on 22, 23, 24, 25, 26, 28, 29, 30 and 31 August, and 1, 2, 4 and 5 September 1911.

16   E. G. Millward, *Ceinion y Gân: Detholiad o Ganeuon Poblogaedd Oes Victoria* (Llandysul, 1983), p. 43 and passim. See also Huw Williams, *Canu'r Bobol* (Dinbych, 1978).

17   *South Wales Daily News*, 24 August 1911.

18   *An Investigation into the Causes of the Continued High Death Rate from TB in Certain Parts of North Wales*, quoted in the source book *The Condition of The People in Nineteenth and Twentieth century Gwynedd* (Caernarfon, 1976), p. 41. See also C. L. Sutherland and S. Bryson, *Report on an Inquiry into the Occurrence of Disease of the Lungs from Dust Inhalation in The Slate Industry in the Gwyrfai District* (London, 1930).

19   See *www.llgc.casglu'rtlysau* (accessed 11 May 2010).

20   Seebohm Rowntree, *How the Labourer Lives: a Study of the Rural Labour Problem* (London, 1913), p. 336. For similar stark views by contemporaries see Maude F. Davies, *Life in an English Village* (London, 1919); E. N. Bennett, *Problems of Village Life* (London, 1914); R. Bishop, *My Moorland Patients* (London, 1922); F. E. Green, *The Tyranny of the Countryside* (London, 1921); and R. Rider Hagard, *Rural England*, 2 vols (London, 1906). In the Welsh context A. W. Ashby has many interesting points to make in 'The Human Side of the Farming Business', *Welsh Journal of Agriculture* (1925) and in 'A View of Rural Society', *The Welsh Outlook* (May 1924).

21   One of the best investigations into living conditions in urban Wales is *The Land: the Report of the Land Enquiry Committee, Vol 11 Urban* (London, 1914).

22 Quoted in Russell Davies, *Secret Sins: Sex, Violence and Society in Carmarthenshire, 1870–1920* (Cardiff, 1995), p. 260.

23 On Welsh housing see John Davies, *The Making of Wales* (Stroud, 2009). Malcolm J. Fisk, *Housing in the Rhondda 1800–1940* (Cardiff, 1996) has a photograph of the painfully named Long Row in Blaenllechau just after the coalman's visit. The mounds of coal would have to be carried from the front pavement, where it was delivered, to the backyard, through the house with serious effects for cleanliness (p. 69). See also Gerallt D. Nash, *Timber-framed Buildings in Wales* (Cardiff, 1995); Eurwyn William, *Home-made Houses: Dwellings of the Rural Poor in Wales* (Cardiff, 1998); and J. B. Lowe, *Welsh Industrial Workers Housing 1775–1875* (Cardiff, 1977). There is a lot of valuable material in Kate Sullivan, '"The Biggest Room in Merthyr": Working Class Housing in Dowlais, 1850–1914', *Welsh History Review*, 17 (2) (1994–5), 155–85. 'What is the biggest room in Merthyr?', asked the *Merthyr Express*, and answered 'the room for improvement.'

24 On the conditions faced by working women in Welsh society see Mari A. Williams, 'Aspects of Women's Working Lives in the Mining Communities of South Wales, c.1891–1939', *Folk Life*, 28 (1999–2000), 56–70; Jane Elliot, 'The Welsh Mam', in Rob Humphreys and Anna-Marie Taylor (eds), *Opening up 'The Keep' by Gwyn Thomas* (Swansea, 1996), pp. 41–4; Deirdre Beddoe, 'Women Between the Wars', in Trevor Herbert and Gareth Elwyn Jones (eds), *Wales Between the Wars* (Cardiff, 1988), pp. 128–60; idem, 'Munitionettes, Maids and Mams: Women in Wales 1914–1939', in Angela V. John (ed.), *Our Mothers' Land: Chapters in Welsh Women's History* (Cardiff, 1991), pp. 189–209; idem, *Out of the Shadows: a History of Women in Twentieth Century Wales* (Cardiff, 2000); and White and Williams, *Struggle or Starve*. See also, for a contemporary view, Margery Spring-Rice (ed.), *Working-class Wives: Their Health and Condition* (Harmondsworth, 1939).

25 E. Williams, 'Pit-Head Baths', in *The Colliery Workers Magazine* (July 1925). On the campaign for pithead baths see Edgar L. Chappell and J. A. Lovall-Fraser, *Pithead and Factory Baths* (Cardiff, 1920), and Neil Evans and Dot Jones, '"A blessing for the Miner's Wife": The Campaign for Pithead Baths in the South Wales Coalfield, 1908–1950', *Llafur*, 6 (3) (1994), 5–28.

26 J. A. Lovat-Fraser, 'Pithead Baths', *Welsh Housing and Development Association Yearbook* (1922), p. 77.

27 For the question on the Rhondda see *Report of the Medical Officer of Health Rhondda Urban District Council 1893* (Porth, 1893), p. 17. See also PP.XXXVII (1896), ARLGB, for 1895 Appendix XII "Report . . . of certain Valleys . . . with Special Reference to . . . the Pollution of Streams",

pp. 11, 115; PP.XXXIII (1874) CRCRP. Fifth Report (Pollution from mining operative and metal manufacturers) 1. Report, pp. vii–viii. For a discussion of atmospheric and environmental pollution see Anthony S. Wohl, *Endangered Lives: Public Health in Victorian Britain* (London, 1874), pp. 205–57.

28   *Aberdare Times*, 16 April 1898, and *Western Mail*, 23 April 1898. Quoted in Croll, 'A Famished Coalfield or a "Healthy Strike"?', 69.

29   The *Western Mail* first reported on slum conditions in Merthyr Tydfil on 8, 9 and 10 December 1898. See also *Western Mail* 27, 28 and 29 June 1907, and George Simms, *Human Wales* (Cardiff, 1908).

30   Hilda Jennings, *Brynmawr: a Study of a Distressed Area* (London, 1934), p. 152. For social conditions in Wales see John Davies, 'The Communal Conscience in Wales in the Inter-War Years', *Transactions of the Honourable Society of Cymmrodorion*, 5 (1998), 145–60.

31   J. P. Howell, 'Economic Depression in Welsh Farming', *The Welsh Journal of Agriculture*, XI (1935), 5–22.

32   Some studies that emphasise a particular, single cause for the improvement are S. Szreter, 'The Importance of Social Intervention in Britain's Mortality Decline c.1850–1914: a Reinterpretation of the Role of Public Health', *Social History of Medicine*, 1 (1988), 119–39, and R. I. Woods, 'The Effects of Population Redistribution on the Level of Mortality in Nineteenth-Century England and Wales', *Journal of Economic History*, 45 (1985), 211–29.

33   Quoted in Mark Girouard, *Victorian Public Houses* (London, 1975), p. 21. For alcohol in Wales see W. R. Lambert, *Drink and Sobriety in Victorian Wales, c.1820–1895* (Cardiff, 1983).

34   The appropriately named Eric Burns has written *The Smoke of the Gods: a Social History of Tobacco* (Philadelphia, 2007). There are many useful insights in John C. Burnham, *Bad Habits: Drinking, Smoking, Taking Drugs, Gambling, Sexual Misbehaviour, and Swearing in American History* (New York, 1993). See also Zhou Xun and Sander L. Gillman, *Smoke: a Global History of Smoking* (London, 2004); Allan M. Brendt, *The Cigarette Century: the Rise, Fall and Deadly Persistence of the Product that Defined America* (Cambridge, Mass., 2007), and M. Hilton, *Smoking in British Popular Culture, 1800–2000* (Manchester, 2000).

35   J. J. Morgan, *Cofiant Edward Matthews, Ewenni* (Abertawe, 1922), p. 210; David Evans, *Atgofion yr Hybarch David Evans Archddeiacon Llanelwy* (Dinbych, 1904), p. 50; see also *Y Casglwr*, 61 (1997), 14–15.

36   For the intrusion of the state into private life see Martin Daunton, *Wealth and Welfare: an Economic and Social History of Britain 1850–1950* (Oxford, 2007), pp. 321–419, 459–574; Jose Harris, *Private Lives, Public Spirit: a Social History of Britain 1870–1914*; J. Winter, *The Great War and*

the British People (Basingstoke, 1986); H. V. Perkin, 'Individualism Versus Collectivism in Nineteenth Century Britain: a False Antithesis', in his *The Structured Crowd: Essays in English Social History* (London, 1981), pp. 170–92; Keith Laybourn and Jack Reynolds, *Liberalism and the Rise of Labour 1890–1918* (London, 1984); and Pat Thorne, *Origins of British Social Policy* (London, 1978).

[37] Such an isolation hospital was located at Flat Holm island. Here victims died of cholera in 1883 and 1893. The last patient to die on the island suffered from the bubonic plague.

[38] For a discussion of the film and its Welsh background see David Berry, *Wales and the Cinema: the First Hundred Years* (Cardiff, 1994), pp. 150–7.

[39] Roy Porter, *The Greatest Benefit to Mankind* (London, 1997); idem, *Blood and Guts: a Short History of Medicine* (London, 2004); W. F. Bynum (ed.), *The Western Medical Tradition* (London, 1995); Stephen Cherry, *Medical Services and the Hospital in Britain, 1860–1939* (London, 1996). For a specific example of rivalry and conflict between medical professionals see J. Donnison, *Midwives and Medical Men: History of Interprofessional Rivalries and Women's Rights* (London, 1977).

[40] On the cholera revival see Davies, *Hope and Heartbreak*, pp. 194–201; C. B. Turner, 'Religion and Popular Revivals in Victorian and Edwardian Wales' (unpublished PhD thesis, University of Wales, Aberystwyth, 1973); and J. J. Morgan, *Dafydd Morgan a Diwygiad 1859* (Mold, 1906).

[41] Max Beloff, *War and Welfare: Britain, 1914–45* (Harmondsworth, 1984); Martin Daunton, *State and Market in Victorian Britain: War, Welfare and Capitalism* (Cambridge, 2008).

[42] James Roy Hay, *Origins of the Liberal Welfare Reforms, 1906–14* (London, 1983).

[43] For a discussion of some of these themes see John Wyn Pritchard, 'Water Supply in Welsh Towns, 1840–1900: Control, Conflict and Development', *Welsh History Review*, 21 (1) (2002), 24–47; Sue Brierly, 'The Politics of Food, Gender, Family, Community and Collective Feeding in South Wales in the General Strike and Miners' walkout of 1926', *Twentieth Century British History*, 18 (1) (2007), 54–77; Charles Webster, 'Health, Welfare and Unemployment During the Depression', *Past and Present*, 109 (1985), 204–30. One figure of visionary genius in the area of architecture and town planning was Arthur Trystan Edwards (1884–1973) of Merthyr Tydfil. In a series of pamphlets for the Hundred New Towns Association (1933–4), Edwards set out a prophetic vision for a greener and pleasanter environment. See his *Second-best Boy: the Autobiography of a Non-Speaker* (London, 1970).

[44] Quoted in J. M. Winter, 'The Impact of the First World War on Civilian Health in Britain', *Economic History Review*, XXX, 3 (1977), 497. The *Daily Telegraph* in reporting the bishop's words noted that 'if we had been more careful for the past fifty years to prevent the unheeded wastage of infant life, we should now have at least half a million more men available for the defence of the country'. The paper urged people to save lives, so more could die in the war.

[45] See Thompson, *Unemployment, Poverty and Health*, pp. 217–40.

[46] *Forty-fourth Annual Report of the Local Government Board, 1914–15: Supplement in Continuation of the Medical Officer for the Board for 1914–15: Containing a Report on Maternal Mortality in Connection with Childbearing and its Relation to Infant Mortality*, 1914–16 [Cd 8085], pp. 109, 118–21.

[47] See J. Barker, *W. H. Davies: Selected Poems* (Oxford, 1985), p. 99. W. H. Davies had been birched for theft in 1885. See also W. H. Davies, *The Adventure of Johnny Walker, Tramp* (London, 1926).

[48] Lionel Rose, *The Massacre of the Innocents: Infanticide in Great Britain 1880–1939* (London, 1986), pp. 93–108; R. W. Ireland, 'Perhaps my Mother Murdered Me: Child Death and the Law in Victorian Carmarthenshire', in Christopher Brooks and Michael Lobban (eds), *Communities and Courts in Britain, 1150–1900* (London, 1997), pp. 229–44 (I am very grateful to Richard for a copy of the article); Keith Wrightson, 'Infanticide in European History', *Criminal Justice History*, III (1982), 1–20; R. Sauer, 'Infanticide and Abortion in Nineteenth-Century Britain', *Population Studies*, 32 (1978), 90–1; A. McLaren, 'Women's Work and Regulation of Family Size: the Question of Abortion in the Nineteenth Century', *History Workshop Journal*, 4 (1977), 79–92.

[49] *South Wales Daily News*, 6 September 1887, 17 December 1886, 7 January 1907, 18 August 1909. See Davies, *Secret Sins: Sex, Violence and Society*, pp. 70–9, 173–5, 302–5.

[50] *South Wales Daily News*, 20 April 1877, 5 December 1895, 3 January 1912.

[51] *South Wales Press*, 10 March 1901.

[52] Davies, *Secret Sins: Sex, Violence and Society*, p. 174.

[53] Davies, *Secret Sins: Sex, Violence and Society*, pp. 302–3.

[54] *Western Mail*, 2 December 1899.

[55] *Western Mail*, 12 July 1873.

[56] *Western Mail*, 25 July 1888.

[57] *Western Mail*, 21 June 1878.

[58] *Western Mail*, 13 February 1899. For other reports see 10 April 1877, 3 August 1888 and 5 December 1888.

[59] *Ministry of Health: Report on Maternal Mortality in Wales* [Cmd 5423] (London, 1937), p. 72.

[60] In another poem Lynette Roberts portrays her body as an incinerator, a destroyer of life: 'I rimmeled, awake before the dressing sun / Above I, pent up incinerator, serf of satellite gloom / Cower around my cradled self'. Patrick McGuinness (ed.), *Collected Poems by Lynette Roberts* (London, 2005), p, 49.

[61] Thompson, *Unemployment, Poverty and Health*, pp. 217–21.

[62] See for example Carol Dyhouse, 'Working-class Mothers and Infant Mortality in England, 1895–1914', *Journal of Social History*, 12, 2 (1978), 248–67; R. I. Woods, P. A. Watterson and J. H. Woodward, 'The Causes of Rapid Infant Mortality Decline in England and Wales 1861–1921', *Population Studies*, 43, 9 (1989), 113–32; and Michael Anderson, 'The Emergence of the Modern Life Cycle in Britain', *Social History*, 10, 1 (1985), 69–87.

[63] Thompson, *Unemployment, Poverty and Health*, pp. 225–6.

[64] Quoted in Dyhouse, 'Working-class Mothers and Infant Mortality in England, 1895–1914', 261. Perhaps one of the most extreme examples of 'class prejudice' against mothers was given by Dr H. R. Jones, who practiced in Liverpool. For Jones, a high diarrhoeal mortality rate served as a 'useful measure of the ignorance of a community, together with the prevalence therein of child neglect . . . The children of women engaged in industrial occupations suffer from the effects of maternal neglect. They are handicapped from the moment of birth in the struggle for existence, and have to contend not only against the inevitable perils of infancy, but also against the perils due to their neglect by mothers, and to the ignorance of those to whose care they are entrusted'. See also Naomi Williams, 'Death in its Season: Class, Environment and the Mortality of Infants in Sheffield', *Social History of Medicine*, 5 (1992), 71–94.

[65] James C. Riley, 'Did Mothers Begin with an Advantage? A Study of Childbirth and Maternal Health in England and Wales, 1778–1929', *Population Studies*, 57, 1 (2003), 5–20; and Robert Millward and Frances Bell, 'Infant Mortality in Victorian Britain: the Mother as Medium', *Economic History Review*, 54, 4 (2001), 699–733. It is important to note that the passage of an Act by Parliament did not lead to any immediate improvements. Often changes took place over a long period. Local medical officers frequently complained that Acts were not being enacted. To quote just one example, the medical officer for Carmarthenshire was still complaining in the 1920s that the Midwife Act of 1908 had not been fully implemented locally.

[66] Thompson, *Unemployment, Poverty and Health*, p. 232, and in Williams, 'Death in its season', 91.

[67] *Ministry of Health Report on Maternal Mortality in Wales*, p. 29.

[68] *South Wales Press*, 8 February 1883.

[69] *Carmarthen Weekly Reporter*, 24 December 1909.

[70] Glyn Jones, *The Dragon Has Two Tongues* (London, 1968), pp. 98–9. Edith Picton-Turbervill was the daughter of the Ewenni Priory estate in Glamorgan. A tireless worker for votes for women, for the rights of women to be priests and the ending of the death sentence being enacted against expectant mothers, she was one of the first female Members of Parliament. She worked in support of navvies and their families in south Wales. See Edith Picton-Turbervill, *Life is Good: An Autobiography* (London, 1939), and *In the Land of My Fathers* (Cardiff, 1946).

[71] See for example in A. Hardy, *The Epidemic Streets: Infectious Diseases and the Rise of Preventative Medicine, 1856–1900* (Oxford, 1993).

[72] Roy Porter, *Blood and Guts: a Short History of Medicine* (London, 2003), passim.

[73] Davies, a fluent Welsh speaker, was devoted to several cultural causes in Wales. Despite being a close friend of Aneurin Bevan, he, as a staunch nonconformist, refused to participate in the newly formed National Health Service in 1945. For his obituary see *The Times*, 19 May 1966. Amongst the Welshmen who became physicians to the Royal family were Sir Noah Thomas, Sir David Davies, David Lloyd Morgan, and Sir John Williams. See Davies, *Hope and Heartbreak*, p. 14.

[74] Letter Florence Nightingale sent to William Rathbone, University of Bangor Archives, item 37618.

[75] Porter, *The Greatest Benefit to Mankind*, p. 443.

[76] On influenza see John H. Barry, *The Great Influenza: the Epic Story of the Deadliest Plague in History* (London, 2004); Mark Honigsbaum, *Living with Enza: the Forgotten Story of the Great Flu Pandemic of 1918* (London, 2009); Gina Kolata, *Flu: The Story of the Great Influenza Pandemic and the Search for the Virus That Caused It* (London, 1999); Alfred Crosby, *Epidemic and Peace, 1918* (London, 1976); and Richard Collier, *The Plague of the Spanish Lady* (London, 1996).

[77] Weekly mortality data compiled by N. P. A. J. Johnson from the supplement to the eighty-first *Annual Report by the Registrar General, Report on the Mortality from Influenza in England and Wales During the Epidemic of 1918–19* at *www.ahds.ac.uk/catalogue/download/.htm?List-4350-1type=col* (accessed 12 April 2006). See also David Killingray and Howard Phillips (eds), *The Spanish Flu Pandemic of 1918–19: New Perspectives* (London, 2001). See also Gerardo Chowell et al., 'The 1918–19 Influenza Pandemic in England and Wales: Spatial Patterns in Transmissibility and Mortality Impact', *Proceedings of the Royal Society B* (2008), 501–9.

[78] *Cambrian Daily Leader*, 5 November 1918. Earlier outbreaks of flu had occurred in Wales, the most notable was the Russian influenza of 1890 that affected thousands of people across Wales and all the 'Coolie sailors in Barry Dock', *Western Mail*, 8 January 1890.

[79] *Cambrian Daily Leader*, 31 October 1918.

[80] *Cambrian Daily Leader*, 23 November 1918.

[81] *Cambrian Daily Leader*, 18 June 1918.

[82] *Cambrian Daily Leader*, 28 November 1918.

[83] *Cambrian Daily Leader*, 22 June 1918.

[84] *Cambrian Daily Leader*, 28 June 1918.

[85] *Cambrian Daily Leader*, 7 October 1918.

[86] *Cambrian Daily Leader*, 20 July 1918.

[87] *Cambrian Daily Leader*, 1 November 1918.

[88] *Cambrian Daily Leader*, 23 November 1918.

[89] *Cambrian Daily Leader*, 21 October 1918.

[90] *Cambrian Daily Leader*, 25 November 1918.

[91] *Cambrian Daily Leader*, 22 and 28 October 1918.

[92] *Cambrian Daily Leader*, 29 November 1918.

[93] *Cambrian Daily Leader*, 14 November 1918.

[94] *Cambrian Daily Leader*, 17 December 1918.

[95] *Cambrian Daily Leader*, 25 and 26 October 1918.

[96] *Cambrian Daily Leader*, 18 May, 1 June, 3 October, 29 October, 11 November, 14 November, 21 November, 22 November, 13 December 1918.

[97] *Cambrian Daily Leader*, 27 June 1918. Rich the Chemist's descendants are probably still busy with chemical solutions to the townspeople's problems.

[98] *Cambrian Daily Leader*, 17 December 1918.

[99] *Cambrian Daily Leader*, 18 May and 11 November 1918.

[100] Watching the reaction to the 2014 Ebola epidemic provided a remarkable insight into how helpless people must have felt in 1918 in face of a threat they could do nothing to prevent.

[101] *Western Mail*, 31 March 1908.

[102] *Western Mail*, 22 March 1900.

[103] One of the few to consider the area is John Davies, *Rhanbarth Ymylol?: y Gogledd Ddwyrain yn Hanes Cymru / A Marginalised Region?: the North-East in the History of Wales* (Caerdydd / Cardiff, 2007).

[104] David Lee Williams, 'A Healthy Place to Be? The Wrexham Coalfield in the Inter-war Period', *Llafur*, 7 (1) (1996), 87–95.

[105] *Wrexham Leader*, 20 January 1933.

[106] Williams, 'A Healthy Place to Be?', 93.

[107] On tuberculosis see 'A Gentle Death: Tuberculosis in the Nineteenth Century', *www.concordma.com/magazine/winter03/tuberculosis.html*

(accessed 4 July 2016); Thomas Domarndy, *The White Death: a History of Tuberculosis* (London, 1999); and Helen Bynnam, *Spitting Blood: the History of TB* (Oxford, 2012).

[108] Sam Adams, *Geraint Goodwin* (Cardiff, 1975).

[109] John Fothergill, *James Dickson Innes, Llanelly, 1887 – Swanley, 1914* (London, 1946). There was a major exhibition of Innes's work at the National Museum Wales in 2012/13.

[110] *Western Mail*, 31 January 1925.

[111] *Ministry of Health: Report of the Committee to Inquire into the Anti-Tuberculosis Service in Wales and Monmouthshire* (London, 1939), pp. 257–60.

[112] *Ministry of Health: Report of the Committee to Inquire into the Anti-Tuberculosis Service in Wales and Monmouthshire*, p. 613.

[113] *Ministry of Health: Report of the Committee to Inquire into the Anti-Tuberculosis Service in Wales and Monmouthshire*, p. 216. On tuberculosis in its wider context see Richard J. Evans, *Death in Hamburg: Society and Politics in the Cholera Years 1830–1910* (Harmondsworth, 1987), pp. 183–9.

[114] Daunton, *Wealth and Welfare*, p. 360.

[115] Pyrs Gruffudd, '"A Crusade Against Consumption": Environment, Health and Social Reform in Wales, 1900–1939', *Journal of Historical Geography*, 21 (1) (1995), 39–54; Lynda Bryder, 'The King Edward VII Welsh National Memorial Association and its Policy Towards Tuberculosis', *Welsh History Review*, 13 (2) (1986), 194–214.

[116] D. H. James, *A Guide to Llanybydder: And a Short History of the Foundation of Alltymynydd Sanatorium* (Pencader, 1908).

[117] There is a superbly evocative oral history of Craig-y-Nos see Ann Shaw and Carole Reeves, *The Children of Craig-y-Nos: Life in a Welsh Tuberculosis Sanatorium 1922–1959* (London, 2009).

[118] Gruffydd, 'A Crusade Against Consumption', 51.

[119] Letter William Fisher, 30 March 1914. Gathering the Jewels item 375, *www.llgc.org/gatheringthejewels* (accessed 15 July 2005).

[120] On Senghenydd disasters in 1901 and 1913 see Michael Lieven, 'Representations of the Working Class Community: the Senghenydd Disaster, 1913', *Llafur*, 5 (2) (1989), 17–29, and idem, *Senghennydd: the Universal Pit Village 1890–1930* (Llandysul, 1994).

[121] The tradition of composing ballads to commemorate disasters continued into the twentieth century. See Ben Bowen Thomas, *Drych y Baledwr* (Aberystwyth, 1958), and Gomer M. Roberts, 'Hen Faledi'r Glowr', *Y Casglwr*, 15 (1981), 13. For a few ballads see for example *Tanchwa yn Tylorstown: Degau wedi eu lladd . . . Explosion at Tylorstown . . . 55 men killed* (Tylerstown, 1896); *Tanchwa Difrifol Mewn Pwll Glo yn y Deheudir* (Bangor University, Rare Books, Cerddi Bangor 31 (95)).

[122] On the presentation of Welsh coal mining in movies see Berry, *Wales and the Cinema: the First Hundred Years*, pp. 127–46, 159–82.

[123] Bill Jones and Beth Thomas, *Teyrnas y Glo / Coal's Domain* (Caerdydd / Cardiff, 1993), p. 37.

[124] Lieven, *Senghennydd: the Universal Pit Village* (the name of the mine in Senghenydd was the Universal Colliery).

[125] Ken Llewellyn, *Disaster at Tynewydd: an account of a Rhondda Mine Disaster, in 1877* (Cardiff, 1975).

[126] A first-hand account was given in *Bywyd o Feirw – sef Hanes y Carcharorion Tanddaearol, Ym Mhwll Tynewydd, Cwm Rhondda, ar Ebrill yr 11eg hyd yr 20fed, 1877, gan David Jenkins a Moses Powell (Dau o'r Carcharorion* (Cwm-afon, 1877); the translation by Revd David Jones, Porthcawl, had a briefer title *Life from the Dead* (Cwm-afon, n.d. [1877?]).

[127] Morien was a fascinating character, who in addition to his journalism, wrote a *History of Pontypridd and the Rhondda Valleys* (Pontypridd, 1903) and works on Druidism such as *Pabell Davydd*. Upon the death of Myfyr Morgannwg, Morien assumed the title of 'archdruid'. *Western Mail*, 16 December 1921. *Who's Who in Wales* (Cardiff, 1921).

[128] For the press reaction to the disaster see Hywel Teifi Edwards, 'The Welsh Collier as Hero: 1850–1950', *Welsh Writing in English: a Yearbook of Critical Essays*, 2, (1996), pp. 6–9, and idem, *Arwr Glew Erwau'r Glo: Delwedd y Glöwr yn Llenyddiaeth y Gymraeg (1850–1950)* (Llandysul, 1994). Such melodrama could, on occasion, descend into pathos and bathos. Although eighty-seven miners lost their lives at the Morfa pit in March 1890, the reporters in the *Western Mail* seemed more concerned at the fate of the horses. *Western Mail*, 25 March 1890.

[129] The detailed statistics are from T. Boyns, 'Work and Death in the South Wales Coalfield, 1874–1914', *Welsh History Review*, 12 (4) (1985), 514–37; N. Woodward, 'Why Did South Wales Miners have High Mortality? Evidence from the Mid-twentieth Century', *Welsh History Review*, 20 (1) (2000), 116–41. See also Kim Howells, 'Victimisation, Accidents and Disease', in David Smith (ed.), *A People and a Proletariat: Essays in the History of Wales 1780–1980* (London, 1980), pp.181–98.

[130] D. Gwenallt Jones, 'Y Meirwon', in *Eples* (Llandysul, 1951), p. 10.

[131] *South Wales Press* and the *Llanelly Mercury*, 30 December 1908.

[132] Bangor University, Llyfrau Prin, Rare Books – Cerddi Bangor 22 (85). Amongst the most famous Welsh people killed in motor accidents in the years 1870–1945 were William Beynon (1864–1932), the British bantam-weight boxing champion, Herbert Benjamin Winfield (1879–1929), the Welsh international rugby fullback who played in the victory against the 1905 All Blacks, the palaeographer and poet Edward Stanton Roberts (1878–1938), and T. E. Lawrence (1888–1935), Lawrence of Arabia.

[133] See *Maritime Review*, 23 July 1910, for the case of the steamship *Selworthy*. See also *The Times*, 21 July 1910 and 22 August 1910.

[134] Dilys Gater, *Historic Shipwrecks of Wales* (Llanrwst, 1992), pp. 22, 27, 75. For the great gale of 1890 see *Western Mail*, 29 January 1890.

[135] Gater, *Historic Shipwrecks*, p. 79.

[136] On Welsh seafarers and the World Wars see Terry Breverton and Phil Carradice, *Welsh Sailors of the Second World War* (Cowbridge, 2007), and J. D. Davies, *Britannia's Dragon: a Naval History of Wales* (Stroud, 2013), pp. 185–249.

[137] See *www.garethhones.org* (accessed 20 October 2017). See also Margaret Siriol Colley, *Gareth Jones: a Manchukuo Incident* (Newark, 2002).

[138] *Western Mail*, 15 March 1889.

[139] *Western Mail*, 9 March 1914.

[140] *Western Mail*, 6 January 1900.

[141] *Western Mail*, 17, 18, and 19 July and 18 November 1878. Another daughter had returned to work on the morning of the murders, otherwise Garcia might well have claimed six victims. Reporters in the *Western Mail* noted that 'many people were alarmed last night, thinking the murderer or murderers were concealed in the district and several old guns and pistols were pitched up and loaded in anticipation of possible attack.' The correspondents blamed 'the tramp question'. *Western Mail*, 19 July 1878.

[142] Quoted in Jane Aaron, *Welsh Gothic* (Cardiff, 2013), pp. 159–60.

[143] For *The Citadel* see Berry, *Wales and the Cinema: the First Hundred Years*, pp. 150–7, and A. J. Cronin, *Adventures in Two Worlds* (Boston, 1952), pp. 261–72.

[144] B. L. Coombes, *Miner's Day* (London, 1945), pp. 124–5.

[145] C. B. Edwards, 'It was like this: Personal Recollections of Garndiffaith in the 1930s', *Gwent Local History*, 77 (1994), 44.

[146] For example see Daunton, *Wealth and Welfare*, p. 360, and S. Szreter, 'The Importance of Social Intervention in Britain's Mortality Decline c.1850–1914: a Reinterpretation of the Role of Public Health', *Social History of Medicine*, 1 (1988), 1–37. Steven Thompson concludes his section on 'Mixed Economy of Medical Services' thus: 'doctors and other practitioners lacked the means to prevent illness or effect cures'. Thompson, *Unemployment, Poverty and Health*, p. 179.

[147] O. Thomas, *Frances Elizabeth Hoggan, 1843–1927* (Brecon, 1970).

[148] Roy Porter, *Quacks: Fakers and Charlatans in English Medicine* (Stroud, 2001); H. Burger, 'The Doctor, the Quack and the Appetite of the Public for Magic in Medicine', *Proceedings of the Royal Society of Medicine*, 17 (1933), pp. 171–6; and J. Camp, *Myth, Magic and Medicine* (London, 1973).

[149] A. Bailey Williams, 'Customs and Traditions Connected with Sickness, Death and Burial in Montgomeryshire in the Late Nineteenth Century', *The Montgomeryshire Collections*, LII (1951–2), 51–61.

[150] Anne E. Jones, 'Folk Medicine in Living Memory in Wales', *Folk Life*, 18 (1980), 58–68. See also Anne Elizabeth Williams, *Meddyginiaethau Gwerin Cymru* (Talybont, 2017).

[151] Marie Trevelyan, *Folk-lore and Folk Stories of Wales* (London, 1909); Timothy Lewis, *A Welsh Leech Book* (Liverpool, 1977).

[152] For the role of women in popular medicine and the 'battle' to establish control of childbirth see J. Donnison, *Midwives and Medical Men: a History of Interprofessional Rivalries and Women's Rights* (London, 1977).

[153] W. F. Bynum and R. Porter (eds), *Medical Fringe and Medical Orthodoxy* (London, 1987).

[154] Quoted in Thompson, *Unemployment, Poverty and Health*, pp. 160–1. Abraham Cohen, 'a quack doctor', was imprisoned for eighteen months with hard labour for theft at Llanddeiniolen in 1872. It appears that he had tricked a local woman into buying two bottles of his medicine. *North Wales Chronicle*, 6 January 1872.

[155] Dewi Williams, 'Anffaeledig Dolenni Dryg Bach y Port', *Y Casglwr* (August 1987); Dafydd Guto, 'Pilenni a chyhoeddiadau'r rhyfeddol Alltud Eifion', *Y Casglwr* (December 1985); Huw Edwards, 'Yr Hen Feddiginiaethau', *Y Casglwr* (March 1981). A similar figure to Alltud Eifion in south Wales was David Gravell (1787–1875), a farmer, herbalist and publisher, of Llandyfaelog, Carmarthenshire. Amongst his unguents was 'Gravell of Cwmfelin's Oil'. Gravell was a close friend of Sir David Daniel Davies, who became the royal physician. See W. A. Griffiths, *Hanes Emynwyr Cymru* (Caernarfon, 1907), pp. 162–3.

[156] *Kelly's Directory of Monmouthshire and South Wales 1921*.

[157] T. D. Gwernogle Evans, *The Cup of Health* (Cardiff, 1922), pp. 9–14. For a study of Gwernogle Evans's influence see P. S. Brown, 'The Vicissitudes of Herbalism in Late Nineteenth and Early Twentieth Century Britain', *Medical History*, 29 (1985), 71–92.

[158] *British Medical Journal*, 2 (1966), 1014.

[159] See for example Alex Owen, *The Darkened Room: Women, Power and Spiritualism in Late Victorian England* (London, 1989); Ronald Pearsall, *The Table-Rappers: the Victorians and the Occult* (Stroud, 2004); and Jennifer Hazelgrove, *Spiritualism and British Society between the Wars* (Manchester, 2000).

[160] *The Western Mail*, 16 June 1927.

[161] The photograph is in the National Library of Wales, item number JTH01681. It can be accessed on the library's excellent website of John

Thomas's photographs (accessed 11 May 2006). It is also in the Casglu'r Tlysau site as item GTJ12857.

162 F. Watson, *The Life of Sir Robert Jones* (London, 1934). Thomas and Jones are treated together in H. Winnett Orr, *On the Contributions of Hugh Owen Thomas of Liverpool, Sir Robert Jones of Liverpool and London and John Ridlow, M.D. of New York and Chicago, to Modern Orthopaedic Surgery* (Springfield, Ill., 1949) – it is typical of the age that no Welsh placename was mentioned in the title.

163 Seth Koven, 'Remembering and Dismemberment, Crippled Children, Wounded Soldiers and the Great War in Great Britain', *The American Historical Review*, 99, 9 (1994), 1125, 1187. For the effectiveness of the Thomas splint see Maurice Sinclair, *The Thomas Splint and its Modifications in the Treatment of Fractures* (London, 1927).

164 *British Medical Journal* (9 May 1953), 1054–5.

165 *The Times*, 19 September 1964.

166 J. Harris, *William Beveridge* (London, 1997), passim.

167 *Who's Who in Wales 1921*(Cardiff, 1922).

168 *Special Papers of the House of Lords Vol LXIX Session 1913, National Insurance, Report Administration of the National Insurance Act, Part 1, Wales* [Cd 6907], p. 507. See also *Report on Administration of National Health Insurance: Welsh Board of Health*, XVII, 1920 [Cmd 978].

169 L. J. Williams, *Digest of Welsh Historical Statistics*, vol. 2 (Cardiff, 1985), p. 152.

170 Steven Thompson, 'A Proletarian Public Sphere: Working-class Self-help and Medical Services and Care in South Wales, c.1900–1948', in Anne Bouray (ed.), *Medicine in Wales c.1800–2000: Public Service or Public Commodity?* (Cardiff, 2003), pp. 86–107; Ray Earwicker, 'Miners' Medical Services before the First World War: the South Wales Coalfield', *Llafur*, 3 (2) (1981), 39–52.

171 Edward Davies, *The North Wales Quarry Hospitals and the Health and Welfare of the Quarrymen* (Gwynedd Archive Services, Caernarfon 2003).

172 Thompson, 'A Proletarian Public Sphere', 95–7.

173 Aneurin Bevan, *In Place of Fear* (London, 1952). As Bevan declared in a speech in 1948: 'All I am doing is extending to the entire population the benefits we had in Tredegar for a generation or more. We are going to "Tredegarise" you'. *The Times*, 7 July 1960.

174 A. Trevor Jones et al., *Hospital Lunacy: the Hospital Services of South Wales and Monmouthshire* (London, 1945).

175 Neil Evans, 'The First Charity in Wales: Cardiff Infirmary and South Wales Society, 1837–1914', *Welsh History Review*, 9 (3) (1979), 319–46.

176 Martin Powell, 'How Adequate Was Hospital Provision Before the NHS? An Examination of the 1945 South Wales Hospital Survey', *Local*

Population Studies, 48 (1992), 29–38; idem, 'Hospital Provision Before the National Health Service: a Geographical Study of the 1945 Hospital Surveys', *Social History of Medicine*, 5, 3 (1992), 483–504. See also the *First Report of the Welsh Consultative Council on Medical and Allied Services in Wales*, HC (1920), xvii [Cmd 703]. There is also a lot of useful detail on 'Wales and Health' in the *Transactions of the Honourable Society of Cymmrodorion* (1939), 55–100.

177   Williams *Digest Historical Statistics*, vol. 2, p. 151.

178   Denis Hayes Crofton (ed.), *The Surgery at Aberffrwd: Some Encounters of a Colliery Doctor Seventy Years Ago by Francis Maylett Smith* (Hythe, 1981). For a similar portrayal of a country practice see R. W. S. Bishop, *My Moorland Patients* (London, 1922).

179   For conditions in rural Wales see T. G. Davies, 'The Highest Triumph: Some Aspects of Pre-twentieth-century Medical Practice in Parts of Montgomeryshire', *Montgomery Collections*, 91 (2003), 89–107; idem, 'And Where Shall She Find a Doctor?: Accidents in the History of Medicine in Gower During the Nineteenth Century', *Morgannwg*, XLV (2001), 29–54; see also the essays in John Cule (ed.), *Wales and Medicine: a Historical Survey* (Llandysul, 1973).

180   The articles appeared in *The Lancet* on 1 February 1879, 30 August 1879, 15 March 1880, 26 March 1881, 17 September 1881, 11 March 1882 and 20 May 1882.

3 Going Gently into that Good Night

1   The best history of suicide is Olive Anderson's *Suicide in Victorian and Edwardian England* (Oxford, 1987).

2   On suicide in Wales see Pamela Michael, 'From Private Grief to Public Testimony: Suicide in Wales, 1832–1914', in Ann Borsay (ed.), *Medicine in Wales c.1800–2000* (Cardiff, 2003), pp. 40–64.

3   Standardised mortality ratio for deaths by suicide in Wales in the decade 1861–70 and 1901–10:

	Males		Females	
	1861–70	1901–10	1861–70	1901–10
North Wales	39	59	22	62
South Wales	49	59	74	81
Glamorgan	53	55	86	69

Registrar General's 35th Annual Report, Supplement, 99.410–45; 75th Annual Report, Part III, p. xcvi, Table XLVI.

4 Anderson, *Suicide in Victorian and Edwardian England*, pp. 98–102.

5 Georgia Noon, 'On Suicide', *Journal of the History of Ideas*, XXXIX (3) (1978), 371–86; Alexander Murray, *Suicide in the Middle Ages: Volume 1: the Violent Against Themselves* (Oxford, 1998); E. Durkheim, *Suicide* (London, 1950); Olive Anderson, 'Did Suicide Increase with Industrialisation in Victorian England?', *Past and Present*, 86 (1980), 149–73; John McManners, *Death and the Enlightenment: Changing Attitudes to Death in Eighteenth Century France* (Oxford, 1985), pp. 409–37; and Barbara T. Gates, *Victorian Suicide: Mad Crimes and Short Histories* (Princeton, NJ, 1988).

6 Elias Owen, *Welsh Folk-lore: a Collection of the Folk-Tales and Legends of North Wales* (Oswestry, 1986), pp. 71–80.

7 For the case of the refusal of a jury to give a suicide verdict in the case of Jane Lewis see P. H. Thomas, 'Medical Men of Glamorgan: William Thomas Edwards (1821–1915)', *The Glamorgan Historian*, viii (1972), 127. Pamela Michael concluded that such practices also operated in Denbighshire. Michael, 'From Private Grief to Public Testimony', p. 57.

8 Kate Gramich, 'The Madwoman in the Harness-Loft: Women and Madness in the Literatures of Wales', in Katie Gramich and Andrew Hiscock (eds), *Dangerous Diversity: the Changing Faces of Wales, Essays in Honour of Tudor Bevan* (Cardiff, 1998), pp. 20–33. See also Margaret Higonnet, 'Speaking Silences: Women's Suicide', in Susan Rubin Suleiman, *The Female Body in Western Culture: Contemporary Perspectives* (London, 1986), pp. 68–83; Howard I. Kushner, 'Suicide, Gender and the Fear of Modernity in Nineteenth-Century Medical and Social Thought', *Journal of Social History* (1993), 461–90; in the Welsh context see Russell Davies, 'Do Not Go Gentle into that Good Night: Women and Suicide in Carmarthenshire, *c*.1860–1920', in Angela V. John (ed.) *Our Mothers' Land: Chapters in Welsh Women's History 1830–1939* (Cardiff, 1991), pp. 93–108. On the links with madness and female suicide see Elaine Showalter, *The Female Malady: Women, Madness and English Culture, 1830–1980* (London, 1987).

9 For the full text of Llew o'r Wern's 'Yr eneth gadd ei gwrthod' see E. G. Millward, *Ceinion y Gân: Detholiad o Ganeuon Poblogaidd Oes Victoria* (Llandysul, 1983), pp. 30–1.

10 See Russell Davies, *People, Places and Passions: a Social History of Wales and the Welsh 1870–1945: Pain and Pleasure Volume 1* (Cardiff, 2015), chapters 2 and 3.

11 *Cambrian Daily Leader*, 11 January 1917.

12 *Llanelly Mercury*, 27 April 1899; for similar cases see *Carmarthen Weekly Reporter*, 5 November 1915; *Carmarthen Journal*, 25 March 1904; *South*

Wales Daily News, 25 November 1897; *South Wales Press*, 1 December 1887.

13   Quoted in Michael Lieven, *Senghennydd: Universal Pit Village 1890–1930* (Llandysul, 1994), p. 129.

14   *Carmarthen Weekly Reporter*, 3 November 1916.

15   *Carmarthen Journal*, 19 January 1905.

16   *South Wales Press*, 8 February 1900; *Carmarthen Journal*, 8 February 1900.

17   *South Wales Press*, 25 November 1918.

18   For suicides linked with marital problems and possible postnatal depression see *South Wales Press*, 28 April 1904 and 29 May 1902; *Carmarthen Journal*, 24 October 1902.

19   *Western Mail*, 9 October 1878.

20   *Western Mail*, 31 March 1908.

21   *Western Mail*, 13 August 1878.

22   I am very grateful to Dr E. G. Millward for this information.

23   R. Lewis and D. Ward, 'Politics, Culture and Assimilation: the Welsh on Teesside, c.1850–1940', *Welsh History Review*, 17 (4) (1994–5), 453–67.

24   Gavin Mortimer, *Double Death: the True Story of Pryce Lewis, the Civil War's Most Daring Spy* (New York, 2010).

25   *South Wales Press*, 17 December 1917.

26   *South Wales Press*, 11 July 1907.

27   *South Wales Press*, 17 January 1907.

28   *South Wales Press*, 14 June 1900.

29   *Carmarthen Weekly Reporter*, 7 June 1909. There was a similar case at Cardiff, *Western Mail*, 30 May 1900.

30   *Western Mail*, 19 February 1864.

31   *Western Mail*, 3 August 1876.

32   Quoted in Michael Lieven, *Universal Pit Village*, pp. 336–7.

33   *Western Mail*, 27 May 1899.

34   Quoted in Michael Lieven, *Universal Pit Village*, pp. 257–9.

35   For a discussion of the treatment of shell-shock and hysteria see Elaine Showalter, *Female Malady*, pp. 167–94; Joanna Bourke, *Dismembering the Male: Men's Bodies, Britain and the Great War* (Chicago, 1996); Michael Micale, *Hysterial Men: the Hidden History of Male Nervous Illnesses* (Cambridge, Mass., 2008); Jessica Meyer, *Men of War: Masculinity and the First World War in Britain* (Basingstoke, 2009); and Michael Roper, *The Secret Battle: Emotional Survival in the Great War* (Manchester, 2009).

36   *Carmarthen Weekly Reporter*, 9 October 1914 and 1 December 1916; *South Wales Press*, 17 October 1917.

37   *Carmarthen Weekly Reporter*, 15 September 1915.

38   *South Wales Press*, 3 July 1918; *Cambrian Daily Leader*, 3 July 1918.

39 *South Wales Press*, 9 August and 18 October 1916.
40 *Carmarthen Weekly Reporter*, 17 August 1917.
41 David Richard Davies, *In Search of Myself* (Swansea, 1961).
42 On George M. Ll. Davies's time in Denbigh hospital see Pamela Michael, *Care and Treatment of the Mentally Ill in North Wales, 1800–2000* (Cardiff, 2003), pp. 105, 186; E. H. Griffiths, *Seraff yr Efengyl Seml* (Caernarfon, 1968); Iorwerth Peate considered Davies 'un o'r dynion mwyaf a welodd yr ugeinfed ganrif' (one of the greatest men the twentieth century ever saw) in *Syniadau* (Llandysul, 1969), p. 117.
43 *Carmarthen Weekly Reporter*, 4 April 1919.
44 *Carmarthen Weekly Reporter*, 6 November 1903; *South Wales Press*, 5 November 1903.
45 *South Wales Press*, 24 May 1906.
46 For some contemporary views of Sarah Jacob see *The Western Mail*, 1 May, 8 September, 20 December 1869, and 13 July and 14 July 1870.
47 *Western Mail*, 21 January 1870, 15 September 1876, and 2 March 1899. On deaths by starvation see *Return on Deaths from Starvation or Accelerated by Privation in England and Wales*. H.M.S.O., Cd 337 (London, 1908), pp. 27, 37, 38.
48 *South Wales Press*, 24 May 1880.
49 A. Alvarez, *The Savage God: a Study of Suicide* (Harmondsworth, 1979). Superfluous to say, the other quotation given is from Dylan Thomas's poem.
50 On Dorothy Edwards see Christopher Meredith's preface to *Rhapsody: Dorothy Edwards* (Cardigan, 2007).
51 *Western Mail*, 16 February 2008.
52 Roy Porter, *A Social History of Madness: Stories of the Insane* (London, 1989), pp. 1–17.
53 Quoted in Russell Davies *Secret Sins: Sex, Violence and Society in Carmarthenshire 1870–1920* (Cardiff, 1995), pp. 96–7, 271; *Carmarthen Weekly Reporter*, 7 August 1908. See also R. S. Stewart, 'The Relationship of Wages, Lunacy and Crime in South Wales', *Journal of Mental Science*, 50 (1904), 64–9.
54 Sarah Wise, *Inconvenient People: Lunacy, Liberty and the Mad-Doctors in Victorian England* (London, 2012).
55 Michael Foucalt, *Madness and Civilization: a History of Insanity in the Age of Reason* (London, 1964).
56 Andrew T. Scull, *Museum of Madness: the Social Organisation of Insanity in Nineteenth-Century England* (Harmondsworth, 1982); and idem, *The Most Solitary of Afflictions: Madness and Society in Britain 1700–1900* (London, 1993). See also Joseph Melling and Bill Forsythe (eds), *Insanity, Institutions and Society, 1800–1914: a Social History of Madness in*

Comparative Perspective (London, 1999); and Barbara Taylor, *The Last Asylum: a Memoir of Madness in Our Time* (London, 2014).

57 T. G. Davies, 'Bedlam yng Nghymru – datblygiad Seiciatreg yn y Bedwaredd Ganrif ar Bymtheg', *Transactions of the Honourable Society of Cymmrodorion* (1980), 105–22; and idem, 'Of all the Maladies: Episodes in the History of Psychiatry in Nineteenth Century Pembrokeshire', *Journal of the Pembrokeshire Historical Society*, 5 (1992–3), 75–90.

58 On Carmarthen see Russell Davies, 'Inside the House of the Mad: the Social Context of Mental Illness, Suicide and the Pressures of Rural Life in South Wales c.1860–1920', *Llafur*, 4 (2) (1985), 20–35; on Cardiff see Ian Beech, 'I Can't Believe it's Not Butter: Industrial Relations in Cardiff City Mental Hospital Before the First World War', *Llafur*, 10 (1) (2008), 32–46; and idem, 'The Universal Khaki: the Impact of the Asylum War Hospital Scheme on Cardiff City Mental Hospital, 1915–20', *Llafur*, 9 (2) (2005), 4–26. On Denbigh see M. Rolf Olsen, 'The Foundation of the Hospital for the Insane Poor, Denbigh', *Transactions Denbighshire Historical Society*, 2–3 (1974), 193–217; and Michael, *Care and Treatment of the Mentally Ill in North Wales, 1800–2000*; on Pen-y-Fal and Veron House see Kerry Davies, 'Sexing the Mind: Women, Gender and Madness in Nineteenth-century Welsh Asylums', *Llafur*, 7 (1) (1996), 29–40.

59 *Western Mail*, 15 April 1908; *South Wales Daily News*, 16 April 1908.

60 Gomer M. Roberts (ed.), *Cyfansoddiadau a Beirniadaethau Eisteddfod Genedlaethol Llandybïe, 1944* (Llandysul, 1944), p. 79. This was also the experience of Helen Thomas, the wife of the poet Edward Thomas, when she visited the musician Ivor Gurney in the 1920s. See Michael Hood, *The Ordeal of Ivor Gurney* (Oxford, 1984), pp. 151–78, especially p. 167. 'We arrived at the asylum which looked like – as indeed it was – a prison. A warder let us in after unlocking a door, and doors were opened and locked behind us as we were ushered into the building . . .' For the custodial view see Pauline Morris, *'Put Away': a Sociological Study of Institutions for the Mentally Retarded* (London, 1969); Andrew T. Scull, *Mad Houses, Mad-Doctors and Mad Men: the Social History of Psychiatry* (Philadelphia, Pa., 1982); Richard W. Fox, *So Far Disordered in Mind: Insanity in California, 1870–1930* (Berkeley, Calif., 1978); and Michael MacDonald, *Mystical Bedlam: Madness, Anxiety and Healing in Seventeenth-Century England* (Cambridge, 1982). For some interesting general points see Lawrence Stone, 'Madness', *New York Review of Books* (16 December 1992), 28–36.

61 For Dr Goodall see Beech, 'I Can't Believe it's Not Butter', 33–7

62 *The Lancet*, 15 June 1963.

63 On Ernest Jones see T. G. Davies, *Ernest Jones 1879–1958* (Cardiff, 1979), and Brenda Maddox, *Freud's Wizard: the Enigma of Ernest Jones* (London, 2006).
64 Michael, *Care and Treatment of the Mentally Ill in North Wales, 1800–2000*, p. 155.
65 Carmarthenshire Records Office, St David's Hospital, no. 14, *Superintendent's Journal*, entry for 8 April 1881.
66 Carmarthenshire Records Office, St David's Hospital, no. 14, *Superintendent's Journal*, entry for 25 November 1882.
67 Carmarthenshire Records Office, St David's Hospital, Annual Reports of the Committee of Visitors, *Twenty-fifth Annual Report* (1898), p. 14; *Thirty-ninth Annual Report* (1904).
68 J. Gwynn Griffiths (ed.), *D. J. Williams – Y Gaseg Ddu a Gweithiau Eraill* (Llandysul, 1970), pp. 3–26.
69 D. H. Tuke, *Chapters in the History of the Insane in the British Isles* (London, 1982), p. 178.
70 *Carmarthen Journal*, 4 April 1873.
71 Carmarthenshire Records Office, St David's Hospital, *Agenda and Minutes*, vol. 6, *Annual Report 1907*, p. 29.
72 Carmarthenshire Records Office, St David's Hospital, vol. 5, *Chaplain's Report* (10 January 1904).
73 Carmarthenshire Records Office, St David's Hospital, no. 17, *Twentieth-Annual Report* (1884), p. 8.
74 For two such suicides see *South Wales Press*, 24 June 1888 (Revd H. Lewis) and *Carmarthen Weekly Reporter*, 6 November 1903.
75 Carmarthenshire Records Office, St David's Hospital, *Agenda and Minutes*, no. 14, *Superintendent's Journal*, entry for 22 December 1883. The Christmas period was often the most difficult for those with religious delusions.
76 Carmarthenshire Records Office, St David's Hospital, *Agenda and Minutes*, vol. 5, *Forty-first Annual Report*, 8 January 1906. For suicides linked to the 1904–5 religious revival see *South Wales Press*, 10 April 1912; and *The Welshman*, 17 February 1905.
77 Charles Williams, *Religion and Insanity* (London, 1908), p. 170. J. S. Bushman, in *Religious Revivals in Relation to Nervous and Mental Disease* (London, 1860), gave the opposite view to Williams and warned against revivals. Charles Williams also wrote about the importance of religion in casting out the devil from mentally ill patients, see his *Demonical Obsession and Possession as Causes of Insanity* (London, 1911).
78 Carmarthenshire Records Office, St David's Hospital, no. 17, *Annual Reports*, vol. 3, *Thirty-fourth Annual Report*, 7 January 1898.

79 *Baner ac Amserau Cymru*, January 1925.

80 Ivor Gurney, *Collected Poems of Ivor Gurney* (Oxford, 1982).

81 Caradog Prichard, *Afal Drwg Adda* (Dinbych, 1973). See also Llwyd, *Rhyfel a Gwrthryfel*, pp. 186–95.

82 Carmarthenshire Records Office, St David's Hospital, no. 14, *Superintendent's Journal* entry for 23 July 1881.

83 Carmarthenshire Records Office, St David's Hospital, no. 14, *Superintendent's Journal* entry for 3 February 1882.

84 Carmarthenshire Records Office, St David's Hospital, no. 14, *Superintendent's Journal* entry for 15 January 1884.

85 Carmarthenshire Records Office, St David's Hospital, no. 14, *Superintendent's Journal* entry for 17 April 1881.

86 Carmarthenshire Records Office, St David's Hospital, no. 14, *Superintendent's Journal* entry for 12 October 1881.

87 Carmarthenshire Records Office, St David's Hospital, no. 14, *Superintendent's Journal* entry for 12 November 1881.

88 Maddox, *Freud's Wizard*, p. 280.

4 Where, When, What Was Wales?

1 One of the first to ponder the issues was the archaeologist and author Glyn Daniel (1914–86) in his *Who Were The Welsh?*, the Sir John Rhŷs Memorial Lecture of 1954. See also Gwyn A. Williams, *When Was Wales? A History of Wales and the Welsh* (London, 1995); idem, *The Welsh in Their History* (London, 1982).

2 Emyr Humphreys, *The Taliesin Tradition: A Quest for the Welsh Identity* (London, 1983). Geraint H. Jenkins turns from chronicler into prophet in his final chapter entitled 'Whither Wales', in which he ponders the future for Wales, in his *A Concise History of Wales* (Cambridge, 2007), pp. 301–7. See also Matthew Cragoe, *Culture, Politics and National Identity in Wales, 1832–1886* (Oxford, 2004); Dai Smith, 'Psychocolonialism', *New Welsh Review*, 66 (2004), 22–9; and H. G. Roberts, *Embodying Identity: Representations of the Body in Welsh Literature* (Cardiff, 2009). Many themes of the national identity are discussed in Tony Curtis (ed.), *Wales: The Imagined Nation – Essays in Cultural and National Identity* (Bridgend, 1996).

3 See for example Chris Williams, 'Problematizing Wales: an Exploration in Historiography and Postcoloniality', in idem and Jane Aaron (eds), *Postcolonial Wales* (Cardiff, 2005), pp. 3–23.

4   Works of particular relevance in the *Writing Wales in English* series include Kirsti Bohata, *Postcolonialism Revisited* (Cardiff, 2004); M. Wynn Thomas, *In the Shadow of the Pulpit: Literature and Nonconformist Wales* (Cardiff, 2010); Damian Walford Davies, *Cartographies of Culture: New Geographies of Welsh Writing in English* (Cardiff, 2012); Daniel G. Williams, *Wales Unchained: Literature, Politics and Identity in the American Century* (Cardiff, 2015); and Jane Aaron, *Welsh Gothic* (Cardiff, 2013). See also Simon Brooks, *Pam na fu Cymru: Methiant Cenedlaetholdeb Cymraeg* (Caerdydd, 2015).

5   For an interesting contemporary view see the article 'Cymru, Cymro a Chymraeg yn 1890' [Wales, Welshmen and Welsh in 1890], *Y Genedl Gymraeg* (2 January 1900).

6   Quoted in Hywel Teifi Edwards, *The National Pageant of Wales 1909* (Llandysul, 2009), p. 60.

7   See also J. V. Morgan, *Welsh Political and Educational Leaders in the Victorian Era* (London, 1908), pp. 149–56.

8   Gwilym Davies, 'Beyond our Frontiers', in *The Welsh Review*, vol. II, no. 1 (March 1939), 45–7. Little seemed to have changed seventy-five years later, for in a trenchant article Simon Jenkins described Wales as 'a nearly nation carelessly slumbering'. *The Guardian*, 30 September 2014.

9   Benedict Anderson, *Imagined Communities* (London, 1991), pp. 127–46.

10   Iwan Meical Jones, *Hen Ffordd Gymreig o Fyw: Ffotograffau John Thomas Photographs* (Aberystwyth, 2009), p. 35.

11   Alan R. Thomas, *The Linguistic Geography of Wales* (Cardiff, 1973).

12   Quoted in Dafydd Roberts, *Y Chwarelwr a'r Sowth* (Caernarfon, 1982), p. 14. The astute Wyn Griffith noted the differences in *The Welsh*: 'The mining valleys of the South are full of life, eager, vivid, mercurial and yet determined, a life somehow Latin in quickness. The North is quieter, slower in pulse, less accustomed to living in large aggregations, less penetrated by different nationalities. In between North and South there lies a thinly populated agricultural area which diminishes the contact between them and acts as a stable centre, a mean between the two extremes. Is there a common factor, something which can be recognised in isolation, in all this variety?' Quoted in Dai Smith, *Wales! Wales?* (London, 1984), p. 9.

13   A. T. Johnson (Draig Glas), *The Perfidious Welshman* (London, 1910), p. 36. For an interesting presentation of the relationships with the English see Mike Parker, *Neighbours from Hell? English Attitudes to the Welsh* (Talybont, 2007).

14   On such themes see Raymond Williams, *The Country and the City* (London, 1975); Gillian Darley, *Villages of Vision* (London, 1977), and

Alun Howkins, 'The Discovery of Rural England', in Robert Colls and Phillip Dodd, *Englishness, Politics and Culture 1880–1920* (London, 1986). For the links between religion and national identity see Dorian Llywelyn, *Sacred Place, Chosen People – Land and National Identity in Welsh Spirituality* (Cardiff, 1999).

[15] Jan Morris, *The Matter of Wales* (London, 1983), p. 69.

[16] Pyrs Gruffudd has been exceptionally active in establishing the importance of geography in the creation of a national identity; see for example his 'Back to the Land: Historiography, Rurality and the Nation in Inter-War Wales', *Transactions of the Institute of British Geographers*, 19 (1994), 61–74; idem, 'The Countryside as Educator: Schools, Rurality and Citizenship in Inter-War Wales', *Journal of Historical Geography*, 22 (4) (1996), 412–23.

[17] D. Gwenallt Jones, 'Rhydcymerau', in *Eples* (Llandysul, 1951), p. 21.

[18] Herbert Hughes, *An Uprooted Community: a History of Epynt* (Llandysul, 1998), pp. 21–5.

[19] Waldo Williams, 'Preseli', *The Peacemakers: Selected Poems*, trans. by Tony Conran (Llandysul, 1997), pp. 112–13.

[20] A significant and important attempt to preserve country life was the Council for the Preservation of Rural Wales. Ironically, the council included many authority figures who were the very antithesis of the simple Welsh-speaking rustic. Amongst the founder members were Herbert Vaughn, estate agent and apologist for the gentry of south-west Wales, Sir Henry Stuart Jones, principal of the university in Aberystwyth, the architect Sir Clough Williams-Ellis, the novelist Richard Hughes, and the landowner Lord Howard de Walden. Their programme was eloquently set out in Clough Williams-Ellis's rant against urban sprawl and commercialisation, *England and the Octopus*, published in 1928.

[21] O. M. Edwards[?] in *Cymru*, XLI (1911), 8. O. M. Edwards's was a geographical, almost an environmental, interpretation of Welsh history. See Neil Evans, 'Finding a New Story: the Search for a Useable Past in Wales, 1869–1930', *Transactions of the Honourable Society of Cymmrodorion*, 10 (2004), 151–3; see also W. T. R. Pryce, 'Region or National Territory? Regionalism and the Idea of the Country of Wales, c.1927–1998', *Welsh History Review*, 23 (2) (2006), 123–52.

[22] See Hywel Teifi Edwards, *O'r Pentre Gwyn i Gwmderi: Delwedd y Pentref yn Llenyddiaeth y Cymry* (Llandysul, 2004).

[23] E. G. Millward, 'Rhywfaint o Anfarwolrwydd', *Ysgrifau Beirniadol*, XIII (Dinbych, 1985), pp. 250–60.

[24] Albert Evans-Jones (Cynan), *Cerddi Cynan* (Liverpool, 1959), pp. 130–48. The great socialist, dentist and poet, T. E. Nicholas, in his

best-selling poem *Meirionnydd*, takes the contrasts between the virtues of the country and the vices of the city (Liverpool in this case) into the realms of bathos. For example, in the city, 'Nwy a thrydan yn goleuo'r caddug megis haul ar dwyn / Minnau yn hiraethu am lewyrch golau cartref cannwyll frwyn' (Gas and electricity light the dusk like the sun at mid-day / I yearned for the glow and homely light of a rush candle), T. E. Nicholas, *Meirionnydd* (Llandysul, 1949), p. 19.

25 David Evans, *Y Wlad: ei Bywyd, ei Haddysg a'i Chrefydd* (Liverpool, 1933), p. 77.

26 D. G. Jones, *Bywyd a Gwaith Islwyn* (Caerdydd, 1948), p. 21. See also John Fordham, 'The Matter of Wales: Industry and Rurality in the work of James Hanly', *Welsh Writing in English*, 5 (1999), 86–100.

27 William Williams (Crwys), 'Gwerin Cymru', in *Cerddi Crwys* (Llanelli, 1920), pp. 1–27. To Alun Llewelyn-Williams, Crwys's work was the pinnacle of the idealisation of rural Wales and 'y werin', see 'Hen Werin y Graith', in *Y Nos, y Niwl a'r Ynys* (Cardiff, 1960), p. 141. See also Prys Morgan, 'Gwerin Cymru – y Ffaith a'r Ddelfryd', *Transactions of the Honourable Society of Cymmrodorion*, part 1 (1967), pp. 117–31.

28 The darker aspects and social tensions of rural Wales are shown in David Pretty, *The Rural Revolt that Failed: Trade Unions in Wales 1889–1950* (Cardiff, 1989).

29 Crwys, *Cerddi Crwys*, p. 39.

30 On Mallt and Gwenffreda Williams see Jane Aaron, 'A National Seduction: Wales in Nineteenth Century Women's Writing', *The New Welsh Review*, 27 (1994), 31–8.

31 Mair I. Davies, *Gwaith Kitchener Davies* (Llandysul, 1980).

32 John Harries (ed.), *My People* (Llandysul, 1987), pp. 7–48.

33 Iorwerth Peate's most famous poetic works are *Y Cawg Aur* (London, 1928), *Plu'r Gweunydd* (Liverpool, 1953) and *Y Deyrnas Goll* (Caerdydd, 1947). He was the founder and inspirer of the Welsh Folk Museum at St Fagans in the late 1930s–40s. His autobiography, *Rhwng Dau Fyd* (Dinbych, 1976) provides a moving account of his life and times. For biographies see C. Stevens, *Iorwerth C. Peate* (Cardiff, 1986), and T. Robin Chapman, *Iorwerth Peate* (Caernarfon, 1987).

34 Quoted in Bill Jones and Aled Jones, *Welsh Reflections: Y Drych and America 1851–2991* (Llandysul, 2001), p. 114.

35 Waldo Williams, 'Yr Heniaith', in *Dail Pren* (Llandysul, 1991).

36 K. O. Morgan, *Rebirth of a Nation: Wales 1880–1980* (Cardiff and Oxford, 1981).

37 Quoted in Smith, *Wales! Wales?*

38 Hywel Teifi Edwards, *O'r Pentre Gwyn i Gwmderi*, p. 117.

[39]   See Russell Davies, *Pain and Pleasure: a Social History of Wales and the Welsh 1870–1945: Volume 1. People, Places and Passions* (Cardiff, 2015), chapter 5.

[40]   Quoted in Margaret Macmillan, *Peacemakers: Six Months that Changed the World* (London, 2001), p. 51.

[41]   See K. O. Morgan, *Wales in British Politics* (Cardiff, 1963), p. 177.

[42]   *Wales and Her Prince: the Investiture and All About It: With a Programme of the Tour of the King and Queen* (London, 1911). See also Edwards, *The National Pageant of Wales 1909*.

[43]   Angus Calder, *The Myth of the Blitz* (London, 1991), p. 68. Chris Williams and M. Cragoe (eds), *Wales and War: Religion, Society and Politics in the Nineteenth and Twentieth Centuries* (Cardiff, 2007), especially pp. 126–64. For a general discussion see M. Howard, *War and the Nation State* (Oxford, 1978), pp. 11–17.

[44]   *Western Mail*, 8 and 9 May 1945.

[45]   J. E. Daniel, *'Torri'r Seiliau Sicr': Detholiad o Ysgrifau John Edward Daniel* (Llandysul, 1993), p. 140.

[46]   T. Robin Chapman, *Un Bywyd o Blith Nifer: Cofiant Saunders Lewis* (Llandysul, 2006), pp. 166, 200.

[47]   Jones, *Eples*, p. 26. 'The Sant' is quoted in Alan Llwyd, *Rhyfel a Gwrthryfel: Brwydr Moderniaeth a Beirdd Modern* (Llandybïe, 2003), p. 292. Lewis Valentine expressed a similar view: 'Yr unig Gymru i fi wedi ei hadnabod, â'r unig Gymru sydd wedi bod i'm tyb i, yw'r Gymru Gristnogol. Onid y genhadaeth Gristnogol a wnaeth Cymru yn genedl ar y cychwyn? A'r genhadaeth Gristnogol sy'n mynd i gadw hi yn genedl hyd byth, gobeithio'. Quoted in D. Denzil Morgan, *Cedyrn Canrif: Crefydd a Chymdeithas yng Nghymru'r Ugeinfed Ganrif* (Caerdydd, 2001), p. 104.

[48]   Morgan, *Cedyrn Canrif*, p. 150. See also D. Denzil Morgan, 'Spirit and Flesh in Twentieth-Century Welsh poetry', *Proceedings of the Harvard Celtic Colloquia*, 23 (2003), 219–31.

[49]   Robert Pope (ed.), *Religion and National Identity: Wales and Scotland c.1700–2000* (Cardiff, 2001); Michael McCabe, *For God and Ireland: the Fight for Moral Superiority in Ireland 1922–1932* (Sallins, 2012); Timothy Lasson, *A People of One Book: the Bible and the Victorians* (Oxford, 2011).

[50]   D. Denzil Morgan, *Wales and the Word: Historical Perspectives on Welsh Identity and Religion* (Cardiff, 2008), p. 213. Morgan suggests that Catholicism might have been the 'truer' religious heritage of Wales. Indeed, in the long term for the development of ideas on Welsh nationality, the Catholic Church served as the inspiration for Saunders Lewis, one of the founders in the early 1920s of Plaid Genedlaethol Cymru (see Morgan, *Wales and the Word*, pp. 222–30). See also Chapman,

Un Bywyd o Blith Nifer, and Trystan Owain Hughes, 'An Uneasy Alliance? Welsh Nationalism and Roman Catholicism', *North American Journal of Welsh Studies*, 22 (Summer 2002), 1–6.

51 J. Lambert Rees, *Timothy Rees of Mirfield and Llandaff, a Biography* (London, 1945), pp. 10–11; see also D. Densil Morgan, *Cedyrn Canfrif: Crefydd a Chymdeithas yng Nghymru'r Ugeinfed Ganrif* (Caerdydd, 2011), pp. 28–68.

52 John Gwynfor Jones, 'Cyfraniad Bedyddwyr Caerdydd i Dwf Ymwybyddiaeth Ddinesig Gymreig yn y Cyfnod Tua 1890–1914', *Trafodion Cymdeithas Hanes y Bedyddwyr* (2004), 1–29.

53 It is noteworthy that there is always a capital 'S' in these portrayals of south Wales. The best portrayals of 'South Wales' are Dai Smith *Wales! Wales?*, and idem, *Aneurin Bevan and the World of South Wales* (Cardiff, 1993).

54 Smith, *Aneurin Bevan and the World of South Wales*, p. 178.

55 The best examination of the literary portrayal of the Welsh miner is Hywel Teifi Edwards, *Arwr Glew Erwau'r Glo: Delwedd y Glowr yn Llenyddiaeth y Gymraeg, 1850–1950* (Llandysul, 1994); and idem, 'Gwaddoliaeth Lenyddol Dai a Shoni', in Geraint H. Jenkins (ed.), *Cof Cenedl X: Ysgrifau ar Hanes Cymru* (Llandysul, 1995), pp. 91–120; see also Huw Walters, *Erwau'r Glo* (Swansea, 1976).

56 For conceptualisations of Welsh women see Deirdre Beddoe, *Out of the Shadows: a History of Women in Twentieth-Century Wales* (Cardiff, 2000).

57 Gwyn Thomas, *A Welsh Eye* (London, 1964), p. 12. The poet Gwenallt, a native of Alltwen near Pontardawe, remembered: 'Glynai ein tadau, hyd yn oed mewn pentref diwydiannol, wrth arferion gwledig . . .' (Our parents, even in industrial villages, adhered to rural customs), quoted in J. E. Meredith (ed.), *Credaf: Llyfr o Dystiolaeth Gristnogol* (Llandysul, 1943), p. 64.

58 W. G. Gruffydd, *Hen Atgofion* (Llandysul, 1964), pp. 11–12.

59 On the Welsh literary heritage of industrial Wales see M. Wynn Thomas, *Corresponding Cultures: the Two Literatures of Wales* (Cardiff, 1999). For the cultural tradition of the valleys of south Wales see the series *Cyfres y Cymoedd*, all edited by Hywel Teifi Edwards: *Cwm Tawe* (Llandysul, 1993), *Nedd a Dulais* (Llandysul, 1994), *Cwm Rhondda* (Llandysul, 1995), *Cwm Aman* (Llandysul 1996), *Llyfni ac Afan, Garw ac Ogwr* (Llandysul, 1998), *Ebwy, Rhymni a Sirhowy* (Llandysul, 1999), *Gwendraeth* (Llandysul, 2000), and *Merthyr a Thaf* (Llandysul, 2001).

60 Alred Zimmern, *My Impressions of Wales* (London, 1927), p. 29. Many historians appear to have been enchanted by the glitter and glitz of American Wales. See for instance Smith's *Wales! Wales?* In many

respects, American Wales was the world of the flickering screens of the golden age of the cinema and sporting endeavours. Ironically, many of the American films appeared to ape and echo the cultural values of high English culture. For these arguments see Robert W. Rydell and Rob Knoes, *Buffalo Bill in Bologna: the Americanisation of the World, 1869–1922* (Chicago, Ill., 2005). The impact of the early cinema in Wales has been well told in David Berry's *Wales and the Cinema, the First Hundred Years* (Cardiff, 1995), Peter Miskell's *The Social History of the Cinema in Wales, 1918–51, Pulpits, Coal Pits and Fleapits* (Cardiff, 2006), and Gwenno Ffrancon's *Cyfaredd y Cysgodion: Delweddau Cymru a'i Phobl ar Ffilm, 1935–51* (Caerdydd, 2003).

[61] E. L. Ellis, *The University College of Wales, Aberystwyth 1872–1972* (Aberystwyth, 1972), p. 75.

[62] Smith, *Wales! Wales?*, p. 1.

[63] Letter from Menna Gallie, February 1927, National Library of Wales [NLW] Ac 2000/76, Women's Archive of Wales. Her friend, the artist Josef Herman, an emigrant from Poland to Ystradgynlais, was equally blunt – 'the miner is the man of Ystradgynlais' – quoted in Patrick Hannan, *Wales and the Wireless* (Llandysul, 1988), p. 53.

[64] NLW MS, T. E. Ellis papers, MS 2134.

[65] M. J. Daunton, *Coal Metropolis Cardiff* (Leicester, 1977).

[66] On Joseph Conrad's period in Cardiff when he lived in the 'Sailors and Fishermen's Home', see John Stape, *The Several Lives of Joseph Conrad* (London, 2007), pp. 36–45, 98.

[67] Bernice Rubens, *When I Grow Up* (London, 2005), pp. 1–5.

[68] On Herbert Swann see D. Swann, *Swann's Way: a Life in Song* (London, 1993); and idem, *The Space between the Bars* (London, 1968).

[69] J. Geraint Jenkins, *Maritime Heritage: the Ships and Seamen of Southern Ceredigion* (Llandysul, 1982).

[70] G. M. Hopkins trained at St Bruno's College, Tremeirchion, near St Asaph. His most prolific period, which included many of his best poems – 'God's Grandeur', 'The Starlit Night', 'Spring', 'The Sea and the Skylark', and 'The Windhover' – were inspired by Wales which was 'always to me a mother of Muses', and 'his true Arcadia of wild beauty'. His views were tempered, however, when an operation for circumcision went wrong and he left Wales. See Alfred Thomas, 'Hopkins, the Jesuits and Barmouth', *Journal of the Merionethshire Historical and Land Society*, X (1964), 360–4; and idem, 'G. M. Hopkins, the Jesuits and Clwyd', *Journal of Welsh Ecclesiastical History*, 2 (1985), 41–54; N. White, *Gerald Manley Hopkins in Wales* (London, 1998), and idem, *Hopkins a Literary Biography* (London, 1992).

[71] On the Irish in Wrexham see Peter Jones, 'The Irish in Wrexham', in Paul O'Leary (ed.), *Irish Migrants in Modern Wales* (Liverpool, 2004), pp. 83–100.

[72] For the importance of mythic and fictional characters see Dan Karlaw et al., *The 101 Most Influential People Who Never Lived: How Characters of Fiction, Myth, Legends, Television and Movies Have Shaped Our Society, Changed Our Behaviour and Set the Course of History* (London, 2006).

[73] In a broader context of the importance of myths for the processes of nation building see Robertson Davies, 'Literature in a Country Without a Mythology', in his *The Merry Heart: Reflections on Reading, Writing and the World of Books* (London, 1996), pp. 40–63. See also Duncan S. Bell, 'Mythscapes: Memory, Mythology and National Identity; *British Journal of Sociology*, 54 (1) (2003), 63–81. It was no coincidence perhaps that the turn of the twentieth century saw a remarkable surge of interest in the folklore and folk tales of Wales. Sir John Rhŷs published widely on such material, for example: 'Welsh Fairytales', *Y Cymmrodor*, 5 (1882), 49–143; 'Welsh Antiquities and Fairytales', *Y Cymmrodor*, 5 (1882), 148–53; and 'Welsh Fairytales', *Y Cymmrodor*, 6 (1883) pp.155–221; see also Juliette Wood, 'Folk Narrative Research in Wales at the Beginning of the Twentieth Century: the Influence of John Rhŷs (1840–1916)', *Folklore*, 116 (3) (2005), 325–41; idem, 'Perceptions of the Past in Welsh Folklore Studies', *Folklore*, 108 (1997), 93–102; and W. J. Gruffydd, *John Rhŷs* (Cardiff, 1954). There is also much useful material in Roslyn Blyn-Ladrew, 'Ancient Bards, Welsh Gypsies, and Celtic Folklore in the Cauldron of Regeneration', *Western Folklore* (Fall, 1998), 225–43.

[74] D. Gwenallt Jones, *Taliesin* (6) (1967), 71.

[75] John K. Bollard, *Companion Tales to the Mabinogi* (Llandysul, 2007).

[76] Michael Holroyd, *Augustus John: the New Biography* (London, 1939), p. 393.

[77] For Burne-Jones see Fiona MacCarthy, *The Last Pre-Raphaelite: Edward Burne-Jones and the Victorian Imagination* (London, 2011), pp. 15–21.

[78] In a broadcast in 1939, Powys expressed his search for 'the occult secret of the most conservative, the most introverted, the most mysterious nation that has ever existed on earth outside China'. John Cowper Powys, *Autobiography* (London, 1968), p. 11; and L. Marlow, *Welsh Ambassadors: Powys Lives and Letters* (London, 1986), p. 79.

[79] C. Lloyd-Morgan, *Margiad Evans* (Cardiff, 1998).

[80] For a detailed discussion see Jane Aaron, *Welsh Gothic* (Cardiff, 2013).

[81] Daryl Jones, 'Borderlands: Spiritualism and the Occult in *Fin de siècle* Edwardian Welsh and Irish horror', *Irish Studies Review*, 17 (1) (2009),

31–44. See also Alex Owen, *The Place of Enchantment: British Occultism and the Culture of the Modern* (London, 2004), and David J. Skal, *Monster by Moonlight: the Immortal Saga of the Wolfman* (Hollywood, 2004).

[82] On the 'wilder' writing of Arthur Machen see Jessica George, 'Mixed-up Creatures: Identity and its Boundaries in Arthur Machen's *Weird Tales*', *Almanac*, 15 (2010–11), 29–46; see also Arthur Machen, *Far Off Things* (London, 1922). For a biography see W. D. Sweetser, *Arthur Machen* (London, 1964).

[83] Caroline G. Bott, *The Life and Works of Alfred Bestall: Illustrator of Rupert Bear* (London, 2003 and 2010).

[84] Roald Dahl, *Boy* (London, 1984); J. Treglown, *Roald Dahl: a Biography* (London, 1994); Donald Sturrock, *Storyteller: the Life of Roald Dahl* (London, 2011).

[85] Llandudno still has a memorial to 'the real' Alice in Wonderland, Alice Liddel, who stayed regularly at the town's Gogarth Abbey Hotel (now, sadly, demolished).

[86] Dimitri Fimi, '"Mad Elves and Elusive Beauty": some Celtic Strands of Tolkein's mythology (1)', *Folklore*, 117 (2) (2006), 156–70; and Carl Phelpstead, *Tolkein and Wales: Language, Literature and Identity* (Cardiff, 2011).

[87] On C. S. Lewis's Welsh links see Grahame Davies, *Real Wrexham* (Bridgend, 2001), pp. 70–1.

[88] Cecil Woodham-Smith, *The Great Hunger: Ireland 1840–1849* (London, 1973).

[89] Holroyd, *Augustus John*, pp. 2–7.

[90] A. S. T. Griffith-Boscawen, *Fourteen Years in Parliament* (London, 1907), and idem, *Memories* (London, 1925). For Dalton see B. Pimlott, *Hugh Dalton* (London, 1985), and H. Dalton, *Call Back Yesterday: Memoirs, 1887–1931* (London, 1953).

[91] On Lord Penrhyn (George Sholto Gordon Douglas-Pennant) see J. Lindsay, *The Great Strike: a History of the Penrhyn Quarry Dispute of 1900–1903* (Cardiff, 1967); R. M. Jones, *The North Wales Quarrymen, 1874–1922* (Cardiff, 1981); B. Owen, *The History of the Welsh Militia and Volunteer Corps, Anglesey and Caernarvonshire* (London, 1989); and the National Trust's *Penrhyn Castle, Gwynedd* (Caernarfon, 1991).

[92] J. V. Morgan, *Welsh Political and Educational Leaders in the Victorian Era* (London, 1908).

[93] On Henry Richard see C. S. Miall, *Henry Richard, MP* (London, 1889); I. G. Jones, *Explorations and Explanations: Essays in the Social History of Victorian Wales* (Llandysul, 1981), pp. 193–214; and idem, *Mid-Victorian Wales: the Observers and the Observed* (Llandysul, 1992), pp. 103–65. See

also D. Ben Rees, *Life and work of Henry Richard: Apostle of Peace* (Nottingham, 2007). The statue stands as a silent witness to Tregaron's goings on and a resting place for the town's pigeons.

94 Hector Bolitho, *Alfred Mond: First Lord Melchett* (London, 1933).

95 G. Williams and D. Smith, *Fields of Praise: a History of the Welsh Rugby Union* (Cardiff, 1989), p. 87. D. Gwenallt Jones in his poems of the 1930s confirmed how rugby had become engrained within the national identity, speaking of how he would 'gwallgofi pan giciai Banroft ei gôl Gymreig / A sgorio Dici Owen ei genedlaethol gais' (Go mad when Bancroft kicked his Welsh penalty / And Dici Owen his national try). On the links between national identity and sport, one of the best histories is David Goldblatt, *Futebol Nation: the Story of Brazil through Soccer* (London, 2014).

96 On Maurice Turnbull see Maurice Allen and Maurice Turnbull, *The Book of Two Maurices* (London, 1930), and *www.scrum.com* (accessed 26 June 2011). On the confusions in national identity and sport see Martin Johnes, 'Eighty Minute Patriots? National Identity and Sport in Modern Wales', *International Journal of the History of Sport*, 17 (2000), 93–110.

97 R. Brangwyn, *Brangwyn* (London, 1978), and R. Charles, *Frank Brangwyn Centenary*, Arts Council of Wales (Cardiff, 1967).

98 Winifred Coombe Tennant was a fascinating figure – a suffragette, journalist, politician, and patron of the arts. Her private life was dominated by emotional anguish following the death of her two children. The revelation, through vivid and sustained psychic experience, of what she believed to be their continued life after death, led her to become the most closely studied psychic medium of her period, working under the pseudonym of 'Mrs Willet'. After her death, she reported on life 'on the other side' on more than forty occasions to other mediums. See Peter Lord's superb *Winifred Coombe Tennant: a Life through Art* (Aberystwyth, 2007).

99 Financial problems were an ever present problem for the university in Aberystwyth. On one occasion when the wolf was closer to the door than usual, the vice-presidents, who included figures such as Sir R. A. Cunliffe Bt, Sir Henry H. Hussey Vivian, His Grace the Duke of Westminster, the Earl of Lisburne and the Rt. Hon. Lord Sudley, each donated £500 to the college. Ellis, *The University College of Wales*, p. 329.

100 Jones, *The Dragon Has Two Tongues.*

101 Jones, *The Dragon Has Two Tongues.*

102 R. Thomas, *Wales in Quotations* (Bridgend, 19910, p. 17.

[103] Thomas, *Wales in Quotations*, p. 18.

[104] Thomas, *Wales in Quotations*, p. 21.

[105] Ceridwen Lloyd Morgan, 'Berta Ruck (1878–1978) of Aberdyfi: Novelist', *Journal of the Merionethshire Historical and Record Society*, XV, 111 (2007), 216.

[106] Quoted in Matthew Hollis, *Now All Roads Lead to France: the Last Years of Edward Thomas* (London, 2011), p. 139.

[107] S. Jones, *Allen Raine* (Carmarthen, 1979); J. Harris, 'Queen of the Rushes', *Planet* 97 (1993), 64–72.

[108] Dafydd Ifans, *Tyred Drosodd* (Pen-y-bont ar Ogwr, 1977), p. ii; see also Jane Aaron, 'Eluned Morgan a'r Angen am Wreiddiau', *Efrydiau Athronyddol*, 61 (1998), 86–103; and R. Bryn Williams, *Eluned Morgan. Bywgraffiad a Detholiad* (Llandysul, 1948). For an interesting account of confused identities transplanted around the globe linked to Eluned's see Michelle Langfield and Peter Roberts, *Welsh Patagonians: the Australian Connection* (Darlinghurst, NSW, 2005). One example from several which is instructive is that of David and Mary Ann Humphreys who married in Merthyr Tydfil in 1876 and had ten children – six born in Wales, and the last four in Argentina. They emigrated to Patagonia on the *Vesta* in 1886 with five children (one child had already died). They lived in Patagonia for twenty-four years until they moved again, to Australia. During these years, five of their children died, and one son, David John, emigrated to Canada in 1902 (p. 49).

[109] L. J. Williams, *A Digest of Welsh Historical Statistics*, vol. 1 (Cardiff, 1985), p. 68.

[110] On Mary Webb (1881–1927) see G. M. Coles, '*The Flower of Light*: a Biographical Introduction and a Bibliography', *Welsh Writing in English*, 11 (2006–7), 69–101.

[111] M. Wynn Thomas, '"A Grand Harliquinade": the Border Writing of Nigel Heseltine', *Welsh Writing in English*, 11 (2006–7), 51–68; Ross Gossedge, 'Tales of the *Boneddigion*: Nigel Heseltine's Gentry Context', *Almanac: a Yearbook of Welsh Writing in English*, 13 (2008–9), 55–80. The best guide to his work on the themes of border belonging is Nigel Heseltine *Capriol for Mother: a Memoir of Peter Warlock and his Family by his Son Nigel Heseltine* (London, 1992).

[112] See for example Hywel Bishop, Nikolas Coupland and Peter Garrett, 'Blood is Thicker Than the Water that Separates us: Dimensions and Qualities of Welsh Identity in the North American Diaspora', *North American Journal of Welsh Studies*, 3, 2 (Summer 2003), 39–54; John Harris, '(Re)Presenting Wales: National Identity and Celebrity in the Postmodern Rugby World', *North American Journal of Welsh Studies*, 6,

2 (Summer 2006), 1–13; R. Merfyn Jones, 'Beyond identity – the Reconstruction of the Welsh', *Journal of British Studies*, 31 (4) (1992), 330–57; Rhys Jones, 'Relocating Nationalism: on the Geographies of Reproducing Nations', *Transactions of the Institute of British Geographers*, 33 (3) (2008), 221–39; and Neil Evans, *National Identity in the British Isles* (Harlech, 1989).

113 The most famous portrayal of Abrahams is given in the 1981 film *Chariots of Fire* in which he is claimed to be an 'English' Jew.

114 Waldo Williams, *Dail Pren* (Llandysul, 1956), p. 67.

115 Jones, *The Dragon Has Two Tongues*, p. 204.

116 Quoted in James Nicholas, *Waldo Williams* (Cardiff, 1975), p. 62. For useful general discussions on these themes of the ethereal and elusive nature of identity see E. Renan, 'What is a Nation?', in S. Woolf (ed.), *Nationalism in Europe: 1818 to the Present: a Reader* (London, 1996), pp. 10–19; S. Berger and C. Lorenz (eds), *The Contested Nation: Ethnicity, Class, Religion and Gender in National Histories* (Basingstoke, 2008); and D. Cannadine, *The Undivided Past: History Beyond our Differences* (London, 2013), pp. 53–92.

5 'The Way of all Flesh'

1 On the history of sex in Wales during the period 1870–1945 see Russell Davies, *Secret Sins: Sex, Violence and Society in Carmarthenshire, 1870–1920* (Cardiff, 1995), and idem, *Hope and Heartbreak: a Social History of Wales and the Welsh, 1776–1871* (Cardiff, 2005), pp. 263–323.

2 Caradoc Evans, National Library of Wales [NLW], MSS 200 33, p. 12.

3 Quoted in Carol Zisowitz Stearns and Peter N. Stearns, 'Victorian Sexuality: Can Historians Do It Better?', *Journal of Social History*, 18 (1985), 625–34, 626.

4 Amongst the best studies are Paul Ferris, *Sex and the British* (London, 1993); Fraser Harrison, *The Dark Angel: Aspects of Victorian Sexuality* (London, 1977); Ronald Pearsall, *The Worm in the Bud: the World of Victorian Sexuality* (Harmondsworth, 1983); Cyril Pearl, *The Girl with the Swansdown Seat* (London, 1956); and Jeffrey Weekes, *Sex, Politics and Society: the Regulation of Sexuality since 1800* (London, 1981).

5 On the themes of the second industrial revolution and the consumer revolution in Wales see Russell Davies, *People, Places and Passions: Pain and Pleasure, a Social History of Wales and the Welsh 1870–1945* (Cardiff, 2015), pp. 55–90. On the sexual life of the Victorians see Stephen Marcus, *The Other Victorians: a Study of Sexuality and Pornography in*

Mid-Nineteenth Century England (New York, NY, 1977); Matthew Sweet, *Inventing the Victorians* (London, 2001), and Michael Mason, *The Making of Victorian Sexuality* (Oxford, 1994).

6 E. Jones, *Essays in Applied Psycho-Analysis Vol.1, Miscellaneous Essays* (London, 1951), pp. 27–39; idem, 'The Future of "Psychoanalysis" ', *International Journal of Psychoanalysis*, 17 (1936), 269–77. For a discussion see Richard Overy, *The Morbid Age: Britain and the Crisis of Civilization, 1919–1939* (London, 2010), 141–52. For a superb biography of Ernest Jones see Brenda Maddox, *Freud's Wizard: the Enigma of Ernest Jones* (London, 2006); also useful is T. G. Davies, *Ernest Jones: 1878–1958* (Cardiff, 1959).

7 Rachel Barrett was born in Carmarthen in 1875, educated at the University College of Wales, Aberystwyth, and then worked for women's suffrage across south Wales and London. See Spartacus – *spartacus-educational.com/women.htm* (accessed 21 May 2015); and also Elizabeth Crawford, *The Women's Suffrage Movement: A Reference Guide 1866–1928* (London, 2003), pp. 35–6. On suffrage in Wales see Ryland Wallace's detailed *The Women's Suffrage Movement in Wales, 1866–1928* (Cardiff, 2009). See also S. Clive, *Radclyffe Hall: a Woman Called John* (London, 1997), p. 172, where the claim of their lesbian relationship is made. See also Diana Souhami, *The Trials of Radclyffe Hall* (London, 2012).

8 Havelock Ellis, *Sexual Inversion* (London, 1897).

9 Lewis Jones, *Cwmardy: the Story of a Welsh Mining Valley*, with an introduction by Dai Smith (London, 1978); and idem, *We Live: the Story of a Welsh Mining Valley*, with an introduction by Dai Smith (London, 1978).

10 For a valuable discussion on the Bolshevik revolution and sexuality see Dan Healy, *Bolshevik Medicine and Russia's Sexual Revolution* at *www.iisg.nl/womhist/healey.doc* (accessed 19 May 2015). Amongst their reforms were secularising marriage, permitting free divorce and abortion on demand and apparently decriminalising homosexuality.

11 For the life of Lewis Jones see David Smith, *Lewis Jones* (Cardiff, 1982).

12 D. Gwenallt Jones, *Ffrwneisiau: Cronicl Blynyddoedd Mebyd* (Llandysul, 1982), pp. 102–3.

13 D. Gwenallt Jones, *Y Mynach a'r Sant: Dwy Awdl* (Aberystwyth, 1928).

14 For a detailed study of each of these see Alan Llwyd, *Rhyfel a Gwrthryfel: Brwydr Moderniaeth a Beirdd Modern* (Llandybïe, 2003), pp. 130–360.

15 For the Newport Nude see *Daily Mirror*, 31 December 1947 and 22 July 2008. The exhibition 'The Art of the Nude' ran at Newport museum between July and September 2008.

16 Carol Dyhouse, *Heartthrobs: A History of Women and Desire* (London, 2017).

[17] Huw Evans and Marian Davies, *'Fyl'na Weden I': Blas ar Dafodiaith Canol Ceredigion* (Llanrwst, 2000), passim.

[18] The most detailed linguistic studies of Wales are Alan R. Thomas, *The Linguistic Geography of Wales: a Contribution to Welsh Dialectology* (Cardiff, 1973); and Alan R. Thomas et al., *The Welsh Dialect Survey* (Cardiff, 2000).

[19] Huw Evans, *Cwm Eithin*, 3rd edn (Lerpwl, 1943).

[20] For a useful discussion of the way folk songs reveal popular sexuality see E. G. Millward, 'Delweddau'r Canu Gwerin' (The Imagery of Folk Song), *Canu Gwerin*, 3 (1980), 11–21.

[21] Gwilym Davies, 'Cyflwr Moesol Cymru', *Y Geninen* (June and July 1909), 201–8, 223–7. The long quotation is on page 226. On Gwilym Davies see Ieuan Gwynedd Jones (ed.), *Gwilym Davies, 1879–1955* (Llandysul, 1972).

[22] H. Elwyn Thomas, *Martyrs of Hell's Highway* (London, 1896) pp. 137–9.

[23] Julie Peakman, *The Pleasure's All Mine: A History of Perverse Sex* (London, 2013), p. 367. On the development of pornography see Lisa Sigel, *Governing Pleasures: Pornography and Social Change in England, 1815–1914* (New Brunswick, 2002).

[24] On sexual scandals in Welsh public schools see Davies, *Hope and Heartbreak*, pp. 118, 321.

[25] Maddox, *Freud's Wizard*, p. 12.

[26] On the rise of the consumer society and its impact on Wales see Davies, *People, Places and Passions*, pp. 55–90. See also K. Theodor Hoppen, *The Mid-Victorian Generation, 1846–1886* (Oxford, 1998), pp. 322–32.

[27] See for example the cases quoted by Matthew Sweet, *Inventing the Victorians* (London, 2001), pp. 215–16, and the luridly pornographic [anon.] *Raped on the Railway: a True Story of a Lady who was first Ravished and Then Flagellated on the Scottish Express* (London, 1875).

[28] Morine Krissdóttir, *Descents of Memory: The Life of John Cowper Powys* (London, 2007), pp. 258, 318–19.

[29] Quoted in Sue Asbee, 'Margiad Evans's *The Wooden Doctor*: Illness and Sexuality', *Welsh Writing in English*, 19 (2004), 33–49.

[30] M. Bryant, *Dictionary of Twentieth-century British Cartoonists and Caricaturists* (London, 2000), entry on H. S. Thomas; and H. Shaw, 'Bert Thomas and his work', *The Strand* (London, 1929), pp. 130–8.

[31] For the saucy postcards of Saundersfoot see Ken Daniels, *Saundersfoot and Tenby: the Archive Photographs Series* (Stroud, 1995), pp. 52–4.

[32] Amongst the Welsh-related items in the collection is a naked lady playing the harp and a topless Britannia. Milford Haven Collection, *Victoria and Albert Museum* X507. The collection was gathered by

George, Second Marquess of Milford Haven. On Welsh postcards in general see William Troughton, 'Y Cerdyn Post Darluniadol yng Nghymru', *Y Casglwr*, 55 (Haf 1995), 11–12; and E. G. Millward, 'Cymry'r Cardiau Post', *Y Casglwr* (Haf 1995), 13–15.

33   Rachel P. Maines, *The Technology of Orgasm: Hysteria, the Vibrator and Women's Sexual Satisfaction* (Baltimore, Md., 1999); Sarah Boxer, 'Batteries Not Included', *New York Times*, 21 March 1999; and Dieca Aitkenhead, 'The Buzz', *The Guardian*, 8 September 2012, 34–8 (*Guardian Weekend*). The story of the 'medical' development of the vibrator was entertainingly told in the 2012 movie *Hysteria* directed by Tanya Wexler.

34   Peter Levi makes this claim in (Walter) David Michael Jones (1895–1974), *Oxford Dictionary of National Biography*, *www.oxforddnb.com/view/article/31294* (accessed 21 January 2015).

35   Caroline Palmer, 'Matthew Lewis Vaughan Davies – ambitious cad or assiduous politician', *Ceredigion – Journal of the Ceredigion Historical Society*, 14 (4) (2004), 73–104.

36   *Y Cymro*, 17 March 1993; T. Robin Chapman, *W. J. Gruffydd* (Caerdydd, 1993).

37   James Williams, *Give Me Yesterday* (Llandysul, 1971), pp. 59–62.

38   I am grateful to the late Dr John Davies for this information.

39   *South Wales Press*, 9 October 1918. For similar cases involving minsters and ministerial candidates see *South Wales Press*, 12 November 1911, and 12 March 1920, and *Llanelly Mercury*, 2 February 1911. William Hughes, a student for the Baptist ministry of Merthyr Tydfil, was imprisoned for seven years in 1880 for the rape of Margaret Ingram. A case was subsequently brought against Margaret for having committed perjury in denying that she had sexual intercourse with Isaac Lewis in the Cwm Pit Engine House in April 1879. Her journey to court was marked by angry crowds who 'hooted her all the way'. *Western Mail*, 22 November 1880. For a fascinating study of religion and sexual scandals in nineteenth-century Wales see R. Elwyn Hughes, *Merched Digon Trafferthus a Chapeli Caerdydd yn Ail Hanner y Bedwaredd Ganrif ar Bymtheg* (Caerdydd, 2011). I am grateful to Elwyn Hughes for a copy of the lecture.

40   *Carmarthen Weekly Reporter*, 6 January 1906.

41   *South Wales Press*, 31 June 1905.

42   *South Wales Press*, 19 August 1907.

43   *South Wales Press*, 1 May 1907.

44   *South Wales Press*, 22 November 1906. Indeed some women appear to have been remarkably careless. Fanny Garland had her thirteenth illegitimate child at Carmarthen workhouse infirmary on 24 July 1917.

See Carmarthenshire Records Office, Abercennen MS5178, *Register of Births at the Workhouse.*

[45] *South Wales Press*, 15 September 1904.

[46] Quoted in Michael Lieven, *Senghennydd: the Universal Pit Village 1890–1930* (Llandysul, 1994), p. 125.

[47] On popular courtship in rural Wales see Russell Davies, '"In a Broken Dream": Some Aspects of Sexual Behaviour and the Dilemmas of the Unmarried Mother in South West Wales, 1887–1914', *Llafur*, 3 (4) (1983), and idem, *Secret Sins*, pp. 156–85.

[48] For a discussion of these customs, see E. W. Jones, 'Carwriaeth y Cymry, Neu Cipdrem Feddygol ar Flynyddoedd Cynnar y Bedwaredd Ganrif ar Bymtheg yng Ngheredigion', *National Library of Wales Journal* (1966), 1–40; reprinted in idem, *Ysgubau'r Meddyg* (Y Bala, 1973), pp. 16–40.

[49] David Jenkins, *The Agricultural Community in South West Wales at the Turn of the Twentieth Century* (Cardiff, 1971), pp. 125–7.

[50] The case against Daniel Rees is reported in the *Carmarthen Weekly Reporter* on 13 November 1905, and that of Evan Jones on 14 December 1906. At the Carmarthenshire Quarter Sessions in October 1909, David Owen was defended on a charge of breaking and entering by William Llewelyn Williams, KC, MP, who argued that Owen had been attempting to enter the maidservants' quarters, not to steal but for the 'Pleasures of Noswedd o Garu' – a tradition that, this notable Welsh historian claimed, dated back to the age of Dafydd ap Gwilym (*Carmarthen Weekly Reporter*, 29 October 1909). In the *South Wales Press* of 7 March 1907, T. R. Ludford described the practice as the 'traditional courtship procedure on local farms'.

[51] Thomas Rees, *Miscellaneous Papers . . . on Subjects Relating to Wales* (London, 1867), pp. 29–37. The most detailed study of illegitimacy in Wales is Anna Brueton, 'Illegitimacy in South Wales 1660–1870' (unpublished PhD, University of Leicester, 2015), available at *https://Lra.le.ac.uk/bitstream/2381/32012/1/2015_BRUETON-AC_PhD. pdf* (accessed 3 May 2014). I am grateful to Dr Huw Walters for this reference.

[52] Gwilym Davies, 'Cyflwr Moesol Cymru', *Y Geninen* (June and July 1909), 201–8, 223–7. On Gwilym Davies, see Ieuan Gwynedd Jones (ed.), *Gwilym Davies 1879–1955* (Llandysul, 1972).

[53] These figures have been calculated from the annual reports of the Registrar General of Births, Deaths and Marriages between 1885 and 1919.

[54] T. C. Smout, 'Aspects of Sexual Behaviour in Nineteenth Century Scotland', in Peter Laslett (ed.), *Bastardy and its Comparative History*

(London, 1980), pp. 192–216, and idem, *A Century of the Scottish People 1830–1950* (chapter VII) (London, 1986), pp. 159–80.

55 L. J. Williams, *Digest of Welsh Historical Statistics*, vol. 1 (Cardiff, 1985), pp. 50–9. The rates of illegitimate births were:

1871 – 35	1930 – 16.7
1880 – 32.8	1939 – 15.2
1890 – 31.3	1940 – 15.6
1900 – 31	1943 – 17.6
1910 – 28.6	1944 – 19.1
1914 – 27	1945 – 17.1
1918 – 21.98	

56 The marriage rate in Wales per 1,000 of population was:

1870 – 14.2	1914 – 16.7
1880 – 14	1915 – 15.8
1890 – 16.4	1930 – 14.6
1900 – 16.2	1940 – 20.8
1910 – 14.2	1945 – 19.6

57 *Carmarthen Weekly Reporter*, 30 April 1915.

58 Gail Graybon and Penny Summerfield, *Out of the Cage: Women's Experiences in Two World Wars* (London, 1987), pp. 108–9.

59 Gerard J. DeGroot, *Blighty: British Society in the Era of the Great War* (London, 1996), pp. 231–4.

60 P. Levine, '"Walking the Streets in a Way No Decent Woman Should": Women Police in World War 1', *Journal of Modern History*, 66 (1994), 44.

61 Quoted in Helen Jones, *Health and Society in Twentieth-Century Britain* (London, 1994), p. 36.

62 See for example Lara Figel, *The Love-charms of Bombs: Restless Lives in the Second World War* (London, 2013), and John Costello, *Love, Sex and War 1939–1945* (London, 1985). For a fictional account of war's effort on the libido see Sarah Waters, *The Night Watch* (London, 2006).

63 Family legend.

64 P. Simkins, 'Soldiers and Civilians: Billeting in Britain and France', in L. Beckett and K. Simpson (eds), *A Nation in Arms* (Manchester, 1985), pp. 175–86.

65 Quoted in D. Roberts, 'The Slate Quarrying Communities of Caernarvonshire and Merioneth 1911–1939' (unpublished PhD, University Colleges of Wales, Aberystwyth, 1982), pp. 345, 410.

66 *House of Lords, Report from Committees: Contagious Diseases Acts (3) Vol IX*, February–December 1882; and *Session 1878–81, Volume VIII*, 1881 (351), pp. 50–61.

67   Gwyn A. Williams, *Fishers of Men: Towards an Autobiography* (Llandysul, 1996), p. 17.

68   For just a few useful studies of prostitution see Lujo Dassermann, *The Oldest Profession: a History of Prostitution* (London, 1967); Raelene Frances, *Selling Sex: a Hidden History of Prostitution* (Sydney, NSW, 2007); Paula Bartley, *Prostitution Prevention and Reform in England, 1860–1914* (London, 2000); Paul McHugh, *Prostitution and Victorian Social Reform* (London, 1980); Frances Finigan, *Poverty and Prostitution: a Study of Victorian Prostitutes in York* (Cambridge, 1979).

69   *Western Mail*, 4 July 1891.

70   *Western Mail*, 8 May 1909.

71   *Western Mail*, 9 May 1909.

72   *Western Mail*, 14 July 1894.

73   *The Times*, 19 July 1884.

74   W. H. Davies, *Young Emma* (London, 1980). On W. H. Davies see L. Hockey, *W. H. Davies* (London, 1971), and Lawrence Normand, *W. H. Davies* (London, 2003).

75   On the estimate of the number of brothels see M. J. Daunton, 'Jack Ashore: Seamen in Cardiff Before 1914', *Welsh History Review*, 9 (2) (1978–9), 176–203, and idem, *Coal Metropolis Cardiff 1870–1914* (Leicester, 1974), p. 220.

76   *Western Mail*, 15 September 1894.

77   On such themes see Neil Larry Shumsky, 'Tacit Acceptance: Respectable American and Segregated Prostitutes, 1870–1910', *Journal of Social History* (Summer 1986), 665–79.

78   *Western Mail*, 12 November 1916.

79   On Undeb Dirwestol Gogledd Cymru see Ceridwen Lloyd Morgan, 'From Temperance to Suffrage?', in Angela V. John (ed.), *Our Mothers' Land: Chapters in Welsh Women's History 1830–1939* (Cardiff, 1991), pp. 135–58.

80   H. C. G. Matthew (ed.), *The Gladstone Diaries*, vol. 10 and vol. 11 (Oxford, 1990), passim. On Catherine Gladstone see J. Marlow, *Mr and Mrs Gladstone* (London, 1977), and P. Gladstone, *Portrait of a Family: the Gladstones, 1839–1889* (London, 1989).

81   The papers of the Cwmdonkin Shelter are in Swansea University's Archives, see GB 0217 LAC/Cwmdonkin Shelter/B2.

82   Quoted in Lesley Hulonce, '"A Social Frankenstein": Inciting Interpretations of Prostitution in Late Nineteenth-Century Swansea', *Llafur*, 9 (4) (2007), 55.

83   Deirdre Beddoe, *Out of the Shadows: A History of Women in Twentieth-Century Wales* (Cardiff, 2000), pp. 38–9. On Mother Shepherd see Charles

Preece, *Woman of the Valleys: the Story of Mother Shepherd* (Port Talbot, 1988).

[84] On the early history of China see Keith Strange, 'In Search of the Celestial Empire: Crime in Merthyr, 1830–60', *Llafur*, 3 (1) (1980), 44–86; and David Jones and Alan Bainbridge, 'The Conquering of China: Crime and an Industrial Community', *Llafur*, 2 (4) (1979), 47–69. Prostitution, especially in the Iron Bridge area of the town also features in the novel by Jack Jones, *Black Parade* (London, 1935), pp. 112–13.

[85] 'A Journal Kept by a Scripture Reader', NLW MS 4, 943B.

[86] Charles Ashton, *Ffeiriau Cymru* (Llanelli, 1881), pp. 8–9.

[87] *Western Mail*, 19 October 1882.

[88] *Western Mail*, 23 January 1894.

[89] See Russell Davies, '"Hen Wlad y Menig Gwynion": Profiad Sir Gaerfyrddin', in Geraint H. Jenkins (ed.), *Cof Cenedl: Ysgrifau ar Hanes Cymru* (Llandysul, 1991), pp. 135, 160.

[90] Quoted in Davies, *Secret Sins*, p. 163.

[91] *Carmarthen Weekly Reporter*, 28 June 1907.

[92] On the policing of Carmarthen see Pat Molloy, *A Shilling for Carmarthen: The Town they Nearly Tamed* (Llandysul, 1980), pp. 107–65.

[93] *Western Mail*, 21 March 1913.

[94] *Wrexham Advertiser, Denbighshire, Flintshire, Cheshire, Shropshire, Merionethshire, and North Wales Register*, 3 March 1875.

[95] *Wrexham Advertiser, Denbighshire, Flintshire, Cheshire, Shropshire, Merionethshire, and North Wales Register*, 3 March 1878.

[96] *Wrexham Advertiser, Denbighshire, Flintshire, Cheshire, Shropshire, Merionethshire, and North Wales Register*, 24 August 1875.

[97] Lewis Lloyd, *The Port of Caernarfon, 1793–1900* (Caernarfon, 1989), pp. 162–3.

[98] *Western Mail*, 7 January 1897.

[99] Jeff Townes, *Dylan Thomas: the Pubs* (Talybont, 2014), pp. 58–61.

[100] Donald Moore (ed.), *Barry: the Centenary Book* (Barry, 1984), p. 291, 321.

[101] *Western Mail*, 25 March 1890.

[102] Davies *Hope and Heartbreak*, pp. 300–3. See also W. R. (Bodwyn) Owen, '"Tiger Bay": the Street of the Sleeping Cats', *Glamorgan Historian*, 7 (1971), 82–5.

[103] *Western Mail*, 29 November 1870.

[104] *Western Mail*, 23 July 1885.

[105] Quoted in Davies, *Hope and Heartbreak*, p. 303.

[106] *Western Mail*, 20 August 1890.

107 Gwyn Thomas, *A Welsh Eye* (London, 1964), p. 156.

108 Thomas, *A Welsh Eye*, pp. 157–8.

109 *Western Mail*, 1 May 1869.

110 This is claimed in 'Methodist Creulon Cas?', *Barn* (January 2009), 33–4. See also John Belcham (ed.), *Liverpool 800: Culture, Character and History* (Liverpool, 2008), pp. 350–1.

111 Hywel Teifi Edwards, *Eisteddfod Ffair y Byd, Chicago 1893* (Llandysul, 1990). After a lucid description of the premises, Hywel Teifi concludes, 'Bordello teilwng o Brifwyl' (A Bordello fit for a major festival), p. 71. On the geography of British prostitution see Philip Howells, *Geographies of Regulation: Policing Prostitution in Nineteenth-Century Britain and the Empire* (Cambridge, 2009).

112 See Paul Morgan, *Good Time Girls of the Alaska-Yukon Gold Rush* (Fairbanks, Alas., 1998). For other histories of Welsh prostitutes in America see Jan Mackell, *Red Light Women of the Rocky Mountains* (Albuquerque, N.Mex., 2009), and Elizabeth Alice Clement, *Love for Sale: Courting, Treating and Prostitution in New York City, 1900–1945* (Chapel Hill, NC, 2006).

113 On Ivor Novello see David Slattery-Christy, *In Search of Ruritania* (London, 2006).

114 Matt Houlbrook, *Queer London: Perils and Pleasures in the Sexual Metropolis, 1918–1957* (Chicago, Ill., 2005), p. 308.

115 On Rhys Davies see Meic Stephens, *Rhys Davies: A Writer's Life* (Cardigan, 2013), pp. 125, 190, 202–3. For Emlyn Williams see Russell Stephens, *Emlyn Williams* (Bridgend, 2000), pp. 114–52.

116 William Cross, *The Abergavenny Witch Hunt: an Account of the Prosecution of Over Twenty Homosexuals in the Welsh Town in 1942* (Newport, 2014).

117 Maddox, *Freud's Wizard*, pp. 74, 90, 160 and 208.

118 Ray Monk, *Bertrand Russell: the Ghost of Madness* (New York, NY, 2001), pp. 104–5.

119 Matt Houlbrook, *Queer London: Perils and Pleasures in the Sexual Metropolis, 1918–1957* (London, 2005), pp. 19–42.

120 Robb Strangers, *Homosexual Love in the Nineteenth Century* (London, 2003), pp. 31–4, 272–5.

121 Dylan Thomas, *A Child's Christmas in Wales* (London, 1993), p. 21.

122 Huw Evans and Marian Davies, '*Fyl'na Weden I*', p. 59.

123 Personal knowledge.

124 Davies, *People, Places and Passions*, pp. 301, 306

125 Christopher Breward, 'Fashion and the Man: From Suburb to City Street: the Species of Masculine Consumption, 1870–1914', *New Formations*, 37 (1999), 49–67; idem, *The Hidden Consumer:*

Masculinities, Fashion and City Life, 1860–1914 (Manchester, 1999); Elizabeth Wilson and Amy de la Haye, *Defining Dress: Dress as Object, Meaning and Identity* (Manchester, 1999); Shaun Cole, *'Don We Now Our Gay Apparel': Gay Men's Dress in the Twentieth Century* (Oxford, 2000).

126 Stephen Bourne, *Brief Encounters: Lesbians and Gays in British Cinema, 1930–71* (London, 1996); James Gardiner, *Who's A Pretty Boy Then? One Hundred and Fifty Years of Gay Life in Pictures* (London, 1997); Jeffrey Richards, *The Age of the Dream Palace: Cinema and Society in Britain, 1930–39* (London, 1989); Malcolm Shifrin, *Victorian Turkish Baths*, http://www.victorianturkishbath.org (accessed 8 June 2015); and Agnes Campbell, *Report on Public Baths and Wash-houses in the United Kingdom* (Edinburgh, 1918).

127 Lionel Rose, *Rogues and Vagabonds: Vagrant Underworld in Britain, 1815–1985* (London, 1988).

128 C. Devlin (ed.), *Gerard Manley Hopkins: the Sermons and Devotional Writings* (London, 1967), pp. 34–7.

129 For a discussion on these themes see Thomas Hughes, *The Manliness of Christ* (London, 1879).

130 *The Times*, 10 April 1902.

131 Jim Perrin, *Menlove: the Life of John Menlove Edwards* (Llandysul, 1985).

132 Michael Holroyd, *Augustus John: the New Biography* (London, 1997), pp. 352–4, 400.

133 *The Times*, 23 March 1973.

134 *The Times*, 28 January 1992.

135 R. Morphet, *Cedric Morris* (London, 1984); B. Tufnell, *Cedric Morris and Lett Haines: Teaching Life and Art* (Cardiff, 2003).

136 K. Deepwell, *Ten Decades: Careers of Ten Women Born 1897–1906* (Norwich, 1992).

137 Angela V. John, *Turning the Tide: the Life of Lady Rhondda* (Cardigan, 2013), passim.

138 Lori Williamson, *Power and Protest: Frances Power Cobbe and Victorian Society* (London, 2005). The 'Homintern' was a portmanteau word, a mash-up of 'Comintern' (the international communist organisation) and 'homosexual'. See Gregory Woods, *Homintern: How Gay Culture Liberated the Modern World* (London, 2016).

139 E. Picton-Turbervill, *Life is Good: An Autobiography* (London, 1939); *The Times*, 3 September 1960.

140 McBean strengthened his reputation as an innovative and creative photographer with a number of LP cover photographs, most notably the Beatles first album *Please, Please Me*. See 'The Curious Mr McBean',

The Times, 11 June 2006; and Adrian Woodhouse, *Angus McBean* (London, 1985).

[141] *Daily Mail*, 27 October 2007; M. Montgomery Hyde, *The Other Love: an Historical and Contemporary Survey of Homosexuality in Britain* (London, 1970), pp. 153–4; *The Times*, 15 March 1905.

[142] Alan Llwyd *Kate: Cofiant Kate Roberts, 1891–1985* (Llandysul, 2011). Alan Llwyd also presented his argument in an S4C documentary, *Kate, Y Cofiant*, in 2011.

[143] On Prosser Rhys see Rhisiart Hincks, *Cofiant E. Prosser Rhys, 1901–1945* (Llandysul, 1980); and Nan Griffiths, 'Prosser Rhys a'r Hen Ferch', *Taliesin*, 128 (2006), 85–108.

[144] For the relationship between Caradog Prichard and Morris T. Williams and Prosser Rhys see Menna Baines, *Yng Ngolau'r Lleuad: Ffaith a Dychymyg yng Ngwaith Caradog Prichard* (Llandysul, 2005), pp. 18–23, 24–7, 29–34, 266–72.

[145] There is a voluminous literature on the life and work of Rhys Davies. On his sexuality the most incisive are M. Wynn Thomas, 'Never seek to kill thy love: Rhys Davies's Fiction', *Welsh Writing in English: a Yearbook of Critical Essays*, 4 (1998), 22–53; Huw Edwin Osborne, 'Rhys Davies, Professional Welshman: Identities in the Market Place', *The North American Journal of Welsh Studies*, 3 (1–2) (2003), 22–32; Meic Stephens, *Rhys Davies: A Writer's Life* (Cardigan, 2013); Rhys Davies, *Print of a Hare's Foot* (London, 1969); for a sample of his work see *The Best of Rhys Davies* (London, 1979). Also useful is David Rees, *Rhys Davies* (Cardiff, 1975).

[146] Meic Stephens (ed.), *Decoding the Hare* (Cardiff, 2001).

[147] The best biographies of Ivor Novello are David Slattery-Christy, *In Search of Ruritania* (London, 2006); and James Harding, *Ivor Novello* (Bridgend, 1997).

[148] John Stuart Roberts, *Siegfried Sassoon* (London, 2005), p. 77. Sassoon's latest biographer outlines how destructive his affair with Novello was. See Jean Moorcroft Wilson, *Siegfried Sassoon: Soldier Poet, Lover, Friend* (London, 2013), pp. 420–1.

[149] This is claimed in an article by Michael Thornton, *Daily Mail*, 31 December 2005.

[150] On Emlyn Williams see Russell Stephens, *Emlyn Williams: the Making of a Dramatist* (Bridgend, 2000).

[151] Emlyn Williams, *Emlyn, an Early Autobiography, 1927–1935* (London, 1973), p. 71.

[152] Williams, *Emlyn, an Early Autobiography*, p. 347.

[153] Williams, *Emlyn, an Early Autobiography*, p. 367.

154 *Welsh Gazette*, 30 November 1944, and *Cambrian News*, 12 January 1945. The events were similar to those portrayed in the infamous novel of Aberystwyth's homosexual underworld forty years later. See Michael Carson, *Sucking Sherbet Lemons* (London, 1988). Also useful in the context of sexual abuse of boys see the horrible goings-on in James Hanley's novel *Boy* (London, 1931). Hanley, who considered himself Welsh lived in Corwen and Llanfechain between 1931 and 1963. In *Boy*, the 'hero', such as he is, escapes the economic exploitation of his family for the sexual humiliation of a ship.

155 The Abergavenny sex scandal has been exhaustively discussed in Cross, *The Abergavenny Witch Hunt*.

156 Cross, *The Abergavenny Witch Hunt*, p. 300.

157 Cross, *The Abergavenny Witch Hunt*, p. 183.

158 On Kilvert's fondness for very young girls see Davies, *Hope and Heartbreak*, pp. 316–17.

159 This is claimed in Richard Perceval Graves, *Richard Hughes: a Biography* (London, 1994), p. 358.

160 John Cowper Powys's *Autobiography* (London, 1934) makes several references to his sadism and to his masochism. For a discussion see Louis Marlow, *Welsh Ambassadors: Powys Lives and Letters* (London, 1971), pp. 25–37.

161 Revd Robert Jones (Trebor Aled), *Pleser a Phoen: Sef Cyfrol o Farddoniaeth yn y Llon a'r Lleddf* (private printing, 1908). For a discussion see Simon Brooks, 'Prolog: Ysgrif Goffa', *Tu Chwith*, 3 (1995), 8–12.

162 *Western Mail*, 19 January 1883 and 31 January 1883.

163 John J. Eddleston, *A Century of Welsh Murders* (Stroud, 2008), passim.

164 *Western Mail*, 1 April 1874.

165 Carmarthen Records Office, Felons Register, Acc. 4,916 case no. 1357. The case is also reported in the *Carmarthen Journal*, 15 July 1870.

166 On Eric Gill see Fiona MacCarthy, *Eric Gill* (London, 2011). David Jones, the war poet and painter, was engaged to Gill's daughter. Gill continues to be a controversial figure. See for example 'Can the art of a paedophile be celebrated?', *www.news.bbc.co.uk* (accessed 14 July 2015) and Rachel Cooke, 'Eric Gill: can we separate the artist from the abuser?', *The Guardian*, 9 April 2017.

167 *Western Mail*, 19 December 1890.

168 *Western Mail*, 17 March 1920.

169 *Western Mail*, 7 June 1909.

6 Love in a Cold Climate

1   Bertrand Russell, *Marriage and Morals* (London, 1929), p. 27.
2   Russell, *Marriage and Morals*, p. 37.
3   Russell, *Marriage and Morals*, p. 49.
4   On these themes in modern society see Simon May, *Love: A History* (London, 2011), and Anthony Giddens, *The Transformation of Intimacy: Sexuality, Love and Emotion in Modern Society* (London, 1993).
5   Wirt Sikes, *Rambles and Studies in Old South Wales* (London, 1881), p. 185.
6   Elinor Glyn, *The Flirt and the Flapper* (London, 1930), p. 11.
7   David Slattery-Christie, *In Search of Ruritania* (London, 2006), passim.
8   Quoted in Peter Miskell, *Pulpits, Coal Pits and Fleapits: a Social History of the Cinema in Wales 1918–1951* (Cardiff, 2006), p. 118.
9   H. G. Cocks, *Classified: the Secret History of the Personal Column* (London, 2009), pp. 56–7, 145–6.
10 Cocks, *Classified*, p. 115.
11 Cocks, *Classified*, p. 120.
12 Bernice Rubens, *I Sent A Letter to My Love* (Cardigan, 2003).
13 Wirt Sikes, *British Goblins* (London, 1880), p. 259.
14 *The Times*, 2 April 1960.
15 Berta Ruck, *A Trickle of Welsh Blood* (London, 1967). Ruck also celebrated her Welsh blood in two works of anecdotal reminiscences, *A Smile from the Past* (1959) and *Ancestral Voices* (1972). The appearance of the *Berta Ruck Birthday Book* (1920) confirmed her place amongst the leading writers of romantic fiction in the first half of the twentieth century. See also Alana Harris and Timothy Willen, *Love and Romance in Britain, 1918–1970* (London, 2015).
16 Gwynn ap Gwilym and Alan Llwyd (eds), *Blodeugerdd o Farddoniaeth Gymraeg yr Ugeinfed Ganrif* (Llandysul, 1987), pp. 1–2. On Sir John Morris Jones see Allan Jones, *John Morris-Jones* (Cardiff, 2011), and John Lasarus Williams, *Syr John Morris-Jones 1864–1929* (Llangefni, 2000).
17 T. M. Owen, *The Story of the Lovespoon* (Swansea, 1973); and Herbert E. Roese, 'Lovespoons in Perspective', *Bulletin of the Board of Celtic Studies*, 35 (1988), 106–16.
18 Bethan Mair (ed.), *Hoff Gerddi Serch Cymru*, pp. 25, 38 and 79.
19 On Whistler see *Financial Times*, 2 December 2012; *Western Mail*, 3 October 2007; Laurence Whistler, *The Laughter and the Urn: the Life of Rex Whistler* (London, 1985); J. Spencer-Smith, *Rex Whistler's War 1939–July 1944: Artist into Tank Commander* (London, 1994); and Hugh Cecil and Mirabel Cecil, *In Search of Rex Whistler* (London, 2012).

[20] The statistics are taken from L. J. Williams, *Digest of Welsh Historical Statistics*, vol. 1 (Cardiff, 1985), p. 61.

[21] Williams, *Digest of Welsh Historical Statistics*, vol.1, p. 61.

[22] Olive Anderson, 'The Incidence of Civil Marriage in Victorian England and Wales', *Past and Present*, 69 (1975), 72–9.

[23] On the impact of the consumer culture and the rise of retail in Wales see Russell Davies, *People, Places and Passions: Pain and Pleasure, a Social History of Wales and the Welsh 1870–1945* (Cardiff, 2015), pp. 55–90.

[24] On the development of marriage see David Cressy, *Birth, Marriage and Death: Ritual, Religion and the Life-cycle in Tudor and Stuart England* (Oxford, 1999), pp. 285–377, and Lawrence Stone, *The Family, Sex and Marriage in England, 1500–1800* (London, 1977). See also Russell Davies, *Hope and Heartbreak: a Social History of Wales and the Welsh, 1776–1870* (Cardiff, 2005), p. 229.

[25] Huw Evans and Marian Davies, *'Fyl'na Weden I': Blas ar Dafodiaith Canol Ceredigion* (Llanrwst, 2000), pp. 169–85.

[26] On Frances Power Cobbe see Sally Mitchell, *Frances Power Cobbe: Victorian Feminist, Journalist, Reformer* (Charlottesville, Va., 2004). See also Peter Gay, *Education of the Senses: Vol.1: The Bourgeois Experience, Victoria to Freud* (New York, NY, 1984), p. 163.

[27] 'Chwaer', in 'Gwersi Angenrheidiol i Ferched Ieuanc', *Y Gymraes*, 3, 28 (1899), 134.

[28] Rhys Gwesyn Jones, *Caru, Priodi a Byw* (Y Bala, 1886).

[29] Other sources of published marriage guidance were Edward Foulkes, *Y Pwysigrwydd o Fynd i'r Ystad Briodasol yn Anrhydeddus* (Caernarfon, 1860), and J. Jones, *Arferion a Defodau Priodas Ymhlith Amryw Genhedloedd y Ddaear* (Trefriw, n.d.). Contemporary women's magazines such as *Y Frythones* and *Y Gymraes* often contained short essays of advice.

[30] M. Hopkins, *Cyn, ac ar ôl Priodi: a'r Fodrwy Briodasol* (Dinbych, 1881).

[31] Anon., 'Addysg Genethod Cymru', *Y Gymraes* (November 1909), 163.

[32] Keith Thomas, 'The Double Standard', *The Journal of the History of Ideas*, 2 (1959), 189–99.

[33] On the themes in the Welsh context see Davies *People, Places and Passions*, pp. 55–120. For a very general survey see David R. Shumway, *Modern Love: Romance, Intimacy and the Marriage Crisis* (New York, NY, 2003).

[34] On masculinity in this period see Kevin White, 'The New Man and Early Twentieth Century Educational Culture in the United States', in Peter Stearns (ed.), *An Emotional History of the United States* (London, 1998), pp. 333–55; John Tosh, 'What Should Historians do with Masculinity? Reflections on Nineteenth-Century Britain', *History*

Workshop, 38 (1994), 179–202; Claudia Nelson, *Boys Will Be Girls: The Feminine Ethic and British Children's Fiction, 1857–1917* (London, 1991); Paul R. Deslandes, 'The Basics of Manhood in Eighteenth-and-Nineteenth-Century Britain', *Gender and History*, 19 (2) (2007), 376–9; John Tosh, *Manliness and Masculinities in Nineteenth-Century Britain: Essays on Gender, Family and Empire* (Harlow, 2005); Angela V. John and Claire Eustance (eds), *The Men's Share? Masculinities, Male Support and Women's Suffrage in Britain, 1890–1920* (London, 1997); E. Anthony Rotundo, 'Romantic Friendship: Male Intimacy and Middle-Class Youth in the Northern United States, 1800–1900', *Journal of Social History* (online edition at *jsh.oxfordjournals.org*; accessed 20 November 2012). On masculinity in Welsh historiography see Paul O'Leary's pathbreaking article 'Masculine Histories: Gender and the Social History of Modern Wales', *Welsh History Review*, 22 (2) (2004), 252–77.

[35] For a more fluid interpretation of fatherhood see Lynn Broughton and Helen Rogers, *Gender and Fatherhood in the Nineteenth Century* (Basingstoke, 2007), and Julie-Marie Strange, *Fatherhood and the British Working Class 1865–1914* (Cambridge, 2015).

[36] Williams, *Digest of Welsh Historical Statistics*, vol. 1, pp. 60–2.

[37] Davies, *People, Places and Passions*, p. 88.

[38] Neil Penlington, 'Masculinity and Domesticity in 1930s South Wales: Did Unemployment Change the Domestic Division of Labour?', *Twentieth Century British History*, 21 (3) (2010), 281–99.

[39] South Wales Miners Library Collection (Swansea University) AUD/180 William Rosser Jones.

[40] Clive Menadue, *The Foxglove Sun: Moments from Childhood Recalled* (Blaengarn, 1996), p. 54.

[41] Quoted in Neil Penlington, 'Masculinity and Domesticity', 292.

[42] Michèle Cohen, *Fashioning Masculinity: National Identity and Language in the Eighteenth Century* (London, 1996).

[43] Graham Dawson, *Soldier Heroes: British Adventure, Empire and the Imaging of Masculinities* (London, 2012); Michael Lieven, 'Heroism, Heroics and the Making of Heroes: the Anglo-Zulu War of 1879', *Albion a Quarterly Journal Concerned with British Studies*, 30, 3 (1988), 419–38; and R. Hyam, *Empire and Sexuality: the British Experience* (Manchester, 1990).

[44] Claudia Nelson, 'Sex and the Single Boy: Ideals of Manliness and Sexuality in Victorian Literature for Boys', *Victorian Studies*, 32, 4 (1989), 525–50.

[45] Peter N. Stearns, 'Girls, Boys and Emotions: Redefinitions and Historical Change', *Journal of American History*, 80, 1 (1993), 36–74.

46 For Graves's view of the encounter see Robert Graves, *Goodbye to All That* (Harmondsworth, 1976), p. 70. For Sassoon's views see Siegfried Sassoon, *Siegfried Sassoon's Diaries 1915–1918* (London, 1983), pp. 44–5, and his *Memoirs of a Fox-hunting Man* (London, 1943), pp. 240–3. On the theme of male friendship see Jean Moorcroft Wilson, *Siegfried Sassoon, Soldier, Poet, Lover, Friend: a Life in One Volume* (London, 2013), pp. 114–43.

47 Alan Llwyd and Elwyn Edwards (eds), *Gwaedd y Bechgyn: Blodeugerdd Barddas o Gerddi'r Rhyfel Mawr, 1914–18* (Llandybïe, 1989), p. 29.

48 John Horne, *A Companion to World War I* (Oxford, 2010), p. 270; Michael Korda, *Hero: the Life and Legend of Lawrence of Arabia* (London, 2011).

49 Judy Girls, *The Parlour and the Suburb: Domestic Identities, Class, Femininity and Modernity* (Oxford, 2004); C. Wouters, 'Etiquette Books and Emotion Management in the Twentieth Century', in Peter Stearns (ed.), *An Emotional History of the United States* (London, 1998), p. 193.

50 Stephen Kern, *Anatomy and Destiny: a Cultural History of the Human Body* (Indianapolis, Ind., 1975), p. 95.

51 Havelock Ellis, 'Auto-Eroticism', in his *Studies in the Psychology of Sex* (London, 1900) pp. 174–5.

52 Ernest Jones, 'The Early Development of Female Sexuality', *International Journal of Psycho-Analysis*, 8 (1927), 459–72. For the correspondence see R. Andrew Paskauskas, *The Complete Correspondence of Sigmund Freud and Ernest Jones* (Cambridge, Mass., 1993), pp. 688–9. See also Brenda Maddox, *Freud's Wizard: the Enigma of Ernest Jones* (London, 2006), pp. 206–8.

53 *Reynold's News*, 21 April 1895. For a discussion of Emily Davies's argument see Eric Trudgill, *Madonnas and Magdalens. The Origins and Development of Victorian Sexual Attitudes* (New York, NY, 1976), pp. 240–3.

54 Russell Davies, *Secret Sins: Sex, Violence and Society in Carmarthenshire, 1870–1920* (Cardiff, 1995), pp. 301–2.

55 *Llanelly Mercury*, 8 February 1901.

56 Quoted in Andrew Lycett, *Dylan Thomas: a New Life* (London, 2003), p. 249. Steven Humphreys and Pamela Gordon, *A Man's World: From Boyhood to Manhood, 1900–1960* (London, 1996), pp. 117–21.

57 See 'Little Kinsey: Mass Observation's Sex Survey of 1949', in Liz Stanley, *Sex Surveyed, 1949–1994: From Mass Observations 'Little Kinsey' to the National Survey and the Hite Report* (London, 1995), p. 124.

58 See Kate Fisher, 'She Was Quite Satisfied with the Arrangements I Made': Gender and Birth Control in Britain 1920–1950', *Past and Present*, 169 (2000), 161–92.

[59] Fisher, 'She Was Quite Satisfied with the Arrangements I Made', 174.

[60] Fisher, 'She Was Quite Satisfied with the Arrangements I Made', 177.

[61] Julie Grier, 'Eugenics and Birth Control: Contraceptive Provision in North Wales 1918–1939', *Journal of the Society for the Social History of Medicine*, 11 (3) (1998), 443–58.

[62] On Marie Stopes's clinics and travelling caravans see A. McLaren, *History of Contraception from Antiquity to the Present* (Oxford, 1990); J. Rose, *Marie Stopes and the Sexual Revolution* (London, 1992); and C. Davey, 'Birth Control in Britain During the Inter-War Years: Evidence from the Stopes Correspondence', *Journal of Family History*, 13, 3 (1988), 329–45.

[63] Quoted in D. Beddoe, 'Women between the Wars', in T. Herbert and G. E. Jones (eds), *Wales Between the Wars* (Cardiff, 1988), p. 153.

[64] Margaret Douglas, 'Women, God and Birth-Control, The First Hospital Birth Control Clinic, Abertillery, 1925', *Llafur*, 6 (4) (1995), 110–22.

[65] *Report on Maternal Mortality in Wales (1937)* (PP, 1936–37, XI, Cmd 5423), pp. 367–524, p. 440.

[66] Quoted in Grier, 'Eugencis and Birth Control', 451–2.

[67] This sorry and shocking tale is told with customary erudition by Gareth Williams, 'Compulsory Sterilisation of Welsh Miners, 1936', *Llafur*, 3 (3) (1982), 67–73 (the quotation is on p. 69).

[68] Davies, *Secret Sins*, p. 173.

[69] *Amman Valley Chronicle*, 11 December 1941. I am very grateful to Dr Huw Walters for this reference. On abortion in Wales see Kate Fisher, '"Didn't stop to think I just didn't want another one: the culture of abortion in inter-war South Wales"', in Franz X. Elder, Lesley Hall and Got Hekma (eds), *Sexual Cultures in Europe: Themes in Sexuality* (Manchester, 1999), pp. 213–32.

[70] *Y Frythones*, November 1909, 163.

[71] For an interesting comparison between the 'enslaved' lives of women and the freer lives of servants see Leonore Davidoff, 'Mastered for Life: Servant and Wife in Victorian and Edwardian England', *Journal of Social History*, 7, 4 (1974), 406–28, idem, *Worlds Between: Historical Perspectives in Gender and Class* (Cambridge, 1995), and idem, *The Family Story: Blood, Contract and Intimacy* (London, 1999). In the Welsh context there is a lot of fascinating detail in R. Tudur Jones, 'Daearu'r Angylion: Sylwadau ar Ferched Mewn Llenyddiaeth, 1860–1900', in J. E. Caerwyn Williams (ed.), *Ysgrifau Beirniadol XI* (Dinbych, 1979), pp. 191–226.

[72] On Bohemia see Virginia Nicholson, *Among the Bohemians: Experiments in Living, 1900–1939* (London, 2003); Michael Flocker, *The Hedonism Handbook: Mastering the Lost Arts of Leisure and Pleasure* (London, 2010);

Elizabeth Wilson, *Bohemians: the Glamorous Outcasts* (London, 2007); Dan Frank, *Bohemian Paris: Picasso, Modigliani, Matisse and the Birth of Modern Art* (London, 2003); Jerrold Seigel, *Bohemian Paris: Culture, Politics, and the Boundaries of Bourgeoisie Life, 1830–1930* (London, 1999); and Sue Roe, *In Montmartre: Picasso, Matisse and Modernism in Paris 1900–1910* (London, 2014).

[73]   Gillian Tindall, *Footprints in Paris: a Few Streets, a Few Lives* (London, 2009), p. 137.

[74]   The quotation is from Andrew Sinclair, *Dylan the Bard: A Life of Dylan Thomas* (London, 1999), p. 80. See also Gabriel Summers, Leonie Summers and Jeff Townes, *Dylan Thomas and the Bohemians: the Photographs of Nora Summers* (Cardigan, 2014), and Jeff Townes, *Dylan Thomas: the Pubs* (Talybont, 2013), p. 120.

[75]   Quoted in Davies, *Hope and Heartbreak*, p. 296.

[76]   P. Pullar, *Frank Harris* (London, 1975); Grahame Davies, *Real Wrexham* (Bridgend, 2007), pp. 143–7.

[77]   S. Roth, *The Private Life of Frank Harris* (London, 1931), p. 49; and Frank Harris, *My Life and Loves* (private printing, 1922).

[78]   This is claimed by Hilary Spurling in her review of John Campbell's *If Love Were All: the Story of Frances Stevenson and David Lloyd George* in *The Guardian*, 4 June 2006.

[79]   On Elinor Glyn see J. Hardwick, *Addicted to Romance: the Life and Adventures of Elinor Glyn* (London, 1994); and M. Etherington-Smith and J. Pilcher, *The It Girls: Lucy, Lady Duff Gordon, the Couturière 'Lucile', and Elinor Glyn, Romantic Novelist* (London, 1986).

[80]   On the relationship between Lloyd George and his wife Dame Margaret see the prolific J. Graham Jones's 'Lloyd George and Dame Margaret 1921–1941', *Transactions of Caernarfonshire History Society*, 67 (2006), 98–127. On the seamier and steamier side of Lloyd George's sex life see John Campbell, *If Love Were All: the Story of Frances Stevenson and David Lloyd George* (London, 2006); John Grigg, *The Young Lloyd George* (London, 1973); Don M. Cregier, *Bounder from Wales* (London, 1976); and Ffion Hague, *The Pain and the Privilege: the Women in Lloyd George's Life* (London, 2008). Ruth Longford strives hard to make the case for Frances Stevenson but is not convincing in *Frances, Countess Lloyd George, More than a Mistress* (Leominster, 1996).

[81]   *The Guardian*, 14 June 2008.

[82]   Spencer Vignes, *Lost in France: the Remarkable Life and Death of Leigh Richmond Roose Football's First Playboy* (London, 2007).

[83]   Hazel Walford Davies, *O. M. Edwards* (Llandysul, 1988).

[84]   Mari Emlyn (ed.), *Llythyrau'r Wladfa 1865–1945* (Llanrwst, 2009), p. 160.

[85] Constantine Fitzgibbon, *The Life of Dylan Thomas* (London, 1965), p. 9. There is much valuable material of life in the Bohemia of the 1930s in Constantine Fitzgibbon's *Through the Minefield – An Autobiography* (London, 1967).

[86] Caitlin Thomas, *Double Drink Story: My Life With Dylan Thomas* (London, 1997), p. 79. Her other volume of memoirs *Leftover Life to Kill* (London, 1957) is even angrier.

[87] Denise Hooker, *Nina Hamnett: Queen of Bohemia* (London, 1986), p. 19.

[88] Quoted in William Fifield, *Modigliani, the Biography* (London, 1968), p. 289.

[89] Quoted in Hooker, *Nina Hamnett*, p. 112.

[90] Hooker, *Nina Hamnett*, p. 191.

[91] Jane Ann Jones, *Pererinion a Storïau'r Hen Ferch* (Pen-y-bont ar Ogwr, 2008); for a review see *Barn*, December 2008/January 2009, 60–1.

[92] Lilian Pizzichini, *The Blue Hour: a Portrait of Jean Rhys* (London, 2009), p. 117.

[93] Nicholson, *Among the Bohemians*, pp. 26–30.

[94] Judith Markrell, *Flappers: Six Women of a Dangerous Generation* (London, 2014); D. J. Taylor, *Bright Young People: the Rise and Fall of a Generation 1918–1940* (London, 2008).

[95] *The Independent*, 3 December 1993; *The Guardian*, 3 December 1993.

[96] John Harris, *Goronwy Rees* (Cardiff, 2011), pp. 36, 41 (for his affair with Rosamond Lehmann) and pp. 35–7 (for the affair with Elizabeth Bowen).

[97] Lara Feigel, *The Love Charms of Bombs: Restless Lives in the Second World War* (London, 2014), p. 95. Selina Hastings, *Rosamond Lehmann* (London, 2002).

[98] Alan Pryce-Jones, *The Bonus of Laughter* (London, 1987), p. 205.

[99] Evan Morgan's life story has been well and exhaustively told in William Cross, *Not Behind Lace Curtains: the Hidden World of Evan, Viscount Tredegar* (Newport, 2013); and idem and Monty Dust, *Aspects of Evan, the Last Viscount Tredegar* (Newport, 2013).

[100] Cross, *Not Behind Lace Curtains*, pp. 137, 225.

[101] Mervyn Horder (ed.), *Ronald Firbank: Memoirs and Critiques* (London, 1977), p. 97.

[102] Robin Bryans, *The Dust Has Never Settled* (London, 1992), p. 343.

[103] Cross, *Not Behind Lace Curtains*, pp. 181, 187, 204.

[104] See *www.ruthincastle.co.uk* (accessed 17 July 2015).

[105] J. F. Cone, *Adelina Patti, Queen of Pearls* (London, 1994).

[106] David N. Thomas, *Dylan Remembered Volume One 1914–1934* (Bridgend, 2003), pp. 297–9.

[107] A. J. Toynbee, *Acquaintances* (London, 1967), p. 31.

108 Zachary Leader, *The Life of Kingsley Amis* (London, 2006), p. 18.

109 Malcolm Bullin, 'The Welshness of William Emrys Williams: Strands from a Biography', *Almanac: A Yearbook of Welsh Writing in English: Critical Essays*, 13 (2008–9), 81–109, especially pp. 85–6.

110 Norman Lewis, *Jackdaw Cake* (Harmondsworth, 1985); Julian Evans, *Semi Invisible Man: the Life of Norman Lewis* (London, 2008).

111 Jennet Conant, *The Irregulars: Roald Dahl and the British Spy Ring in Wartime Washington* (London, 2008); *The Sunday Times*, 31 August 2008; see also Donald Sturrock, *Storyteller: the Life of Roald Dahl* (London, 2008).

112 T. Robin Chapman, *W. J. Gruffydd* (Caerdydd, 1993), pp. 137–60; see also the review in *Y Cymro* by Glyn Evans, 14 July 1993.

113 Eluned Phillips, *The Reluctant Redhead* (Llandysul, 2007), p. 67. This autobiography promised much but revealed little. See also Menna Elfyn, *Optimist Absoliwt: Cofiant Eluned Phillips* (Llandysul, 2016).

114 Eluned Phillips, *Dewi Emrys* (Llandysul, 1971), p. 267.

115 Phillips, *Reluctant Redhead*, p. 108.

116 Michael Holroyd, *Augustus John: the New Biography* (London, 1997), pp. 415–16.

117 Andrew Sinclair, *Dylan the Bard: A Life of Dylan Thomas* (London, 1999), p. 180. See also Fitzgibbon, *The Life of Dylan Thomas*.

118 Fitzgibbon, *The Life of Dylan Thomas*, p. 56.

119 Andrew Lycett, *Dylan Thomas: A New Life* (London, 2003), p. 69.

120 Lycett, *Dylan Thomas: A New Life*, p. 245.

121 Lycett, *Dylan Thomas: A New Life*, pp. 136, 178.

122 Caitlin Thomas, *Leftover Life to Kill* (London, 1998), and idem, *Double Drink Story*.

123 Holroyd, *Augustus John*, p. 236.

124 For the effect of a Bohemian upbringing see Romilly John's *The Seventh Child* (London, 1975). Romilly was much teased for considering himself the seventh child when he was, in fact, the sixth. See Nicholson, *Among the Bohemians*, p. 69.

125 Holroyd, *Augustus John*, p. 150.

126 See Sue Roe, *Gwen John: A Life* (London, 2002), pp. 44–6.

127 The obsession with the Bohemians continues. In 2015 the BBC and ITV both had series on them whilst the most recent addition at the time of writing to the Bloomsburian-Bohemian world is Sarah Knights's *Bloomsbury's Outsider: A Life of David Garnett* (London, 2015).

128 D. J. Taylor, *Bright Young People*, p. 225. For Augustus John's reminiscences see *Chiaroscuro* (London, 1952) and *Finishing Touches* (London, 1964).

Notes

7 Religion and Superstition

[1] The quote is from R. B. Jones, *Rent Heavens: the Revival of 1904, Source of its Hidden Springs and Permanent Results* (London, 1931), p. 7. On Richard Owen see W. Pritchard, *Cofiant a Phregethau y Parch. Richard Owen, Y 'Diwygiwr'* (Holyhead, 1889), and *Y Traethodydd* (1888), 296–310. On revivals see David Bebbington, *Victorian Religious Revivals: Culture and Piety in Social and Global Contexts* (Oxford, 2012); John Kent, *Holding the Fort: Studies in Victorian Revivalism* (London, 1978); J. E. Orr, *The Second Evangelical Awakening in Britain* (London, 1949); Janice Holmes, *Religious Revivals in Britain and Ireland, 1859–1905* (Dublin, 2000); and Callum Brown, *Religion and Society in Twentieth Century Britain* (Harlow, 2006).

[2] On the religious revivalistic tradition in Wales see C. B. Turner, 'Revivals and Popular Religion in Victorian and Edwardian Wales' (unpublished PhD, University College of Wales, Aberystwyth, 1971), especially pp. 282–340. If ever a thesis deserved to be published then this is it; the 'Studies in Welsh History' series of the University of Wales Press would be stronger with it. See also G. M. Roberts, 'Y Cyffroadau Mawr', *Y Goleuad*, 24 June, 22 October 1953.

[3] *Y Tyst*, 16 May 1890. Three years later Iolo Caernarfon echoed his call for the Holy Ghost to be more active: 'mae angen i'r Ysbryd Glân i wrthweithio cynydd llygredigaeth yr oes' (there is a need for the Holy Ghost to counteract the increasing corruption of our age), *Y Drysorfa* (1893), 90.

[4] The best history of Welsh religion in this period is R. Tudur Jones, *Ffydd ac Argyfwng Cenedl: Hanes Crefydd yng Nghymru 1890–1914: 1, Prysurdeb a Phryder* (Abertawe, 1981), and idem, *Ffydd ac Argyfwng Cenedl: Hanes Crefydd yng Nghymru 1890–1914: 2, Dryswch a Diwygiad* (Abertawe, 1982). This work has been translated and is available as *Faith and the Crisis of a Nation* (Cardiff, 2004).

[5] The statistics from the denominational yearbooks have been compiled by the indefatigable L. J. Williams in *Digest of Welsh Historical Statistics*, vol. 2 (Cardiff, 1985), pp. 256–354. There is also much detail in the statistical tables and appendices in the *Report of the Royal Commission on the Church of England and Other Religious Bodies in Wales and Monmouthshire*, 1911, Cd 5437, 6 vols.

[6] Quoted in Russell Davies, *Secret Sins: Sex, Violence and Society in Carmarthenshire 1870–1920* (Cardiff, 1995), p. 171.

[7] There are several excellent denominational histories in Wales, see for example T. M. Bassett, *Bedyddwyr Cymru* (Abertawe, 1977), translated

as *Welsh Baptists* (Swansea, 1977); R. Tudur Jones, *Hanes Annibynwyr Cymru* (Abertawe, 1966) and idem, *Yr Undeb: Hanes Undeb yr Annibynwyr Cymreig 1872–1972* (Abertawe, 1975).

8   On the church in Wales see D. T. W. Price, *A History of the Church in Wales in the Twentieth Century* (Cardiff, 1990).

9   On the Unitarians see J. Eric Jones, *The Good Ground* (Llandysul, 2006), and Euros Meredydd Lloyd, *Datblygiad Undodiaeth y Smotyn Du* (unpublished MPhil, Aberystwyth University, 2008).

10   *Y Cymro*, 15 July 1933. On the persistence of anti-Catholicism see Trystan Owain Hughes, 'Anti-Catholicism in Wales 1900–1960', *Journal of Ecclestial History*, 53, 2 (2002), 312–25; and idem, *Winds of Change: the Roman Catholic Church and Society in Wales 1916–62* (Cardiff, 1999). On Catholic immigration into Wales see Paul O'Leary, *Immigration and Integration: the Irish in Wales* (Cardiff, 2000), pp. 95–100, 306–7.

11   On Saunders Lewis's conversion to Catholicism see T. Robin Chapman, *Un Bywyd o Blith Nifer: Cofiant Saunders Lewis* (Llandysul, 2006), pp. 119–20, 163–6, 282–3, 327–9.

12   *Seren Gomer* (1899), 131.

13   *Y Diwygiwr* (1901), 6.

14   Quoted in Russell Davies, *People, Places and Passions: Pain and Pleasure: A Social History of Wales and the Welsh, 1870–1945* (Cardiff, 2015), p. 274.

15   *Y Drysorfa* (1899), 282.

16   R. S. Thomas coined the phrase. For an excellent synopsis of the history of religion in modern Wales see D. Densil Morgan, *Cedyrn Canrif: Crefydd a Chymdeithas yng Nghymru'r Ugeinfed Ganrif* (Caerdydd, 2001), and idem, *The Span of the Cross: Christian Religion and Society in Wales*, 2nd edn (Cardiff, 2011). See also Robert Pope, *Codi Muriau Dinas Duw: Anghydffurfwyr ac Anghydffurfiaeth Cymru'r Ugeinfed Ganrif* (Bangor, 2005), and idem, *Building Jerusalem: Nonconformity, Labour and the Social Question in Wales, 1906–1936* (Cardiff, 1998).

17   On humour in Daniel Owen see Glyn Tegai Hughes, *Daniel Owen a Natur y Nofel* (Mold, 1991); and Ioan Williams, *Capel a Chomin: Astudiaeth o Ffug-chwedlau Pedwar Llenor Fictoraidd* (Caerdydd, 1989).

18   On the religious artistic tradition in Wales see John Harvey *The Art of Piety: the Visual Culture of Welsh Nonconformity* (Cardiff, 1995) and idem *Image of the Invisible: the Visualisation of Religion in the Welsh Nonconformist Tradition* (Cardiff, 1999). See also Peter Lord, *The Visual Culture of Wales: Imaging the Nation* (Cardiff, 2000) and idem *The Visual Culture of Wales: Industrial Society* (Cardiff, 1998). See also Martin O'Kane and John Morgan-Guy *Biblical Art from Wales* (Sheffield, 2010).

[19] On Edward Burne-Jones see Fiona MacCarthy, *The Last Pre-Raphaelite: Edward Burne-Jones and the Victorian Imagination* (London, 2011), and Alistair Carew-Cox, *Edward Burne-Jones: Stained Glass in Birmingham* (London, 1998).

[20] T. J. Morgan, *Diwylliant Gwerin* (Llandysul, 1972), and Huw Walters, *Canu'r Pwll a'r Pulpud* (Abertawe, 1987) are valuable studies of the breadth of the cultural life of Welsh religion.

[21] On chapel architecture see Anthony L. Jones, *Welsh Chapels* (Stroud, 1996); and D. Huw Owen, *Capeli Cymru* (Talybont, 2005), and idem *The Chapels of Wales* (Bridgend, 2011).

[22] R. W. Dale, *Life and Letters of John Angell James* (London, 1961), p. 60.

[23] E. T. Davies, *Religion in the Industrial Revolution in South Wales* (Cardiff, 1965), p. 148.

[24] *Carmarthen Weekly Reporter*, 5 December 1902.

[25] *Carmarthen Weekly Reporter*, 17 April 1903.

[26] Gwyn Thomas, *A Welsh Eye* (London, 1964), pp. 122–3.

[27] On church building see Ieuan Gwynedd Jones, *Communities: Essays in the Social History of Victorian Wales* (Llandysul, 1987), especially for church building in Flintshire, north Cardiganshire, Llanrhystud, Aberystwyth and Aberdare; idem, *Religion and Politics: the Rebuilding of St Michael's Church, Aberystwyth and its Political Consequences* (Aberystwyth, 1973); idem *Mid-Victorian Wales: the Observers and the Observed* (Cardiff, 1985); and idem, *Explorations and Explanations Essays in the Social History of Victorian Wales* (Llandysul, 1981), especially chapter 1: denominationalism in Caernarfonshire (pp. 17–52) and chapter 2: denominationalism in Swansea and district (pp. 53–82).

[28] For the R. T. Jenkins quote see *Y Llenor*, Spring, 1939.

[29] On the crisis in preaching see Jones, *Ffydd ac Argyfwng Cenedl*, vol. 1, pp. 86–121. There are some very barbed, bitchy comments about the capabilities of some preachers in R. A. Griffith et al., *The Welsh Pulpit: Diverse Notes and Opinions* (London, 1894).

[30] Jones, *Ffydd ac Argyfwng Cenedl*, vol. 1, p. 144.

[31] On the musical traditions of Wales see Gareth Williams, *Valleys of Song: Music and Society in Wales, 1840–1914* (Cardiff, 2003); and idem, 'How's the Tenors in Dowlais?': the Choral Culture of the South Wales Coalfield', *Transactions of the Honourable Society of Cymmrodorion*, 11 (2004), 170–88. On the danger of religion becoming too involved in entertainment see Dominic Erdozain, *The Problem of Pleasure: Sport, Recreation and the Crisis of Victorian Religion* (Woodbridge, 2010).

[32] Rhidian Griffiths and Alun Roberts, 'O! Ganu Bendigedig', *Y Traethodydd*, July 2011; *Western Mail*, 9 December 1940.

33 On the general impact of hymns see Ian Bradley, *Abide with Me: the World of Victorian Hymns* (London, 1997); see also Lionel Adey, *Hymns and the Christian 'Myth'* (Vancouver, 1986). In the Welsh context there is still much of value in H. Elvet Lewis, *Sweet Singers of Wales: a Story of Welsh Hymns and their Authors: With Original Translations* (London, 1889).

34 Huw Williams, *Canu'r Bobol* (Dinbych, 1978), and E. Wyn James, *Dechrau Canu: Rhai Emynau Mawr a'u Cefndir* (Pen-y-bont ar Ogwr, 1987).

35 J. E. Jones, *Ieuan Gwyllt: ei Fywyd, ei Lafur, ei Athrylith, ei Nodweddion a'i Ddylanwad ar Gymru* (Treffynnon, 1881); J. Owen, *Traethawd ar Fywyd ac Athrylith y Parchedig John Roberts (Ieuan Gwyllt)* (Pwllheli, 1879).

36 Williams, *Valleys of Song*, p. 121.

37 Ken Llewellyn, *Disaster at Tynewydd: an Account of the Rhondda Mine Disaster in 1877* (Bridgend, 1992). See also chapter 2 above.

38 Richard Holmes, *'Tommy': The British Soldier on the Western Front, 1914–1918* (London, 2005), pp. 502–4.

39 C. H. Dudley Ward, *History of the Welsh Guards* (London, 1920), p. 393.

40 Quoted in Davies, *People, Places and Passions*, pp. 294–5.

41 *Cambria Daily Leader*, 12 March 1920.

42 Edwin C. Lewis, *Mil a Mwy o Ddyfyniadau* (Llandysul, 2007), p. 259.

43 D. Gwenallt Jones, 'Y Capel yn Sir Gaerfyrddin', *Gwreiddiau* (Llandysul, 1975), p. 41.

44 Laura Schwartz, *Infidel Feminism: Secularism and Women's Emancipation, England 1830–1914* (Mancheter, 2012).

45 Quoted in Davies, *People, Places and Passions*, p. 239.

46 Rosina Davies, *The Story of My Life* (Llandysul, 1942), pp. 27, 31. Although she laboured in a 'man's world' of religion, Rosina did reserve herself one feminine prerogative, this lady did not disclose her date of birth in her autobiography.

47 Edith Picton-Tubervill, *Life is Good: An Autobiography* (London, 1939), p. 83. The title of the autobiography and the year of publication appear, with hindsight, to be somewhat ironic.

48 On these points see Sue Morgan and Jacqueline de Vries, *Women, Gender and Religious Cultures in Britain, 1900–1940* (Abingdon, 2010), and Jennifer Lloyd *Women and the Shaping of British Methodism: Persistent Preachers, 1807–1907* (Manchester, 2010).

49 For a few autobiographies and biographies of these figures see T. M. Rees, *Seth Joshua and Frank Joshua* (Wrexham, 1926); W. Morris, *Deg o Enwogion* (Abertawe, 1965); W. Nantlais Williams, *Y Deugain Mlynedd Hyn* (Rhydaman, 1921); Davies, *The Story of My Life*; E. Morgan

Humphreys, *Gwŷr Enwog Gynt* (Aberystwyth, 1953). On conversion see Peter Mullen, *Strange Gifts? A guide to Christian Renewal* (Oxford, 1984).

50 On the international reach of the revival see Noel Gibbard, *On the Wings of a Dove: the International Effects of the 1904–05 Revival* (Bridgend, 2002). The revival reached France, Germany, Norway, Sweden, Denmark, Russia, Holland, the USA, Argentina, Patagonia, the West Indies, South Africa, Madagascar, India, China, Korea, Manchuria, Japan, Australia, New Zealand, and an estimated eighty-six other countries around the world. See also Mrs John Roberts, *The Revival in the Khasia Hills* (Caernarfon, 1906).

51 There are several histories of the revival, see for example T. Francis, *Y Diwygiad a'r Diwygwyr: Hanes Toriad Gwawr Diwygiad 1904–05* (Dolgellau, 1906); J. Vyrnwy Morgan, *The Welsh Religious Revival 1904–05 a Retrospect and a Criticism* (London, 1909); S. Evans and G. M. Roberts, *Cyfrol Goffa Diwygiad 1904–05* (Caernarfon, 1954) – this includes an useful bibliography; Eifion Evans, *The Welsh Revival of 1904* (Bridgend, 1969); W. T. Stead, *The Revival in the West* (London, 1905); M. Holyoak, *The Afterglow: Gleanings from the Welsh Revival* (London, 1907); Awstin, *The Religious Revival in Wales*, six pamphlets (Cardiff, 1904–5); H. Fleming, *The Story of the Welsh Revival* (New York, NY, 1905); Geraint Fielder, *Grace, Grit and Gumption: Spiritual Revival in South Wales* (Bridgend, 2000); John Gwynfor Jones, 'Ebychiad Mawr Olaf Anghydffufiaeth yng Nghymru', *Transactions of the Honourable Society of Cymmrodorion*, II (2005), 105–43; Noel Gibbard, *Fire on the Altar: A History and Evaluation of the 1904–05 Revival in Wales* (Bridgend, 2005); C. R. Williams, 'The Welsh Religious Revival of 1904', *British Journal of Sociology*, 3 (1953), 242–59. By far the best accounts are Jones *Ffydd ac Argyfwng Cenedl*, vol. 2, pp. 122–228, and the contemporary works of Henri Bois, *Le Reveil au Pays de Galles* (Toulouse, 1905), and J. Rogues de Fursac, *Un Movement Mystique Contemporain: Le Reveil Religieux du Pays de Galles 1904–1905* (Paris, 1907).

52 For a few local studies see Constance L. Maynard, *Between College Terms* (London, 1910); Richard Matthews, 'Diwygiad 1094–05', in Hugh Owen (ed.), *Braslun o Hanes M.C. Môn* (Liverpool, 1937); H. Elvet Lewis, *With Christ Amongst the Miners* (London, 1906); R. Mills, *Y Diwygiad yn Rhosllanerchrugog* (Rhosllanerchrugog, 1905). There is an interesting timeline for some areas on the website *www.churchmodel.org.uk/Timeline2W04.pdf* by John Hayward (accessed 21 January 2016).

[53] On the revival in Carmarthenshire see Davies, *Secret Sins: Sex, Violence and Society in Carmarthenshire 1870–1920*, pp. 193–210; for the events in Cardiganshire see David Jenkins, *The Agricultural Community in South-West Wales at the Turn of the Twentieth Century* (Cardiff, 1971), pp. 219–79.

[54] On Jessie Penn-Lewis see Mary Garrard, *Mrs Penn-Lewis: A Memoir* (The Shoals, Indiana, 2014); Brynmor Pierce Jones, *Jessie Penn-Lewis* (London, 2002). For Evan Roberts's theology see Robert Pope, 'Evan Roberts in Theological Context', *Transactions Honourable Society of Cymmrodorion*, II (2005), 144–69. See also Karen Lowe, *Carriers of Fire: the Women of the Welsh Revival of 1904–05* (Llanelli, 2004).

[55] Awstin, *The Religious Revival in Wales*, p. 17.

[56] *Llais Llyfrau* (Hydref, 1995).

[57] D. M. Phillips's *Evan Roberts a'i Waith* (Dolgellau, 1912) is still the best biography. There is also much of value in Idrisyn, *Y Diwygiad a'r Diwygiwr: Taith Gyntaf Evan Roberts* (Caerdydd, 1905); A. Sheldrick, *Evan Roberts: An Examination an Appreciation and a Vindication* (London, 1905); and a contemporary eyewitness account with a rather premature title, J. Tudor Rees, *Evan Roberts His Life and Work* (London, 1905).

[58] See for example works such as Morgan, *The Welsh Religious Revival 1904–05 a Retrospect and a Criticism*; Thomas Jones, *Yr Adfywiad a'i Wersi* (Caerdydd, 1906); T. Pritchard, *Y Diwygiad a'r Hyn a Ddylai ei Ddilyn* (Rhosllanerchrugog, 1906); Henry Jones, *Y Diwygiad: A'r Hyn a All Ddod Ohono* (Caernarfon, 1905); and Ilsley W. Charlton, *The Revival in Wales: Some Facts and Some Lessons* (London, 1905).

[59] For a superb study see the comments on Evan Roberts and the revival see M. Wynn Thomas, *In the Shadow of the Pulpit: Literature and Non-conformist Wales* (Cardiff, 2010). See also Robert Pope, 'Demythologising the Evan Roberts Revival, 1904–05', *Journal of Ecclesiastical History*, 3 (2006), pp. 515–34. See also D. I. Davies, 'Y Darlun o'r Weinidogaeth yn Llenyddiaeth Cymru: Astudiaeth o Weinidogion a Chlerigwyr yn y Nofel, y Ddrama ac mewn Barddoniaeth o 1750 hyd 1950' (unpublished MA, University of Swansea, 1966).

[60] Rhys Davies, *The Withered Root* (London, 1927), p. 115.

[61] For a study of Rhys Davies's novel see Stephen Knight, 'On Strong Ground: Rhys Davies's *The Withered Root* (1927)', in Katie Gramich (ed.), *Mapping the Territory: Critical Approaches to Welsh Fiction in English* (Cardigan, 2010), pp. 11–34. For other novels set in and around the revival see Max Bearing, *A Prophet of Wales: a Novel of the Welsh Revival* (London, 1905); and W. Margam Jones, *The Stars of the Revival* (London, 1910). See also Katie Gramich, 'Dehongli'r Diwygiad: Ymateb Awduron Cymreig i Ddiwygiad 1904–05', *Taliesin*, 128 (2006), 12–28.

[62] Davies, *Secret Sins: Sex, Violence and Society in Carmarthenshire, 1870–1920*, p. 194.

[63] Jones, *Ffydd ac Argyfwng Cenedl*, vol. 2, p. 170. On the effects of the highly influential Keswick missions see J. C. Pollock, *The Keswick Story: The Authorised History of the Keswick Convention* (London, 1964).

[64] Davies, *Secret Sins: Sex, Violence and Society in Carmarthenshire, 1870–1920*, p. 194. On the efforts of such meetings see Anthropos, *Perlau'r Diwygiad: sef Perl-ddywediadau am y Cyfarfod Gweddi, y Seiat Brofiad, y Pulpud* (Caernarfon, 1906).

[65] Jenkins, *The Agricultural Community in South-West Wales*, p. 196.

[66] Jenkins, *The Agricultural Community in South-West Wales*, p. 196.

[67] *Y Geninen* (1909), 157; my translation.

[68] Davies, *Secret Sins: Sex, Violence and Society in Carmarthenshire 1870–1920*, p. 196.

[69] David Davies, *Reminiscences of My Country and People* (Cardiff, 1925), p. 61.

[70] *Western Mail*, 31 January 1905.

[71] T. M. Rees, *Seth and Frank Joshua: the Renowned Evangelists* (Wrexham, 1925), p. 5

[72] H. Elvet Lewis, *With Christ Amongst the Miners* (London, 1905), p. 180.

[73] *Y Goleuad*, 16 December 1964; my translation.

[74] *South Wales Daily News*, 26 November 1904. On the earlier sightings at previous revivals see T. Gwyn Jones, *Welsh Folk Life and Folk-Culture* (London, 1930), pp. 49–50. For other phenomena (angelic voices) see *South Wales Daily News*, 26 November 1904, and *South Wales Daily News*, 10 December 1904. On speaking in tongues see Cyril G. Williams, 'Glossolalia as a religious phenomenon: "Tongues" at Corinth and Pentecost', *Religion*, 5 (1), (1975), 16–32, and idem, *Tongues of the Spirit: Study of Pentecostal Glossolalia and Related Phenomena* (Cardiff, 1981). See also Rene Noorbergen, *Glossolalia: Sweet Sounds of Ecstasy* (London, 1973).

[75] Phillips, *Evan Roberts a'i Waith*, p. 221.

[76] *South Wales Daily News*, 26 November 1904.

[77] *South Wales Daily News*, 1 December 1904.

[78] *South Wales Daily News*, 17 January 1905.

[79] *South Wales Daily News*, 6 February, 21 February, 2 March 1905.

[80] *South Wales Daily News*, 2 March 1905.

[81] J. T. Job in T. Francis, *Y Diwygiad a'r Diwygiad: Hanes Toriad Gwawr Diwygiad 1904–5* (Dolgellau, 1906), pp. 217, 219.

[82] *Y Drysorfa*, March 1905, 118.

[83] G. G. Johnson, 'A Centenary Celebration for Pastor Daniel Powell Williams 1882–1982', *Riches of Grace*, 6 (51) (May 1982), 68–9; see also

Rees Evans, *Precious Jewels from the 1904 Revival in Wales* (London, 1910); Thomas Napier Turnbull, *Brothers in Arms* (London, 1963); and idem, *What God Hath Wrought: a Short History of the Apostolic Church* (Pen-y-groes, 1959). On Pentecostalism in general see David Martin, *Pentecostalism: the World Their Parish* (Oxford, 2002); and Allan Anderson, *An Introduction to Pentecostalism: Global Charismatic Christianity* (London, 2014).

[84] *South Wales Daily News*, 12 April 1906.

[85] *South Wales Daily News*, 14 April 1906.

[86] *South Wales Daily News*, 12 April 1906. Evan Roberts was attributed with similar attributes. See Jones, *Ffydd ac Argyfwng Cenedl*, vol. 2, pp. 137–9.

[87] *Carmarthen Weekly Reporter*, 19 April 1906.

[88] *Carmarthen Weekly Reporter*, 19 April 1906.

[89] *Carmarthen Weekly Reporter*, 19 April 1906. Brynmor Thomas, later minister of Milo (Carmel) and Mynydd Seion Pen-y-groes, two chapels profoundly moved by the revival, recalled Sarah Jones in the revial meetings: 'Weithiau cerddai'n araf, arall yn ôl a blaen ar hyd ale'r capel gyda'r ystum o fam yn magu'i baban. Yr argraff a gai'r gynulleidfa oedd y Fendigaid Fair yn magu'r Iesu. Siaradai ag ef yn ôl dull mam yn siarad â'i hanwylyd bach gyntafanedig. Canai'n dawel iddo, a'i alw'n "Anwylyd y Tad", "Rhosyn Saron", "Lili'r Dyffrynnoedd", "Eneiniog yr Arglwydd" ' (Sometimes she would walk slowly, other times she would walk down the aisle with gestures of a mother holding a baby. The impression the congregation had was of Mary cradling the infant Jesus. She talked in the tones of a mother addressing her dearest first-born child. She sang quietly to him and called him "Father's Dearest", "Rose of Sharon", the "Lily of the Valley", the "Anointed of the Lord"). Brynmor Thomas, *Llwybrau Llafur* (Abertawe, 1970), p. 96. For more on Sarah Jones see Jones, *Ffydd ac Argyfwng Cenedl*, vol. 2, p.187, ff.123.

[90] *South Wales Daily News*, 18 and 21 April 1906.

[91] *South Wales Daily News*, 21 April 1906.

[92] *South Wales Daily News*, 13 April 1906. He continued with warnings against spiritualism and mesmerism, and 'strong delusions', which were becoming increasingly powerful.

[93] *Western Mail*, 5 June 1906; *Carmarthen Weekly Reporter*, 8 June 1906. See Davies, *Secret Sins: Sex, Violence and Society in Carmarthenshire 1870–1920*, pp. 100–1.

[94] These cases are taken from the excellent website *www.madnessofnorthwales. com/case-notes* (accessed 14 October 2015). See also S. C. Linden,

M. Harris, C. Whitaker and D. Healy, 'Religion and Psychosis: the effects of the Welsh Religious Revival in 1904–05', *Psychological Medicine*, 40 (8) (2010), 1317–23.

[95] On Caradog Prichard see Menna Baines, *Yng Ngolau'r Lleuad: Ffaith a Dychymyg yng Ngwaith Caradog Prichard* (Llandysul, 2005); and Alan Llwyd, *Rhyfel a Gwrthryfel: Brwydr Moderniaeth a Beirdd Modern* (Llandybïe, 2003), pp. 186–292.

[96] There is much valuable information on Mary Jones and the Egryn lights on the website *www.inamidst.com/lights/egryn* (accessed 14 October 2015).

[97] *Daily Mirror*, 10, 13, 14, 15, 17 February and 6, 14, 21 April 1905.

[98] Davies, *Secret Sins: Sex, Violence and Society in Carmarthenshire, 1870–1920*, p. 209.

[99] D. P. Williams, *Souvenir: The Apostolic Church Commemorating the Opening of the Apostolic Temple* (Llanelli, 1913), p. 9. People in Carmarthenshire continued to witness remarkable visions well after the stories of 1904–6 abated. On 1 July 1915, at the Lakefield Mission Room, Llanelli, massive crowds gathered when a vision of 'the man of Sorrows' appeared on the wall. More than 100 converts were claimed and several spoke in tongues. One of them wrote in the *South Wales Press* with a conviction that was common to them all: 'Do not run away with the idea that we were deceived by a little dampness on the wall; what we saw was a reality. We saw the face of Christ whether you believe it or not.' (*South Wales Press*, 15 July 1914). See also *South Wales Press*, 14 March 1914, and *Cambria Daily Leader*, 29 July 1914. For later scenes of revival activity in the Park Place Mission see *South Wales Press*, 31 December 1919.

[100] Percy Bysshe Shelley, *The Poems of Shelley*, ed. Geoffrey Matthews and Kelvin Everest, vol. 1 (London, 1989), p. 79.

[101] Robert Darnton, *Mesmerism and the End of the Enlightenment* (Cambridge, Mass., 1968); Derek Forrest, *Hypnotism: A History* (Harmondsworth, 2000); David De Giustino, *Conquest of Mind: Phrenology and Victorian Social Thought* (London, 1975); Alison Winter, *Mesmerized: Powers of Mind in Victorian Britain* (London, 1998); Arthur Conan Doyle, *The History of Spiritualism* (London, 1926).

[102] Ronald Pearsall, *The Table-Rappers: the Victorians and the Occult* (London, 2004), pp. 9–11. Robert Owen, *The Life of Robert Owen by Himself* (London, 1857); G. D. H. Cole, *Robert Owen* (London, 1925), p. 271–7. See also Phillip Hoare, *England's Lost Eden: Adventures in Victorian Utopia* (London, 2005), pp. 136, 350–7.

[103] Hoare, *England's Lost Eden*, pp. 136, 350–7.

[104] Owen, *The Life of Robert Owen by Himself*; Cole, *Robert Owen*, pp. 271–7.

[105] For the denigration of Alfred Russel Wallace's reputation see Roy Davies, *The Darwin Conspiracy: the Origins of a Scientific Crime* (Golden Square Books, private, no place of publication, 2008). See also Ted Benton, *Alfred Russel Wallace: A Thinker for Our Own Times?* (Manchester, 2013). There is a wealth of material on the website *www.wallacefund. info* (accessed 13 March 2015) established to mark the centenary of Wallace's death. See also Alfred Russel Wallace, *The World of Life* (London, 1911), p. 279.

[106] Quoted in Antonio Melechi, *Servants of the Supernatural: the Night Side of the Victorian Mind* (London, 2009), p. 169.

[107] Alfred Russel Wallace, *On Miracles and Modern Spiritualism: Three Essays* (London, 1875), pp. 190–1; one essay on 'Spiritualism and Human Evolution' is published in Jane R. Camerivi, *The Alfred Russel Wallace Reader: a Selection of Writings from the Field* (Baltimore, Md., 2002), pp. 163–87.

[108] On this theme see Roger Clarke, *A Natural History of Ghosts: 500 Years of Hunting for Proof* (London, 2012).

[109] On spirit photography see John Harvey, 'Revival, Revisions, Visions and Visitations: the Resurgence and Imaging of Supernatural Religion, 1850–1940', *Welsh History Review*, 23 (2) (2006), 78, 86–92.

[110] Louie Harris, *They Walked Amongs Us* (London, 1980).

[111] Harry Edwards, *The Mediumship of Jack Webber* (London, n.d.). Edwards was himself a talented medium who could heal the sick.

[112] On her mediumship see G. W. Balfour, 'Some Recent Scripts Affording Evidence of Personal Survival', *Proceedings Psychical Society*, 27, 49 (1914). See also *www.survivalafterdeath.org* – 'the Willet Scripts' (accessed 14 March 2007). See also Peter Lord, 'Winifred Coombe Tennant: "Bridging Worlds" ', *Planet* (October/November 2007), 32–45.

[113] Doris Stokes, *Voices in My Ear* (London, 1980). Doris Stokes published another seven volumes of ghost-written autobiography/biography each with 'voices' in its title.

[114] Norman Lewis, *Jackdaw Cake* (Harmondsworth, 1986), pp. 1–17.

[115] For spiritualism in Llandysul see *Cardigan and Tivyside Advertiser*, 3 June 1903. Dr Charles Williams attended several séances in south Wales. He claimed that the spiritualism movement was widespread in the area, with local libraries stocking its magazine; see Charles Williams, *Spiritualism: Its True Nature and Results* (London, 1910), p. 41. Harry Edwards, *The Mediumship of Jack Webber* (London, 1940?), pp. 38–9.

[116] Jessie Penn-Lewis, *The War on the Saints* (Leicester, 1912), pp. 7–8. See also idem, *The Leading of the Lord: A Spiritual Autobiography* (London, 1903).

[117] R. B. Jones, *Spiritism in Bible Light: A Series of Addresses* (Cardiff, 1920), p. iii.

[118] Robert Graves, *Goodbye to All That* (Harmondsworth, 1983).

[119] *Cambrian Daily Leader*, 5 November 1918.

[120] *South Wales Press*, 19 September 1917.

[121] *The Times*, 27 September 1999.

[122] Andrew Lycett, *Dylan Thomas: a New Life* (London, 2005), p. 232.

[123] On the history of poltergeists see Roger Clarke, *A Natural History of Ghosts* (London, 2012), pp. 270–310. Owen Davies, *The Haunted: the Social History of Ghosts* (London, 2007). In the Welsh context see the excellent study by J. Towyn Jones, *Rhag Ofn Ysbrydion: Chwilio am y Gwir am Straeon Ysbryd* (Aberystwyth, 2008), pp. 95–120.

[124] The story is related in Gomer M. Roberts, 'Ysbrydion', *Y Geninen*, 27, 3 (1977), 130–2. There are many interesting anecdotes in the highly entertaining memoir by J. Aelwyn Roberts, *Holy Ghostbuster: A Parson's Encounter With the Paranormal* (E. Clement Books, 1996).

[125] For an eyewitness account of the Kidwelly ghost in action see *South Wales Press*, 24 January and 7, 21 and 28 February 1917. See also *Western Mail* 7 and 21 February 1917. On the activities of ghost hunters such as J. Arthur Hill see Deborah Blum, *Ghost Hunters: William James and the Search for Scientific Proof of Life After Death* (London, 2007), and Peter Lamont, *The First Psychic: The Peculiar Mystery of a Notorious Victorian Wizard* (London, 2006), and Joanna Timms, 'Ghost-Hunters and Psychical Research in Interwar England', *History Workshop Journal*, 74 (2012), 88–104.

[126] For Adeleina Patti's ghost see Ann Shaw and Carole Reeves, *The Children of Craig-y-Nos: Life in a Welsh Tuberculosis Sanatorium, 1922–1959* (Milton Keynes, 2009), p. 16.

[127] See Richard Holland, *Haunted Wales: a Survey of Welsh Ghostlore* (Ashbourne, 2005); Peter Underworld, *The Ghosts of Wales* (Llandybïe, 1978); and Margaret R. Shanahan, 'Ghosts of Glamorgan', *Port Talbot Historical Society Transactions* (1963), 32–44. The publications by South Wales Paranormal Research are valuable; see for example *Haunted Cardiff and the Valleys* (Stroud, 2007); *Haunted Newport and the Valleys* (Stroud, 2010); and *Haunted Swansea and Beyond* (Stroud, 2008).

[128] Elias Owen, 'Folk-Lore, Superstition or What-Not in Montgomeryshire and Elsewhere', *Montgomeryshire Collections*, XXIXX (1896), 68–74.

[129] *Y Gofdail Fethodistaidd*, III (1884), 387. For a discussion on angels in Wales see R. Tudur Jones's superb article 'Hapus Dyrfa: Nefoedd Oes

Victoria' in J. E. Caerwyn Williams (ed.), *Ysgrifau Beirniadol* (Dinbych, 1976), pp. 236–77. On angels see H. Desroches, *Jacob and the Angel: An Essay in the Sociology of Religion* (Cambridge, Mass., 1973); and David Albert Jones, *Angels: A Very Short Introduction* (Oxford, 2011); A. Walsham and P. Marshall, *Angels in the Early Modern World* (Cambridge, 2006); and Henry Mayer-Harting, *Perceptions of Angels in History* (Oxford, 1998).

[130] Frank Richards, *Old Soldiers Never Die* (Eastbourne, n.d. [1964?]), p. 19.

[131] See James Hayward, *Myths and Legends of the First World War* (Stroud, 2002). Interestingly the myths and legends of the Second World War do not have the supernatural aspects as did those that circulated in the First World War. See idem, *Myths and Legends of the Second World War* (Stroud, 2006).

[132] David Clarke, *The Angel of Mons: Phantom Soldiers and Ghostly Guardians* (Chichester, 2005).

[133] On the atmosphere of paranoia see Davies, *People, Places and Passions*, pp. 275–86.

[134] This was published as Arthur Machen, *'The Angel of Mons': The Bowmen and other Legends of the War* (London, 1915). The title indicates that, despite his denials, even Machen was prepared to give the angels precedence over archers. Perhaps when you suddenly have a bestseller it is best to swim with the tide. For a biography see Mark Valentine, *Arthur Machen* (Bridgend, 1995). Machen did receive considerable criticism. See for example the outraged reactions in Harold Begbie, *On the Side of the Angels: The Story of the Angels at Mons, an Answer to 'The Bowmen'* (London, 1915).

[135] Robert Graves had a similar but much less well-known story to Arthur Machen's 'The Bowmen' entitled 'The Legion'. In the story he imagines a legendary Greek legion as a metaphor for his own in France. See Norman Vance, *The Victorians and Ancient Greece* (Oxford, 1997), pp. 122–3. Arthur Machen also tried to recreate his earlier success in a story 'Drake's Drum', which had the Elizabethan sailor appear at the naval battle of Scappa Flow.

[136] Quoted in Davies, *People, Places and Passions*, p. 286.

[137] Clarke, *The Angel of Mons*, pp. 163–4.

[138] Quoted in Father Ignatius, *Mission Sermons and Orations* (London, 1886).

[139] On Father Ignatius see D. Attwater, *Father Ignatius of Llanthony* (London, 1931), and A. Calder-Marshall, *The Enthusiast* (London, 1962). See also 'The Apparitions at Llanthony', *Brycheiniog*, XIX (1980–1).

140 For contemporary studies of Welsh fairies see W. Jenkyn Thomas, *The Welsh Fairy Book* (London, 1912); P. H. Emerson, *Welsh Fairy Tales and Other Stories* (London, 1894); idem, *Tales from Welsh Wales, Founded on Fact and Current Tradition* (London, 1894); and Joseph Jacobs, *Celtic Fairy Tales* ([1891]; reprinted London 1970); and John Owen Huws, *Y Tylwyth Teg* (Llanrwst, 1987).

141 Wirt Sikes, *British Goblins: Welsh Folk Lore, Fairy Mythology, Legends and Traditions* (Boston, 1881), p. 2.

142 Jonathan Caredig Davies, *Folk Lore of West and Mid Wales* (Aberystwyth, 1911), p. 148.

143 Byron Rogers, *The Bank Manager and the Holy Grail* (London, 2005), p. 5.

144 Rogers, *The Bank Manager and the Holy Grail*, p. 10.

145 For the photographs see Hilary Woolen and Alistair Crawford, *John Thomas, 1838–1905 Photographer* (Llandysul, 1977), pp. 15, 40. See also Juliette Wood, 'Filming Fairies: Popular Film, Audience Response and Meaning in Contemporary Fairy Lore', *Folklore*, 117 (2006), 279–96.

146 For several tales of the impact of fairies on humanity see Jonathan Ceredig Davies, *Folk-Lore of West and Mid-Wales* (Aberystwyth, 1911), pp. 88–147. The fairies even played football against the inhabitants of Caio and Pencarreg. For valuable insights into fairy tales see A. S. Byatt, 'The Wild Ones', *The Guardian*, 24 November 2007.

147 John Rhŷs, *Celtic Folklore: Welsh and Manx*, vol. 11 (London, 1907), pp. 160–1. He also adds that a mermaid was reportedly caught off Fishguard in 1858, adding another element to the supernatural maritime fauna of Wales. See also Marie Curtis, *The Antiquities of Laugharne, Pendine and their Neighbourhoods* (London, 1880), p. 216.

148 St Fagans National Museum of History in St Fagans has a remarkable series of interviews with eyewitnesses who saw the fairies. William John Jones, Drws-y-Coed, near Beddgelert, in an interview recorded on 16 August 1974, recalled as a terrified child he and his brother: 'We saw the fairies dancing round the stone – little things dressed in the daintiest many-coloured clothes you ever saw. They were like a garden of flowers . . . We were frightened in the most awful way, afraid to disturb them, so we were quiet as mice. Grandfather had warned us that if we showed ourselves . . . we would vanish.' Considering his fear, the interviewee concludes with remarkable understatement: 'As I grow older I think a lot about these pleasant things'. St Fagans MWL4367 (recorded 16 August, 1974). D. Rhys Phillips claimed that the Vale of Neath was the 'Home of the Fairies' in *History of the Vale of Neath* (private printing, 1925), p. 572.

149 See the detailed arguments in Ronald Hutton, 'Witch Hunting in Celtic Societies', *Past and Present*, 212 (2011), 43–71.

150 See most notably J. Gwynn Williams, 'Witchcraft in Seventeenth-Century Flintshire', *Flintshire Historical Society Transactions*, xxvi (1973–4), 16–33l, and xxvii (1875–6), 5–35; Geraint H. Jenkins, 'Popular Beliefs in Wales from the Restoration to Methodism', *Bulletin Board of Celtic Studies*, xxvii (1977), 70–99, and Richard Suggett, *A History of Magic and Witchcraft in Wales* (Stroud, 2008).

151 See for example William Butler Yeats, 'Irish Fairies, Ghosts, Witches . . .', in *Unsolved Prose* by W. B. Yeats, ed. John P. Frayne (London, 1970), pp. 130–7; and Éilis Ni Dhuibhne, '"The Old Woman as Hare": Structure and Meaning in an Irish Legend', *Folklore*, civ (1993), 17–31. For an influential and insightful study of witchcraft in communities see E. E. Evans-Pritchard, *Witchcraft, Oracles and Magic among the Azande* (Oxford, 1937).

152 For a mystic national identity see the sub-section 'Weird Wales' in chapter 4 above. See also Katie Trumpener, *Bardic Nationalism: the Romantic Novel and the British Empire* (Princeton, NJ, 1997).

153 On Mary Webb's mysticism see G. M. Coles, *The Flower of Light: A Biography of Mary Webb* (London, 1978), and G. M. Coles, *Mary Webb* (London, 1990). On Hilda Vaughan see C. W. Newman, *Hilda Vaughan* (Bridgend, 1981).

154 Mark Valentine, *Arthur Machen* (Bridgend, 1995), p. 46. Machen's dark stories are rivalled by *The House on the Borderland* (1908), a work of theosophical horror by the fabulist and bodybuilder William Hope Hodgson. It is a compendium of occult and spiritualist themes and ideas, from the two-world hypothesis and actual journeys of the spiritualists, to the theosophical 'Esoteric Buddhism' of Madame Blatavsky, to the Occult Celtic Hermetic Order of the Golden Dawn. The novel is set in that well-known domain of the living dead – Borth, Cardiganshire. See also Katie Bohata, 'Apes and Cannibals in Cumbria: Images of Racial and Gendered other in Gothic Writing in Wales', *Welsh Writing in English: A Yearbook of Critical Essays*, 6 (2000), 119–43.

155 See also Jane Aaron, *Welsh Gothic* (Cardiff, 2013), pp. 78–9.

156 The most measured studies of modern witchcraft and wizardry are Owen Davies, *Witchcraft, Magic and Culture 1736–1951* (Manchester, 1999); idem, 'Methodism, the Clergy, and the Popular Belief in Witchcraft and Magic', *History*, 82, 266 (1997), 252–65; and idem, 'Cunning-Folk in England and Wales during the Eighteenth and Nineteenth Centuries', *Rural History*, 8, 1 (1997), 91–107. See also Stuart Clark,

'Inversion, Misrule and the Meaning of Witchcraft', *Past and Present*, 87 (1980), 82–127.

[157] For the Welsh context see John Humphries Davies, *Rhai o Hen Ddewiniaid Cymru* (London, 1901), and Jane Pugh, *When the Devil Roamed Wales* (Llanrwst, 1988). There are also many fascinating articles in *Llafar Gwlad*, for example Eirlys Gruffydd, 'Y Diafol a'r Werin', 2 (1983–4); idem, 'Y Diafol a'i Ddilynwyr', 4 (1984); idem, 'Eithr Gwared Ni Rhag Drwg', 6 (1984). Eirlys Gruffydd, *Gwrachod Cymru* (Caernarfon, 1980); and idem, *Gwrachod Cymru Ddoe a Heddiw* (Llanrwst, 1998); Kate Boss Griffiths, *Byd y Dyn Hysbys: Swyngyfaredd yng Nghymru* (Talybont, 1977); Jane Pugh, *Welsh Witches and Warlocks* (Llanrwst, 1987). See also Eirlys Gruffydd, 'Mari Berllan Biter', *Llafar Gwlad*, 5 (1984), and idem, 'Hela 'Sgwarnogod', *Llafur Gwlad*, 1 (1983).

[158] Jessie Penn-Lewis, *The War on the Saints* (Liverpool, 1912), p. 11.

[159] Wayland D. Hand, *Magical Medicine: the Folkloric Component of Medicine, Belief, Custom, and Ritual of the Peoples of Europe and America* (Berkley, Calif., 1980). Welsh folk museum, St Fagans, photographs F.2055 and F.9254. I am very grateful to Dr Robin Gwyndaf for copies of several of the sources used in this and the previous section.

[160] L. Winstanley and H. J. Rose, 'Collectanea', *Folk Lore*, LXXXVI (1926), 172.

[161] Winstanley and Rose, 'Collectanea', 166–7.

[162] For some other warnings about February – 'Os yn Chwefror y tyf y pawr / Drwy'r flwyddyn wedyn ni thyf fawr'; 'Chwefror a chwyth, ni chwyd neidr oddiar ei nyth'; 'Mae pob mis o'r flwyddyn yn melltithio Chwefror teg'; or 'Chwefror teg yn difetha'r unarddeg' – see Twm Elias, 'Dywediadau am y Tywydd', *Llafar Gwlad*, 3 (1984).

[163] Twm Elias 'Dywediadau am y Tywydd', *Llafar Gwlad*, 12 (1986).

[164] Lyn Davies, 'Aspects of Mining Folklore in Wales', *Folklife*, 9 (1971), 80–102.

[165] Lyn Davies, 'Coelion y Glowyr', *Llafar Gwlad*, 9 (1987).

[166] D. Rhys Phillips, *The History of the Vale of Neath* (Swansea, 1925), p. 589.

[167] *South Wales Weekly News*, 14 September 1901.

[168] *Westminster Gazette*, 4 October 1901.

[169] *South Wales Echo*, 15 July 1902.

[170] Davies, 'Aspects of Mining Folklore in Wales', 87–8.

[171] Davies, 'Aspects of Mining Folklore in Wales', 94.

[172] *Western Mail*, 11 March 1871.

[173] For a full discussion see Anne E. Jones, 'Folk Medicine in Living Memory in Wales', *Folk Life*, 18 (1980), 58–68, and Anne Elizabeth Williams, *Meddyginiaethau Gwerin Cymru* (Talybont, 2017). See also David Hoffman, *Welsh Herbal Medicine* (Abercastle, n.d.).

174 Davies, *Folk-Lore of West and Mid-Wales*, p. 301.

175 L. J. Williams, *Digest of Welsh Historical Statistics*, vol. 2, pp. 253–4.

176 On these themes see Robin Gwyndaf, 'Religion in Everyday Life in Wales: Belief, Norms and Behaviour', in Nils-Arvid Bringéus (ed.), *Religion in Everyday Life* (Stockholm, 1994), pp. 15–185; idem, '"The Sorrow of All People": Death, Grief and Comfort in a Welsh Rural Community', *Folk Life*, 36 (1997–8); Tristam Potter Coffin, *Our Living Traditions* (London, 1968); and Alec Owen, *The Place of Enchantment: British Occultism and the Culture of the Modern* (Chicago, Ill., 2004).

177 For the tradition see Dafydd Evans, *Cân Newydd o Hanes Dafydd Williams o Swydd Benfro yr hwn a gafodd ei Argyhoeddi wrth weld Cannwyll Gorph ei Hun Bedwar Mis Cyn ei Farw a fu Ebrill 1, 1833* (Llanrwst, 1833/4?) – note the date.

178 In a letter to a friend Thomas Henry Thomas, Wallace criticised his paper on 'Some Folklore of south Wales' (1903) for not including information about the Corpse Candle. Wallace recalled that his belief in spiritualism had affected his view of the many eyewitness accounts he had heard about the 'Corpse Candle' and he stated that 'although at the time I could not accept them as facts, I can now'. See Christabel Hutching, '"Men of Monmouthshire": Letters from Alfred Russel Wallace (1823–1913) to Thomas Henry Thomas (1839–1915)', *Monmouthshire Antiquity*, XXIII (2007), 87–94. M. J. Wallace, 'Ghostly Lights', *Folk-Lore*, V (1894), 293–8.

179 See also St Fagans 63.70/100 MS Book of Horoscopes from Montgomeryshire; and 63.152/19.

180 Keith Thomas published his influential work *Religion and the Decline of Magic* in 1972. The central argument was that magic declined in the seventeenth century as Britain became more religious. For highly entertaining views on the longevity and value of tales see David Cressy, *Agnes Bowker's Cat: Travesties and Transgressions in Tudor and Stuart England* (Oxford, 2000), and Darren Oldridge, *Strange Histories: The Trial of the Pig, the Walking Dead and Other Matters of Fact From the Medieval and Renaissance Worlds* (Abingdon, 2005).

181 Dr R. Tudur Jones subtitled the first volume of his superb study of Welsh religion in the period 1890–1914 'prysurdeb a phryder'. See R. Tudur Jones, *Ffydd ac Argyfwng Cenedl: Hanes Crefydd yng Nghymru 1890–1914*, 2 vols (Abertawe, 1981 and 1982).

182 For a discussion see Derec Llwyd Morgan, 'Ffydd a Gwyddoniaeth yng Ngweithiau Beirdd Oes Victoria', *Llên Cymru*, 21 (1998), 88–139.

183 Davies, *Secret Sins: Sex, Violence and Society in Carmarthenshire 1870–1920*, p. 71.

[184] Quoted in Jones, *Ffydd ac Argyfwng Cenedl*, vol. 2, p. 65.

[185] Jones, *Ffydd ac Argyfwng Cenedl*, vol. 2, p. 90.

[186] For the links between religion and politics see Kenneth O. Morgan, *Rebirth of a Nation: Wales 1880–1980* (Cardiff and Oxford, 1981).

[187] John Owen and O. Madoc Roberts (eds), *Pregethau (Emrys ap Iwan)* (Dinbych, 1926).

[188] Bertrand Russell, *Why I am Not a Christian* (London, 1927), p. 27.

[189] Jones, 'Hapus Dyrfa: Nefoedd Oes Victoria'; David Albert Jones, *Angels: A Very Short Introduction* (Oxford, 2011); Henry Mayr-Harting, *Perceptions of Angels in History* (Oxford, 1998); and Darren Oldridge, *Strange Histories: the Trial of the Pig, the Walking Dead, and Other Matters of Fact from the Medieval and Renaissance Worlds* (London, 2005), pp. 20–39.

[190] David Berry, *Wales and the Cinema: The First Hundred Years* (Cardiff, 1994), p. 62.

[191] Berry, *Wales and the Cinema*, p. 184.

[192] Berry, *Wales and the Cinema*, p. 148.

[193] Berry, *Wales and the Cinema*, p. 125.

[194] *Cardiganshire and Tivyside Advertiser*, 13 February 1914.

[195] *South Wales Press*, 15 October and 17 December 1913.

[196] Carmarthenshire Records Office, *Education Book* 340, 12 December 1877.

[197] Quoted in Richard Overy, *The Morbid Age: Britain and the Crisis of Civilization, 1919–1939* (London, 2009), p. 4. On similar pessimistic themes to the twentieth century see Ian Kershaw, *To Hell and Back: Europe, 1914–1949* (St Ives, 2015), and Mark Greif, *The Age of the Crisis of Man: Thought and Fiction in America 1933–1973* (Princeton, NJ, 2015).

[198] Richard Perceval Graves, *Richard Hughes: A Biography* (London, 1994), p. 77.

[199] Gareth W. Williams, 'The Disenchantment of the World: Innovation, Crisis and Change in Cardiganshire *c*.1880–1910', *Ceredigion*, IX (1983), 314–15.

[200] For John Cowper Powys see Morine Krissdóttir, *Descents of Memory: the Life of John Cowper Powys* (London, 2007), pp. 79–110.

[201] Hedd Wyn, 'Rhyfel', in *Cerddi'r Bugail* (Wrecsam, 1931), p. 1.

[202] Gwenallt, *Ysgubau'r Awen* (Llandysul, n.d. [1957?]).

8 The Pursuit of Pleasure

1   Title of a song by Gracie Fields's accompanist, Briton Ferry-born musical prodigy Harry Parr-Davies (1914–1955).

2   On Tommy Cooper see John Fisher, *Tommy Cooper: Always Leave Them Laughing* (London, 2006).

3   On these themes see Egon Friedell, *A Cultural History of the Modern Age*, 3 vols (London, 2008, 2009, and 2010 editions).

4   On Raymond Williams see Dai Smith, *Raymond Williams: A Warrior's Tale* (Cardigan, 2008).

5   Raymond Williams, *Culture and Society 1780–1950* (New York, NY, 1960), p. xiv. There is a digital facsimile copy at *www.archive.org* (accessed 7 December 2005).

6   Arnold had considerable sympathy for Welsh culture: 'When I see the enthusiasms these Eisteddfods can awaken in your whole people, and then think of the tastes, the literature, the amusements of our own [i.e. English] lower and middle class, I am filled with admiration'. But the language was another matter: 'the sooner the Welsh language disappears as an instrument of the practical, political, social life of Wales, the better, the better for England, the better for Wales itself'. Matthew Arnold, *On the Study of Celtic Literature* (London, 1866), pp. 290, 294. His advice on the study of Celtic literature could have been more succinct – 'don't!'

7   On this theme in the British Empire see Russell Davies, *People, Places and Passions: Pain and Pleasure, a Social History of Wales and the Welsh 1870–1945* (Cardiff, 2015), pp. 247–58.

8   T. J. Morgan, *Diwylliant Gwerin* (Llandysul, 1972); Huw Walters, *Canu'r Pwll a'r Pulpud: Portread o'r Diwylliant Barddol Cymraeg yn Nyffryn Aman* (Llandybïe, 1987); idem, *Cynnwrf Canrif: Agweddau ar Ddiwylliant Gwerin* (Llandybïe, 2004), and idem, *Erwau'r Glo* (Abertawe, 1976); Hywel Teifi Edwards (ed.), *Cwm Rhondda* (Llandysul, 1995); idem, *Cwm Aman* (Llandysul, 1996); idem, *Cwm Tawe* (Llandysul, 1993); idem, *Llyfni ac Afan, Garw ac Ogwr* (Llandysul, 1998), and idem, *Cwm Gwendraeth* (Llandysul, 2000). Together, the authors provide ample evidence of the rich Welsh-language cultural 'heritage' of 'industrial' Wales.

9   On Peate's wider cultural importance see T. Robin Chapman, *Iorwerth Peate* (Caernarfon, 1987), and for his role in St Fagans see Catrin Stevens, *Iorwerth C. Peate* (Cardiff, 1986), and R. Alun Evans, *Bro a Bywyd Iorwerth Cyfeiliog Peate* (Caernarfon, 2003). See also *Y Cymro*, 26 October 1982, for an obituary.

10   John Ceiriog Hughes, *Gweithiau Ceiriog*, 2 vols (Wrecsam, 1890), vol. 1, p. 70.

11   On these themes see Russell Davies, *Hope and Heartbreak: a Social History of Wales and the Welsh, 1776–1871* (Cardiff, 2005), pp. 38–48.

12   On the impact of technology on society and culture see Stephen Kern, *The Culture of Time and Space, 1880–1918* (Harvard, Mass., 2003); G. R. Searle, *A New England? Peace and War, 1886–1918* (Oxford, 2004), pp. 107–11, 529–663; and Philipp Blom, *The Vertigo Years Change and Culture in the West, 1900–1914* (London, 2008), and idem, *Fracture: Life and Culture in the West, 1918–1938* (New York, NY, 2015).

13   Quoted in Peter Miskell, *Pulpits, Coal Pits and Fleapits: A Social History of the Cinema in Wales, 1918–1951* (Cardiff, 2006), p. 18.

14   On these themes see the discussion on work in Davies, *People, Places and Passions*, pp. 99–106.

15   On education see the related discussion in Davies *People, Places and Passions*, pp. 106–19.

16   It is perhaps worth noting that although the Minister for Education, Foster, is given the credit for the 1870 Education Act, its real father was H. A. Bruce, later enobled as Lord Aberdare.

17   G. R. Searle, *A New England?*, p. 571.

18   E. C. Baker, *Sir William Preece F.R.S. Victorian Engineer Extraordinary* (London, 1976).

19   Wyn Thomas, 'Y Ffonograff a Byd Cerddoriaeth Draddodiadol yng Nghymru', *Canu Gwerin*, 29 (2006), 49.

20   David Edgerton, *The Shock of the Old: Technology and Gobal History since 1900* (London, 2008).

21   On these themes see the intriguing, infuriating and inspiring arguments in Jay Griffiths, *Pip Pip: A Sideways Look at Time* (London, 1999).

22   See *www.davidedwardhughes.com* (accessed 11 December 2015).

23   Peter Doggett, *Electric Shock: From the Gramaphone to the iPhone 125 Years of Pop Music* (London, 2015); see also Bill C. Malone, *Singing Cowboys and Musical Mountaineers* (Athens, Ga., 1993).

24   *Cardigan and Tivyside Advertiser*, 5 May 1925.

25   On the 'carefree' aspect of interwar culture see Martin Pugh, *We Danced All Night: A Social History of Britain Between the Wars* (London, 2009); Robert Graves and Alan Hodge, *The Long Weekend: A Social History of Great Britain 1918–1939* (London, 1995); and D. J. Taylor, *Bright Young People: the Rise and Fall of a Generation, 1918–1940* (London, 2007).

26   Paddy Scannell and David Cardiff, *Serving the Nation: a Social History of British Broadcasting; Volume 1, 1922–1939* (Oxford, 1991); John Davies, *Broadcasting and BBC in Wales* (Cardiff, 1994); and Lucas Rowland, *The*

Voice of a Nation? The BBC in Wales, 1923–1973 (Llandysul, 1981). For some useful examples of the material actually broadcast see Patrick Hannan, *Wales on the Wireless: a Broadcasting Anthology* (Llandysul, 1988).

27 On the 'Americanisation' of Wales see Daniel Williams, *Black Skin, Blue Books: African Americans and Wales, 1845–1945* (Cardiff, 2012); and idem, *Aneurin Bevan a Paul Robeson: Sosialaeth, Dosbarth a Hunaniaeth* (Caerdydd, 2010).

28 On William Haggar see Peter Yorke, *William Haggar (1851–1925): Fairground Film Maker* (Bedlinog, 2007). The bible of the history of the cinema and 'moving pictures' in Wales is David Berry, *Wales and the Cinema: the First Hundred Years* (Cardiff, 1994). Reading Berry's comprehensive compendium is probably the closest a sedentary activity like reading comes to weight training.

29 Quoted in Berry, *Wales and the Cinema*, pp. 185–8.

30 Jack Jones *Rhondda Roundabout* (London, 1949), p. 113.

31 Kern, *The Culture of Time and Space*, pp. 117–18.

32 H. Tours, *Parry Thomas: Designer-Driver* (London, 1959); and M. Berresford, *Parry Thomas and Pendine* (Cardiff, 1985).

33 V. Bruce, *Nine Lives Plus: Record Breaking on Land, Sea and in the Air, an Autobiographical Account* (London, 1977); Virginia Scharff, *Taking the Wheel: Women and the Coming of the Motor Age* (New York, NY, 1991); and Georgina Clarsen, *Eat My Dust: Early Women Motorists* (Baltimore, MD, 2008).

34 Raymond Williams, *The Politics of Modernism* (London, 1989), p. 33. See also Terry Eagleton, *Culture* (London, 2016).

35 On these themes see James Walvin, *Leisure and Society, 1830–1950* (London, 1978), especially pp. 47–57, 'Useful Pleasures'; see also Joanathan Rose, *The Intellectual Life of the British Working Classes* (London, 2001).

36 Philip Henry Jones, 'Two Welsh Publishers of The Golden Age: Gee a'i Fab a Hughes a'i Fab', in Philip Henry Jones and Eiluned Rees (eds), *A Nation and its Books: a History of the Book in Wales* (Aberystwyth, 1998), p. 173; see also, '"We only publish what we think will pay for publishing": agweddau ar Hanes Hughes a'i Fab, Wrexham, 1820–1920', *Transactions of the Honourable Society of Cymmrodorion*, 3 (1997), 118–35; and T. Gwynn Jones, *Cofiant Thomas Gee* (Dinbych, 1913), pp. 130–4. For Gee's business acumen see Ieuan Wyn Jones, *Y Llinyn Arian: Agweddau ar Fywyd a Chyfnod Thomas Gee* (Dinbych, 1997).

37 W. J. Gruffydd, *Cofiant Owen Morgan Edwards* (Aberystwyth, 1937); see also Owen M. Edwards, *Detholiad o Ysgrifau* (Wrecsam, 1932).

38   Huw Walters, 'The Periodical Press to 1914', in Jones and Rees (eds), *A Nation and its Books*, pp. 197–208.

39   The definitive work on Welsh periodicals and magazines is Huw Walters, *Llyfryddiaeth Cylchgronnau Cymreig: A Bibliography of Welsh Periodicals 1850–1900* (Abersytwyth, 2003).

40   Dafydd Arthur Jones, *Thomas Levi* (Caernarfon, 1996).

41   Menna Phillips, 'Children's Literature in Welsh to 1950', in Jones and Rees (eds), *A Nation and its Books*, pp. 379–86.

42   R. M. Jones, *Llenyddiaeth Gymraeg, 1936–1972* (Llandybïe, 1975), pp. 157–64.

43   Margaret Haig Thomas, *D. A. Thomas: Viscount Rhondda* (London, 1921).

44   *Western Mail*, 24 May 1928 and 16 December 1940; Lord Hartwell, *William Camrose: Giant of Fleet Street* (London, 1992); and D. Hartt-Davies, *The House the Berry's Built: Inside the Telegraph, 1928–1986* (London, 1990).

45   Glyn Jones, *The Dragon Has Two Tongues* (London, 1968), p. 64.

46   Mark Valentine, *Arthur Machen* (Bridgend, 1995); Christopher Palmer (ed.), *The Collected Arthur Machen* (London, 1988); see also Arthur Machen, *The Autobiography of Arthur Machen* (London, 1951).

47   Quoted in John Harris, 'Queen of the Rushes: Allen Raine and Her Public', *Planet*, 97 (1993), 64.

48   Harris, 'Queen of the Rushes', 65–72; for a biography of Allen Raine see Sally Jones, *Allen Raine* (Cardiff, 1979).

49   John Harris, 'Anglo-Welsh Literature', in Jones and Rees (eds), *A Nation and its Books*, pp. 355–70.

50   Philip Henry Jones, 'Welsh Public Libraries to 1914', in Jones and Rees (eds), *A Nation and its Books*, p. 277.

51   C. M. Baggs, 'The Miner's Institute Libraries of South Wales 1875–1939', in Jones and Rees (eds), *A Nation and its Books*, pp. 297–306.

52   Thomas Jones, *Leeks and Daffodils* (Newtown, 1942), p. 137.

53   South Wales Miners' Library tape: Mrs Agnes Jones, Tumble (Swansea University Archives). See also South Wales Miners' Library final report (Swansea, 1974).

54   On these themes see Richard Hoggart, *The Uses of Literacy* (London, 1957).

55   R. F. Harrod, *The Life of John Maynard Keynes* (London, 1951), p. 257.

56   On the eisteddfod and drama in the early twentieth century see Alan Llwyd, *Hanes Eisteddfod Genedlaethol Cymru: Prifysgol y Werin 1900–1918* (Barddas, 2008); idem, *Blynyddoedd y Locustiaid: Hanes Eisteddfod Genedlaethol Cymru 1919–1936* (Llandybïe, 2007); and idem, *Y Gaer*

Fechan Olaf: Hanes Eisteddfod Genedlaethol Cymru 1937–1950 (Llandybïe, 2006).

[57] Anton Gill, *The Great Escape: the Full Dramatic Story* (London, 2001), pp. 188–90. See also Davies, *People, Places and Passions*, p. 358.

[58] On Hugh Owen see the hagiographic W. E. Davies, *Sir Hugh Owen, His Life and Work* (London, 1885).

[59] On the Welsh in Australia see Bill Jones, 'Representatives of Australia in Welsh Emigrant Literature: "Gwlad yr Aur" ', *Welsh History Review*, 23/2 (2006), 51–74; and idem, 'Cymry Gwlad yr Aur: Ymfudwyr Cymreig yn Ballarat, Awstralia', *Llafur*, 8/2 (2001), 41–62.

[60] For a scathing criticism of the 'social science section', see Hywel Teifi Edwards, *Gŵyl Gwalia: Yr Eisteddfod yn Oes Aur Victoria, 1858–1868* (Llandysul, 1980).

[61] Ioan Williams, *Y Mudiad Drama yng Nghymru* (Caerdydd, 2006).

[62] On Kitchener-Davies see M. Wynn Thomas, *James Kitchener Davies* (Cardiff, 2002). For the arguments over the play *Cwm Glo* see Manon Rhys, 'Atgyfodi Cwm Glo, Kitchener Davies', in Hywel Teifi Edwards (ed.), *Cwm Rhondda* (Llandysul, 1995), pp. 276–300.

[63] Hazel Walford Davies, *Saunders Lewis a Theatr Garthewin* (Llandysul 1995).

[64] Ioan Williams (ed.), *Dramau Saunders Lewis: Y Casgliad Cyflawn* (Caerdydd, 1996), p. 77.

[65] Cecil Price, *The Professional Theatre in Wales* (Swansea, 1984).

[66] *Llanelly Star*, 23 April 1910; and *Llanelly Mercury*, 23 March 1910.

[67] Cecil Price, 'Portable Theatres in Wales, 1843–1914', *National Library of Wales Journal*, IX (1955–6), 64–92.

[68] Thomas Jones, *Rhymney Memories* (Newtown, 1938), p. 56.

[69] Hettie Glyn Davies, *Hanes Bywyd John Glyn Davies, 1870–1953* (Lerpwl, 1965).

[70] See *www.meucymru.co.uk/music/Songs/Caneuon.html* (accessed 18 January 2016).

[71] Dulais Rhys, *Bachgen Bach o Ferthyr* (Llandysul, 1998).

[72] Gareth Williams, *Valleys of Song: Music and Society in Wales 1840–914* (Cardiff, 1998), pp. 76–91.

[73] Lyn Davies, *David Vaughan Thomas (1873–1934)* (Caerdydd, 2004).

[74] Lyn Davies, *Morfydd Owen (1891–1918)* (Caerdydd, 2004); Rhian Davies, '"O can it be she sleeps?" Morfydd Owen: a Centenary Lecture', *Transactions of the Honourable Society of* Cymmrodorion (1991), 249–65.

[75] Gareth Williams, '"How's the Tenors in Dowlais?": the choral culture of the south Wales coalfield c.1880–1930', *Transactions of the Honourable Society of Cymmrodorion*, 11 (2004–5), 170–88.

[76] Robin Williams, *Y Tri Bob* (Llandysul, 1970); Dyfnallt Morgan (ed.), *Babi Sam: yn Dathlu Hanner Can Mlynedd o Ddarlledu o Fangor, 1935–1985, Atgofion a Gobeithion Penblwydd* (Caerdydd, 1985).

[77] John Davies, *Broadcasting and the BBC in Wales* (Cardiff, 1994).

[78] On the Welsh escapades (culturally) in Chicago see Hywel Teifi Edwards, *Eisteddfod Ffair y Byd: Chicago* (Llandysul, 1990).

[79] Williams, *Valleys of Song*, pp. 79–81.

[80] *South Wales Daily Post*, 19 November 1929.

[81] Williams, *Valleys of Song*, pp. 81–2.

[82] Quoted in David R. A. Evans, *The Golden Years: the Llanelli Town Band 1884–1898* (unpublished typescript). I am very grateful to David Evans for a copy of the lecture).

[83] Jen Wilson, 'Doing the Plantation Walkaround Skedaddle', *Planet*, 177 (2006), 7–83.

[84] Wilson, 'Doing the Plantation Walkaround Skedaddle', 82. See also R. E. Lotz, *Black People, Entertainers of African Descent in Europe and Germany* (London, 1997).

[85] *Musical Times*, 40 (1989), 513–18.

[86] Megan Lloyd Ellis, *Hyfrydlais Leila Megáne* (Llandysul, 1979).

[87] D. Peers, *Pathway* (London, 1951); *The Times*, 10 August 1953.

[88] *The Times*, 25 April 1995.

[89] D. Parker and J. Parker, *The Story Not The Song* (London, 1979).

[90] S. Wilson, *Ivor* (London, 1975); J. Harding, *Ivor Novello* (London, 1987); P. Noble, *Ivor Novello: Man of the Theatre* (London, 1951); and R. Rose, *Perchance to Dream: the World of Ivor Novello* (London, 1974).

[91] Peter Yorke, *William Haggar, 'Fairground Film Maker': the Biography of a Pioneer of the Cinema* (Bedlinog, 2007).

[92] Kevin Brownlow, *The Parades Gone By: the Early Years of the Cinema* (London, 1992). For the way cinema has changed our attitudes to love, identity, desire and responsibility see David Thomson, *The Big Screen: the Story of the Movies and What they Did to Us* (London, 2010).

[93] Richard Schickel, *D. W. Griffith: an American Life* (New York, NY, 1984), p. 71. See also David Robinson, *Hollywood in the Twenties* (New York, NY, 1968); Iris Barry and Eileen Bowser, *D. W. Griffith: American Film Master* (New York, NY, 1965); and William M. Drew, *D. W. Griffith's 'Intolerance': Its Genesis and Its Vision* (Jefferson, NJ, 1986).

[94] *South Wales Echo*, 13 March 1941.

[95] Jones, *Leeks and Daffodils*, p. 137.

[96] Quoted in Stephen Ridgwell, 'South Wales and the Cinema in the 1930s', *Welsh History Review*, 17 (1994–5), 608–9.

[97] Iris Barry, *Let's Go to the Pictures* (London, 1926), p. 31.

[98] On the links between the British Empire and sport see Brian Dobbs, *Edwardians at Play: Sport, 1890–1914* (London, 1973); John Nauright and Timothy J. L Chandler, *Making Men: Rugby and Masculine Identity* (London, 1996); J. A. Mangan, *The Games Ethic and Imperialism* (London, 2013); and Ronojoy Sen, *Nation at Play: A History of Sport in India* (London, 2015).

[99] See *www.britishempire.co.uk* (accesed 27 January 2016); and *www.rugby-pioneers.blogs.com/rugby/2009/02/the-other-calcutta.html* (accessed 27 January 2016).

[100] Martin Pugh, *We Danced All Night: a Social History of Britain between the Wars* (London, 2009), pp. 259–60.

[101] Martin Johnes, *A History of Sport in Wales* (Cardiff, 2005).

[102] R. J. Moore-Colyer, 'Field Sports, Conservation and the Countryside in Georgian and Victorian Wales', *Welsh History Review*, 16, 3 (1993), 310–29.

[103] D. J. V. Jones, 'The poacher: a Study in Victorian Crime and Protest', *Historical Journal* 22, 4 (1977), pp.825–60; Russell Davies, *Secret Sins: Sex, Violence and Society in Carmarthenshire, 1870–1920* (Cardiff, 1996), pp. 128–31. See also Leslie Baker-Jones, *Princelings, Privilege and Power: The Tivyside Gentry in their Community* (Llandysul, 1999).

[104] D. Sahrhage and Johannes Lundbeck, *A History of Fishing* (London, 1992); and Derek Mills, ' *The Fishing Here is Great': A Light Hearted Discourse on the Social History of Angling* (London, 1985).

[105] R. J. Moore-Colyer, 'Gentlemen, Horses and the Turf in Nineteenth Century Wales', *Welsh History Review*, 6, 1 (1992), 40–59.

[106] Robin Campbell, *All Bets Are Off: Horse Racing in Swansea* (Llandysul, 2004), pp. 68–9.

[107] *The Cambrian*, 5 August 1887.

[108] *The Cambrian*, 22 April 1887.

[109] *The Cambrian*, 22 April 1887.

[110] Carl Chinn, *Better Betting With a Decent Feller: a Social History of Book-making* (London, 2004), pp. 146–7.

[111] Peter Miskell, *Pulpits, Coal Pits and Fleapits: A Social History of the Cinema in Wales, 1918–1951* (Cardiff, 2006), p. 20.

[112] Climbing accidents were inevitable but there is something truly tragic about the death of Muriel Gwendoline Jones (née Edwards) and her husband, the great climber Owen Glynn Jones. A guide, tied to the honeymooning couple stumbled and the trio were swept to their death on a glacier over a thousand feet below. See Merfyn Jones, 'The Mountaineering of Wales, 1880–1925', *Welsh History Review*, 19, 1 (1998–9), 44–67.

[113] Martin Johnes, 'Archery, Romance and Elite Culture in England and Wales c.1780–1840', *History*, 89, 2 (2004), 193–208.

[114] Gwilym Usher, 'The Society of Royal British Bowmen', *Denbighshire Historical Society Transactions*, 4 (1955), 89.

[115] Quoted in Johnes, *Sport in Wales*, p. 13.

[116] Johnes, *Sport in Wales*, pp. 38–9.

[117] D. M. C. Pritchard, *The History of Croquet* (London, 1986), pp. 177–9.

[118] Quoted in *www.oxforddnb.com/view/article/65059* (accessed 29 June 2005).

[119] See *www.tennisfame.com/hall-of-famers/inductees/major-walter-clopton-wingfield/* (accessed 28 January 2016).

[120] Stephen Thompson, 'Welsh Cyclists: Heroes or Villains', *Western Mail*, 7 April 2011, 22–5. See also S. P. Cooke, 'Triumph and Tragedy: the Aberdare Cyclists', in *Old Aberdare 5* (Aberdare, 1988), pp. 54–73; and Stephen Thomson, 'The Bicycling Craze of the 1890s in Wales', *Transactions of the Honourable Society of Cymmrodorion*, 14 (2008), 114–26.

[121] Lawrence Davies, *Mountain Fighters: Lost Tales of Welsh Boxing* (Cardiff, 2011), p. 153.

[122] Davies, *Mountain Fighters*, pp. 66–77.

[123] Alan Llwyd, *Out of the Fires of Hell: Welsh Experience of the Great War in Poetry and Prose* (Llandysul, 2008), p. 117.

[124] Davies, *People, Places and Passions*, pp. 116–17.

[125] For an excellent study of boxing in Wales see Andrew Gallimore, *Occupation Prizefighter: The Freddie Welsh Story* (Bridgend, 2006). For the boxing tradition in west Wales see Gareth Jones, *The Boxers of Wales: Swansea and Llanelli* (Cardiff, 2015).

[126] Johnes, *Sport in Wales*, p. 43.

[127] F. Deakin, *Tommy Farr* (London, 1989).

[128] On some of these themes see Gareth Williams, *1905 And All That* (Llandysul, 1991).

[129] For the history of Swansea Town/City AFC see Geraint H. Jenkins, *Proud to Be a Swan: The History of Swansea City AFC, 1912–2012* (Talybont, 2012).

[130] Dannie Abse, *Perfect Pitch*, quoted in Gareth Williams (ed.), *Sport* (Cardigan, 2008), pp. 77–89. On the history of football in Wales see Martin Johnes, *Soccer and Society: South Wales, 1900–1939* (Cardiff, 2002).

[131] Derek Birley, *A Social History of English Cricket* (London, 1999).

[132] The story is told in Ron Jones and Joe Lovejoy, *The Auschwitz Goalkeeper: A Prisoner of War's True Story* (Llandysul, 2013).

133 The history of Welsh rugby has been told with the excitement of the best sports commentaries in David Smith and Gareth Williams, *Fields of Praise: The Official History of the Welsh Rugby Union* (Cardiff, 1980).

134 For these themes see Huw Richards, Peter Stead and Gareth Williams (eds), *Heart and Soul: the Character of Welsh Rugby* (Cardiff, 1998).

135 Richards, Stead and Williams (eds), *Heart and Soul*, p. 119.

136 Quoted in Johnes, *Sport in Wales*, p. 61.

137 Johnes, *Sport in Wales*, p. 61.

138 On the history of women in Welsh sport see Emma Lile, 'Menywod a Chwaraeon: Athletwragedd yng Ngholeg Prifysgol Cymru, Aberystwyth *c*.1880–1914', *Ceredigion*, 4 (2000), 59–72.

139 Johnes, *Sport in Wales*, p. 37.

140 *South Wales Daily News*, 18 December 1905.

141 Rory Waterman (ed.), *W. H. Davies: The Time Traveller, A Reader* (London, 2015); see also 'All in June', the quotation is from *www.poemhunter.com* (accessed 17 January 2015).

142 The history of brewing has been well told and titled by Brian Glover in *Prince of Ales: the History of Brewing in Wales* (Stroud, 1993); the quotations are on pp.7, 21.

143 John William Davies, *Cider Making in Wales* (Cardiff, 1984), p. 45.

144 Glover, *Prince of Ales*, pp. 133–4.

145 Glover, *Prince of Ales*, pp. 148–57.

146 'Gwaith Wisgi'r Fron-Goch', *Llafar Gwlad*, 23 (2004?).

147 Davies, *Hope and Heartbreak*, p. 402.

148 J. M. Stubbs, 'The Wreck of a "Whisky Ship" the *Stewart* Re-visited', *Cymru a'r Môr / Maritime Wales*, 5 (1980), 112–14.

149 Ivor Waters, *Inns and Taverns of Chepstow and the Lower Wye Valley* (Chepstow, 1976), p. 42.

150 Alun Rees et al., *Historical and Hysterical Tales of Pontarddulais Public Houses* (Pwllheli, 2008). For some other histories of pubs see Peter Johnson and Catherine Jefferies, *Conwy and District Pubs* (Stroud, 2016); Brian Davies, *Mumbles and Gower Pubs* (Stroud, 2006); Frank Olding, *Abergavenny Pubs* (Stroud, 2005); Brian Glover, *Cardiff Pubs and Breweries* (Stroud, 2005); and John Eisel and Frank Benett, *Pubs of Hay-on-Wye and the Golden Valley* (Longaston, 2005).

151 On the subject of women in pubs see Mass-Observation, *The Pub and the People: A Worktown Study* (London, 1938).

152 Rees et al., *Historical and Hysterical*, p. 214, p. 32.

153 Waters, *Inns and Taverns of Chepstow*, p. 78.

154 On the role of women in Welsh temperance see Ceridwen Lloyd Morgan, 'From Temperance to Suffrage?', in Angela V. John (ed.), *Our*

Mothers' Land: Chapters in Welsh Women's History, 1830–1939 (Cardiff, 1999, republished 2014), pp. 135–58. See also B. Harrison, *Drink and the Victorians: The Temperance Question in England, 1815–1872* (Keele, 1994); N. Longmate, *The Water Drinkers: A History of Temperance* (London, 1968); A. E. Dingle, *The Campaign for Prohibition in Victorian England* (London, 1980); and John Greenaway, *Drink and British Politics since 1830: a Study in Policy Making* (Basingstoke, 2003). For Wales, the story has been well told in W. R. Lambert, *Drink and Sobriety in Wales, 1820–1895* (Cardiff, 1983), and idem, 'The Welsh Sunday Closing Act, 1881', *Welsh History Review*, 6 (1972–3), 161–89.

155 Glover, *Prince of Ales*.

156 David W. Gutzke, *Protecting the Pub: Brewers and Publicans Against Temperance* (Woodbridge, 1989).

157 J. O. Jones, *The History of the Caernarfonshire Constabulary* (Caernarfon, 1963), p. 88.

158 *Report on the Select Committee of the House of Lords on Intemperance*, P.P. 1887, pp. 747 and 586–9.

159 Davies, *Secret Sins: Sex, Violence and Society in Carmarthenshire, 1870–1920*, pp. 120–1.

160 Quoted in Deborah Jones, '"Drunk and Riotous in Pontypridd": Women, the Police Courts and the Press in South Wales Coalfield Society 1899–1914', *Llafur*, 8 (3) (2002), 11.

161 Jones, 'Drunk and Riotous in Pontypridd', 11.

162 *The Cambrian*, 31 December 1890.

163 *Parliamentary Reports on Welsh Sunday Closing*, 1890, vol. XL [c.5994], p. 427.

164 David Davies, *The Welsh Sunday Closing Act* (Cardiff, 1889), p. 112.

165 Lambert, 'The Welsh Sunday Closing Act', 176.

166 *Western Mail*, 11 April 1889.

167 *Carmarthen Weekly Reporter*, 2 August 1901.

168 *Western Mail*, 27 February 1889.

169 A. F. Harvey, *The Royal Commission and Sunday Closing in Wales, Scotland and Ireland* (Manchester, 1894), p. 4.

170 *Western Mail*, 7 March 1889.

171 For the effects of wartime legislation against drinking see Gerard J. DeGroot, *Blighty: British Society in the Era of the Great War* (London, 1996), pp. 236–9; Derek H. Aldcroft, 'Control of the Liquor Trade in Great Britain 1914–21', in W. H. Chalnoner and Barrie M. Ratcliffe, *Trade and Transport: Essays in Economic History in Honour of T. S. Williams* (Manchester, 1977), pp. 242–57; Ian Donnaclie, 'World War, and the Drink Question: State Control of the Drink Trade', *Journal of the Scottish*

Labour History Society, 17 (1982), 19–26; Michael E. Rose, 'The Success of Social Reform? The Central Control Board (Liquor Traffic) 1915–21', in M. R. D. Foot (ed.), *War and Society: Historical Essays in Honour and Memory of J. R. Western* (London, 1973), pp. 71–84, 298–304.

[172] On complaints against legislation against 'treating' of soldiers see Davies, *Secret Sins: Sex, Violence and Society in Carmarthenshire, 1870–1920*, pp. 120–1.

[173] *The Dragon and the Eagle* (app published by Thud Media, April 2015). This is an interactive history of the Welsh in the USA by Colin Thomas.

[174] For the career of Hiram Wesley Evans (1881–1966) see David Mark Chalmers, *Hooded Americanism: the History of the Ku Klux Klan* (Durham, NC, 1981); Thomas R. Pegram, *One Hundred Percent American: the Rebirth and Decline of the Ku Klux Klan in the 1920s* (Littlefield, 2011); and Wyn Craig Wade, *The Fiery Cross: the Ku Klux Klan in America* (Oxford, 1998). Hiram Wesley Evans appeared on the front cover of *Time* magazine on 23 June 1924. As leader of the Ku Klux Klan he saw membership expand to around six million and addressed a convention of more than 200,000 people on 4 July 1923. His views are given in *The Menace of Modern Immigration* (1923), *The Klan of Tomorrow* (1924), *Alienism in the Democracy* (1927) and *The Rising Storm* (1929). Even within an organisation beset with corruption and criminality, Evans stood out for seeking to leverage as much financial profit as possible for himself.

[175] On Humphreys see John Morgan, *No Gangster More Bold: Murray Humphreys, the Welsh Political Genius who Corrupted America* (London, 1985). Amongst other things, Murray Humphreys organised the St Valentines Day's Massacre that wiped out the Capone gang's main rivals.

[176] For some of these themes see the wonderfully appropriately named A. Barr, *Drink: a Social History* (London, 1998); and J. Burnett, *Liquid Pleasures: a Social History of Drink in Modern Britain* (London, 1999). See also Henry Jeffreys, *Empire of Booze: British History Through the Bottom of a Glass* (London, 2015). For the glorification see Robert Sellers, *Hellraisers: the Life and Inebriated Times of Richard Burton, Richard Harries, Peter O'Toole and Oliver Reed* (London, 2009). The book also mentions Dylan Thomas's drinking partner, the 'notorious boozer and general mad old bastard, actor Hugh Griffith (1912–1980) of Marian Glas, Anglesey. Taking a naked stroll down a corridor in the ultra-posh George V Hotel in Paris, Griffith had modestly placed a 'Do Not Disturb' sign over his genitals, but had altered it to read 'Do Disturb'.

Griffith was also asked whether he was a 'method actor', to which he replied, 'No, but I am a Methodist' (p. 54).

177 The link between the creative artist, particularly the writer and drink, is well told in Olivia Laing, *The Trip to Echo Spring: Writers and Drinking* (Edinburgh, 2014). Tennessee Williams features prominently in this excellent book. On the individual writer's drinking see Daniel Jones, *My Friend Dylan Thomas* (Littlehampton, 1977), Gwen Watkins, *Dylan Thomas: Portrait of a Friend* (Swansea, 2005), and Menna Baines, *Yng Ngolau'r Lleuad: Ffaith a Dychymyg yng Ngwaith Caradog Prichard* (Llandysul, 2005). For how 'y felan' hit him hardest see pp. 53–6. An excellent guide for a great pub crawl is provided by Jeff Towns, *Dylan Thomas: the Pubs* (Talybont, 2013), p. 12.

178 On these themes see Russell Davies, '"Inside the House of the Mad": the Social Context of Mental-Illness, Suicide and the Pressures of Life in Rural South-West Wales c.1860–1920', *Llafur*, 4, 2 (1985), 20–35; see also idem, *Hope and Heartbreak*, pp. 142–50, 470–2.

179 On the history of humour in Wales see Davies, *Hope and Heartbreak*, pp. 414–33. For samples of Welsh jokes see Dilwyn Phillips, *Welsh Jokes* (Talybont, 2003), and idem, *More Welsh Jokes* (Talybont, 2005).

180 On the history of jokes and humour see Vic Gatrell, *City of Laughter: Sex and Satire in Eighteenth Century London* (London, 2006); Marjolein t'Hart and Dennis Bos, *Humour and Social Protest: International Review of Social Hsitory; Supplement 15* (Cambridge, 2007); and Jan Bremmer and Herman Roodenbury, *A Cultural History of Humour* (London, 1997). Some of the finest research on humour has been done in two countries not usually associated with jokes, Germany and Russia; perhaps such research was more needed there. See, for example, F. K. M. Hillenbrand, *Underground Humour in Nazi Germany, 1933–1945* (London, 1995); and M. R. Townsend, *Forbidden Laughter: Popular Humour and the Limits of Repression in Nineteenth Century Russia* (Ann Arbor, MI, 1992); and Ben Lewis, *Hammer and Tickle: A History of Communism Told Through Communist Jokes* (London, 2008). An excellent study of the joke is Jimmy Carr and Lucy Greeves, *The Naked Jape: Uncovering the World of Jokes* (London, 2006).

181 On Ernest Jones see Brenda Maddox, *Freud's Wizard: Ernest Jones and the Transformation of Psychoanalysis* (London, 2006). On humour, as so much else, Jones's starting point was his master's views, see Sigmund Freud, *Jokes and Their Relation to the Unconscious* (London,1916).

182 *The Observer*, 20 July 1930; Catherine Gomez, *Through Dread of Crying you will Laugh Instead: Disillusionment in World War 1* (San Francisco, 1999); Esther MacCallum-Stewart, *Satirical Magazines of the First World*

War: Punch and the Wipers Times, to be found at *FirstWorldWar.com* (accessed 17 March 2017). Ian Hislop wrote a play in 2017 based on the newspaper.

[183] Quoted in Davies, *People, Places and Passions*, p. 301. On the use of humour in wartime see Edward Madigan, 'Sticking to a Hateful Task: Resilience, Humour and British Understanding of Combat Courage, 1914–18', *War in History*, 20, 1 (2013), 76–98; and Clémentine Tholas-Dissat and Karen A. Ritzenhoff, *Humour, Entertainment, and Popular Culture During World War One* (London, 2015).

[184] The quotations in this paragraph are all in Nancy McPhee, *The Book of Insults* (London, 1978), pp. 16, 135–6.

[185] John Bengston, *Silent Visions: Discovering Early Hollywood and New York Through the Films of Harold Lloyd* (Santa Monica, 2011), and Tom Dardis, *Harold Lloyd: The Man on the Clock* (Harmondsworth, 1983).

[186] William Robert Faith, *Bob Hope: a Life in Comedy* (Cambridge, Mass., 2003).

[187] Davies, *People, Places and Passions*, pp. 348–9.

[188] Harry Secombe, *Arias and Raspberries: An Autobiography* (London, 1989), p. 139.

[189] Quoted in John Fisher, *Tommy Cooper: Always Leave Them Laughing* (London, 2006), p. 21.

[190] Fisher, *Tommy Cooper*.

[191] John Harris (ed.), *Caradoc Evans: Morgan Bible* (Aberystwyth, 2006).

[192] On the Cardi see Emyr Llewelyn, *Hiwmor y Cardi* (Talybont, 2006).

[193] Peter Hughes Griffiths, *Hiwmor Sir Gâr* (Talybont, 2006), p. 77.

[194] Emyr Edwards (ed.), *Yr Awen Lawen: Blodeugerdd Barddas o Gerddi Ysgafn a Doniol* (Llandybïe, 1989), p. 243.

[195] Edwards (ed.), *Yr Awen* Lawen, p. 519.

[196] Edwards (ed.), *Yr Awen* Lawen, p. 268.

[197] Edwards (ed.), *Yr Awen* Lawen, p. 258.

[198] Edwards (ed.), *Yr Awen* Lawen, p. 608.

[199] Idwal Jones, *Cerddi Digri a Rhai Pethau Eraill* (Llandysul, 1936), and idem, *Cerddi Digri Newydd a Phethau o'r Fath* (Llandysul, 1937). For a biography see D. Gwenallt Jones, *Cofiant Idwal Jones Llanbedr Pont Steffan* (Aberystwyth, 1958), and Tegwyn Jones, 'Idwal Jones: Dramodydd a Digrifwr', *Ceredigion*, XII, 4 (1996), 59–80.

[200] See for example *North Wales Chronicle*, 7 February 1879, 7 April 1883, 28 April 1883, 30 September 1898.

[201] Ronald Pearsall, *Collapse of Stout Party: Victorian Wit and Humour* (London, 1975).

[202] Michael Parnell, *Laughter from the Dark: A Life of Gwyn Thomas* (Bridgend, 1997), p. 117.

203 John Fordham, 'The Matter of Wales: Industry and Rurality in the Work of James Hanley', *Welsh Writing in English: A Yearbook of Critical Essays* (1997), p. 94.

204 'Llysenwau Ynys-y-bŵl', *Llafar Gwlad*, 14 (2004); D. Leslie Chamberlain, *Welsh Nicknames* (Penygroes, 1981); *Western Mail*, 20 February 2013; Bedwyr Lewis Jones, 'Glasenwau Gogleisiol', *Llafar Gwlad*, 3 (1984); 'Swyn Llysenwau', *Llafar Gwlad*, 23 (1989). I am grateful to Dr Robin Gwyndaf for several of these references.

Conclusion

1 *By-Gones*, 26 September 1897.

2 Stanley Bligh, *The Direction of Desire* (Oxford, 1911), p. 39.

3 Dylan Thomas, *Under Milk Wood: The Definitive Edition*, eds Walford Davies and Ralph Maud (London, 1995), p. 71.

4 C. S. Lewis, *The Four Loves* (London, 1960), pp. 113, 124 and 127–32. On his Welsh links see Grahame Davies, *Real Wrexham* (Bridgend, 2001), pp. 70–1.

5 John Fisher, *Tommy Cooper: Always Leave Them Laughing* (London, 2006), p. 394.

6 The anecdote about Bertrand Russell, the purpose of life and the taxi driver was first told by T. S. Eliot's widow Valerie in *The Times*, 8 February 1970. For a discussion see Terry Eagleton, *The Meaning of Life* (Oxford, 2007). See also Peter Hennessy, *Distilling the Frenzy: Writing the History of One's Own Times* (London, 2013).

7 T. H. Parry-Williams's 'Dychwelyd', in Gwynn ap Gwilym and Alan Llwyd (eds), *Blodeugerdd o Farddoniaeth Gymraeg yr Ugeinfed Ganrif* (Llandysul, 1987), p. 58.

Index